Microsoft Excel 2013: Building Data Models with PowerPivot

Alberto Ferrari and Marco Russo

ISBN: 978-0-7356-7634-3

Third Printing: December 2014

Printed and bound in the United States of America.

Microsoft Press books are available through booksellers and distributors worldwide. If you need support related to this book, email Microsoft Press Book Support at *mspinput@microsoft.com*. Please tell us what you think of this book at *http://www.microsoft.com/learning/booksurvey*.

Microsoft and the trademarks listed at *http://www.microsoft.com/about/legal/en/us/IntellectualProperty/ Trademarks/EN-US.aspx* are trademarks of the Microsoft group of companies. All other marks are property of their respective owners.

The example companies, organizations, products, domain names, email addresses, logos, people, places, and events depicted herein are fictitious. No association with any real company, organization, product, domain name, email address, logo, person, place, or event is intended or should be inferred.

This book expresses the author's views and opinions. The information contained in this book is provided without any express, statutory, or implied warranties. Neither the authors, O'Reilly Media, Inc., Microsoft Corporation, nor its resellers, or distributors will be held liable for any damages caused or alleged to be caused either directly or indirectly by this book.

Acquisitions and Developmental Editor: Kenyon Brown

Production Editor: Christopher Hearse

Editorial Production: S4 Carlisle Publishing Services

Technical Reviewer: Javier Guillen

Indexer: Ellen Troutman Zaig

Cover Design: Twist Creative • Seattle

Cover Composition: Zyg Group, LLC

Illustrator: S4 Carlisle Publishing Services

Contents at a Glance

Contents

What do you think of this book? We want to hear from you!

Microsoft is interested in hearing your feedback so we can continually improve our
books and learning resources for you. To participate in a brief online survey, please visit:

microsoft.com/learning/booksurvey

Chapter 5   Publishing to SharePoint   117

Chapter 6   Loading data   133

What do you think of this book? We want to hear from you!

Microsoft is interested in hearing your feedback so we can continually improve our
books and learning resources for you. To participate in a brief online survey, please visit:

microsoft.com/learning/booksurvey

Introduction

Microsoft Excel is the world standard for performing data analysis. Its ease of use and power make the Excel spreadsheet the tool that everybody uses, regardless of the kind of information being analyzed.

You can use Excel to store your personal expenses, your current account information, your customer information or a complex business plan, or even your weight-loss progress during a hard-to-follow diet. The possibilities are infinite—we are not even going to try to start enumerating all the kind of information you can analyze with Excel. The fact is that if you have some data to arrange and analyze, your chances are excellent that Excel will be the perfect tool to use. You can easily arrange data in a tabular format, update it, generate charts, PivotTables, and calculations based on it, and make forecasts with relatively limited knowledge of the software. With the advent of the cloud, now you can use Excel on mobile devices like tablets and smart phones, too, using Internet to have constant access to your information. Also, in earlier versions of Excel, there was a limit of 65,536 rows per single worksheet, and the fact that so many customers asked Microsoft to increase this number (which Microsoft did, raising the limit to 1 million rows in Excel 2007) is a clear indication that users want Excel to store and analyze large amounts of data.

Besides Excel users, there is another category of people dedicating their professional lives to data analysis: business intelligence (BI) professionals. BI is the science of getting insights from large amounts of information, and, in recent years, BI professionals have learned and created many new techniques and tools to manage systems that can handle the range of hundreds of millions or even billions of rows. BI systems require the effort of many professionals and expensive hardware to run. They are powerful, but they are expensive and slow to build, which are serious disadvantages.

Before 2010, there was a clear separation between the analysis of small and large amounts of data: Excel on one side and complex BI systems on the other. A first step in the direction of merging the two worlds was already present in Excel because the PivotTable tool had the ability to query BI systems. By doing that, data analysts could query large BI systems and get the best of both worlds because the result of such a query can be put into an Excel PivotTable, and thus they could use it to perform further analysis.

In 2010, Microsoft made a strong move to break down the wall between BI professionals and Excel users by introducing xVelocity, a powerful engine that drives large BI solutions directly inside Excel. That happened when Microsoft SQL Server 2008

R2 PowerPivot for Excel was released as a free add-in to Excel 2010. The goal was to make the creation of BI solutions so easy that Excel would start to be not only a BI client, but also a BI server, capable of hosting complex BI solutions on a notebook. They called it *self-service BI*.

Microsoft PowerPivot has no limits on the number of rows it can store: if you need to handle 100 million rows, you can safely do so, and the speed of analysis is amazing. PowerPivot also introduced the DAX language, a powerful programming language aimed to create BI solutions, not only Excel formulas. Finally, PowerPivot is able to compress data in such a way that large amounts of information can be stored in relatively small workbooks. But this was only the first step.

The second definitive step to bring the power of BI to users was the introduction of Excel 2013. PowerPivot is no longer a separate add-in of Excel; now it is an inherent part of the Excel technology and brings the power of the xVelocity engine to every Excel user. The era of self-service BI started in 2010, and it has advanced in 2013.

Because you are reading this introduction, you are probably interested in joining the self-service BI wave, and you want to learn how to master PowerPivot for Excel. You will need to learn the basics of the tool, but this is only the first step. Then, you will need to learn how to shape your data so that you can execute analysis efficiently: we call this *data modeling*. Finally, you will need to learn the DAX language and master all its concepts so you can get the best out of it. If that is what you want, then this is the book for you.

We are BI professionals, and we know from experience that building a BI solution is not easy. We do not want to mislead you: BI is a fascinating technology, but it is also a hard one. This book is designed to help you take the necessary steps to transform you from an Excel user to a self-service BI modeler. It will be a long road that will require time and dedication to travel, and you will find yourself making the adaptations you need to learn new techniques. However, the results you will be able to accomplish are invaluable.

The book is not a step-by-step guide to PowerPivot for Excel 2013. If you are looking for a *PowerPivot for Dummies* book, then this is not the book for you. But if you want a book that will go with you on this long, satisfying journey, from the first simple workbooks to the complex simulations you will be creating soon, then this is your ultimate resource.

When writing this book, we decided to focus on concepts and real-world examples, starting at zero and bringing you to mastering the DAX language. We do not cover every single feature, and we do not explain each operation in a "Click this, and then do that" fashion. On the other hand, we packed in this single book a huge amount of information so that, once you finished studying the book, you will have a great background in the new modeling options of Excel.

This last sentence highlights the main characteristic of this book: it is a book to study, not just to read. Get prepared for a long trip—but we promise you that it will be well worth it.

> **Note** The PowerPivot and Power View features are included only with specific configurations of Office 2013. The PowerPivot feature, which was available in all versions of Excel 2010, is available only in Office 2013 Professional Plus, SharePoint 2013 Enterprise Edition, SharePoint Online 2013 Plan 2, and the E3 or E4 editions of Office 365. The Power View feature, new in Excel 2013, is included with the same versions as PowerPivot. Fortunately, the Excel Data Model is supported in all configurations of Excel 2013. Be aware, however, that the variety of available configurations may change.

Who this book is for

The book is aimed at Excel users, project managers, and decision makers who wish to learn the basics of PowerPivot for Excel 2013, master the new DAX language that is used by PowerPivot, and learn advanced data modeling and programming techniques with PowerPivot.

Assumptions about you

This book assumes that you have a basic knowledge of Excel 2010 or Excel 2013. You do not need to be a master of Excel; just being a regular user is fine. We will cover what is needed to make the transition from Excel to PowerPivot, but we do not cover in any way the fundamentals of Excel, like entering a formula, writing a *VLOOKUP* function, or other basic functionalities.

No previous knowledge of PowerPivot is needed. If you already tried to build a data model by yourself, that is fine, but we will assume that you never opened PowerPivot before reading the book.

Organization of this book

The book is designed to be read from cover to cover. Trying to jump directly to the solution of a specific problem, skipping some content, will probably be the wrong choice. In each chapter, we introduce concepts and functionalities that you will need to understand the subsequent chapters. Moreover, we wrote some chapters knowing that you will need to read them more than once, because the theoretical background they provide is hard to take in at a first read.

The book is divided into 16 chapters:

Chapter 1, "Introduction to PowerPivot," offers a guided tour of the basic features of PowerPivot for Excel 2013. By following a step-by-step guide, we show the main benefits of using PowerPivot for your analytical needs. We show how to create a simple Power View report as well.

Chapter 2, "Using the unique features of PowerPivot," shows the features that are available only if you enable the PowerPivot for Excel add-in. This includes calculated columns, calculated fields, hierarchies, and some other basic features. It is the logical continuation (and conclusion) of Chapter 1.

In Chapter 3, "Introducing DAX," we start covering the DAX language, including its syntax and the most basic functions. We highlight the difference between a calculated column and a calculated field, and at the end, we show a first practical example of DAX usage.

Chapter 4, "Understanding data models," is a theoretical chapter, covering the basics of data modeling and showing the different modeling options in a Power-Pivot database. We describe several concepts that are not evident for Excel users, like normalization and denormalization, the structure of a SQL query, how relationships work and why they are so important, the structure of data marts, and data warehouses.

In Chapter 5, "Publishing to SharePoint," we cover the process of publishing workbooks to Microsoft SharePoint to do team BI. Moreover, we introduce the concept of PowerPivot for SharePoint being a server-side application that you can program and extend using Excel and PowerPivot.

Chapter 6, "Loading data," is dedicated to the many ways to load data inside PowerPivot. For each data source, we show the way it works and provide many hints and best practices for that specific source.

Chapter 7, "Understanding evaluation contexts," and Chapter 8, "Understanding CALCULATE," are the theoretical core of the book. There, we introduce the concepts of evaluation contexts, relationships, and the *CALCULATE* function. These are the pillars of the DAX language, and you will need to master them before writing advanced data models with PowerPivot.

Chapter 9, "Using hierarchies," shows how to create and manage hierarchies. It covers basic hierarchy handling, how to compute values over hierarchies, and finally, it shows how to manage parent/child hierarchies by using the concepts learned in Chapters 7 and 8.

Chapter 10, "Using Power View," is dedicated to the new reporting tool in Excel 2013: Power View. There, we show the main feature of this tool, how to create simple Power View reports, and how to filter data and build reports that are pleasant to look at and provide useful insights in your data.

Chapter 11, "Shaping the reports," covers several advanced topics regarding reporting. It includes Key Performance Indicators (KPIs), how to write them, and how to use them to improve the quality of your reporting system. We also cover the Power View metadata layer in PowerPivot, drill-through, sets in Excel or in MDX, and perspectives.

Chapter 12, "Performing date calculations in DAX," deals with time intelligence. Year to Date (YTD), Quarter to Date (QTD), Month to Date (MTD), working days versus non-working days, semiadditive measures, moving averages, and other complex calculations involving time are all topics covered here.

Chapter 13, "Using advanced DAX," is a collection of scenarios and solutions, all of which share the same background: they are hard to solve using Excel or in any other tool, whereas they are somewhat easier to manage in DAX, once you gain the necessary knowledge from the previous chapters in the book. All these examples come from real-world scenarios and are among the top requests we see when we do consultancy or look at forums on the web.

Chapter 14, "Using DAX as a query language," is dedicated to using DAX as a query language (as you might guess). It covers the various functionalities of DAX when used to query a database. It also shows advanced functionalities, like reverse-linked and linked-back tables, which greatly enhance the capabilities of PowerPivot to build complex data models.

Chapter 15, "Automating operations using VBA," discusses using Microsoft Visual Basic for Applications (VBA) to manage PowerPivot workbooks in a programmatic way, automating a few common tasks. We provide some code examples and show how to solve some of the common scenarios where VBA might be useful.

Chapter 16, "Comparing Excel and SQL Server Analysis Services," compares the functionalities of the three flavors of PowerPivot technology: PowerPivot for Excel, PowerPivot for SharePoint, and SQL Server Analysis Services (SSAS). The goal of this final chapter is to give you a clear picture of what can be done with PowerPivot for Excel, when you need to move a step further and adopt PowerPivot for SharePoint, and what extra features are available only in SSAS.

Conventions

The following conventions are used in this book:

- **Boldface** type is used to indicate text that you type.

- *Italic* type is used to indicate new terms, calculated fields and columns, and database names.

- The first letters of the names of dialog boxes, dialog box elements, and commands are capitalized. For example, the Save As dialog box.

- The names of ribbon tabs are given in ALL CAPS.

- Keyboard shortcuts are indicated by a plus sign (+) separating the key names. For example, Ctrl+Alt+Delete mean that you press Ctrl, Alt, and Delete keys at the same time.

About the companion content

We have included companion content to enrich your learning experience. The companion content for this book can be downloaded from the following page:

http://go.microsoft.com/FWLink/?Linkid=279953

The companion content includes the following:

- A Microsoft Access version of the *AdventureWorksDW* databases that you can use to build the examples yourself.

- All the Excel workbooks that are referenced in the text (that is, all the workbooks that are used to illustrate the concepts). Note you need to have Excel 2013 to open the workbooks.

Acknowledgments

We have so many people to thank for this book that we know it is impossible to write a complete list. So thank you so much to all of you who contributed to this book—even if you had no idea that you were doing it. Blog comments, forum posts, email discussions, chats with attendees and speakers at technical conferences, and so much more have been useful to us, and many people have contributed significant ideas to this book. That said, there are people we need to cite personally here because of their particular contributions.

We want to start with Edward Melomed: he inspired us, and we probably would not have started our journey with PowerPivot without a passionate discussion that we had with him several years ago.

We have to thank Microsoft Press, O'Reilly Media, and the people who contributed to the project: Kenyon Brown, Christopher Hearse, and many others behind the scenes.

The only job longer than writing a book is the studying you must do in preparation for writing it. A group of people that we (in all friendliness) call "ssas-insiders" helped us get ready to write this book. A few people from Microsoft deserve a special mention as well because they spent precious time teaching us important concepts about PowerPivot and DAX. Their names are Marius Dumitru, Jeffrey Wang, and Akshai Mirchandani. Your help has been priceless, guys!

We also want to thank Amir Netz, Ashvini Sharma, and T. K. Anand for their contributions to the discussion about how to position PowerPivot. We feel they helped us in some strategic choices we made in this book.

Finishing a book in the age of the Internet is challenging because there is a continuous source of new inputs and ideas. A few blogs have been particularly important to our book, and we want to mention their creators here: Chris Webb, Kasper de Jonge, Rob Collie, Denny Lee, and Dave Wickert.

Finally, a special mention goes to the technical reviewer, Javier Guillen. He double-checked all the content of our original text, searching for errors and giving us invaluable suggestions on how to improve the book. If the book contains fewer errors than our original manuscript, it is because of Javier. If it still contains errors, it is our fault, of course.

Thank you so much, folks!

Support and feedback

The following sections provide information on errata, book support, feedback, and contact information.

Errata

We have made every effort to ensure the accuracy of this book and its companion content. Any errors that have been reported since this book was published are listed on our Microsoft Press site:

http://aka.ms/Excel2013DataModelsPP/errata

If you find an error that is not already listed, you can report it to us through the same page.

If you need additional support, email Microsoft Press Book Support at mspinput@microsoft.com.

Note that product support for Microsoft software is not offered through these addresses.

We Want to Hear from You

At Microsoft Press, your satisfaction is our top priority, and your feedback our most valuable asset. Please tell us what you think of this book at

http://www.microsoft.com/learning/booksurvey

The survey is short, and we will read every one of your comments and ideas. Thanks in advance for your input!

Stay in Touch

Let's keep the conversation going! We are on Twitter: *http://twitter.com/MicrosoftPress.*

CHAPTER 1

Introduction to PowerPivot

Microsoft PowerPivot for Microsoft Excel 2013 is a technology aimed at providing self-service business intelligence (BI), which is a real revolution inside the world of data analysis because it gives the final user all the power needed to perform complex data analysis without requiring the intervention of BI technicians. PowerPivot is an Excel add-in that implements a fast, powerful, in-memory database that can be used to organize data, detect interesting relationships, and provide the fastest way to browse information.

Some of the most interesting features of PowerPivot are the following:

- The ability to organize tables for the PivotTable tool in a relational way, freeing the analyst from the need to import data as Excel sheets before analyzing them.

- The availability of a fast, space-saving, columnar database that can handle huge amounts of data without the limitations of Excel sheets.

- DAX, a powerful programming language that defines complex expressions on top of the relational database. It makes it possible to define surprisingly rich expressions compared to those standards in Excel.

- The ability to integrate different sources of data, such as databases, Excel sheets, and data sources available on the Internet, and virtually any kind of data.

- Amazingly fast in-memory processing of complex queries over the whole database.

Some people might think of PowerPivot as a simple replacement for the PivotTable, while others might use it as a rapid development tool for complex BI solutions, and still others might believe that it is a real replacement for a complex BI solution. PowerPivot is not a replacement for large and complex BI solutions like the ones built on top of Microsoft Analysis Services, but it is much more than a simple replacement for the Excel PivotTable, and it is a great tool for exploring the BI world and implementing end-to-end BI solutions.

PowerPivot fills the gap between an Excel sheet and a complete BI solution, and it has some unique characteristics that make it appealing for both Excel power users and seasoned BI analysts. This book analyzes all the features of PowerPivot, but, as with any big project, we need to start from the beginning. This chapter starts with a simple introduction to the basic features of PowerPivot. We suggest that you follow the step-by-step instructions so you can see on your own computer the results that we show in the book. Later, in the following chapters, we will not use step-by-step instructions anymore because we think that it is better to focus the book on concepts rather than on "click Next" instructions for more advanced topics.

Even though this book is about PowerPivot for Excel 2013, it is a good idea to start with a short review of how PowerPivot was born and how it worked in Excel 2010, so you can better appreciate the new features and understand some of the peculiarities of this add-in.

Using a PivotTable on an Excel table

Let's start by going backward, into the past. Since the release of Excel 97, it has been possible to analyze data using PivotTables. Prior to the availability of PowerPivot, using PivotTables was the main way to analyze data. The PivotTable is an easy and convenient way to browse huge amounts of data that you collect into Excel sheets. This book does not explain in detail how the PivotTable tool works; there are a lot of good descriptions available from other sources. However, it is helpful to recall the main features of the PivotTable to compare them with those of PowerPivot.

Suppose you have a standard Excel table, imported from a query run against a database, that contains all the data that you want to analyze. To get this data, you probably asked IT to provide some means to access the database and a specific query to retrieve the information. Your Excel sheet would look like the one in Figure 1-1. Because the table contains raw data, it is very difficult to analyze. You can look at this worksheet in the companion workbooks under the name "CH01-01-Classical Excel PivotTable.xlsx."

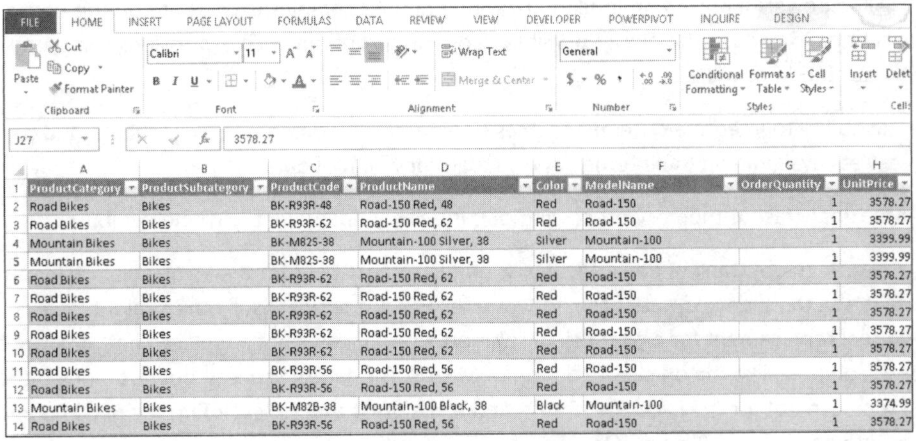

ProductCategory	ProductSubcategory	ProductCode	ProductName	Color	ModelName	OrderQuantity	UnitPrice
Road Bikes	Bikes	BK-R93R-48	Road-150 Red, 48	Red	Road-150	1	3578.27
Road Bikes	Bikes	BK-R93R-62	Road-150 Red, 62	Red	Road-150	1	3578.27
Mountain Bikes	Bikes	BK-M82S-38	Mountain-100 Silver, 38	Silver	Mountain-100	1	3399.99
Mountain Bikes	Bikes	BK-M82S-38	Mountain-100 Silver, 38	Silver	Mountain-100	1	3399.99
Road Bikes	Bikes	BK-R93R-62	Road-150 Red, 62	Red	Road-150	1	3578.27
Road Bikes	Bikes	BK-R93R-62	Road-150 Red, 62	Red	Road-150	1	3578.27
Road Bikes	Bikes	BK-R93R-62	Road-150 Red, 62	Red	Road-150	1	3578.27
Road Bikes	Bikes	BK-R93R-62	Road-150 Red, 62	Red	Road-150	1	3578.27
Road Bikes	Bikes	BK-R93R-62	Road-150 Red, 62	Red	Road-150	1	3578.27
Road Bikes	Bikes	BK-R93R-56	Road-150 Red, 56	Red	Road-150	1	3578.27
Road Bikes	Bikes	BK-R93R-56	Road-150 Red, 56	Red	Road-150	1	3578.27
Mountain Bikes	Bikes	BK-M82B-38	Mountain-100 Black, 38	Black	Mountain-100	1	3374.99
Road Bikes	Bikes	BK-R93R-56	Road-150 Red, 56	Red	Road-150	1	3578.27

FIGURE 1-1 Here, you see some sample data we can use to create a new PivotTable.

Now that you have all the data available in a sheet, you can choose to insert a PivotTable using the PivotTable button of the Insert tab of the Excel ribbon. The wizard prompts for the table to use as the source of the Pivot and for where to put the PivotTable, and then it provides the standard Excel PivotTable interface shown in Figure 1-2.

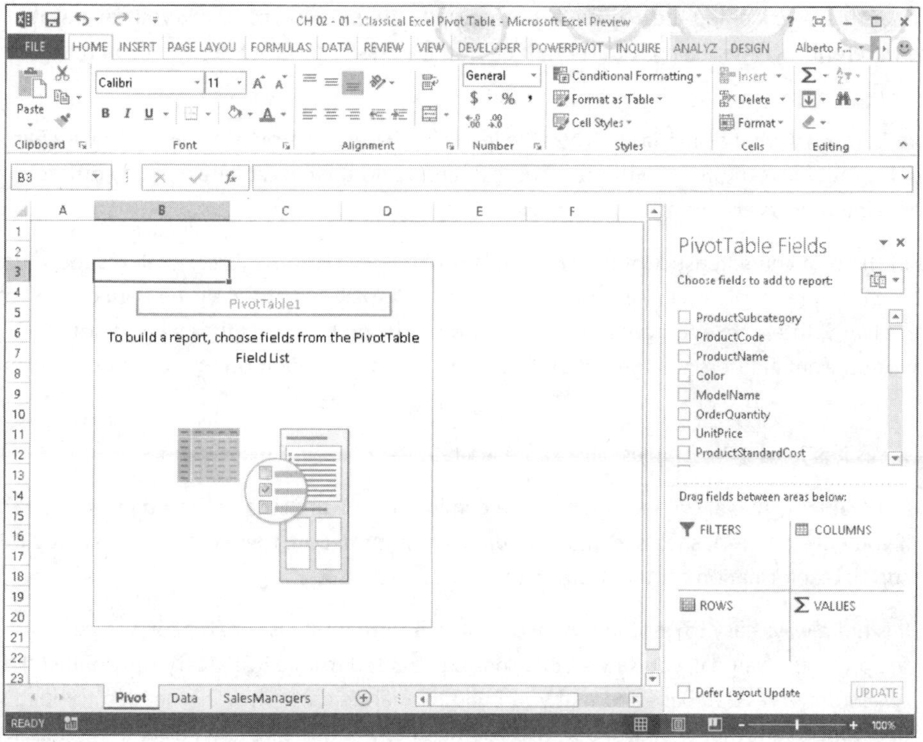

FIGURE 1-2 This is the standard PivotTable interface in Excel.

From here, you can choose to take the Year (to cite one example) and put it as a column and the ProductCategory as a row, displaying the SalesAmount at the intersection of rows and columns. After properly formatting your numbers, you get a nice report (as shown in Figure 1-3) showing how each category performed over time.

Sum of SalesAmount	Column Labels				
Row Labels	2005	2006	2007	2008	Grand Total
Bike Racks			16,440.00	22,920.00	39,360.00
Bike Stands			18,921.00	20,670.00	39,591.00
Bottles and Cages			23,280.27	33,517.92	56,798.19
Caps			7,956.15	11,731.95	19,688.10
Cleaners			3,044.85	4,173.75	7,218.60
Fenders			19,408.34	27,211.24	46,619.58
Gloves			14,228.69	20,792.01	35,020.70
Helmets			92,583.54	132,752.06	225,335.60
Hydration Packs			16,771.95	23,535.72	40,307.67
Jerseys			70,370.46	102,580.22	172,950.68
Mountain Bikes	585,973.27	1,562,456.76	3,989,638.48	3,814,691.06	9,952,759.56
Road Bikes	2,680,400.39	4,967,886.77	3,952,029.21	2,920,267.67	14,520,584.04
Shorts			30,445.65	40,874.16	71,319.81
Socks			2,229.52	2,876.80	5,106.32
Tires and Tubes			103,259.76	142,269.56	245,529.32
Touring Bikes			1,417,434.93	2,427,366.12	3,844,801.05
Vests			13,017.50	22,669.50	35,687.00
Grand Total	3,266,373.66	6,530,343.53	9,791,060.30	9,770,899.74	29,358,677.22

FIGURE 1-3 Here is an example of a report created with the PivotTable tool.

It is clear that by changing the way data is organized into rows and columns, you can easily produce different and interesting reports with an intuitive, fast interface that helps you navigate the information.

Figure 1-3 shows what a standard PivotTable looks like. Users all around the world have been utilizing this tool for many years with great success, analyzing their Excel data in many different ways and producing reports according to their needs.

One of the best characteristics of the PivotTable tool is its ease of use. Excel analyzes the source table, detects numeric values, and provides the ability to display their total slicing data over all other columns. Clearly, totals are aggregated using the *SUM* function because this is what is normally needed. If you want a different aggregation function, you can choose it using the various PivotTable options.

As easy as it is to use, PivotTables have some limitations:

- PivotTables can analyze only information coming from a single table stored in an Excel sheet. If you have different sheets, containing different information, there is not an easy way to correlate information coming from them.

- It is not always easy to get the source data into a format that is suitable for analysis. In the previous example, you saw a table that is extracted from a SQL query run against the *AdventureWorks* database and that you build to analyze data. The skills needed to build such a query are somewhat technical because you need to know the SQL syntax and the underlying database structure, and this often raises the problem of asking your IT department to develop such queries before you even start the analysis process.

- Because only one table can be analyzed at a time, you can often end up building the queries needed for a specific analysis and, if for any reason you want to perform a different analysis, then you will need to build different queries. For example, if you have a query that returns sales at the "month" level, you cannot use that same query to perform further analysis at the "day of week" level. To do that, you will need a new query. This, in turn, might involve the need to contact IT again, which can become expensive if IT charges based on the amount of work it performs.

When PivotTables are not enough, as is the case for medium-sized companies, it is very common to start a complete BI project with products like SQL Server Analysis Services, which will provide the same pivoting features on complex data structures known as *OLAP cubes*. OLAP cubes are difficult to build but provide the best solution to the complexity of free analysis of the company data. OLAP cubes will be discussed briefly later in this book, in Chapter 4, "Understanding data models"; at this point, it is enough to point out that they are the definitive solution to BI requirements, but they are expensive and still require great effort from the IT department.

Using PowerPivot in Microsoft Office 2013

PivotTables based on standard Excel tables are a pretty handy tool. Nevertheless, to let you analyze more complex data, Microsoft introduced a feature called "self-service BI." The goal of this technology is to let you build complex data structures and analyze them with PivotTables, removing the current limitations of PivotTables. PowerPivot is the primary tool available from Microsoft to handle self-service BI, along with its companion Power View, which you will learn to use later in this chapter.

PowerPivot enables the user to analyze data without needing to contact IT to produce complex queries. Furthermore, it removes the limitation that a PivotTable can analyze only a single table because you will be able to query more tables at the same time, producing reports that easily integrate information coming from different sources.

Working with the *AdventureWorks* sample database

In order to provide examples, we will use the *AdventureWorks* database throughout this book. We have chosen *AdventureWorks* because it is well known, freely available on the web, and contains sample data that you can easily use for complex analysis. The database contains information about Adventure Works Cycles, which is a large multinational, fictitious company that manufactures and sells metal and composite bicycles to North American, European, and Asian commercial markets.

You can download the *AdventureWorks* database from *http://www.codeplex.com/SqlServerSamples*, where you will find different versions of the database, depending on the release of Microsoft SQL Server that you have installed. If you do not have SQL Server on your PC, then you can use the Microsoft Access version of *AdventureWorks* that is provided in the companion material. Moreover, all the demos in this book are available in the companion material as Excel workbooks. Thus, you will be able to follow most of the examples even if you do not have access to a database.

Moreover, for the interested reader, Microsoft provides sample data in Excel workbooks that can be used to test PowerPivot at *http://tinyurl.com/PowerPivotSamples*. Even if we do not use these files in this book, you might be interested in loading them to have some data to perform your tests.

In 2010, PowerPivot for Excel 1.0 was released as an add-in for Excel 2010. PowerPivot is a powerful columnar database that does not work with classical Excel tables. Rather, it works with data stored inside its proprietary database, and it can be queried using the DAX language or a PivotTable. Although this information seems to be just a curiosity about the history of PowerPivot, it is in reality very important: for PowerPivot to work, the data should not be stored inside Excel tables, it needs to be stored inside the PowerPivot database. Keep this fact in mind; it will come in handy later.

Note The PowerPivot database is also referred to as the "Excel data model." The two terms relate to the very same technology: the Excel data model is, in reality, a PowerPivot database; and the PowerPivot database is stored inside the Excel workbook. In this book, we will refer to it using both names, depending on the context. If we believe that it is important to separate PowerPivot from Excel, then we will refer to it as the PowerPivot database; otherwise, we adhere to the more standard terminology and call it the Excel data model.

At the beginning, the PowerPivot database was somewhat separated from Microsoft Office, meaning that all its features were available only to users who decided to download and install the add-in. If an Excel workbook containing PowerPivot data was opened on a PC where the add-in was not installed, it simply did not work, even if the data contained in Excel sheets is always visible.

In Office 2013, PowerPivot comes preinstalled and should only need to be activated. Moreover, in Office 2013, the PowerPivot engine is fully integrated into the Excel code and starts to work even before being activated. Some features are immediately available, whereas others have to be manually activated, as you will learn later in this chapter.

In order to start using PowerPivot, we are going to take the easy way: we will create PowerPivot tables (remember—they are different from Excel tables) without even activating the add-in. This happens smoothly as soon as you activate some of the advanced features of Excel for the analysis of data, such as

- Power View reports
- Relationships between tables
- PivotTables over more than one table

Adding information to the Excel table

Let's start making the analysis slightly more complex. The dataset provided by our Excel table contains information about product categories. Assume that at AdventureWorks, each product category is assigned to a salesperson and this information is not stored in the database, so you do not have the option to modify the original query to grab this information. Because Excel is available, you can fill another Excel table with this information, as shown in Figure 1-4.

Category	SalesManager	Office
Bike Racks	Maurizio Macagno	Redmond
Bike Stands	Maurizio Macagno	Redmond
Bottles and Cages	Maurizio Macagno	Redmond
Caps	Maurizio Macagno	Redmond
Cleaners	Alberto Ferrari	Seattle
Fenders	Alberto Ferrari	Seattle
Gloves	Alberto Ferrari	Seattle
Helmets	Alberto Ferrari	Seattle
Hydration Packs	Alberto Ferrari	Seattle
Jerseys	Marco Russo	Redmond
Mountain Bikes	Marco Russo	Redmond
Road Bikes	Marco Russo	Redmond
Shorts	Marco Russo	Redmond
Socks	Marco Russo	Redmond
Tires and Tubes	Marco Russo	Redmond
Touring Bikes	Louis Bonifaz	Seattle
Vests	Louis Bonifaz	Seattle

FIGURE 1-4 The SalesManager Excel table will prove useful to show performance of managers instead of categories.

In order to use this new information in the PivotTable, you need to bring the SalesManager column into the original data model and, as you probably already know, VLOOKUP is invaluable here. Add a column to our original table with this formula:

```
=VLOOKUP([@ProductCategory],SalesManagers,2)
```

You will end up with a new dataset that now contains the sales manager, as shown in Figure 1-5.

B2	✕ ✓ fx	=VLOOKUP([@ProductCategory],SalesManagers,2)		
	A	B	C	D
1	ProductCategory	SalesManager	ProductSubca	ProductCode
2	Road Bikes	Marco Russo	Bikes	BK-R93R-48
3	Road Bikes	Marco Russo	Bikes	BK-R93R-62
4	Mountain Bikes	Marco Russo	Bikes	BK-M82S-38
5	Mountain Bikes	Marco Russo	Bikes	BK-M82S-38
6	Road Bikes	Marco Russo	Bikes	BK-R93R-62
7	Road Bikes	Marco Russo	Bikes	BK-R93R-62
8	Road Bikes	Marco Russo	Bikes	BK-R93R-62
9	Road Bikes	Marco Russo	Bikes	BK-R93R-62
10	Road Bikes	Marco Russo	Bikes	BK-R93R-62
11	Road Bikes	Marco Russo	Bikes	BK-R93R-56
12	Road Bikes	Marco Russo	Bikes	BK-R93R-56
13	Mountain Bikes	Marco Russo	Bikes	BK-M82B-38
14	Road Bikes	Marco Russo	Bikes	BK-R93R-56
15	Mountain Bikes	Marco Russo	Bikes	BK-M82B-44

FIGURE 1-5 Using VLOOKUP, we have been able to bring the sales manager into the original table.

With the new dataset, the PivotTable can be easily re-created, adding the SalesManager to the rows. This results in the desired report, as shown in Figure 1-6.

Sum of SalesAmount	Column Labels				
Row Labels	2005	2006	2007	2008	Grand Total
⊟ Alberto Ferrari			146,037.37	208,464.78	354,502.15
Cleaners			3,044.85	4,173.75	7,218.60
Fenders			19,408.34	27,211.24	46,619.58
Gloves			14,228.69	20,792.01	35,020.70
Helmets			92,583.54	132,752.06	225,335.60
Hydration Packs			16,771.95	23,535.72	40,307.67
⊟ Louis Bonifaz			1,430,452.43	2,450,035.62	3,880,488.05
Touring Bikes			1,417,434.93	2,427,366.12	3,844,801.05
Vests			13,017.50	22,669.50	35,687.00
⊟ Marco Russo	3,266,373.66	6,530,343.53	8,147,973.08	7,023,559.47	24,968,249.73
Jerseys			70,370.46	102,580.22	172,950.68
Mountain Bikes	585,973.27	1,562,456.76	3,989,638.48	3,814,691.06	9,952,759.56
Road Bikes	2,680,400.39	4,967,886.77	3,952,029.21	2,920,267.67	14,520,584.04
Shorts			30,445.65	40,874.16	71,319.81
Socks			2,229.52	2,876.80	5,106.32
Tires and Tubes			103,259.76	142,269.56	245,529.32
⊟ Maurizio Macagno			66,597.42	88,839.87	155,437.29
Bike Racks			16,440.00	22,920.00	39,360.00
Bike Stands			18,921.00	20,670.00	39,591.00
Bottles and Cages			23,280.27	33,517.92	56,798.19
Caps			7,956.15	11,731.95	19,688.10
Grand Total	3,266,373.66	6,530,343.53	9,791,060.30	9,770,899.74	29,358,677.22

FIGURE 1-6 The SalesManager column is now visible in the PivotTable.

This technique works fine, but if you now want to slice data using the Office column from the SalesManager table, you need to repeat the operation of using VLOOKUP to put the Office column in the original table. Even if it does not mean a huge amount of work in this specific example, it is better to move to the next level and learn some of the new features of Excel 2013.

Creating a data model with many tables

Instead of using VLOOKUP to populate a single dataset, as in the previous example, you now want to add the SalesManager table to the PivotTable, so that all its columns can be used. You are moving from a classical single-table analysis to a more advanced multi-table one. Doing this is very easy. At the bottom of the PivotTable fields list is the MORE TABLES... option (see Figure 1-7).

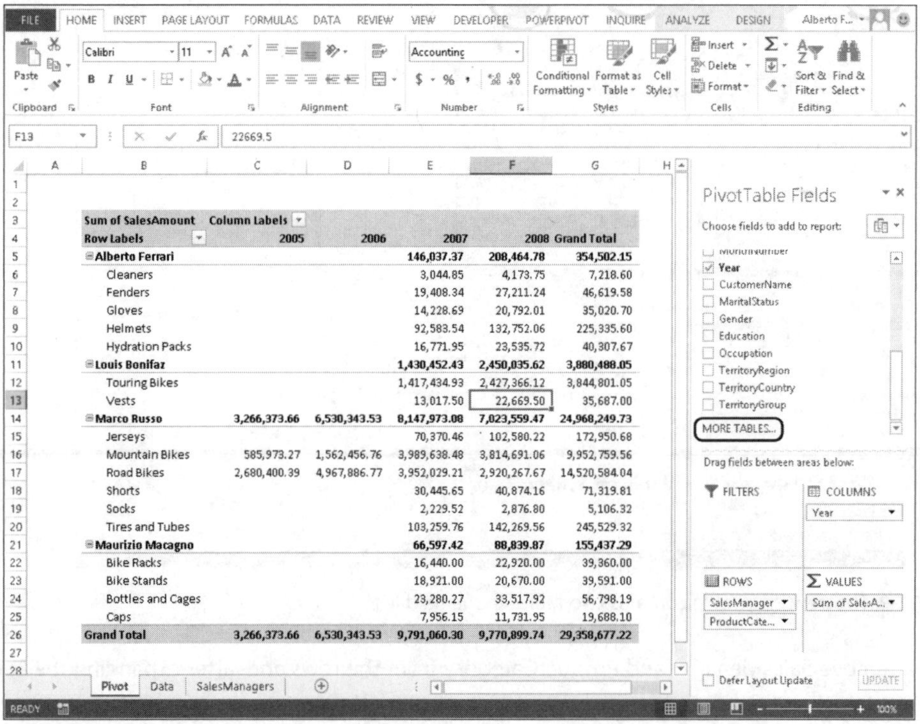

FIGURE 1-7 The MORE TABLES... option lets you add more tables to a single PivotTable report.

If you click MORE TABLES..., you will see an information message that asks you to confirm whether you want to continue creating a new PivotTable. The dialog box, shown in Figure 1-8, contains some very useful information about what is happening, including a reference to something new: the data model.

FIGURE 1-8 As simple as it is, this confirmation window contains a good deal of useful information.

If you click Yes, Excel creates a new PivotTable, with a structure that is identical to the current one but with more tables. You can see the result in Figure 1-9, where the field list now contains two tables.

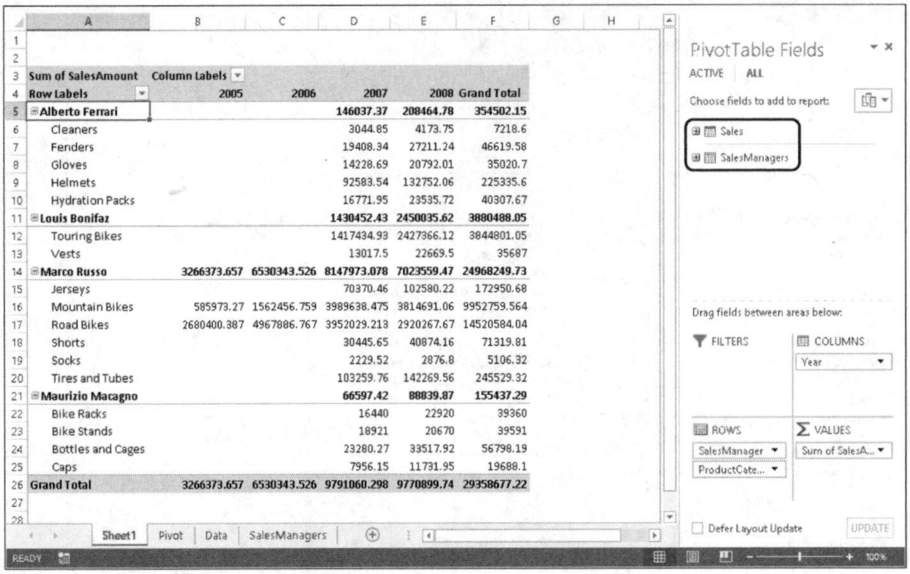

FIGURE 1-9 The new PivotTable contains two tables in the field list.

Now remove SalesManager and ProductCategory from the rows and, after expanding the Sales-Managers table, add Office to the rows. The result is *not* what you might expect. In fact, as Figure 1-10 shows, it seems that all the offices (two, in this example) have exactly the same sales, which is clearly false. The PivotTable seems to detect the same wrong situation because a warning appears in the Field List: "Relationships Between Tables May Be Needed." There is also an inviting CREATE... button.

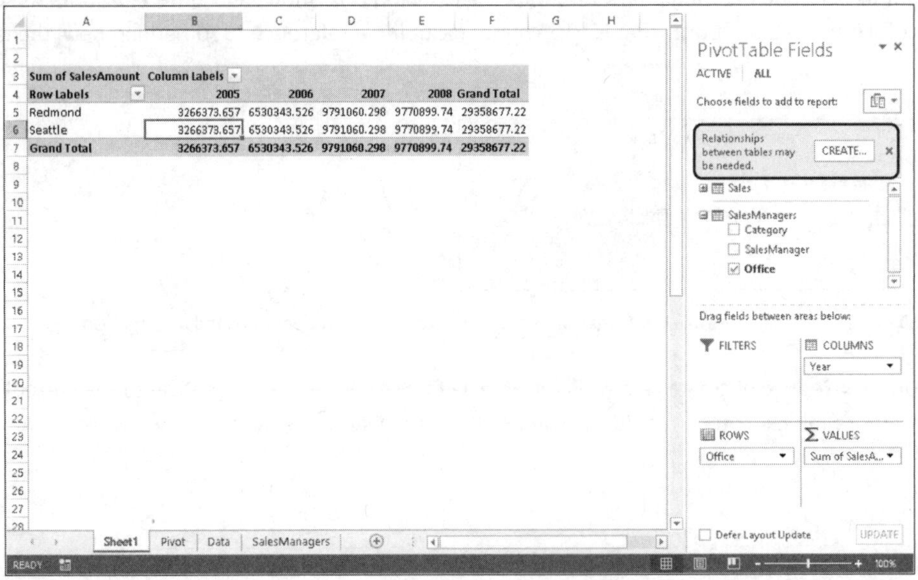

FIGURE 1-10 Adding the Office column to the PivotTable shows incorrect results and a warning about relationships.

As you might imagine, creating the relationship is the key to make the PivotTable show correct values. However, before doing it, it is worth learning more about what a relationship is.

Understanding relationships

At this point, there are two tables: Sales and SalesManagers. Each sale concerns a product, and the product has a category. Each category has a sales manager, and the relationship between a category and its sales manager is stored in the SalesManagers table. In order to bring a sales manager's name into the sales table, you previously used VLOOKUP to search for the category name in the SalesManagers table and, after it found the category, grab the associated sales manager's name.

In more technical terms, we can say that there is a relationship between the Sales and the SalesManagers tables, based on the Category column. To be more precise, the relationship is defined as follows:

- **Source Table** The source table from where the relationship starts. In this example, it is the Sales table, which contains only the ProductCategory column.

- **Foreign Key Column** The column in the source table that contains the value to search. In this example, the column is ProductCategory, the category of the product, which we have used as the first parameter of VLOOKUP.

- **Related Table** The table that contains the values to look for. In this example, the related table is the SalesManager table, which contains both the product category and the sales manager's name, along with that person's office.

- **Related Column** The column in the related table containing the value that should match the foreign key column. In the example, the column is Category, in the SalesManager table.

Think of a relationship as a sort of automatic VLOOKUP. In fact, the parameters of a relationship are very similar to the parameters of VLOOKUP. The only information missing is the value of the column to retrieve because, once a relationship is in place, it allows you to retrieve any of the columns in the related table without needing to specify which ones (as was the case with VLOOKUP, which retrieved only a single column from the related table).

With this new information, click the CREATE... button and create the relationship, filling the boxes with the values shown in Figure 1-11.

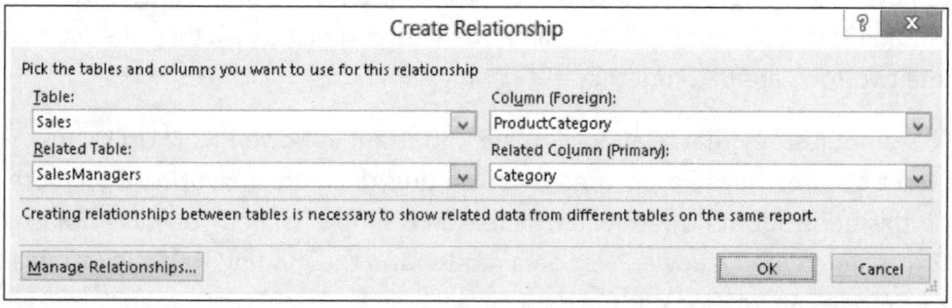

Create Relationship

Pick the tables and columns you want to use for this relationship

Table:
Sales

Column (Foreign):
ProductCategory

Related Table:
SalesManagers

Related Column (Primary):
Category

Creating relationships between tables is necessary to show related data from different tables on the same report.

Manage Relationships...   OK   Cancel

FIGURE 1-11 Here are the correct parameters to enter to create the relationship.

Note PowerPivot for Excel 2010, the previous version of this add-in, had an engine that automatically detected relationships, making life easier in some cases. Unfortunately, the detection algorithm used a heuristic to check for the existence of relationships, and in some rare cases, it could detect the relationship incorrectly. For this reason, no automatic detection happens in Excel 2013; it is up to you to define the relationship. Although this characteristic might seem to be a downgrade, it really is a welcome development: it is always better to be safe when creating a relationship, and in this case, the human brain is much better than a heuristic algorithm.

Clicking OK will make Excel create the relationship and update the content of the PivotTable, which now shows correct values arranged by office. Figure 1-12 shows the result, where the SalesManager column from the SalesManagers table is placed on the rows.

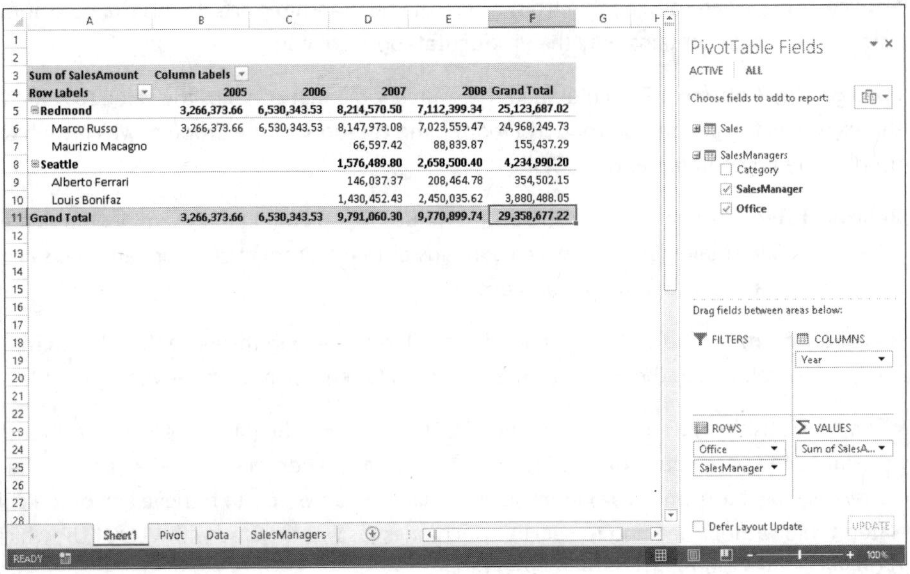

FIGURE 1-12 The PivotTable shows the correct results once the relationship is set.

Relationships play a very important role in PowerPivot, and you will learn a lot more about them from this book. For now, it is enough to think of a relationship as a way to tie together two tables, using a column in both. If two columns share the same value for a specific row, then the relationship has a match, and the two rows are tied together.

But . . . wait! Did we not just say that relationships are important in PowerPivot? Up to now, you have not used PowerPivot—you have simply used Excel features to create a PivotTable on more than one table. So why is this book about PowerPivot? The reason is simple: even if you have not explicitly used PowerPivot, Excel has created a PowerPivot data model, and the multiple-table PivotTable is, in reality, browsing that model. So let's look at the data model.

Understanding the data model

As Figure 1-8 previously demonstrated, the confirmation window asked you to create a new PivotTable using the data model. It did not explain what a data model is, nor why it is needed if you want to show more than one table in the PivotTable, but it was clear about the fact that the new PivotTable would use the data model. Thus, it is interesting to understand better what the data model is before diving into more advanced topics.

Excel tables are exactly what their name suggests: they are tables. You can have hundreds of tables in an Excel workbook, but each table is separated from the others. This is why you can create a PivotTable over a single table: adding more than one table to a PivotTable is meaningless because they share nothing. The key to turn a set of tables into a data model is the existence of relationships. If many tables are connected by relationships, then it is useful to show them all together inside a PivotTable because filtering a table, as a side effect, filters other, related tables as well.

In this example, putting a filter on the Office column of the SalesManagers table included a filter on the Sales table. In fact, rows with information about the Seattle office showed only values about categories that are handled by Seattle personnel. The reason why the Sales table is filtered by Office is because each sale is pertinent to a sales manager who works in an office. The relationship between the two tables makes this mechanism work. Thus, the following is true:

- A set of tables is nothing but a set of separate tables.

- A set of tables with relationships holding among them is a data model.

Excel 2013 introduced the concept of a data model as one of the tools available to users to analyze data. Each Excel table can belong to the data model: it is automatically added to the data model as soon as a relationship is defined on the table, either as the source or as the target of the relationship.

All this seems fine, but what has PowerPivot got in common with this description of a data model? The data model in Excel is, in reality, a PowerPivot data model. Whenever you add a table to the data model, you are really adding the table to the PowerPivot database that lives inside the Excel workbook.

The PowerPivot data model and the Excel table are two distinct entities. If you add an Excel table to the data model, you are not transforming the Excel table into a PowerPivot one. What happens is that the data in the Excel table is copied into a PowerPivot table. The two tables are then linked, so that if you update the original Excel table and refresh the PivotTable, the updates are imported into the PivotTable data model. But, from the point of view of storage, the data is really duplicated in two places: the original table in Excel and a copy in PowerPivot.

Creating a data model is very simple. It happens automatically as soon as Excel detects that it needs to create a data model to solve your specific needs. In this case, Excel turned the tables into a PowerPivot data model as soon as it was necessary to create a PivotTable with more than one table. To accomplish this task, Excel created a PowerPivot data model for use, effectively eliminating the need to completely understand what is happening under the surface.

Nevertheless, it is important to understand that by using these automatic features, you are using only a very small portion of the real power of PowerPivot. In order to exploit all PowerPivot features, you will need to learn how to work with the PowerPivot data model by itself, without simply relying on the automatic usage of the PowerPivot engine, as Excel does.

Querying the data model

In the previous section of this chapter, you learned that, by means of creating relationships among tables, you can create a PowerPivot data model inside your Excel workbook. Once the data model has been created for the first time, it can be queried with many PivotTables, without the need to add more tables to the same model. This section discusses how to perform this operation, which, although not very easy to find, is very convenient.

If you create a new PivotTable, Excel prompts you with the Create PivotTable dialog box, shown in Figure 1-13.

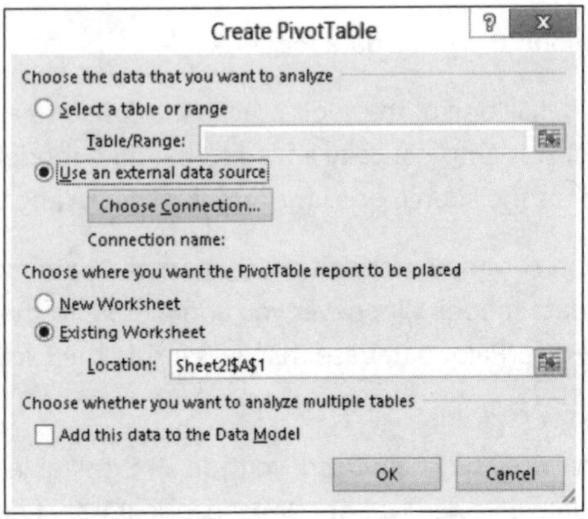

FIGURE 1-13 The Create PivotTable dialog box prompts you for the parameters of a new PivotTable.

From this dialog box, instead of choosing a range, as you are probably used to doing, you should choose Use An External Data Source and then click Choose Connection. Excel shows the external connection that can be used and, on the Tables tab, lists both the Excel tables and the data model, as shown in Figure 1-14.

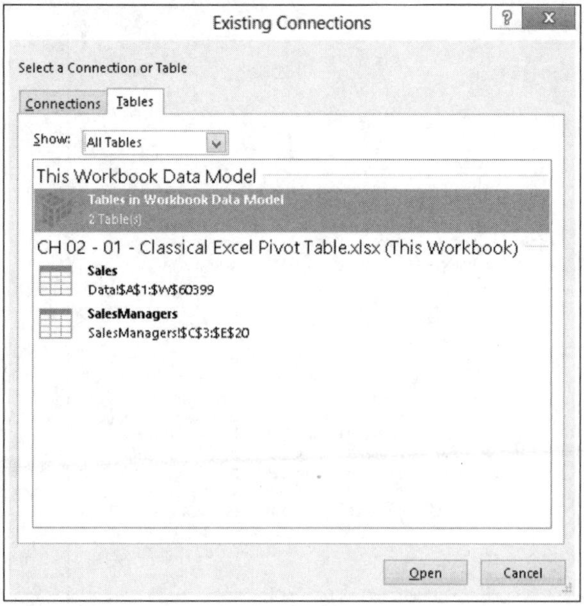

FIGURE 1-14 The list of external tables contains the Workbook data model, which is also the PowerPivot data model.

Selecting the Workbook data model and confirming everything up to the end of the PivotTable creation process leads you to a new PivotTable connected to the same data model that you previously created, based on the original Excel tables.

The PowerPivot add-In

In the previous sections of this chapter, you learned that the new features of Excel 2013 require you to create a PowerPivot data model to work with, and that this data model can be created without enabling the PowerPivot add-in, which comes preinstalled but disabled. Once the data model has been created, you can query it with a PivotTable (or, as you will see later in this chapter, with Power View). If, on the other hand, you want to look at the data model, Excel does not offer a way to analyze it or simply look at its content. In order to see the data model, you need to enable the PowerPivot add-in, as you are going to learn in this section.

To enable the PowerPivot add-in, you need to open the Excel options, select Add-Ins, and choose the COM Add-Ins, as shown in Figure 1-15.

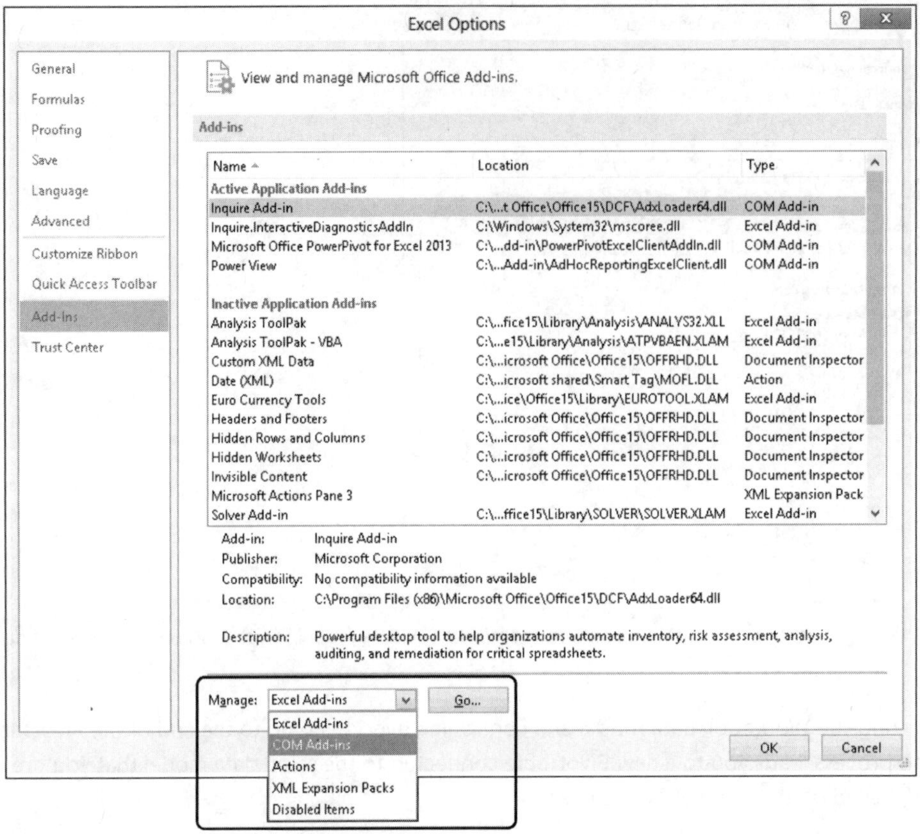

FIGURE 1-15 You will need to enable the PowerPivot add-in to use the new PowerPivot features.

Once you have selected COM Add-Ins, click Go to open the list of COM add-ins available, as shown in Figure 1-16.

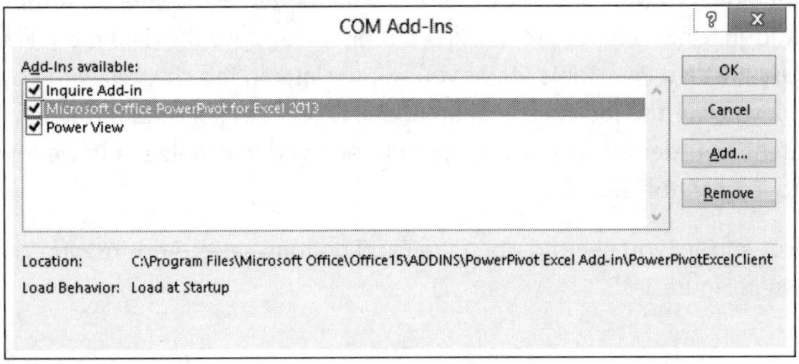

FIGURE 1-16 In the list of COM add-ins, you can enable or disable the PowerPivot add-in.

To enable the PowerPivot add-in, you simply have to select the Microsoft Office PowerPivot For Excel 2013 check box and then click OK. While you are here, it is a good idea to enable the Power View add-in (if it's disabled), which is going to come in handy shortly. To do this, simply select the

Power View check box. Power View is another great addition to your Excel analytical experience, and it works with the PowerPivot data model too.

Once the PowerPivot add-in has been enabled, you will see a new tab on the Excel ribbon named PowerPivot, which you can see in Figure 1-17.

FIGURE 1-17 The PowerPivot tab on the Excel ribbon is enabled as soon as you enable the PowerPivot add-in.

From here, you will be able to use a wide number of exciting functions, which this book is going to explain. For now, we are interested only in opening the PowerPivot window and taking a very quick tour of the data model that you just created. In order to open the PowerPivot window, you need to click the Manage button on the ribbon, which opens the main PowerPivot window, as Figure 1-18 shows.

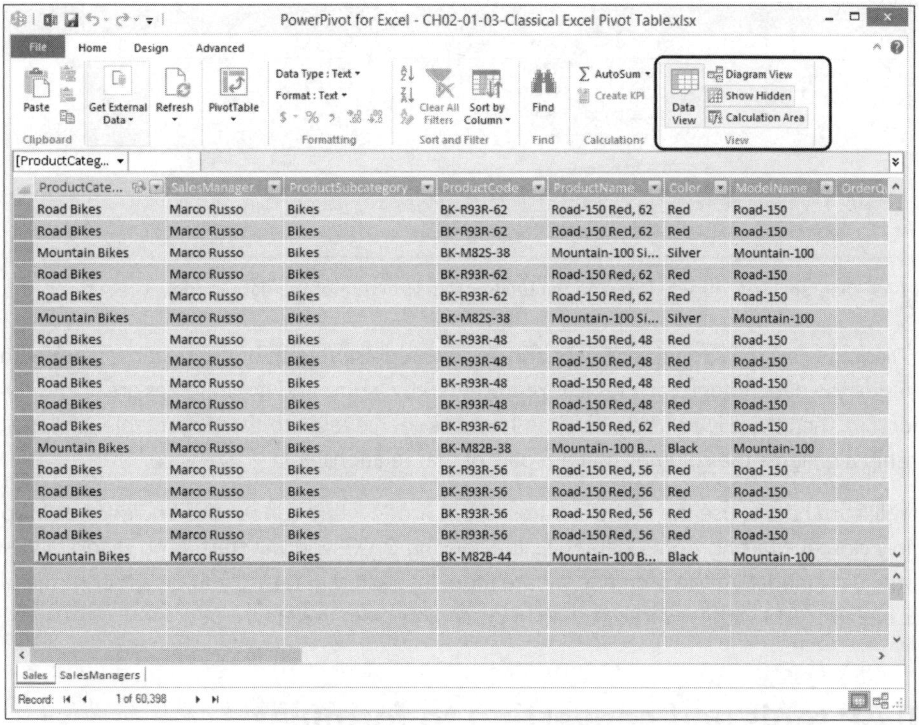

FIGURE 1-18 The PowerPivot window is the main window that lets you use PowerPivot advanced features.

The PowerPivot window opens by default in Data view, showing the content of the PowerPivot tables that are present in the model. You can browse the rows and, at the bottom of the window, you can see the tabs of the tables already loaded in the data model. For now, we are not interested in exploring all the features of this window. We want to use it to take only a brief look at the data model. In order to look at the data model, you need to click the Diagram View button on the ribbon.

As a result, the PowerPivot window switches from Data view to Diagram view is a very convenient way of visualizing the data model because, instead of focusing on the content of the tables, it shows the structure of the relationships, making it easier to represent relationships graphically, as shown in Figure 1-19.

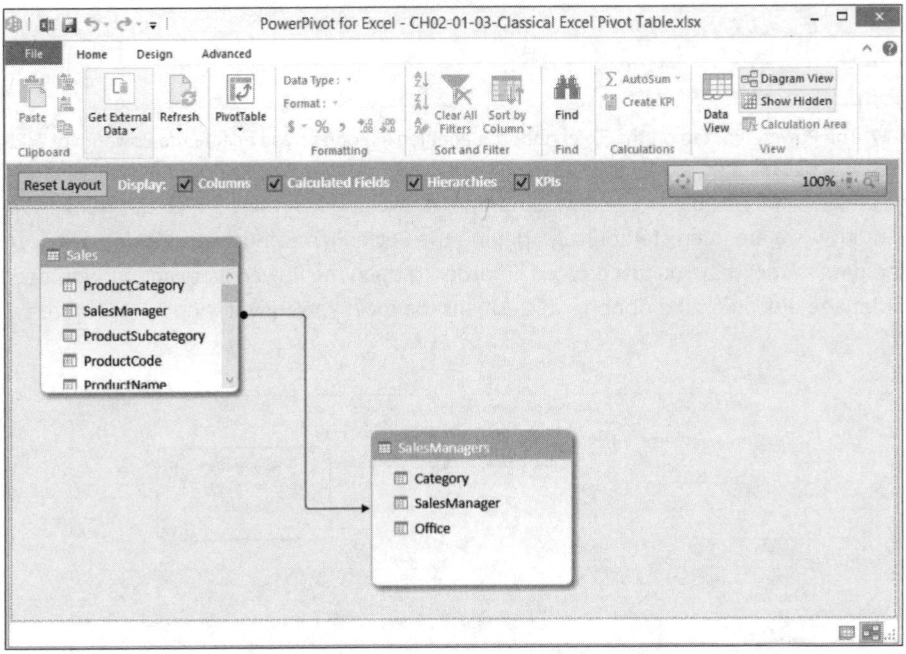

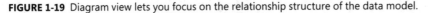

FIGURE 1-19 Diagram view lets you focus on the relationship structure of the data model.

The Diagram view is a canonical "boxes and arrows" representation of the relational model that is stored inside the data model. Each table is represented by a box, and if two tables are linked through a relationship, then there is an arrow running from the source table to the target table. Clicking a relationship highlights the columns that are part of that relationship.

You will learn how to use the many features of this window throughout this book; for now, you can simply close it. Starting from Chapter 3, "Introducing DAX," you will start using Diagram view to modify the data model. At the moment, we are more interested in taking you on a tour of the main features of Excel 2013 with PowerPivot than in describing them in detail.

Using OLAP tools and converting to formulas

One of the new features of Excel, which is available on the data model but not on the single-table PivotTable, is the OLAP Tools section. This set of features was originally available only on PivotTables built on top of OLAP databases (hence its name), but because of the nature of the data model, which is in reality a PowerPivot database, the feature is now available with the data model too.

PivotTables are really powerful tools to explore data. Nevertheless, they very often serve as the first step in the production of complex reports that gather data from PivotTables, perform computations and formatting, and provide the final results in compact reports, sometimes called *dashboards*. Roughly speaking, a dashboard is nothing but a report containing several pieces of information (each one taken from a query to the database), resulting in a very compact representation of the company status.

Suppose that you want to produce a report containing total sales, the growth in percentage of total sales, and the percentage of Internet and reseller sales of the last three years. The report should contain information divided by region, so that you can use it to find which regions need your attention.

Figure 1-20 shows such a report in its final form, which you can find in the workbook "CH01-02-Dashboard.xlsx."

	Total Sales			Growth		2006		2007		2008	
	2006	2007	2008	2007	2008	Internet	Resell	Internet	Resell	Internet	Resell
Europe	1,478,106	4,757,754	13,553,399	222%	185%	100%		40%	60%	41%	59%
France	414,245	2,061,420	4,772,398	398%	132%	100%		31%	69%	33%	67%
Germany	513,353	593,247	3,768,095	16%	535%	100%		100%		47%	53%
United Kingdom	-	2,103,087	5,012,905		138%			33%	67%	43%	57%
North America	19,313,719	26,826,465	33,182,889	39%	24%	16%	84%	6%	94%	20%	80%
Canada	3,652,908	5,920,180	6,771,829	62%	14%	16%	84%	5%	95%	16%	84%
United States	15,660,811	20,906,285	26,411,060	33%	26%	16%	84%	7%	93%	21%	79%
Central	2,024,176	2,812,658	3,072,175	39%	9%		100%	0%	100%	0%	100%
Northeast	1,182,920	3,354,277	2,402,177	184%	-28%		100%	0%	100%	0%	100%
Northwest	4,181,083	4,006,507	7,887,187	-4%	97%	22%	78%	15%	85%	27%	73%
Southeast	2,857,048	2,483,826	2,538,667	-13%	2%		100%	0%	100%	0%	100%
Southwest	5,415,584	8,249,017	10,510,854	52%	27%	28%	72%	10%	90%	32%	68%
Pacific	2,568,701	2,099,585	5,977,815	-18%	185%	100%		100%		73%	27%
Australia	2,568,701	2,099,585	5,977,815	-18%	185%	100%		100%		73%	27%

FIGURE 1-20 Here, you can see a simple dashboard created from a PivotTable.

We are not interested in these specific results; the focus here is on the technique. So, having a clear idea of the results you want to produce, let's take a closer look at the problems you will need to solve:

- The first issue concerns the geographical slicing. In the final report, you have data at the group, country, and region levels, but countries with only one region have been compacted to remove the region level, which is useless. This is something that the PivotTable will not handle by itself, even though it is a very common request for reports.

- The headers contain total sales and growth divided by year (and the selection of years in the two columns is different, since growth is not shown for 2006). Moreover, in the columns header, you want to show years divided by sales type (Internet and reseller). This mixed kind of slicing is not something that can be realized with a PivotTable.

- Data inside the cells is a mix of Internet and reseller sales for some cells (the total sales ones); other cells display the ratio of Internet or reseller sales to the total.

- Moreover, via the Conditional Formatting option in Excel, the report shows cells of various colors that will direct the reader's attention to the most interesting data. Clearly, the conditional formatting uses different formulas for different cells.

- Needless to say, you cannot produce such a report by using any type of PivotTable. Nevertheless, you surely can produce the original values needed to compute each single cell by using one or more PivotTables. All you need to do is to create some PivotTables that perform the computation and then use standard Excel formulas to move the original piece of data inside the dashboard.

You can start building this dashboard by creating the PivotTable shown in Figure 1-21, using a simple PivotTable that shows sales amounts from the FactResellerSales table.

Sum of SalesAmount	Column Labels		
Row Labels	2006	2007	2008
⊟ Europe		2,834,512.33	8,036,022.46
⊟ France		1,428,020.38	3,179,517.56
France		1,428,020.38	3,179,517.56
⊟ Germany			1,983,988.04
Germany			1,983,988.04
⊟ United Kingdom		1,406,491.96	2,872,516.87
United Kingdom		1,406,491.96	2,872,516.87
⊟ North America	16,288,441.77	25,087,158.18	26,610,126.86
⊟ Canada	3,079,806.81	5,615,169.14	5,682,949.64
Canada	3,079,806.81	5,615,169.14	5,682,949.64
⊟ United States	13,208,634.95	19,471,989.04	20,927,177.22
Central	2,024,175.80	2,810,586.67	3,071,245.71
Northeast	1,182,920.47	3,352,228.07	2,397,693.48
Northwest	3,255,251.43	3,386,959.80	5,792,864.77
Southeast	2,857,047.77	2,480,188.69	2,530,179.76
Southwest	3,889,239.48	7,442,025.82	7,135,193.50
⊟ Pacific			1,594,335.38
⊟ Australia			1,594,335.38
Australia			1,594,335.38
Grand Total	16,288,441.77	27,921,670.52	36,240,484.70

FIGURE 1-21 This PivotTable is the starting point for this dashboard.

This PivotTable, together with a very similar one built on top of Internet sales, contains the basic information needed to build the dashboard. Now, since this is a PowerPivot workbook, you might expect to build a very complex DAX formula that will magically build the dashboard, but this is not the case. PivotTables are useful to explore data in an interactive way, but there is no need to push them too far from their natural inclinations. Once you have data available, Excel moves it inside the dashboard and performs further computations.

You can start building your dashboard based on the PivotTable that you just made, creating formulas that move information from the PivotTable to the dashboard. Nevertheless, PivotTables are dynamic by their very nature. They can change their size if new values appear inside the source tables. Thus, if you reference directly the cells inside a PivotTable, you are at risk of needing to update formulas as the source data is updated. It would be much better if you found a way to fix the PivotTable so that it cannot change its size dynamically.

Luckily, Excel has an option that will help you to convert the dynamic PivotTable in a set of static formulas that show the same data, but without the PivotTable's dynamic nature. You will lose the ability to navigate through your data, but on the other hand, you will gain the immobility of cells.

On the ANALYZE tab of the Excel ribbon, there is a button called OLAP Tools, which contains several features. One of these is Convert To Formulas, as shown in Figure 1-22.

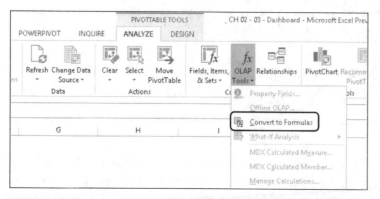

FIGURE 1-22 The Convert To Formulas option is available for PivotTables based on the data model.

If you choose this option, the PivotTable is deleted and returns as a standard Excel worksheet that contains a formula for each of the original cells (see Figure 1-23).

Sum of SalesAmount	Columns Labels			
Row Labels	2005	2006	2007	2008
Europe			2,834,512.33	8,036,022.46
France			1,428,020.38	3,179,517.56
France			1,428,020.38	3,179,517.56
Germany				1,983,988.04
Germany			1,406,491.96	1,983,988.04
United Kingdom			1,406,491.96	2,872,516.87
United Kingdom			1,406,491.96	2,872,516.87
North America		16,288,441.77	25,087,158.18	26,610,126.86
Canada		3,079,806.81	5,615,169.14	5,682,949.64
Canada		3,079,806.81	5,615,169.14	5,682,949.64
United States		13,208,634.95	19,471,989.04	20,927,177.22
Central		2,024,175.80	2,810,586.67	3,071,245.71
Northeast		1,182,920.47	3,352,228.07	2,397,693.48
Northwast		3,255,251.43	3,386,959.80	5,792,864.77
Southeast		2,857,047.77	2,480,188.69	2,530,179.76
Southwest		3,889,239.48	7,442,025.82	7,135,193.50
Pacific				1,594,335.38
Australia				1,594,335.38
Australia				1,594,335.38
Grand Total		16,288,441.77	27,921,670.52	36,240,484.70

FIGURE 1-23 The worksheet that contained PivotTable, after Convert To Formulas has been applied.

Now it is worth taking a look at the formulas inside the cells. They are of two different types:

- **CUBEMEMBER** This type of formula is used for the headers of both columns and rows. It returns an object, called a *member*, which is basically the value of a column in a table. For example, the formula inside the "2008" header contains:

```
=CUBEMEMBER("ThisWorkbookDataModel","[DimTime].[FiscalYear].&[2008]")
```

This can be read as: Return the value of the column FiscalYear in table DimTime where the value is "2008."

The formula might be confusing because its return value is "2008" and we provide "2008" as the parameter, which doesn't seem to make sense. This has to do with the internals of PowerPivot, which reasons in terms of members and values of an OLAP cube. Moreover, it might be worth noting at this point that the syntax used for the expressions in CUBEMEMBER and CUBEVALUE is not DAX syntax—it is MDX. Excel still uses MDX to interact with PowerPivot.

- **CUBEVALUE** This type of formula is used for the cells inside the table. Each cell asks for a value giving the set of members that form the coordinates of the requested value. For example, in the case of sales in North America for 2009, the coordinates are:

  - [Measures].[Sum of SalesAmount]

  - [DimTime].[FiscalYear].&[2009]

  - [DimSalesTerritory].[SalesTerritoryGroup].&[North America]

The result is the value of the measure SalesAmount in 2009 for North America.

Readers used to OLAP databases will recognize in these formulas the standard set of coordinates used to navigate over OLAP cubes. In fact, at the very end, PowerPivot stores its data inside cubes that are automatically processed by PowerPivot itself, which is something that we are going to show later in this chapter.

Now, it is not important to take this digression too far. The real interesting aspect of this is that the worksheet is now composed of formulas (the PivotTable disappeared) and the formulas can be moved wherever you want. Moreover, even if the source data changes, Excel will not change the position of any cell.

You can now create a new worksheet and proceed to write your dashboard, referencing the values inside this new set of cells. The only caution is that if a cube does not return any data, it is returned by CUBEMEMBER as an empty string. Thus, whenever you need to reference its value, you need to surround it with an IF, as in the cell Total Sales in Europe for 2006 in Figure 1-20, which contains this formula:

```
= IF( Internet!D5 = "", 0, Internet!D5 ) + IF( Resellers!D5 = "", 0, Resellers!D5 )
```

The only precaution to take when using values coming from an OLAP cube is to remember that empty values are empty strings, not numbers. The remaining part of the dashboard can be easily created by using standard Excel formulas and some formatting, all of which is already well known and documented.

> **Note** Results from OLAP cubes are always strings, so the *ISBLANK* function in Excel will not help here.

The really interesting part of this section is not the dashboard itself, but the fact that, by converting a PivotTable into formulas, you can use data from PowerPivot as the first brick of a more complex workbook, which uses the original data to provide values, indicators, and other information that can be processed later with the full power of Excel at hand.

Understanding PowerPivot for Excel 2013

Now that you have used the PowerPivot data model for the first time, it is worthwhile to learn some basics about what the PowerPivot engine is before delving into all its features. This section of the chapter will give you a general understanding of this topic. It is not strictly required to use PowerPivot, at least at a basic level; however, we believe that it is interesting. You can consider it as a small digression, just to give you some general background on the topic of columnar databases.

PowerPivot for Excel 2013 is, in reality, the Tabular engine of SQL Server Analysis Services 2012, running in process inside Excel. The PowerPivot engine is called the xVelocity analytics engine, and it is a space-saving columnar database running completely in memory.

Most databases, including SQL Server, are row-oriented databases, and they are easy to understand because they work in a very natural way: every table of the database stores data row by row, exactly the way you see data on the screen.

For example, consider the following table of data:

ID_Author	FirstName	LastName	Blog	Posts
1	Alberto	Ferrari	http://sqlblog.com/blogs/alberto_ferrari	27
2	Maurizio	Macagno	http://adventureworks.com/blogs/mmacagno	43
3	Marco	Russo	http://sqlblog.com/blogs/marco_russo	38

A row-oriented database physically stores data row by row. For example, the second item in the list contains all the columns of the row describing Maurizio's data, in a way that can be expressed in this table:

Row ID	Row Data
1	1, Alberto, Ferrari, http://sqlblog.com/blogs/alberto_ferrari, 27
2	2, Maurizio, Macagno, http://adventureworks.com/blogs/mmacagno , 43
3	3, Marco, Russo, http://sqlblog.com/blogs/marco_russo, 38

The physical implementation depends on the database product. For example, SQL Server divides the storage space into pages and every page stores one or more rows. Other databases might use different techniques, but the important point is that data is stored row-wise.

In general, a row-oriented database requires a full scan of all the rows of a table if you want to query all the values of a single column of a table (that is, to compute an aggregation). The cost of a complete table scan is the same regardless of the number of columns requested.

A column-oriented database uses a different approach. Instead of considering the row of a table as the main unit of storage, it considers every column as a separate entity and stores data for every column in a separate way. For example, you might imagine that data of our initial table is logically stored in this way:

Column Name	Column Data
ID_Author	1, 2, 3
FirstName	Alberto, Maurizio, Marco
LastName	Ferrari, Macagno, Russo
Blog	http://sqlblog.com/blogs/alberto_ferrari, http://adventureworks.com/blogs/mmacagno, http://sqlblog.com/blogs/marco_russo
Posts	27, 43, 38

This makes it very fast to query data for a single column, but it requires a higher computational effort to retrieve data for several columns of a single row. The worst-case scenario is the request of all the columns from a row, which requires access to the storage of all the rows. For example, to retrieve Maurizio's data, Maurizio must be identified in the FirstName column. Because it is the second element in the column, getting the second element from every other column will retrieve all of Maurizio's data. Moreover, to calculate the total number of posts of all the authors, it will be necessary to access only the Posts column data.

From the point of view of data retrieval, a column-oriented database might be faster because data access is optimized for many query scenarios. In fact, the most frequent requests in an analytical system require data from only a few columns, usually to aggregate data from a column by grouping results according to the value of other columns.

In Figure 1-24, you can see a comparison between row-based and column-based storages.

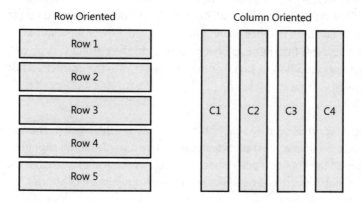

FIGURE 1-24 Row-oriented vs. column-oriented databases.

PowerPivot is also an in-memory database. This means that it has been designed and optimized on the assumption that the whole database is loaded into memory. To store more data and improve performance, data is kept compressed in memory as well, and it is dynamically uncompressed during each query.

Creating a Power View report

Power View is a great reporting tool that is integrated into Excel 2013 as an add-in. It needs to be activated following the very same procedure that you used previously to enable the PowerPivot add-in. Once it is activated, you will have the option to create Power View reports based on the PowerPivot data model.

Power View does not work with Excel tables; it only works with the data model. Thus, if you create a Power View report, all the tables you use in the report will be automatically added to the data model, same as with the PivotTable, when you added more than one table to the PivotTable report. Because Power View works only with the data model, when you create a Power View report, you don't have the option to choose the source of data—it is the data model by default. You can find the Power View reports built in this section in the companion workbook: "CH01-03-Power View Report.xlsx."

To create a Power View report once the add-in has been activated, you need to use the Power View button on the INSERT tab of the Excel ribbon, as shown in Figure 1-25.

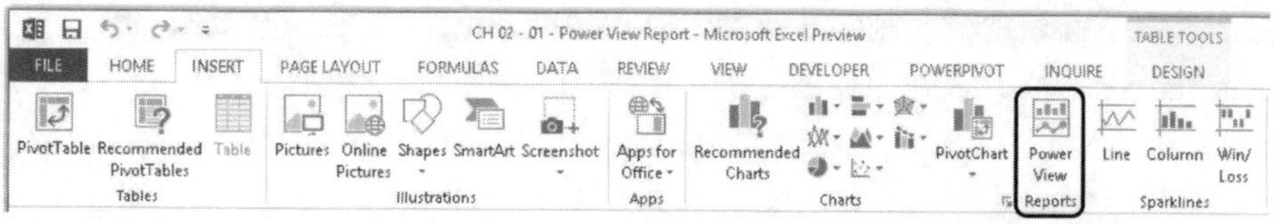

FIGURE 1-25 You can use the Power View button to create a new Power View report.

> **Note** Power View requires the Silverlight component to be installed on your system. If you have never installed Silverlight, Power View will prompt you to do so, directing you to the website where you can download it. Once Silverlight is installed, Power View will work fine. You will need to use Microsoft Internet Explorer to download the correct version of Silverlight; downloading it using a different browser might not activate the correct version of Silverlight that Excel needs.

Now you will create a simple report using the same workbook created in this chapter. The Power View environment is designed to be simple: most of its features require a single mouse click to be activated, and you do not have all the configuration options available in classical Excel charts. The major benefit of Power View is that it can create beautiful reports with a minimum of effort.

Once the Power View report is opened, you will see an empty canvas on the left of the window and the list of tables in the data model in the right panel, which resembles the PivotTable Field list. To start creating your first report, expand the Sales table and select the ProductCategory column. You will see the list of categories in a new table in the canvas. Then, selecting the SalesAmount column, Power View will add the total sales amount to each row of the table, showing the total sales for each category. At this point, the Excel window will look like Figure 1-26.

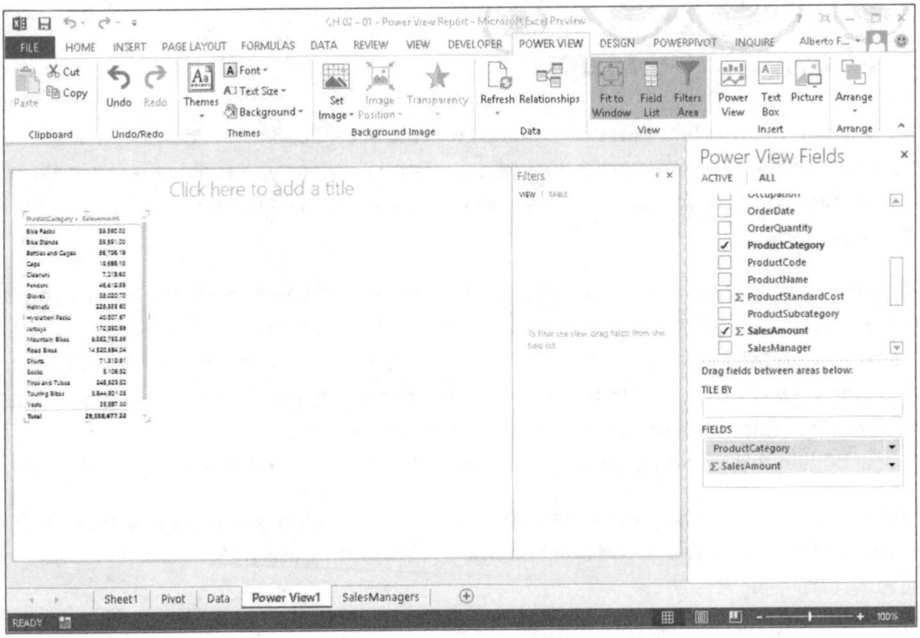

FIGURE 1-26 The Power View report shows categories and sales.

The idea of Power View is to start with data and decide only later what format you want to use for them. For example, suppose that you are interested in creating a report that shows the total sales for each category (which you already did) and, beside them, a report that shows the sales divided by geographical area.

Because you already have completed the first step, you now need to create a new table containing the country of sale, along with the total sales amount. This can be easily done by clicking in the empty area of the Power View canvas and then selecting the TerritoryCountry column first, and then the SalesAmount column. At this point, your report should look like the one in Figure 1-27.

Sales by Category and Geography

ProductCatagory ▲	SalesAmount		TerritoryCountry	SalesAmount
Bike Racks	39,360.00		Australia	9,061,000.58
Bike Stands	39,591.00		Canada	1,977,844.86
Bottles and Cages	56,798.19		France	2,644,017.71
Caps	19,688.10		Germany	2,894,312.34
Cleaners	7,218.60		United Kingdom	3,391,712.21
Fenders	46,619.58		United States	9,389,789.51
Gloves	35,020.70		Total	29,358,677.22
Helmets	225,335.60			
Hydration Packs	40,307.67			
Jerseys	172,950.68			
Mountain Bikes	9,952,759.56			
Road Bikes	14,520,584.04			
Shorts	71,319.81			
Socks	5,106.32			
Tires and Tubes	245,529.32			
Touring Bikes	3,844,801.05			
Vests	35,687.00			
Total	29,358,677.22			

FIGURE 1-27 The Power View report shows tabular data by default.

Although the data is there, it does not look very appealing. The tabular representation of information is less than wonderful—you need a way to show the same information with charts. Let's start with the geography. It would be much better to show the sales on a map. To perform this operation, simply select the table containing the TerritoryCountry and use the Map button on the DESIGN tab of the Excel ribbon, as shown in Figure 1-28. The table is immediately transformed into a map, where the total sales are shown by the size of the points on the map.

Tip You need an active Internet connection for the map to work because the map itself and the geographical resolution of the countries is created through the Bing web service.

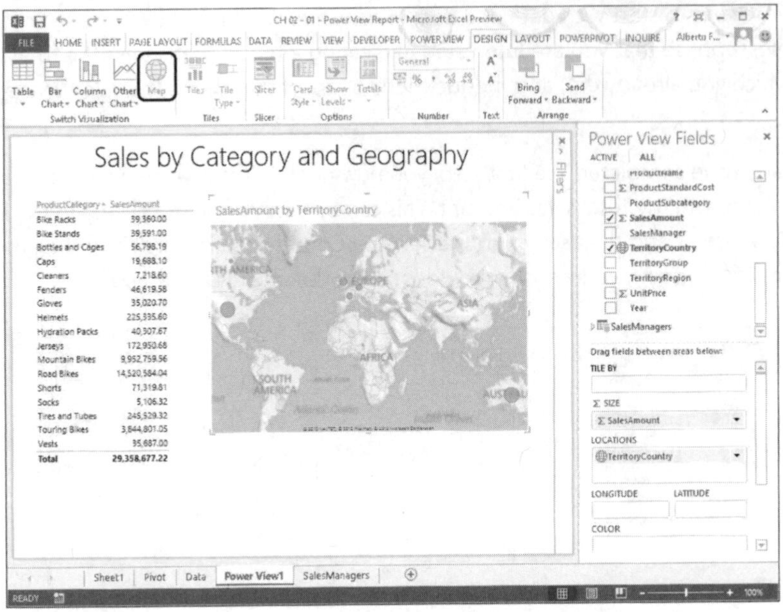

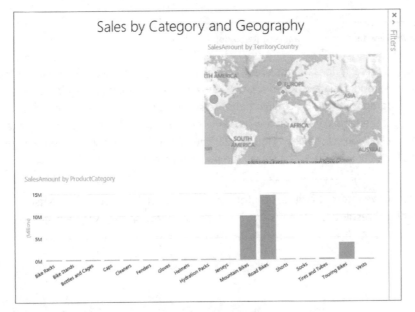

FIGURE 1-28 The Map button transforms the tabular representation into a map.

At this point, you can follow the same procedure to transform the Categories table into a Column chart, resize it, and put it below the map. You have seen that the idea of Power View is first the data, then the graphical representation. The chart, at this point, looks like the one in Figure 1-29.

FIGURE 1-29 The Categories table is now a column chart.

> **Note** Now that you started using it, it is worthwhile to discuss briefly what Power View is. Power View is a graphical data exploration tool designed to let you investigate data using charts instead of PivotTables. In this way, you can easily look at pictures instead of numbers, and when you discover something worth investigating further, then you can continue using a PivotTable, drilling down to explore the details. Power View is not a sophisticated charting environment. Its goal is to let you create charts very quickly and look at data in different formats in a simple way.

Now you can click on an empty space of the report and, following the same steps, add two tables: one with the Office column from the SalesManagers table and another one with the SalesManager column from the same table. As you might have noticed, you need to click on empty space to create a new table because if you have a table already selected, the columns on which you click will be added to the selected table.

The chart, at this point, has two tables, one map and a column chart, as shown in Figure 1-30.

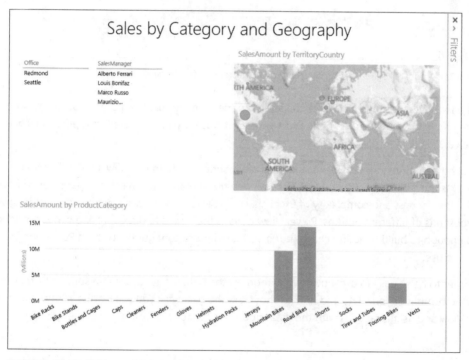

FIGURE 1-30 The Office and Salesmanager tables have been added to the report.

Finally, you can convert the last two tables into slicers, using the Slicer button on the DESIGN tab of the Excel ribbon. Converting a table into a slicer lets you use them to filter the report. As soon as you click a row of a slicer, the full report will show data using that slicer as a filter. In Figure 1-31, you can now see the final report, where we have selected the Seattle office and Alberto Ferrari as the Sales Manager.

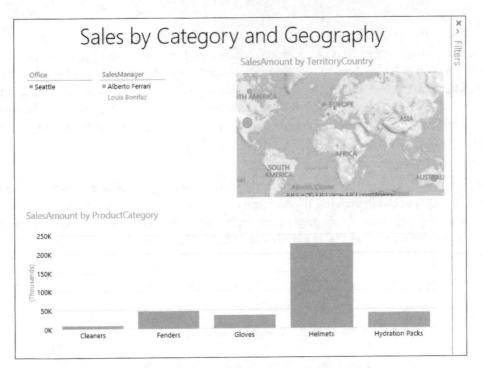
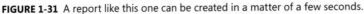

FIGURE 1-31 A report like this one can be created in a matter of a few seconds.

It is impossible to explain in a book the feeling of performing these steps live, but we are sure that the simplicity of these operations and how easy it was for you to create this report speak for themselves.

Creating beautiful graphical views of data is really simple with Power View. Remember that simplicity is the leitmotif of Power View. Do not even try to search the charting capabilities of Power View for the richness and complexity of Excel charts. Excel lets you create any type of chart by giving you thousands of different options. Power View goes in the opposite direction: a few mouse clicks are always enough to build beautiful charts, but if you need more configurability, then Power View is not the tool to use.

In order to be so easy to use, Power View requires the data model to contain some information about the content of your data and how to show it in the best way. You will learn a lot more about Power View and its interactions with the data model in Chapter 10, "Using Power View."

CHAPTER 2

Using the unique features of PowerPivot

In the previous chapter, you learned the basics of the data model in Microsoft Excel 2013, and you have seen that the key to exploiting some of the most interesting new features of Excel 2013 is the creation of a Microsoft PowerPivot data model. Finally, you learned that the PowerPivot engine works even if you do not enable the PowerPivot add-in because the xVelocity in-memory analytics engine is integrated into Excel 2013, and it starts working as soon as you create a PivotTable working on more than a single table or Power View chart.

You might be wondering at this point why you would want to enable the add-in at all, if the PowerPivot engine can be executed without using it. The reason is that Excel makes available only a small fraction of the features of PowerPivot by default. Most of the advanced, more interesting features are available only through the add-in. In this chapter, you will learn what some of these features are. Each feature will be analyzed and described in great detail later in the book. In this chapter, the goal is only to give you an overview of the most important features of PowerPivot that are available only through the add-in.

Loading data from external sources

In the examples from the previous chapters, you loaded data into Excel and then, from there, you created the PowerPivot data model. You have already learned that PowerPivot storage is different from Excel storage. Thus, by creating the data model in this way, you effectively use more than twice the space needed to work with your data.

You use more than twice the space because the PowerPivot data model uses xVelocity storage, which is highly compressed when data are loaded in memory, whereas Excel does not compress data for its tables in memory and uses a less efficient compression technique when data is stored on disk. Moreover, PowerPivot is capable of storing hundreds of millions of rows in memory, whereas Excel still is limited to 1 million of rows for a table. Thus, by loading data first in Excel and only later in the data model, you are not making good use of resources: you are hitting the limits of Excel long before you hit the limits of PowerPivot.

One of the most interesting features of PowerPivot is its ability to load data directly inside the data model, without Excel even knowing it. Doing this, you are loading data only once and in its best format (highly compressed). To give you a rough idea of what this means, note that the sales table you used in Chapter 1, "Introduction to PowerPivot," to analyze sales resulted in an Excel workbook of around 10 MB. The same table, loaded directly inside PowerPivot without the extra step of Excel loading, resulted in a workbook that was only 1 MB in size (that is, 10 times smaller).

To load data directly into the data model, you need to open the PowerPivot window from the PowerPivot tab on the ribbon by clicking the MANAGE button. Once the PowerPivot window is open, you can load data using the From Database button on the Home tab of the PowerPivot ribbon, as shown in Figure 2-1.

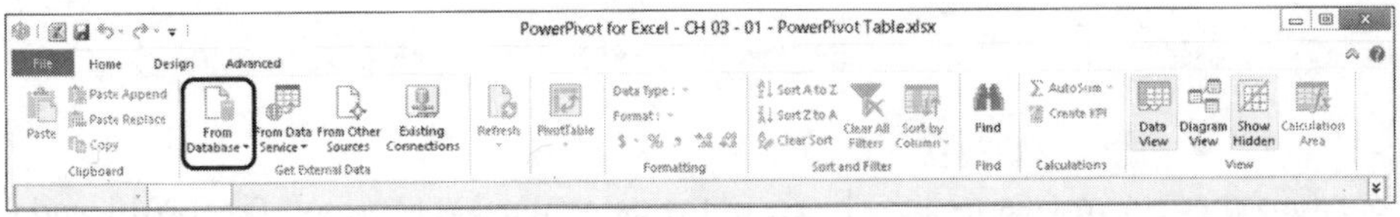

FIGURE 2-1 The From Database button lets you load data directly inside the PowerPivot data model.

A lot of different drivers can be used to load data from different databases, and they are all explained in detail in Chapter 6, "Loading Data." For the purposes of this small demonstration, we are going to use the Microsoft SQL Server connection. Thus, from the drop-down list of databases, you will need to choose From SQL Server.

At this point, PowerPivot opens the Table Import Wizard, which will guide you through the full process of data loading. The first page of the wizard (see Figure 2-2) prompts you for the connection parameters: you need to specify the name of the server that hosts the database (Demo, in this example) and the database name (AdventureWorks DW2012). You can find the workbook with data already loaded in the companion workbook: "CH02-01-PowerPivot Data Model.xlsx."

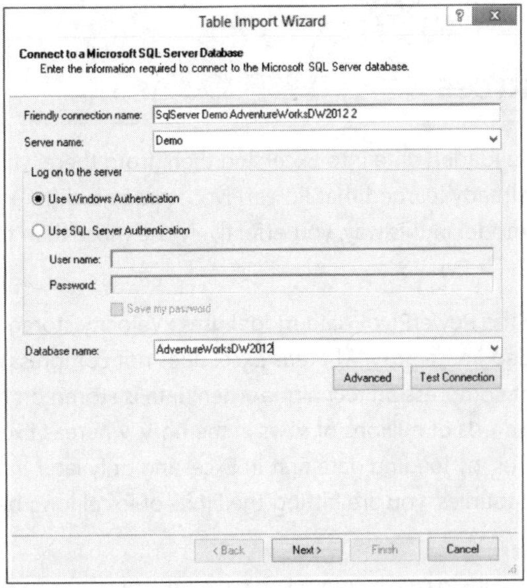

FIGURE 2-2 The Table Import Wizard asks for the basic information that is needed to perform the loading procedure.

Clicking Next takes you to the second page of the wizard, where you need to decide whether you want to load from a list of tables or from a query, as shown in Figure 2-3.

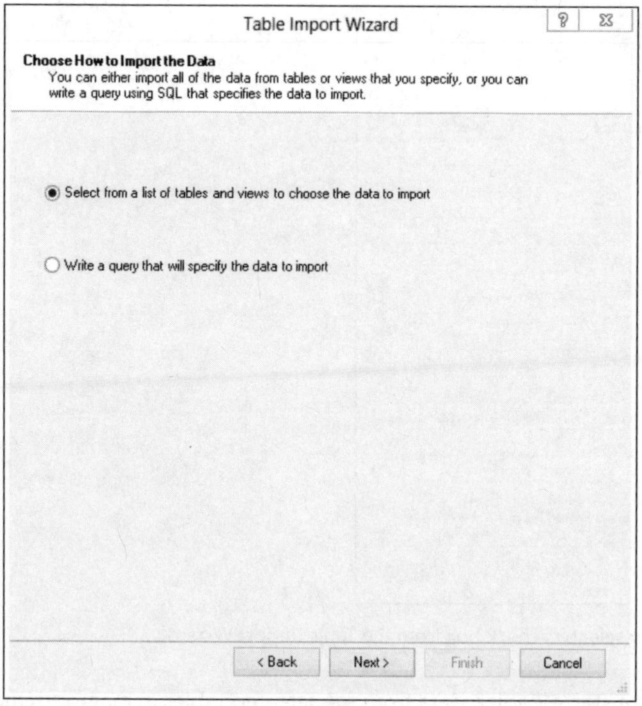

Table Import Wizard

Choose How to Import the Data
You can either import all of the data from tables or views that you specify, or you can write a query using SQL that specifies the data to import.

◉ Select from a list of tables and views to choose the data to import

○ Write a query that will specify the data to import

[< Back] [Next >] [Finish] [Cancel]

FIGURE 2-3 You can choose to load data from tables or to write an SQL query.

Loading from a query is slightly more complex because you need to know the SQL language. Thus, for this small example, it is better to choose the Select From A List Of Tables And Views To Choose The Data To Import option. The wizard shows, at this point, a list of all the tables that are available in the database, as shown in Figure 2-4.

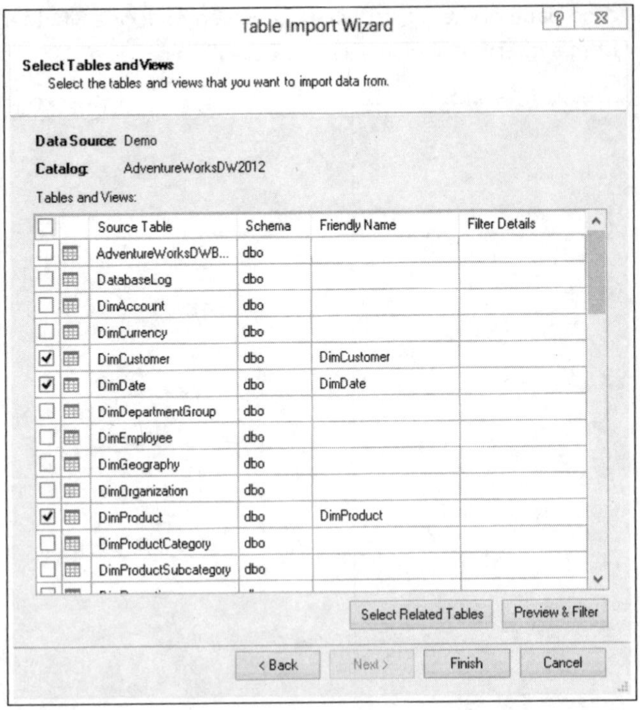

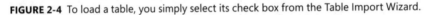

FIGURE 2-4 To load a table, you simply select its check box from the Table Import Wizard.

Once you click Finish, PowerPivot starts loading data from the selected tables in memory. Once it finishes, it shows a summary report and returns you to the PowerPivot window, which now shows all the data loaded into the PowerPivot data model.

It is interesting to note that, when PowerPivot loads tables from a server, it not only loads the data, but it also performs an extra step that analyzes any existing relationship in the database, and if the relationship can be loaded in PowerPivot, it automatically creates it.

> **Note** Situations occur where PowerPivot cannot load a relationship into the data model or when the relationship can be loaded but not activated. It is beyond the scope of this chapter to go into more detail about the specific scenarios. We will investigate this topic more in Chapter 6.

In the example, we have loaded four tables: DimProduct, DimCustomer, FactInternetSales, and DimDate. If you switch to Diagram view right after loading these tables, as shown in Figure 2-5, you will notice that several relationships are automatically created during the loading procedure because PowerPivot detected their presence in the database.

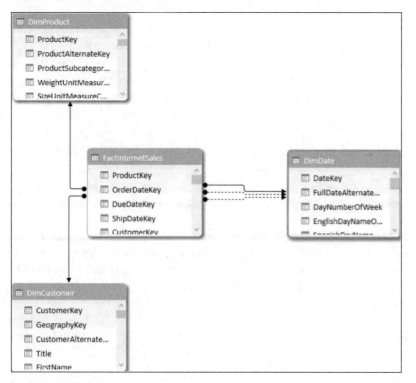

FIGURE 2-5 Relationships are automatically loaded in the data model if they are present in the source database.

As you have seen, loading data directly inside the PowerPivot data model is straightforward—incredibly, it is even easier than loading data into an Excel table. Nevertheless, there are some drawbacks to not performing the extra step of Excel loading: PowerPivot tables are read-only. Read that last sentence twice and digest it before moving on, because this is a big limitation that you always need to keep in mind when deciding whether it is better to load a table in Excel and then in PowerPivot or to skip the extra step of Excel loading.

If you load a table in Excel, then you have all Excel editing features available. If the table is loaded into PowerPivot directly, then no editing is permitted. For example, you cannot add Excel-calculated columns. That does not mean that you cannot make changes, though. In fact, with PowerPivot, you have an impressive number of calculations that can be easily performed on your table, and you can add new columns to the original tables using the DAX language. But you will not be able to modify the original content in any way. This feature might be also an advantage: it keeps you from modifying data by mistake. Either way you look at it, it remains a feature to consider when building your report.

Creating a PowerPivot PivotTable

You can create a new PivotTable on the PowerPivot data model directly from inside the PowerPivot window, by clicking the PivotTable button on the Home tab of the PowerPivot ribbon and selecting PivotTable, as shown in Figure 2-6.

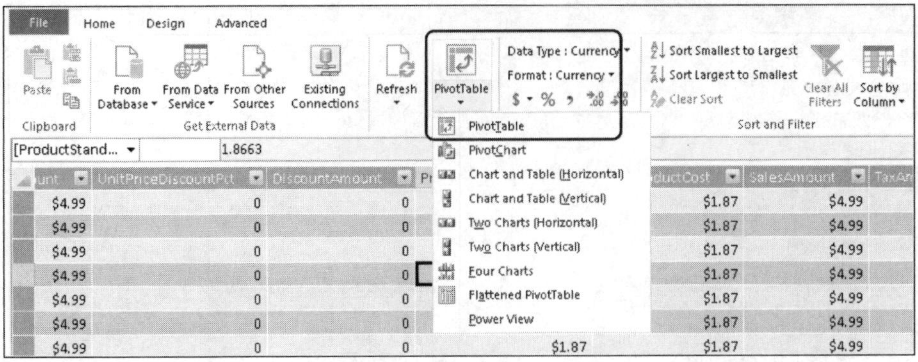

FIGURE 2-6 You can create a PivotTable from the PowerPivot window using the PivotTable button.

The dialog box that opens as soon as you select the option is a very simple one, much simpler than the one used by Excel (see Figure 2-7). The reason is that a PivotTable created from inside the PowerPivot window is—by default—a PivotTable over the PowerPivot data model. Thus, there is no need to ask for the data source or any other parameter: Excel already knows that you want to query the PowerPivot data model.

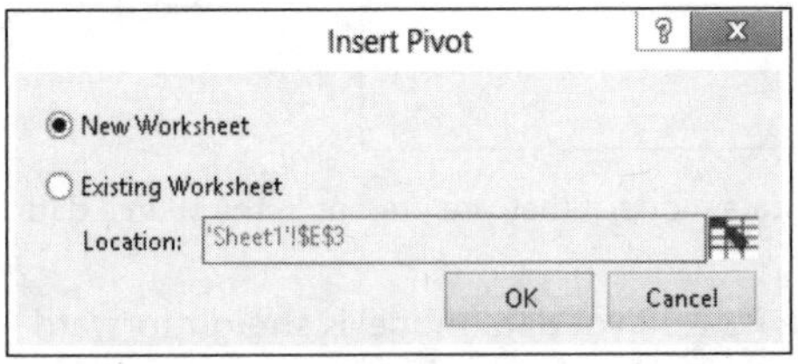

FIGURE 2-7 PivotTables created from inside PowerPivot work only on the PowerPivot data model.

Clicking OK creates a new PivotTable in a new worksheet. You can now put the Color column from the DimProduct table on the rows, the Year column from the DimDate table on the columns, and the SalesAmount column on the Values area. The resulting PivotTable is shown in Figure 2-8.

Sum of SalesAmount	Column Labels				
Row Labels	2005	2006	2007	2008	Grand Total
Black	345815.493	1728251.554	3851090.661	2913254.25	8838411.958
Blue			860380.78	1418715.5	2279096.28
Multi			42099.32	64371.42	106470.74
NA			184354.22	250762.47	435116.69
Red	2634959.004	3935630.74	953203.05	200537.73	7724330.524
Silver	285599.16	720397.3572	2044406.894	2062985.67	5113389.082
White			2229.52	2876.8	5106.32
Yellow		146063.875	1853295.853	2857395.9	4856755.628
Grand Total	3266373.657	6530343.526	9791060.298	9770899.74	29358677.22

FIGURE 2-8 This PivotTable aggregates and slices values using different tables, thanks to relationships.

It is interesting to note that with minimum effort, you have been able to aggregate and slice values from different tables, producing an interesting report from your data model. The magic that happens under the surface is due to the usage of relationships: thanks to them, you can divide sales in the FactInternetSales table using the product color and the calendar year, which are columns of other related tables.

Using the DAX language

Many chapters in this book are dedicated to the DAX language. In this introduction of the unique features of the PowerPivot add-in, you will learn why DAX is so important and the main usages of DAX.

DAX, which stands for Data Analysis eXpression language, is the language of PowerPivot and of SQL Server Analysis Services Tabular. It originated with PowerPivot for Excel 1.0, which was included in Excel 2010. In the new version of PowerPivot, it has many interesting improvements. It has been designed to be easy for Excel users to learn because it has many functions that share both name and behavior with Excel. However, it is not identical to the Excel language because the two languages work on completely different data structures.

Excel is focused on cell calculation. You define a cell and, inside the formula, you reference other cells by using their coordinates. Thus, a formula like A2+B10 is a valid formula in Excel because A2 and B10 are the coordinates of a cell. DAX is focused on tables and columns because its environment is the PowerPivot data model, which is not built on top of cells but on top of tables. You will learn the basics of DAX beginning with Chapter 3, "Introducing DAX."

Even before you know everything about DAX, you can start using it in a very simple way, by creating the two kinds of formulas that exist in the PowerPivot data model: calculated columns and calculated fields. Both kinds of calculation can be created only by using the add-in; there is no way to create calculated columns or calculated fields with the default Excel user interface.

Creating a calculated column

The easiest calculation that can be created in DAX is a calculated column. *Calculated columns* are columns stored in the data model that can extend the content of a table. They are very similar to new columns defined with formulas in an Excel table.

Let's start with the PivotTable shown previously in Figure 2-8. There, you have aggregated the sales amount, dividing it by color and year. If you are interested in profitability, the sales amount is only one term of the equation—you need to take into account at least the product cost in order to determine the margin. Thus, you can add the TotalProductCost column from the FactInternetSales table to the values area of the PivotTable, and the result is a single PivotTable showing both values side by side, as shown in Figure 2-9.

Column Labels				
	2005		2006		2007
Row Labels	Sum of SalesAmount	Sum of TotalProductCost	Sum of SalesAmount	Sum of TotalProductCost	Sum of SalesAmount
Black	345815.493	195784.9111	1728251.554	1001103.186	3851090.661
Blue					860380.78
Multi					42099.32
NA					184354.22
Red	2634959.004	1598361.906	3935630.74	2397388.037	953203.05
Silver	285599.16	160620.9696	720397.3572	396577.3682	2044406.894
White					2229.52
Yellow			146063.875	88424.7832	1853295.853
Grand Total	3266373.657	1954767.787	6530343.526	3883493.375	9791060.298

FIGURE 2-9 By default, new values are shown side by side, making the report sometimes hard to read.

Depending on the kind of report you want to build, having the two fields side by side can be good or bad. In this example, they are not very easy to read when positioned in this way. It would be much better to show them one on top of the other, better resembling the subtraction we want to perform next. To position the fields on the rows rather than on the columns, you need to locate the $\sum$ Values item that is now in the COLUMNS area of the PivotTable (see Figure 2-10), and drag it to the ROWS area.

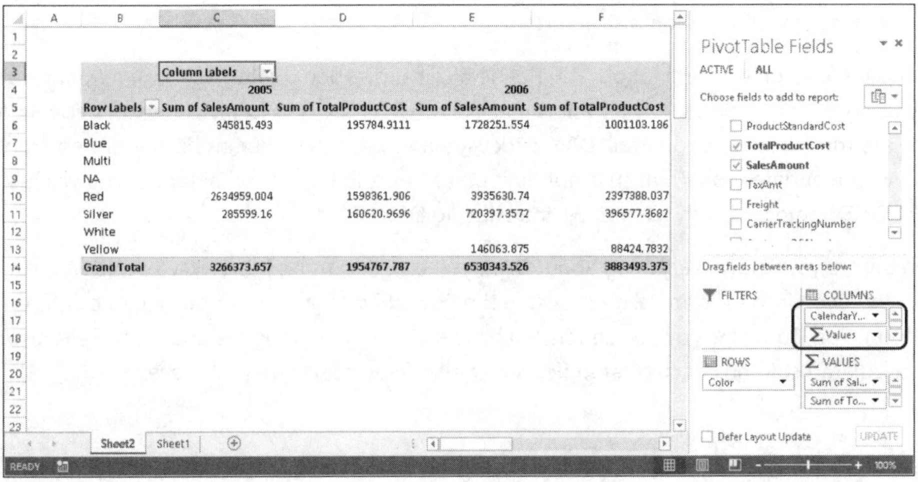

FIGURE 2-10 The $\sum$ VALUES field lets you move the values to rows or to columns.

In Figure 2-11, you can see the resulting PivotTable, which is much easier to read.

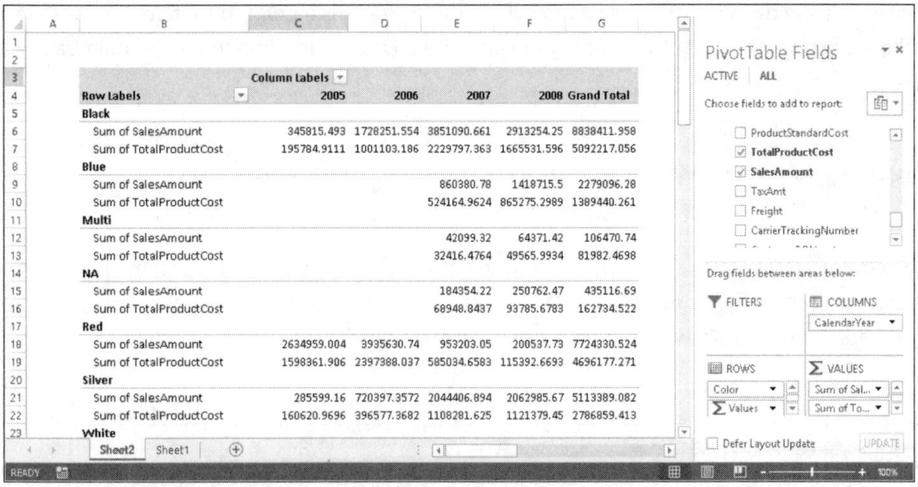

FIGURE 2-11 Showing the measures one on top of the other makes the report easier to read.

Now, even though the report shows both values, we are still missing the most important one: the gross margin, which can be computed by subtracting the total product cost from the sales amount. If we were in an Excel worksheet, this computation would have been very easy to make, but doing it inside a PivotTable is a much greater challenge. PivotTables are very good at showing aggregates of columns from tables, but the problem here is that we do not have a column in FactInternetSales that contains the gross margin.

It is time for DAX. You are going to use DAX to add a column to FactInternetSales that contains the desired computation. First, go back to the PowerPivot window, switch to Data view, and move to the FactInternetSales table using the bottom tabs. At this point, go to the Design tab of the ribbon and click Add, which is highlighted in Figure 2-12.

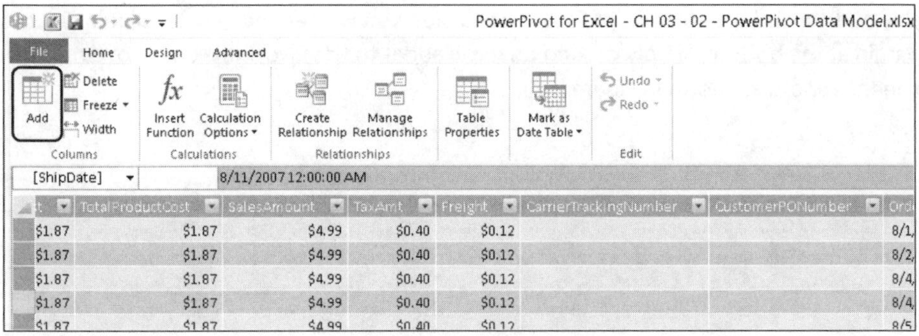

FIGURE 2-12 Use Add to create a new calculated column in the PowerPivot window.

The new column does not belong to the source database. It is a column that you are adding to satisfy the reporting needs. At this point, you can write a DAX expression in the formula bar. In this case, the expression is very simple:

```
= FactInternetSales[SalesAmount] - FactInternetSales[TotalProductCost]
```

Even without knowing DAX, the meaning of this expression is straightforward: the product cost is being subtracted from the sales amount. Once you confirm the expression, PowerPivot computes the values and adds them to a new column, which is named CalculatedColumn1 by default. You can see the result in Figure 2-13.

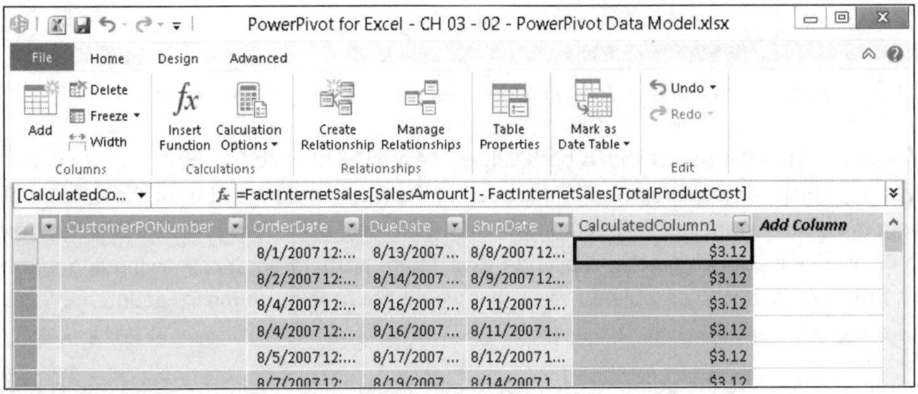

FIGURE 2-13 The new calculated column is added as the rightmost one and given a default name.

To rename the column, right-click the column header, choose Rename Column, and type the new name of the column. In this example, it will be GrossMargin. If, at this point, you go back to the PivotTable and expand the columns of FactInternetSales, you will see the new calculated column GrossMargin at the bottom. Simply clicking on it will add it to the PivotTable and show the new column in the report, as shown in Figure 2-14.

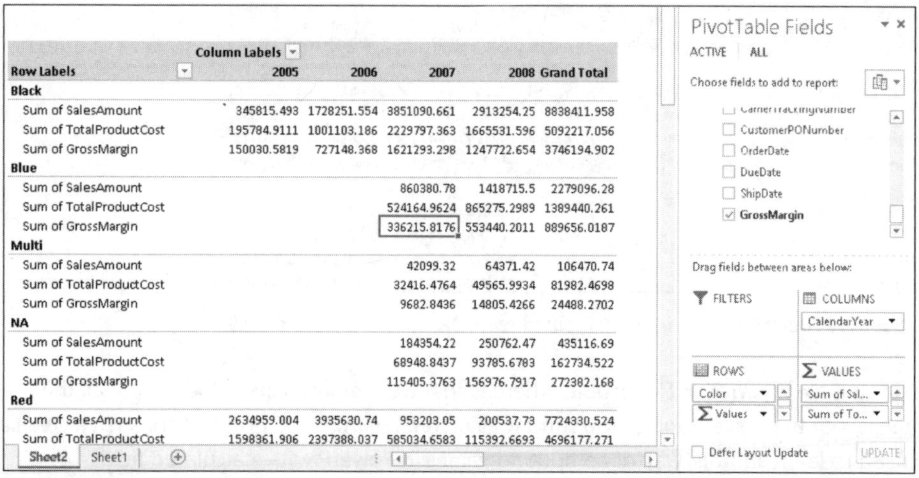

FIGURE 2-14 Once a calculated column is added to the data model, it shows in the PivotTable Fields list.

You have seen that creating a new calculated column in the data model is very easy to do and greatly enhances the reporting power of Excel. As you will learn in the next chapters, by using DAX, you will be able to solve much more complex scenarios than this simple one: DAX will be your best friend in the building of your self-service business intelligence (BI) reports.

Creating a calculated field

As you have learned in the previous section, calculated columns are very useful whenever you want to perform a calculation for each row of a table and then aggregate its value in a PivotTable. But there are some formulas that cannot be computed on a row-by-row basis; they should be computed at the aggregate level.

If you want to compute the gross margin not as a value, but as a percentage of the sales amount, you can create a very simple calculated column containing this expression:

```
GrossMarginPct = FactInternetSales[GrossMargin] / FactInternetSales[SalesAmount]
```

This calculation works fine at the row level, giving you the percentage of margin for a single row. However, when it comes to computing it at the aggregate level, this expression is not going to work anymore. In fact, if you add this column to the model and then put it in a PivotTable, you will get the result shown in Figure 2-15, which is incorrect.

	Column Labels ▼				
Row Labels ▼	2005	2006	2007	2008	Grand Total
Black					
Sum of SalesAmount	345815.493	1728251.554	3851090.661	2913254.25	8838411.958
Sum of TotalProductCost	195784.9111	1001103.186	2229797.363	1665531.596	5092217.056
Sum of GrossMargin	150030.5819	727148.368	1621293.298	1247722.654	3746194.902
Sum of GrossMarginPct	65.53332736	360.6291298	2137.918725	2440.121774	5004.202956
Blue					
Sum of SalesAmount			860380.78	1418715.5	2279096.28
Sum of TotalProductCost			524164.9624	865275.2989	1389440.261
Sum of GrossMargin			336215.8176	553440.2011	889656.0187
Sum of GrossMarginPct			854.3894099	1313.157337	2167.546747

FIGURE 2-15 The GrossMarginPct is not computed correctly at the aggregate level.

The result is clearly wrong. The problem here is that we are performing the sum of all the percentages, not the percentage of the sums. Calculated columns will not help for such a calculation, so you need to learn another way of computing values in PowerPivot—calculated fields.

> **Note** The name *calculated field* has been introduced in Excel 2013. In PowerPivot for Excel 2010, these calculations were called *measures*. It is useful to know this information because when you read blog posts and other forms of documentation, you might see the term *measure* used to refer to calculated fields and this could confuse you if you did not know they are the same thing.

A calculated field is a DAX expression that is not computed on a row-by-row basis. Instead, it is computed at the aggregate level. To create a new calculated field, you can use the PowerPivot tab of the Excel ribbon and click the button Calculated Fields button (see Figure 2-16).

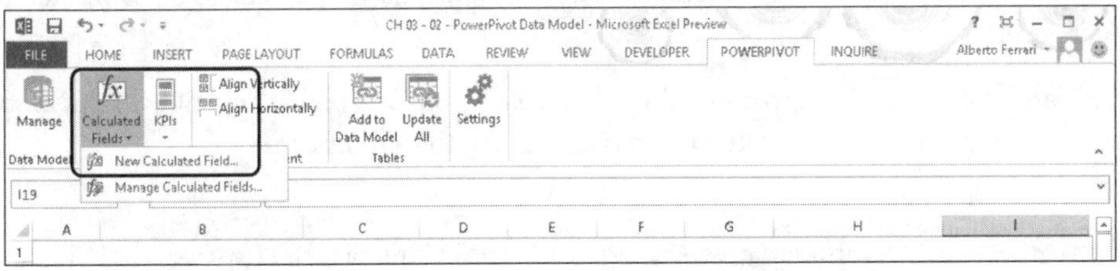

FIGURE 2-16 The Calculated Field button on the PowerPivot tab of the ribbon lets you create calculated fields.

When you select New Calculated Field..., a dialog box opens, from which you can create the DAX formula, give the new field a name, put in a format string, and, in general, set all the properties of the new field. You can see the dialog box in Figure 2-17.

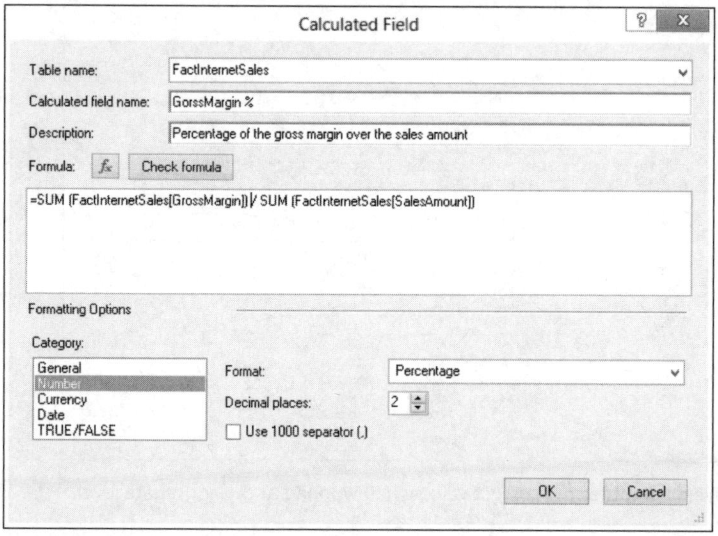

FIGURE 2-17 The Calculated Field dialog box lets you set all the parameters of a calculated field.

In the example, the formula used for the calculated field is the following one:

```
= SUM ( FactInternetSales[GrossMargin] ) / SUM ( FactInternetSales[SalesAmount] )
```

If you compare with the same formula for the calculated column, you will notice that this time we used the *SUM* function before the column names, both for the GrossMargin and the SalesAmount columns. You will learn in Chapter 3 why this is needed and how the syntax for calculated columns and calculated fields are different.

In the calculated field, you have the opportunity to set the number format. In this example, you have used the Percentage as the number format, so that numbers will show as percentages. When you click OK, the calculated field is added to the PowerPivot data model and is available in the PivotTable. You can add it to the PivotTable simply by clicking it to obtain the result shown in Figure 2-18.

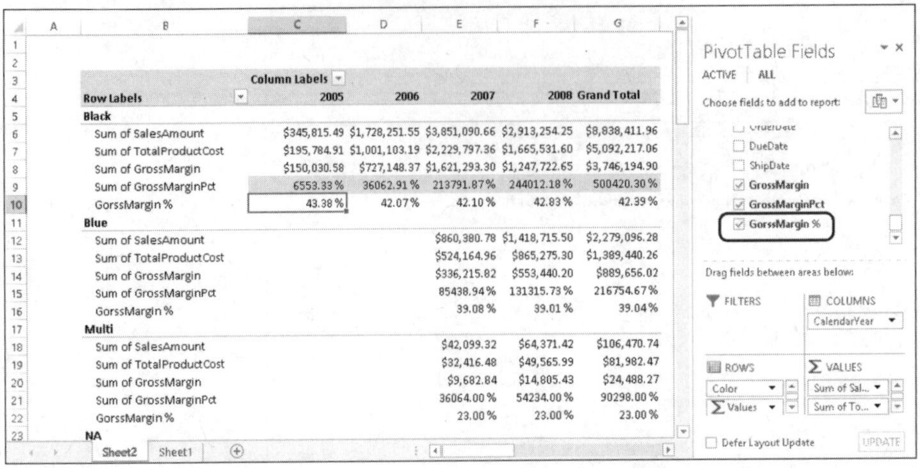

FIGURE 2-18 The Calculated Field computes the correct value when working at the aggregate level.

Calculated fields are very useful because they let you create complex expressions, store them inside the PowerPivot data model, and then use them in any PivotTable. In fact, the calculated field is not local to the PivotTable into which it is being placed. It belongs to the data model and will be available in any PivotTable or report that you create on your data model.

It is interesting to note that the calculated field contains the format string too, freeing the user from the need to always choose the correct formatting for the PivotTable cells. Creating calculated fields in your data model will allow you to create PivotTables quickly and easily. Given their reusable nature, only the time needed to click the calculated fields would be required when generating a new report.

You are building a data model, not only a report

When you work with the PowerPivot data model, you are not working on a single report, as you are probably used to doing in Excel. You are a creating a data model that will be useful for many reports, each one built with PivotTables. This requires a shift in your mind: having the attitude of being a good data modeler is a different skill from that of being able to create a good report. Several chapters in this book will help you to move to that next level, the most important of which is Chapter 4, "Understanding Data Models."

Computing complex aggregations like Distinct Count

One of the most interesting feature of calculated fields is the ability to compute complex aggregations, which are available in the DAX language but not in the standard set of Excel functions. As an example, you are learning how to create a distinct count field in DAX. You can find the data in the workbook "CH02-02-Distinct Count.xlsx."

We start with a very simple PivotTable containing sales amount divided by product color (see Figure 2-19).

Row Labels ▾	Sum of SalesAmount
Black	$8,838,411.96
Blue	$2,279,096.28
Multi	$106,470.74
NA	$435,116.69
Red	$7,724,330.52
Silver	$5,113,389.08
White	$5,106.32
Yellow	$4,856,755.63
Grand Total	$29,358,677.22

FIGURE 2-19 Computing the sum of sales amounts, as you have already seen, is very easy.

Now, presume that you want to count the number of products in each color that determined the sales. Clearly, if a single product has been sold 1,000 times, it should count only once because it is always the same product. This kind of aggregation is known as the *distinct count* of products.

The first trial could be that of dragging the ProductKey from the DimProduct table to the VALUES area. The resulting PivotTable is shown in Figure 2-20.

Row Labels ▾	Sum of SalesAmount	Sum of ProductKey
Black	8838411.958	50742
Blue	2279096.28	14058
Grey		446
Multi	106470.74	4830
NA	435116.69	48136
Red	7724330.524	18016
Silver	5113389.082	20444
Silver/Black		3815
White	5106.32	1400
Yellow	4856755.628	22034
Grand Total	29358677.22	183921

FIGURE 2-20 Dragging the ProductKey to the VALUES area produces the sum of the keys, not the count.

As you can easily see from both the result and the column header, this is not the desired result: Excel computed the sum of the product keys, not their count. After all, the product key is an integer value, so it is reasonable that Excel would sum it—but you do not want that information.

Luckily, there is a feature in Excel that lets you change the way that data is aggregated. To activate it, you need to open the options of the Sum of ProductKey column in the VALUES area and choose Value Field Settings, as displayed in Figure 2-21.

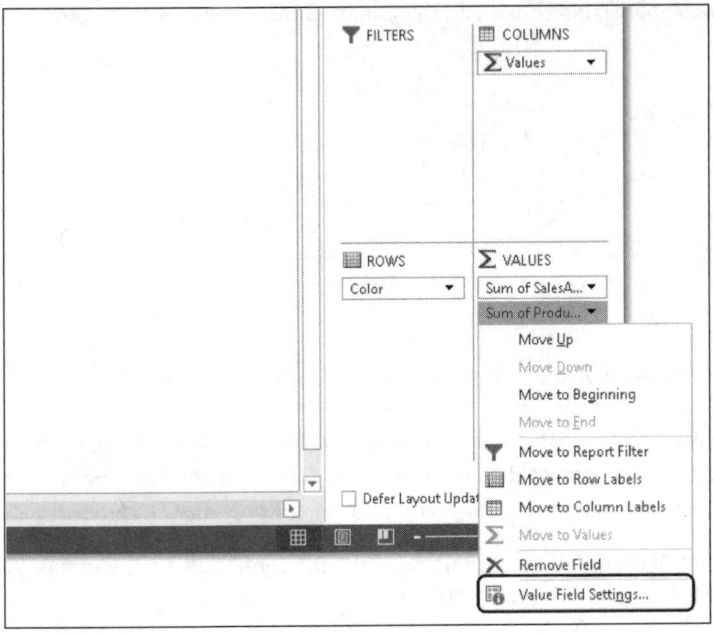

FIGURE 2-21 The Value Field Setting menu option lets you change various properties of a value.

Choosing this option opens the Value Field Settings window, from where you can change many options for the calculation. Right now, we are interested in changing the aggregate function. If you go down the list of functions, you will discover an inviting one called Distinct Count, as shown in Figure 2-22.

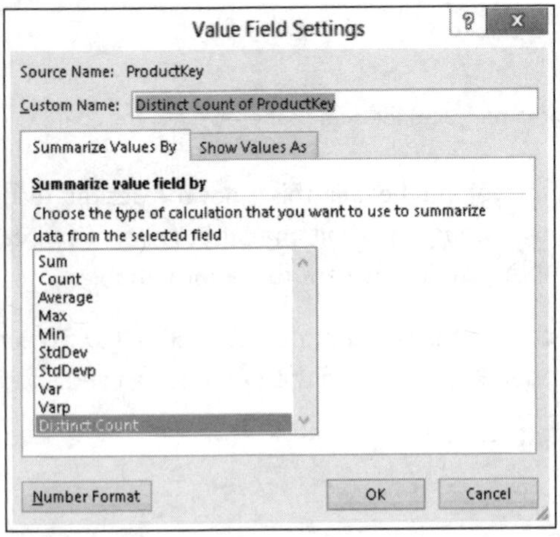

FIGURE 2-22 The Value Field Setting window has a *Distinct Count* aggregate function available.

Note The same window, from the same menu option, is also available for a PivotTable based on an Excel table. However, even if they look very similar, they do not work in the same way. In fact, the set of aggregate functions available for Excel tables is different from the set of aggregate functions in a PivotTable over the PowerPivot data model. Distinct Count, for example, is available only for PowerPivot because it includes some features that are just available in PowerPivot.

Selecting the Distinct Count option and clicking OK will perform the magic: instead of using the *SUM* aggregation, now the PivotTable is using *Distinct Count,* counting the products. In Figure 2-23, you can see the final result.

Row Labels	Sum of SalesAmount	Distinct Count of ProductKey
Black	8838411.958	133
Blue	2279096.28	28
Grey		1
Multi	106470.74	18
NA	435116.69	254
Red	7724330.524	63
Silver	5113389.082	52
Silver/Black		7
White	5106.32	4
Yellow	4856755.628	46
Grand Total	**29358677.22**	**606**

FIGURE 2-23 The ProductKey is now aggregated using *Distinct Count.* Yet, something still is not correct here.

If you look carefully at the result, though, you will understand that something is still not working right. In the two highlighted rows, there are no sales, but there is a count for the products. This should not happen if we want to count the number of distinct products that are responsible for the sales.

In fact, it turns out that we have picked the wrong column to aggregate. Because we chose the ProductKey in the DimProduct table, we are really counting the number of products, not the number of products sold. If a product has never been sold, then we do not want to count it. The correct column to count is not the ProductKey in DimProduct, but the ProductKey in the FactInternetSales.

If you repeat the same procedure using the correct column, you will get the desired result, which is shown in Figure 2-24.

Row Labels	Sum of SalesAmount	Distinct Count of ProductKey
Black	8838411.958	46
Blue	2279096.28	17
Multi	106470.74	5
NA	435116.69	18
Red	7724330.524	23
Silver	5113389.082	20
White	5106.32	2
Yellow	4856755.628	27
Grand Total	**29358677.22**	**158**

FIGURE 2-24 Using ProductKey from FactInternetSales results in the correct report, shown.

You might be asking at this point why we decided to take you through a wrong procedure before showing you the final result, with the correct column aggregated. The reason is that we wanted to show not only how to aggregate values with distinct count, but also how easy it is to make the wrong choice, having many tables in the data model and not taking into account the increased complexity of the model.

The mistake of using the wrong column for distinct count happens very often, even to seasoned modelers. For this reason, it is important that you always check the numbers before assuming they are correct. We know you already do it but . . . since you well might have to deal with increasingly complex data models, we just want to warn you once more.

Refreshing the PowerPivot data model

Up to now, you have learned that the PowerPivot data model can load tables from a database without using Excel as an intermediate step. Because the database content is very dynamic by nature, you will want to refresh the content of your data model to reflect any newly added or updated rows in the database tables.

To refresh the content of the data model, you need to use the Refresh button on the Home tab of the PowerPivot ribbon from inside the PowerPivot window, as shown in Figure 2-25.

FIGURE 2-25 The Refresh button in the PowerPivot window lets you reload the content from the database.

You have the option to refresh all the tables or only the one that is currently shown in the PowerPivot window. For example, if you select Refresh All, PowerPivot will start collecting all the data again from all the databases from where you have loaded data, and it will automatically update all the calculated columns that you have defined in the model. Calculated fields need not be recomputed, however, because they are not stored in the PowerPivot data model. Rather, they are calculated only as needed.

Keep in mind that refreshing the data model means reloading everything from the database. There is no way to load only updated rows: whenever you issue a Refresh command, the content of the tables is read again from the source databases. If your data model is huge (containing, say, tens or hundreds of millions of rows), this operation can last several minutes. In some real-world scenarios, where you work in the range of hundreds of thousands of rows, the operation is very quick, usually taking just a few seconds. But this is a consideration you should always keep in mind.

In Chapter 15 "Automating operations using VBA" you will learn that the refresh operation can be automated by using VBA code and the Excel programming model, creating in this way reports that are automatically updated, for example, upon opening the reports or by clicking a button that you design.

CHAPTER 3

Introducing DAX

Now that you have seen some of the features of Microsoft PowerPivot for Microsoft Excel 2013, it is time to learn the fundamentals of the DAX language. PowerPivot has its own syntax for defining calculation expressions. It is conceptually similar to an Excel expression, but it has specific functions that allow you to create more advanced calculations on data stored in multiple tables. (The PowerPivot language is called the Data Analysis eXpressions language, but we always use the shorter DAX acronym.)

In this chapter, you will learn the basics of DAX and how to use it to solve some typical problems in business scenarios.

Understanding DAX calculations

Just like Excel, any calculation in DAX begins with the assignment operator. The main difference is that DAX never uses cell coordinates like A1, C2, and so on. In DAX, you always specify coordinates using column and table names. Moreover, DAX does not support the concept of range as Excel does: to use DAX efficiently, you need to learn to work with columns and tables.

> **Note** In a DAX expression, you can get the value of a column for only a single row or for the whole table—that is, you cannot get access to a specific row inside a table. To get a range, you need to use DAX functions that filter a table, thus returning a subset of the rows of the original table that corresponds to the needed range.

To express complex formulas, you need to learn the basics of DAX, which includes the syntax, the different data types that DAX can handle, the basic operators, and how to refer to columns and tables. In the next few sections, we are going to introduce these concepts.

DAX syntax

A relatively simple way to understand how DAX syntax works is to start with an example. Suppose that you have a PowerPivot table like the one shown in Figure 3-1. Two columns, SalesAmount and TotalProductCost, are useful in this particular instance. You can find this data model in the companion workbook "CH03-01-SalesExample.xlsx."

FIGURE 3-1 We will use this table to demonstrate DAX syntax.

Using this data, you now want to calculate the margin by subtracting the TotalProductCost from the SalesAmount. To do that, you need to write the DAX formula shown in Figure 3-2 in a new column, which you can call GrossMargin.

FIGURE 3-2 You can enter the definition of GrossMargin into the formula bar.

This new formula is repeated automatically for all the rows of the table, resulting in a new column in the table. In this example, you are using a DAX expression to define a calculated column. (Later in this chapter, we will show that DAX is used also to define calculated fields.) This DAX expression handles numeric values and returns a numeric value, too.

DAX data types

You saw in the previous formula how to handle numeric values. DAX can perform computations with seven numeric types:

- *Integer*

- *Real*

- *Currency*

- *Date* (*datetime*)

- *TRUE/FALSE* (Boolean)

- *String*

- *BLOB* (which stands for "binary large object")

PowerPivot has a powerful type-handling system, so you do not have to worry much about data types: when you write a DAX expression, the resulting type is based on the type of the terms used in the expression. You need to be aware of this in case the type returned from a DAX expression is not the expected one; then you must investigate the data type of the terms used in the expression itself. For example, if one of the terms of a sum is a date, the result is also a date; if the same operator is used with integers, the result is an integer. This is known as *operator overloading*, and you can see an example of its behavior in Figure 3-3, where the DatePlusOneWeek column is calculated by adding 7 to the value in the Date column. The result: a date.

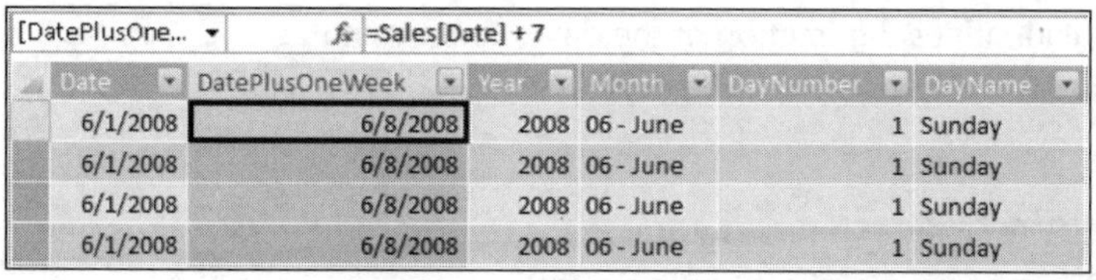

FIGURE 3-3 Adding an integer to a date results in a date being increased by the corresponding number of days.

In addition to operator overloading, PowerPivot automatically converts strings into numbers and numbers into strings whenever the operator requires it. For example, if you use the & operator, which concatenates strings, PowerPivot automatically converts its arguments into strings. If you look at the formula:

```
= 5 & 4
```

it returns a "54" string result. On the other hand, the formula:

```
= "5" + "4"
```

returns an integer result with the value of 9.

As you have seen, the resulting value depends on the operator and not on the source columns, which are converted following the requirements of the operator. But even if this behavior is convenient, in the "Handling errors in DAX expressions" section later in this chapter, you will see what types of errors might happen during these automatic conversions.

DAX operators

A list of the operators available in DAX is shown in Table 3-1.

Moreover, the logical operators are available also as DAX functions, with syntax very similar to Excel syntax. For example, you can write:

```
AND ([Country] = "USA", [Quantity] > 0)
OR ([Country] = "USA", [Quantity] > 0)
NOT ([Country] = "USA")
```

that corresponds, respectively, to:

```
[Country] = "USA" && [Quantity] > 0
[Country] = "USA" || [Quantity] > 0
! ([Country] = "USA")
```

TABLE 3-1 Operators

Operator type	Symbol	Use	Example
Parenthesis	()	Precedence order and grouping of arguments	(5 + 2) * 3
Arithmetic	+	Addition	4 + 2
	-	Subtraction/negation	5 − 3
	*	Multiplication	4 * 2
	/	Division	4 / 2
Comparison	=	Equal to	[Country] = "USA"
	<>	Not equal to	[Country] <> "USA"
	>	Greater than	[Quantity] > 0
	>=	Greater than or equal to	[Quantity] >= 100
	<	Less than	[Quantity] < 0
	<=	Less than or equal to	[Quantity] <= 100
Text concatenation	&	Concatenation of strings	"Value is " & [Amount]
Logical	&&	*AND* condition between two Boolean expressions	[Country] = "USA" && [Quantity] > 0
	||	*OR* condition between two Boolean expressions	[Country] = "USA" || [Quantity] > 0
	!	*NOT* operator on the Boolean expression that follows	! ([Country] = "USA")

DAX values

You have already seen that you can use a value directly in a formula (for example, USA or 0). When such values are used in this way, they are called *literals* and, although using literals is straightforward, the syntax for referencing a column should be looked at. Here is the basic syntax:

```
'Table Name'[Column Name]
```

The table name can be enclosed in single quotes. Most of the time, though, the quotes can be omitted if the name does not contain any special characters, such as spaces. In the following formula, for example, the quotes can be omitted:

```
TableName[Column Name]
```

The column name, on the other hand, always needs to be enclosed in square brackets. Note that the table name is optional. If the table name were omitted, the column name would be searched in the current table, which is the one to which the calculated column or measure belongs. However, we strongly suggest that you always specify the complete name (table and column) to avoid any confusion.

IntelliSense

Whenever you write a formula in Excel or PowerPivot, a special help feature called IntelliSense shows all the possible function names and references that you can use in a formula. When you write a formula in the PowerPivot window, if you type an opening square bracket, IntelliSense shows only the columns of the current table (the one in which you are defining the calculated column or the calculated field). If you type the first letters of a table name, you will see both table name and column names in IntelliSense. In Figure 3-4, you can see the list of columns of the current table displayed when the opening square bracket is typed into the calculated column formula.

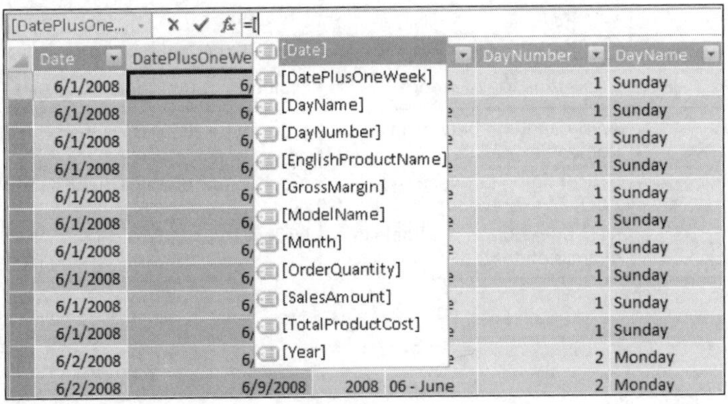

FIGURE 3-4 IntelliSense shows all the fields of the current table when you type the opening square bracket into the PowerPivot window.

Understanding calculated columns and fields

Now that you know the basics of DAX syntax, you need to learn one of the most important concepts in DAX: the difference between calculated columns and calculated fields. Even though they might appear similar initially because you can make some calculations both ways, they are in reality very different. Understanding the differences between them is a key to unlocking the true power of DAX.

Calculated columns

In Chapter 2, "Using the unique features of PowerPivot," you learned how to define a calculated column. You can do this by using the Add button on the Design tab of the ribbon, or you can simply move to the last column, which is named Add Column, and start writing the formula. The DAX expression has to be inserted into the formula bar, and IntelliSense helps you write the expression.

A calculated column is just like any other column in a PowerPivot table. It can be used in rows, columns, filters, or values of a PivotTable. The DAX expression defined for a calculated column operates in the context of the current row of the table that it belongs to. Any reference to a column returns the value of that column in the current row. You cannot access directly the values of other rows.

> **Note** As you will see in the "Aggregate functions" section later in this chapter, there are DAX functions that aggregate the value of a column for the whole table. The only way to get the value of a subset of rows is to use DAX functions that return a table and then operate on it. In this way, you can aggregate column values for a range of rows, or get a single value from another row and operate on it. Using DAX, you can make a reference to a table and apply filters so that only the desired rows are retrieved.

Calculated columns are easy to create and use. You already saw in Figure 3-2 how to define the Gross Margin column to compute the amount of the gross margin:

```
[Gross Margin] = Sales[SalesAmount] - Sales[TotalProductCost]
```

The expression of the calculated column is evaluated for each row, and its result is stored in the table as if it were a column retrieved from the database. Calculated columns are familiar to Excel users because they behave in a very similar way to Excel table columns.

Calculated fields

You might remember from Chapter 2 that the definition of gross margin as a value works fine with calculated columns, but if you want to compute the gross margin as a percentage, then you will need to define a calculated field. It is now time to deepen your understanding of calculated fields and the syntax needed to write them.

A calculated field is a DAX expression that uses the same syntax as a calculated column; the difference is the context of evaluation. A calculated field is evaluated in the context of the cell of the PivotTable, whereas a calculated column is computed at the row level of the PowerPivot table. The cell context depends on the user selections on the PivotTable. When you use *SUM (SalesAmount)* in a calculated field, you mean the sum of all the rows that are aggregated under the PivotTable cell, whereas when you use *Sales[SalesAmount]* in a calculated column, you mean the value of SalesAmount in this row.

When you create a calculated field, you can define a value that changes according to the filter that the user applies to a PivotTable. In this way, you can solve the problem of calculating the gross margin percentage.

To define a calculated field, you can choose New Calculated Field drop-down menu item displayed by clicking the Calculated Fields button on the PowerPivot tab of the Excel ribbon (see Figure 3-5) when a cell in a PivotTable is selected.

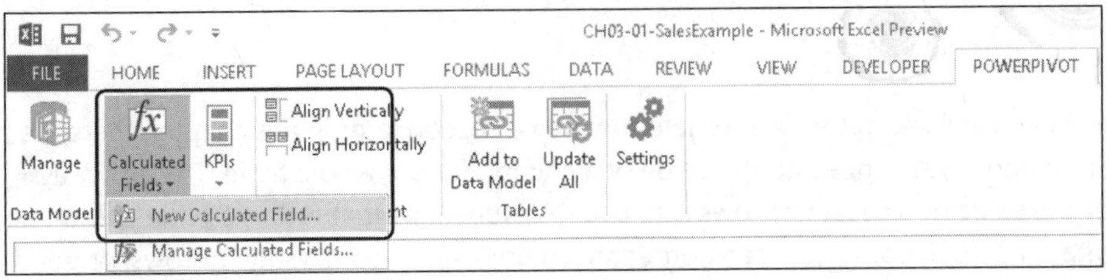

FIGURE 3-5 The New Calculated Field option on the PowerPivot ribbon.

At this point, the Calculated Field dialog box (see Figure 3-6) opens, and you can choose the table name that contains the new calculated field, its name, a description, and finally, the DAX formula and the format string.

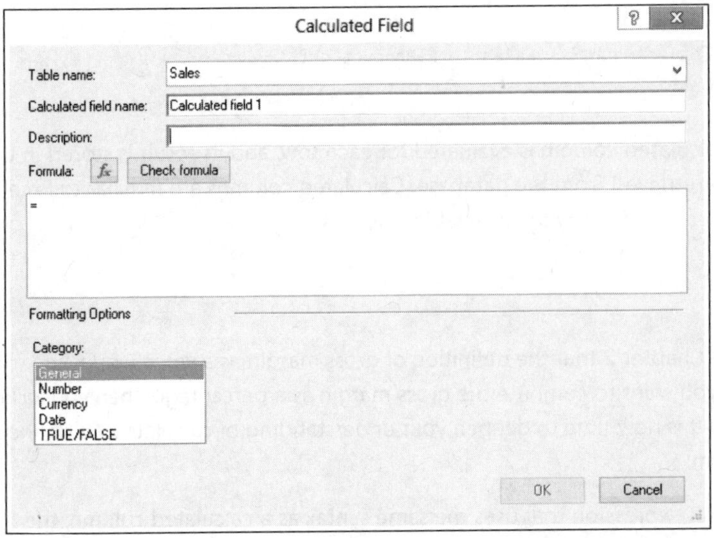

FIGURE 3-6 Here, you can see the Calculated Field window, which is useful for creating a new calculated field.

Now, let's focus on the formula to define a new measure. In a first attempt, you might define it by using the same DAX expression used in the calculated column, but you would get the error shown in Figure 3-7.

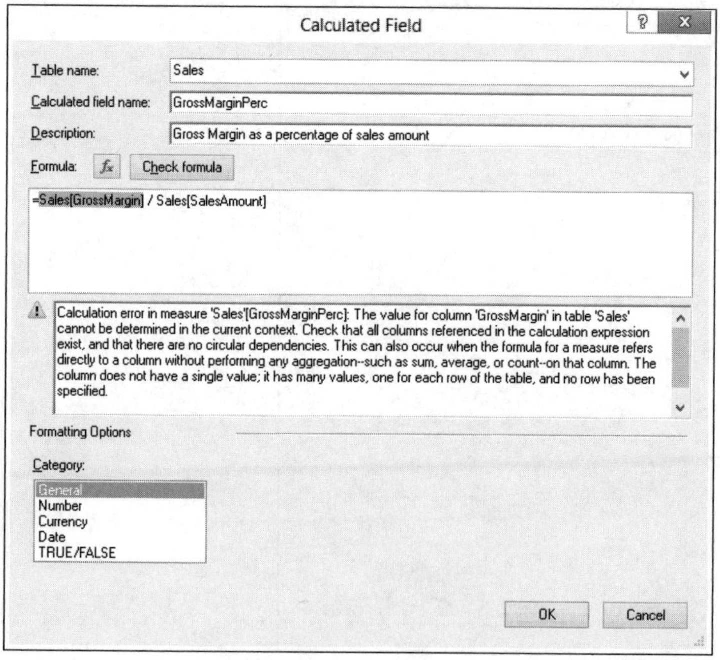

FIGURE 3-7 If you define the GrossMarginPerc calculated field with the same DAX expression as a calculated column, you get an error message.

You display the error message by clicking Check Formula. The reason for this error is that the context of execution is not a single row, but a group of rows. That group corresponds to the selection that is implicitly defined by the cell that has to be calculated in the PivotTable. In such a context, which contains multiple rows, there is no way to refer to the value of the column Sales[SalesAmount] because a column has a value only when it is used in the context of a single row.

To avoid this error, you need to define an expression that divides the sum of the gross margin by the sum of the sales. This expression makes use of the *SUM* function, which aggregates all the rows filtered by the current selection in the PivotTable (which will be the year, as we said before). The following is the correct DAX expression for the measure calculated field; it is also shown in Figure 3-8.

```
= SUM ( Sales[Gross Margin] ) / SUM ( Sales[SalesAmount] )
```

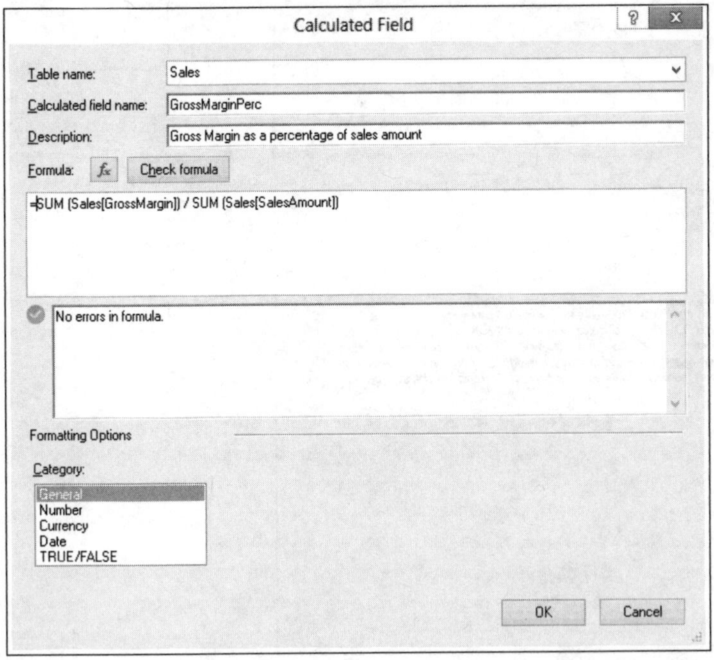

FIGURE 3-8 The correct definition of the GrossMarginPerc measure calculated field.

Differences between calculated columns and calculated fields

Even if they look similar, there is a big difference between calculated columns and calculated fields. The value of a calculated column is computed during data refresh and uses the current row as a context; it does not depend on user activity on the PivotTable. A calculated field operates on aggregations of data defined by the context of the current cell: source tables are filtered according to the coordinates of the cell, and data is aggregated and calculated using these filters. In other words, a calculated field always operates on aggregations of data in the evaluation context, and for this reason the default execution mode does not reference any single row. The evaluation context is explained further in Chapter 7.

Choosing between calculated columns and measures

Now that you have seen the difference between calculated columns and calculated fields, you might be wondering when it is better to use one or the other. Sometimes either is an option, but in most situations, your computation needs determine your choice.

You have to define a calculated column (in the PowerPivot table grid window) whenever you want to do the following:

- Place the calculated results in an Excel slicer or see results in rows or columns in a PivotTable (as opposed to the Values area).

- Define an expression that is strictly bound to the current row. (For example, Price * Quantity cannot work on an average of the two columns.)

- Categorize text or numbers (for example, a range of values for a measure such as customer age, such as 0–18, 18–25, and so on).

However, you must define a calculated field whenever you want to display the resulting calculation values that reflect PivotTable selections made by the user and see them in the Values area of PivotTables. For example:

- When you calculate profit percentage of a PivotTable selection

- When you calculate ratios of a product compared to all products but filter both by year or region

Some calculations can be covered both by calculated columns and calculated fields, even if different DAX expressions must be used in these cases. For example, you can define the GrossMargin as a calculated column as follows:

```
= Sales[SalesAmount] - Sales[TotalProductCost]
```

but it can be defined as a calculated field too:

```
= SUM ( Sales[SalesAmount] ) - SUM ( Sales[TotalProductCost] )
```

The final result is exactly the same. We suggest that you favor the calculated field in this case because, being evaluated at query time, doing so does not consume memory and disk space. However, this factor is really important only in large datasets. When the size of the workbook is not an issue, you can use the method you are more comfortable with.

Cross-references

It is obvious that a calculated field can refer to one or more calculated columns. It might be less intuitive that the opposite is also true: A calculated column can refer to one or more calculated fields. In this way, it forces the calculation of a field for the context defined by the current row. This operation transforms and consolidates the result of a calculated field into a column, which will not be influenced by user actions. Obviously, only certain operations can produce meaningful results because usually a calculated field makes computations that strongly depend on the selection made by the user in the PivotTable.

Handling errors in DAX expressions

Now that you have seen some basic formulas, you should learn how to handle invalid calculations gracefully if (or should we say when?) they happen. A DAX expression might contain invalid calculations because the data that it references is not valid for the formula. For example, you might have a division by zero or a column value that is not a number being used in an arithmetic operation such as multiplication. You must learn how these errors are handled by default and how to intercept these conditions if you want to handle them in a special way.

Before you learn how to handle errors, it is worth describing the different kinds of errors that might appear during a DAX formula evaluation. They are:

- Conversion errors

- Arithmetical operations

- Empty or missing values

Conversion errors

The first kind of error that we analyze is the conversion error. As you have seen before in this chapter, DAX values are automatically converted between strings and numbers whenever the operator requires it. To review the concept, all of these are valid DAX expressions:

```
"10" + 32 = 42
"10" & 32 = "1032"
10 & 32 = "1032"
DATE (2010,3,25) = 3/25/2010
DATE (2010,3,25) + 14 = 4/8/2010
DATE (2010,3,25) & 14 = "3/25/201014"
```

These formulas are always correct because they operate with constant values. But what about the following one?

```
SalesOrders[VatCode] + 100
```

Because the first operator of this sum is obtained by a column (which, in this case, is a text column), you must be sure that all the values in that column are numbers to ascertain whether they will be converted and the expression will be evaluated correctly. If some of the content cannot be converted to suit the operator's needs, you will incur a conversion error. Here are typical situations:

```
"1 + 1" + 0          = Cannot convert value '1+1' of type string to type real
DATEVALUE ("25/14/2010") = Type mismatch
```

To avoid these errors, you need to write more complex DAX expressions that contain error detection logic to intercept error conditions and always return a meaningful result.

Arithmetical operations

The second category of errors is arithmetical operations, such as division by zero or the square root of a negative number. These kinds of errors are not related to conversion; they are raised whenever you try to call a function or use an operator with invalid values.

In PowerPivot, division by zero requires a special handling because it behaves in a way that is not very intuitive (except for mathematicians). When you divide a number by zero, PowerPivot usually returns the special value *Infinity*. Moreover, in the very special cases of 0 divided by 0 or *Infinity* divided by *Infinity*, PowerPivot returns the special *NaN* (not a number) value. Because this is a strange behavior for Excel users to encounter, we have summarized it in Table 3-2.

TABLE 3-2 Special result values for division by zero

Expression	Result
10 / 0	*Infinity*
7 / 0	*Infinity*
0 / 0	*NaN*
(10 / 0) / (7 / 0)	*NaN*

It is important to note that *Infinity* and *NaN* are not errors, but special values in PowerPivot. In fact, if you divide a number by *Infinity*, the expression does not generate an error; rather, it returns 0 (note that in the following expression, 7/0 results in *Infinity*):

```
9954 / (7 / 0)    = 0
```

Apart from this special situation, arithmetical errors might be returned when calling a DAX function with a wrong parameter, such as the square root of a negative number:

```
SQRT ( -1 )    = An argument of function 'SQRT' has the wrong data type
               or the result is too large or too small
```

If PowerPivot detects errors like this, it blocks any further computation of the DAX expression and raises an error. You can use the special DAX *ISERROR* function to check if an expression leads to an error, something that you will use in the "Intercepting errors" section later in this chapter. Finally, even if special values like *NaN* are displayed in this way in the PowerPivot window, they are displayed as errors when shown in an Excel PivotTable and will be detected as errors by the error detection functions.

Empty or missing values

The third category is not a specific error condition. Rather, it is the presence of empty values, which might result in unexpected results or calculation errors when combining those empty values with other elements in a calculation. You need to understand how these special values are treated in PowerPivot.

DAX handles missing values, blank values, and empty cells in the same way; using the value *BLANK*. *BLANK* is not a real value but a special way to identify these conditions. The value *BLANK* can be obtained in a DAX expression by calling the *BLANK* function, which is different from an empty string. For example, the following expression always returns a blank value, which is displayed as an empty cell in the PowerPivot window:

```
= BLANK ()
```

On its own, this expression is useless, but the *BLANK* function becomes useful every time you want to return an empty value. For example, you might want to display an empty cell instead of 0, as in the following expression that calculates the total discount for a sale transaction and leaves the cell blank if the discount is 0:

```
= IF ( Sales[DiscountPerc] = 0, BLANK (), Sales[DiscountPerc] * Sales[Amount] )
```

If a DAX expression contains a *BLANK*, it is not considered an error, but an empty value. So an expression containing a *BLANK* might return a value or a blank, depending on the calculation required. For example, the following expression:

```
= 10 * Sales[Amount]
```

returns *BLANK* whenever Sales[Amount] is *BLANK*. In other words, the result of an arithmetic product is *BLANK* whenever one or both terms are *BLANK*. This propagation of *BLANK* in a DAX expression happens in several other arithmetical and logical operations, as shown in the following examples:

```
BLANK () + BLANK ()    = BLANK ()
10 * BLANK ()          = BLANK ()
BLANK () / 3           = BLANK ()
BLANK () / BLANK ()    = BLANK ()
BLANK () || BLANK ()   = FALSE
BLANK () && BLANK ()   = FALSE
```

However, the propagation of *BLANK* in the result of an expression is not produced by all formulas. Some calculations do not propagate *BLANK*, but return a value depending on the other terms of the formula. Examples of these are addition, subtraction, division by *BLANK*, and a logical operation between a *BLANK* and a valid value. In the following expressions, you can see some examples of these conditions, along with their results:

```
BLANK () - 10          = -10
18 + BLANK ()          = 18
4 / BLANK ()           = Infinity
0 / BLANK ()           = NaN
FALSE || BLANK         = FALSE
FALSE && BLANK         = FALSE
TRUE || BLANK          = TRUE
TRUE && BLANK          = FALSE
```

Empty values in Excel

Excel has a different way of handling empty values. In Excel, all empty values are considered 0 whenever they are used in a sum or in multiplication, but they return an error if they are part of division or of a logical expression.

Understanding the behavior of empty or missing values in a DAX expression and using *BLANK* to return an empty cell in a calculation are also important skills that control the results of a DAX expression. You can often use *BLANK* as a result when you detect wrong values or other errors, as you are going to learn in the next section.

Intercepting errors

Now that you have seen the various kinds of errors that can occur, you can learn a technique to intercept errors and correct them or, at least, show an error message that contains some meaningful information. The presence of errors in a DAX expression frequently depends on the value contained in tables and columns referenced in the expression itself. So you might want to control the presence of these error conditions and return an error message. The standard technique is to check whether an expression returns an error and, if so, replace the error with a message or a default value. A few DAX functions have been designed to do this.

The first of them is the *IFERROR* function, which is very similar to the *IF* function, but instead of evaluating a *TRUE/FALSE* condition, it checks whether an expression returns an error. You can see two typical uses of the *IFERRROR* function here:

```
= IFERROR ( Sales[Quantity] * Sales[Price], BLANK () )
= IFERROR ( SQRT ( Test[Omega] ), BLANK () )
```

In the first expression, if either Sales[Quantity] or Sales[Price] are strings that cannot be converted into a number, the returned expression is an empty cell; otherwise the product of Quantity and Price is returned.

In the second expression, the result is an empty cell every time the Test[Omega] column contains a negative number.

When you use *IFERROR* this way, you follow a more general pattern that requires the use of *ISERROR* and *IF*:

```
= IF (
    ISERROR ( Sales[Quantity] * Sales[Price] ),
    BLANK (),
    Sales[Quantity] * Sales[Price]
  )

= IF (
    ISERROR ( SQRT ( Test[Omega] ) ),
    BLANK (),
    SQRT ( Test[Omega] )
  )
```

You should use *IFERROR* whenever the expression that has to be returned is the same one that is being tested for an error; you do not have to duplicate the expression in two places, and the resulting formula is more readable and easier to fix later without introducing errors. You should use *IF*, however, when you want to return the result of a different expression when there is an error.

For example, *ISNUMBER* can be used to detect whether a string (the price in the first line) can be converted to a number and then calculate the total amount; otherwise, an empty cell can be returned.

```
= IF ( ISNUMBER ( Sales[Price] ), Sales[Quantity] * Sales[Price], BLANK () )
= IF ( Test[Omega] >= 0, SQRT ( Test[Omega] ), BLANK () )
```

The second example simply detects whether the argument for *SQRT* is valid or not, calculating the square root only for positive numbers and returning *BLANK* for negative ones.

A particular case is the test against the empty value. The *ISBLANK* function detects an empty value condition, returning *TRUE* if the argument is *BLANK*. This is important especially when a missing value has a meaning different from a value set to 0. In the following example, we calculate the cost of shipping for a sales transaction, using a default shipping cost for the product if the weight is not specified in the sales transaction:

```
= IF (
    ISBLANK ( Sales[Weight] ),
    RELATED ( Product[DefaultShippingCost] ),
    Sales[Weight] * Sales[ShippingPrice]
)
```

If we had just multiplied product weight and shipping price, we would have gotten an empty cost for all the sales transactions with missing weight data.

Formatting DAX code

Before continuing with the explanation of the DAX language, it is useful to cover a very important aspect of DAX: formatting the code. DAX is a functional language, meaning that no matter how complex it is, a DAX expression is always a single function call with some parameters. The complexity of the code is reflected in the complexity of the expressions that are passed as parameters to the outermost function.

For this reason, it is normal to see expressions that span 10 lines or more. Seeing a 20-line DAX expression may seem strange to you, but it is normal, and you will get used to it. Nevertheless, as formulas start to grow in length and complexity, it is extremely important that you learn how to write them correctly so that they are readable by humans.

There is no "official" standard to format DAX code, yet we believe that it is important to describe the standard that we used with our code. It is probably not perfect, and you might prefer something different. The only thing you need to remember when formatting your code is: "Do not write everything on a single line, or you will get in trouble before you know it."

To demonstrate why formatting is so important, we show here a formula that you will use in Chapter 12, "Performing date calculations in DAX" It is somewhat complex to learn, but not the most complex formula you will create. Here is what the expression looks like if you do not format it in some way:

```
IF (COUNTX (BalanceDate, CALCULATE (COUNT( Balances[Balance] ), ALLEXCEPT
( Balances, BalanceDate[Date] ))) > 0, SUMX (ALL ( Balances[Account] ), CALCULATE
(SUM( Balances[Balance] ), LASTNONBLANK (DATESBETWEEN (BalanceDate[Date],
BLANK(),LASTDATE( BalanceDate[Date] )), CALCULATE ( COUNT( Balances[Balance]
)))))), BLANK ())
```

Trying to understand what this formula computes is nearly impossible because you have no idea which is the outermost function and how the different function calls are merged to create the complete flow of execution. We have seen too many examples of formulas written this way by customers that, at some point, ask for help in understanding why the formula returns incorrect results. Guess what? The first thing we do is format the expression—only then can we start working on it.

The same expression, properly formatted, looks like this:

```
=IF (
    COUNTX (
        BalanceDate,
        CALCULATE (
            COUNT ( Balances[Balance] ),
            ALLEXCEPT ( Balances, BalanceDate[Date] )
        )
    ) > 0,
    SUMX (
        ALL ( Balances[Account] ),
        CALCULATE (
            SUM ( Balances[Balance] ),
            LASTNONBLANK (
                DATESBETWEEN (
                    BalanceDate[Date],
                    BLANK (),
                    LASTDATE ( BalanceDate[Date] )
                ),
                CALCULATE ( COUNT ( Balances[Balance] ) )
            )
        )
    ),
    BLANK ()
)
```

The code is the same, but now it is much easier to identify the three parameters of *IF* and, most important, to follow the blocks that raise naturally from the indented lines and see how they create the complete flow of execution. Yes, the code is still hard to read, but now the problem is with DAX, not the formatting. And you are shortly going to learn how to read and manage DAX.

Thus, this is the set of rules that we use in this book and the associated workbooks:

- Keywords like *IF, COUNTX,* and *CALCULATE* are always separated from any other term with a space, and they are always written in uppercase.

- All column references are written in the form TableName[ColumnName], with no space between the table name and the opening square bracket.

- Commas are always followed by a space and are never preceded by a space.

- If the formula fits one single line, then no other rule need to be applied.

- If the formula does not fit on a single line, then the following applies:

  - The function name stands on a line by itself, with the opening parenthesis.

  - All the parameters are on separate lines, indented with four spaces and with a comma at the end of the expression.

  - The closing parenthesis is aligned with the function call and stands on a line by itself.

These are the basic rules that we use. If you find a way to express formulas that best fits your reading attitude, then use it. The goal of formatting is to make the formula easier to read, so use the way that works best for you. The most important thing to remember when defining your personal set of formatting rules is that you always need to see errors as soon as possible. If, on the unformatted code shown earlier, DAX alerts you to a missing closing parenthesis, you will have a very hard time spotting the error. On the other hand, it is much easier to see how the closing parenthesis matches the opening function calls in the formatted code.

Help with formatting DAX

Formatting DAX is not easy because you need to write it using a small font in a text box, and unfortunately, Excel does not provide an editor for it. Nevertheless, a few hints might help you when writing your DAX code:

- If you want to make the text bigger, you can use Ctrl + the mouse wheel to increase the font size, making it easier to see the code.

- If you want to add a new line to the formula, you can press Shift+Enter.

- If editing in the text box is really difficult, you can always copy the code into another editor, like Notepad, make your changes, and then paste the formula into the text box again.

Finally, whenever you look at a DAX expression, it is hard to understand at first glance whether it is a calculated column or a calculated field. Thus, we use an equals sign (=) in this book to define a calculated column and the assignment operator (:=) to define calculated fields:

```
CalcCol = SUM ( Sales[SalesAmount] )        is a calculated column
CalcFld := SUM ( Sales[SalesAmount] )       is a calculated field
```

Common DAX functions

Now that you have learned about the fundamentals of DAX and how to handle error conditions, let's take a brief tour through its most commonly used functions and expressions. Writing a DAX expression is often similar to writing an Excel expression because many functions are similar, if not identical. Excel users often find using PowerPivot very intuitive, thanks to their previous knowledge of Excel. In the remaining part of this chapter, you will see some of the most frequently used DAX functions, which you are likely to use to build your own PowerPivot data models.

You can see all the formulas shown in this section in the companion workbook "CH03-02-Aggregation Functions.xlsx."

Aggregate functions

Almost every PowerPivot data model needs to work on aggregated data. DAX offers a set of functions that aggregate the values of a column in a table and return a single value. We call this group of functions *aggregate functions*. For example, the expression:

```
= SUM ( Sales[Amount] )
```

calculates the sum of all the numbers in the Amount column of the Sales table. This expression aggregates all the rows of the Sales table if it is used in a calculated column, but it considers only the rows that are filtered by slicers, row, columns, and filter conditions in a PivotTable whenever it is used in a measure.

The main four aggregate functions (*SUM, AVERAGE, MIN,* and *MAX*) operate only on numeric values. These functions are identical to the corresponding Excel functions both in name and in behavior: any data that is not numeric is ignored in the operation. In PowerPivot, these functions work only if the column passed as an argument is of numeric or date type. In Figure 3-9, you can see an example of calculated fields defined by these aggregate functions.

Values	Column Labels				
	2005	2006	2007	2008	Grand Total
SUM of SalesAmount	3,266,373.66	6,530,343.53	9,791,060.30	9,770,899.74	29,358,677.22
AVG of SalesAmount	3,224.46	2,439.43	400.57	302.83	486.09
MIN of SalesAmount	699.10	699.10	2.29	2.29	2.29
MAX of SalesAmount	3,578.27	3,578.27	2,443.35	2,443.35	3,578.27

FIGURE 3-9 In this PivotTable, you can see different calculated fields using statistical functions that aggregate SalesAmount values.

As in Excel formulas, DAX offers an alternative syntax to these functions to make the calculation on columns that can contain both numeric and non-numeric values, such as text columns. That syntax simply adds the suffix A to the name of the function to get the same name and behavior as the same function in Excel. However, these functions are useful only for columns containing *TRUE/FALSE* values because *TRUE* is evaluated as 1 and *FALSE* as 0. Any value for a text column is always considered to be 0. Empty cells are never considered in the calculation. So even if these functions can be used in non-numeric columns without retuning an error, their results are not always the same as Excel because there is no automatic conversion to numbers for text columns. These functions are named *AVERAGEA, COUNTA, MINA,* and *MAXA,* and Figure 3-10 displays an example of their usage in measures operating in a *TRUE/FALSE* column of the sample table shown in the same worksheet. The table is used as a linked table in PowerPivot, and the lower part of the screenshot is a PivotTable based on that PowerPivot data.

Category	Product	IsActive
Drink	Milk	TRUE
Drink	Soda	FALSE
Drink	Cofee	
Snacks	Chips	FALSE
Snacks	Peanuts	FALSE

Values	Drink	Snacks	Grand Total
	Column Labels		
AVERAGEA Active	0.5	0	0.25
MINA Active	0	0	0
MAXA Active	1	0	1
COUNTA Active	2	2	4

FIGURE 3-10 *TRUE/FALSE* is evaluated as 1/0 in *A*-suffixed statistical functions.

Even though these aggregate functions have the same name, there is a difference in the way they are used in DAX and Excel. In PowerPivot, a column has a type, and its type determines the behavior of aggregate functions in that column. Excel handles a type for each cell, whereas PowerPivot handles a type for each column. PowerPivot deals with data in tabular form (technically called *relational data*) with well-defined types for each column, whereas Excel formulas work on heterogeneous cell values without well-defined types. If a column in PowerPivot is of a number type, all the values can be only numbers or empty cells. If a column is of a text type, these functions behave as if it were always 0 (except for *COUNTA*), even if the text can be converted to a number, whereas in Excel, the value is considered a number on a cell-by-cell basis. For these reasons, these DAX functions are not very useful for text-type columns.

The only interesting function in the group of *A*-suffixed functions is *COUNTA*. It returns the number of cells that are not empty and works on any type of column. If you are interested in counting all the cells in a column containing an empty value, you can use the *COUNTBLANK* function. Finally, if you want to count all the cells of a column regardless of their content, you want to count the number of rows of the table, which can be obtained by calling the *COUNTROWS* function. (It gets a table as a parameter, not a column.) In other words, the sum of *COUNTA* and *COUNTBLANK* for the same column of a table is always equal to the number of rows of the same table, as shown in Figure 3-11.

```
COUNTROWS( Sales ) = COUNTA ( Sales[SalesPersonID] )
                   + COUNTBLANK ( Sales[SalesPersonID] )
```

FIGURE 3-11 The *COUNTROWS* function returns the sum of *COUNTA* and *COUNTBLANK* of the same column.

So you can use four functions to count the number of elements in a column or table:

- *COUNT* operates only on numeric columns

- *COUNTA* operates on any type of columns

- *COUNTBLANK* returns the number of empty cells in a column

- *COUNTROWS* returns the number of rows in a table

There is still another very important counting function. *DISTINCTCOUNT,* which does exactly what its name suggests: it counts the distinct values of a column, which it takes as its only parameter. *DISTINCTCOUNT* counts the *BLANK* value as one of the possible values. Thus, as shown in Figure 3-12, the *DISTINCTCOUNT* of the IsActive column for category Drink is 3 because *BLANK* is a possible value.

FIGURE 3-12 *DISTINCTCOUNT* counts the *BLANK* value as a valid value.

> **Note** *DISTINCTCOUNT* is a function introduced in the 2012 version of PowerPivot. To compute the number of distinct values of a column in the previous version of PowerPivot, you had to use *COUNTROWS(DISTINCT(ColName))*. The two patterns return the very same result, but *DISTINCTCOUNT* is easier to read, requiring only a single function call.

A last set of statistical functions can apply an expression to each row of a table and then operate an aggregation on that expression. This set of functions is very useful, especially when you want to make calculations using columns of different related tables. For example, if a Sales table contains all the sales transactions and a related Product table contains all the information about a product, including its cost, you might calculate the total internal cost of a sales transaction by defining a calculated field with this expression:

```
Cost := SUMX ( Sales, Sales[Quantity] * RELATED ( Product[StandardCost] ) )
```

This function calculates the product of Quantity (from the Sales table) and the StandardCost of the sold product (from the related Product table) for each row in the Sales table, and it returns the sum of all these calculated values.

Generally, all the aggregate functions ending with an *X* behave in the following way: they calculate an expression (the second parameter) for each of the rows of a table (the first parameter) and return a result obtained by the corresponding aggregate function (*SUM, MIN, MAX,* or *COUNT*) applied to the result of those calculations.

Evaluation context is important for understanding how this calculation works. You will learn more about this behavior in Chapter 7, "Understanding evaluation contexts." The *X*-suffixed functions available are *SUMX, AVERAGEX, COUNTX, COUNTAX, MINX,* and *MAXX.*

Logical functions

Sometimes you may want to build a logical condition in an expression—for example, to implement different calculations depending on the value of a column or to intercept an error condition. In these cases, you can use one of the logical functions in DAX. In the section, "Handling Errors in DAX Expressions," earlier in this chapter, you learned the two most important functions of this group, which are *IF* and *IFERROR*. All of these functions are very simple and do what their names suggest: *AND, FALSE, IF, IFERROR, SWITCH, NOT, TRUE,* and *OR*. If, for example, you want to compute the Amount as Quantity multiplied by Price only when the Price column contains a correct numeric value, you can use the following pattern:

```
Amount := IFERROR ( Sales[Quantity] * Sales[Price], BLANK () )
```

If you did not use *IFERROR* and the *Price* value contains an invalid number, the result for the calculated column would be an error because if a single row generates a calculation error, that error is propagated to the whole column. The usage of *IFERROR*, however, intercepts the error and replaces it with a blank value.

Another interesting function in this category is *SWITCH*, which is useful when you have a column containing a low number of distinct values and you want to get different behaviors depending on the value. For example, the Size column in the DimProduct table contains L, M, S, and XL, and you might want to decode this value in a more meaningful column. You can obtain the result by using nested *IF* calls:

```
SizeDesc :=
    IF ( DimProduct[Size] = "S", "Small",
        IF ( DimProduct[Size] = "M", "Medium",
            IF ( DimProduct[Size] = "L", "Large",
                IF ( DimProduct[Size] = "XL", "Extra Large", "Other" ) ) ) )
```

A more convenient way to express the same formula using *SWITCH* is:

```
SizeDesc :=
    SWITCH (
        DimProduct[Size],
        "S", "Small",
        "M", "Medium",
        "L", "Large",
        "XL", "Extra Large",
        "Other"
    )
```

The code in this expression is more readable, even though it is not faster, because, internally, *SWITCH* statements are translated into nested *IF*.

> **TIP** Because *SWITCH* is converted into a set of nested *IF*, where the first one that matches takes precedence, you can test multiple conditions in the same expression using this pattern:
>
> ```
> SWITCH (
>     TRUE (),
>     DimProduct[Size] = "XL" && DimProduct[Color] = "Red", "Red and XL",
>     DimProduct[Size] = "XL" && DimProduct[Color] = "Blue", "Blue and XL",
>     DimProduct[Size] = "L" && DimProduct[Color] = "Green", "Green and L"
> )
> ```
>
> Using *TRUE* as the first parameter means "Return the first result where the condition evaluates to true."

Information functions

Whenever you need to analyze the type of an expression, you can use one of the information functions in DAX. All of these functions return a *TRUE/FALSE* value and can be used in any logical expression. They are *ISBLANK, ISERROR, ISLOGICAL, ISNONTEXT, ISNUMBER,* and *ISTEXT*.

It is important to note that when a table column is passed as a parameter, the functions *ISNUM-BER, ISTEXT,* and *ISNONTEXT* always return *TRUE* or *FALSE,* depending on the data type of the column and on the empty condition of each cell. In Figure 3-13, you can see how the column Price (which is of Text type) affects the result of these calculated columns.

```
ISBLANK         = ISBLANK ( Sales[Price] )
ISNUMBER        = ISNUMBER ( Sales[Price] )
ISTEXT          = ISTEXT ( Sales[Price] )
ISNONTEXT       = ISNONTEXT ( Sales[Price] )
ISERROR         = ISERROR ( Sales[Price] + 0 )
```

Product	Price	ISBLANK	ISNUMBER	ISTEXT	ISNONTEXT	ISERROR
Bike	100	FALSE	FALSE	TRUE	FALSE	FALSE
Clock		TRUE	FALSE	FALSE	TRUE	FALSE
Hat	15	FALSE	FALSE	TRUE	FALSE	FALSE
Notebook	399	FALSE	FALSE	TRUE	FALSE	FALSE
Gadget	N/A	FALSE	FALSE	TRUE	FALSE	TRUE

FIGURE 3-13 The results from information functions are based on column type.

You might be wondering whether *ISNUMBER* can be used with a text column just to check whether a conversion to a number is possible. Unfortunately, you cannot use this approach; if you want to test whether a text value can be converted to a number, you must try the conversion and handle the error if it fails. For example, to test whether the column Price (which is of type *String*) contains a valid number, you must write:

```
IsPriceCorrect = ISERROR ( Sales[Price] + 0 )
```

To get a *TRUE* result from the *ISERROR* function, for example, DAX tries to add a zero to the Price to force the conversion from a text value to a number. The conversion fails for the N/A price value, so you can see that *ISERROR* is *TRUE.*

Suppose, however, that you try to use *ISNUMBER,* as in the following expression:

```
IsPriceCorrect = ISNUMBER ( Sales[Price] )
```

In this case, you will always get *FALSE* as a result because, based on metadata, the Price column is not a number but a string.

Mathematical functions

The set of mathematical functions available in DAX is very similar to the same set in Excel, with the same syntax and behaviors. The most commonly used mathematical functions are *ABS, EXP, FACT, LN, LOG, LOG10, MOD, PI, POWER, QUOTIENT, SIGN,* and *SQRT.* Random functions include *RAND* and *RANDBETWEEN.* Finally, there are several functions to round numbers that deserve an example; in fact, you might use several approaches to get the same result. Consider these calculated columns, along with their results in Figure 3-14:

```
FLOOR        = FLOOR ( Tests[Value], 0.01 )
TRUNC        = TRUNC ( Tests[Value], 2 )
ROUNDDOWN    = ROUNDDOWN ( Tests[Value], 2 )
MROUND       = MROUND ( Tests[Value], 0.01 )
ROUND        = ROUND ( Tests[Value], 2 )
CEILING      = CEILING ( Tests[Value], 0.01 )
ISO.CEILING  = ISO.CEILING ( Tests[Value], 0.01 )
ROUNDUP      = ROUNDUP ( Tests[Value], 2 )
INT          = INT ( Tests[Value] )
FIXED        = FIXED ( Tests[Value], 2, TRUE )
```

Test	Value	FLOOR	TRUNC	ROUNDDOWN	MROUND	ROUND	CEILING	ROUNDUP	INT	FIXED	ISO.CEILING
A	1.12345	1.12	1.12	1.12	1.12	1.12	1.13	1.13	1	1.12	1.13
B	1.265	1.26	1.26	1.26	1.26	1.27	1.27	1.27	1	1.27	1.27
C	1.265001	1.26	1.26	1.26	1.27	1.27	1.27	1.27	1	1.27	1.27
D	1.499999	1.49	1.49	1.49	1.5	1.5	1.5	1.5	1	1.50	1.5
E	1.51111	1.51	1.51	1.51	1.51	1.51	1.52	1.52	1	1.51	1.52
F	1.000001	1	1	1	1	1	1.01	1.01	1	1.00	1.01
G	1.999999	1.99	1.99	1.99	2	2	2	2	1	2.00	2

FIGURE 3-14 A summary of different rounding functions.

As shown, *FLOOR, TRUNC,* and *ROUNDDOWN* are very similar, except in the way that you can specify the number of digits to round to. *CEILING* and *ROUNDUP* are very similar in their results, but in the opposite way. You can see a few differences in the way the rounding is done between the *MROUND* and *ROUND* functions. Finally, it is important to note that *FLOOR* and *MROUND* functions do not work on negative numbers, whereas other functions do.

Text functions

Almost all the text functions available in DAX are similar to those available in Excel, with only a few exceptions: *CONCATENATE, EXACT, FIND, FIXED, FORMAT, LEFT, LEN, LOWER, MID, REPLACE, REPT, RIGHT, SEARCH, SUBSTITUTE, TRIM, UPPER,* and *VALUE.* These functions are useful for manipulating text and extracting data from strings that contain multiple values. For example, in Figure 3-15, you can see an example of the extraction of first and last name from a string containing these values separated by commas, with the title in the middle that we want to remove.

Name	Comma1	Comma2	SimpleConversion	FirstLastName
Russo, Mr., Marco	6	11	Marco Russo	Marco Russo
Ferrari, Mr., Alberto	8	13	Alberto Ferrari	Alberto Ferrari
Ferrari, Alberto	8		Ferrari, Alberto Ferrari	Alberto Ferrari

FIGURE 3-15 Here, you can see an example of extracting first and last names using text functions.

You start by calculating the position of the two commas, and then you use these numbers to extract the right part of the text. The SimpleConversion column implements a formula that might return wrong values if there are fewer than two commas in the string (and it raises an error if there are no commas at all), whereas the FirstLastName column implements a more complex expression that does not fail in the case of missing commas. In fact, you can see in Figure 3-15 that the last row shows an incorrect value in the SimpleConversion column, whereas the FirstLastName column shows a correct conversion.

```
Comma1 = IFERROR ( FIND ( ",", People[Name] ), BLANK () )
Comma2 = IFERROR ( FIND ( ",", People[Name], People[Comma1] + 1 ), BLANK () )
SimpleConversion = MID ( People[Name], People[Comma2] + 1, LEN ( People[Name] ) )
                 & " " & LEFT ( People[Name], People[Comma1] - 1 )
FirstLastName = TRIM (
                  MID (
                      People[Name],
                      IF (
                          ISNUMBER ( People[Comma2] ),
                          People[Comma2],
                          People[Comma1]
                      ) + 1,
                      LEN ( People[Name] )
                  )
              )
              & IF (
                  ISNUMBER ( People[Comma1] ),
                  " " & LEFT ( People[Name], People[Comma1] - 1 ),
                  ""
              )
```

The FirstLastName column is defined by a long DAX expression, but you must use it to avoid possible errors that would propagate to the whole column if even a single value generated an error.

Conversion functions

You learned at the beginning of this chapter that DAX converts data types automatically to adjust them to the needs of the operators. Even if this happens automatically, a set of functions still can perform explicit conversion of types.

CURRENCY can transform an expression into a currency type, whereas *INT* transforms an expression into an integer. *DATE* and *TIME* take the date and time parts as parameters and return a correct *DATETIME*. *VALUE* transforms a string into a numeric format, whereas *FORMAT* gets a numeric value as the first parameter and a string format as its second one and can transform numeric values into strings.

Date and time functions

In almost every type of data analysis, handling time and date is an important aspect. PowerPivot has a large number of functions that operate on date and time. Some of them correspond to similar functions in Excel and make simple transformations to and from a *datetime* data type. The date and time functions are *DATE, DATEVALUE, DAY, EDATE, EOMONTH, HOUR, MINUTE, MONTH, NOW, SECOND, TIME, TIMEVALUE, TODAY, WEEKDAY, WEEKNUM, YEAR,* and *YEARFRAC*. To make more complex operation on dates, such as comparing aggregated values year over year or calculating the year-to-date value of a measure, there is another set of functions called Time Intelligence functions, which will be described later in the book in Chapter 12.

As mentioned before in this chapter, a *datetime* data type internally uses a floating-point number wherein the integer part corresponds to the number of the day (starting from December 30, 1899) and the decimal part indicates the fraction of the day in time. (Hours, minutes, and seconds are converted into decimal segments of the day.) So adding an integer number to a *datetime* value increments the value by a corresponding number of days. However, most of the time the conversion functions are used to extract day, month, and year from a date. The following example demonstrates how to extract this information from a table containing a list of dates (see Figure 3-16 for the result of the code):

```
Day     = DAY ( Calendar[Date] )
Month   = FORMAT ( Calendar[Date], "MM - mmmm" )
Year    = YEAR ( Calendar[Date] )
```

Date	Day	Month	Year
1/1/2010	1	01 - January	2010
1/2/2010	2	01 - January	2010
1/3/2010	3	01 - January	2010
1/4/2010	4	01 - January	2010
1/5/2010	5	01 - January	2010
1/6/2010	6	01 - January	2010

FIGURE 3-16 Here, you can see an example of extracting date information using date and time functions.

As Figure 3-16 shows, the Month column is calculated using the *FORMAT* function, which is classified as a text function but is very useful for building a string that keeps the right sort order of the months by placing the month number before the month name. (The Day and Year columns are sorted in the right order because of their numeric data type.)

Relational functions

Two useful functions that enable you to navigate through relationships inside a DAX formula are *RELATED* and *RELATEDTABLE*. In Chapters 7 and 8, you learn all the details of how these functions work, but for now, it is worthwhile to discuss them briefly here.

You already know that a calculated column can reference column values of the table in which it is defined. Thus, a calculated column defined in FactResellerSales can reference any column of the same table. But what can you do if you must refer to a column in another table? In general, you cannot use columns in another table unless a relationship is defined between the two tables. However, if the two tables are in a relationship, then the *RELATED* function enables you to access columns in the related table.

For example, you might want to compute a calculated column in the FactResellerSales table that checks whether the product that has been sold is in the Bikes category and, if so, apply a reduction factor to the standard cost. To compute such a column, you must write an *IF* function that checks the value of the product category, which is not in the FactResellerSales table. Nevertheless, a chain of relationships starts from FactInternetSales, reaching DimProductCategory through DimProduct and DimProductSubcategory, as Figure 3-17 shows.

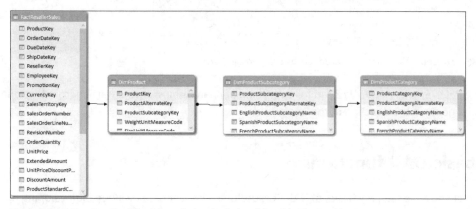

FIGURE 3-17 FactResellerSales has a chained relationship with DimProductCategory.

It does not matter how many steps are necessary to travel from the original table to the related one, DAX will follow the complete chain of relationships and return the related column value. Thus, the formula for the AdjustedCost column can be expressed as follows:

```
=IF (
    RELATED ( DimProductCategory[EnglishProductCategoryName] ) = "Bikes",
    [ProductStandardCost] * 0.95,
    [ProductStandardCost]
)
```

In a one-to-many relationship, *RELATED* can access the "one" side from the "many" side because, in that case, only one row in the related table exists, if any. If no row is related with the current one, *RELATED* simply returns *BLANK*. This is different than Excel *VLOOKUP* function, which returns an error if there is no match.

If you are on the "one" side of the relationship and you want to access the "many" side, *RELATED* is not helpful because many rows from the other side might be available for a single row in the current table. In that case, *RELATEDTABLE* will return a table containing all the related rows. For example, if you want to know how many products are in each category, you can create a column in DimProductCategory with this formula:

```
= COUNTROWS ( RELATEDTABLE ( DimProduct ) )
```

This calculated column will show the number of products that are related for each product category, as shown in Figure 3-18.

ProductCategoryKey	EnglishProductCategoryName	NumOfProducts
1	Bikes	125
2	Components	189
3	Clothing	48
4	Accessories	35

FIGURE 3-18 Count the number of products by using *RELATEDTABLE*.

Like *RELATED*, *RELATEDTABLE* can follow a chain of relationships, always starting from the "one" side and going in the direction of the "many" side.

Using basic DAX functions

Now that you have seen the basics of DAX, it is useful to check your knowledge of developing a sample reporting system. With the limited knowledge you have so far, you cannot develop a very complex solution. Nevertheless, even with a basic set of functions, you can already build something interesting.

Start loading the following tables from *AdventureWorksDW* into a new Excel workbook: DimDate, DimProduct, DimProductCategory, DimProductSubcategory, and FactResellerSales. The resulting data model is shown in Figure 3-19. You can find this workbook under the name "CH03-05-Final Exercise. xlsx."

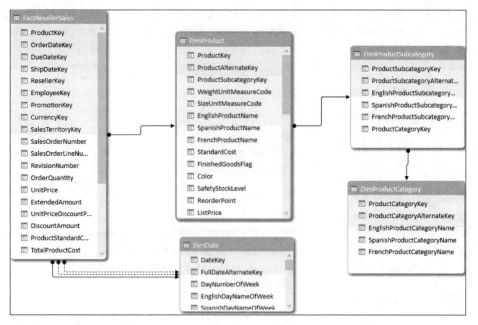

FIGURE 3-19 The Diagram view shows the structure of the demo data model.

To test your new knowledge of the DAX language, let's start solving some reporting problems with this data model.

First, count the number of products and enable the user to slice them by category and subcategory, so long as it is with any of the DimProduct columns. It is clear that you cannot rely on calculated columns to perform this task; you need a measure that simply counts the number of products, called NumOfProducts. The code is as follows:

```
NumOfProducts := COUNTROWS ( DimProduct )
```

Although this measure seems very easy to write, there is one problem. Because DimProduct is a slowly changing dimension of type 2 (that is, it can store different versions of the same product to track changes), the same product might appear several times in the table, and you want to count it only once. This common scenario can be solved easily by counting the number of distinct values in the natural key of the table. The natural key of DimProduct is the ProductAlternateKey column. Thus, the correct formula to count the number of products is

```
NumOfProducts := DISTINCTCOUNT ( DimProduct[ProductAlternateKey] )
```

You can see in Figure 3-20 that although the number of rows in the table is 606, the number of products is 504. This number correctly takes into account different versions of the same product, counting them only once.

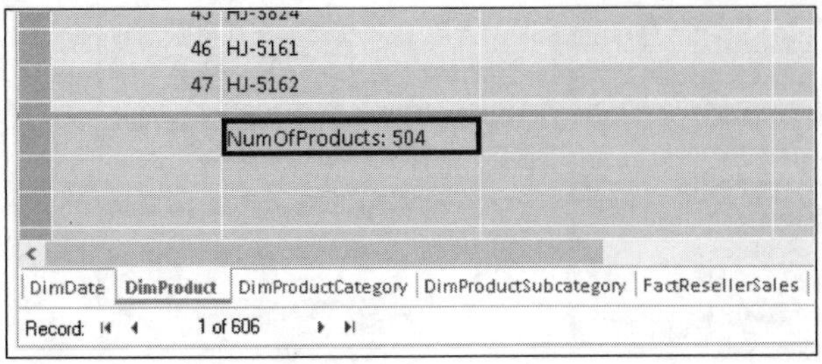

FIGURE 3-20 *DISTINCTCOUNT* is a useful and common function for counting.

This measure is very useful and, when browsed through a PivotTable, slicing by category and subcategory produces a report like the one shown in Figure 3-21.

Row Labels	NumOfProducts
Accessories	**29**
Bikes	**97**
Mountain Bikes	32
Road Bikes	43
Touring Bikes	22
Clothing	**35**
Components	**134**
(blank)	**209**
Grand Total	**504**

FIGURE 3-21 A sample report using NumOfProducts.

In this report, the last row is blank because there are products without a category and subcategory. After investigating the data, you discover that many of these uncategorized products are nuts, whereas other products are of no interest. Thus, you decide to override the Category and Subcategory columns with two new columns following this pattern:

- If the category is not empty, then display the category.
- If the category is empty and the product name contains the word "nut," show "Nuts" for the category and "Nuts" for the subcategory.
- Otherwise, show "Other" as both category and subcategory.

Because you must use these values to slice data, this time you cannot use calculated fields; you must create some calculated columns. You will put these two calculated columns in the DimProduct table and call them ProductCategory and ProductSubcategory. The code is as follows:

```
ProductSubcategory =
    IF (
        ISBLANK ( DimProduct[ProductSubcategoryKey] ),
        IF (
            ISERROR ( FIND ( "Nut", DimProduct[EnglishProductName] ) ),
            "Other",
            "Nut"
        ),
        RELATED ( DimProductSubcategory[EnglishProductSubcategoryName] )
    )
```

This formula is interesting because it uses several of the functions you have just learned. The first *IF* checks whether the ProductSubcategoryKey is empty and, if so, it searches for the word "Nut" inside the product name. *FIND* returns an error if there is no match, which is why you must surround it with the *ISERROR* function, which intercepts the error and enables you to take care of it. If *FIND* returns an error, the result is "Other"; otherwise, the formula computes the subcategory name from the DimProductSubcategory by using the *RELATED* function.

> **Tip** The *ISERROR* function can be slow in such a scenario because it raises errors if it does not find a value. Raising thousands if not millions of errors is a time-consuming operation. In such a case, it is often better to use the fourth parameter of the *FIND* function (which is the default return value if there is no match) to always get a value back, avoiding the error handling. In this formula, we are using *ISERROR* for educational purposes. In a production data model, it is always best to take care of performance speed and use the fourth parameter.

With this calculated column, you have solved the issue with ProductSubcategory. The very same code, by replacing ProductSubcategory with ProductCategory, yields to the second calculated column, which makes the same operation with the category (the difference between the formulas is indicated in bold):

```
ProductCategory =
    IF (
        ISBLANK ( DimProduct[ProductSubcategoryKey] ),
        IF (
            ISERROR ( FIND ( "Nut", DimProduct[EnglishProductName] ) ),
            "Other",
            "Nut"
        ),
        RELATED ( DimProductCategory[EnglishProductCategoryName] )
    )
```

Note that you still must check whether ProductSubcategoryKey is empty because this is the only available column in DimProduct to test if the product has a category. In fact, because of the way data is shaped in *AdventureWorks*, all subcategories have a category, and a product does not have a category if it does not have a subcategory. In different data models, you might face different scenarios, so that, for example, you might need to check ISBLANK (RELATED (DimProductCategory[ProductCategoryKey])).

If you now browse this new data model in a PivotTable and use the newly created calculated column on the rows, you get the result shown in Figure 3-22.

Row Labels	NumOfProducts
⊞ Accessories	29
⊟ Bikes	97
Mountain Bikes	32
Road Bikes	43
Touring Bikes	22
⊞ Clothing	35
⊞ Components	134
⊟ Nut	79
Nut	79
⊟ Other	130
Other	130
Grand Total	504

FIGURE 3-22 You can build a report with the new product category and subcategory.

As you have seen, creating a report and shaping it to fit your analytical needs is easy with a basic knowledge of the DAX language. DAX is the key to many complex reports that you will be able to build with PowerPivot for Excel. You have a long way to go before you become a real DAX master, but the ability to create this report alone, without help from anybody else, is already very rewarding.

CHAPTER 4

Understanding data models

The first chapters of this book introduced some basic Microsoft PowerPivot features for generating interesting reports from existing data. In several examples, you discovered the need to model your data to make them easier to understand and manage. Nevertheless, because all the examples were introductive ones, data modeling was not an issue. It is now time to perform a deeper analysis of data modeling, so you can learn what it is and how to handle different data models.

Data modeling is not a new concept for database analysts and administrators. These technicians already know that a good data model is the foundation of a good database solution. In the world of Microsoft Excel, the same applies: a good data model is definitely the foundation of a good reporting system.

On the other hand, the problem of data modeling is somewhat new to Excel users. Until the introduction of the data model, Excel users could query only one table at a time, so the very concept of relationship was missing. The Excel data model is a sophisticated columnar database that can store huge amounts of data. It is a real database. Because you are handling a database, you need to understand how different tables are related to each other and which model is the easiest and most effective regarding your needs. In short, you need to learn the basics of data modeling.

You have already learned about the concept of relationship, which is the foundation of data modeling in the previous chapters. Nevertheless, because we believe that relationships and data models need to be well understood by the Excel analysts who are willing to create self-service business intelligence (BI) reporting, we are going to dedicate this full chapter to data modeling. At the beginning, we repeat some concepts that you have already encountered in Chapter 1, "Introduction to PowerPivot," but this time, we are trying to be more precise and follow a complete path that will help you learn how to become a good data modeler.

Understanding the basics of data modeling

You have learned in Chapter 1 that there are two ways to merge information coming from two different tables into a single, coherent view of data:

- Using single-table PivotTables, you need to use *VLOOKUP* to bring data from several tables into a single one, so that the PivotTable can work on only one table and let you analyze data.

- Using the multi-table data model, you do not need to use *VLOOKUP*. You use the creation of relationships between tables so that the PivotTable (and Power View) can analyze data coming from different tables in a single view.

The first method is easy and intuitive, but it falls short as soon as the number of tables you need to analyze grows to more than three or four. Handling and managing all the *VLOOKUP* functions end in a very complex work if *VLOOKUP* is the only available tool in your hands. On the other hand, the second method is much better, but it requires you to understand what a relationship is and how it works.

In reality, *VLOOKUP* and relationships behave much in the same way. The big difference is that *VLOOKUP* is an operation, meaning that you instruct Excel to perform a specific calculation (that is, search for a value in a table where a condition is met), whereas a relationship is a declaration (that is, you instruct Excel on how to search for values when they will be needed). But you do not ask it to perform an operation—you simply declare the existence of a relationship.

This is the big difference between using *VLOOKUP* and using relationships. When creating a relationship, you tell Excel: "Whenever you will need to merge values coming from these two tables in a computation, search for matching values between the two tables using these two columns, which need to be equal in the two tables to make a match." You can think of a relationship as a set of "virtual *VLOOKUPs*," where the lookup operation will happen only when needed for the columns requested.

Now let's learn more about the power of relationships by looking at how to handle a simple scenario with both Excel and PowerPivot. Suppose that you want to count the number of products for each category and subcategory by using a PivotTable. In the *AdventureWorks* database, you have three tables:

- **DimProduct**   Contains information about products and a column called ProductSubcategoryKey, which is the code of the subcategory of the product

- **DimProductSubcategory**   Contains all the product subcategories and, for each category, the code of the category it belongs to, in a column called ProductCategoryKey

- **DimProductCategory**   Contains information about categories

Producing a report without a data model

If you want to create a single Excel table to hold the information of the three database tables, you start by loading the three sets of data in three Excel tables similar to the ones you see in Figure 4-1, where we have removed many columns from the tables, to highlight the useful ones.

You can find this data model in the companion workbook "CH04-01-Understanding Relationships.xlsx."

ProductKey	ProductAlternateKey	ProductSubcategoryKey	EnglishProductName
553	HB-T721	4	LL Touring Handlebars
554	HB-T928	4	HL Touring Handlebars
555	FB-9873	6	Front Brakes
556	CS-4759	8	LL Crankset
557	CS-6583	8	ML Crankset
558	CS-9183	8	HL Crankset
559	CH-0234	7	Chain
560	BK-T44U-60	3	Touring-2000 Blue, 60
561	BK-T79Y-46	3	Touring-1000 Yellow, 46
562	BK-T79Y-50	3	Touring-1000 Yellow, 50

ProductSubcategoryKey	ProductSubcategoryAlternateKey	EnglishProductSubcategoryName	ProductCategoryKey
1	1	Mountain Bikes	1
2	2	Road Bikes	1
3	3	Touring Bikes	1
4	4	Handlebars	2
5	5	Bottom Brackets	2
6	6	Brakes	2
7	7	Chains	2

ProductCategoryKey	ProductCategoryAlternateKey	EnglishProductCategoryName
1	1	Bikes
2	2	Components
3	3	Clothing
4	4	Accessories

FIGURE 4-1 Here, you can see the three tables containing the datasets of products, categories, and subcategories.

If you want to bring all the information from the three tables into a single one, you will need to perform these steps:

1. Create a new *VLOOKUP* operation column in DimProductSubcategory to store the ProductCategoryName taken from the DimProductCategory table by searching for the ProductCategoryKey:

```
= VLOOKUP( [@ProductCategoryKey], DimProductCategory, 3 )
```

2. Create two *VLOOKUP* operations in DimProduct to store both the product subcategory name and the product category name, taken from the DimProductSubcategory table using the ProductSubcategoryKey as the value to search for:

```
= VLOOKUP( [@ProductSubcategoryKey], DimProductSubcategory, 5 )
= VLOOKUP( [@ProductSubcategoryKey], DimProductSubcategory, 3 )
```

At the end, you created a single table containing all the columns you need, as shown in Figure 4-2.

ProductKey	ProductAlternateKey	ProductSubcategoryKey	EnglishProductName	ProductCategory	ProductSubcategory
207	TO-2301		Top Tube	#N/A	#N/A
208	TP-0923		Tension Pulley	#N/A	#N/A
209	RC-0291		Rear Derailleur Cage	#N/A	#N/A
210	FR-R92B-58	14	HL Road Frame - Black, 58	Components	Road Frames
211	FR-R92R-58	14	HL Road Frame - Red, 58	Components	Road Frames
212	HL-U509-R	31	Sport-100 Helmet, Red	Accessories	Helmets
213	HL-U509-R	31	Sport-100 Helmet, Red	Accessories	Helmets
214	HL-U509-R	31	Sport-100 Helmet, Red	Accessories	Helmets
215	HL-U509	31	Sport-100 Helmet, Black	Accessories	Helmets
216	HL-U509	31	Sport-100 Helmet, Black	Accessories	Helmets
217	HL-U509	31	Sport-100 Helmet, Black	Accessories	Helmets
218	SO-B909-M	23	Mountain Bike Socks, M	Clothing	Socks

FIGURE 4-2 The DimProduct table now contains all the necessary columns to create a PivotTable.

If you want to create a PivotTable based on this table, you then insert a new PivotTable using the DimProduct table as the source. You can put ProductCategory in the rows, but when it comes to producing the count of products, there is a problem. Producing the sum of any numeric value is as easy as dragging the column name to the VALUES area, but counting rows is somewhat more difficult. To do this, follow these instructions.

First, drag the ProductKey to the VALUES area. After that, you will obtain the sum of ProductKey, which is meaningless because there is no point in summing a key. Nevertheless, Excel uses *SUM* as the default aggregate function for any numeric column. Then, click the Field Settings button on the ANALYZE tab of the ribbon, as shown in Figure 4-3.

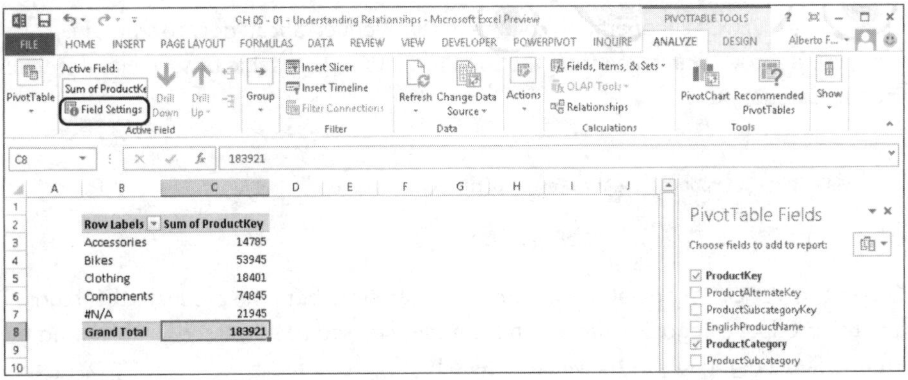

FIGURE 4-3 The Field Settings button lets you modify the way that values are shown in the PivotTable.

Excel will open the Field Settings dialog box (see Figure 4-4), where you can modify the way that values from the ProductKey column are summarized. To count products, you simply need to choose the Count function, as shown in Figure 4-4.

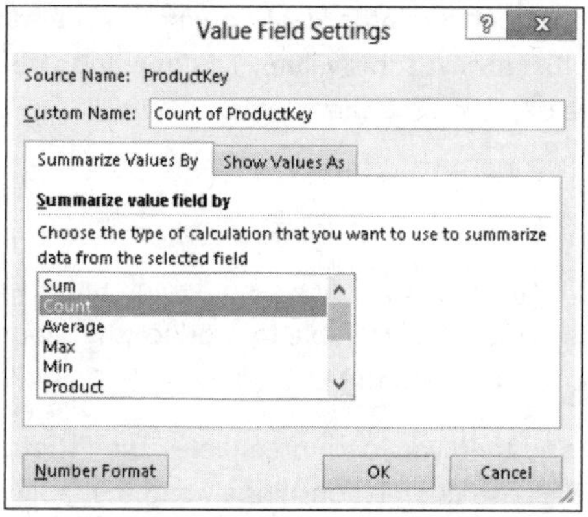

FIGURE 4-4 In the Field Settings dialog box, choose the Count function to count the number of products.

Using the *Count* function to aggregate values, the PivotTable will now show the desired report, as shown in Figure 4-5.

Row Labels	Count of ProductKey
Accessories	35
Bikes	125
Clothing	48
Components	189
#N/A	209
Grand Total	**606**

FIGURE 4-5 The PivotTable now shows the count of products instead of the sum of ProductKey.

Clearly, because the information about how to aggregate the ProductKey column is local to the PivotTable, if you want to create a similar report in another worksheet, you will need to repeat the operation. This is not a major issue with small reports, but it might be annoying if you create a very large workbook that covers complex analysis.

Now, let's recall briefly what we have covered so far. The relevant points of this technique are as follows:

- The product category name takes two steps to be brought into the products table. To reach it, you need to bring it first to the product subcategory table and, from there, to the products table. Another technique would have been to use a nested *VLOOKUP*, making the formula harder to read and modify later.

- To bring two columns from the product subcategory table to the product table, you have to create two columns, with two different formulas (although they are very similar), in the products table.

- If you are working with small tables, then speed and memory occupations are not an issue. But as soon as you try loading hundreds of thousands of rows, using multiple *VLOOKUP* functions will start slowing your workbook, and the table size will use up a lot of memory.

- When you need to count the products, instead of performing a *SUM,* you modify the way the PivotTable aggregates data because, by default, it always sums values. This operation needs to be executed for any PivotTable that you create based on the same table.

Building a data model

Producing the same report in PowerPivot is not more difficult; it just follows a different path. Using PowerPivot, you will first create a data model, and then create a PivotTable to produce the report. You can find this data model in the companion workbook "CH04-02-Data Model.xlsx."

To do this, first, you open the PowerPivot window and then you load three tables: DimProduct, DimProductCategory, and DimProductSubcategory. Because the relationships among the tables are already present in the database, PowerPivot creates them during the loading process. If, at this point, you switch to Diagram view, you will see the data model shown in Figure 4-6.

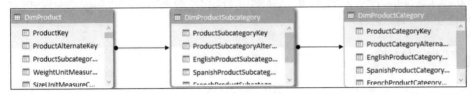

FIGURE 4-6 This data model diagram is created by PowerPivot by detecting existing relationships among tables.

You can immediately create a PivotTable based on this data, but this time, it is better to create the required calculated field in advance because we already know that we are interested in counting the number of products.

Using the measure grid, you can enter this calculated field definition:

```
NumOfProducts := COUNTROWS ( DimProduct )
```

At this point, you can simply create a new PivotTable, put the category name from the DimProductCategory table into the rows, and choose the calculated field NumOfProducts for the values. The result (see Figure 4-7) is very similar to the one obtained with the previous technique.

Row Labels	NumOfProducts
Accessories	35
Bikes	125
Clothing	48
Components	189
(blank)	209
Grand Total	**606**

FIGURE 4-7 The PivotTable working on the data model looks very similar to the previous one.

What are the main differences between the two approaches?

- Using the data model approach, you did not need to use *VLOOKUP* to create columns. Rather, you declared the existence of relationships and then, when the PivotTable needed to slice products using the category name, it had to follow a relationship.

- Having a chain of relationships between tables is not an issue: even if the product category needs two steps to reach the products table (one from products to subcategories and one from subcategories to categories), the data model knows how to handle them in a simple way.

- The definition of the calculated field NumOfProducts is not local to the PivotTable. It is defined in the model and, if you need to use the same calculation in many different PivotTables based on the same data model, you do not need to create the definition in each PivotTable.

- Regarding speed and memory usage, the data model is capable of holding hundreds of millions of rows and computing very complex PivotTables in a matter of seconds.

Having reached this point, it is now time to be more precise. So, what is a data model? A data model is nothing but a group of tables tied together by a set of relationships with some calculated fields and, possibly, some calculated columns.

Thus, it is correct to say that you already know everything that you need to build a data model. Nevertheless, being able to build a data model does not mean that you know how to build a good one. The art of data modeling is complex and, as you are going to learn in the rest of this book, a good data model is the key to producing easy and maintainable DAX code. Thus, the rest of this chapter is dedicated to concepts and topics that will help you build better data models.

More about relationships

You can look at relationships via the diagram view in the PowerPivot window. Graphically, a relationship between tables is represented as an arrow starting from one table and pointing to another one. Being an arrow, a relationship has a direction. At this point, look at Figure 4-8, which shows the data model that you have built right now.

FIGURE 4-8 Relationships are shown as arrows running from one table to another.

Let's focus on the arrow between DimProduct and DimProductSubcategory:

- DimProduct is the source table (that is, the table at which the relationship originates).

- DimProductSubcategory is the target table (that is, the table that contains values related to the source table).

- The ProductSubcategoryKey column in the DimProduct table is the foreign key. It contains the value that needs to be searched in DimProductSubcategory to find the related row.

- The ProductSubcategoryKey column in the DimProductSubcategory table is the primary key. It needs to have a unique value for each row in the table. This is a requirement because, for each row in the DimProduct table, there can be only one related row in the DimProductSubcategory table. If a target table does not have unique values on the column that is used to establish the relationship, this relationship cannot be created.

Because there can be only one subcategory for each product, whereas for a single subcategory there can be many products, we sometimes refer to the tables using different names. The source table is called the "many side" of the relationship, whereas the target table is called the "one side" of the relationship. For this reason, we refer to this kind of relationship as a "one-to-many relationship." Later in this chapter, we will discuss about different kinds of relationships, like many-to-many relationships.

To better understand the direction of this relationship between DimProduct and DimProductSubcategory, you can try to delete and re-create it. To delete the relationship, switch to Diagram view, click the arrow, and hit the Del key. Excel opens a box for you to confirm the deletion. After you click Delete From Model, the relationship will be deleted.

Then, to re-create it, click the Create Relationship button on the Design tab of the PowerPivot ribbon. The Create Relationship dialog box will open and you can fill it in, as shown in Figure 4-9.

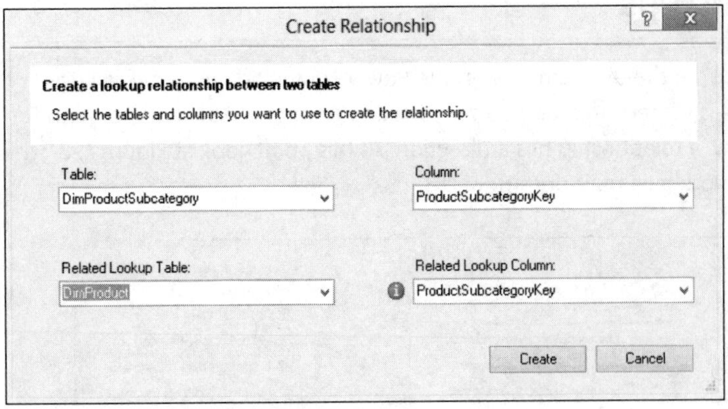

FIGURE 4-9 When you create a relationship in the wrong direction, PowerPivot automatically reverses it.

In the figure, you can see an information circle beside the Related Lookup Column. By placing the mouse on top of it, you will see this message:

The relationship cannot be created in the requested direction. When you click create, the direction of the relationship will be reversed.

PowerPivot analyzed the data in your data model and verified that ProductSubCategoryKey is a primary key in the DimProductSubcategory and is not in the DimProductTable. Thus, the relationship cannot have DimProduct as the target table. It needs to have DimProductSubcategory as the target and DimProduct as the source. For this reason, the relationship will be created in the opposite direction you have requested. This is not only a simple warning: You are going to learn that the direction of a relationship is very important because some DAX function will work only when invoked from the correct side of the relationship.

> **Note** Rare cases do exist where you have a column that is a primary key in both tables. For example, you might have a DimProduct table with several columns and a DimProductAdditionalInfo table, containing additional information for the product. In such a scenario, the ProductKey is a primary key in both columns. This relationship is known as an identity relationship because if the relationship holds, both tables are on the "one" side. Nevertheless, in the PowerPivot data model, all relationships are always one-to-many, and you will need to decide which is the one side and which is the many side. This task is not easy because DAX evaluates the formulas in different ways depending on the side of a relationship where you write the calculation. You will learn more about this topic in Chapter 7, "Understanding evaluation contexts."

Understanding normalization and denormalization

Now that you have taken a first look at what a data model is, you need to learn the difference between the physical and the logical data model. To do that, we are going to show an example of a physical data model, describe its limitations and issues, and introduce the new concept of a logical data model.

The data model containing products, categories, and subcategories is shown again in Figure 4-10.

FIGURE 4-10 This is an example of a normalized data model, each table containing a single entity.

This data model contains three tables, and each table contains a single entity. But there is a tendency to believe that a product category should not be in a table by itself, but is nothing but an attribute of the product. So, why is it stored inside a table instead of being a column in the DimProduct table? You are facing a very common issue that happens whenever users and technicians deal with a database:

- Users think in a logical way. They divide the database into entities and concepts that are directly related to their view of the topics, which are closely related to the real world. In this example, they see products as entities and categories and subcategories as simple textual descriptions of the products. Users do not need to think of a table as containing all the categories, nor do they understand why there should be a relationship between these two tables.

- Technicians, on the other hand, think in a physical way. They divide the database into technical entities that are closely related to the physical representation of data on disk. In the technical world, it is obvious that if products have categories and subcategories, the most effective way to store this information is by creating a set of relationships among three different tables. The physical representation on disk aims at reducing data duplication to avoid inconsistencies. This technique is known as *data normalization*. Data normalization is the reason to have so many tables in a relational database. You will learn more about normalization in the next part of this text.

Thus, there are always at least two distinct ways to look at a database. We will refer to the two views as *logical* (user) versus *physical* (technician). Because the database is normally created by technicians, you can expect to have to manage normalized data models. Nevertheless, because we want to analyze it, we need a way to turn the normalized data model into a denormalized one, reducing the number of tables and increasing the model readability.

To reduce the normalization of the data model, you create two calculated columns in the DimProduct table, and then you hide the product category and subcategory tables from the model. First, create a calculated column in the DimProduct table with these DAX expressions:

```
ProductCategory    = RELATED ( DimProductCategory[EnglishProductCategoryName] )
ProductSubcategory = RELATED ( DimProductSubcategory[EnglishProductSubcategoryName] )
```

You end up with a DimProduct table that looks like the one shown in Figure 4-11.

EnglishProductName	Color	ListPrice	ProductCategory	ProductSubcategory
Long-Sleeve Logo Jerse...	Multi	$48.07	Clothing	Jerseys
Long-Sleeve Logo Jerse...	Multi	$48.07	Clothing	Jerseys
Long-Sleeve Logo Jerse...	Multi	$49.99	Clothing	Jerseys
LL Fork	NA	$148.22	Components	Forks
ML Fork	NA	$175.49	Components	Forks
HL Fork	NA	$229.49	Components	Forks
LL Mountain Handlebars	NA	$40.49	Components	Handlebars
LL Mountain Handlebars	NA	$44.54	Components	Handlebars
LL Mountain Front Wheel	Black	$60.75	Components	Wheels
ML Mountain Front Wh...	Black	$209.03	Components	Wheels
HL Mountain Front Wh...	Black	$300.22	Components	Wheels
Touring Front Wheel	Black	$218.01	Components	Wheels

FIGURE 4-11 The DimProduct table contains denormalized columns.

The column values from their tables have been brought to the DimProduct one using the *RELATED* function. At this point, there is no need to show the DimProductCategory and DimProductSubcategory tables in the PivotTables because their content is now available in the DimProduct table. For this reason, it is better to hide them from the data model. To do so, select the table in Diagram view, right-click it, and choose Hide From Client Tools, as shown in Figure 4-12.

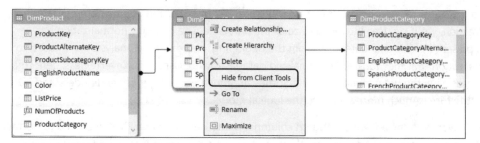

FIGURE 4-12 Technical tables should be hidden using the Hide From Client Tools function.

Performing the same operation for both DimProductCategory and DimProductSubcategory, you will reach the optimal situation, where the normalized tables, although still present in the data model, are no longer visible in the PivotTable. We refer to tables like those, which are needed for the data model but can be safely hidden, as *technical tables* (tables that exist for technical reasons but that are useless from an analytical point of view).

It is worth noting at this point that there also are technical columns (that is, columns that are needed for the data model but that have no analytical significance). For example, if you look at the ProductSubcategoryKey in the DimProductTable, it is useless to see it inside a PivotTable, even if it is necessary because it is the foreign key of the relationship with the DimProductSubcategory table. Following the same procedure, you can right-click the column and hide it from the client tools. The same can be done with many other columns as well. Hiding technical columns from the data model and removing normalization is one of the first and most important operations that improve the usability of a data model.

Recall what has been discussed so far: if you think of the possible ways to store products, categories, and subcategories on a disk file, you have these two options:

- You can store the textual descriptions of category and subcategory inside each product, as the logical model requires. If you do this, you will end up repeating the same description for each product with a specific category.

- On the other hand, you can store the textual description of each category only once and then reference it from subcategories using a number, which is usually shorter than the description. Moreover, you can perform the same operation with each subcategory, storing its description only once in the subcategory table and using a reference from products that links to the subcategory. This technique, in databases like Microsoft SQL Server, leads to less space being used on disk, even if it will be harder to read.

The first option is required by the logical data model. It is clear that, due to the nature of the method, the logical model contains a lot of redundancy. Because the description of a category is the same for many different products, the logical model is not optimized due to the high level of data duplication. The technical model, on the other hand, is optimized because redundancy is removed, which leads to taking up less disk size and memory and, in general, to a higher level of database performance for daily operation. In other words, the technical model is normalized (redundancy removed) and the logical one is denormalized (redundancy present).

Normalization is a process that increases the number of tables needed to store the same information, yet it reduces the overall size of the database. The need for normalization has been present in relational databases from the beginning, and database analysts are so used to normalization that they look at denormalized databases with suspicion. Nevertheless, denormalized databases have the great characteristic that they are much easier to query and understand because their structure is much more similar to the logical model.

Moreover, with the advent of modern columnar databases like PowerPivot, the need to normalize tables is greatly reduced, if not removed completely. If a single value is repeated several times in a table, PowerPivot will not store the value as is. Instead, it will provide a kind of automatic normalization by removing the long description and replacing it with numbers that just refer to it. In other words, the process of normalization is carried on internally by the PowerPivot database even if you load a denormalized table.

Is normalization the correct technique?

Note that normalization is neither good nor bad. The same applies for its opposite, denormalization. The need to normalize data comes from the very nature of the database and follows technical rules that are too complex to cover here and yet are very important. An operational database should be normalized, whereas a data model that the user can browse directly should be denormalized.

When considering logical vs. technical data models, you should avoid the temptation to think that one model is "more correct" than the other. Each one could be right or wrong, depending on the kind of operations that you need to perform on it. The point here is that, when you load data from an operational database, you will probably find normalized data. Because you will need to show that information to a user, you will need techniques to remove normalization and produce a denormalized data model, which is the correct one for the analysis.

Finally, even if denormalized data models are normally easier to query, you need to be aware that sometimes you end up over-denormalizing a data model (that is, reaching a point where denormalization starts to be a major issue) because your data model is losing its original shape. We will cover over-denormalization in the "Understanding over-denormalization" section later in this chapter because it happens very often and needs specific handling.

Denormalizing within SQL queries

In order to get acquainted with the concept of denormalization, you now will learn how to denormalize a data model using the SQL editor instead of using the *RELATED* function from inside the data model.

The *RELATED* technique is easy to use and understand, but it has the disadvantage of being annoying to implement for the many normalized columns that normally appear in an operational database. It might be interesting to learn at least one different technique to perform the same operation.

This new technique requires you to use the query builder of PowerPivot to denormalize the original data, loading information inside PowerPivot in an already denormalized way. Thus, we are shifting from denormalization inside PowerPivot (the previous technique) to denormalization outside PowerPivot (the new one).

Having more than one technique to solve the same problem will later raise the issue of deciding when to use each one, but that will come up later in this book. You can find this simple data model in the companion workbook "CH04-03-Understanding Normalization.xlsx."

The PowerPivot query designer

If you want to remove normalization from a data model, you can use the PowerPivot query designer to produce denormalized datasets. Nevertheless, before you start designing a query, it is important to understand a SQL query.

A *SQL query* is a statement written in a special language called SQL, which is understood by most modern relational databases. This book is not going to describe in detail how to write an SQL query. Here, we are interested in discussing the usage of the PowerPivot query designer, which requires you to understand just the basics of SQL and handles much of the hard work for you.

A very simple SQL query looks like this:

```
SELECT
    ProductKey,
    EnglishProductName AS ProductName,
    EnglishProductSubcategoryName AS ProductSubcategory
FROM
    dbo.DimProduct AS Prod
    INNER JOIN dbo.DimProductSubcategory AS Sub
        ON Prod.ProductSubcategoryKey = Sub.ProductSubcategoryKey
WHERE
    Sub.EnglishProductSubcategoryName = 'Helmets'
```

Let's look at this example in greater detail. A query is composed of several parts, the most common and important of which are the following:

- **SELECT**   In the first part of the query, you will declare which columns you are interested in reading. You can refer more than one table in the column list of *SELECT*, which is particularly useful when you need to get data from tables with relationships between them.

- **FROM**   In this second part of the query, you declare which tables you want the database to read to gather the columns declared in the *SELECT* section. If more than one table is referenced, as is the case in this example, then you should specify how to follow relationships through the different tables. This is done using the *JOIN* predicate.

- **WHERE**   The last part of the query lets you create filtering conditions so as not to retrieve all the rows. In the example, the code asks for rows that contain "Helmets" as the subcategory name.

Now that you have seen the overall structure of a query, you are going to create this query and load its data inside PowerPivot so you can appreciate the difference between the query result and the original tables.

Building a query is always a complex step because it requires a good knowledge of the data model to query. SQL technicians normally write queries using a standard text editor because they already know how to retrieve data. You are probably not an SQL technician, however, so you will be interested in using the PowerPivot query designer, which is a tool that lets you build an SQL query through a visual interface. Even if the query designer will handle the hard work for you, understanding the final query structure will let you understand better what the query designer is asking of you.

To open the query designer, go to the PowerPivot window and start the loading procedure to take data from a database. When choosing how to import data, instead of selecting from a list of tables, you will choose the Write A Query That Will Specify The Data To Import option, as shown in Figure 4-13.

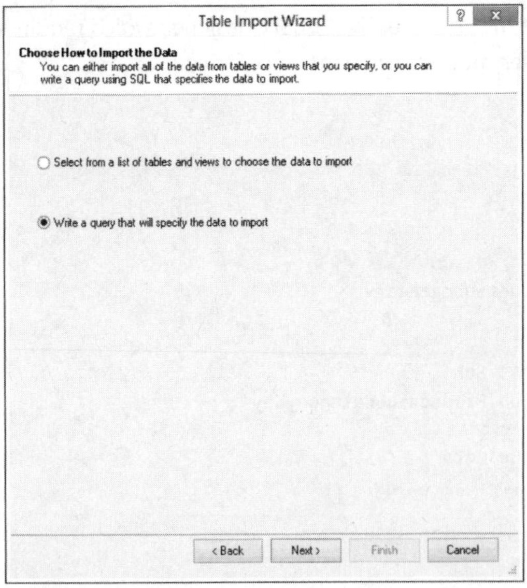

FIGURE 4-13 Choose the right option to start the query editor.

Once you click Next, the Table Import Wizard will open the SQL query editor (see Figure 4-14).

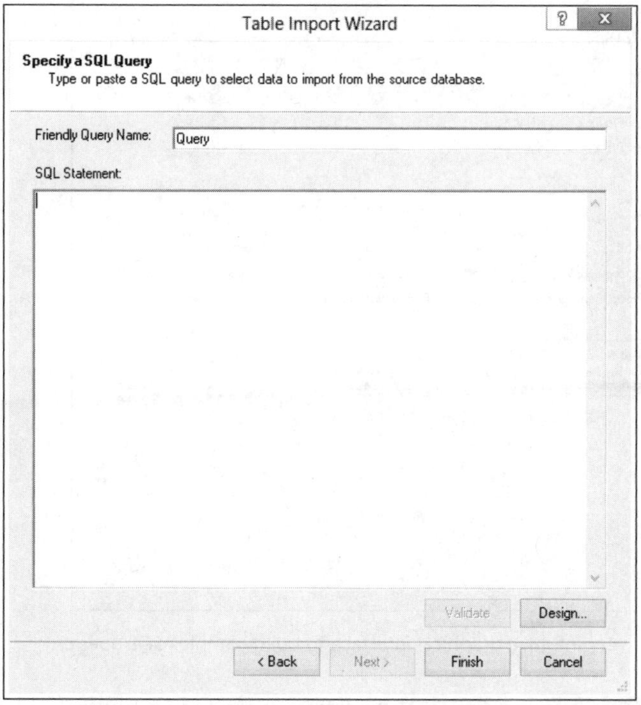

FIGURE 4-14 The SQL query editor lets you write your SQL code in a simple text box.

The query editor is a simple text editor where you can start to write the SQL query and give it a user-friendly name. Because you are probably not an SQL expert, it is much better to click Design to open the query designer.

In the query designer shown in Figure 4-15, the three tables, Product, ProductSubcategory, and ProductCategory, are already selected, and the Relationship pane has been expanded to describe it. The relationship panel is hidden by default; to expand it, you need to use the double-arrow button that appears right below the Selected Fields panel.

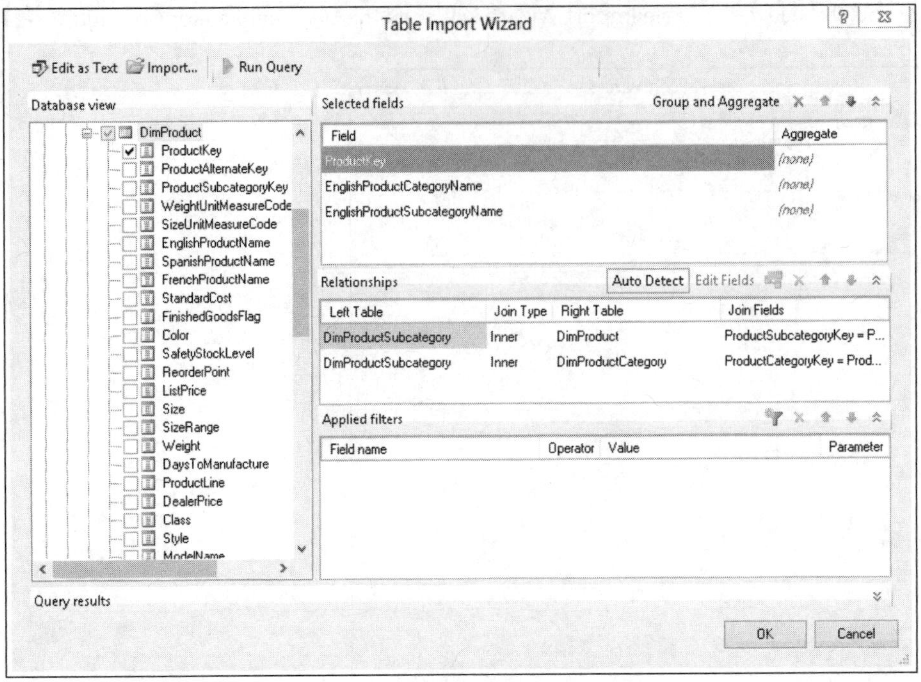

FIGURE 4-15 The query designer has a very intuitive graphical interface to build complex SQL queries.

Let's explore the query designer in more detail now. In the left pane, you can select the tables to add to the query and, expanding the table, you can select the single columns inside them. In the right part of the window, you can see the list of all the columns selected (the SELECT part of the query), the list of the tables involved, along with their relationships (the FROM part of the query) and, in the lower part, the list of filters to apply (the WHERE part of the query).

In the example, we selected a very small number of columns, to make the screenshots easy to read. In the real world, the number of columns to retrieve is normally much higher.

The less intuitive part of the query designer is the Relationship pane. You can see that, having selected three tables, the designer detected the existence of relationships between them: one between DimProduct and DimProductSubcategory and one between DimProductSubcategory and DimProductCategory. Those relationships have been automatically detected by the engine because they are stored inside the database metadata.

To understand how relationships work, you need to understand the following:

- A relationship exists between two tables only. It does not matter how many tables are involved in a query—a single relationship relates only two of them at a time.

- The two tables are ordered: one is called "Left table," and the other is "Right table." This is very important, as the next part of this text will show, because a wrong table ordering might lead to an incorrect query.

- A relationship has a type (the middle column in the relationship pane) that indicates how to retrieve rows from the database. You definitely need to understand how different types of relationships affect the query result to get the data you need.

Thus, reading the result of the auto detection algorithm, you can see that it detected both relationships and has chosen the *INNER* type of relationship for both.

In a few lines, we will analyze how different types of relationships return different results in the query designer. For the moment, though, it is enough to click OK to see the query that gets built. PowerPivot returns to the query editor, which is now filled with a complex query that the designer has written, as shown in Figure 4-16.

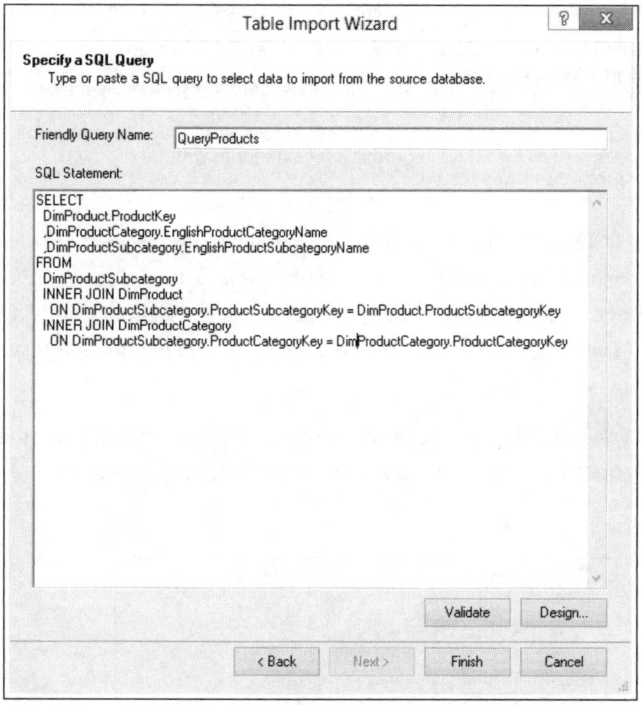

FIGURE 4-16 The SQL query editor, with a query written by the designer.

If you click Finish, you start the loading process, which means that the query is executed against the database and all the rows are imported into the PowerPivot database. Nevertheless, if you look at the number of rows returned, you may not like what you see: only 397 rows have been loaded, whereas the DimProducts table effectively contains 606 different products.

Something is wrong here why has PowerPivot lost 209 rows during the loading process? The reason is that the designer is able to understand that a relationship exists between two tables, but it is not as good in determining the type of relationship, and, having selected the wrong one, the database failed to return all the products. It is definitely time to understand better which kind of relationships you can set and how they affect the final result.

When relating the left and right tables (in this example, we will use left for DimProducts and right for DimProductSubcategory), you have four different options, listed in Table 4-1. The big difference among all the types of *JOIN* is in the handling of *NULL* values in the left or right table.

TABLE 4-1 Different types of relationships

Relationship	Result
INNER JOIN	Only the rows where there is a match between the left and right table are returned. In this example, the query will return only the products that have a subcategory, discarding the ones with the ProductSubcategoryKey column set to *NULL*.
LEFT OUTER JOIN	The left table is preserved. This means that rows coming from the left table that do not have corresponding rows in the right one will be returned anyway, leaving all the columns for the right table as *NULLs*. In the example, all products would be returned and, if they have no subcategory, the subcategory name column would be left as *NULL*.
RIGHT OUTER JOIN	The right table is preserved. In the example, all the subcategories would be returned, even the ones where there are no products inside them. Moreover, because the left table is not preserved, the products that have no subcategory will not be returned.
FULL OUTER JOIN	Both tables are preserved. In this example, you would receive all the products and all the subcategories with *NULL* values in products for categories without products, and in categories for products without categories.

If you carefully read Table 4-1, it will be clear how the error happened. The query designer chose the *INNER JOIN* type for the relationship between Products and Subcategory, thus discarding all the products that do not have a subcategory set. In other words, all the products that contained *NULL* in the ProductSubCategoryKey column will not be returned by the query because no subcategory exists with *NULL* in the key column.

To load all the products, you will need to change the relationships to *OUTER*. You can edit the query again by clicking the Table Properties button in the PowerPivot window, as shown in Figure 4-17.

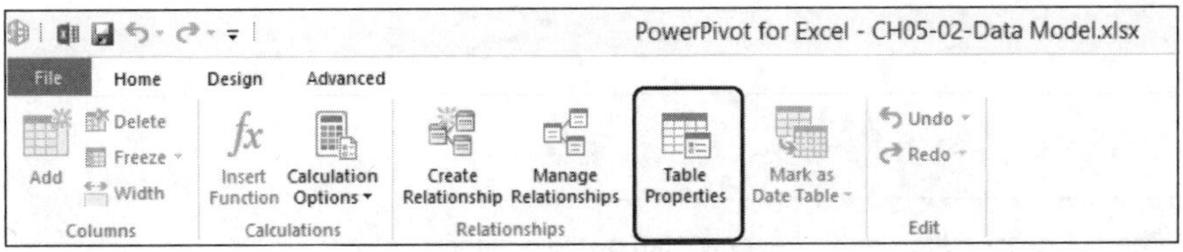

FIGURE 4-17 The Table Properties button lets you modify the properties of a table.

Using the Table Properties button, PowerPivot will open again the query editor and, from here, you can recall the query designer.

In Figure 4-18, you can see the query designer again, this time with the correct relationships set.

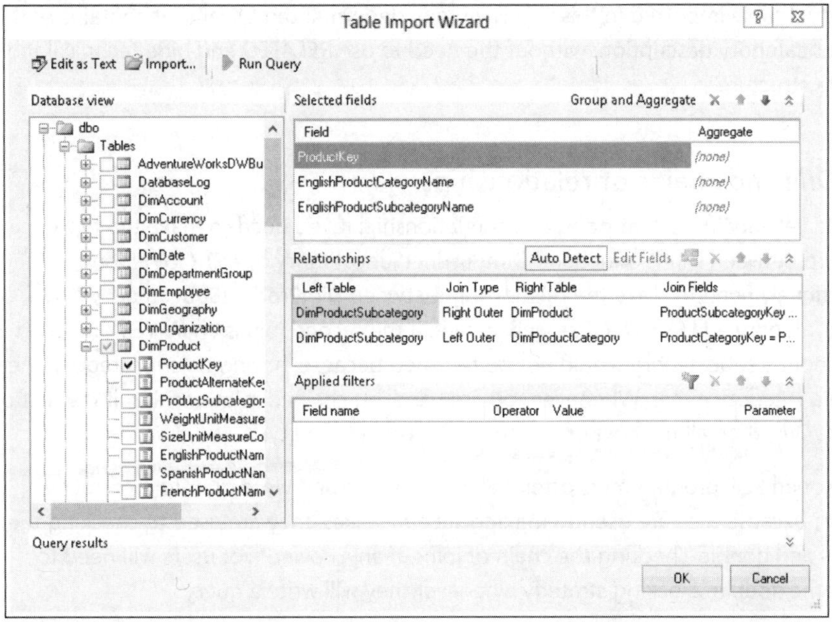

FIGURE 4-18 Here, you can see the SQL query designer, this time with the correct relationships set.

At this point, let's review the relationship definition:

- The first relationship is between DimProductSubcategory and DimProduct. Note that DimProductSubCategory is the left table, and you want to get all the products, even the ones that contain *NULL* in the ProductSubcategoryKey column. Thus, you need a *RIGHT OUTER JOIN* between the two tables, so that the right table (DimProduct) is preserved.

- The second relationship is between DimProductSubcategory and DimProductCategory. The DimProductSubcategory table is again the left one, but now you want all the subcategories, even if they do not have any category. Thus, here you need a *LEFT OUTER JOIN* type so that the left table (DimProductSubcategory) is preserved.

If you now save this query and refresh the table, you will get all 606 products inside your PowerPivot database, even those that do not have any category or subcategory set. This is the desired result.

> **Note** *LEFT* and *RIGHT* outer joins are somewhat interchangeable because both types of join save the rows from one table (the left or right one, depending on the type of join). If you swap the two tables, then you will need to change the join type. We find that it is better to have only one kind of join (that is, left or right, and usually, left is our preference) in a query definition because it makes it easier to follow the chain. In this example, we would prefer to swap the tables in the first relationship so that we follow a chain that starts from Products, then *LEFT OUTER JOINs* to ProductSubcategory, and finally *LEFT OUTER JOINs* to ProductCategory. Unfortunately, if you rely on the auto detection algorithm, it will choose the left and right tables individually, making your work a bit harder.

The DimProduct table imported in this way is already denormalized because it contains both the category and subcategory description, without the need to use *RELATED* and hide technical tables to simplify the data structure.

OUTER JOIN and chains of relationships

Note a subtle yet very important point about relationship: if you need to make the type of relationship between DimProduct and DimProductSubcategory a *LEFT OUTER* one, then you definitely need to make the relationship between DimProductSubcategory and DimProductCategory a *LEFT OUTER* as well. In fact, if the second join is an *INNER* one, then all the rows without a subcategory would not be returned because, having no subcategory, they do not have a category either. Whenever you are handling chained relationships, if the first one is an *OUTER JOIN*, then all the next ones need to be of the same type.

Even seasoned SQL programmers often fall into this trap and write queries incorrectly. Nevertheless, because they are used to making such mistakes, they are used to checking the query results and double-checking the chain of joins, if any. PowerPivot users will need to follow the same double-checking strategy whenever they will write a query.

You have seen that using the SQL query designer, you can write queries to the database that transform a simple table into a complex structure, which resolves the relationships at the database level and returns a denormalized table to PowerPivot. Thus, the SQL designer is a very interesting tool that you can use to perform denormalization when needed.

When to denormalize tables

Now that you have learned two distinct techniques to perform denormalization, an interesting question arises: "When do I need to denormalize tables inside queries, and when is it better to perform the same operation in PowerPivot?" Unfortunately, as with many interesting questions, there is no definitive answer. (Maybe this is why we find it interesting.)

In the example of DimProductCategory, the answer is very simple: it is much better to denormalize the column inside a query because this operation leads to a data model that is easier to query and reduces the number of tables inside PowerPivot. The rationale behind this is that the DimProductCategory table has one sole purpose: to provide a description of product categories. Therefore, when you fulfill this requirement by adding a ProductCategory column inside the Products table, the DimProductCategory table can be safely removed from the data model without changing the features of the model. The same, obviously, applies to DimProductSubcategory.

This situation (tables being needed only to provide descriptions) is amazingly common in the world of relational databases. Thus, you will encounter many cases where the application of this simple rule will drastically reduce the number of tables needed and simplify the PowerPivot data model. For simple lookup tables, the denormalization through SQL queries is by far the easiest tool.

On the other hand, when a table contains more information than a simple description, then it is much more difficult to decide whether it is better to import the table and perform the denormalization inside PowerPivot or to perform the denormalization inside a query and import the result of that query. If, for example, the DimProductSubcategory table contained more columns, then you need to add all these columns to the DimProduct table, which might result in a complex product table that is difficult to use. These situations need to be handled delicately to make sure that you make the correct decisions and produce an easy-to-use model.

Finally, complex tables that represent business entities are the pillars of data models and therefore should not be denormalized. For instance, the relationship between sales and products should not be denormalized at all because orders and products are different business entities. Both the entities and their relationships should exist in the PowerPivot database, and denormalizing it would produce an incorrect data model.

The rationale behind this approach is that you might be interested in analyzing products without relating them to sales. Think about this: if you denormalize the product name inside sales, you might want to count the number of products to produce a report. But if you see the product name only inside sales, then you will be able to count only sold products, not all the products. If a product has never been sold, then it will not even appear in the sales table because no sales row exists for it. If you reach the point where you over-denormalize the structure, you might end up creating a data model that returns incorrect results.

> **Note** One of the most frequent causes of over-denormalization is the fact that you sometimes do not have access to the original database. All you have available are prebuilt queries or reports coming from a source system. If these queries already denormalize data, they might do that for reasons that are different from yours when analyzing data. For example, you might have access to a query that returns products and sales in the same dataset, but you do not have a query for products only. Handling these scenarios is always a problem because although normalization is easy to remove, over-denormalization is much more complex.

As a rule of thumb, you will denormalize tables when the number of useful columns inside the table is very small (for lookup tables, it is often only one) and you will not denormalize tables when the number of useful column exceeds three. For two or three columns, it is up to the data modeler (that is, you) to choose the best denormalization strategy.

Keep in mind that the task of defining a data model is very complex, and denormalization is just one of the many tough decisions that need to be made. As a PowerPivot user, you are going to create data models more and more, so get ready to make lots of difficult decisions; and do not worry too much about making the wrong ones. Even seasoned BI experts often have a hard time deciding whether to keep an attribute normalized or not.

Understanding over-denormalization

Now that you have a solid background of what data modeling is and what normalization and denormalization are, it is time to delve into a complex situation that often happens when there is the need to create self-service BI reports.

Over-denormalization is simply excess denormalization (as you might assume from the name). You have already learned that denormalization works to create a user-friendly database; but over-denormalization is way too much of a good thing. This example shows why.

Figure 4-19 displays a simple data model based on the *AdventureWorks* database.

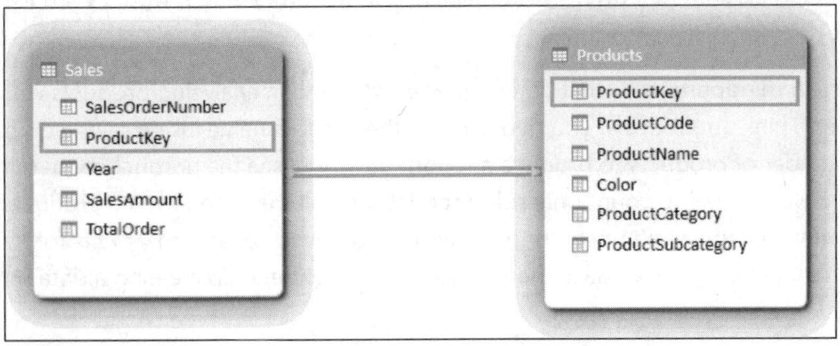

FIGURE 4-19 A very simple, yet over-denormalized data model.

Both tables have been loaded from SQL queries, and their content is as follows:

- The Products table contains products, categories, and subcategories that already have been denormalized. Moreover, many columns have been removed from the tables, so as to focus on the most important ones.

- The Sales table contains all the sales from the FactInternetSales table. In this table, a column has been added, TotalOrder, which contains the total of the order. Thus, SalesAmount contains the sales of the specific product (as indicated by ProductKey), whereas TotalOrder is the total sales of the order containing that specific row.

> **Note** This is an ad-hoc example, created just for this demonstration. Nevertheless, queries like this one occur very often when taking data from predefined queries used to build reports (to cite just one scenario). In fact, it is often the case that a whole dataset is stored in a single table, so that products, categories, and subcategories all belong to a single table. However, we used two tables in this example. The limitation of previous versions of Excel that required data to be stored in a single table to pivot over them has probably contributed to the spread of over-denormalization.

What is the problem with this data model? It is not in the Products table, where denormalization has been applied correctly. Rather, the problem is in the Sales table. In fact, the TotalOrder column is not additive. If, for example, you create a simple PivotTable like the one shown in Figure 4-20, you immediately see the problem.

Row Labels	Sum of SalesAmount	Sum of TotalOrder
Black	8,838,411.96	11,736,713.49
Blue	2,279,096.28	4,496,968.50
Multi	106,470.74	2,932,191.11
NA	435,116.69	17,848,527.87
Red	7,724,330.52	9,629,604.09
Silver	5,113,389.08	5,880,293.60
White	5,106.32	412,379.28
Yellow	4,856,755.63	6,290,502.98
Grand Total	**29,358,677.22**	**59,227,180.92**

FIGURE 4-20 Over-denormalization often leads to non-additive columns.

Although the sum of sales amounts is correct, the sum of total orders is not, and you can easily check this by looking at the Grand Total row. The reason is that the total order data is stored at the order level and, thus, it is repeated for all the rows of a single order. If you want to analyze, for example, the percentage of a category or of a color against the total of the order, this data model is of no help.

> **Note** We have spent a lot of time consulting with companies that wanted to create specific reports and failed to complete them. In our experience, we can roughly estimate that 80 percent of the time, the problem was with an incorrect data model and about 50 percent of those problems were caused by over-denormalization. Although it is possible to create very complex DAX code that handles over-denormalization, the formulas tend to become so complex that we rarely trust any scenario where over-denormalization happens. It is always better to stop, rebuild the data model using the correct normalization level, and then write simpler DAX code.

In this specific case, the correct solution is not to denormalize the orders. The correct data model contains one table for the orders, as shown in Figure 4-21.

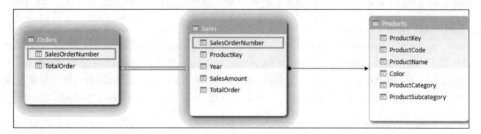

FIGURE 4-21 Here, you can see the correct, more normalized data model.

Now that the TotalOrder in the correct table, there is a many-to-many relationship between products and orders, so you will need to know how to use many-to-many relationships (which will be discussed in Chapter 13, "Advanced DAX"). However, with the correct formulas in place, you can easily build a report like the one shown in Figure 4-22, where the non-additive nature of the TotalOrder field is clear: the grand total is not the sum of the order total value repeated for each product on that same order (which would incorrectly overstate the actual order total).

Row Labels	Sum of SalesAmount	SumOfTotalOrder
Black	8,838,411.96	10,805,254.37
Blue	2,279,096.28	4,109,309.77
Multi	106,470.74	2,749,799.81
NA	435,116.69	9,533,098.49
Red	7,724,330.52	9,594,581.35
Silver	5,113,389.08	5,639,690.09
White	5,106.32	412,379.28
Yellow	4,856,755.63	5,621,153.54
Grand Total	29,358,677.22	29,358,677.22

FIGURE 4-22 With the correct data model, the results are as expected, and the formulas are still easy to create.

What is the lesson here? As an Excel user, you are not expected to be a professional data modeler. But because you need to work with data models, you must learn and finally master at least the basics of data modeling. If you do not, sooner or later you will encounter a data model that does not return the correct results.

Being able to quickly detect over-denormalization and find a good solution to the issue will help you most of the time, but there are very rare cases where the model will be much more complicated than this simple example. You will learn how to handle most of the complex scenarios in Chapter 13.

Understanding OLTP and data marts

The task of creating a data model is taxing. Many decisions need to be made, and it is normal to be missing some of the information you need. Creating a model is more an art than a science; it requires a lot of experience and foresight. Nevertheless, a good data model is the key to producing good analysis, and this is why we believe that a good PowerPivot analyst needs to understand data modeling.

As you have already discovered, there are at least two different ways to look at a data model:

- **Technical view**   This is a very compact and normalized way to look at data. It is the best way to model data when it needs to be used by software. Normalized data models are used by OLTP software, which is—more or less—the software that handles everyday tasks for a company. Handling such models is not your job—there are technicians who do this all day long. Nevertheless, you will probably need to read data this way at some time or another.

- **User view**   This is a highly denormalized view of data, much simpler to query and to analyze. As a side effect, however, it contains a lot of redundancy, generates bigger databases, and is very hard for software to update. Denormalized data models are normally present when the company has a data warehouse—that is, a database that contains all the data about the company in a structured way that is useful for querying.

The task of building a data warehouse usually involves several years of labor by highly specialized technicians, whose job it is to build both the data warehouse model and the software systems that fill it with the information found in the various OLTP systems around the company each day. An OLTP system is a transactional database like the one you use in your daily work to do accounting, manage sales, send invoices, and so on.

This is not a book about data warehouse modeling, so we are not going to go into a complete discussion about how this is done. Instead, we would like to give to you a sense of what a data warehouse is and the differences between querying an OLTP system and querying a data warehouse.

Querying the OLTP database

The denormalization process that you have seen up to now works well with simple tables that follow simple or chained relationships. In order to show this, we use the OLTP version of the *AdventureWorks* database, which contains the original OLTP database from which the *AdventureWorks* data warehouse is built. The *AdventureWorks* OLTP database, like any other relational database, often contains much more complex relationships, which will test your judgment.

> **Note** This is the only time where we show data from the OLTP version of *AdventureWorks* instead of loading data from the *AdventureWorks* data warehouse, which is much simpler to use. You can download both versions of *AdventureWorks* from the links provided in Chapter 1.

As an exercise, we are going to use a diagram for the Customer table, which is implemented in *AdventureWorks* in a complex way (see Figure 4-23). The purpose of this example is to show how complex the querying of a database might be, so it is a deliberately difficult sample. You can find this model in the companion workbook "CH04-04-Querying OLTP.xlsx."

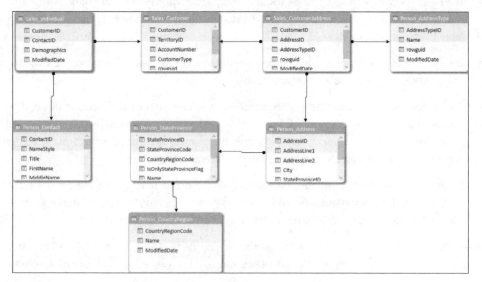

FIGURE 4-23 Here, you can see the complex relationship diagram for Customer.

You can see that the business entity Customer is represented by several tables that have complex relationships among them:

- Sales_Customer has a relationship with Sales_Individual, which stores some demographic information about the customer.

- Sales_Individual, in turn, refers to Person_Contact through the ContactID column. Person_Contact contains the personal data of any contact, and from the database point of view, a customer is a contact. Thus, Sales_Customer is in a chained relationship with Person_Contact.

- A customer row might have different addresses, so the table Sales_CustomerAddress contains all the addresses of a Sales_Customer row.

- All addresses have a related Person_AddressType, which categorizes the address. The main address of the customer has a type (a value in AddressTypeID field) called Primary.

- Other information about the address (that is, address line, ZIP code, and so on) are stored in the Person_Address table, which has a relationship with Sales_CustomerAddress, which in turn has a relationship with Sales_Customer, forming a complex relationship that looks very similar to a chained one.

- Person_Address refers to Person_StateProvince, which in turn is in relation to Person_CountryRegion. They form a chained relationship that lets us recover the name of the country through a couple of steps, from Person_Address to Person CountryRegion.

You cannot expose such complexity through PowerPivot because the PivotTable would become a nightmare. Moreover, some tables expose a many-to-many relationship (like CustomerAddress) and will not work without some complex DAX code. So you should start the analysis of this topic to understand what to do to make the model easier to query:

- The Sales_Individual table contains some demographic information. When the information is useful, it should be added to the Sales_Customer table, thus removing the Sales_Individual table from our data model.

- The Person_Contact information can be denormalized in the Sales_Customer table so that it is available directly in the Sales_Customer table.

- The Person_AddressType table is a simple descriptive one, so it can be denormalized, if you need to do that. Moreover, if (as we are supposing) we are not interested in having all the addresses of a customer, we can take only the primary address of a customer and then denormalize all the address information in the Sales_Customer table.

- Because we need to denormalize the address, we denormalize all the chained relationships, starting from the Person_Address and reaching Person_CountryRegion; we move all the information from those tables directly into the Sales_Customer table.

When the starting data model is complex, as this one is, the best (if not the only) option is to use SQL queries. Moreover, the query will be complex because it involves a high number of *JOINs*, all of which need to be *LEFT OUTER JOIN* because you want to include all customers, whether or not they have an address stored in the database.

Here is the final result of the query:

```sql
SELECT
    Customer.CustomerID AS CustomerID,
    Customer.AccountNumber AS AccountNumber,
    Customer.CustomerType AS CustomerType,
    Contact.FirstName AS FirstName,
    Contact.LastName AS LastName,
    Contact.MiddleName AS MiddleName,
    Contact.EmailAddress AS EmailAddress,
    Contact.Phone As Phone,
    Address.AddressLine1 AS AddressLine1,
    Address.AddressLine2 AS AddressLine2,
    Address.City AS City,
    StateProvince.StateProvinceCode AS StateProvinceCode,
    StateProvince.Name As StateProvince,
    cr.CountryRegionCode AS CountryRegionCode,
    cr.Name AS CountryRegionName
FROM
    Sales.Customer AS Customer
    LEFT OUTER JOIN Sales.Individual AS Individual
        ON Individual.CustomerID = Customer.CustomerID
    LEFT OUTER JOIN Person.Contact AS Contact
        ON Contact.ContactID = Individual.ContactID
    LEFT OUTER JOIN Sales.CustomerAddress AS CustomerAddress
        ON CustomerAddress.CustomerID = Customer.CustomerID
    LEFT OUTER JOIN Person.AddressType AS T
        ON CustomerAddress.AddressTypeID = T.AddressTypeID
            AND T.Name = 'Primary'
    LEFT OUTER JOIN Person.Address AS Address
        ON Address.AddressID = CustomerAddress.AddressID
    LEFT OUTER JOIN Person.StateProvince AS StateProvince
        ON StateProvince.StateProvinceID = Address.StateProvinceID
    LEFT OUTER JOIN Person.CountryRegion AS CR
        ON CR.CountryRegionCode = StateProvince.CountryRegionCode
```

Although it is possible to write such a query using the query designer, we believe that these kinds of queries are beyond the scope of business analysts. Writing such complex SQL code should be done only by database professionals because the chances of making errors are too high.

We made this example complex on purpose. Our goal is not to scare you, or to direct you to one of the many good SQL books that are on the market. Instead, the focus here is the fact that there is a big difference between how data is stored in the source data model and how you want to handle it for your analytical purposes. Having data in the correct form makes it easier to produce interesting queries because they are easier to write using the PivotTable. Moreover, if you ever are faced with such a complex architecture, it might be wisest to ask for help from a SQL technician—you might even want to ask that person to write the query for you.

Data marts, facts, and dimensions

You have seen that querying an OLTP database could turn into a nightmare. It is now worth spending some time describing the difference between an operational database and a data warehouse, which requires us to describe how a data warehouse is composed.

The *AdventureWorks* data warehouse follows the Kimball methodology. There is not room here to provide a full description of the Kimball methodology—at this point, we just want to discuss the basic principles of this methodology to clarify some names and concepts that are present in the *AdventureWorks* database. In Kimball methodology, tables are divided into two big categories: *facts* and *dimensions*. Facts and dimensions are tied together into business units that are called, in Kimball's terminology, *data marts*. Let's quickly review what facts and dimensions are.

The core organizing principle of the data mart structure is that the database is composed of two distinct types of entities:

■ **Dimension** A *dimension* is an analytical object. It can be the list of products or customers, the time space, or any other entity used to analyze numbers.

- Dimensions have attributes. An attribute of a product may be its color, its manufacturer, or its weight. An attribute of a date may be simply its weekday or its month name.

- Dimensions have both natural keys and surrogate keys. The natural key is the original product code, customer ID, or real date. The surrogate key is an independent integer used in the data marts to uniquely identify a dimension entity, joining it to related facts.

- A dimension has relationships with facts. Its purpose is to add qualitative information to the numeric measures of an event contained in facts. Sometimes a dimension might reference other dimensions, or it might correlate to other dimensions, even if its main purpose is that of joining to facts.

■ **Fact** A *fact* is something that happened or that has been measured. A fact may be the sale of a single product to a single customer or the total amount of sales of a specific item during a month. From our point of view, a fact is an event (usually represented by a number) that we want to aggregate in several forms to generate our reports.

- We normally relate a fact to several dimensions, but we do not relate facts in any way with other facts.

- Facts definitely have relationships with dimensions via the surrogate keys. This is one of the foundations of Kimball's methodology.

> **Note** Now that you have seen the two main entities in the data warehouse world (that is, facts and dimensions), it should be clear why the tables we have used so far from the *AdventureWorks* data warehouse always have a prefix of either *Fact* or *Dim*. *Dim* stands for dimension and *Fact*, not surprisingly, stands for fact.

Star schemas

Having seen what facts and dimensions are, you are now ready to learn about a very well-known structure called a star schema. A *star schema* is the shape taken by data warehouse diagrams. When you define dimensions and create relationships between facts and dimensions, a star schema is the natural result. The fact table is always at the center of the schema, with the dimensions related to the fact table placed around it. Because the fact table is directly related only to the dimensions, you get a shape resembling a star (see Figure 4-24, which shows a piece of the schema of the *AdventureWorks* data warehouse). You can find this model in the workbook "CH04-05-Star Schemas.xlsx."

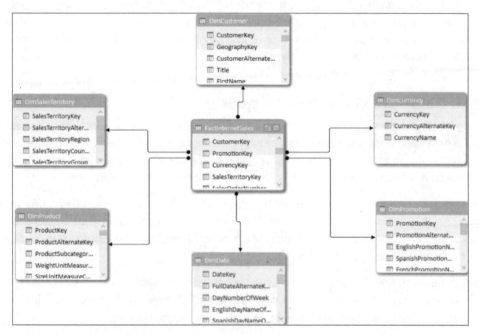

FIGURE 4-24 A star schema has a fact table at the center and dimensions around it.

Looking at this image, you can easily understand that a Customer bought a Product with a specific Currency. The sale is pertinent to a specific Territory. Star schemas are easily understandable by almost anybody at first glance.

So long as a data warehouse contains only star schemas created in accordance with the Kimball methodology, it gains several other very useful characteristics:

- There are no chained relationships. Because relationships exist only between facts and dimensions, the maximum depth of a relationship is 1. This makes it easy to generate relationships in PowerPivot because you know that a dimension is always related to a fact.

- All information is highly denormalized. This means that you never need (apart from some very specific cases) to use the *RELATED* function to load a column from a table into another one.

- If the model is well written, all descriptions in attributes are user-friendly. This means that no columns contain *NULLs* and the user can slice the data by using attributes in a very easy way.

Moreover, we figure that most of the reporting needs in the company are already fulfilled by the data warehouse. When you get your data from there, chances are better that personal reports will be comparable with the corporate ones. If, on the other side, you create your personal reports from scratch, you are in danger of producing computation that differs from that produced by the data warehouse.

Last, but not least, is the fact that by directly querying the OLTP system, we rely on its data model to remain the same over time. Although people building the data warehouse know that their data structure is queried by analysts, OLTP programmers normally do not think that someone is poking around at their data, and so they feel free to change data structure as their needs change, so long as their software works. However, if the underlying OLTP data model changes, you discover it only when someone refreshes your reports for the first time. Chances are that you would need to perform a lot of work to re-create the data model in PowerPivot.

Which database is the best to query?

Deciding whether is it better to load data from the OLTP system or the data warehouse is not easy. Using the data warehouse, you receive data already cleaned up and organized, which reduces the hard work of creating your personal data model. On the other hand, data is already organized, so you cannot model it as you would like because a lot of operations have been already carried out.

If you have a data warehouse, we suggest that you start using it. If this is enough to satisfy your reporting needs, you have completed your work with a minimum of effort. If, on the other hand, you still lack some information, you should import new data into PowerPivot tables and try to relate it with the data warehouse facts and dimensions.

Directly querying the OLTP should be seen as a very last resort because the work of creating a clean data model from an OLTP database is not easy. You could spend most of your time cleaning the model, reducing the time you might prefer to dedicate to analyzing the data.

Using advanced relationships

You have learned that the data warehouse is, by far, the best source for your data analysis. That said, even a data warehouse often hides some complexities. In this section, you are going to learn about some examples of complex relationships and how to handle them.

The first example you need to discover is multiple-column relationships. Up to now, we have said that a relationship holds between two tables and it is based on a single column, which creates the relationship when the two tables are equal. In reality, a relationship can be created between two tables using more than one column.

A good example of this is the relationship between FactInternetSales and FactInternetSalesReason in the *AdventureWorks* data warehouse, which is based on two columns. You can find this example in the companion workbook "CH04-06-Advanced Relationships.xlsx."

Note You might notice at this point that after a long digression about fact tables never being related each other, we are now introducing an example of two fact tables that share a relationship. What is happening here? Nothing special, really. The fact is that in the real world, there are many data warehouses that ignore the strict rules of Kimball methodology, and they do it for good reasons. Sometimes the real world cannot be modeled using only facts and dimensions and, in such cases, strange relationships start to appear, as the one we are showing in this section.

In *AdventureWorks*, each line of an order can have one or many sales reasons associated. For this reason, there is a table (FactInternetSalesReason) that contains a row for each reason linked to a specific sale.

In Figure 4-25, you can see the FactInternetSalesReason table, with the dimension DimSalesReason.

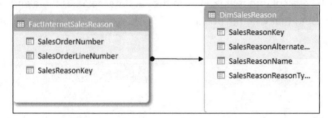

FIGURE 4-25 FactInternetSalesReason is a fact table linked to a single dimension, which is the sales reason.

FactInternetSalesReason, by itself, does not contain any interesting numbers. It contains two other columns, SalesOrderNumber and SalesOrderLineNumber, which are useful to create a relationship with the FactInternetSales table, which contains the same two columns. This time, the only issue is the fact that the relationship is based on two keys, not only one.

In PowerPivot, there is no way to create a relationship between two tables based on more than a single column. This limitation exists due to the columnar nature of the database in PowerPivot. In other databases, like SQL Server or Microsoft Access, this limitation does not exist. For this reason, you are likely to encounter several relationships based on more than one column. These relationships will not be automatically loaded inside PowerPivot.

The key to handle such a scenario is to create a single column out of the two ones present in the original tables. The easiest way to do this is to create a calculated column that uses string concatenation to merge the two columns into a single one. You can create in FactInternetSales a new calculated column with this expression:

```
InternetSalesKey =
FactInternetSalesReason[SalesOrderNumber]
& "_"
& FactInternetSalesReason [SalesOrderLineNumber]
```

The resulting table will look like Figure 4-26.

SalesOrderNumber	SalesOrderLineNumber	SalesReaso...	InternetSalesKey
SO51176	1	1	SO51176_1
SO51178	1	1	SO51178_1
SO51179	1	1	SO51179_1
SO51180	1	1	SO51180_1
SO51181	1	1	SO51181_1
SO51182	1	1	SO51182_1
SO51183	1	1	SO51183_1
SO51184	1	1	SO51184_1
SO51185	1	1	SO51185_1
SO51187	1	1	SO51187_1
SO51189	1	1	SO51189_1

FIGURE 4-26 The new InternetSalesKey is a string concatenation of the two columns used in the relationship.

You need to perform the same operation in the FactInternetSales table, using the columns with the same names. At this point, you will have a column that is a key in the FactInternetSales table and you will be able to create a relationship using that column. In Figure 4-27, you can see the resulting data model.

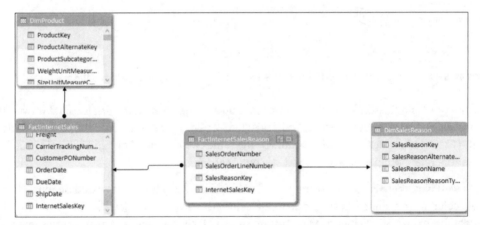

FIGURE 4-27 Here, you can see the data model, with a single column built from the two original ones.

As you have seen, even if the original data model was not perfect for the Excel data model, by means of using simple techniques and calculated columns, you have been able to make it work. You often will encounter scenarios like this one, where some modeling skills are required to design a data model that fits the needs of PowerPivot.

Nevertheless, after all this hard work, there still is a subtle problem. If you create a PivotTable and put the SalesReasonName on rows and some colors on the columns, projecting the SalesAmount on the values, you will get a PivotTable similar to the one shown in Figure 4-28.

Sum of SalesAmount	Column Labels 🔻					
Row Labels 🔻	Black	Blue	Multi	White	Yellow	Grand Total
Demo Event	8,838,411.96	2,279,096.28	106,470.74	5,106.32	4,856,755.63	16,085,840.93
Magazine Advertisement	8,838,411.96	2,279,096.28	106,470.74	5,106.32	4,856,755.63	16,085,840.93
Manufacturer	8,838,411.96	2,279,096.28	106,470.74	5,106.32	4,856,755.63	16,085,840.93
On Promotion	8,838,411.96	2,279,096.28	106,470.74	5,106.32	4,856,755.63	16,085,840.93
Other	8,838,411.96	2,279,096.28	106,470.74	5,106.32	4,856,755.63	16,085,840.93
Price	8,838,411.96	2,279,096.28	106,470.74	5,106.32	4,856,755.63	16,085,840.93
Quality	8,838,411.96	2,279,096.28	106,470.74	5,106.32	4,856,755.63	16,085,840.93
Review	8,838,411.96	2,279,096.28	106,470.74	5,106.32	4,856,755.63	16,085,840.93
Sponsorship	8,838,411.96	2,279,096.28	106,470.74	5,106.32	4,856,755.63	16,085,840.93
Television Advertisement	8,838,411.96	2,279,096.28	106,470.74	5,106.32	4,856,755.63	16,085,840.93
Grand Total	8,838,411.96	2,279,096.28	106,470.74	5,106.32	4,856,755.63	16,085,840.93

FIGURE 4-28 The PivotTable shows incorrect results when slicing with the sales reason.

You can see that the same number is repeated for all the rows. The PivotTable correctly slice data using the color of the product, but it repeats the numbers for all the reasons.

The reason why this happens is that the relationship between DimSalesReason and FactInternet-Sales is not a one-to-many relationship, as the ones you have learned so far have been. Indeed, this is a many-to-many relationship; that is, a single sale reason can be related to many sales but, at the same time, a single line in the FactInternetSales can be related to many rows in DimSalesReasons. PowerPivot does not handle many-to-many relationships without DAX coding. Chapter 13 will cover how to work correctly with many-to-many relationships.

For now, it is enough to recognize that many-to-many relationships often appear in data models and, when they are part of the model, you will need some advanced DAX code to solve them. In reality, the code is not difficult to write—it is only hard to understand. We want to show here, in advance, the formula:

```
SalesM2M :=
CALCULATE (
    SUM ( FactInternetSales[SalesAmount] ),
    FactInternetSalesReason
)
```

Using this new calculated field, the PivotTable now shows correct results, as shown in Figure 4-29.

SalesM2M	Column Labels 🔻					
Row Labels 🔻	Black	Blue	Multi	White	Yellow	Grand Total
Manufacturer		199,293.05			241,430.44	440,723.49
On Promotion	2,494,836.60	545,315.31	8,254.88	665.26	977,700.45	4,026,772.50
Other	130,100.26	16,636.88	6,270.95	206.77	8,354.84	161,569.70
Price	3,899,986.11	1,328,163.92	106,470.74	5,106.32	2,438,305.38	7,778,032.47
Review	98,775.71	3,129.66			460,265.20	562,170.57
Television Advertisement	2,169.38	1,994.43			8,368.45	12,532.26
Grand Total	5,720,481.28	1,576,767.19	106,470.74	5,106.32	3,433,412.64	10,842,238.17

FIGURE 4-29 Using the many-to-many pattern, the PivotTable now shows correct results.

By looking carefully at the numbers, you will see that many-to-many relationships are non-additive, meaning that the total of the columns is not the sum of the single cells. The reason is that a single sale can be related to more than one reason, and thus, it will be accounted more than once for each row, while counting it only once for the grand total. Moreover, keep in mind that this formula uses several advanced features of DAX. We have shown the formula here because we wanted to give you the feeling of what a many-to-many relationship is and that it can be safely used in DAX.

> **Note** Many-to-many relationships often appear due to over-denormalization of your model. In such a case, it is better not to rely on the many-to-many pattern but to remove over-denormalization from the model, creating a correct data model.

CHAPTER 5

Publishing to SharePoint

In the previous chapters of this book, you learned the foundations of Microsoft PowerPivot, the DAX language, and some basic concepts of data modeling. In a world where you were the only consumer of your data, this book would continue by discussing other interesting topics about PowerPivot. Nevertheless, once you have created an interesting report with Microsoft Excel, chances are that you want to share it with your colleagues and, in the world as it is now, teamwork on reports means using a network (either the intranet or the Internet) to deploy the report on a server so that other users can have access to it directly from their PCs.

In the Microsoft BI stack, this server is Microsoft SharePoint. SharePoint is one of the major building blocks of a complete business intelligence (BI) solution because it lets people share their reports and build an information repository that is always up to date with the latest information that your team will use to make decisions.

Moreover, once a report is deployed on SharePoint, it is really moved into a next-level experience: it is no longer only an Excel report, it is a data model hosted inside a server (the SharePoint server, for instance) that can be used to create further analysis by loading data from there. Finally, Power View is also available on SharePoint, which lets users without Excel create exciting Power View reports directly on SharePoint using a web interface instead of relying on the local Power View engine of Excel.

All right—maybe we are going too fast at this point. It is better to start from the beginning and leave the more advanced topics for later in this chapter. So join us in the discovery of the amazing world of SharePoint integration of PowerPivot.

SharePoint 2013 and PowerPivot integration

SharePoint 2013 is a platform that makes it easier for people to work together. It offers a set of services for sharing information, managing workflows, publishing reports, and so on. You can save your Microsoft Office files to a SharePoint site and, more important, you can publish an Excel workbook on SharePoint, which means that the workbook is shown as a webpage that can be read using just a web browser. The service that allows this publishing is called Excel Services, and it is included in SharePoint 2013. Your IT department can add PowerPivot for SharePoint to a SharePoint 2013 installation. With that installed, you also can publish Excel workbooks that contain PowerPivot data.

An Excel workbook that contains a data model can be published to a SharePoint site, either in a standard document library or in a special library called the PowerPivot Gallery. If you save the workbook in a standard document library, your document does not preview any of its content but shows just a line that includes the document name and some other information. On the other hand, if you use the PowerPivot Gallery, then you will have a very nice preview of the content of the workbook, as well as some more advanced features of SharePoint, like the ability to run a Power View report on top of your data model.

Licensing and setup

In this chapter, you are not going to learn how to set up a SharePoint server or PowerPivot for SharePoint. Covering those topics would require a full, separate chapter filled with technical details and utterly complicated topics: the kind of arguments that are interesting to system administrators, but not to users. We only want to point out a couple of points that you might find useful:

- SharePoint 2013 requires an Enterprise Client Access License to use Excel Services. PowerPivot for SharePoint also requires a license for Microsoft SQL Server 2012 Business Intelligence.

- SharePoint is accessed through a web interface; thus, it has an address. In this book, we use a server located at *http://sp2013*. In your company, the address will probably be different, as there will be some differences in authentication mode and in the way security is handled. Please contact your system administrator if you need help on this.

Publishing a workbook to SharePoint

The first step of learning about SharePoint integration is saving a workbook on SharePoint. Office 2013 has a strong integration with SharePoint. In fact, you can save a document to a SharePoint server directly from inside Excel, without needing to open a browser and upload the file manually.

To save a document to SharePoint, you can open the usual Save As dialog box and enter the SharePoint address in the File Name textbox, as if it were a standard folder on your local PC. You can see in Figure 5-1 the dialog box that opens after you enter the server address.

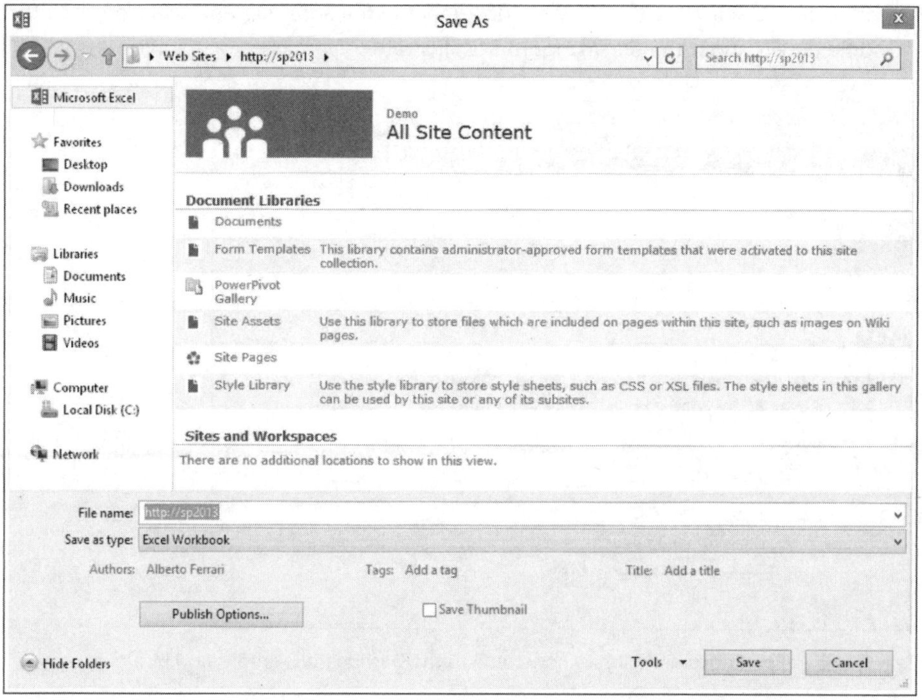

FIGURE 5-1 The Save As dialog box as it appears when saving to a SharePoint server.

The document libraries in SharePoint are listed as if they were folders. Double-clicking Documents lists the documents present in the library and, at this point, you can follow the standard Excel saving procedure. The file will not be saved on your disk; rather, it will be uploaded to SharePoint, and from this point on, it will be visible in the SharePoint document library. The document we are using here is the dashboard example you have learned in Chapter 2, "Using the unique features of PowerPivot," which is composed of four worksheets: one PivotTable, two PivotTables converted to formulas, and a colored dashboard. We are saving this as "Dashboard Example" in the SharePoint database.

> **Note** By default, Excel Services does not let you open documents bigger than 10 MB. Although this limit looks fine for standard Excel workbooks, it is actually too low for many workbooks containing an Excel data model. The limit can be increased using the configuration page of Excel Services in SharePoint. If you need to increase this value, you can ask your SharePoint administrator to handle this for you.

A user connected to SharePoint will see the document in the library as an Excel icon, with the name and some details about the file, as Figure 5-2 illustrates.

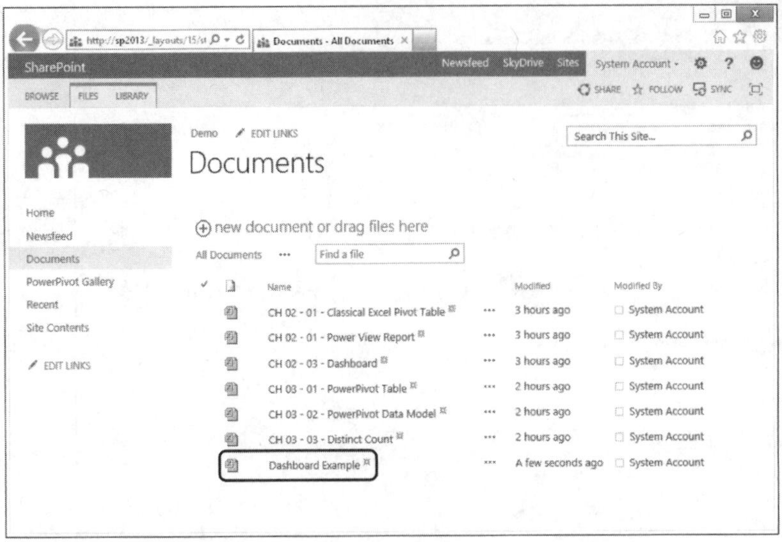

FIGURE 5-2 The SharePoint document library now contains the Dashboard Example workbook.

Clicking the document will make SharePoint open the Dashboard Example workbook using Excel Services, which is the service responsible for creating a web representation of the workbook. In fact, as soon as users open the file in the browser, they will see the Excel report surfaced as an HTML page, as shown in Figure 5-3.

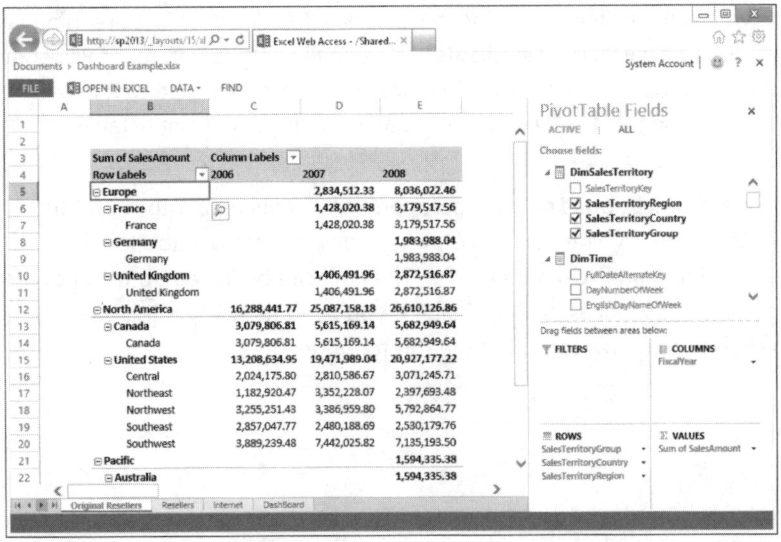

FIGURE 5-3 The Excel workbook is shown from inside Microsoft Internet Explorer, thanks to SharePoint and Excel Services.

There are a few interesting points to note here:

- All the content of the workbook is visible as a webpage. However, there may be cases in which you do not want the full content of the workbook to be visible. For example, in this case, the content of the Resellers and Internet worksheets is better hidden. This is possible through the Browser View Options window in Excel, which is explained next.

- The PivotTable is fully functional. This is a new feature of SharePoint 2013. There was a very similar feature in SharePoint 2010, but the PivotTable was static, meaning that you did not have the option to add fields to rows, columns, or filters. In SharePoint 2013, a PivotTable can be dynamically updated from inside the browser, which greatly increases the usability of the report.

If you want to limit the visibility of some items in the workbook, before publishing it, you can use the Browser View Options button, which can be activated from the Save As dialog box shown in Figure 5-1. The Browser View Options dialog box is displayed in Figure 5-4.

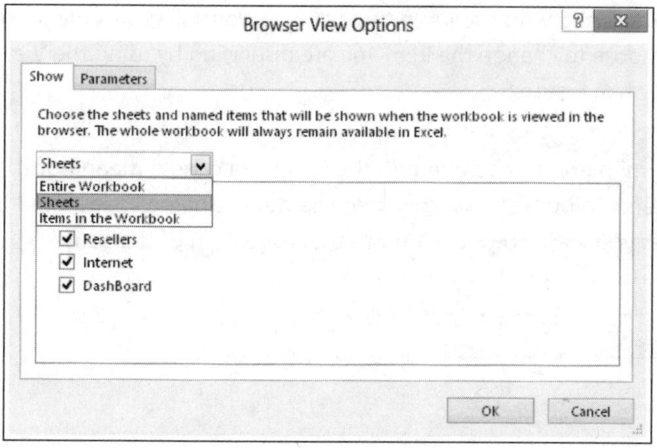

FIGURE 5-4 You can choose to make only some items of your total workbook visible.

The Parameters tab in the Publish Options dialog box

The Parameters tab allows you to select what parameters to make available to the user in the web browser. A parameter is a named range corresponding to a single cell of the workbook, which is usually used in other Excel calculations. For example, imagine a loan amortization table that is calculated on a base interest rate. You might want to give the user the option to change this interest rate in the web browser, showing the updated table without the user needing to open the workbook in Excel. This is not a feature directly related to PowerPivot, but it can be used for some of the calculations made in a dashboard that is published to SharePoint.

The Show tab allows you to select the parts of the workbook that you want to publish after the document is opened in SharePoint. You can choose among these options:

- **Entire Workbook**   This is the default for any new document. Each of the worksheets of the Excel workbook is shown as a worksheet when SharePoint displays it inside the browser.

- **Sheets**   Using this option, you can choose the worksheets that you want users to see after SharePoint displays the workbook in the browser. The default selection is All Sheets (which corresponds to the Entire Workbook option), but you can choose to make visible or invisible every single worksheet. You have to choose at least one worksheet to be visible.

- **Items In The Workbook**   This option allows you to select only a few items of the workbook, such as a selection of Tables, Charts, Named Ranges, and so on. PivotTables and PivotCharts are also items that you can publish.

Whenever you choose to publish Entire Workbook or a selection of Sheets, you see in the web browser the same arrangement of columns, rows, and worksheets that you are used to seeing in Excel. However, choosing to publish any number of items in the workbook produces a different result, removing the display of columns, rows, and worksheets. In this example, you will show only one item in the web browser, and you can choose to change the item you are displaying by using the View list to select the item you want, as shown in Figure 5-5.

> **Tip** Be sure to give a meaningful name to each item in the Excel workbook; meaningful names help you select what items to publish and to show. The default names generated by Excel are less helpful whenever you want to publish more than one item of the same type in a workbook.

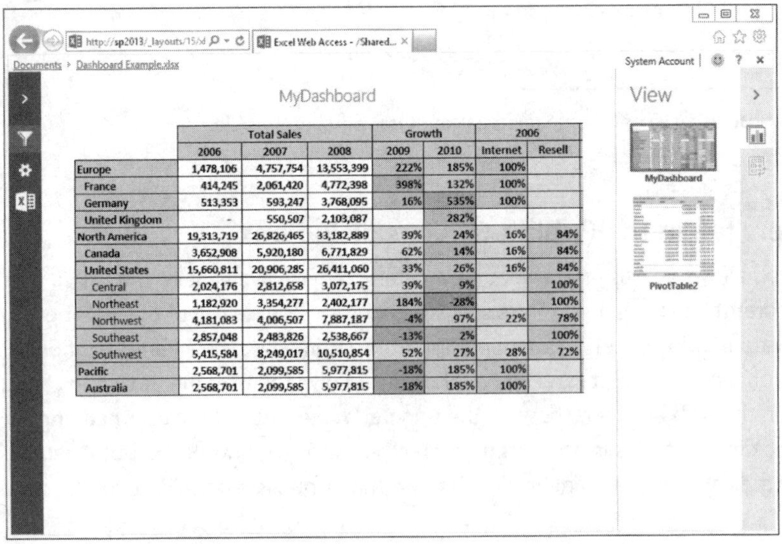

FIGURE 5-5 When only some items are selected, the rendering of the webpage is different.

Note Publish Options are saved in the Excel workbook whether or not the file is saved to SharePoint. In other words, if you save the file in your local Documents folder after you choose the item to publish and then plan to upload the document to a SharePoint document library without using Excel, the Publish Options that you set still will be considered by SharePoint.

Using the PowerPivot Gallery

You have learned how to save a workbook in a normal document library in SharePoint. There is another special gallery among the ones available in SharePoint, which is the PowerPivot Gallery. This gallery is optimized to work with Excel workbooks containing data models and offers some unique features, like opening a Power View report on top of the Excel data model.

To the user, the PowerPivot Gallery looks very good. It shows a preview of the content of the report, which might be useful if you want to get a sneak preview of what you are going to open. There are several different ways to show the preview. In Figure 5-6, you can see the Gallery theme.

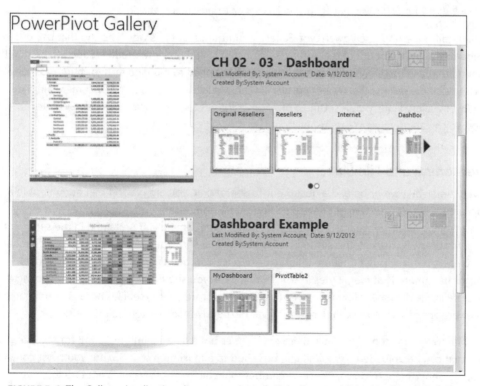

FIGURE 5-6 The Gallery visualization shows a preview of all the items published in the workbooks.

In Figure 5-7, you can see another representation of the same content, named Carousel view.

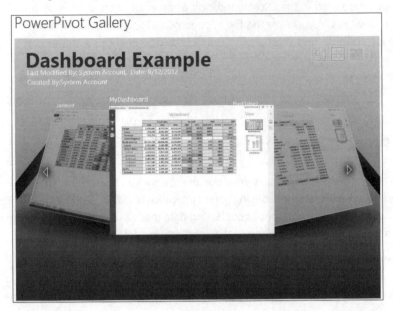

FIGURE 5-7 The Carousel view is interactive and focuses on a single report at a time.

Graphically speaking, the PowerPivot Gallery is intriguing, but it is worth noting that using this visualization, a huge amount of real estate is dedicated to the preview, greatly reducing the number of reports that can be seen on the screen at once. If you need to manage tens (or hundreds) of reports in a single gallery, then reverting to a simpler visualization (called All Documents in the PowerPivot Gallery Library view settings) provides a format that is similar to the classical document library, which can greatly increase usability.

Versioning and File Size

Every time you save or upload a document to SharePoint, you are placing that document in a document library, which might have a setting that automatically creates a new version every time a file is saved. In other words, older versions of the same file are retained in the same document library. By default, this setting is disabled in a PowerPivot Gallery, but it can be changed to be as it is in any other document library. An Excel workbook containing PowerPivot data might be hundreds of megabytes in size. In that case, you should be careful about enabling this feature in the document library in which you want to store your Excel files because retaining all the versions of such a workbook might be very expensive for the storage on the server.

Moreover, also consider that a SharePoint server has a default limit of 50 MB for the size of a file that can be uploaded. That limit can be raised to a maximum of 2 GB, but you must contact your IT department to do so. Please remember that changing this value is not enough; you need to take into account the maximum size of Excel files rendered by Excel Services, which should be increased to the same extent.

Connecting Excel to a SharePoint Excel data model

The PowerPivot Gallery has a couple of interesting features that are worth mentioning. The first is the ability to open Excel with a connection to another workbook, saved in SharePoint, which contains an Excel data model. As already said in the introduction of this chapter, once a workbook is saved in SharePoint, it is not only an Excel workbook, but it is also transformed into a data model hosted by the PowerPivot server inside SharePoint. You have the option to connect to it as if it were a database. An example might help in clarifying this.

This dashboard example was created by loading some tables from SQL Server inside the Excel data model and then building some PivotTables on top of the model. Now that the Excel file is saved inside SharePoint, you can query the data model without needing to reload the data in Excel. In fact, there is a button in the PowerPivot Gallery, highlighted in Figure 5-8, that performs this operation.

FIGURE 5-8 Here, you can see the Open New Excel Workbook button as it is shown in the Gallery visualization.

This button is available in all the PowerPivot Gallery visualizations. By clicking it, you will receive a warning about whether you want to download an .odc file from the site. This small file contains information about how to connect to the Excel workbook hosted inside SharePoint, and Excel will read it to manage the connection. Selecting Open will open Excel, which is directly connected with the data model. In Figure 5-9, you can see a PivotTable that analyzes sales divided by color and year.

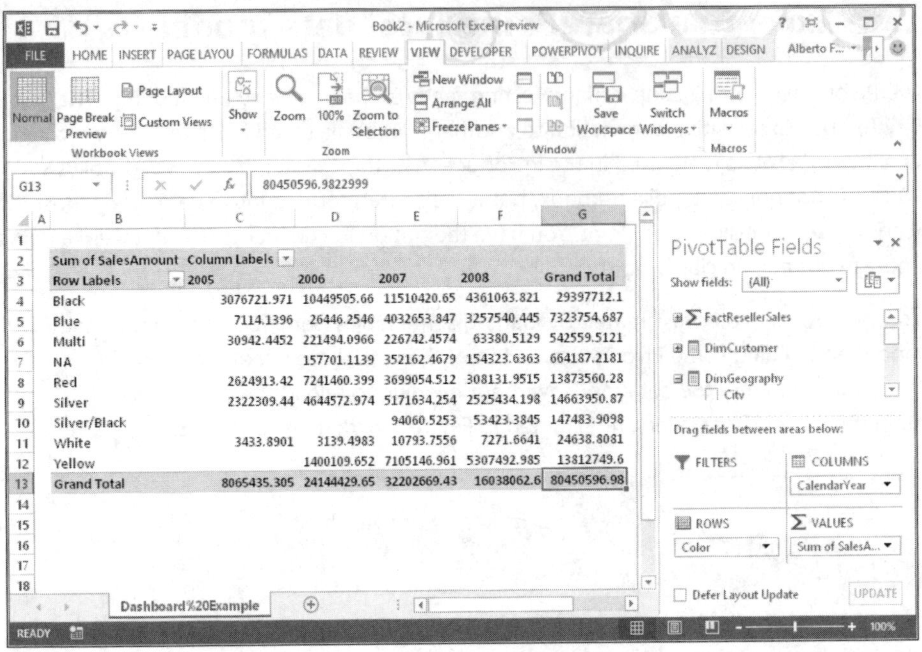

FIGURE 5-9 This PivotTable is connected to an Excel data model hosted in a SharePoint server.

This PivotTable is not connected to the Excel data model of the local workbook; rather, it is connected to the Excel data model of the workbook stored in the SharePoint server.

> **Note** Technically, the PowerPivot data model of the SharePoint workbook is hosted inside the Analysis Services instance dedicated to SharePoint and behaves exactly as if it were an Analysis Services Tabular database. There are some minor differences in the way data is organized; for instance, instead of tables and calculated fields, you will interact with measure groups and dimensions. However, the overall experience is very similar. Using this feature, you will be able to use Excel to build complex solutions and data models that can be further used to perform analysis without having the need to load data in all of the workbooks you will create.
>
> Obviously, this new workbook can be saved to SharePoint later. Thus, at the end, you can have both server workbooks and client workbooks in SharePoint, the former directly connected to the database that hosts the original data, and the latter connected to the server.

Finally, it is worth noting that the feature of using an Excel workbook saved to SharePoint as an SQL Server Analysis Services database is available to any client tool. Thus, you are not limited to using Excel as a client tool; you can choose from the many third-party software programs that connect to SQL Server Analysis Services to build complex deployment scenarios.

Creating a Power View report

You have already seen that you can create a Power View report in Excel. Later, in Chapter 11, "Shaping the reports," you will learn more advanced techniques. In this chapter, it is interesting to look at another feature that is available in SharePoint—Power View for SharePoint.

Users need only a web browser to read and manage reports in SharePoint, Excel is not needed. Power View is no exception here, but it requires a SilverLight runtime on the web browser, so Power View reports are only supported on web browser that can run Silverlight (currently, only Windows x86 x64 and Mac OS 10.5/10.5). In Figure 5-10, you can see the report built in Chapter 2 rendered inside Internet Explorer.

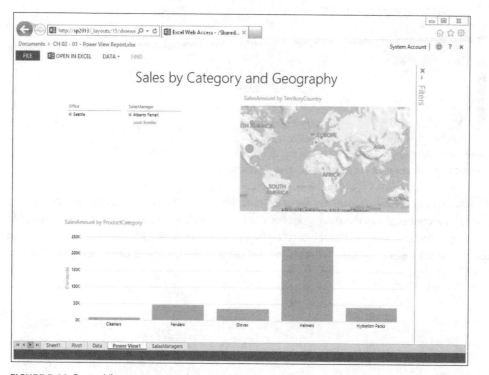

FIGURE 5-10 Power View reports are shown in the Internet Explorer browser as part of an Excel report rendering.

Unlike PivotTables, the Power View reports inside an Excel workbook are read-only. If you want to modify them, you will need to open the workbook in Excel, update the report, and then publish it again in SharePoint.

But there is more to the process than this. Using SharePoint, you will be able to write a whole new Power View report and save it to the document library. In this way, users who do not have Excel 2013 will be able to create Power View reports by using just SharePoint.

> **Note** Power View in SharePoint comes as a part of Reporting Services in SharePoint mode, which is one of the features available in SQL Server 2012. If you need Power View in SharePoint and do not have it enabled on your SharePoint server already, you can ask IT to install the feature.

Figure 5-11 again shows the three buttons in the PowerPivot Gallery. The second one is dedicated to creating a Power View report.

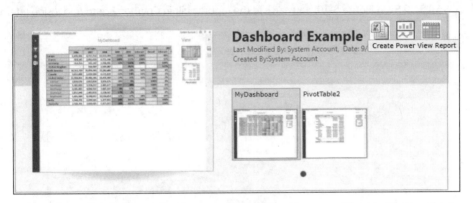

FIGURE 5-11 The PowerPivot Gallery lets you create a Power View report from inside SharePoint.

Simply clicking Create Power View Report opens the Power View application inside SharePoint. The report will be connected to the data model of the Excel workbook, exactly as if it were created from inside Excel. The only notable difference is the fact that, this time, the Power View report is a separate report. Once the report has been created, you will see it in the gallery as one of the documents, as shown in Figure 5-12.

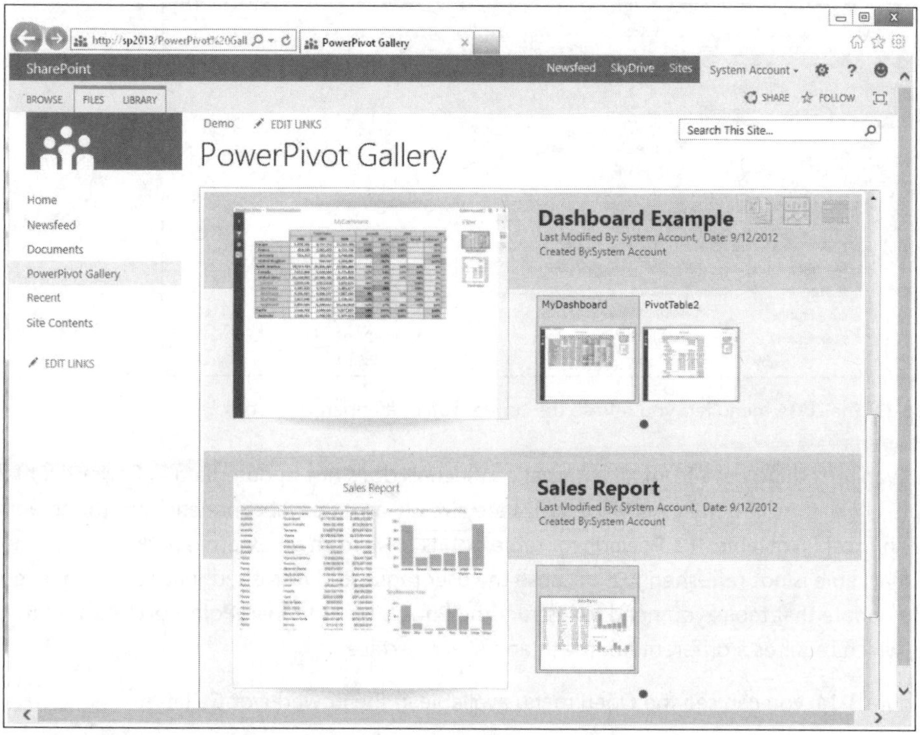

FIGURE 5-12 Power View reports created inside SharePoint are separate documents.

Managing the PowerPivot data refresh

Once you have published a report on SharePoint, you will probably want to refresh its content periodically, so that users connecting to it always see the most recent data. A sales report built in February and opened in May should show the sales up to and including May, not just what was put into the report initially.

Each time you want to view an Excel workbook in the browser, you can ask (through the Data menu that you can see in Figure 5-13) to refresh data coming from external connections. This allows you to recalculate the workbook on demand.

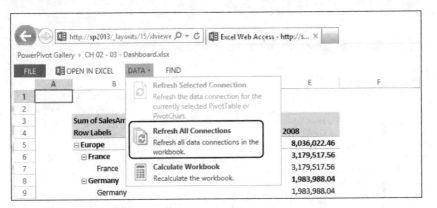

FIGURE 5-13 The DATA menu lets you refresh the connection of an open workbook.

However, refreshing data from an external connection does not update data in PowerPivot tables. Conceptually, data stored in PowerPivot tables are already an external connection, from the point of view of an Excel PivotTable. If a PowerPivot table got its rows from an external database, such as SQL Server, that table is not refreshed just because the user requested refreshed data for a connection in Excel. To update that table, you need to instruct the PowerPivot for SharePoint service to do that job for you, which requires a different approach and user interface.

In Figure 5-14, you can see the Open menu available in the PowerPivot Gallery.

![The Manage Data Refresh button in the PowerPivot Gallery showing the Dashboard Example.]

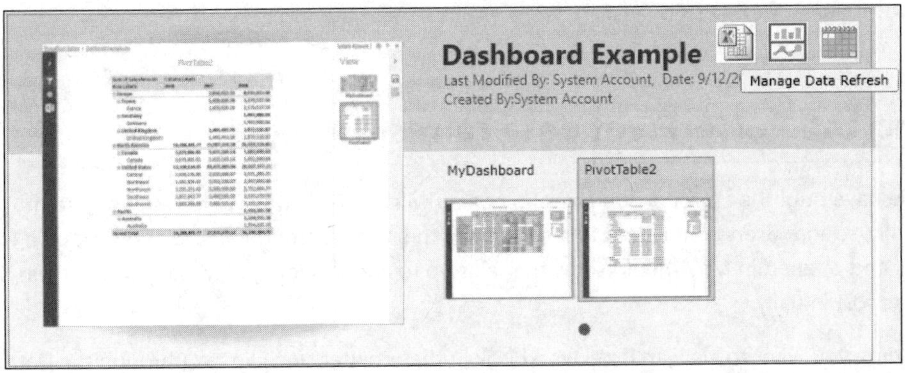

FIGURE 5-14 The Manage Data Refresh button in the PowerPivot Gallery.

The Data Refresh operation is not enabled by default in a workbook published to SharePoint. The first check box in the configuration window, shown in Figure 5-15, is just this setting, which must be enabled to schedule an automatic refresh of PowerPivot tables contained in the workbook data model.

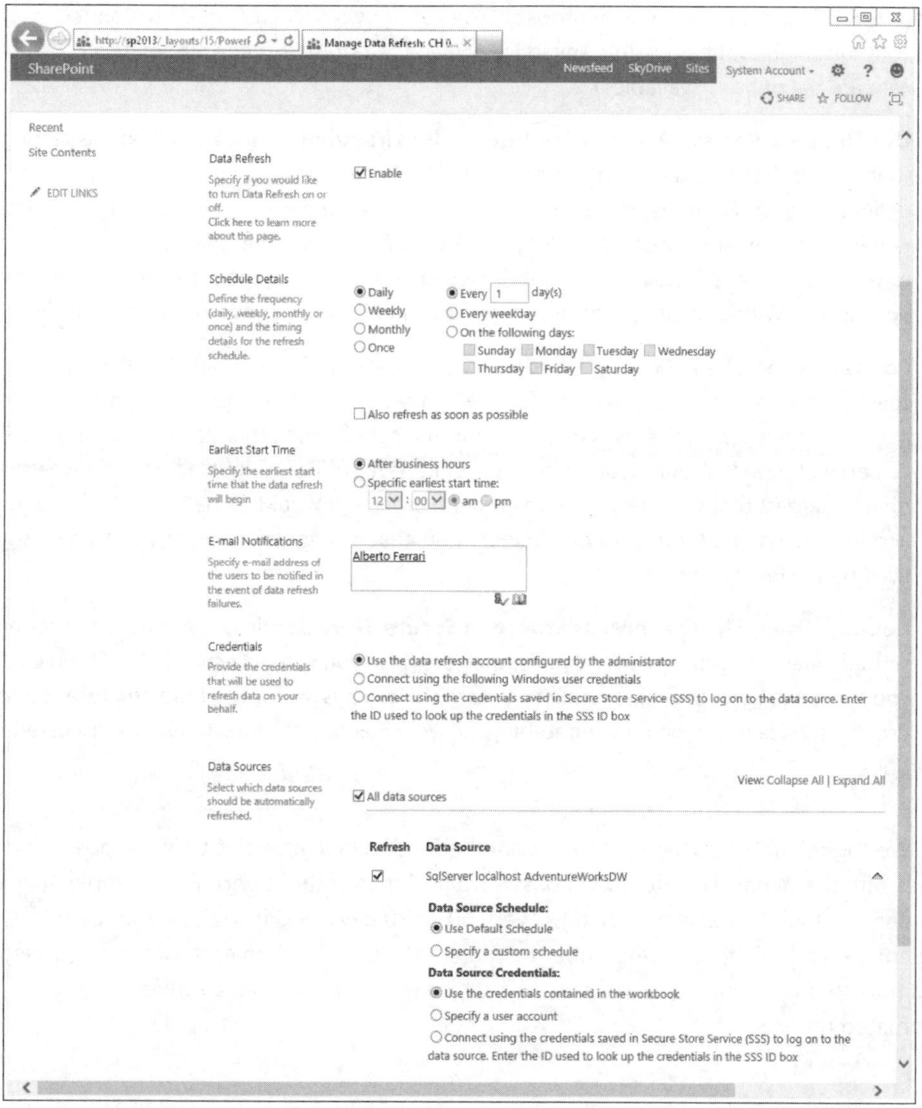

FIGURE 5-15 The Data Refresh configuration.

The Schedule Details section controls the time interval of data refresh operations. You can also choose the Also Refresh As Soon As Possible check box if you want an immediate data refresh of PowerPivot tables. The word *immediate* means that Refresh usually starts within a minute. Select this check box if you want to verify that the data refresh will run properly.

The E-mail Notifications section simply defines users who have to receive automated e-mail from SharePoint every time a data refresh is completed (with or without errors).

The most important section is Credentials, which defines the credentials that you need to connect to the data source for PowerPivot tables. You have to pay attention to this setting because when you created the PowerPivot tables, you probably used your own user credentials to connect to data sources, but this might not be possible any longer when the refresh is made automatically by the server. Here are the options available:

- **Use The Data Refresh Account Configured By The Administrator**   When this setting, which is the default, is selected, the connection to data sources is made by using a user defined by SharePoint system administrators. It is called the PowerPivot Unattended Data Refresh Account, and you have to ask your IT department whether this user is able to connect to your data source. Usually, this account can be used just to connect to data sources that do not support Windows Integrated authentication and have their own authentication system.

- **Connect Using The Following Windows User Credentials**   This setting allows you to specify a user name and a password for users to connect to the data source. In theory, you might use your own credentials to connect to the data sources that you used to build the PowerPivot model because your account should have sufficient rights to do that. However, we do not suggest that you use your own credentials here. It would be better to use a dedicated account provided by your system administrators that has rights of access only to data sources used by the Excel workbook.

- **Connect Using The Credentials Stored In Secure Store Services**   You have to use this setting whenever your system administrator provides you with a Secure Store ID, which allows you to enable users to access required data without a password. The infrastructure required to use this service has to be configured by your system administrators and is not discussed in this book.

> **Tip** We suggest that you avoid storing your credentials in SharePoint to avoid possible issues with the handling of your own password and that of the report. For example, many companies require a password change every 60 or 90 days, and if you use your own credentials, you will have to remember to change the password on each of the scheduled data refresh operations under your user ID, which is not an ideal situation for fully automated reports.

In the lowest part of Figure 5-15, you can choose, for each of the data sources of your model, whether to use the default settings that you defined in the previous section of the configuration window or to use a custom schedule or system credential. You can disable the refresh of a single data source by clearing the corresponding check box.

CHAPTER 6

Loading data

As you learned in previous chapters, the key to producing reports with the Microsoft Excel data model is to load information from one source or many sources and then integrate them, building the data model that will produce your reports. This chapter will describe the data loading options available in Microsoft PowerPivot. You have already used some of the loading features of PowerPivot to prepare the earlier examples. Now it is time to move a step further and analyze in detail all the PowerPivot options for loading data so you can figure out which ones you need to use and how to get the best from them.

Probably no single user will ever need all the different features of data loading available in PowerPivot. Nevertheless, we think that it is better to look at all of these features so that you know in advance what can and cannot be loaded in PowerPivot.

> **Note** In this chapter, the focus is only on data loading directly inside PowerPivot. You can, of course, load data in Excel using one of the many features available and then add the Excel table in the data model, but these features are not covered here.

Understanding data sources

When you need to load data inside PowerPivot, you do so using a data source. *Data sources* are interfaces between PowerPivot and external data that provide the layer that PowerPivot needs to communicate with many different media. PowerPivot provides several kinds of data sources, which can be roughly divided into these categories:

- **Relational databases**   PowerPivot can load data hosted inside a relational database, like Microsoft Access, Microsoft SQL Server, or another relational database. The data sources in this category will let you load tables, views, and queries from the server. This is the most commonly used category of data sources.

- **Multidimensional sources**   You can load data in PowerPivot from an OLAP cube hosted inside databases like SQL Server Analysis Services using this kind of data source. Currently, SQL

Server Analysis Services is the only Multidimensional database for which exists a PowerPivot data source. The same data source can also load data from queries issued to PowerPivot data contained into an Excel workbook published in SharePoint.

- **Data feeds**   This category of data sources let you load data from dynamic feeds, like Really Simple Syndication (RSS) feeds from the Internet, data feeds tied to reports stored inside SQL Server Reporting Services, or any other kind of data feed.

- **Text files**   Data sources in this category can load data that is stored in comma-separated value or fixed-length text files, Excel files, or any other specific file format that can be interpreted by PowerPivot (like the Excel one).

In any PowerPivot data model, you will normally have more than a single data source, because PowerPivot's task is to let you integrate information coming from different sources. Once data passes through the data source and reaches PowerPivot, it becomes a table and is added to the data model. Thus, the choice of the data source is useful only during the loading process; once data is inside PowerPivot, it does not matter from where it came.

If you want to see the complete list of all the data sources available in PowerPivot, you can open the Table Import Wizard, which can be found by clicking the From Other Sources button on the PowerPivot ribbon (see Figure 6-1).

FIGURE 6-1 The Table Import Wizard lists all available data sources.

Inside the Table Import Wizard, you will find all the data sources available in PowerPivot. This includes a lot of sources that are not available on the ribbon, like Oracle, Teradata, and many others. Each data source has specific parameters, which we are not going to cover in full detail since their descriptions would require too much detail for this book. However, it is interesting to look at the differences between a text file and a SQL Server data source, though it is not useful at all to investigate the subtle differences between SQL Server and Oracle, which are both relational database servers.

Data source limitations for refreshing data

If you want to publish an Excel workbook on SharePoint and you want to schedule the refreshing of data directly on the server, you have to be aware of the existing limitations of the available data sources. For example, if you import data from text or Excel files stored in a local directory, these files will be not accessible by SharePoint, and refreshing these data will be impossible on the server. Moreover, if you are using a 32-bit version of Excel and you access a database using a third-party provider, you have to be sure that the corresponding 64-bit version is installed on the SharePoint server. Finally, pasting data from the Clipboard is an operation that cannot be refreshed on the client or the server.

Loading from a database

We are now going to describe the first option to load data—using the From Database button. This option is probably the most common for loading data into PowerPivot. This is not fortuitous, since the vast majority of the databases around the world are in relational databases.

Note In the rest of this section, we will show examples using SQL Server since this is probably the most frequently used database for PowerPivot users. If you want to connect to a different server, you might need different connection parameters, which you can get from your IT department.

As soon as you select From SQL Server, PowerPivot opens the Table Import Wizard, as shown in Figure 6-2.

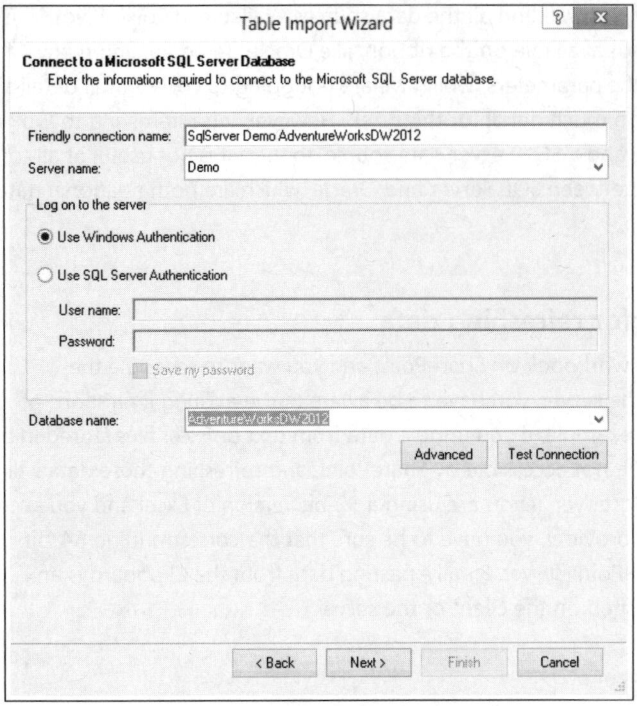

FIGURE 6-2 The Table Import Wizard asks for the parameters to connect to SQL Server.

The options on the first page of the Table Import Wizard for Microsoft SQL Server are as follows:

- **Friendly Connection Name** This is a name that you can assign to the connection so you can recall it later. We suggest overriding the default name that PowerPivot suggests because using a meaningful name will make your life easier later, when you will need to recall the same connection (for example, to load another table from the same database).

- **Server Name** This is the name of the computer running SQL Server to which you want to connect. In all the examples here, we will use "demo," which is the name of our test environment. In your specific environment, you need to write the name of the computer running SQL Server, which your IT department will provide you.

- **Database Name** In this box, you need to specify the name of the database to which you want to connect. A single computer running SQL Server normally hosts many databases, so you need to provide the name of the specific database you want. Again, you will need the IT department to give you the name of the database that contains your data and give you read access to it.

Before you continue, it is a good practice to test the connection with the Test Connection button, to be sure that there are no problems with the connection parameters. If the connection test runs well, then you can safely save this connection and proceed with the next steps. If, on the other hand, there is any kind of problem, then it is better to discover it now and solve it immediately.

Clicking Next in this first window will bring you to the next window of the wizard (see Figure 6-3), where you need to make an important choice: whether you want to load data directly from tables or views or whether you want to write a SQL query to perform advanced data loading.

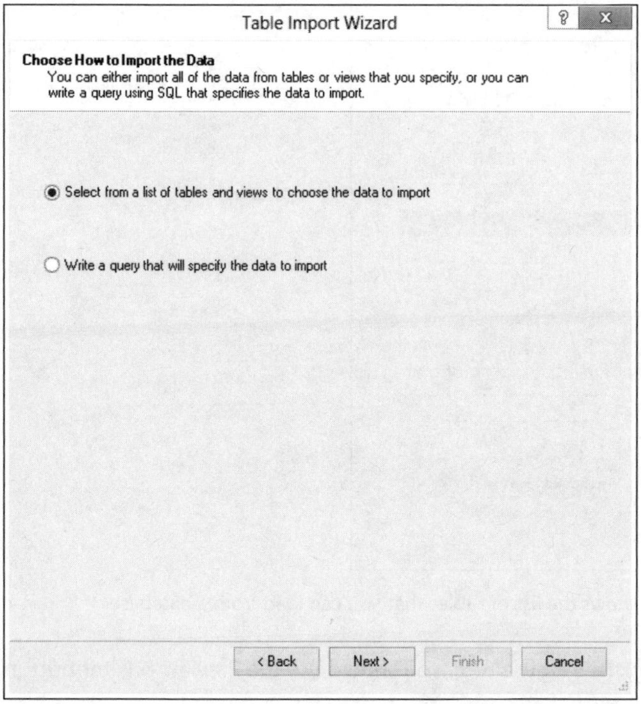

FIGURE 6-3 From here, you can choose the right loading method from the database.

These two options will lead you to completely different loading paths, which will be described in the following sections.

Loading from a list of tables

If you choose to select the tables from a list, then PowerPivot will read from the computer running SQL Server the list of tables and views available in the database and provide you the option to choose which one to load, as shown in Figure 6-4.

When you select a table for import, you can give it a friendly name, which is the name that PowerPivot will use for the table after it will have been imported. If you want, you can provide filtering to reduce the number of rows read from the table. Filtering is useful when you face a large table and you are interested in analyzing only a portion of it.

FIGURE 6-4 The Table Import Wizard shows the list of tables that you can load from a database.

To access the filtering dialog box (see Figure 6-5), you should use the Preview & Filter button (shown previously in Figure 6-4).

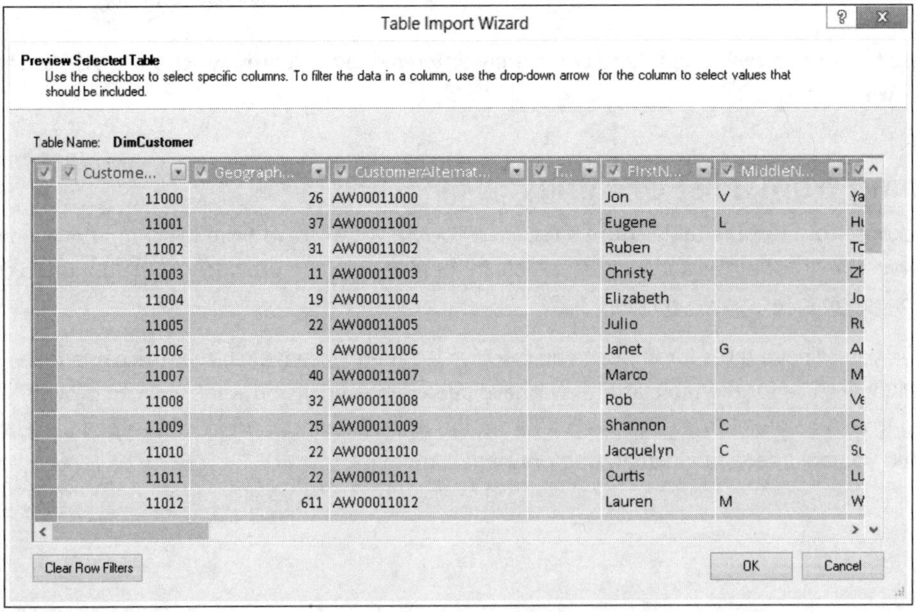

FIGURE 6-5 You can preview and filter a table before importing it.

To limit the content of the table that will be loaded, you can apply two different kinds of filters:

- **Column filtering**: You can choose a selection of all the columns of the table for loading. This is convenient when the source table contains technical columns, which are not needed for your analysis. To select or remove a column, you must select the small check box that appears before each column title in the grid.

- **Data filtering**: You can also choose to load only a subset of the rows of the table, specifying a condition that will filter the unwanted rows. In Figure 6-6, you can see the data filtering area, open for the CustomerAlternateKey column.

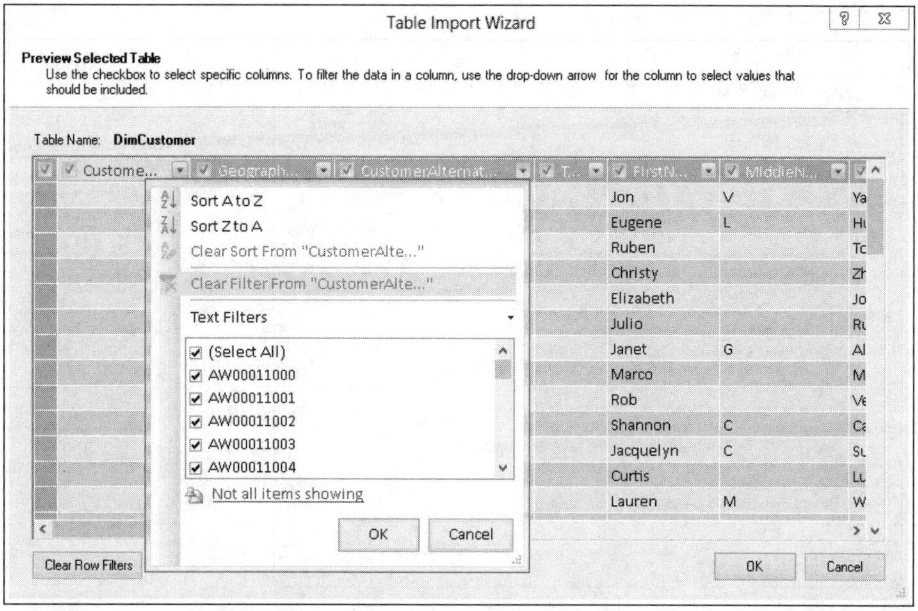

FIGURE 6-6 Here, you can see the data filtering for text columns.

Data filtering is powerful and easy to use. You can use the list of values automatically provided by PowerPivot, or if there are too many values, you can use the Text Filters option and provide a set of rules in the form "greater than," "less or equal than," and so on.

> **Note** Both column and data filters are saved in the PowerPivot table definition, so when you refresh the table from inside the PowerPivot window, they will be applied again.

Loading relationships

When you finish filtering the table, clicking OK makes PowerPivot load the tables. As soon as PowerPivot finishes loading the data, it looks for any relationships among the tables. Since relational databases are able to store not only data, but also information about existing relationships, PowerPivot will query the database to see if there are relationships stored, and if some exist, it will replicate them inside its internal database.

The relationship detection occurs only when you load data directly from more than one table. When loading a single table or a query (a topic that we will discuss in the "Loading from a SQL query" section later in this chapter), no relationship detection takes place.

You can see in Figure 6-7 that at the end of the Table Import Wizard there is an additional step called Data Preparation, which indicates that relationship detection has taken place.

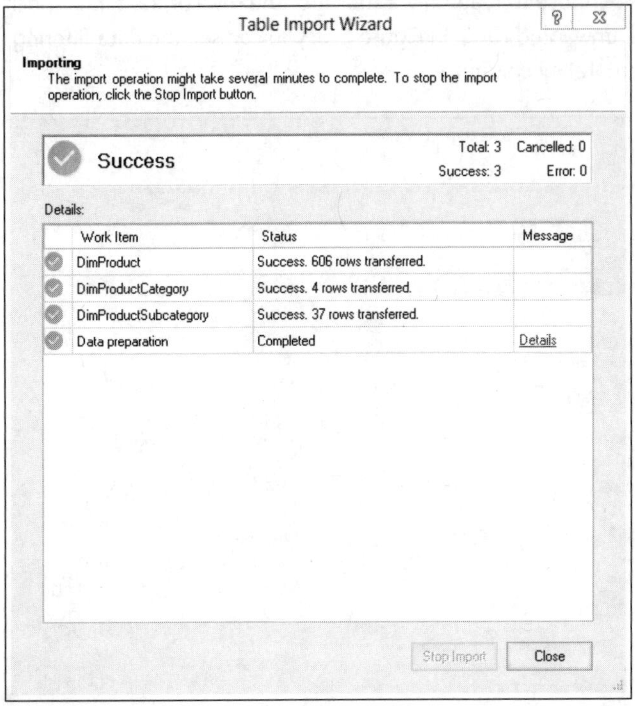

FIGURE 6-7 The final step in the loading process is data preparation, when relationships are detected.

If you want to see more details about the relationships found, you can use the Details hyperlink to open a small window that summarizes the relationships created.

Selecting related tables

During the loading process that we have discussed up to now, we chose not to focus on another useful button in the Table Import Wizard—Select Related Tables (see Figure 6-8). Now it is time to talk about it.

PowerPivot is able to analyze the relationships between tables stored in the database and automatically select all the tables that have some kind of relationship to the ones already selected. For example, if you select only the DimProduct table, you will see a page similar to Figure 6-8.

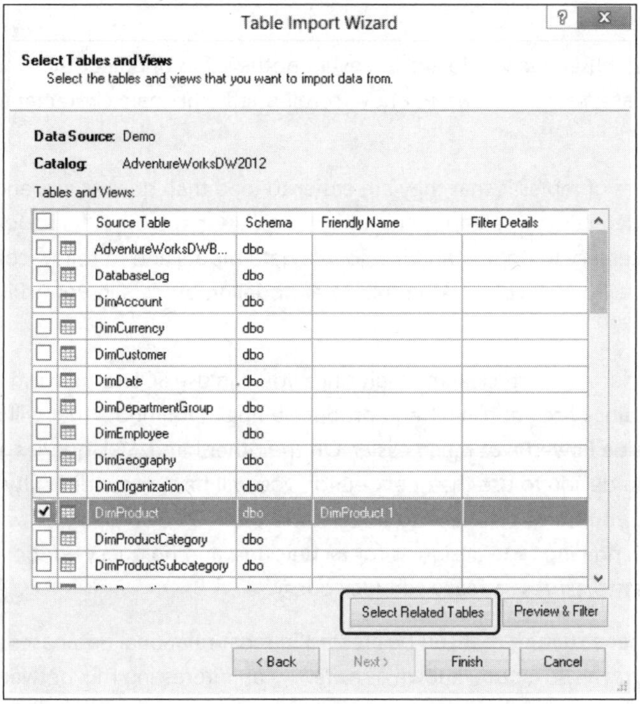

FIGURE 6-8 PowerPivot let us quickly select all tables related to the selected ones.

If you click Select Related Tables, PowerPivot will scan all the tables inside the database, and it will automatically select the ones related to the DimProduct table.

Loading from a SQL query

In the previous sections, we have completed the description of the loading process from a relational database. In the first step of the Table Import Wizard, you have chosen to select some tables and then followed all the steps until you reach the end. But there is another option: Write A Query To Specify The Data To Import (see Figure 6-3), which we will discuss now.

As you might recall from Chapter 4, "Data Models," SQL is a standard programming language for reading information from a database and, if you select the second option in Figure 6-3, PowerPivot will open the query editor.

You already read a description of how the query designer works in Chapter 4, so we are not going to repeat that information here. The relevant part of all of this is the fact that, when working with SQL databases, you always have the option to load tables or queries—whichever works better in your specific data model.

Loading from views

Before leaving the topic of SQL databases, we would like to cover another kind of object that you can use to load data from a SQL database: namely, views. For now, recall briefly the main characteristics of the two means we have used so far:

- **Tables** The big advantages of tables is that they are easier to load than queries are, and that PowerPivot is able to detect most relationships automatically. On the other hand, loading tables directly makes it necessary to understand the source data model and to follow complex chains of relationships inside PowerPivot, making this data modeling process in PowerPivot slightly complex.

- **Queries** SQL queries produce a much cleaner result since you can use SQL to perform denormalization, follow chains of relationships, and produce a final data model that will make querying the data from inside PowerPivot much easier. On the other hand, SQL queries are not easy to write, and if you decide to use the query editor, you will have some difficulty expressing the exact query you want. You need to understand that SQL has not been written for users—it is a programming language designed for technicians, and no query editor will ever be able to make it easy to express a really complex query.

With all that said, there is another structure that can be created in most relational databases and used by client tools like PowerPivot. This structure, known as a *view,* is an interesting mix between a SQL query and a table.

A view is just a SQL query stored inside the database that has a name. From the PowerPivot point of view, a view is like a table: it contains rows divided into columns. The only difference is that when PowerPivot asks for the data, the database does not return rows stored inside a table. Instead, it executes the SQL query and returns its result.

What makes views so great is that they are the missing link between database technicians and power users. Since the task to write SQL queries is better accomplished by IT, you can ask the IT department to provide you with a set of views that handle the complexities of SQL and expose a more user-friendly data model to you.

Moreover, your IT staff will really appreciate that you are reading data from views since, from their perspective, the sole existence of a view represents an interface between the database and the user asking for data (in this case, you). By looking at views, they will be aware of what data you are using.

The usage of views is highly recommended since it acts as a perfect bridge between the complexity of SQL queries (which is left to the IT department) and the simplicity of tables.

Opening existing connections

The previous section covered all the features of data loading, creating a connection from the beginning. Once you have created a connection with a data source, it will be saved inside the PowerPivot workbook so that you can open it again without needing to provide the connection information. To reopen an existing connection, you can use the Existing Connections button on the Home tab on the PowerPivot ribbon, as shown in Figure 6-9.

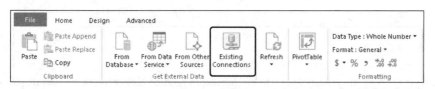

FIGURE 6-9 You can use the Existing Connections button on the Home tab on the PowerPivot ribbon to reopen a connection.

If you click this button, PowerPivot opens the Existing Connections window shown in Figure 6-10, where you can select both the connections saved in the Excel workbook or any local connections previously saved in your document library.

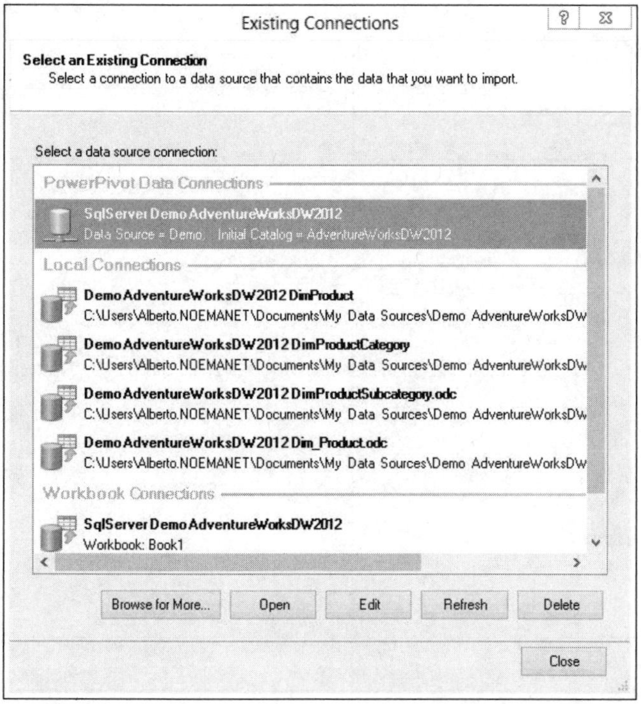

FIGURE 6-10 The Existing Connections lists all available connections.

Moreover, if you need to change the properties of a saved connection, you can use Edit to open the Edit Connection window again and update its configuration.

Note It is very important that you get used to reopening existing connections whenever you need to import more tables from the same database. If you create a new connection each time you want to load some data instead of reopening an existing one, you end up with many connections in the same workbook and, in the case that you have to modify some of the connection parameters, you need to make some extra and unneeded work to update all the different connections.

Loading from Access

Now that you have seen all the features of data loading from relational databases, we can describe other data sources, including the Access data source. Many Microsoft Office users are accustomed to storing information inside Access databases. PowerPivot provides a data source that can load data from Access much as you do from SQL Server.

Clearly, when you open the Table Import Wizard with an Access data source, the connection parameters will be slightly different because Access databases are stored in files on disk instead of being hosted in server databases. In Figure 6-11, the Table Import Wizard is asking for an Access file.

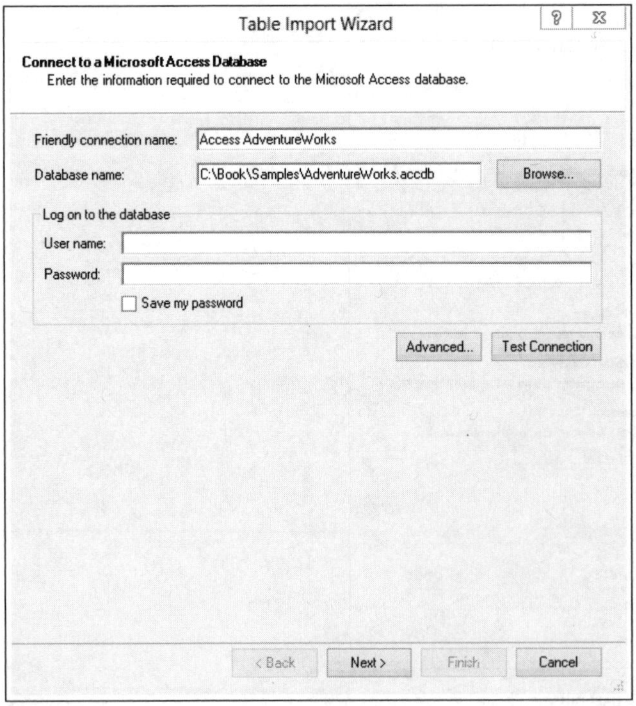

FIGURE 6-11 The Table Import Wizard is asking for Access connection parameters.

There is no practical difference between Access and a relational database when it comes to loading tables. On the other hand, the SQL designer of Access is very limited because it does not offer a visual designer for the SQL query. When querying Access, you need to write the query in a plain-text editor, as shown in Figure 6-12.

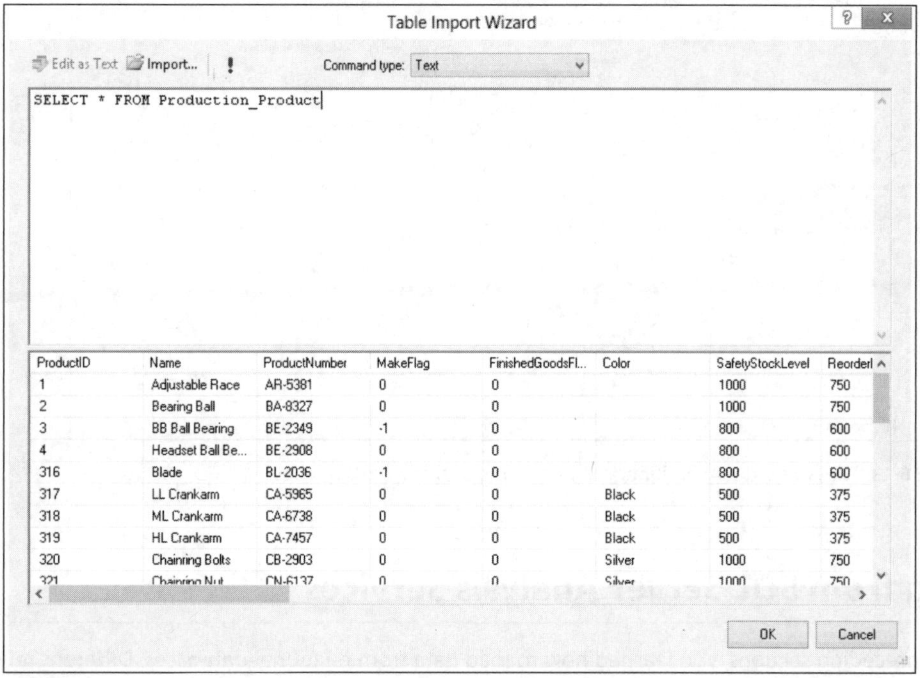

FIGURE 6-12 The Access query designer inside PowerPivot has few features.

Since the query designer of Access is so limited, if you need to load data from Access and need help with SQL, then it might be useful to write the query using the Access query designer directly inside Access, as shown in Figure 6-13. Then, after the query has been built inside Access, you can load the data by selecting the query.

It might be useful to recall that once data is loaded inside PowerPivot, there are no differences between SQL Server, Access, or any other database that we have used to import data. All PowerPivot tables can be used together and related to each other.

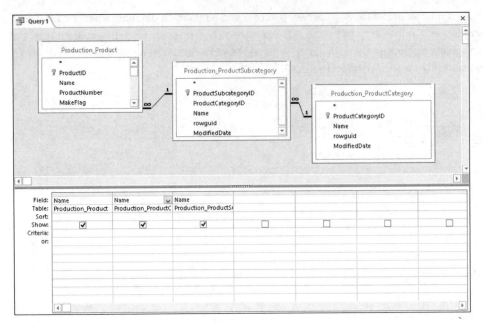

FIGURE 6-13 The Access query designer can be used to design Access queries.

Loading from SQL Server Analysis Services

In the preceding sections, you learned how to load data from relational databases. Different relational data sources might have some slight differences among them, but the overall logic of importing from a relational database is the same. PowerPivot allows you to load data from other data sources, which are completely different kinds of databases. This section describes one of these sources, SQL Server Analysis Services, which has some unique features.

It might seem strange to have the option to load data from SQL Server Analysis Services (whose main purpose is the construction of PivotTables) into PowerPivot (whose purpose is to build PivotTables)! You might wonder why you ever would need to load data from a SQL Server Analysis Services database when you already can create PivotTables directly from the original source.

Once again, the reason is data integration. Even if you can easily create PivotTables on a SQL Server Analysis Services OLAP cube, it is not at all easy to integrate different pieces of information into the same PivotTable. With PowerPivot, you can load data coming from the SQL Server Analysis Services database, integrate this information with other tables coming from other databases (including your personal Excel workbooks), and then use PowerPivot to create new and useful PivotTables, as you will do in later chapters.

To connect to SQL Server Analysis Services, you need to select the From Analysis Services Or PowerPivot option of the From Database button on the Home tab of the PowerPivot ribbon.

The Table Import Wizard opens again (see Figure 6-14), and you need to provide the server name and the database to which you want to connect. This time, you also need to direct the system to a valid SQL Server Analysis Services database.

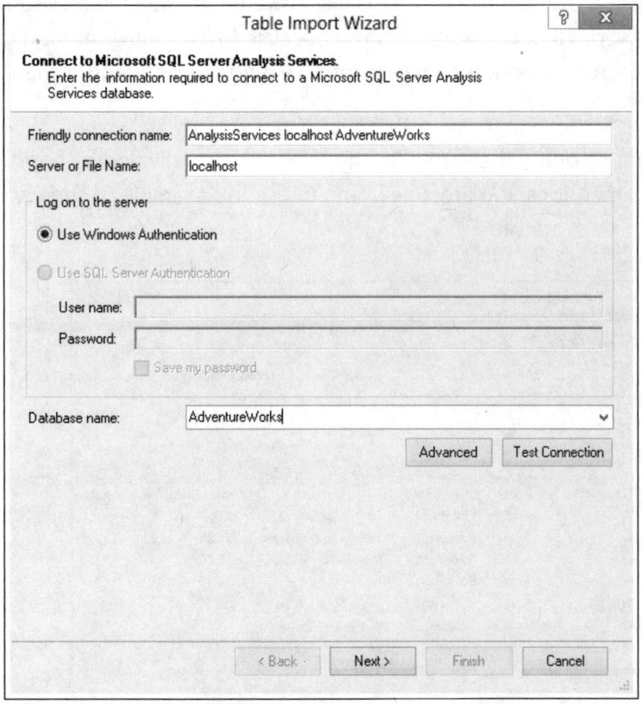

FIGURE 6-14 The Table Import Wizard asking for a SQL Server Analysis Services connection.

Clicking Next brings you to the MDX query editor. The MDX editor is similar to the SQL editor, but this time, the language that you need to use to query the database is not SQL but MDX, which is the query language for OLAP cubes. As with the SQL editor, you do not need to know the language to build a query: PowerPivot contains an MDX query designer, which you can open by clicking Design.

Note As you might have noticed, you cannot import tables from a SQL Server Analysis Services database; the only way to load data from a SQL Server Analysis Services database is to write a query. The reason is very simple: OLAP cubes do not contain tables, so there is no space for a table selection. OLAP cubes are composed of measure groups and dimensions, and the only way to retrieve data from there is to create an MDX query that creates a dataset to import. Although this is true for Multidimensional cubes, if you need to connect to a Tabular database, then you can use the DAX language to query it and, in that case, you will be able to load tables, as you are going to learn later in this section.

Using the MDX editor

Designing an MDX query with the MDX editor is much easier than designing a SQL query. The reason stems partly from their purposes: whereas SQL is a query language intended to be used by IT people, MDX has been created to be easily integrated into rich clients like PowerPivot. Moreover, as strange as it might seem, MDX editors are powerful and convenient to use because MDX is much more difficult to write than SQL; as a consequence, much more effort went into creating the MDX editor than into creating the SQL editor.

In Figure 6-15, you can see a sample query that provides the sales amounts divided by region, category, subcategory, and other dimensions. We are now going to use this example to show some of the most interesting features of the MDX editor.

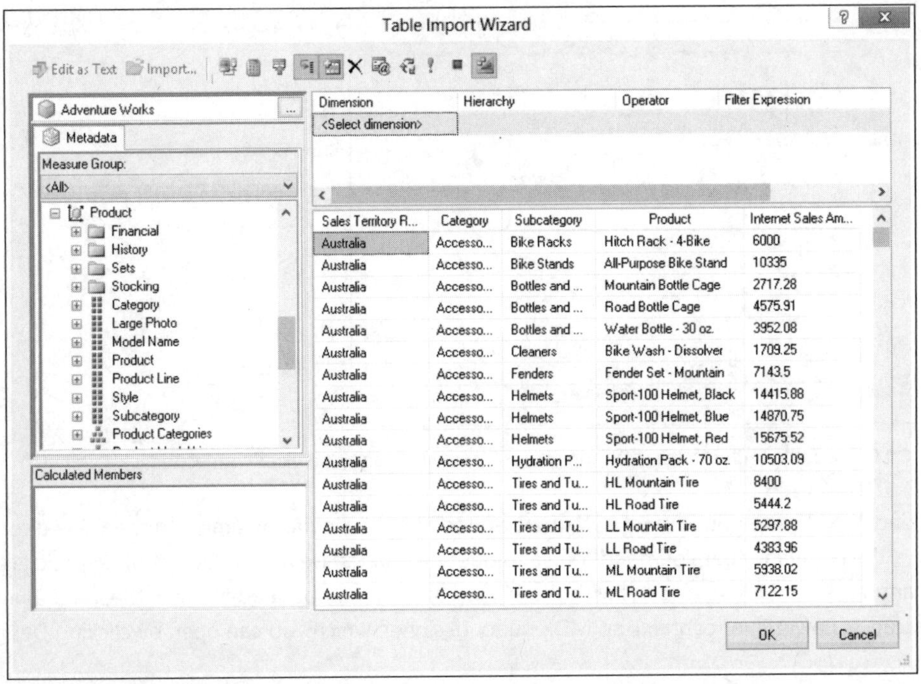

FIGURE 6-15 The MDX editor is a powerful tool to build MDX queries graphically.

The first interesting feature is the measure group selector, which allows you to choose a measure group from which you want to load data. It is very useful because if the cube contains several dimensions, not all of which are linked to all measure groups, selecting a specific measure group hides all the dimensions that are not linked to that measure group. If, for example, you select the Sales Target measure group (see Figure 6-16), all the dimensions that are not related to the sales targets are hidden. This makes it easier to build the query by reducing the number of visible dimensions.

FIGURE 6-16 The measure group selection automatically filters unrelated dimensions (the Sales Targets measure group in this example).

Using the MDX editor is pretty simple, and it works much in the same way as using the PivotTable. To build the query, it is enough to drag measures, dimension attributes, or complete hierarchies from the selector to the query area. The wizard immediately refreshes the query, showing you a preview of the dataset that you are about to query. The only noticeable difference is that you cannot put data items in columns; you can retrieve items only in rows. You can better understand it if you compare Figure 6-17 to Figure 6-18, in which you can see the same query using Excel. In Figure 6-17, the calendar years are placed in columns, as you are probably used to seeing them.

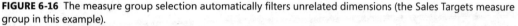

Internet Sales Amount	Column Labels		
Row Labels	CY 2007	CY 2008	Grand Total
⊟**Accessories**	**$293,709.71**	**$407,050.25**	**$700,759.96**
⊞Bike Racks	$16,440.00	$22,920.00	$39,360.00
⊞Bike Stands	$18,921.00	$20,670.00	$39,591.00
⊞Bottles and Cages	$23,280.27	$33,517.92	$56,798.19
⊞Cleaners	$3,044.85	$4,173.75	$7,218.60
⊞Fenders	$19,408.34	$27,211.24	$46,619.58
⊞Helmets	$92,583.54	$132,752.06	$225,335.60
⊞Hydration Packs	$16,771.95	$23,535.72	$40,307.67
⊞Tires and Tubes	$103,259.76	$142,269.56	$245,529.32
⊞**Bikes**	**$9,359,102.62**	**$9,162,324.85**	**$18,521,427.47**
⊞**Clothing**	**$138,247.97**	**$201,524.64**	**$339,772.61**
Grand Total	**$9,791,060.30**	**$9,770,899.74**	**$19,561,960.04**

FIGURE 6-17 In an Excel PivotTable, you are used to slice data using both rows and columns.

If you put the calendar year information in PivotTable rows instead of columns (see Figure 6-18), you get a result that is identical to that produced by the query editor, except for the fact that the data is shown in a hierarchical way, whereas the query designer uses a simpler list.

Row Labels	Internet Sales Amount
⊟ **Accessories**	**$700,759.96**
⊞ Bike Racks	**$39,360.00**
CY 2007	$16,440.00
CY 2008	$22,920.00
⊞ Bike Stands	**$39,591.00**
CY 2007	$18,921.00
CY 2008	$20,670.00
⊞ Bottles and Cages	**$56,798.19**
CY 2007	$23,280.27
CY 2008	$33,517.92

FIGURE 6-18 You can obtain the same data in Figure 6-17 using only rows to slice data, as the MDX Editor does.

You can see that there is no difference at all between the two representations in terms of data; it is just a matter of how data is presented.

> **Note** The MDX editor does not let you slice on columns because it needs to define the number of columns in the destination table. For example, if you put the date in columns, the number of columns of the resulting table might vary, depending on when you execute the query (as the number of years increases, so does the number of columns). When you impose the restriction of putting dimensions on rows only, the MDX editor grants that the number of columns is invariant and can be used to determine the structure of the PowerPivot destination table, which needs a fixed number of columns.

After you have designed the query and clicked OK, the user interface returns to the query editor, showing the complex MDX code that executes the query against the server. At this point, it is unnecessary, and not particularly interesting, for you to understand the complexities of MDX; you can safely trust that the strange code shown in Figure 6-19 will indeed return the correct values.

If you now click Finish, PowerPivot begins loading the data.

Handling of keys in the OLAP cube

You have seen that by using the MDX editor, you can easily load data from SQL Server Analysis Services. Nevertheless, when loading data from an OLAP cube, you need to tackle a subtle problem. OLAP cube programmers often design the cube structure so that it is easy for people to query. The programmers tend to expose textual attributes that are easy to understand from a human point of view and hide all the more technical attributes, which are not useful when you are pivoting data. In other words, they follow the same process of hiding technical columns that you already learned. This data model is well suited for pivoting data, but it is seldom the best one for further processing, as you want to do in PowerPivot.

An example should help to clarify this concept. If you want to load the average unit price per year for each product, you can easily create a query that returns a table like the one shown in Figure 6-20.

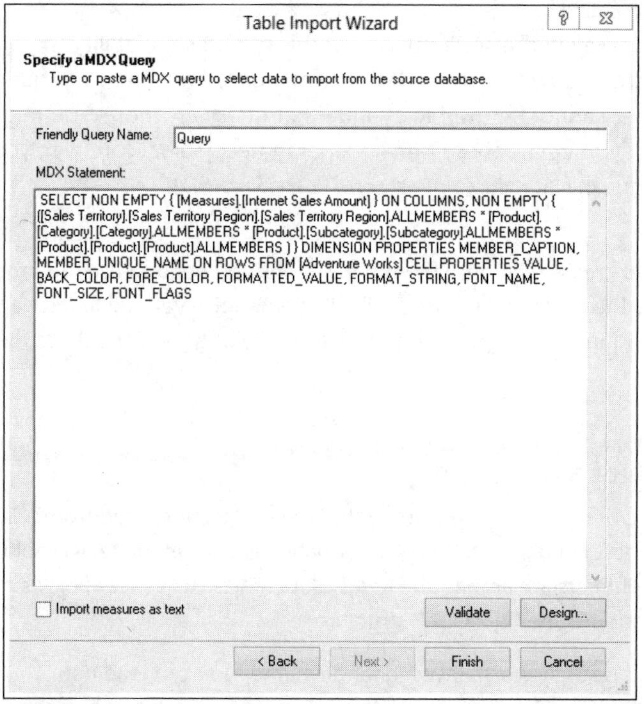

FIGURE 6-19 The Table Import Wizard shows the MDX code generated by the designer.

Product Name	Year	Average Unit Price
All-Purpose Bike Stand	CY 2007	$159.00
AWC Logo Cap	CY 2007	$5.18
AWC Logo Cap	CY 2007	$8.16
Bike Wash - Dissolver	CY 2007	$6.72
Cable Lock	CY 2007	$15.00
Chain	CY 2007	$12.14
Classic Vest, L	CY 2007	$61.41
Classic Vest, M	CY 2007	$44.37

FIGURE 6-20 This table computed the average unit price per product and year.

You probably created this table to integrate its information with other tables in the same PowerPivot workbook. Nevertheless, to relate this table to other ones—for example, by product—you need a product key. The OLAP cube lets you easily load the product name because this is how people will identify a product. On the other hand, in a typical database as in PowerPivot, we tend to join tables using keys like the ProductKey for the relationship. The ProductKey is not useful in reporting, so cube designers do not normally show this instance of data, even if they store it in the database for technical reasons.

> **Tip** You can include the ProductKey in the MDX query, but this requires the ability to change the MDX query code created by the query designer manually and, after that query has been modified, the designer cannot be used to change that query anymore. You might ask your IT department to help you create these MDX queries, if necessary. Moreover, you can find more information about this at *http://tinyurl.com/PowerPivotSSAS*.

All this means that if you want to create relationships with this table, you need to use the product name, not the product ID, because the product ID is not available. Sometimes you will find it hard to detect a valid key to create relationships; that depends on the availability of good candidates for the key column in OLAP cubes.

Investigate the presence of a data mart

If you can load data from an OLAP cube, it is highly likely that the OLAP cube is fed from a SQL data mart. Normally, the data mart contains a lot more information than that made available through the cube, and table identifiers are among the items. Data marts store identifiers as the internal key even if they are hidden in the final OLAP structure.

If you face such a situation, it is surely worth investigating whether you can load data directly from the data mart so that you can have access to all the technical information and create relationships using identifiers.

Loading from a tabular database

As you have learned, you can use the SQL Server Analysis Services data source to load data from a Multidimensional database. An interesting and perhaps less obvious feature of the data source is that you also can use it to load data from a Tabular data model. The Tabular model can be either a Tabular database in SQL Server Analysis Services or a PowerPivot workbook hosted in PowerPivot for SharePoint, like the ones you have learned how to publish in Chapter 5, "Publishing to SharePoint."

To load data from a Tabular data model, you just connect to a Tabular database in the same way you connect to a Multidimensional one. The MDX editor shows the Tabular database as if it were a Multidimensional one, exposing the data in measure groups and dimensions even if no such concept exists in a Tabular model.

Because the native programming and querying language of Tabular is DAX, you might be wondering at this point whether a Tabular database can be queried in DAX as well. It turns out that this feature is indeed available, though it is well hidden.

The MDX editor is not capable of authoring or understanding DAX queries. Nevertheless, because the SQL Server Analysis Services server in Tabular mode understands both languages, you can write a DAX query directly in the Table Import Wizard in place of an MDX statement, as displayed in Figure 6-21.

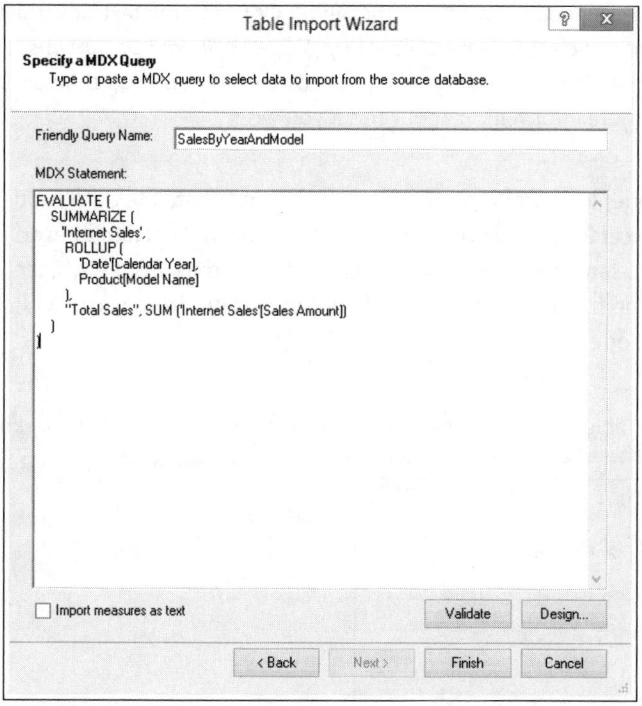

FIGURE 6-21 You can use DAX instead of MDX when querying a Tabular data model.

The query shown in Figure 6-21, which is written in DAX syntax, is very simple. It loads the sales data aggregated by year and model name. In Chapter 14, "DAX as a query language," you will learn how to use DAX to create complex queries.

Writing the DAX query inside the small text box provided by the Table Import Wizard is not convenient. Nevertheless, you can prepare the DAX query in a text editor and then paste the code inside the text box.

Loading from SharePoint

You learned in the previous chapter that SharePoint is an important part of the Microsoft BI offering for Self-Service BI because it lets you upload workbooks to the server and share them with your team. But SharePoint usefulness goes beyond this. A workbook uploaded to SharePoint really becomes a database, and you have the option to load data from SharePoint as if it is a SQL Server Analysis Services Tabular database (which it actually is).

To load data from SharePoint, you only need to know the workbook name and the folder where it has been saved. In Chapter 5, you saved a workbook named "Dashboard Example" in the documents library (which is named, in SharePoint terminology, "Shared Documents"). If you want to connect to the data model stored in that workbook, all you need to do is to choose the From Database menu from the PowerPivot ribbon and select the From Analysis Services Or PowerPivot option.

In the Table Import Wizard, you will need to specify, in the Server Or File Name text box, the full path of the workbook in SharePoint, which in this example is *http://sp2013/Shared Documents/Dashboard Example.xlsx*. In your SharePoint installation, the path can be different. You can consult your SharePoint administrator for more information about this if you wish.

> **Note** To load from a data model in SharePoint, the workbook must contain a data model created with PowerPivot for Excel 2013. A workbook containing only a PivotTable based on an Excel table will not offer the same functionality. You can still load data from any Excel workbook in SharePoint, but the functionality will be limited to loading from Excel, without the ability to query the data model.

In Figure 6-22, you can see the Table Import Wizard ready to load from the SharePoint workbook.

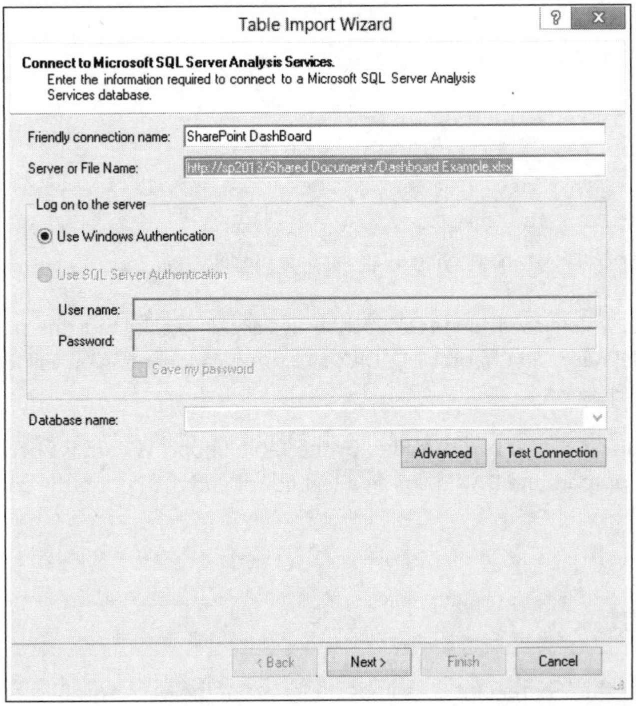

FIGURE 6-22 You can load from a workbook saved in SharePoint using the Table Import Wizard.

> **Tip** It is always good to test the connection before moving on because it is somewhat easy to misspell the file name in the text box. In fact, since you do not have the option to browse for the file name, you will need to enter it manually.

After you specify the workbook path, the procedure is identical to the one you learned previously in this chapter to load data from SQL Server Analysis Services. In Figure 6-23, for example, you can see the Table Import Wizard shows a sample query made on the Excel data model created for your dashboard.

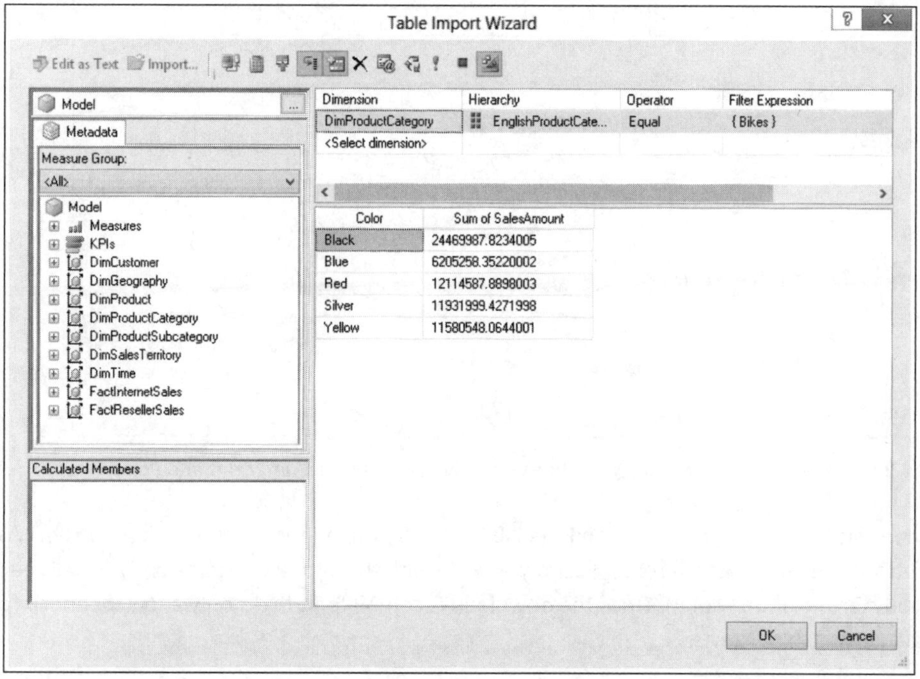

FIGURE 6-23 The Excel data model in a PowerPivot workbook is a Tabular database.

It is interesting at this point to make a small digression and talk about the capabilities that you can exploit using this feature. In fact, using SharePoint and PowerPivot, you can not only load data inside a data model to create reports, you can actually create your personal set of data models, which can be used later to build more sophisticated reports. For example, you can create an accounting data model, then a budgeting one, and finally merge them into a single report, without the need to repeat all the steps that made the first data model work.

Even if you do not have the full power of the tools used by BI professionals to create a complex data warehouse, Excel and SharePoint together are powerful and simple tools to start creating your personal data warehouse. Then, if the data model becomes too complex or your needs increase, you will always have the option to create a full-featured data warehouse later.

Using SharePoint, you have other loading options. Any list in SharePoint can be exported as a data feed (that is, a flow of information that can be loaded in PowerPivot). Imagine, for example, that you want to create a report based on the workbooks that have been uploaded in SharePoint. You start from the SharePoint folder where these reports are, as shown in Figure 6-24.

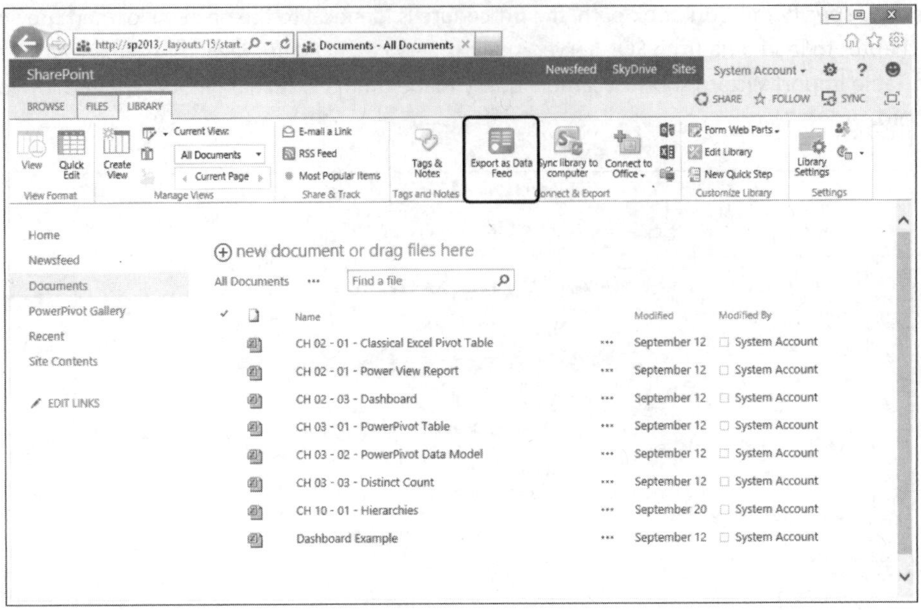

FIGURE 6-24 You can export any SharePoint library as a data feed and then import it into PowerPivot.

To load this list, you will need to open the LIBRARY tab and, on the ribbon, click the Export As Data Feed button. This will make SharePoint send you a file with the .atomsvc extension (you will see a download starting at this point). Once the download is complete (it takes only a few seconds), you can open the file and Excel starts.

> **Note** In previous versions of PowerPivot, .atmosvc were automatically associated to Excel to make this loading process easier. In Excel 2013, this association is not created by the setup program and, if you want to make Excel open these files, you will need to make the association by yourself.

Depending on your security setup, Excel can open a Security Notice window, like the one shown in Figure 6-25, because the data connection created by SharePoint looks like an Internet one. Knowing that you are connecting to SharePoint, you can enable the connection without much worry.

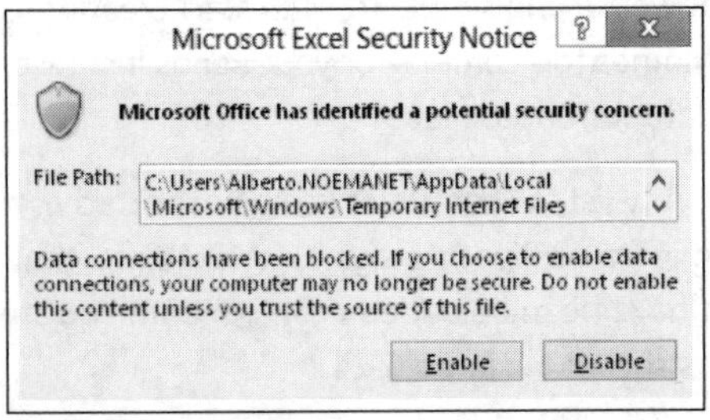

FIGURE 6-25 The .atmosvc connection created by SharePoint can cause a security warning in Excel.

After you enable the connection, you will have the option to choose how you want this data feed to be used in Excel. The Import Data dialog box (see Figure 6-26) shows you several options, from which you can choose the one that best fits your needs.

FIGURE 6-26 A data feed can be used to supply many Excel sources.

In this example, you are loading the data inside a table. Confirming the window will create an Excel table containing all the details about the workbooks in the list. In Figure 6-27, you can see some of the most relevant columns in the table.

	J	K	L	M	N
1	Path	CheckedOutToId	Name	VirusStatus	IsCurrentVersion
2	/Shared Documents		CH 02 - 01 - Classical Excel Pivot Table.xlsx	10553318	TRUE
3	/Shared Documents		CH 02 - 01 - Power View Report.xlsx	10608948	TRUE
4	/Shared Documents		CH 02 - 03 - Dashboard.xlsx	3852858	TRUE
5	/Shared Documents		CH 03 - 01 - PowerPivot Table.xlsx	1133987	TRUE
6	/Shared Documents		CH 03 - 02 - PowerPivot Data Model.xlsx	5787187	TRUE
7	/Shared Documents		CH 03 - 03 - Distinct Count.xlsx	5797680	TRUE
8	/Shared Documents		CH 10 - 01 - Hierarchies.xlsx	5622211	TRUE
9	/Shared Documents		Dashboard Example.xlsx	3710906	TRUE

FIGURE 6-27 The file list imported into Excel contains a great deal of compelling information.

It is interesting to note that the table has already been imported into the data model too. If you open the PowerPivot window, you will see that the table is there. In this way, you avoid the need to add it manually to the data model.

Using linked tables

The next topic of this chapter deals with linked tables, which are probably the easiest way to load data into PowerPivot, even if they do not belong to the family of data sources. If you need a table that is not already loaded into any of your databases, you can simply create an Excel table, load data into it, and then link the table to a PowerPivot table.

Because creating a linked table is so easy, we want to show you not only how to create one, but also how you can use linked tables to immediately update the data model and produce interactive reports. You can find this sample file with the name "CH06-01-Linked Tables.xlsx."

Suppose that at the start of the year, you performed an analysis of the predicted sales increase, month by month, over last year's amounts, computing values based on your personal experience, external market analysis, and meetings with your sales departments. You ended up with an Excel worksheet that contains, for each month, a percentage that indicates how you thought sales would vary during the year (see Figure 6-28).

Month	Increase
January	5%
February	5%
March	6%
April	7%
May	7%
June	5%
July	4%
August	-2%
September	-3%
October	0%
November	2%
December	5%

FIGURE 6-28 You can create a simple Excel table with predictive sales and then use it in the data model.

Now you would like to use this information to create a PivotTable that applies these predictive factors to the sales in the previous year to make a projection of the sales. The first step is to load sales into PowerPivot to have a starting set of figures. For example, you can query the OLAP cube to get the last year's sales amount, producing a table that contains the value for each month, category, and subcategory. The resulting table is shown in Figure 6-29.

Month	Category	Subcategory	Product	Sales
January	Bikes	Touring Bikes	Touring-1000 Blue, 46	$40,529.19
January	Bikes	Touring Bikes	Touring-1000 Blue, 50	$28,608.84
January	Bikes	Touring Bikes	Touring-1000 Blue, 54	$33,376.98
January	Bikes	Touring Bikes	Touring-1000 Blue, 60	$30,992.91
January	Bikes	Touring Bikes	Touring-1000 Yellow, 46	$38,145.12
January	Bikes	Touring Bikes	Touring-1000 Yellow, 50	$38,145.12
January	Bikes	Touring Bikes	Touring-1000 Yellow, 54	$23,840.70
January	Bikes	Touring Bikes	Touring-1000 Yellow, 60	$38,145.12
January	Bikes	Touring Bikes	Touring-2000 Blue, 46	$8.503.95

FIGURE 6-29 An Excel table containing last year's sales, as gathered from the database.

To use the predictive values in the data model, you need to load the table shown in Figure 6-28 into PowerPivot and then make several computations to get the prediction to work. To load the table in PowerPivot, you just have to put the cursor in it and click the Add To Data Model button on the

PowerPivot ribbon (see Figure 6-30). This immediately loads the table into the PowerPivot database and gives it the same name as the table in Excel.

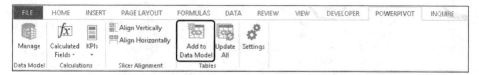

FIGURE 6-30 The Add To Data Model button is located on the PowerPivot tab of the ribbon.

The resulting table, once loaded in the data model, can be seen in Figure 6-31.

Month	Increase
January	0.05
February	0.05
March	0.06
April	0.07
May	0.07
June	0.05
July	0.04
August	-0.02
Septemb...	-0.03
October	0
November	0.02
December	0.05

FIGURE 6-31 The prediction table is now a linked table in the data model.

At this point, the missing link is a relationship between the Sales and the Predictions tables so you can use the predictive factor in the Sales table. You can do that in Diagram view by dragging the Month column of Sales to the Month column of Predictions. The resulting data model is shown in Figure 6-32.

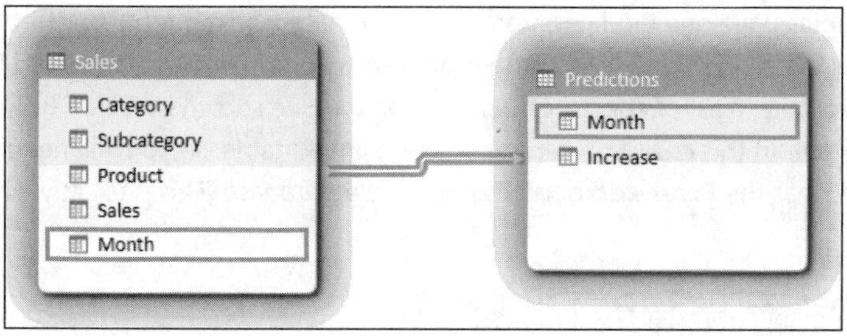

FIGURE 6-32 The resulting data model mixes database tables with Excel tables.

At this point, you can use simple math and the *RELATED* function to create a new calculated column in the Sales table that contains the predicted sales:

```
[Predicted Sales] = Sales[Sales] * ( 1 + RELATED ( Predictions[Increase] ) )
```

The resulting table, containing predicted sales, is shown in Figure 6-33.

M...	Category	Subcategory	Product	Sales	Predicted Sales
January	Bikes	Touring Bikes	Touring-1000 Blue, 46	$40,529.19	$42,555.65
January	Bikes	Touring Bikes	Touring-1000 Blue, 50	$28,608.84	$30,039.28
January	Bikes	Touring Bikes	Touring-1000 Blue, 54	$33,376.98	$35,045.83
January	Bikes	Touring Bikes	Touring-1000 Blue, 60	$30,992.91	$32,542.56
January	Bikes	Touring Bikes	Touring-1000 Yellow, 46	$38,145.12	$40,052.38
January	Bikes	Touring Bikes	Touring-1000 Yellow, 50	$38,145.12	$40,052.38
January	Bikes	Touring Bikes	Touring-1000 Yellow, 54	$23,840.70	$25,032.74
January	Bikes	Touring Bikes	Touring-1000 Yellow, 60	$38,145.12	$40,052.38
January	Bikes	Touring Bikes	Touring-2000 Blue, 46	$8,503.95	$8,929.15
January	Bikes	Touring Bikes	Touring-2000 Blue, 50	$9,718.80	$10,204.74

FIGURE 6-33 Computing predicted sales in the Predicted Sales column.

You have seen that linked tables are a convenient way of putting data inside the data model directly from Excel. At this point, you might wonder what is the difference between tables automatically added to the model by Excel (because of creating a relationship, for example) and tables added using PowerPivot linked tables. After all, they seem to perform exactly the same operation. Well, that is not quite true. The difference is subtle and, to be honest, you will not notice it most of the time.

Excel tables added to the data model need to be refreshed manually by clicking Refresh. Linked tables, on the other hand, are refreshed as soon as you open the PowerPivot window or refresh the PivotTable, making them slightly more interactive. Apart from this small difference, they behave much the same, and both are valid means to load data from Excel inside the data model.

Loading from Excel files

You have learned that if a table is stored in an Excel file, it can be used to create PowerPivot linked tables. Nevertheless, linked tables have one big limitation: you can create a linked table only if the table resides in the same Excel file as the PowerPivot data model. You might have another Excel file containing some data—for example, a list of special offers, such as the one shown in Figure 6-34, that you want to load into PowerPivot. In this case, you cannot create a linked table, so you will need to use the Excel data source and treat the Excel workbook as if it were a database. This is exactly what we are going to show now.

Special Offer	Start	End	Category	Discount
Christmas Gifts	12/1/2005	12/31/2005	Accessory	25%
Christmas Gifts	12/1/2005	12/31/2005	Bykes	12%
Christmas Gifts	12/1/2005	12/31/2005	Clothing	24%
Summer Specials	8/1/2005	8/15/2005	Clothing	10%
Summer Specials	8/1/2005	8/15/2005	Accesory	10%

FIGURE 6-34 Special offers planned for the year are stored in an external Excel file.

In this example, the Excel range containing data (shown in Figure 6-34) has been formatted as a table to make it easier to refer to in other worksheets because we can use the table name instead of the cell range. Suppose that you have saved this table in the CH06-02-2005Plans.xlsx file, which contains several tables with your thoughts about the budget, and now you want to import the data into PowerPivot. By the way, this Excel file is part of the book's companion material, so you can use the companion workbook to follow this example.

To begin the loading process, you need to click the From Other Sources button in the PowerPivot window. Then you open the Table Import Wizard and then, under the Text Files section, select Excel File, which is near the end of the list. When you click Next, PowerPivot opens the Table Import Wizard for Excel files (see Figure 6-35).

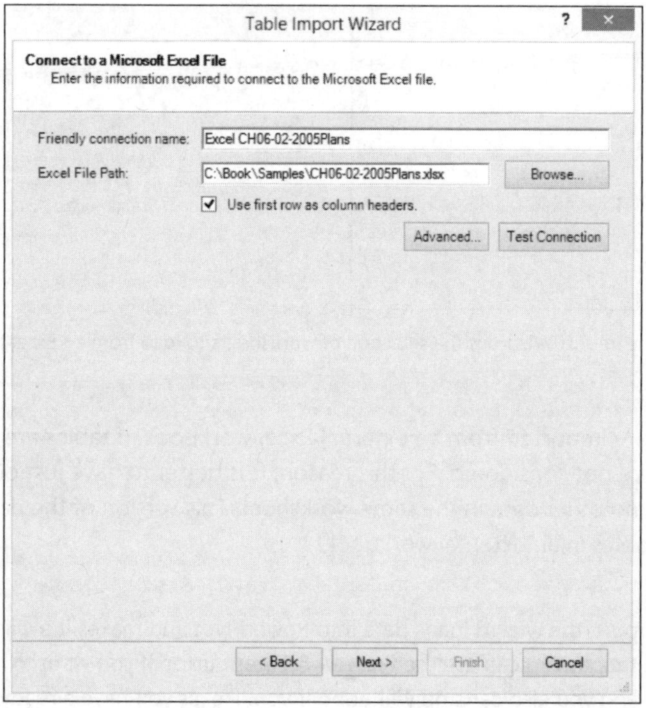

FIGURE 6-35 The Table Import Wizard, asking for the parameters of an Excel file.

You need to provide the file path of the Excel workbook containing the data to load from. An important check box is Use First Row As Column Headers. If your table contains column names in the first row (as is the case in the example), you need to select this check box so PowerPivot automatically detects the column names of the table that you are about to load. If you now click Next, the wizard opens the Excel file, searches for worksheets in it, and allows you to choose which one to load, as shown in Figure 6-36.

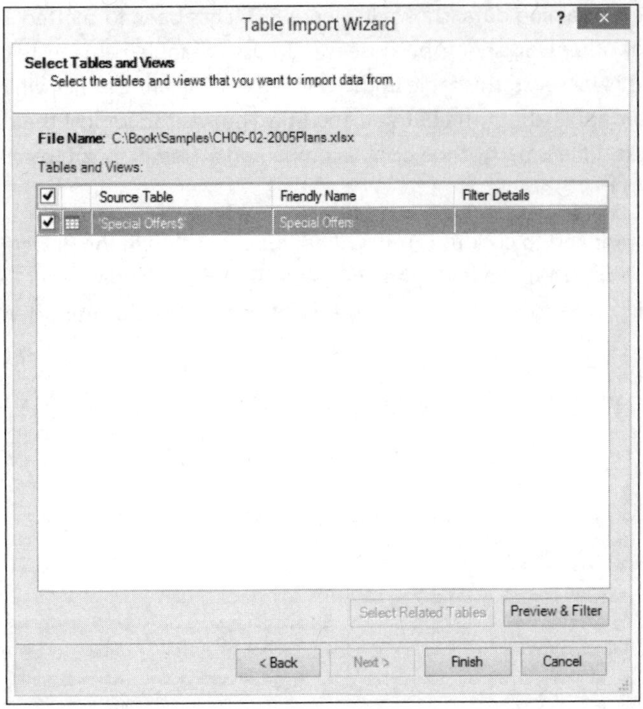

FIGURE 6-36 The next step in the Table Import Wizard is the selection of worksheets to load from an Excel file.

> **Important** Only worksheets are imported from an external Excel workbook. If tables are defined in an Excel file, they are not considered. For this reason, it is better to have just one table for each worksheet and no other data in the same worksheet. This version of the data source cannot detect single tables in an external workbook.

After you select the table to import, the wizard loads data into PowerPivot and makes it available for performing any kind of computation. You can use the Preview & Filter button if you want to look at the data before the data loads, and you also can apply filtering if you like, as you have already learned to do with relational tables.

> **Note** At this point, let's review the difference between a linked table and an Excel import. Linked tables need to be in the same Excel workbook in which the PowerPivot database is stored, which might be a limitation when you already have files containing all the relevant information. On the other hand, when you use the Excel import feature, you can load data that resides in different Excel workbooks. Always keep in mind that loading data does not create a link between the two files: the process of importing data into PowerPivot creates a copy of it, so data is not refreshed when you update the original Excel file. If you want to refresh data, you need to do it manually by using the Refresh button in PowerPivot or through an automated data refresh in SharePoint.

Loading from text files

The list of possible data sources for PowerPivot is growing quickly. The PowerPivot development team has spent a lot of time making it possible for you to load data from many different sources. This is because one of the main goals of PowerPivot is data integration. It is now time to analyze another possible source of data: text files.

Data can be stored in text files in a format known as Comma Separated Values (CSV). This popular format represents data as normal text lines, each one containing a row. Each row contains columns, separated by commas (hence the name).

If you have a CSV file containing some data (see the companion file CH06-03-2005_Plans.txt), you can import it into PowerPivot using the text file data source. Suppose that our CSV file contains the special offers planned for the year 2005 (the same data that we used to show the Excel data source). It looks like this:

```
Special Offer,Start,End,Category,Discount
Christmas Gifts,12/1/2005,12/31/2005,Accessory,25%
Christmas Gifts,12/1/2005,12/31/2005,Bikes,12%
Christmas Gifts,12/1/2005,12/31/2005,Clothing,24%
Summer Specials,8/1/2005,8/15/2005,Clothing,10%
Summer Specials,8/1/2005,8/15/2005,Accesory,10%
```

You can see that each line contains a row, and each row contains columns, each separated from the next by a comma. Usually CSV files contain the column header in the first row of the file so that the file contains both the data and the column names. This is the same standard we normally use with Excel tables.

To load this file into PowerPivot, you need to use the From Text button in the PowerPivot window. This action opens the Table Import Wizard for text files (see Figure 6-37), for which you need to provide several parameters.

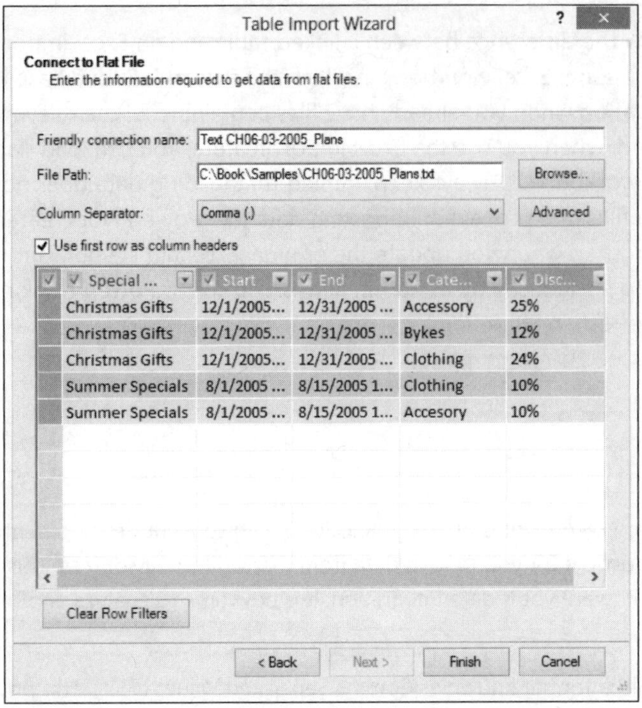

FIGURE 6-37 The Table Import Wizard is loading data from a flat file.

You can choose the column separator (which is a comma by default) from a list that includes a colon, a semicolon, a tab, and several other separators. The right choice depends on the format of the file.

Handling more complex CSV files

You might encounter a CSV file that contains separators that are not listed in the wizard's user interface. In those cases, you might find that the Table Import Wizard cannot correctly load it because you cannot choose just any characters for the separators and file properties. It might be helpful to use the Schema.ini file, in which you can define advanced properties of the CSV file. Consult *http://tinyurl.com/MsSchemaIni* to learn this advanced technique for loading complex data files.

The Use First Row As Column Headers check box indicates whether the first row of the file contains the column names, and it works the same as in the Excel data source. By default, this check box is cleared even if many CSV files follow this convention and contain the column header.

As soon as you fill in the parameters, the grid shows a preview of the data as it will look in PowerPivot. You can use the grid to select or clear any column and to set row filters, as you can with any other data source you have seen up to now. When you are done with the setup, click Finish to start the loading process.

After the loading is finished, you still need to check whether the column types have been correctly detected. For instance, CSV files do not contain the type of each column, so PowerPivot tries to guess the types by analyzing the file content. Clearly, as with any guess, it might fail to detect the correct type sometimes.

In the example, PowerPivot detected the correct type of all the columns except the Discount column. PowerPivot missed that one because the flat file included the percentage symbol after the number, so PowerPivot treated it as a character string and not as a number. If you need to change the column type, you can always do that later by using the PowerPivot ribbon.

> **Tip** If the content of the CSV file needs to be adjusted (as in the sample file we have been discussing, in which you would like to remove the percentage symbol from the Discount column), you can always load the file into the Excel worksheet using the standard Excel functions and then create a linked table. Having the data in an Excel file allows you to modify the data to suit your needs. Always remember that PowerPivot tables are not updatable, so if you need to make any kind of change, you can always use Excel tables as an intermediate step.

Loading from the Clipboard

Now we will analyze a way to load data without using any data source: the Clipboard. By using the Clipboard, we can load data into PowerPivot from any application, so long as we are able to copy data from that application to the Clipboard.

Suppose that you have a Microsoft Word table like the one shown in Figure 6-38 (which you can also find in the companion Word document CH06-05-Word table.docx).

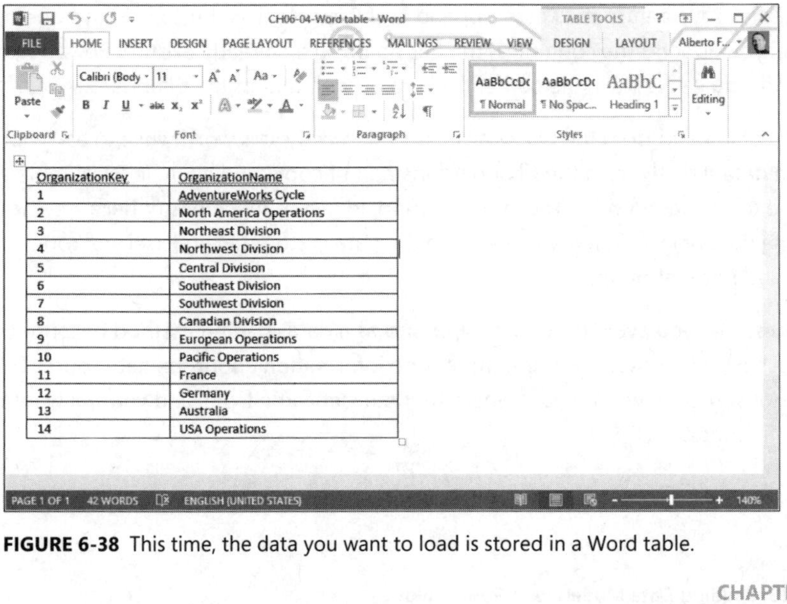

FIGURE 6-38 This time, the data you want to load is stored in a Word table.

Even if PowerPivot has no data source to load from Word documents, you can load this table into PowerPivot by selecting the full table, copying it to the Clipboard, and then clicking the Paste button in the PowerPivot window. PowerPivot opens the Paste Preview dialog box, shown in Figure 6-39.

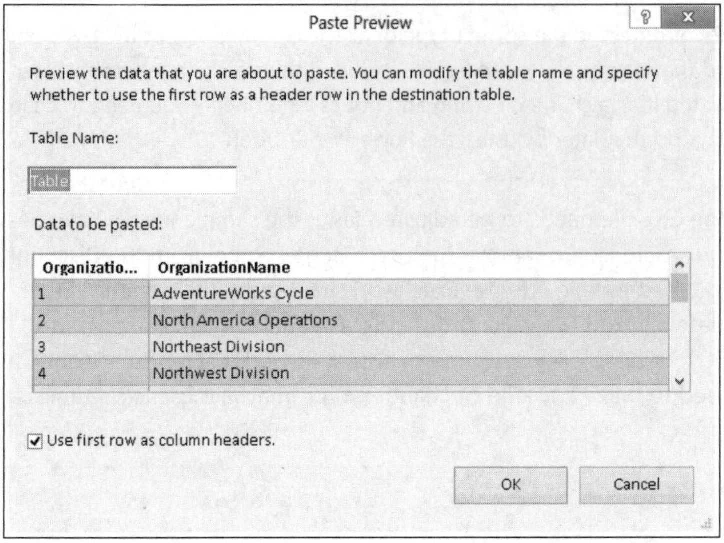

FIGURE 6-39 The Paste Preview dialog box is shown before you can paste data from the Clipboard.

Using this window, you can give the table a friendly name and preview the data before you import into PowerPivot. Clicking OK ends the loading process and places the table in the PowerPivot database.

The same process can be initiated by copying a selection from an Excel worksheet or any other software that is able to copy data in tabular format to the Clipboard.

It is worth noting that you can use the Paste Append and Paste Replace buttons in this operation. With the first button, you append the content of the Clipboard to an already existing PowerPivot table; with the second, you can replace the content of a table with that of the Clipboard.

Even if the feature of loading from the Clipboard works flawlessly, it is worthwhile to ask yourself why you should load data directly from the Clipboard instead of copying data in an Excel table and then linking the table to the data model. The latter method, in fact, is much better because it lets you see the content of the data being loaded and, because the data is stored in an Excel workbook, it lets you add comments and notes about it.

We strongly suggest that you avoid using the Clipboard as a data-loading method because the data cannot be refreshed and, most important, there is no information about the data source. Sooner or later, you will ask (or someone will ask you) where that dataset came from, and you will want to have notes to consult about it.

Loading from a report

When you work for a company, you are likely to have many reports available to you. You might want to import part of or all the data of an existing report into your model, using it as a data source for your own report. Most of the time, you import such data by copying it manually or by using the copy-and-paste technique. However, these methods mean that you always load the final output of the report, not the original data that was used to make the calculations. Moreover, if you use the copy-and-paste technique, you often have to delete formatting values (such as separators and labels) from the real data. In this way, building a report that is able to automatically refresh data extracted from another report is hard, if not impossible and, most of the time, you end up repeating the import process.

If you have access to reports published by SQL Server Reporting Services 2008 R2 and SQL Server Reporting Services 2012, PowerPivot is able to connect directly to the data used by the report. This way, you have access to a more detailed data model that can also be refreshed, and you do not have to worry about the presence of separators or other decorative items. You get only the data. In fact, you can use a report as a special case of Data Feed, a more general type of data source described in the next section. Because this is a particular case of Data Feed, there is a dedicated user interface to select data coming from a report.

Look at Figure 6-40: the URL points to a sample Reporting Services report. (The URL can be different depending on the installation of Reporting Services sample reports, which you can download from *http://msftrsprodsamples.codeplex.com/*.)

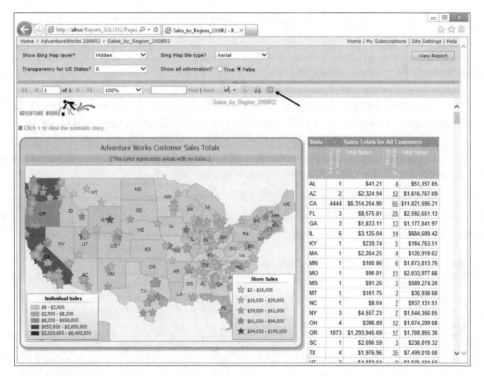

FIGURE 6-40 Here, you can see the Sales by Region report in Reporting Services 2012.

This report shows sales divided by region and by individual stores, using a map and a table. Clicking the NumberofStores entry for a state, the report scrolls down to the list of shops in the corresponding state. So you see another table (not shown in Figure 6-40), which appears when you scroll down the report. If you click the Export To Data Feed icon (see the arrow in Figure 6-40), your browser asks you to open or save a file with a name that has the .atomsvc extension.

> **Note** The .atomsvc file contains technical information about the source data feeds. Technically, this file is a data service document in an XML format that specifies a connection to one or more data feeds.

If you choose to save this file, you can open it from the PowerPivot window by using the Get External Data From Data Feeds feature discussed in the next section. However, if you choose to open this file, the same importing feature is activated automatically, and you see the Select Table window, shown in Figure 6-41.

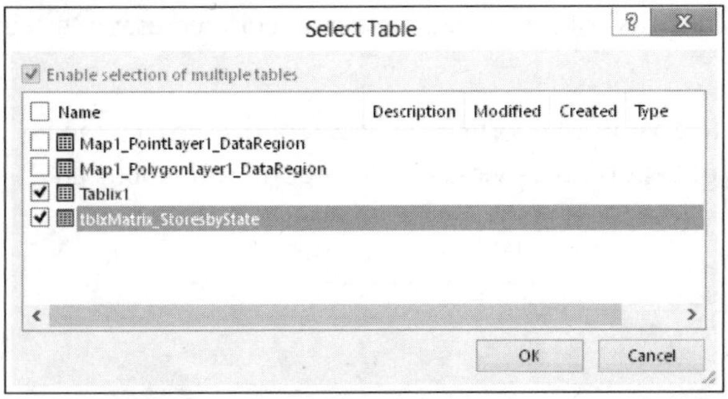

FIGURE 6-41 The Select Table window lets you select tables to import from a data feed (a report, in this case).

The report of the example contains four data tables. The first two contain information about the graphical visualization of the map on the left side of the report. The other two are more interesting: Tablix1 is the source of the table on the right side, which contains sales divided by state, and tblMatrix_StoresbyState contains the sales of each store for each state. If you select the latter two tables and click OK, you will be prompted for the destination of the loading process. The default is PivotTable Report, which will load the tables in the model and automatically create a PivotTable base on the tables.

Once the data has been loaded, you can look at it using the PowerPivot window. In Figure 6-42, for example, you can see the content of the Tablix1 table.

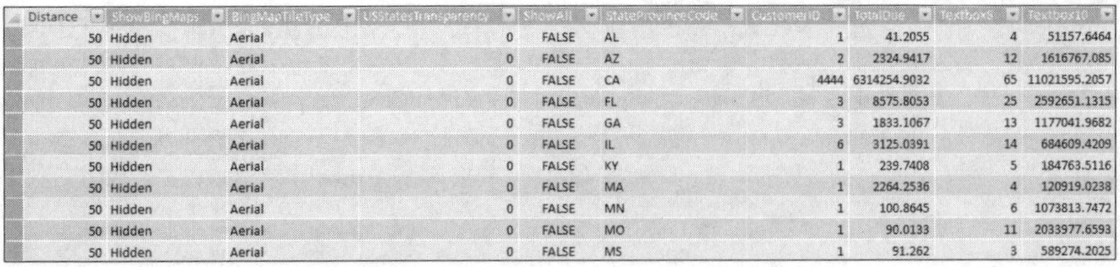

Distance	ShowBingMaps	BingMapTileType	USStatesTransparency	ShowAll	StateProvinceCode	CustomerID	TotalDue	Textbox8	Textbox10
50	Hidden	Aerial	0	FALSE	AL	1	41.2055	4	51157.6464
50	Hidden	Aerial	0	FALSE	AZ	2	2324.9417	12	1616767.085
50	Hidden	Aerial	0	FALSE	CA	4444	6314254.9032	65	11021595.2057
50	Hidden	Aerial	0	FALSE	FL	3	8575.8053	25	2592651.1315
50	Hidden	Aerial	0	FALSE	GA	3	1833.1067	13	1177041.9682
50	Hidden	Aerial	0	FALSE	IL	6	3125.0391	14	684609.4209
50	Hidden	Aerial	0	FALSE	KY	1	239.7408	5	184763.5116
50	Hidden	Aerial	0	FALSE	MA	1	2264.2536	4	120919.0238
50	Hidden	Aerial	0	FALSE	MN	1	100.8645	6	1073813.7472
50	Hidden	Aerial	0	FALSE	MO	1	90.0133	11	2033977.6593
50	Hidden	Aerial	0	FALSE	MS	1	91.262	3	589274.2025

FIGURE 6-42 Here, you can see the content of the Tablix1 table imported from the report.

The first time you import data from a report, you might not know the content of each of the tables available. In this case, you can import everything and then remove from the data model all the tables and columns that do not contain useful data.

> **Note** You can see in Figure 6-42 that the last two columns do not have meaningful names. These names really depend on the discipline of the report author and, because they are usually just internal names not visible in a report, it is pretty common to have undescriptive names. In such cases, you should rename these columns before you use these numbers in PowerPivot.

Now that you have imported report data into the data model, each time you refresh the model, the report is executed again and updated data is imported into the selected tables, overriding previous data.

Until now, you have seen how to import data starting from the report displayed in a browser, opening Excel and PowerPivot automatically. However, you can import data from a report when you are using PowerPivot, by using the Report data source available in the From Other Sources list. The Table Import Wizard asks you for the Report Path, as shown in Figure 6-43.

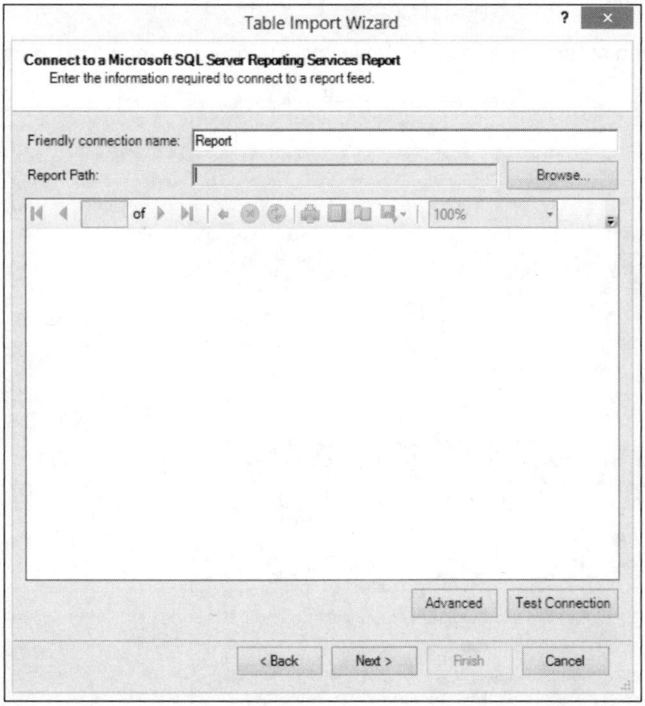

FIGURE 6-43 Here, you can see Table Import Wizard importing data from a report.

When you click Browse, you can choose the report to use, as shown in Figure 6-44.

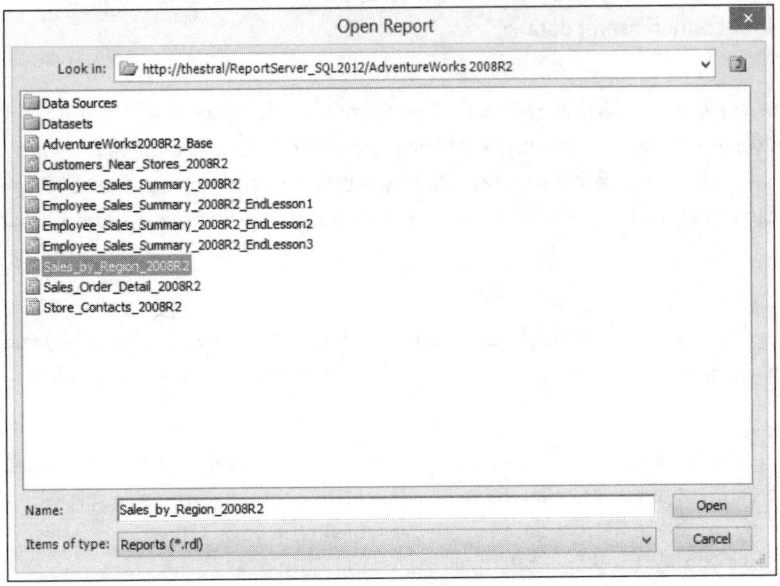

FIGURE 6-44 You can select a report from a list of available reports in Reporting Services.

When you click Open, the selected report appears in the Table Import Wizard, as shown in Figure 6-45.

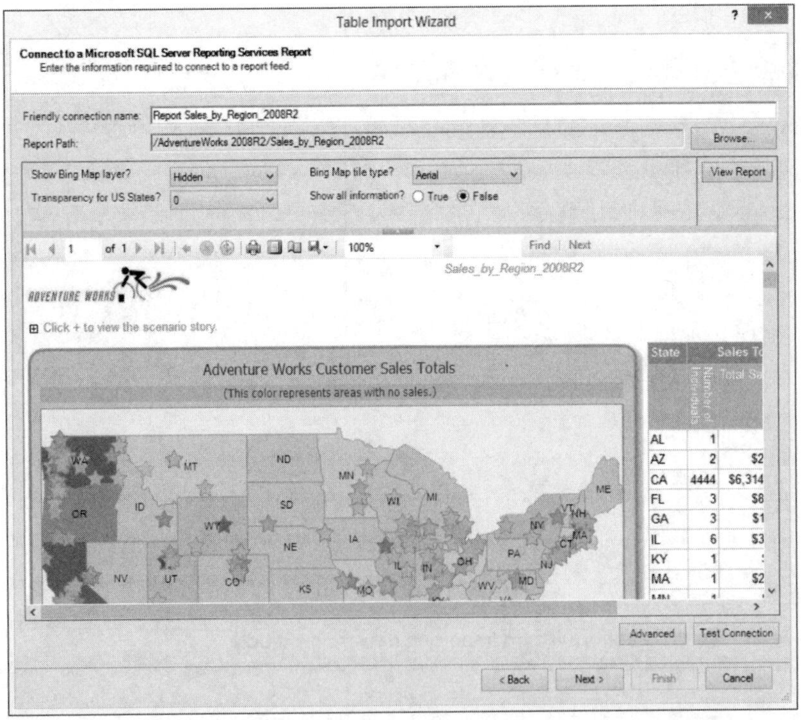

FIGURE 6-45 Before importing data, you can see a preview of a report from Reporting Services.

At this point, when you click Next, you see exactly the same request as in Figure 6-41 because you are at the same point: you just selected a report, and now you have to select the tables to import from that report.

> ### Report path names
>
> In Figure 6-45, you saw the selection of the same report previously used in Figure 6-40. However, you should note that the URL is different.
>
> The difference is that the URL used by PowerPivot when loading with the Table Import Wizard is a direct pointer to the report, which bypasses the user interface of Report Manager that you used earlier when you started from Reporting Services and requested data as a data feed. You should ask your IT department to help you get the right URL for your reports because its name can change due to many different options selected at setup time.

Loading from a data feed

In the previous section, you learned how to load a data feed exported by Reporting Services into PowerPivot. In fact, Reporting Services makes data available to PowerPivot by exporting it as a data feed. However, this technique is not exclusive to Reporting Services and can be used to get data from many other services, including Internet sources that support the Open Data Protocol (also known as OData), and data exported as a data feed by SharePoint 2010 and SharePoint 2013, described in the next section.

You can click the From Data Service button on the ribbon in the PowerPivot window and then select the From OData Data Feed option to start the loading operation. The Table Import Wizard dialog box (displayed in Figure 6-46) asks for the Data Feed URL. You saw this dialog box in Figure 6-43 when you were getting data from a report. This time, however, the Data Feed URL text box can be modified and does not have a fixed value provided by the report itself.

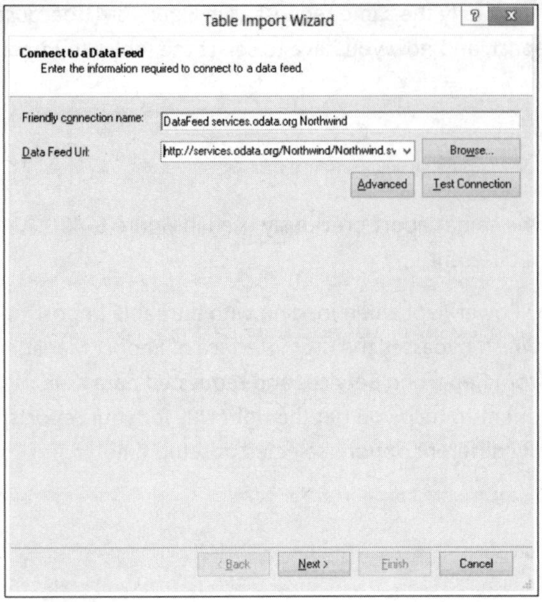

FIGURE 6-46 The Table Import Wizard can load data from OData feeds too.

You can use the following URL to test this data source:

http://services.odata.org/Northwind/Northwind.svc/

After you click Next, you can select the tables to import, as shown in Figure 6-47. Here, only the Customers, Order_Details, Orders, and Products tables have been selected.

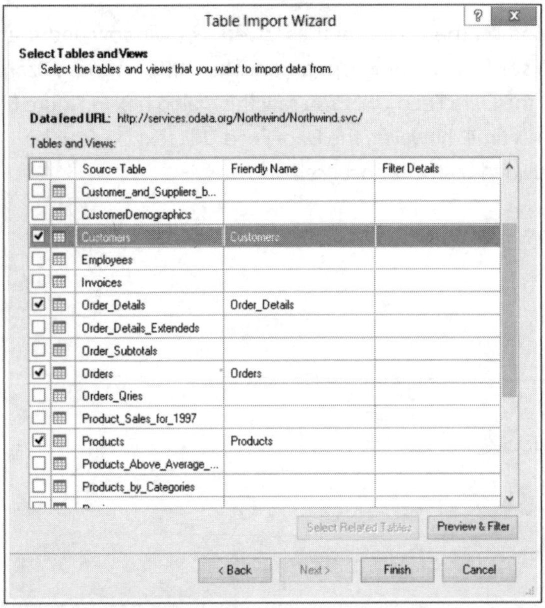

FIGURE 6-47 You can select the tables to import from the *Northwind* database used as the example.

After you click Finish, the selected tables are imported into the Excel data model. This operation can take a long time when you have a high volume of data to import and the remote service providing data has a slow bandwidth. When the process ends, you see a report of the import, and the imported data is available as PowerPivot tables, as shown in Figure 6-48.

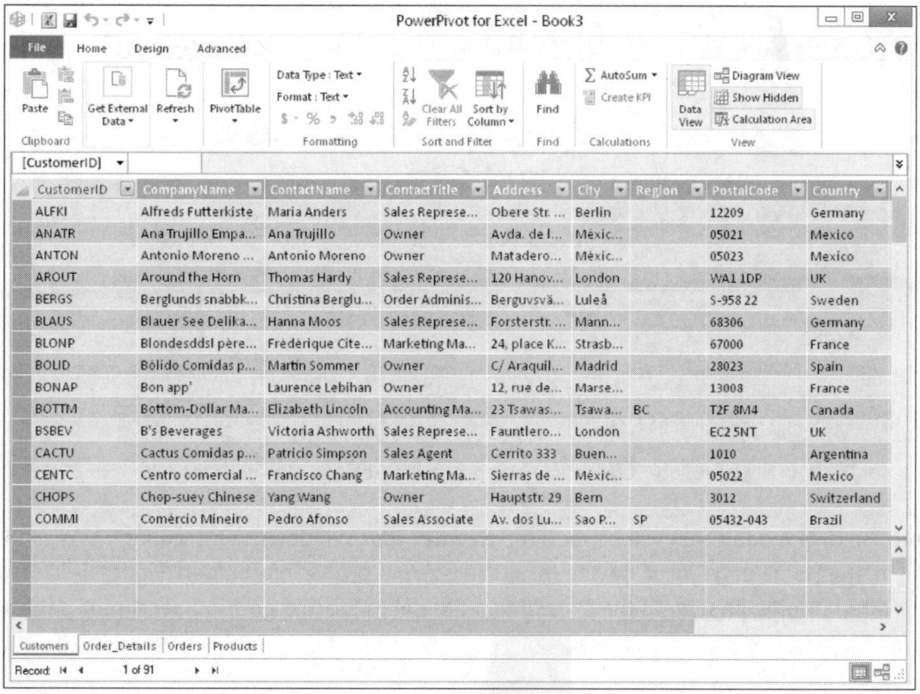

FIGURE 6-48 You can see some of the tables from the *Northwind* database imported into PowerPivot by means of a Data Feed.

Loading from Windows Azure Marketplace

Another powerful OData producer is the Windows Azure Marketplace, an online market for buying and selling finished Software as a Service (SaaS) applications and premium datasets. In the Azure Marketplace, you can find both paid and free data sources that can be loaded inside your Excel data model to expand your analytics opportunities.

To browse the Azure Marketplace, you can go to *https://datamarket.azure.com*, where you must log on using a Windows Live account. You can browse many data sources without being logged on, but to subscribe to any data feed, you must log on and create an account key. You can also browse the Azure Marketplace directly by clicking the From Data Service button in the PowerPivot window and then selecting the From Windows Azure Marketplace option. The Table Import Wizard shows the Windows Azure Marketplace home screen (see Figure 6-49).

FIGURE 6-49 The Azure Marketplace offers many interesting datasets to use in your models.

To browse data models, you will be required to enter your Windows Live account ID. As soon as you sign in, the Home page will show the results using your profile information. Figure 6-50 shows Alberto Ferrari's Home page, with the *DateStream* dataset in the first position because it is the most used one.

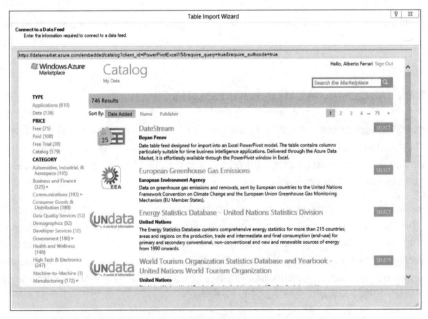

FIGURE 6-50 The Home page of the Azure Marketplace is personalized using a particular user's account information.

As an example for the book, you are going to use an interesting available OData called *DateStream.DateStream* provides a simple yet effective table that contains dates and many useful columns to create a calendar table in your data model. By clicking a data source, you get a sample of its content, as shown in Figure 6-51.

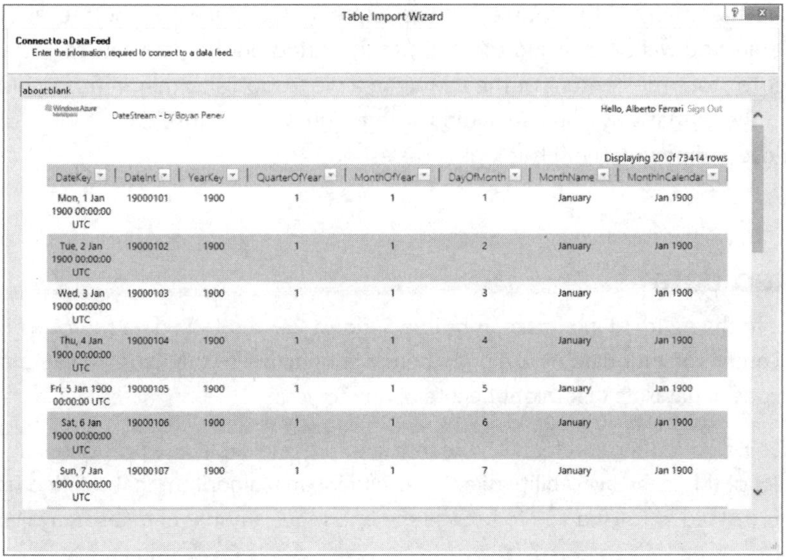

FIGURE 6-51 The sample of *DateStream* contains dates starting from January 1900.

If you scroll this sample window to the bottom, you have the option to select the tables you want to load, as well as a SELECT QUERY button that makes the Table Import Wizard move to the next window, where you can set the friendly connection name for this data source (see Figure 6-52).

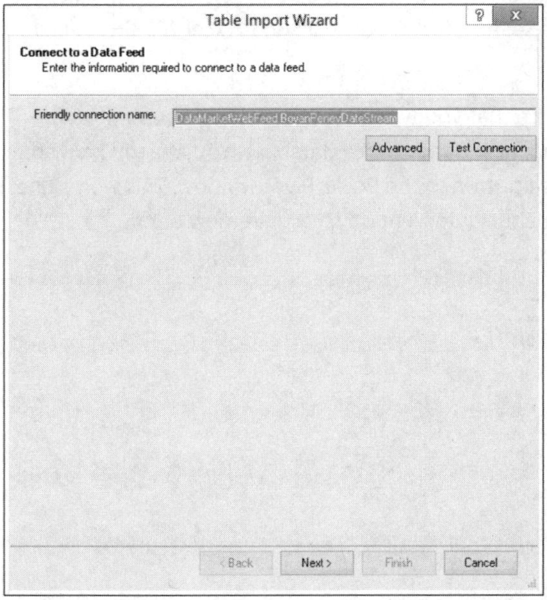

FIGURE 6-52 You can change only the friendly connection name from this step of the Table Import Wizard.

From this point on, the loading procedure is identical to all the others. The interesting point, for the Azure Marketplace, is not the technical side of how to load data, but the availability of a large market of data that you can use to expand your analytical possibilities.

Warning Be aware that many of the sources on the Azure Marketplace are not free, and if you refresh a table, you will be charged the amount indicated on the data source page. It might be better to store the content of the source in a workbook and then refresh your data models from there; that way you can avoid paying high bills because data is loaded from the market every time your workbook gets refreshed.

Suggest related data

You also can connect to the Azure Marketplace using the Suggest Related Data data source. This data source analyzes the content of your data model and opens a connection to the Azure Marketplace with a set of suggestions of datasets that might be interesting to you.

The process of loading data using this feature is identical to the one explained previously; again, the significative aspect of this is the availability of an automatic search algorithm that will find useful opportunities for you, instead of forcing you to browse the enormous amount of datasets available in the marketplace.

Refreshing connections

Before we close this chapter on data loading, there is still an important topic to cover, which is related to all the data loading procedures you have seen so far: the capability of Excel 2013 to refresh the data coming from a connection automatically.

If you load data from a source, chances are that you will want to refresh the content of the PowerPivot database to reflect the latest changes in the source database. You already know that you can perform this operation using the Refresh button in the PowerPivot window. This works fine, but it is not very convenient because it requires manual intervention to acquire new data.

Excel has the capability to perform automatic refreshes at specified intervals during any connection. Moreover, you can instruct Excel to perform a data refresh operation every time the workbook is opened so that you will always see the latest information from the database anytime you open your workbook.

To set this behavior, once you loaded data from a data source, you need to click the Connections button on the DATA tab of the Excel ribbon, as shown in Figure 6-53.

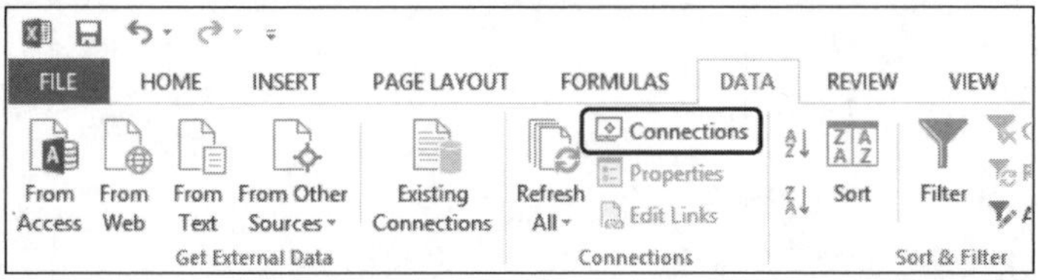

FIGURE 6-53 The Connections button opens the Workbook Connections dialog box.

Clicking Connections opens the Workbook Connections dialog box (see Figure 6-54), where you can change the properties of all the existing connections.

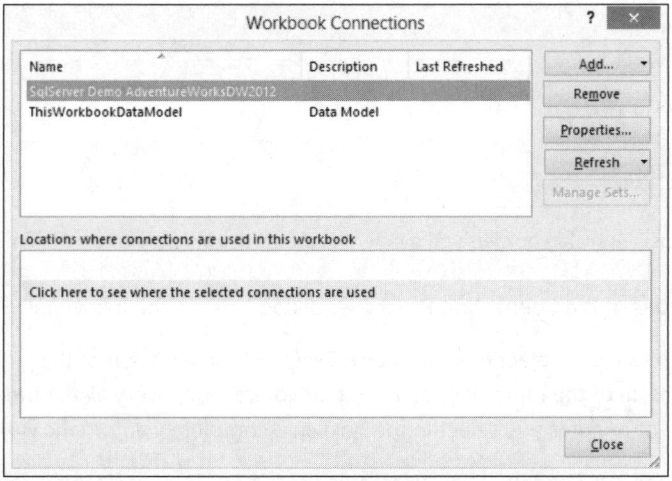

FIGURE 6-54 The Workbook Connections lists all the connections created in the current workbook.

You can create, remove, or modify any connection from this dialog box. An important aspect of this is the Properties button, which will open the Connection Properties dialog box for the selected connection. You can see the Connection Properties dialog box for the connection to the *AdventureWorksDW* database in Figure 6-55.

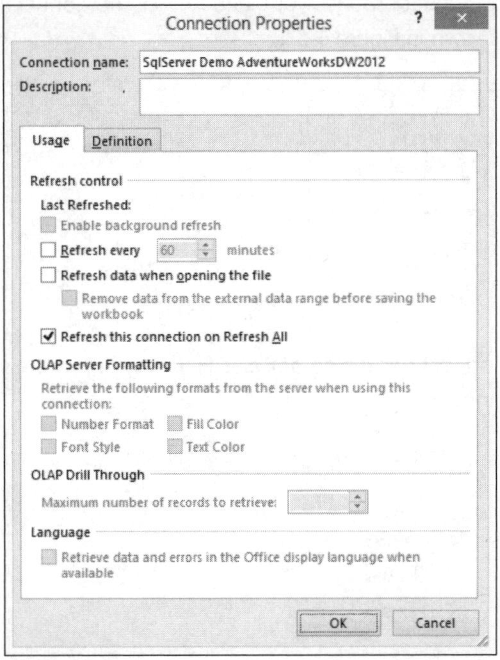

FIGURE 6-55 The Connections Properties dialog box lets you modify the properties of a single connection.

The most interesting properties of the Connection Properties dialog box are the following:

- **Refresh Every *xx* Minutes** If you select this check box, Excel will run a refresh of the connection (which means all of the tables loaded from that connection) every *xx* minutes (where *xx* is the number of minutes you select in the box), in a completely automatic way.

- **Refresh Data When Opening The File** If you select this check box, Excel performs a refresh of the tables in the connection when a file opens.

- **Refresh This Connection On Refresh All** You can invoke a data refresh from inside Excel by clicking the Refresh All button on the DATA tab of the Excel ribbon. If, for any reason, you do not want a connection to be refreshed when Refresh All is executed, clear this check box. For example, you might want to avoid refreshing connections from the Azure Marketplace, which might be slow and/or expensive to refresh several times a day.

You can choose any combination of these check boxes to make automated refreshes of your workbook, or if you want to always perform refreshes manually, clear them all.

CHAPTER 7

Understanding evaluation contexts

At this point, you have learned many features of Microsoft PowerPivot, as well as the basics of the DAX language. You know how to create a calculated column and a calculated field, and you have a good understanding of the basic functions of DAX. In this chapter, you will learn how to move to the next level in DAX: here, we give you a solid theoretical background about the DAX language, and by using that, you will be able to become a real DAX master.

With the knowledge you gained so far, you can already create many reports, but in order to build more complex ones, you really need to learn evaluation contexts. All of the advanced features of DAX are based on evaluation contexts.

We want to give a few words of warning to our readers before we go any further. The concept of evaluation context is easy, and you will learn and understand it soon. But there are some subtle considerations that you need to understand really well; otherwise, at a certain point as you are learning DAX, you will feel lost. We have taught DAX to many users in public and private classes during our careers, and we have found that this is absolutely normal. You may have the feeling that formulas are like magic: they work, but you do not understand why. If so, you are in good company: most DAX students feel that way. It simply means that evaluation contexts are not clear enough to you yet. The solution is easy: come back to this chapter and read it again. You probably will find something new that you missed during your first read.

Moreover, evaluation contexts play an important role in the usage of the function *CALCULATE*, which is probably the most powerful and hard-to-learn function in DAX. We will introduce *CALCULATE* in the next chapter and then use it through the rest of the book. Understanding *CALCULATE* without having a solid background in evaluation context is impossible, but on the other hand, understanding the importance of evaluation contexts without having ever tried to use *CALCULATE* is nearly impossible. Thus, this chapter and the subsequent one are the ones that, in our experience with the previous edition, are always full of well-worn pages.

Finally, this chapter is a theoretical one (as the next one is as well). You need to focus on theory before you can apply the techniques discussed here in the real world. We will show some calculations and examples that might look not intuitive or useful. Do not focus on the meanings of the formulas; rather, focus on what the formulas need to compute and how to write the calculations. Once you master the technique, we will teach useful formulas in the chapters that follow. By that time, we will assume that you have a good grasp of the theory. As with any long trip, the learning of DAX begins in a simple way: one step at a time. There is no need to run too fast.

Introduction to evaluation contexts

What is an evaluation context? Any DAX expression is evaluated inside a context. The context is the "environment" within which the formula is evaluated. For example, consider a simple formula like this:

```
= SUM ( FactInternetSales[SalesAmount] )
```

You already know what this formula computes: the sum of all the values of the [Sales Amount] column in the FactInternetSales table. You can use this formula in a calculated field, defining a calculated field named *Sum of SalesAmount*. Then you put this calculated field into a PivotTable and look at the results (see Figure 7-1). You can find the sample data model in the companion workbook "CH07-01-Evaluation Contexts.xlsx."

FIGURE 7-1 Sum of SalesAmount, without a context, shows the grand total of sales.

This number alone does not look interesting at all, does it? However, if you think carefully, the formula computes exactly what it is supposed to compute: the sum of all sales amounts, which is a big number with no real significance. This PivotTable improves as soon as we slice the grand total into columns and start investigating them. For example, if you take the product color and put it on the rows, the PivotTable suddenly becomes much more meaningful, as shown in Figure 7-2.

Row Labels	Sum of SalesAmount
Black	$8,838,411.96
Blue	$2,279,096.28
Multi	$106,470.74
NA	$435,116.69
Red	$7,724,330.52
Silver	$5,113,389.08
White	$5,106.32
Yellow	$4,856,755.63
Grand Total	**$29,358,677.22**

FIGURE 7-2 Sum of SalesAmount, sliced by color, looks much more interesting.

The grand total is still there, but now it is the sum of smaller values, and each value, considered with all the others, has a much more relevant meaning. But, if you think carefully again, you should note that something weird is happening here: the formula is not computing what we asked.

We supposed that the formula meant "the sum of all values on the sales amount column," but inside each cell of the PivotTable, the formula is not computing the sum of all sales. It is only computing the sum of sales of a specific color. Yet, we never specified that the computation had to be performed on a subset of the data model—or at least the formula does not specify that it can work on subsets of data.

Why is the formula computing different values in different cells of the PivotTable? The answer is simple: it is because of the evaluation context in which the formula is computed. The evaluation context of a formula can be thought of as the surrounding area for the formula.

Because the product color is on the rows, each row in the PivotTable is able to see, out of the whole database, only the subset of products of that specific color. This is the surrounding area of the formula; that is, a set of filters applied to the database prior to the formula evaluation. Then, when the formula computes the sum of all sales amounts, it does not compute it over the whole database because it does not have the option of looking at all the rows. If the formula is computed for the White row, then only white products are visible; because of that, only sales pertinent to white products are calculated. Thus, the sum of all sales amounts, when computed for a row in the PivotTable that shows only white products, becomes the sum of all sales of white products.

You have seen that any DAX formula specifies a calculation, but this calculation is then performed in a context that defines the real value computed. The formula behavior is always the same, but it is executed against different subsets of data.

The only case where the formula behaves in the way it has been defined is in the grand total cell. At that level, no filter happens, and the entire database is visible.

Now, put the year on the columns to give the PivotTable more meaning. The report becomes the one shown in Figure 7-3.

Sum of SalesAmount	Column Labels				
Row Labels	2005	2006	2007	2008	Grand Total
Black	$345,815.49	$1,728,251.55	$3,851,090.66	$2,913,254.25	$8,838,411.96
Blue			$860,380.78	$1,418,715.50	$2,279,096.28
Multi			$42,099.32	$64,371.42	$106,470.74
NA			$184,354.22	$250,762.47	$435,116.69
Red	$2,634,959.00	$3,935,630.74	$953,203.05	$200,537.73	$7,724,330.52
Silver	$285,599.16	$720,397.36	$2,044,406.89	$2,062,985.67	$5,113,389.08
White			$2,229.52	$2,876.80	$5,106.32
Yellow		$146,063.88	$1,853,295.85	$2,857,395.90	$4,856,755.63
Grand Total	$3,266,373.66	$6,530,343.53	$9,791,060.30	$9,770,899.74	$29,358,677.22

FIGURE 7-3 Sum of SalesAmount is now sliced by color and year.

The situation should be clear at this point: each cell has a different value even if the formula is always the same. This is because the context now is defined by both the row and the column of the PivotTable. In fact, sales for white products in the year 2005 are different than sales for white products in 2008. Moreover, because you can put more than one field in both rows and columns, it is better to say that the context is defined by the set of fields on the rows and the set of fields on the columns. Figure 7-4 makes this more evident.

Sum of SalesAmount	Column Labels				
Row Labels	2005	2006	2007	2008	Grand Total
Black	$345,815.49	$1,728,251.55	$3,851,090.66	$2,913,254.25	$8,838,411.96
Half-Finger Gloves			$14,228.69	$20,792.01	$35,020.70
Mountain-100	$300,374.11	$411,748.78			$712,122.89
Mountain-200		$430,310.62	$1,907,464.54	$1,693,702.62	$4,031,477.78
Mountain-500			$54,538.99	$81,538.49	$136,077.48
Road-250		$737,368.13	$1,357,106.40	$581,517.30	$2,675,991.83
Road-650	$45,441.38	$148,824.03	$129,976.34		$324,241.75
Road-750			$326,153.96	$453,051.61	$779,205.57
Sport-100			$31,176.09	$41,778.06	$72,954.15
Women's Mountain Shorts			$30,445.65	$40,874.16	$71,319.81
Blue			$860,380.78	$1,418,715.50	$2,279,096.28
Classic Vest			$13,017.50	$22,669.50	$35,687.00
Sport-100			$29,986.43	$44,367.32	$74,353.75
Touring-1000			$536,415.75	$975,084.63	$1,511,500.38
Touring-2000			$195,590.85	$256,333.35	$451,924.20
Touring-3000			$85,370.25	$120,260.70	$205,630.95

FIGURE 7-4 The context is defined by the set of fields on rows and on columns.

Each cell has a different value and, because there are two fields on the rows, the context is defined by the complete set. For example, the highlighted cell has a context for product model Road-650, color Black, in 2005.

> **Note** It is not important whether a field is on the rows or on the columns (or on the slicer and/or filter, as you are about to learn). All of these filters are used to define a single context, which is used to evaluate the formula. In fact, you can put the year on the rows, too, and not all the values will be affected by this decision. Putting a field on rows or columns has some aesthetic consequences, but the way values are computed does not change at all.

Let's look at the full picture now. In Figure 7-5, we have put the Size on a slicer, from which we selected 38 and 40, and the month name on a filter, from which we selected February.

EnglishMonthName	February			

Size		Sum of SalesAmount	Column Labels			
		Row Labels	2006	2007	2008	Grand Total
(blank)		⊟Black	$13,499.96	$32,785.57	$101,924.51	$148,210.04
38		Mountain-100	$13,499.96			$13,499.96
40		Mountain-200		$32,785.57	$98,684.57	$131,470.14
42		Mountain-500			$3,239.94	$3,239.94
44		⊟Silver	$13,599.96	$35,214.13	$106,507.32	$155,321.41
46		Mountain-100	$13,599.96			$13,599.96
48		Mountain-200		$35,214.13	$83,519.64	$118,733.77
50		Mountain-400-W			$18,467.76	$18,467.76
		Mountain-500			$4,519.92	$4,519.92
		⊟Yellow		$11,004.81	$65,393.52	$76,398.33
		Road-350-W			$34,019.80	$34,019.80
		Road-550-W		$11,004.81	$31,373.72	$42,378.53
		Grand Total	$27,099.92	$79,004.52	$273,825.35	$379,929.79

FIGURE 7-5 In a typical report, the context is defined in many ways, including by slicers and filters.

It is clear at this point that the values computed in each cell have a context that is defined by rows, columns, slicers, and filters. All these entities contribute to the definition of a set of filters that is applied to the data model prior to the formula evaluation. Moreover, it is important to realize that not all the cells have the same set of filters, not only in terms of values, but even in terms of fields. For example, the grand total of the columns contains only the filter for size, month, and year, but it does not contain the filter for color and model because color and model are on the rows and they do not filter the grand total. The same applies to the subtotal for color inside the PivotTable: for those cells, there is no filter on the model. The only valid filter coming from the rows is the color.

This context (the filter coming from the PivotTable) is known as the *filter context* and, as its name suggests, is a context that filters tables. Any formula you ever write will have a different value depending on the filter context that is applied prior to its evaluation. This behavior, although it is intuitive, needs to be well understood. Now that you have learned what a filter context is, you know that the DAX expression:

```
= SUM ( FactInternetSales[SalesAmount] )
```

should be read as "the sum of all sales amounts in the current filter context."

You will learn later how to read, modify, or clear the filter context. As of now, it is enough to have a solid understanding of the fact that the filter context is always present for any cell of the PivotTable, and its definition mainly comes from the user selection in the PivotTable.

Understanding the row context

The filter context is one of the two contexts in DAX. Its companion is the row context, and in this section, you will learn what that is and how it works.

This time, we consider a different formula:

```
= FactInternetSales[Sales Amount] + FactInternetSales[DiscountAmount]
```

You are likely to write such an expression in a calculated column to compute the gross total before discounts. This formula tells DAX to sum two fields, and this is well known. But as soon as you define this formula in a calculated column, you will get the table shown in Figure 7-6.

ProductKey	SalesOrderLineNumber	SalesAmount	DiscountAmount	GrossAmount
484	3	$7.95	0	7.95
487	3	$54.99	0	54.99
478	3	$9.99	0	9.99
529	3	$3.99	0	3.99
487	3	$54.99	0	54.99
541	3	$28.99	0	28.99
489	3	$53.99	0	53.99
473	3	$63.50	0	63.5

FIGURE 7-6 The definition of GrossAmount is computed for all the rows of the table.

The formula is computed for all the rows of the table and, for each row, it computed a different value. In order to understand the row context, we need to be pedantic in our reading of the formula: we asked to sum two fields, but where did we say from which row of the table to get the values of the fields? You might say that the row to use is implicit because if it is a calculated column, it will be computed row by row, and for each row, it will return a different value, which is the value of the calculated column. This is absolutely correct, but, from the point of view of the DAX expression, the information about the row to use is still missing.

In fact, the row to use to perform a calculation is not stored inside the formula. Rather, it is defined by another kind of context: the row context. When you defined the calculated column, DAX started from the first row of the table. It created a row context containing that row only and evaluated the expression. The result has been stored for the first row, and then it moves to the second row and evaluates the expression again. This happens for all the rows in the table, and if you have 1 million rows, it is as though DAX created 1 million row contexts to evaluate the formula 1 million times. Clearly, due to some optimizations in the code, this is not exactly what is happening (otherwise DAX would be a slow language), but from the logical point of view, this is exactly how you should think of it.

Let's try to be more precise. A row context is a context that always contains a single row, and it is automatically defined during the creation of calculated columns. It can be created using other techniques, which you are going to learn soon, but the easiest way to work with row contexts is to look at calculated columns, where its creation is handled automatically by the engine.

> ### There are always two contexts
>
> So far, you have learned what about the row context and the filter context. They are the only kind of contexts in DAX. Thus, they are the only way to modify the result of a formula. Any formula will be evaluated under two distinct contexts: the row context and the filter context.
>
> Both contexts are called *evaluation contexts* because they are contexts that change the way a formula is evaluated, providing different results for the same formula. This point is important and hard to focus on at the beginning: there are always two contexts, and the result of a formula depends on both. At this stage of your DAX learning, you probably think that this is obvious and natural. You are probably right, but throughout this book, you will find formulas that will be a challenge to understand if you do not remember the coexistence of two context expressions, each of which changes the result of the formula evaluation.

Testing your evaluation context understanding

Before we move on with more complex discussions about evaluation contexts, we would like to test your understanding of contexts with a couple of examples. Please do not look at the explanation immediately. Rather, stop after the question and try to answer it, and then read the explanation.

Using *SUM* in a calculated column

The first test is simple. What happens if you define a calculated column, in FactInternetSales, with this code:

```
= SUM ( FactInternetSales[SalesAmount] )
```

Because it is a calculated column, it will be computed row by row, and for each row, you will obtain a result. What number do you expect to see? Choose one of these options:

1. The value of SalesAmount for a particular row, which is different for each row.

2. The total of SalesAmount for all the rows, which is the same value for all the rows.

3. I cannot use SUM inside a calculated column, so this does not work at all.

Now, let's elaborate on what is happening when the formula is evaluated. You already have learned that the formula means: "the sum of all sales amount as seen in the current filter context." Now, the formula is going to be evaluated row by row, so DAX creates a row context for the first row and then invokes the formula evaluation. The formula computes the sum of all sales amount values in the current filter context. What is the current filter context? It is the full database because the formula is being evaluated outside of any PivotTable. It is evaluated during the definition of the calculated column, when no filter is active.

There is a row context, but *SUM* ignores the row context, using only the filter context, and the filter context right now is the full database. Thus, the right answer is 2: you will get the grand total of SalesAmount, which is the same value for all the rows of FactInternetSales, as shown in Figure 7-7.

ProductKey	SalesOrderLineNumber	SalesAmount	DiscountAmount	SumOfSalesAmount
528	1	$4.99	0	$29,358,677.22
528	1	$4.99	0	$29,358,677.22
528	1	$4.99	0	$29,358,677.22
528	1	$4.99	0	$29,358,677.22
528	1	$4.99	0	$29,358,677.22
528	1	$4.99	0	$29,358,677.22
528	1	$4.99	0	$29,358,677.22
528	1	$4.99	0	$29,358,677.22
528	1	$4.99	0	$29,358,677.22

FIGURE 7-7 Sum of SalesAmount, in a calculated column, is computed based on the full database.

This example clearly shows that the two contexts work together. They both work on the final result of a formula, but in different ways. Aggregate functions like *SUM, MIN,* and *MAX* feel the context defined by the filter context and completely ignore the row context. If you answered 1, as many students normally do, it is perfectly normal. The point is that you are not yet thinking that the two contexts are working together, changing the formula result in different ways. Answering 1 is the most common and intuitive logic, but it is the wrong one, and now you know why.

Using fields in a calculated field

The second test we propose is slightly different. Imagine that you want to define the formula for GrossAmount not in a calculated column, but in a calculated field. You might want to write the following expression inside a calculated field:

```
= FactInternetSales[Sales Amount] + FactInternetSales[DiscountAmount]
```

You can try this, of course, using the Calculated Field dialog box of PowerPivot, as shown in Figure 7-8.

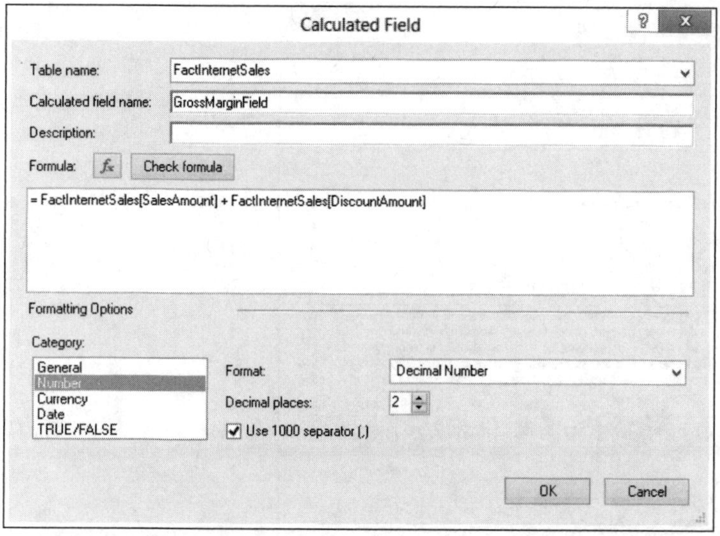

FIGURE 7-8 You can write a DAX expression using the plus operator on fields in a calculated field.

What result should we expect at this point?

1. The expression works correctly, we will need to test the result in a PivotTable.

2. I cannot even write this formula.

3. I can define the formula, but it will give an error when used in a PivotTable.

In the formula, we used FactInternetSales[SalesAmount], which is a field name (that is, the value of SalesAmount in FactInternetSales). Is this definition lacking something? You should recall, from previous discussions, that the small piece of information that is missing here is the row from which to get the current value of SalesAmount. When this code is used inside a calculated column, the row to use is implicitly defined by the engine when it computes the expression, thanks to the row context. But what happens for a calculated field? There is no iteration, there is no current row, and there is no row context. Calculated fields operate on tables (or on subsets of them, if there is a filter context), not on single rows.

Thus, the correct answer is number 2. The formula cannot be written; it is syntactically wrong, and PowerPivot will raise an error if you try to confirm it, as Figure 7-9 illustrates.

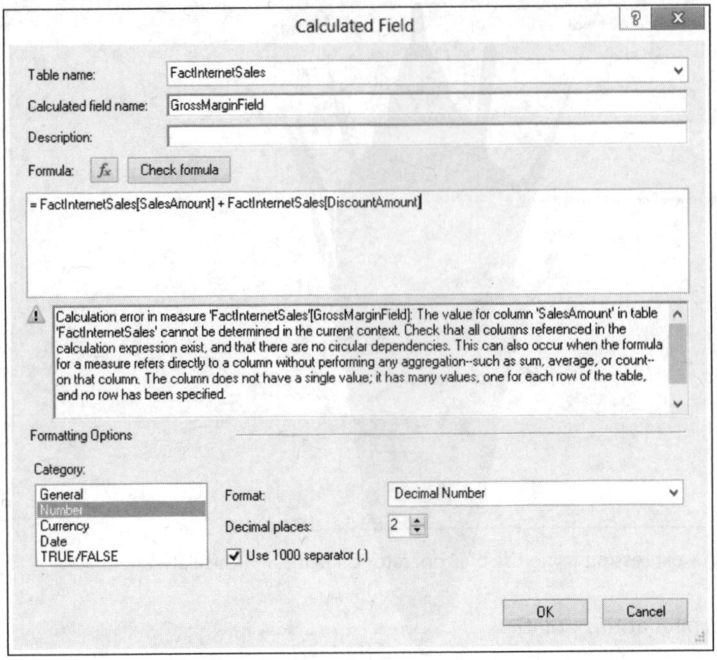

FIGURE 7-9 Trying to access a column name in a calculated field results in an error because no row context exists there.

The core meaning of the error message is in the last two sentences:

This can also occur when the formula for a measure refers directly to a column without performing any aggregation—such as sum, average, or count—on that column. The column does not have a single value; it has many values, one for each row of the table, and no row has been specified.

A column does not have one value; it has a different value for each row of a table. Thus, if you want a single value, you need to specify the row to use. The only way to specify which row to use for a calculation is to use the row context, and inside this calculated field, there is no row context. Thus, the formula is incorrect and will not be accepted.

The correct way to specify this calculation in a calculated field is to use aggregate functions, as in:

```
= SUM ( FactInternetSales[SalesAmount] ) + SUM ( FactInternetSales[DiscountAmount] )
```

Using this formula, we are now asking for an aggregation through *SUM*. Thus, this latter formula does not depend on the existence of a row context. It only requires a filter context and will provide the correct result.

Creating a row context with iterators

You have learned that a row context is automatically created when you define a calculated column because, in that case, the DAX expression is evaluated on a row-by-row basis. Now it is time to learn how to create a row context inside a DAX expression by using iterators.

You might recall from Chapter 3, "Introduction to DAX," that all functions that end in *X* are iterators; that is, they iterate a table and evaluate an expression for each row, finally aggregating the results using different algorithms. For example, look at the following DAX expression:

```
= SUMX ( FactInternetSales, FactInternetSales[SalesAmount] * 1.1 )
```

SUMX is an iterator. It iterates the FactInternetSales table and, for each row of the table, it evaluates the sales amount plus 10 percent, finally returning the sum of all these values. In order to evaluate the expression for each row, *SUMX* creates a row context on the FactInternetSales table and uses it during the iteration so that the inner expression (the second parameter of *SUMX*) is evaluated in a row context that contains the currently iterated row.

It is important to note that different parameters of *SUMX* use different contexts during the full evaluation flow. Let's now look closer at the same expression:

```
= SUMX (
    FactInternetSales,    ← External contexts
    FactInternetSales[SalesAmount] * 1.1   ← External contexts + new Row Context
)
```

The first parameter, FactInternetSales, is evaluated using the context from the caller (for example, it might be a PivotTable cell or another calculated field), whereas the second parameter (the expression) is evaluated using both the external context and the newly created row context.

All iterators behave in the same way, as follows:

1. Create a new row context on the table received as the first parameter.

2. Evaluate the second parameter inside the newly created row context, for each row of the table.

3. Aggregate the values computed during step 2, if needed by the iterator. There are some iterators like FILTER and ADDCOLUMNS that do not perform this step.

It is important to remember that the original contexts are still valid inside the expression. Iterators only add a new row context; they do not modify existing ones in any way. This rule is almost always valid, but there is an important exception: if the previous contexts already contained a row context for the same table, then this row context is hidden by the newly created row context.

This scenario might seem rare, but in reality, it happens very often. Suppose that you want to count, for each product in the DimProduct table, the number of products that have a higher price. To solve this exercise, we need to introduce a new iterator, which is *FILTER*. *FILTER* is an iterator that loops all the rows of a table and returns a table containing only the ones that satisfy a specific condition, which you define with the second parameter. Thus, *FILTER* is a function that receives a table as the first parameter and returns a table. It is the first time that we have used functions that return tables, but as you will learn in the book, there are many of them, and they are useful to perform complex computations. For example, if you want to retrieve the table of products with a price higher than $100, you can use

```
FILTER ( DimProduct, DimProduct[ListPrice] > 100 )
```

As you have seen, *FILTER* is harder to describe than to understand. Reading the expression, it is easy to grasp its behavior, even without knowing the exact way it works. The careful reader should note that *FILTER* needs to be an iterator because the expression DimProduct[ListPrice]>100 can be evaluated if and only if a valid row context exists for DimProduct. Otherwise the effective value of ListPrice would be indeterminate. *FILTER* creates a row context that makes the evaluation of the condition possible.

Now, let's go back to our original problem: counting the number of products that have a higher price than the current one. You want to define this value as a calculated column. If you named the price of the current product *PriceOfCurrentProduct*, then it is easy to understand that this DAX formula would do what you need:

```
1.   ListPriceRank=
2.   COUNTROWS (
3.       FILTER (
4.           DimProduct,
5.           DimProduct[ListPrice] > PriceOfCurrentProduct
6.       )
7.   )
```

FILTER will filter only the product with a price higher than the current one, and *COUNTROWS* simply counts the number of rows in the table returned by *FILTER*. The only remaining issue is how to express the price of the current product, replacing PriceOfCurrentProduct with a valid DAX syntax. (By "current," we mean the current row for the calculated column.) Doing this is harder than you might think, and you will probably need to read the next paragraphs more than once before you grasp them completely.

The problem is that this calculated column is defined inside the DimProduct table. Thus, the DAX code is evaluated inside an already-existing row context defined in the DimProduct table. But the expression creates a new row context on DimProduct due to the iteration introduced by *FILTER*. Moreover, because there is no filter context, *FILTER* iterates the entire table. In fact, the

DimProduct[ListPrice] used in line 5 of the previous expression is the value of the list price for the current row iterated by *FILTER*. Thus, the row context in *FILTER* is nested inside the original row context introduced by the calculated column, which results in the outer filter (the calculated column one) being hidden in the innermost expression. This happens because *FILTER* created a new row context based on the same table. Do you see the issue? Here, we want to access the current value of the list price, but not using the last introduced row context. Instead, we want to get the value in the previous row context, which refers to the value of [ListPrice] on the current row of the PowerPivot table.

There is a function that makes this happen: *EARLIER*. *EARLIER* retrieves the value of a column by using not the last row context, but the previous one. Thus, the value of PriceOfCurrentProduct can be expressed using EARLIER (DimProduct[ListPrice]).

EARLIER is one of the strangest functions in DAX. Many users feel intimidated by *EARLIER*, because they do not think in terms of row contexts and they do not take into account the fact that row contexts can be nested by creating multiple iterations over the same table. In reality, *EARLIER* is a simple and useful function that will come in handy many times. The code that solves this problem is the following:

```
ListPriceRank=
COUNTROWS (
     FILTER (
         DimProduct,
         DimProduct[ListPrice] > EARLIER ( DimProduct[ListPrice] )
     )
) + 1
```

In Figure 7-10, you can see the calculated column defined in DimProduct, where the table has been sorted using ListPrice descending.

	[ListPriceRank] ▼	f_x =COUNTROWS (FILTER (DimProduct, DimProduct[ListPrice] > EARLIER (DimProduct[ListPrice])))+1					
▲	ProductKey ▼	ProductAlternateKey ▼	ListPrice ▼	ListPriceRank ▼	Color ▼	ModelName ▼	Add Column
	310	BK-R93R-62	$3,578.27	1	Red	Road-150	
	311	BK-R93R-44	$3,578.27	1	Red	Road-150	
	312	BK-R93R-48	$3,578.27	1	Red	Road-150	
	313	BK-R93R-52	$3,578.27	1	Red	Road-150	
	314	BK-R93R-56	$3,578.27	1	Red	Road-150	
	344	BK-M82S-38	$3,399.99	6	Silver	Mountain-100	
	345	BK-M82S-42	$3,399.99	6	Silver	Mountain-100	
	346	BK-M82S-44	$3,399.99	6	Silver	Mountain-100	
	347	BK-M82S-48	$3,399.99	6	Silver	Mountain-100	
	348	BK-M82B-38	$3,374.99	10	Black	Mountain-100	
	349	BK-M82B-42	$3,374.99	10	Black	Mountain-100	
	350	BK-M82B-44	$3,374.99	10	Black	Mountain-100	

FIGURE 7-10 ListPriceRank is a useful example of how *EARLIER* is useful for navigating in row contexts.

Because there are five products with the same list price, their rank is always 1, and the sixth product has a rank of 6, shared with other four products with the same price. We suggest that you study and understand this small example very well, because it is a good test of your ability to use and understand row contexts, how to create them using iterators (*FILTER*, in this case), and how to access values outside of them through the usage of *EARLIER*.

> **Note** *EARLIER* accepts a second parameter, which is the number of steps to skip, so that you can skip two or more row contexts. Moreover, there is another function named *EARLIEST* that lets you access directly the outermost defined row context for a table. To be honest, neither the second parameter of *EARLIER* nor that of *EARLIEST* is used often. Although having two nested row contexts is common, having three or more of them is something that happens rarely.

Understanding *FILTER*, *ALL*, and context interactions

In the preceding example, we have introduced *FILTER* as a convenient way of filtering a table to access only part of it. *FILTER* is commonly used whenever you want to apply a filter that is added to the existing context. You can find the sample data model in the companion workbook "CH07-02-Context Interactions.xlsx."

Imagine that you want to create a calculated field that counts the number of red products. With the knowledge you have gained so far, the formula is easy:

```
NumOfRedProducts :=
COUNTROWS (
    FILTER (
        DimProduct,
        DimProduct[Color] = "Red"
    )
)
```

This code works fine, and you can use it inside a PivotTable (for example putting the ModelName on the rows) to produce the report shown in Figure 7-11.

Row Labels	NumOfRedProducts
HL Road Frame	16
LL Road Frame	12
ML Road Frame	5
Road-150	5
Road-250	5
Road-450	5
Road-650	12
Sport-100	3
Grand Total	**63**

FIGURE 7-11 Counting the number of red products is an easy task using *FILTER*.

Before continuing with this example, it is useful to stop for a moment and think carefully about how these values are computed. The NumOfRedProducts formula is computed, inside each cell, in a context defined by the model name on the rows. Thus, each cell computes the number of red products that also have the model name indicated by the corresponding row. This happens because when you ask to iterate the DimProduct table, you are really asking to iterate the DimProduct table as visible in the current filter context, which contains only products with that model name. It might seem trivial, but it is better to repeat it to yourself again and again than take a chance of forgetting it.

This becomes clearer if you put a slicer on the worksheet containing the color. In Figure 7-12, we have created two identical PivotTables with the slicer on color. You can see that the left one has the Red color selected, and the numbers are the same as in Figure 7-11, whereas in the right one, the PivotTable is empty because Blue has been selected.

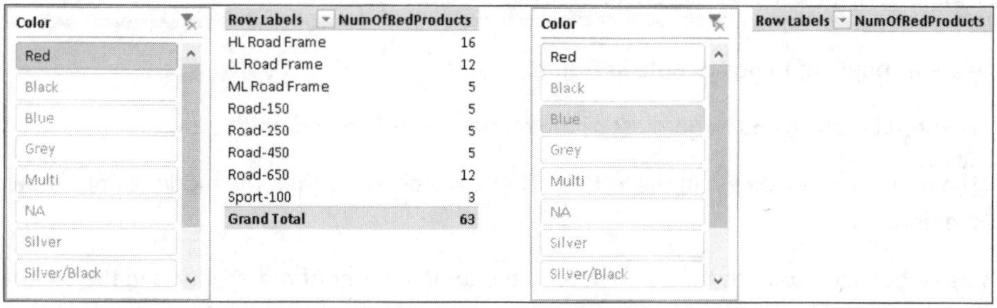

FIGURE 7-12 NumOfRedProducts is evaluated, taking into account the query context.

The reason for the empty PivotTable is that the DimProduct table used inside *FILTER* shows only blue products and, because there are no products that can be blue and red at the same time, it always evaluates to *BLANK*.

The important part of this example is the fact that we have, in the same formula, a filter context coming from the outside (the PivotTable cell, which feels the slicer selection) and a row context introduced in the formula. Both contexts work at the same time and modify the formula result.

At this point, you might want to define a formula that returns the number of red products regardless of the selection made by the slicer. Thus, you want to ignore the selection made by the slicer and always return the number of the red products.

This introduces a new function: *ALL*. *ALL* is a table function that returns the table content ignoring the existing filter context; that is, it always returns all the rows of a table. You can define a new calculated field, NumOfAllRedProducts, by using this expression:

```
COUNTROWS (
    FILTER (
        ALL ( DimProduct ),
        DimProduct[Color] = "Red"
    )
)
```

This time, instead of referring only to DimProduct, we use ALL (DimProduct), meaning that we want to ignore the existing filter context and always iterate over all products. The result is definitely not what we would expect, and you can see it in Figure 7-13.

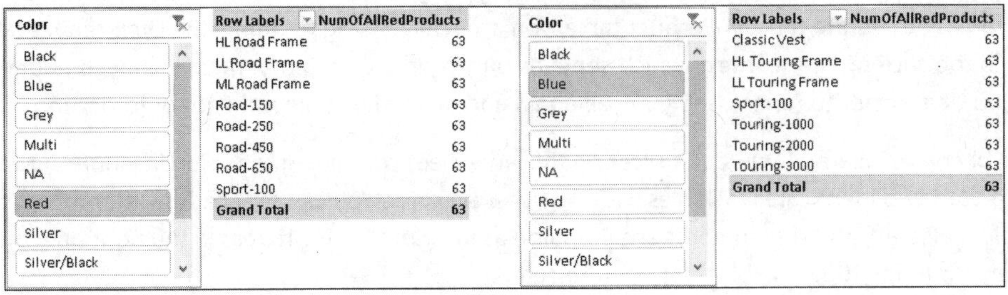

FIGURE 7-13 Here, NumOfAllRedProducts returns strange results.

There are a couple of things to note in Figure 7-13:

- The result is always 63, regardless of the model name selected on the rows.

- The model names shown in the left PivotTable are different than the model names shown in the right one.

Let's delve deeper into both topics. First, 63 is the total number of red products in the database. Having used *ALL*, we have removed all the filters from the DimProduct table; that is we have removed not only the filter on color, but also the filter on model name. This is an unwanted effect, but unfortunately, with the limited knowledge we have of DAX at this point, we have no other option. *ALL* is powerful, but it is an all-or-nothing function: if used, it removes all the filters. It has no option to remove only part of them. To be more specific, we wanted to remove only the filter on color, leaving all other filters untouched. In the next chapter, with the introduction of *CALCULATE*, we will learn how to solve this issue.

The second point is easier to understand: because we have selected Blue, we are seeing the model names of blue products, not the model names of all the products. Thus, the rightmost PivotTable shows blue model names with the total of red products in the database. This happens because the list of model names, which is used to populate the axis of the PivotTable, is computed in the original filter context, which in turn contains a filter on color that equals blue. Then, once the axes have been computed, the values are computed, always returning 63 as a result.

We do not want to solve this scenario right now. The solution will come later when you will learn about *CALCULATE*, which has specific options to solve scenarios like this one. For now, we have used this example to show that you might find strange results coming from relatively simple formulas because of context interactions and the coexistence, in the same expression, of filter and row contexts.

Working with many tables

Using context has led us to some interesting (and surprising) results up to now. However, you might have noticed that we deliberately used only one table: namely, DimProduct. With only one table, you need to worry about only interactions between row context and filter context in the same expression.

Very few useful data models contain one single table; it is most likely that you will have many tables in your data model, linked by relationships. Thus, a good question is: How do the two contexts behave regarding relationships? Moreover, because relations have a direction, we need to understand what happens on the one and on the many side of a relationship.

If you create a row context on a table on the many side of the relationship, do you expect it to let you use columns on the one side? And what if you create it on the one side, do you expect to be able to access columns from the many side? Finally, what about the filter context? Do you expect to put a filter on the many side of the table and see it propagated in some way to the one side? Any answer could be correct depending on the situation, but we are interested in learning how DAX behaves in these situations (that is, understand how the DAX language defines propagation of contexts through relationships). As you are going to learn, there are some subtle interactions between contexts and relationships and learning them requires some patience.

In order to examine this scenario, we use a data model containing five tables, which you can see in Figure 7-14. You can find this example in the companion workbook "CH07-03-Contexts and Relationships.xlsx."

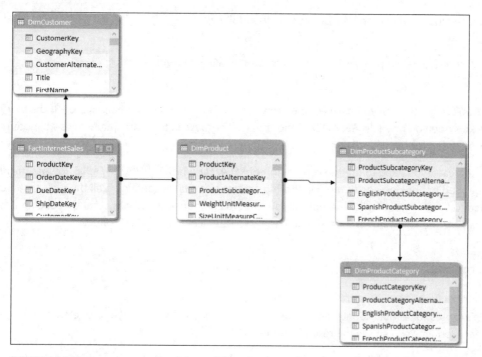

FIGURE 7-14 Here, you can see the data model used to learn about interactions between contexts and relationships.

Row contexts and relationships

The behavior of row contexts and relationships is easy to understand because there is nothing *to* understand: they do not interact in any way, at least not automatically.

Imagine that you want to create a calculated column on FactInternetSales containing the difference between the unit price stored in the fact table and the product list price stored in the DimProduct table, just to verify that data is correctly computed. You could try using this formula:

```
= FactInternetSales[UnitPrice] - DimProduct[ListPrice]
```

This expression uses two columns from two different tables and will be evaluated in a row context that iterates over FactInternetSales only, because the calculated column is defined within that table. DimProduct is on the one side of a relationship with FactInternetSales (which, obviously, is on the many side), so you might expect to be able to gain access to the list price of the related row. Unfortunately, this does not happen. The row context on FactInternetSales is not propagated to DimProduct, and the formula will return an error if you try to create a calculated column with it.

If, from the table on the many side, you want to access columns in the one side, as is the case in this example, you can use the *RELATED* function. *RELATED* accepts a column name as the parameter and retrieves the value of the column in a corresponding row that is found by following existing relationships in the many-to-one direction, starting from the current row context.

The previous formula can be easily corrected as follows:

```
= FactInternetSales[UnitPrice] - RELATED ( DimProduct[ListPrice ] )
```

RELATED works when you have an open row context on the table on the many side. If the row context is open on one side, *RELATED* cannot be used because in that case, many rows will potentially be detected following the relationships.

In this case, you need to use the companion of *RELATED,* which is *RELATEDTABLE. RELATEDTABLE* can be used on the one side of the relationship and returns a table containing all the rows that are related to the current one. For example, if you want to compute the number of sales of each product, you can use the following formula, defined as a calculated column on DimProduct:

```
= COUNTROWS ( RELATEDTABLE ( FactInternetSales ) )
```

This expression simply counts the number of rows in FactInternetSales that are related to the current product. You can see the result in Figure 7-15.

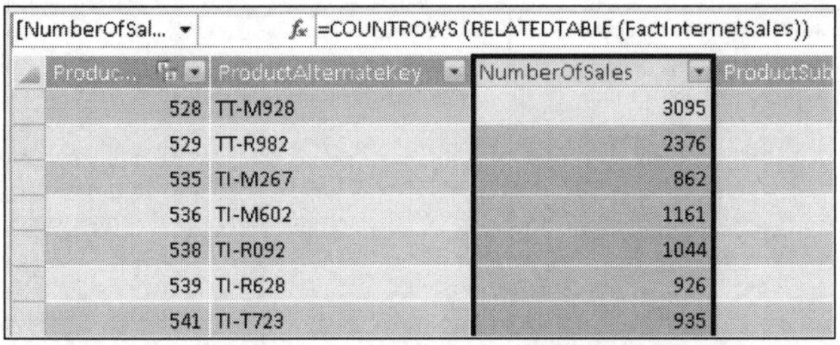

[NumberOfSal... ▼]	f_x =COUNTROWS (RELATEDTABLE (FactInternetSales))		
Produc... ▼	ProductAlternateKey ▼	NumberOfSales ▼	ProductSub
528	TT-M928	3095	
529	TT-R982	2376	
535	TI-M267	862	
536	TI-M602	1161	
538	TI-R092	1044	
539	TI-R628	926	
541	TI-T723	935	

FIGURE 7-15 *RELATEDTABLE* is useful when you have a row context on the one side of the relationship.

It is worth noting that both *RELATED* and *RELATEDTABLE* can traverse a long chain of relationships to achieve their result—they are not limited to a single hop. The only limitation is that the chain should be composed of relationships of the same type (that is, one-to-many or many-to-one), all of which are going in the same direction. If you have two tables related through one-to-many and then many-to-one, with an intermediate bridge table in the middle, then neither *RELATED* nor *RELATEDTABLE* will work.

Let's make this concept clearer with an example. You might think that DimCustomer is related to DimProduct because there is a one-to-many relationship between DimCustomer and FactInternet-Sales, and then a many-to-one relationship between FactInternetSales and DimProduct. Thus, the two tables are linked through a chain of relationships, but they are not in the same direction.

This scenario is known as a many-to-many relationship; that is, a customer is related to many products (the ones bought) and a product is related to many customers (the ones who bought the product). Unfortunately, this scenario is not natively supported by DAX. You will learn how to handle it in Chapter 13, "Advanced DAX," because it requires a better understanding of both evaluation contexts and, most important, of the *CALCULATE* function.

In fact, suppose that you define a calculated column in DimCustomer with this formula:

```
NumOfBoughtProducts = COUNTROWS ( RELATEDTABLE( DimProduct ) )
```

The result will always be 606 (that is, the total number of products in the database), as shown in Figure 7-16.

[NumOfBoug... ▾	*fx* =COUNTROWS (RELATEDTABLE(DimProduct))		
FirstName ▾	MiddleName ▾	LastName ▾	NumOfBoughtProducts ▾
Larry		Gill	606
Geoffrey		Gonzalez	606
Blake		Collins	606
Alexa		Watson	606
Jacquelyn		Dominguez	606
Casey		Gutierrez	606
Colleen		Lu	606
Jeremiah		Stewart	606
Leah		Li	606
Frank		Ramos	606
Candice		He	606
Andrea		Cox	606

FIGURE 7-16 *RELATEDTABLE* does not work if you try to traverse a many-to-many relationship.

Filter context and relationships

You have learned that row context does not interact with relationships, and that, if you want to traverse relationships, you have two distinct functions to use, depending which side of the relationship you are located on while accessing the target table.

Filter contexts behave in a different way: they interact with relationships automatically and they have different behaviors depending on the side of the relationship to which the filter is applied. The general rule is as follows:

A filter context applied to a table is automatically propagated to all related tables that are on the many side of a one-to-many relationship. On the other hand, if the table is the one side of a many-to-one relationship, the automatic propagation does not flow from the many side to the one side, but only from the one side to the many side of a relationship.

This behavior is easy to understand by looking at a simple PivotTable with a few calculated fields. Figure 7-17 displays a PivotTable browsing the data model we have used so far, with three simple calculated fields. The calculated fields have this definition:

```
NumOfSales      := COUNTROWS ( FactInternetSales )
NumOfProducts   := COUNTROWS ( DimProduct )
NumOfCustomers  := COUNTROWS ( DimCustomer )
```

Color		Row Labels	NumOfSales	NumOfProducts	NumOfCustomers
Black		⊟ Cycling Cap	2,190	3	18,484
Blue		AWC Logo Cap	2,190	3	18,484
Grey		⊟ Long-Sleeve Logo Jersey	1,736	12	18,484
Multi		Long-Sleeve Logo Jersey, L	452	3	18,484
NA		Long-Sleeve Logo Jersey, M	442	3	18,484
		Long-Sleeve Logo Jersey, S	429	3	18,484
Red		Long-Sleeve Logo Jersey, XL	413	3	18,484
Silver		⊟ Men's Bib-Shorts		3	18,484
Silver/Black		Men's Bib-Shorts, L		1	18,484
		Men's Bib-Shorts, M		1	18,484
		Men's Bib-Shorts, S		1	18,484
		Grand Total	3,926	18	18,484

FIGURE 7-17 Here, you can see the behavior of filter context and relationships.

The filter is on the product color. DimProduct is the source of a one-to-many relationship with FactInternetSales, so the filter context is propagated from DimProduct to FactInternetSales. You can see this because the NumOfSales measure counts only the sales of multicolored products. Moreover, both the model name and product name put on the rows are fields of the DimProduct table, and the NumOfSales measure obeys the filter because of the automatic propagation of the filter to FactInternetSales.

On the other hand, the NumOfCustomers measure, which counts customers, is not filtered. This is because DimCustomers is the one side of a many-to-one relationship starting from FactInternetSales. Even if FactInternetSales is filtered, the filter is applied to the many side of the relationship and the context is not further propagated.

As it happened with the row context, it is not important how many steps you need to traverse to reach a table: so long as there is a chain of one-to-many relationships, automatic propagation happens. For example, if you put a filter on DimProductCategory, the filter is propagated to DimProductSubcategory (one-to-many) and, from there, to FactInternetSales (one-to-many again). Then, the propagation stops because all the relationships that start from FactInternetSales are many-to-one, so the chain is broken and propagation stops.

It is worth noting that neither row contexts nor filter contexts work with many-to-many relationships. In order to handle them, you will need to learn some more advanced topics about the DAX language.

Finally, it is important to note that there are no functions available to access columns or values from tables following the chain of filter contexts because propagation of the filter context happens automatically, whereas propagation of row contexts does not, and it is required to specify the propagation using *RELATED* and *RELATEDTABLE*.

Introducing *VALUES*

The previous example was interesting because we tried to compute the number of customers who bought a product and failed. This was because we still do not master the full power of DAX. Nevertheless, if you are interested only in counting the number of customers, there is a handy alternative that we are going to show to introduce a new and powerful function: *VALUES*.

VALUES is a table function that returns a table of only one column, containing all the possible values of a column that are visible in the current filter context. There are many advanced usages of *VALUES* which we will introduce later in this book, but, for the moment, it is useful to start using *VALUES* to get acquainted with its behavior.

In the previous PivotTable, you can modify the definition of NumOfCustomers with the following DAX expression:

```
NumOfCustomers := COUNTROWS ( VALUES ( FactInternetSales[CustomerKey] ) )
```

This expression does not count the number of customers in the DimCustomertable. It counts the number of unique values visible in the current filter context for the CustomerKey column in the FactInternetSales. Thus, the expression does not use the relationship between FactInternetSales and DimCustomers; it uses only the FactInternetSales table.

Now, FactInternetSales is filtered because of the propagation of the filter from DimProduct to FactInternetSales. Thus, not all the values of CustomerKey will be visible—only the ones that belong to rows that pertain to sales of the filtered products.

The meaning of the expression is "Count the number of unique customer keys for the sales records related to the selected products." Because a customer key represents a customer, the expression effectively counts the number of customers who bought those products, as shown in Figure 7-18.

Color		Row Labels	NumOfSales	NumOfProducts	NumOfCustomers
Black		⊟ **Cycling Cap**	**2,190**	**3**	**2,132**
Blue		AWC Logo Cap	2,190	3	2,132
Grey		⊟ **Long-Sleeve Logo Jersey**	**1,736**	**12**	**1,684**
Multi		Long-Sleeve Logo Jersey, L	452	3	449
NA		Long-Sleeve Logo Jersey, M	442	3	436
Red		Long-Sleeve Logo Jersey, S	429	3	426
Silver		Long-Sleeve Logo Jersey, XL	413	3	409
Silver/Black		⊟ **Men's Bib-Shorts**		**3**	
		Men's Bib-Shorts, L		1	
		Men's Bib-Shorts, M		1	
		Men's Bib-Shorts, S		1	
		Grand Total	**3,926**	**18**	**3,488**

FIGURE 7-18 Using the new formula, we now can compute the number of customers who bought some products.

Beware of the fact that even if it might seem so, we have not yet been able to correctly traverse the many-to-many relationship. We have been able to use the *COUNTROWS* function to count the number of customers, but we did it by using a simple trick; that is, avoid traversing a relationship and using only the available information in FactInternetSales (the customer key in this example). You will learn how to manage many-to-many relationships in Chapter 13.

Most important, you have learned a first usage of *VALUES*. *VALUES* is a powerful and useful function that you will use often during your DAX writing, both to count values and to use values as filters.

Introducing *ISFILTERED* and *ISCROSSFILTERED*

A couple of other functions are useful and might help you better understand the propagation of filter contexts. Moreover, learning them is a good way to introduce one of the most useful concepts of PivotTable computation: detection of the level for which you are computing a value from inside DAX.

The following functions help you understand whether all the values of a column are visible or not in the current filter context:

- **ISFILTERED** Returns true or false, depending whether the column passed as an argument has a direct filter on it; that is, it has been put on rows, columns, on a slicer or filter, and the filtering is happening for the current cell.

- **ISCROSSFILTERED** Returns true or false depending whether the column is filtered not because of a direct filter, but because of automatic propagation of another filter.

These functions are somewhat advanced, and you will learn to use them later with some more complex formulas. In this section, we are interested in using the functions to better understand the propagation of filter contexts. Thus, we are going to create dummy expressions, which are only useful as learning tools.

Start with an empty PivotTable that contains the color on rows and a slicer for DimProduct[ModelName]. Then, create a new calculated field with this definition:

```
ModelFilter = ISFILTERED ( DimProduct[ModelName] )
```

This simple calculated field returns the value of the *ISFILTERED* function applied to the model name. Then, create a second calculated field that makes the same operation with the color. Thus, the code will be:

```
ColorFilter = ISFILTERED ( DimProduct[Color] )
```

If you add both calculated fields to the PivotTable, the result will be similar to Figure 7-19.

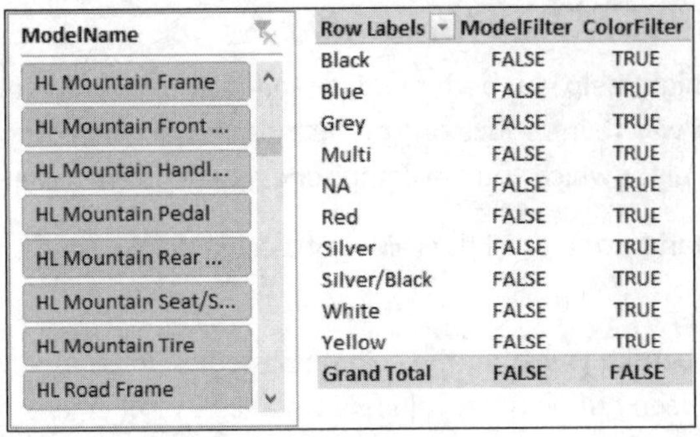

FIGURE 7-19 You can see that ModelName is never filtered and Color is filtered everywhere but on the grand total.

The significant part of this is that the ModelName is never filtered because even if we added a slicer, we did not filter it. Color, on the other hand, is always filtered on rows (because color is on the rows) and not on the grand total because there, the filter context coming from the rows is not applied.

> **Note** This behavior of the grand total (that is, no filter is applied from the ones coming from rows and columns) will be useful whenever you want to modify the behavior of a formula so that, at the grand total level, it shows a different value. In fact, you will check *ISFILTERED* for a column present in the report to understand if the cell that you are evaluating is in the inner part of the PivotTable or if it is at the grand total level.

If you select some values from the ModelName slicer, the result changes because now the model is always filtered, as shown in Figure 7-20. In fact, the filter context introduced by the slicer is effective even at the grand total level.

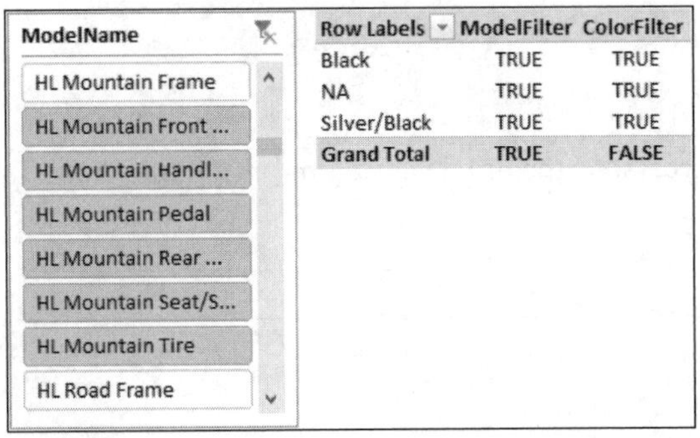

FIGURE 7-20 The filter introduced by the slicer works at the grand total level too.

Now, you may notice something strange about the result of *ISFILTERED*. In fact, you can see that the PivotTable shows fewer colors than before. Blue, Grey, and many others are no longer visible. Why is that the case if no filter is being applied to the table? Because the filter on the model name indirectly filters the color too. In fact, there are no blue products with the selected model names; therefore, the list of values for the Color column is reduced due to an indirect filter.

This operation (indirect filtering of a column due to a filter set on another one) is called *cross-filtering*. In this case, we say that color is being cross-filtered by model name. The *ISCROSSFILTERED* function returns exactly this information. If you add two new calculated fields to the data model that check *ISCROSSFILTERED* for color and model name and add them to the PivotTable, you will see the result shown in Figure 7-21. The two new calculated fields are defined as follows:

```
ModelCross = ISCROSSFILTERED ( DimProduct[ModelName] )
ColorCross = ISCROSSFILTERED ( DimProduct[Color] )
```

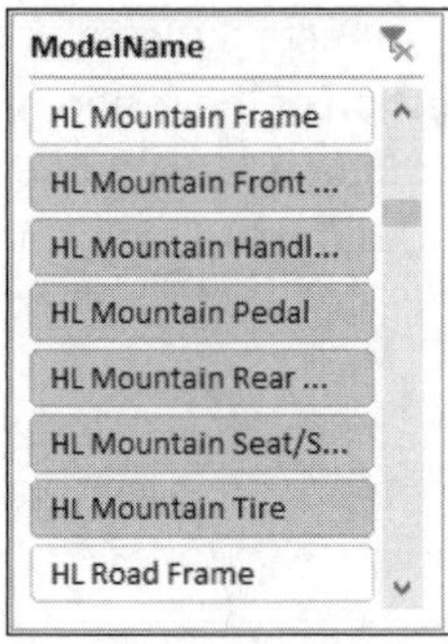

ModelName
HL Mountain Frame
HL Mountain Front ...
HL Mountain Handl...
HL Mountain Pedal
HL Mountain Rear ...
HL Mountain Seat/S...
HL Mountain Tire
HL Road Frame

Row Labels	ModelFilter	ColorFilter	ModelCross	ColorCross
Black	TRUE	TRUE	TRUE	TRUE
NA	TRUE	TRUE	TRUE	TRUE
Silver/Black	TRUE	TRUE	TRUE	TRUE
Grand Total	**TRUE**	**FALSE**	**TRUE**	**TRUE**

FIGURE 7-21 Cross-filtering is visible using the *ISCROSSFILTERED* function.

You can see that both model and color are cross-filtered. In reality, when a table has one filtered column, all of the other columns in the table, including the filtered one, are cross-filtered. Thus, you can think of *ISCROSSFILTERED* as a function that works at the table level even if it accepts a column as an argument.

Now, because you know that the DimProduct table has a relationship with FactInternetSales, you might be interested in looking at the value of *ISCROSSFILTERED* for the FactInternetSales table. You already know that no direct filter is applied, but because of filter context propagation, the FactInternetSales table inherits a filter from DimProduct.

Adding a new calculated field (*FactCross*) that checks *ISCROSSFILTERED* (FactInternetSales[SalesAmount]), you will see the result shown in Figure 7-22.

ModelName		Row Labels	ModelFilter	ColorFilter	ModelCross	ColorCross	FactCross
HL Mountain Frame		Black	TRUE	TRUE	TRUE	TRUE	TRUE
HL Mountain Front ...		NA	TRUE	TRUE	TRUE	TRUE	TRUE
HL Mountain Handl...		Silver/Black	TRUE	TRUE	TRUE	TRUE	TRUE
HL Mountain Pedal		Grand Total	TRUE	FALSE	TRUE	TRUE	TRUE
HL Mountain Rear ...							
HL Mountain Seat/S...							
HL Mountain Tire							
HL Road Frame							

FIGURE 7-22 The FactInternetSales table inherits a cross-filter from DimProduct due to filter context propagation.

The last test is to check what happens to the DimCustomer table (just to cite one example). DimCustomer has no direct relationship with DimProduct, but it has one with FactInternetSales. Is it going to be filtered? You already know the answer (no) because of the direction of the relationship. The filter propagates from the one side (DimProduct) to the many side (FactInternetSales) but does not propagate from the many side (FactInternetSales) to the one side (DimCustomer). Using a new calculated field will confirm this intuition, as shown in Figure 7-23.

```
CustomerCross = ISCROSSFILTERED ( DimCustomer[CustomerKey] )
```

ModelName		Row Labels	ModelFilter	ColorFilter	ModelCross	ColorCross	FactCross	CustomerCross
HL Mountain Frame		Black	TRUE	TRUE	TRUE	TRUE	TRUE	FALSE
HL Mountain Front ...		NA	TRUE	TRUE	TRUE	TRUE	TRUE	FALSE
HL Mountain Handl...		Silver/Black	TRUE	TRUE	TRUE	TRUE	TRUE	FALSE
HL Mountain Pedal		Grand Total	TRUE	FALSE	TRUE	TRUE	TRUE	FALSE
HL Mountain Rear ...								
HL Mountain Seat/S...								
HL Mountain Tire								
HL Road Frame								

FIGURE 7-23 DimCustomer is not cross-filtered from the slicer because of the direction of relationships.

In this section, you have seen many instances of *ISFILTERED* and *ISCROSSFILTERED*. These examples were mainly for educational purposes, because you used them only to get a better understanding of how filter context propagates through relationships. Later, in more advanced DAX code, you will learn why these two functions are so useful.

Evaluation contexts recap

Let's recap what we have discussed about evaluation contexts thus far:

- Evaluation context is the context that modifies the value of a DAX expression by filtering the data model (filter context) and providing the concept or current row (row context) when it is needed to access a column value.

- The evaluation context comprises two parts: the row context and the filter context. They co-exist, and they are present for all the formulas that are evaluated. To understand the behavior of a formula, you always need to take into account both contexts because they operate in different ways.

- Row contexts are automatically created when defining a calculated column and can be created programmatically by using iterators. All iterators define a row context.

- Row contexts can be nested and, in such a case, the *EARLIER* function can be used to get access to the previous row context.

- Filter context are created by using fields on rows, columns, slicers, and filters. There is a way to create filter contexts programmatically by using *CALCULATE,* but we have not covered it yet. At this point, however, we hope that you are curious about it, because you will learn about it soon.

- Row context does not propagate through relationships. Propagation happens manually by using *RELATED* and *RELATEDTABLE*. These functions need to be used on the correct side of a one-to-many relationship: *RELATED* on the many side, *RELATEDTABLE* on the one side.

- Filter context is automatically propagated from the one side of the relationship to the many side, whereas it is not propagated from the many side to the one side. Thus, there are no functions available to propagate it manually: everything happens inside the engine automatically.

- *VALUES* returns a table containing a one-column table with all the distinct values of the column that are visible in the current filter context. Being a table, it can be used as a parameter to any iterator.

At this point, you have learned the most complex topics of the DAX language. These points rule all the evaluation flows of your formulas, and they are the pillars of the DAX language. Whenever you see an expression that does not compute what you want, the chances are excellent that this happened because you still have not mastered these rules.

> **Note** We said that the filter context propagation happens automatically, and there is no way to force this behavior. This is not completely true. In reality, you can manipulate filter context with DAX functions obtaining an effect similar to the propagation of a filter context from the many side to the one side. For example, data models with many-to-many relationships between entities use this technique to calculate measures correctly. More details on these advanced data models are available in Chapter 13 and in the white paper "The Many-to-Many Revolution 2.0," which you can find in the author's company website (SQLBI.com) at *http://www.sqlbi.com/articles/many2many/*.

As was stated in the introduction of this chapter, all these topics look very simple at first. And in fact, they are. What makes them complex is the fact that these simple rules can be used in complex expressions, and a single expression can have different contexts in different subformulas. Being able to follow them is an attitude that you will gain only with experience.

Once that you have written several DAX formulas, it will be natural to follow the contexts as they are created and destroyed during computation. At that point, you will have earned the title of DAX master.

Creating a parameter table

In this chapter, you have learned many theoretical concepts about evaluation contexts. It is now time to use some of them to solve an interesting scenario and learn a useful technique: the usage of parameter tables.

The idea of a parameter table is to create a table that is unrelated to the rest of the data model but is used internally by DAX functions to modify their behavior. An example might help to clarify this concept. Imagine that you have created a report that shows the sum of sales amounts and, because your company sells a large quantity of goods, the numbers shown in the report are big. Because the *AdventureWorks* database does not suffer from this problem, instead of using the SalesAmount column, we have created a new column called BigSalesAmount, which is simply SalesAmount squared, so that numbers are bigger and the scenario is more evident. You can find the sample data model in the companion workbook "CH07-04-Parameter Table.xlsx." In Figure 7-24, you can see this report.

Row Labels	Sum of BigSalesAmount
Black	18,328,560,571.51
Blue	4,310,060,723.26
Multi	4,515,260.19
NA	18,765,758.47
Red	24,345,540,726.06
Silver	11,309,839,383.85
White	45,905.82
Yellow	8,021,400,259.57
Grand Total	**66,338,728,588.73**

FIGURE 7-24 Reading reports with large numbers is sometimes hard.

The issue with this report is that the numbers are large, and they tend to be hard to read: are they millions, billions, or trillions? Moreover, they take up a lot of space in the report without delivering much information. A common request for this kind of report is to show the numbers using a different scale. For example, you might want to show the values divided by 1,000 or 1 million so that they result in smaller numbers that still carry the useful information.

The issue is easily solved by modifying the calculated field and dividing it by 1,000. The only problem is that, depending on the relative scale of these numbers, you might want to see them as real values (if they are small enough), divided by thousands or millions. Creating three measures seems cumbersome at this point, and we want to find a better solution that removes the need to create many different measures. Now that you have become a DAX master, you can devise such a solution.

The idea is to let the user decide which scale to use for the report using a slicer. In Figure 7-25, you can see an example of the report that we want to build.

ShowValueAs		Row Labels ⯆	SumOfBigSalesAmount
Real Value		Black	18,328.56
Thousands		Blue	4,310.06
Millions		Multi	4.52
		NA	18.77
		Red	24,345.54
		Silver	11,309.84
		White	0.05
		Yellow	8,021.40
		Grand Total	66,338.73

FIGURE 7-25 Rather than filtering values here, the slicer is used to change the way that numbers are shown.

The remarkable idea of the report is that the ShowValueAs slicer is not used to filter data. Instead, you will use it to change the scale used by the numbers. If the user selects Real Value, you will show the actual numbers; if he selects Thousands, then you will show the numbers divided by 1,000, and so on.

To create this report, the first thing that you need is a table containing the values you want to show on the slicer. This is as easy as creating an Excel table (as in Figure 7-26) and loading it into the data model.

ShowValueAs	DivideBy
Real Value	1
Thousands	1,000
Millions	1,000,000

FIGURE 7-26 This Excel table is the source for the slicer in the report.

Obviously, you cannot create any relationship with this table because the FactInternetSales table does not contain any column that can be used to relate to ShowValueAs. Nevertheless, once the table is in the model, you can use the ShowValueAscolumn as the source for a slicer. At first, you end up with a slicer that does nothing. But, then, you can use some DAX code that will perform the last step: reading what the user has selected in the slicer and modifying the content of the report accordingly, showing real numbers (thousands or millions) so that the slicer becomes useful.

The DAX expression that you need to use for SumOfBigSalesAmount is the following:

```
SumOfBigSalesAmount =
IF (
    HASONEVALUE ( ShowValueAs[ShowValueAs] ),
    SUM ( FactInternetSales[BigSalesAmount] ) / VALUES ( ShowValueAs[DivideBy] ),
    SUM ( FactInternetSales[BigSalesAmount] )
)
```

There are two points to note about this formula:

- The condition tested by the *IF* function is HASONEVALUE (ShowValueAs[ShowValueAs]). This pattern is very common: you check if the column of your parameter table has only one value visible. If the user has not selected anything in the slicer, then all the values of the column are visible in the current filter context; that is, *HASONEVALUE* will return *FALSE* (because the column has three different values). If, on the other hand, the user selected a single value, then only that value is visible, and *HASONEVALUE* will return *TRUE*. Thus, the condition reads as "If the user has selected a single value for *ShowValueAs*."

- If a single value is visible, then you know this. Thus, you can compute VALUES (ShowValueAs[DivideBy]), and you can be sure that the resulting table contains only one row (the one visible in the filter context). *VALUES* will convert the one-row-one-column table into a single value because of this special condition. If you try to use *VALUES* to read a single value when the result is a multi-row table, you will get an error. But in this specific scenario, you are sure that there will be only one value returned because of the previous condition tested by *IF*.

Thus, you can read the expression as "If the user has selected a single value in the slicer, then show the sum of sales amounts divided by the corresponding denominator; otherwise, show the total of the sales amounts."The final result is a report that changes the values shown interactively, using the slicer as if it were a button. Clearly, because the report uses only standard DAX formulas, it will work when deployed on Microsoft SharePoint too.

Parameter tables are useful when building reports. We have shown a simple (yet common) example, but the only limit to using these tools is your imagination. You can create parameter tables to modify the way a number is computed, change parameters for a specific algorithm, or perform other complex operations that change the values returned by your calculated fields.

CHAPTER 8

Understanding CALCULATE

In this chapter, we continue to explore the power of the DAX language with a detailed explanation of a single function: *CALCULATE*. It might seem strange to dedicate a full chapter to a single function, but this is necessary because of the richness and side effects of this particular one. *CALCULATE* is by far the most important, useful, and complex function of the DAX language. In reality, the function is easy: it performs only a few tasks, but the number of scenarios where *CALCULATE* is necessary and the complexity of the formulas that can be written with *CALCULATE* make a full chapter absolutely justified.

Like the previous chapter, this chapter is about a complex subject. We strongly suggest to read it once, get a general feeling of *CALCULATE,* and move on to the remaining part of the book. Then, as soon as you feel lost with a specific formula, come back here and read the chapter again from the beginning. You will probably discover new information each time you read it.

Why is *CALCULATE* needed?

As stated in the previous chapter, there are two different contexts: row context and filter context. You have learned that the row context can be created programmatically by using iterators, and you learned about a function (*ALL*) that lets you ignore the filter context.

The missing piece of this puzzle is a way to alter the filter context by adding or removing filters to it. *ALL* is a first step in this direction, but it lets you ignore all the filters in the context. It does not help in these scenarios:

- You want to ignore part of the filter context, not all of it.

- You want to add a condition to the filter context or modify an existing condition.

An example might help, as usual. Imagine that you have built the report shown in Figure 8-1, which contains categories, subcategories, and the sum of the sales amounts. You can find this example in the companion workbook "CH08-01-Why CALCULATE.xlsx."

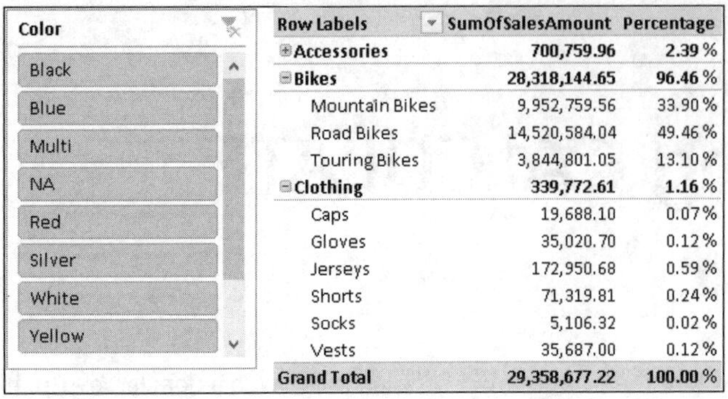

Row Labels	SumOfSalesAmount	Percentage
⊞Accessories	**700,759.96**	**2.39 %**
⊟Bikes	**28,318,144.65**	**96.46 %**
Mountain Bikes	9,952,759.56	33.90 %
Road Bikes	14,520,584.04	49.46 %
Touring Bikes	3,844,801.05	13.10 %
⊟Clothing	**339,772.61**	**1.16 %**
Caps	19,688.10	0.07 %
Gloves	35,020.70	0.12 %
Jerseys	172,950.68	0.59 %
Shorts	71,319.81	0.24 %
Socks	5,106.32	0.02 %
Vests	35,687.00	0.12 %
Grand Total	**29,358,677.22**	**100.00 %**

FIGURE 8-1 Here, you can see a simple report showing sales divided by category and subcategory.

The report shows the percentage of each row to the grand total. While this can be easily computed using Microsoft Excel PivotTable features, you are interested in computing this value as a calculated field, so that users have it handy whenever they want to add it to a PivotTable.

A naive solution is the following:

```
Percentage :=
    SUM ( FactInternetSales[SalesAmount] )
    /
    SUMX ( ALL ( FactInternetSales ), FactInternetSales[SalesAmount] )
```

The numerator is simply the *SUM* of SalesAmount; the denominator ignores the filter context and always returns the grand total of SalesAmount, regardless of filter. This formula works so long as you do not select anything from the slicer. For example, if you select the color Black, then the values are wrong, because the percentage of the grand total is 30.10 percent instead of 100 percent. This is because the denominator used for the Percentage calculation is a higher number, as Figure 8-2 shows.

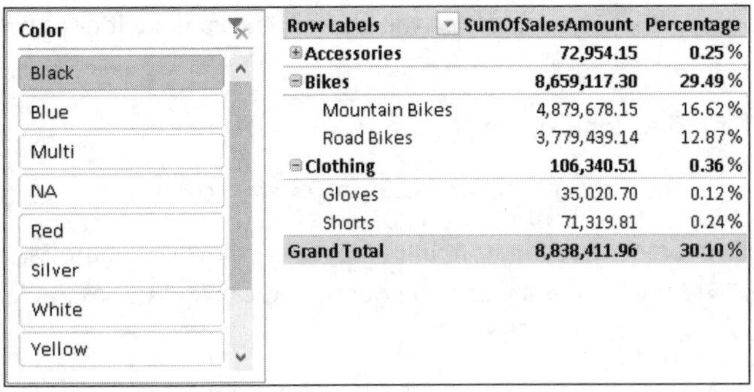

Row Labels	SumOfSalesAmount	Percentage
⊞Accessories	**72,954.15**	**0.25 %**
⊟Bikes	**8,659,117.30**	**29.49 %**
Mountain Bikes	4,879,678.15	16.62 %
Road Bikes	3,779,439.14	12.87 %
⊟Clothing	**106,340.51**	**0.36 %**
Gloves	35,020.70	0.12 %
Shorts	71,319.81	0.24 %
Grand Total	**8,838,411.96**	**30.10 %**

FIGURE 8-2 Selecting a color from the slicer shows incorrect percentage results.

The problem here is easy to understand: By using *ALL,* we are completely ignoring the existing filter context. Thus, the denominator is always the grand total of all sales, whereas if a color is selected, we want to keep the filter on color, clearing only the filters on category and subcategory. *ALL* and iterators are not useful here. Rather, we need something more powerful: *CALCULATE*.

CALCULATE (with its companion, *CALCULATETABLE*, which you will learn about in the "Filtering with Complex Conditions" section later in this chapter) is the only function that is capable of modifying the filter context. In reality, *CALCULATE* creates a new filter context and then evaluates an expression in that context. It helps in this case because we will create a new filter context in which we will remove the filter on category and subcategory, keeping all other filters in place and then computing the sum of the sales amounts.

Let's start examining the syntax of *CALCULATE:*

```
CALCULATE ( Expression, Condition1, … ConditionN )
```

CALCULATE accepts as many conditions as you want, and the only mandatory parameter is the first one (that is, the expression to evaluate).

Remember that the filter context of a calculation is defined by the set of filters currently being applied to any given cell, which are a function of the pivot table filters, slicers, rows, and columns. *CALCULATE* does the following:

- It takes the current filter context and makes a copy of it into a new filter context.

- It evaluates each condition, and for each one:

  - If it uses a column that is not already filtered in the original context, it adds such a condition to the newly created filter context.

  - If, on the other hand, it uses a column already filtered in the original filter context, then it replaces the existing filter with the new condition on that column, effectively removing the existing condition.

- Once evaluated, all the conditions are put in a logical *AND* to create the new filter context. Once the new filter context is defined, the expression is evaluated under the newly created context.

> **Note** *CALCULATE* does another important task: it transforms any existing row context into an equivalent filter context. That topic is discussed in much more detail in the "Using *CALCULATE* inside a row context" section later in this chapter, but the reason we cite it here is that it will be more meaningful once you read this section a second time.

CALCULATE accepts two filter types:

- Boolean conditions, like DimProduct[Color] = "White". These filters need to work on a single column and specify a condition that replaces the existing one in the same column.

- List of values to be considered as valid, presented in the form of a table. In that case, you provide the exact list of values you want to see in the new filter context, and all the columns in that table are part of the filter.

To see *CALCULATE* in action, you can define a new calculated field with this formula:

```
PercentageWithCalculate :=
    SUM ( FactInternetSales[SalesAmount] )
    /
    CALCULATE (
        SUM ( FactInternetSales[SalesAmount] ),
        ALL ( DimProductCategory ),
        ALL ( DimProductSubcategory )
    )
```

Let's focus on the denominator of this formula. It uses *CALCULATE*. The expression to compute is always the same: the sum of sales amounts. But we already know that a formula by itself can have many different values, depending on the context under which it is evaluated. Because the expression is being computed inside *CALCULATE,* we know that the context of the expression will not be the same as for the original calculated field. We only need to understand what the context is going to be, and this information comes from the additional parameters of *CALCULATE*.

The first parameter is ALL (DimProductCategory). *ALL* is a table function that returns all the rows in a table (all the categories in this case). Thus, *CALCULATE* receives a list of rows of the DimProductCategory table and looks at the current filter context. Because it contains a filter on the product category name, it removes it and replaces it with the new filter. The new filter returns all the rows. Thus, at the end, by using *ALL,* you are effectively removing all filters from the DimProductCategory table.

The second parameter is ALL (DimProductSubcategory) and the behavior is identical to the previous filter, but this time, instead of clearing the filter from DimProductCategory, it is the filter on DimProductSubcategory that is cleared.

If we focus on a single cell (for example, the one containing Mountain Bikes), then the original filter context of the cell is <Black, Bikes, Mountain Bikes>. The new filter context has removed the filter on Bikes and Mountain Bikes, and it reads now as <Black>. Do you see the point? We have not removed the filter from the color; we only removed the part of the filter that we wanted to remove, leaving the rest untouched.

Using this new formula inside the PivotTable shows correct values, as shown in Figure 8-3.

Color		Row Labels	SumOfSalesAmount	Percentage	PercentageWithCalculate
Black	^	⊞ Accessories	72,954.15	0.25 %	0.83 %
Blue		⊟ Bikes	8,659,117.30	29.49 %	97.97 %
Multi		Mountain Bikes	4,879,678.15	16.62 %	55.21 %
NA		Road Bikes	3,779,439.14	12.87 %	42.76 %
Red		⊟ Clothing	106,340.51	0.36 %	1.20 %
Silver		Gloves	35,020.70	0.12 %	0.40 %
White		Shorts	71,319.81	0.24 %	0.81 %
Yellow	v	Grand Total	8,838,411.96	30.10 %	100.00 %

FIGURE 8-3 The Percentage figures computed with *CALCULATE* show correct values.

At this point, the careful reader should think: "Well, this does not make sense. You have removed the filter from DimProductCategory and DimProductSubcategory, but you are summing values from the FactInternetSales table. Who removed the filter from that table?" That is a good question, indeed. In fact, our description is missing something important: once *CALCULATE* computed the new filter context, it applied it to the data model prior to compute the expression.

Now, if a filter context is applied to a table, we already know from the previous chapter that this filter is propagated through relationships from the one side of the relationship to the many side. It turns out that we removed the filter from both DimProductCategory and DimProductSubcategory and, when the new filter is applied to the tables, it is propagated to the fact table, which is on the many side of the chain of relationships starting at DimProductCategory and ending at FactInternetSales. By removing the filters from DimProductCategory and DimProductSubcategory, we also removed their correspondent propagated filters on FactInternetSales.

CALCULATE examples

Now that you have seen the basics of *CALCULATE* (or at least learned why it is so useful), the rest of the chapter is dedicated to various examples of how to use it.

Filtering a single column

The simplest way to use *CALCULATE* is to filter a single column. As an example, assume that you want to create a calculated field that always returns the amount of black products sold, regardless of the selection made in the Color column by the user. The formula is easy to write:

```
SalesAmountBlack :=
    CALCULATE (
        SUM ( FactInternetSales[SalesAmount] ),
        DimProduct[Color] = "Black"
    )
```

If you use the previous formula in a PivotTable, you will get the result shown in Figure 8-4. You can find this example in the companion workbook "CH08-02-CALCULATE - Single Column.xlsx."

Row Labels	SumOfSalesAmount	SalesAmountBlack
Black	8,838,411.96	8,838,411.96
Blue	2,279,096.28	8,838,411.96
Grey		8,838,411.96
Multi	106,470.74	8,838,411.96
NA	435,116.69	8,838,411.96
Red	7,724,330.52	8,838,411.96
Silver	5,113,389.08	8,838,411.96
Silver/Black		8,838,411.96
White	5,106.32	8,838,411.96
Yellow	4,856,755.63	8,838,411.96
Grand Total	29,358,677.22	8,838,411.96

FIGURE 8-4 SalesAmountBlack always shows the sales of black products, regardless of the current filter context.

You can see that the *SalesAmountBlack* field always returns the sales for black products, even if the filter context selects different colors on the rows.

If you focus on the second row (Blue), this is what happened: the formula started the evaluation in a filter context where the color selected was Blue. Then, *CALCULATE* evaluated a new condition (Color = Black) and, when it came the time to apply it to the new filter context, it replaced the existing condition, removing the filter on Blue and replacing it with the filter on Black. This happened for all the colors, and this is why you see the same number for all the rows.

Clearly, because the only column for which *CALCULATE* overrides the selection is the color, other columns maintain their filters. If, for example, you put ProductCategoryName on the columns, you see that the result is always the same for all the colors, but it changes for different categories, as shown in Figure 8-5.

SalesAmountBlack	Column Labels			
Row Labels	Accessories	Bikes	Clothing	Grand Total
Black	72,954.15	8,659,117.30	106,340.51	8,838,411.96
Blue	72,954.15	8,659,117.30	106,340.51	8,838,411.96
Grey	72,954.15	8,659,117.30	106,340.51	8,838,411.96
Multi	72,954.15	8,659,117.30	106,340.51	8,838,411.96
NA	72,954.15	8,659,117.30	106,340.51	8,838,411.96
Red	72,954.15	8,659,117.30	106,340.51	8,838,411.96
Silver	72,954.15	8,659,117.30	106,340.51	8,838,411.96
Silver/Black	72,954.15	8,659,117.30	106,340.51	8,838,411.96
White	72,954.15	8,659,117.30	106,340.51	8,838,411.96
Yellow	72,954.15	8,659,117.30	106,340.51	8,838,411.96
Grand Total	72,954.15	8,659,117.30	106,340.51	8,838,411.96

FIGURE 8-5 SalesAmountBlack overrides only the color, but it still obeys the filtering on other columns.

Filtering a single column is straightforward. A less evident fact is that you can filter only one column at a time. For example, you might want to create a calculated field that computes the sales amount for only the products where the list price is at least twice the standard cost. You can try this formula:

```
HighProfitabilitySales :=
    CALCULATE (
        SUM ( FactInternetSales[SalesAmount] ),
        DimProduct[ListPrice] >= DimProduct[StandardCost] * 2
    )
```

You can see that this time, the condition involves two columns: StandardCost and ListPrice. Even if the condition can be easily evaluated for each product, this syntax is not allowed. The reason is that during its evaluation algorithm, *CALCULATE* cannot determine whether the condition should replace any existing filter on ListPrice, on StandardCost, or on neither of them. In fact, if you try to write the formula above, you will get an error as a result:

Calculation error in measure 'FactInternetSales'[HighProfitabilitySales]: The expression contains multiple columns, but only a single column can be used in a True/False expression that is used as a table filter expression.

There is no way to create such a formula using the *TRUE/FALSE* syntax. If you need to invoke *CALCULATE* using more than one column in the condition, you need to use a different syntax; that is, providing a list of values instead of a *TRUE/FALSE* condition.

The correct way to write the previous formula is to use this syntax:

```
HighProfitabilitySales := CALCULATE (
    SUM ( FactInternetSales[SalesAmount] ),
    FILTER ( DimProduct, DimProduct[ListPrice] >= DimProduct[StandardCost] * 2 )
)
```

Instead of using a *TRUE/FALSE* expression, this time we have used the "list of values" syntax for *CALCULATE*. Moreover, we have not filtered a single column; rather, we have filtered the entire DimProduct table. This way of writing conditions is an extension of the same technique that you used previously using the *ALL* function. There, you used *ALL* on a single column, whereas here, you are using *FILTER* on a complete table. Both functions return a table as a result; the difference is only in the number of columns returned. *ALL* on a single column returns a table with a single column, while *FILTER* on a table returns a table containing all the columns of the filtered table.

What happens is that the condition is evaluated: the result of *FILTER* is a table containing multiple columns (it really contains all the columns of the DimProduct table, since it is a *FILTER* on DimProduct). Thus, when the new condition is inserted into the filter context, in reality all the existing conditions on DimProductare replaced with this new filter. In other words, by using the actual table as the first parameter of the *FILTER* function, we effectively replace all conditions on all the columns of that table.

In Figure 8-6, you can see the HighProfitabilitySales calculated field in action.

Row Labels	SumOfSalesAmount	HighProfitabilitySales
Black	8,838,411.96	179,294.66
Blue	2,279,096.28	110,040.75
Multi	106,470.74	
NA	435,116.69	435,116.69
Red	7,724,330.52	78,027.70
Silver	5,113,389.08	40,307.67
White	5,106.32	5,106.32
Yellow	4,856,755.63	
Grand Total	**29,358,677.22**	**847,893.79**

FIGURE 8-6 HighProfitabilySales shows the sales of only the products with a sufficiently high profit margin.

Having read the previous explanations, you should observe that something is not completely clear here. We said that the *FILTER* expression in *CALCULATE* replaces all the previously existing filters on the DimProduct table, because the table returned by *FILTER* contains all the columns of DimProduct. Nevertheless, the value returned by our formula is different for each and every row.

On the Blue row, for example, HighProfitabilitySales returns the sales of blue products with high profitability, even if it should return the sales of *all* the products, regardless of the color. Either the filter on color has not been replaced, or something more complex is happening. Because we already know that the filter on color has been replaced, we need to investigate more to better understand the flow of evaluation. The following code is the formula for our calculated field (we have numbered the lines to make it easier to refer to the various parts of the formula):

```
1.    HighProfitabilitySales :=
2.    CALCULATE (
3.        SUM ( FactInternetSales[SalesAmount] ),
4.        FILTER (
5.            DimProduct,
6.            DimProduct[ListPrice] >= DimProduct[StandardCost] * 2
7.        )
8.    )
```

The first function is *CALCULATE*. We know that *CALCULATE* evaluates the conditions as its first step. Thus, before doing anything else, *CALCULATE* evaluates the *FILTER* expression starting at line 4.

FILTER is an iterator, and it iterates the DimProduct table (see line 5). We already know that it might not be able to see all theDimProduct table, due to the presence of a filter context. Now, the big question is: Under which filter context is DimProduct at line 5 evaluated? Remember that *CALCULATE* has still not created its new evaluation context. You can deduce, at this point, that the filters of *CALCULATE* are evaluated under the original filter context, not under the filter context created by *CALCULATE*. Although it might seem obvious, this simple consideration is one of the main sources of errors in DAX formulas.

On line 5, the reference to DimProduct really means the portion of DimProduct that is visible under the original filter context that, for the Blue line, shows only the blue products. Thus, *FILTER* will return only blue products with high profitability. Then, *CALCULATE* will remove the filter for the color, but this filter is already incorporated into the result of *FILTER*, leading to the behavior that you are observing. It is important to understand correctly the flow of filters and, most important, to understand that the filter on color is replaced inside *CALCULATE,* but not inside the filters of *CALCULATE.*

To get a complete picture, you can check the following formula:

```
1.  HighProfitabilityALLSales :=
2.  CALCULATE (
3.      SUM ( FactInternetSales[SalesAmount] ),
4.      FILTER (
5.          ALL ( DimProduct ),
6.          DimProduct[ListPrice] >= DimProduct[StandardCost] * 2
7.      )
8.  )
```

This time, at line 5, instead of using FILTER (DimProduct), we used FILTER (ALL (DimProduct)). *FILTER* will not iterate only the blue products, it will always iterate all the products, and the filter on color is replaced inside *CALCULATE.* The resulting behavior is shown in Figure 8-7.

Row Labels	SumOfSalesAmount	HighProfitabilitySales	HighProfitabilityALLSales
Black	8,838,411.96	179,294.66	847,893.79
Blue	2,279,096.28	110,040.75	847,893.79
Grey			847,893.79
Multi	106,470.74		847,893.79
NA	435,116.69	435,116.69	847,893.79
Red	7,724,330.52	78,027.70	847,893.79
Silver	5,113,389.08	40,307.67	847,893.79
Silver/Black			847,893.79
White	5,106.32	5,106.32	847,893.79
Yellow	4,856,755.63		847,893.79
Grand Total	**29,358,677.22**	**847,893.79**	**847,893.79**

FIGURE 8-7 HighProfitabilyALLSales shows that the filter on color is effectively replaced inside *CALCULATE.*

HighProfitabilityALLSales always shows the sales of all high-profitability products, effectively ignoring the preexisting filter on color.

Let's start drawing some conclusions from this first simple example:

- You can use *TRUE/FALSE* conditions inside *CALCULATE,* but, in order to use them, you need to refer only one column in the expression. Otherwise, you will get a syntax error.

- You can use *FILTER* or any other table function as a filter parameter in CALCULATE. In this case, all the columns in the table are part of the new filter context. This means that any existing filter on the same columns will be replaced by the table parameter.

- If you use *FILTER,* then *FILTER* is evaluated in the original filter context. If, on the other hand, you use the *TRUE/FALSE* condition, then the existing filter context is replaced only for the affected column.

Filtering with complex conditions

Because you can use many filters in *CALCULATE*, all of them are put in a logical *AND* when they are used to create the new filter context. Thus, if you want to filter all the black versions of the Mountain-200 bike, you can use an expression like this:

```
CalculateVersion := CALCULATE (
    SUM ( FactInternetSales[SalesAmount] ),
    DimProduct[ModelName] = "Mountain-200",
    DimProduct[Color] = "Black"
)
```

Because the two conditions are put in *AND,* you might think that this formulation of the expression is equivalent:

```
[FILTER Version] = CALCULATE (
    SUM ( FactInternetSales[SalesAmount] ),
    FILTER (
        DimProduct,
        AND (
            DimProduct[ModelName] = "Mountain-200",
            DimProduct[Color] = "Black"
        )
    )
)
```

In reality, the two expressions are different, and this section is dedicated to understanding the reason for this. You have already learned it, but it is worth repeating because of the importance of the underlying concepts and the complexity of the topic. In the formula with *TRUE/FALSE* expressions, the filter context is ignored for both the ModelName and the Color, whereas in the formula with *FILTER*, the filter context prior to the formula being applied is considered for both columns.

Thus, CalculateVersion will always return the sales amount for black Mountain-200 bikes, whereas [FILTER Version] will return the black bikes only when they are already selected in the preexisting context. Otherwise, it will return an empty value. You can observe this behavior in Figure 8-8. You can find this example in the companion workbook "CH08-03-CALCULATE - OR Conditions.xlsx."

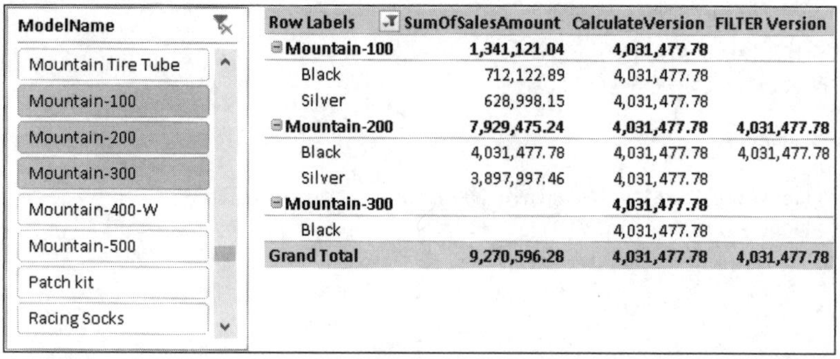

ModelName
Mountain Tire Tube
Mountain-100
Mountain-200
Mountain-300
Mountain-400-W
Mountain-500
Patch kit
Racing Socks

Row Labels	SumOfSalesAmount	CalculateVersion	FILTER Version
Mountain-100	1,341,121.04	4,031,477.78	
Black	712,122.89	4,031,477.78	
Silver	628,998.15	4,031,477.78	
Mountain-200	7,929,475.24	4,031,477.78	4,031,477.78
Black	4,031,477.78	4,031,477.78	4,031,477.78
Silver	3,897,997.46	4,031,477.78	
Mountain-300		4,031,477.78	
Black		4,031,477.78	
Grand Total	9,270,596.28	4,031,477.78	4,031,477.78

FIGURE 8-8 The two formulas result in different computations, as shown in the Mountain-200 row.

The difference is due to the fact that the external filter context is used by *FILTER*. In general, you can look at the following formula:

```
CALCULATE (
    SUM ( FactInternetSales[SalesAmount] ),
    DimProduct[ModelName] = "Mountain-200"
)
```

as equivalent to the next one:

```
CALCULATE (
    SUM ( FactInternetSales[SalesAmount] ),
    FILTER (
        ALL ( DimProduct[ModelName] ),
        DimProduct[ModelName] = "Mountain-200"
    )
)
```

In the second formula, by using ALL (DimProduct[ModelName]), we are explicitly asking to ignore the current filter context, just as for the ModelName column. We cannot overstress the importance of understanding the behavior of these formulas. In fact, even though the expressions used here are only academic, you will encounter similar scenarios when writing your own expressions, and you can be sure that, sooner or later, you will see strange results, whose meaning can be completely understood and corrected only by carefully looking at the context behavior.

Working in a single column, the equivalence stated above works fine. In our example, we have two columns, and you might be tempted to extend the equivalence to a multicolumn scenario with the following formulation:

```
[FILTER ALL Version] = CALCULATE (
    SUM ( FactInternetSales[SalesAmount] ),
    FILTER (
        ALL ( DimProduct ),
        AND (
            DimProduct[ModelName] = "Mountain-200",
            DimProduct[Color] = "Black"
        )
    )
)
```

This time, we tried to use ALL (DimProducts), so as to ignore the filter context on both columns by means of ignoring the filter context on the entire table. Unfortunately, even this formula does not achieve our goal because, by ignoring the filter context on the entire table, we still get a different behavior even if, in order to correctly understand it, we need to make the PivotTable more complex.

In Figure 8-9, we added the category name on the rows and filtered two different models, belonging to two different categories: Accessories and Bikes.

ModelName		Row Labels	SumOfSalesAmount	CalculateVersion	FILTER Version	FILTER ALL Version
Mountain Tire Tube		Accessories	7,307.39			4,031,477.78
Mountain-100		⊟Mountain-200				4,031,477.78
Mountain-200		Black				4,031,477.78
Mountain-300		Silver				4,031,477.78
Mountain-400-W		⊟Patch kit	7,307.39			4,031,477.78
Mountain-500		NA	7,307.39			4,031,477.78
Patch kit		⊟Bikes	7,929,475.24	4,031,477.78	4,031,477.78	4,031,477.78
Racing Socks		⊟Mountain-200	7,929,475.24	4,031,477.78	4,031,477.78	4,031,477.78
		Black	4,031,477.78	4,031,477.78	4,031,477.78	4,031,477.78
		Silver	3,897,997.46	4,031,477.78		4,031,477.78
		⊟Patch kit		4,031,477.78		4,031,477.78
		NA		4,031,477.78		4,031,477.78
		Grand Total	7,936,782.63	4,031,477.78	4,031,477.78	4,031,477.78

FIGURE 8-9 Using *FILTER* and *ALL* on the DimProduct table still does not solve the scenario.

As shown in Figure 8-9, the FILTER ALL Version ignores the filter context on the entire table, showing the value even for the Accessories category, for which the CALCULATE version shows a blank value. The reason is that the CALCULATE version ignores the filter context for the color and model name only, whereas the ALL version ignores the filter context on the entire table, ignoring the category too.

In order to find the correct formula, we need to think about the exact result we want to compute. We need to provide to *FILTER* neither the DimProduct table (because it contains the full original filter context) nor the ALL(DimProduct) result (because it contains too many rows). We need to compute a DimProduct table-based result in which the filters on ModelName and Color have been removed, but any other existing filter is still active. We already know a function that lets us work on the filter context in this granular way: it is *CALCULATE*. The only problem is that *CALCULATE* needs an expression that returns a single value, and this time, we want to return a full table because we need it as a parameter of the *FILTER* function. Luckily, there is a companion to *CALCULATE*, called *CALCULATETABLE*, which returns a table instead of a single value.

CALCULATETABLE works in an identical way to CALCULATE, the only difference is in the type of result. The next formula performs exactly what we need: it removes the filter context from both ModelName and Color, letting other filters flow inside the FILTER function:

```
[CALC TABLE] := CALCULATE (
    SUM ( FactInternetSales[SalesAmount] ),
    FILTER (
        CALCULATETABLE (
            DimProduct,
            ALL ( DimProduct[ModelName] ),
            ALL ( DimProduct[Color] )
        ),
        AND (
            DimProduct[ModelName] = "Mountain-200",
            DimProduct[Color] = "Black"
        )
    )
)
```

As shown in Figure 8-10, this last formula computes the correct value.

ModelName (slicer): Mountain Tire Tube, Mountain-100, Mountain-200, Mountain-300, Mountain-400-W, Mountain-500, Patch kit, Racing Socks

Row Labels	CalculateVersion	FILTER Version	FILTER ALL Version	CALC TABLE
Accessories			4,031,477.78	
Mountain-200			4,031,477.78	
Black			4,031,477.78	
Silver			4,031,477.78	
Patch kit			4,031,477.78	
NA			4,031,477.78	
Bikes	4,031,477.78	4,031,477.78	4,031,477.78	4,031,477.78
Mountain-200	4,031,477.78	4,031,477.78	4,031,477.78	4,031,477.78
Black	4,031,477.78	4,031,477.78	4,031,477.78	
Silver	4,031,477.78		4,031,477.78	4,031,477.78
Patch kit	4,031,477.78		4,031,477.78	4,031,477.78
NA	4,031,477.78		4,031,477.78	4,031,477.78
Grand Total	4,031,477.78	4,031,477.78	4,031,477.78	4,031,477.78

FIGURE 8-10 The usage of CALCULATETABLE results in correct values being computed.

Why is this digression about equivalent results so important? Because knowing the correct technique to transform a TRUE/FALSE filter into a FILTER equivalent will greatly help you with conditions that are more complex. For example, if you wanted to express an OR condition instead of AND, you need to use this technique, because different TRUE/FALSE arguments in CALCULATE are always considered an AND condition.

In this section you have seen that, as soon as you use more than one column or when you want to slightly update a formula or make more complex conditions, the results become hard to understand. Even seasoned DAX programmers often find it hard to follow the evaluation path. Thus, do not be scared by the complexity of this section. Only experience will lead you to a natural path where you will learn how to read formulas at first glance.

Using *CALCULATE* inside a row context

We have previously discussed in this chapter that *CALCULATE* does another important task; that is, it transforms any existing row context into an equivalent filter context. This behavior is not very intuitive and often makes the flow of evaluation harder to understand. Nevertheless, once you master this feature of *CALCULATE,* you will find that it is really useful. You can look at this example in the companion workbook "CH08-04-CALCULATE - Context Transition.xlsx."

To illustrate the behavior, you are going to create a calculated column (inside which, as we already know, there is a row context) containing a *CALCULATE* expression. Let's start in an easy way. You define a calculated column, in the DimProduct table, containing the following DAX expression:

```
SumOfListPrice = SUM ( DimProduct[ListPrice] )
```

There is nothing special in this expression; it sums all the list prices of all the products. You have learned in the previous chapter that because the expression is evaluated within a row context and without a filter context, it returns the grand total of the list prices for all the products, not the list price of the product on which it is evaluated. You can see the behavior in Figure 8-11.

[SumOfListPri... ▾		*fx* =SUM (DimProduct[ListPrice])			
Produc.. 🔒 ▾	ProductAlternateKey ▾	EnglishProductName ▾	ListPrice ▾	SumOfListPrice ▾
1	AR-5381	Adjustable Race		$295,326.40
2	BA-8327	Bearing Ball		$295,326.40
12	CR-9981	Crown Race		$295,326.40
14	DC-8732	Decal 1		$295,326.40
15	DC-9824	Decal 2		$295,326.40
22	FW-1000	Flat Washer 1		$295,326.40

FIGURE 8-11 SumOfListPrice, computed inside a calculated column, returns the grand total of list prices.

Now you are going to create a new calculated column with a slightly modified version of the expression, this time involving *CALCULATE:*

```
SumOfListPriceCalc = CALCULATE ( SUM ( DimProduct[ListPrice] ) )
```

What is this? *CALCULATE* has a single expression parameter? Where have the filters gone? Nowhere. In fact, we are using *CALCULATE* in its simplest form. We said earlier that the only mandatory parameter of *CALCULATE* is the first one, so it is perfectly legal to invoke CALCULATE without any filters. In such a case, *CALCULATE* does not change the existing filter context with other conditions, but it still maintain the behavior you are learning now; it takes the existing row context and transforms it into an equivalent filter context.

Thus, *CALCULATE* searches for existing row contexts, and it finds that there is one, on the DimProduct table, coming from the fact that it is being executed inside a calculated column definition. *CALCULATE* takes this row context, removes it, and replaces it with a filter context that contains only the row currently iterated by the row context (this is done by applying a filter on every column corresponding to the value of that column in the current row). We refer to this behavior as a *context transition*. Generally, we say that *CALCULATE* performs a context transition, from row to filter, for all the row contexts existing before its invocation.

What happens, at this point, to the result of the calculated column? This time, the expression *SUM* (DimProduct[ListPrice]) is computed inside a filter context, which contains only the current row of the row context, and the row context is no longer active because of the context transition performed by *CALCULATE*. It turns out that the result this time is the list price of the product, as shown in Figure 8-12.

[SumOfListPri... ▾		*fx* =CALCULATE (SUM (DimProduct[ListPrice]))				
Produc... ▾	ProductAlternateKey ▾	EnglishProductName ▾	ListPrice ▾	SumOfListPrice ▾	SumOfListPriceCalc ▾
231	LJ-0192-M	Long-Sleeve Logo Jerse...	$49.99	$295,326.40	$49.99
232	LJ-0192-L	Long-Sleeve Logo Jerse...	$48.07	$295,326.40	$48.07
233	LJ-0192-L	Long-Sleeve Logo Jerse...	$48.07	$295,326.40	$48.07
234	LJ-0192-L	Long-Sleeve Logo Jerse...	$49.99	$295,326.40	$49.99
235	LJ-0192-X	Long-Sleeve Logo Jerse...	$48.07	$295,326.40	$48.07
236	LJ-0192-X	Long-Sleeve Logo Jerse...	$48.07	$295,326.40	$48.07
237	LJ-0192-X	Long-Sleeve Logo Jerse...	$49.99	$295,326.40	$49.99

FIGURE 8-12 Using *CALCULATE*, the row context has been transformed into a filter context, changing the result.

The first time you observe this behavior, you may find it hard to understand why it has been designed in this way. After you will start using this feature, however, it is something you will love because of the powerful formulas you will be able to create thanks to it.

Moreover, there is another interesting side effect of context transition. As you might remember from the previous chapter, filter context and row context behave in different ways regarding relationships: the row context does not automatically propagate through relationships, whereas the filter context propagates from the one side of the relationship to the many side. Thus, when the context transition happens, it might be the case that other tables are filtered because of the transition. You can observe this behavior if, instead of summing the list price, you create two new calculated columns, still in the DimProduct table, with these definitions:

```
SalesAmount      = SUM ( FactInternetSales[SalesAmount] )
SalesAmountCalc  = CALCULATE ( SUM ( FactInternetSales[SalesAmount] ) )
```

In Figure 8-13, you can see the result, which is obviously different.

Produc...	ProductAlternateKey	EnglishProductName	ListPrice	SalesAmount	SalesAmountCalc
312	BK-R93R-48	Road-150 Red, 48	$3,578.27	$29,358,677.22	$1,205,876.99
310	BK-R93R-62	Road-150 Red, 62	$3,578.27	$29,358,677.22	$1,202,298.72
313	BK-R93R-52	Road-150 Red, 52	$3,578.27	$29,358,677.22	$1,080,637.54
314	BK-R93R-56	Road-150 Red, 56	$3,578.27	$29,358,677.22	$1,055,589.65
311	BK-R93R-44	Road-150 Red, 44	$3,578.27	$29,358,677.22	$1,005,493.87
361	BK-M68B-42	Mountain-200 Black, 42	$2,294.99	$29,358,677.22	$979,960.73
353	BK-M68S-38	Mountain-200 Silver, 38	$2,319.99	$29,358,677.22	$979,035.78

FIGURE 8-13 Context transition induced by *CALCULATE* affects the filtering of related tables.

Because this time we sum rows from the sales table, which has a relationship with the products, the presence of *CALCULATE* and the related context transition filters the sales table, showing only the sales of the product in the considered row. Thus, the SalesAmount column contains the grand total of all sales and the SalesAmountCalc one contains the sales of the current product.

Please note that context transition happens for all active row contexts when *CALCULATE* is executed. You might have more than one row context on different tables. For example, if you use *SUMX* to iterate the customers in a calculated column created in the DimProduct table, then both row contexts will be converted to filter contexts and the sales table will feel the filter of both. Look at the following expression:

```
SalesWithSUMX = SUMX (
    DimCustomers,
    CALCULATE ( SUM ( FactInternetSales[SalesAmount] ) )
)
```

In this code, the *SUM* inside *CALCULATE* is executed in a filter context that shows only the sales of the current customer and of the current product. The easiest way to remember this rule is to think that inside *CALCULATE* there is no row context. Rather, only a filter context is present.

Understanding this behavior is important because of another hidden aspect of DAX. Up to now, we have always written the expression inside *CALCULATE* using functions and columns. But, as we know, the DAX definition contains calculated fields too. You can invoke a calculated field from inside a calculated column. Thus, suppose that you define a calculated field SumOfSalesAmount in this way:

```
SumOfSalesAmount := SUM ( FactInternetSales[SalesAmount] )
```

Then you can redefine the SalesWithSUMX calculated column using this simpler code:

```
SalesWithSUMX = SUMX (
    DimCustomers,
    CALCULATE ( [SumOfSalesAmount] )
)
```

The presence of *CALCULATE* suggests that context transition happens. The issue is that, in DAX, whenever you invoke a calculated field from inside a DAX expression, the calculated field is always called inside an automatic *CALCULATE* that is added by DAX itself. Thus, the previous expression has a behavior that is identical to the following one:

```
SalesWithSUMX = SUMX (
    DimCustomers,
    [SumOfSalesAmount]
)
```

This time, no *CALCULATE* is visible in the formula, and yet context transition happens because of the automatic *CALCULATE* added by DAX.

This is the reason why it is important that you get used to writing your code in a way that differentiates between columns and calculated fields. The de facto standard used by DAX authors is to avoid putting the table name in front of measures and always prefix columns with the table name. In fact, in the previous formula, the absence of the table name before SumOfSalesAmount makes it clear that SumOfSalesAmount is a calculated field, and because of that, you know that context transition happens.

We will use these features extensively in the next chapters, when we will start to write complex DAX code to solve specific scenarios.

Understanding circular dependencies

When you design a data model, you should pay attention to a complex topic, which is that of circular dependencies in formulas. In this section, you are going to learn what circular dependencies are and how to avoid them in your workbook.

Before speaking about circular dependencies, it is worth discussing simple, linear dependencies. Let's look at an example with the following calculated column:

```
DimProduct[Profit] = DimProduct[ListPrice] - DimProduct[StandardCost]
```

The new calculated column depends on two columns of the same table. In such a case, we say that the column Profit depends on ListPrice and StandardCost. You might then create a new column, like ProfitPct, with the following formula:

```
DimProduct[ProfitPct] = DimProduct[Profit] / DimProduct[ListPrice]
```

It is clear that ProfitPct depends on Profit and ListPrice. Thus, when Microsoft PowerPivot needs to compute the calculated columns in the table, it recognizes that ProfitPct will be computed only after Profit has been calculated and stored. Otherwise, it will not be able to recover a valid value for the formula.

Linear dependency is not something you should normally worry about. It is used internally to detect the correct order of computation of calculated columns during the data model refresh. On a normal data model, with many calculated columns, the dependency of calculations turns into a complex graph that, again, the engine handles gracefully.

Circular dependency is when a loop appears in this graph. For example, a clear situation where circular dependency appears is if you try to modify the definition of Profit to this formula:

```
DimProduct[Profit] := DimProduct[ProfitPct] * DimProduct[ListPrice]
```

Because ProfitPct depends on Profit and, in this new formula, Profit depends on ProfitPct, PowerPivot refuses to modify the formula, returning the error shown in Figure 8-14:

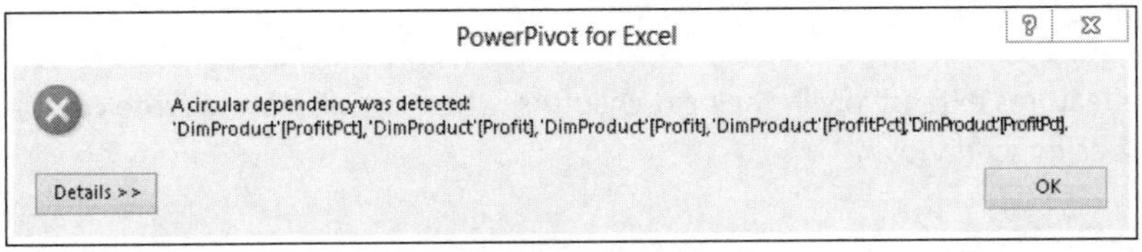

FIGURE 8-14 When circular dependencies are found, PowerPivot shows an error message.

Up to now, you have learned what circular dependencies are from the point of view of columns; that is, you have detected the existence of a dependency by looking at the expression, without paying attention to the table content. Nevertheless, there is a more subtle and complex type of dependency that is introduced by the usage of *CALCULATE* and/or filters inside any expression. Let's examine this topic with an example, starting from a subset of columns of DimProduct, as shown in Figure 8-15. You can find this in the companion workbook "CH08-05-CALCULATE – Circular Dependency.xlsx."

ProductKey	ProductAlternateKey	ListPrice	StandardCost
314	BK-R93R-56	$3,578.27	2171.2942
313	BK-R93R-52	$3,578.27	2171.2942
312	BK-R93R-48	$3,578.27	2171.2942
311	BK-R93R-44	$3,578.27	2171.2942
310	BK-R93R-62	$3,578.27	2171.2942
347	BK-M82S-48	$3,399.99	1912.1544
346	BK-M82S-44	$3,399.99	1912.1544
345	BK-M82S-42	$3,399.99	1912.1544
344	BK-M82S-38	$3,399.99	1912.1544
351	BK-M82B-48	$3,374.99	1898.0944

FIGURE 8-15 This subset of columns of DimProduct is useful to understand circular dependencies.

We want you to understand the dependency list for a new calculated column that uses the *CALCULATE* function, like the following one:

```
SumOfListPrice := CALCULATE ( SUM( DimProduct[ListPrice] ) )
```

At first glance, it may seem that the column depends only on ListPrice, as this is the only column used in the formula. Nevertheless, we used *CALCULATE* to transform the current row context into a filter context. Thus, if we expand the meaning of the *CALCULATE* call, the formula really says:

Sum the value of ListPrice for all the rows in the DimProduct table that have the same value for ProductKey, ProductAlternateKey, StandardCost, and ListPrice.

If you read the formula in this way, it is now clear that the formula depends on all the columns of DimProduct because the newly introduced filter context will filter all the columns of the table. The resulting table is shown in Figure 8-16.

ProductKey	ProductAlternateKey	ListPrice	StandardCost	SumOfListPrice
314	BK-R93R-56	$3,578.27	2171.2942	$3,578.27
313	BK-R93R-52	$3,578.27	2171.2942	$3,578.27
312	BK-R93R-48	$3,578.27	2171.2942	$3,578.27
311	BK-R93R-44	$3,578.27	2171.2942	$3,578.27
310	BK-R93R-62	$3,578.27	2171.2942	$3,578.27
347	BK-M82S-48	$3,399.99	1912.1544	$3,399.99
346	BK-M82S-44	$3,399.99	1912.1544	$3,399.99
345	BK-M82S-42	$3,399.99	1912.1544	$3,399.99
344	BK-M82S-38	$3,399.99	1912.1544	$3,399.99
351	BK-M82B-48	$3,374.99	1898.0944	$3,374.99
350	BK-M82B-44	$3,374.99	1898.0944	$3,374.99
349	BK-M82B-42	$3,374.99	1898.0944	$3,374.99

FIGURE 8-16 Here, you can see the DimProduct table with the SumOfListPrice calculated column.

Now, we might try to define a new calculated column, using the very same formula, in the same table. Thus, we try to add NewSumOfListPrice with the following formula, which is identical to the previous one:

```
NewSumOfListPrice := CALCULATE ( SUM ( DimProduct[ListPrice] ) )
```

Surprisingly, PowerPivot refuses to create this new formula and returns the error shown in Figure 8-17.

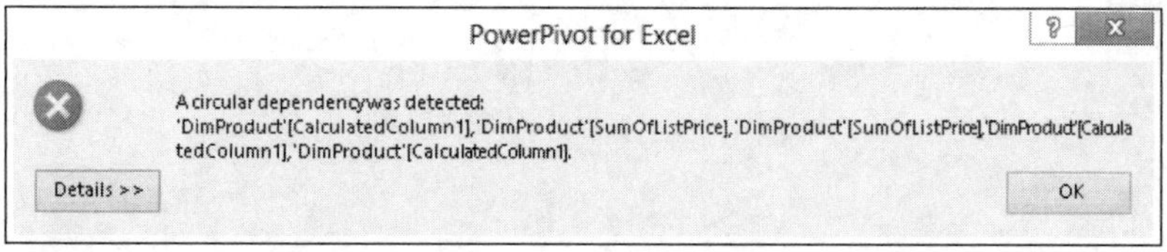

PowerPivot for Excel

A circular dependency was detected:
'DimProduct'[CalculatedColumn1], 'DimProduct'[SumOfListPrice], 'DimProduct'[SumOfListPrice],'DimProduct'[CalculatedColumn1], 'DimProduct'[CalculatedColumn1].

Details >>   OK

FIGURE 8-17 Adding a new *CALCULATE* on the same table raises an error.

PowerPivot has detected a circular dependency in the formula that it did not detect before. We did not change anything in the formula, so the error seems strange. But it turns out that something has changed: it is the number of columns in the table. If we were able to add NewSumOfListPrice to the table, we would reach a situation where the two formulas have these meanings:

- **SumOfListPrice** Sum the value of ListPrice for all the rows in the DimProduct table that have the same value for ProductKey, ProductAlternateKey, StandardCost, ListPrice, and NewSumOfListPrice.

- **NewSumOfListPrice** Sum the value of ListPrice for all the rows in the DimProduct table that have the same value for ProductKey, ProductAlternateKey, StandardCost, ListPrice, and SumOfListPrice.

Any calculated column added to the data model becomes part of the filter context introduced by *CALCULATE* and, as a consequence, all the calculated columns are part of the dependency list. Reading the previous definition, it is clear that there is a circular dependency between the two formulas, and this is the reason why PowerPivot refuses to allow the creation of the NewSumOfListPrice column.

Understanding this error is not easy. But, on the other hand, finding a solution is pretty straightforward, even if not intuitive. The problem is that any calculated column containing *CALCULATE* (or a call to any measure, which adds an automatic *CALCULATE*) creates a dependency from all the columns of the table. The scenario would be different if the table had a row identifier (a primary key, in database terms). If the table has a column that acts as a row identifier, then all columns containing a *CALCULATE* could depend on just the row identifier, reducing their dependency list to a single column.

In the DimProduct table, there is a column that can uniquely identify each row: namely, ProductKey. To mark the ProductKey as a row identifier, you have two options:

- You can create a relationship between any table and DimProduct using ProductKey as the destination column. Performing this operation will ensure that ProductKey is a unique value for DimProduct.

- You can manually set the Row Identifier property for ProductKey using the Table Behavior button on the Advanced tab of the PowerPivot window, as shown in Figure 8-18.

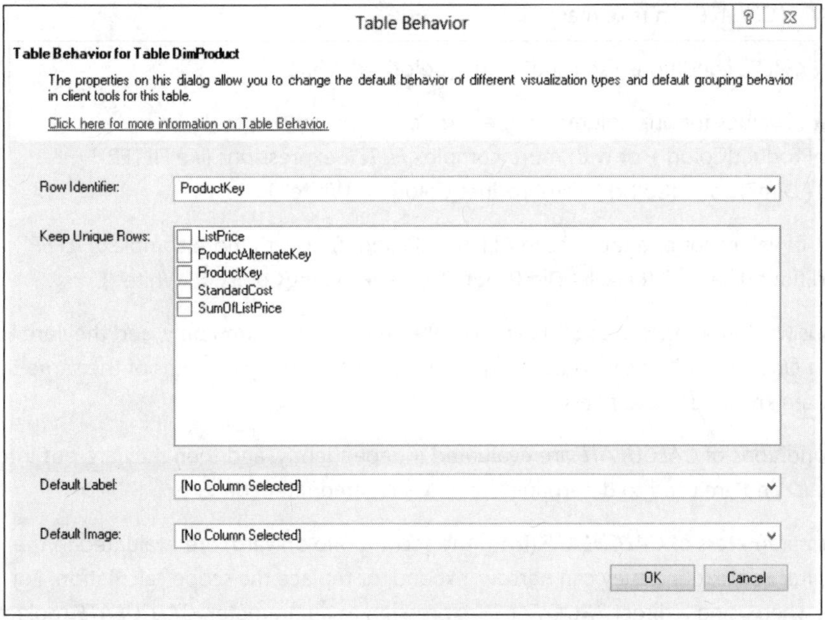

FIGURE 8-18 You can update the Row Identifier property in the Table Behavior window.

One of these operations will make PowerPivot learn that the table has a row identifier and, in such a scenario, you will be able to define the NewSumOfListPrice column avoiding circular dependency.

As a final point, it is always a good idea to set the Row Identifier property of a table if such a column exists in the data model, because PowerPivot will use this information to optimize all calculations. This does not mean that you need to add a row identifier to all your tables. In fact, if you do so, you might end up wasting precious memory with unused columns. Set the row identifier property if the column is already in the database and you need it for calculations; otherwise, skip this step.

CALCULATE rules

It is useful, at this point, to recap the way *CALCULATE* works. You can use this set of rules to test your knowledge of *CALCULATE:* If you can read and understand all of them, then you are on the right track to becoming a real DAX master.

1. *CALCULATE* and *CALCULATETABLE* are the only functions in DAX that operate on the filter context, modifying it so that expressions can be computed in different filter contexts.

2. *CALCULATE* has only one required parameter, which is the expression to evaluate. Other parameters are filters that will be used to build the new filter context. They could be omitted if you only want to invoke *CALCULATE* to perform context transition.

3. Filters in *CALCULATE* can take many shapes:

   a. *TRUE/FALSE* conditions like DimProduct[Color] = "White".

   b. A list of values for one column, in the form of a one-column table, as in ALL (DimProduct[Color]), or with more complex *FILTER* expressions like FILTER (ALL (DimProduct[Color]), DimProduct[Color] = "White").

   c. A list of values for one table, as in ALL (DimProduct) or with more complex *FILTER* conditions, like FILTER (ALL (DimProduct), DimProduct[Color] = "White").

4. Conditions written using 3(a) or 3(b) can operate on a single column only, and they are known as *column filters.* Conditions written using 3(c) can work on many columns of the same table, and they are known as *table filters.*

5. All the conditions of *CALCULATE* are evaluated independently, and then they are put into a logical *AND* and are used to determine the newly created filter context.

6. The filter parameters of *CALCULATE* (from the second one onward) are evaluated in the original filter context and they can narrow, expand, or replace the scope calculation. For example, when using a direct *TRUE/FALSE* expression as a parameter, *CALCULATE* replaces the original filter context, whereas when passing an expression that uses *FILTER* on a table, *CALCULATE* takes the original filter context into account.

7. The first parameter of *CALCULATE* (the expression to evaluate) is evaluated in the newly created filter context after the evaluation of other *CALCULATE* arguments (filter parameters).

Understanding *ALLSELECTED*

ALLSELECTED is a function that is useful whenever you want to perform computations using the selection in the PivotTable as one of the parameters. Imagine, for example, that you want to build a report like the one shown in Figure 8-19. You can find this example in the companion workbook "CH08-06-ALLSELECTED.xlsx."

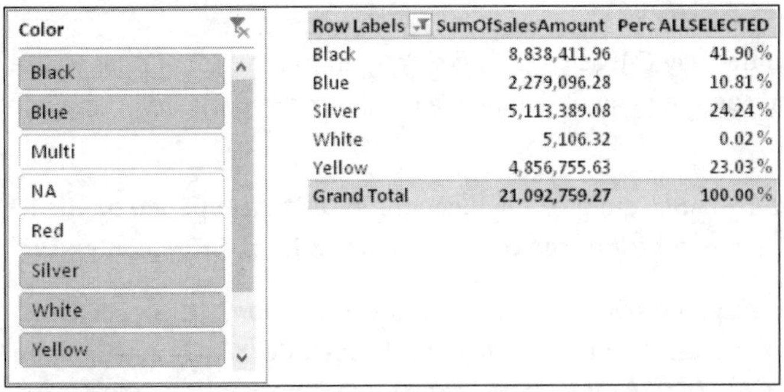

FIGURE 8-19 The *Perc ALLSELECTED* calculated field shows the percentage against the total of the column.

The report shows the percentage of the current row value against the total of the column. What makes this percentage difficult to compute is the fact that the product color is used both as a slicer (in the example, we removed Multi, NA, and Red from the available colors) and on the rows. If you use the knowledge gained so far, you might try this formula:

```
PercALL :=
[SumOfSalesAmount]
/
CALCULATE (
    [SumOfSalesAmount],
    ALL ( DimProduct[Color] )
)
```

Using ALL (DimProduct[Color]), you remove constraints from the Color column and try to compute the total at the column level. Unfortunately, *ALL* removes all the constraints, both the one coming from the row and the one coming from the slicer, resulting in a wrong percentage. In Figure 8-20, you can see the *Perc ALL* formula in the PivotTable.

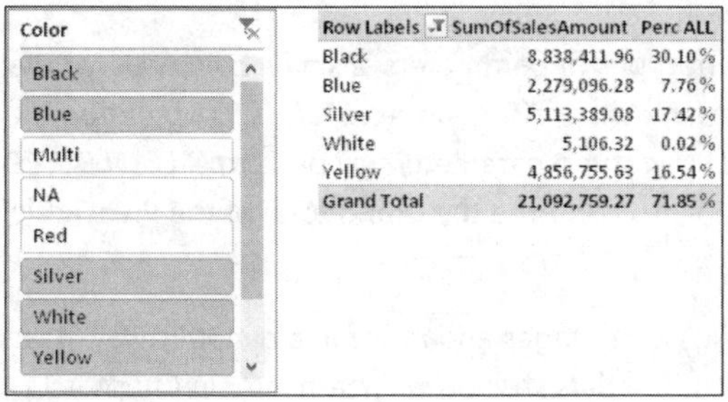

Color		Row Labels	SumOfSalesAmount	Perc ALL
Black		Black	8,838,411.96	30.10%
Blue		Blue	2,279,096.28	7.76%
Multi		Silver	5,113,389.08	17.42%
NA		White	5,106.32	0.02%
Red		Yellow	4,856,755.63	16.54%
Silver		Grand Total	21,092,759.27	71.85%
White				
Yellow				

FIGURE 8-20 The percentage computed by *Perc ALL* is not correct here because it is a percentage against *ALL* colors.

The issue here is that the denominator is computed for all the colors, even if the user has selected only some of them with the slicer. Thus, for each row, you compute the percentage of that line against a denominator that is bigger than the total shown in the PivotTable.

What you need here is a function that does not return all the colors, but only the ones selected by the user in the original filter context (that is, the filter context from the complete PivotTable). This kind of computation is known as VisualTotals because it uses as the total not the total of the data model, but the one selected by the user. This function is called *ALLSELECTED*. Suppose that you write the formula in this way:

```
PercALLSELECTED :=
[SumOfSalesAmount]
/
CALCULATE (
    [SumOfSalesAmount],
    ALLSELECTED ( DimProduct[Color] )
)
```

The result will be correct, as shown in Figure 8-21.

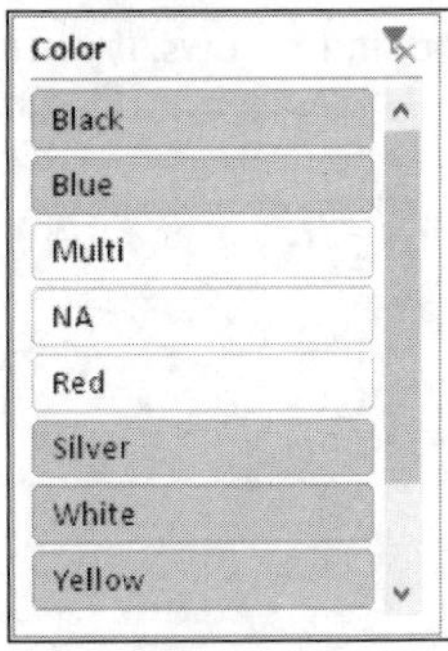

Color		Row Labels	SumOfSalesAmount	Perc ALL	Perc ALLSELECTED
Black		Black	8,838,411.96	30.10%	41.90%
Blue		Blue	2,279,096.28	7.76%	10.81%
Multi		Silver	5,113,389.08	17.42%	24.24%
NA		White	5,106.32	0.02%	0.02%
Red		Yellow	4,856,755.63	16.54%	23.03%
Silver		Grand Total	21,092,759.27	71.85%	100.00%
White					
Yellow					

FIGURE 8-21 Using *ALLSELECTED*, you can easily compute the total against the user-selected color values.

ALLSELECTED does not return all the values for a column; instead, it returns only the values that are visible in the original filter context; that is, that of the PivotTable. In other words, *ALLSELECTED* ignores filters on the rows and columns of the PivotTable and considers the ones used to compute the grand total.

ALLSELECTED can be used with three different types of parameters: a single column, a whole table, or no parameter at all. ALLSELECTED (DimProduct) will perform an *ALLSELECTED* operation on all the columns of the table, whereas *ALLSELECTED ()* with no parameter will perform *ALLSELECTED* on all the tables in the data model, making it possible to compute the grand total of the PivotTable with no filters on rows and columns.

ALLSELECTED is mainly used when computing percentages and ratios in a dynamic way. It is also useful to create dynamic Key Performance Indicators (KPIs), as you will learn later in Chapter 11, "Shaping reports."

CHAPTER 9

Using hierarchies

In the previous chapters, you have learned both basic and advanced features of Microsoft PowerPivot for Excel, and, in the meantime, you have learned the basics of data modeling. Being a good data modeler is one of the attitudes that is required to become a real PowerPivot master. Before now, we have described the data model as the set of tables and relationships that you have loaded into PowerPivot. In reality, the term *data model* has a broader meaning: The data model contains tables and relationships, but it also contains calculated columns and calculated fields, which are entities that you create in Microsoft Excel and that enrich the data model, delivering a better user experience. Other entities belong to the data model, like hierarchies, perspectives, and other information, that are useful to create beautiful reports.

In this chapter, you will learn how to enrich your data model by using standard hierarchies and parent/child (P/C) hierarchies. Understanding these topics is not mandatory if all you need is a simple report, but if you plan to create a report that will be shared on Microsoft SharePoint by many users who expect to be able to browse data in a simple way, then you will need to consider adding hierarchies to the data model and handling P/C hierarchies correctly.

Understanding hierarchies

You already know the way an Excel model appears to a user and the way that the distinct values in each column in your data model are put on the rows or columns of a PivotTable. This provides a flexible way of building queries. The only issue is that every new level of nesting that you add to the row or column axis requires some effort: first, you must find what you want to add, and then you need to click and drag it to where you want it to appear.

Hierarchies provide a solution to these problems by providing a convenient way to do a one-click selection that shows the full analytical path. *Hierarchies* are predefined pathways through your data that help you move from one level to another in a meaningful way. A typical example of a hierarchy would be in a Date table, where you often want to view data at the Year level, then move on to Quarter, Month, and Date; a hierarchy allows you to define just such a path. Figure 9-1 shows what a hierarchy looks like in an Excel PivotTable. You can find this data model in the companion workbook "CH09-01-Hierarchies.xlsx."

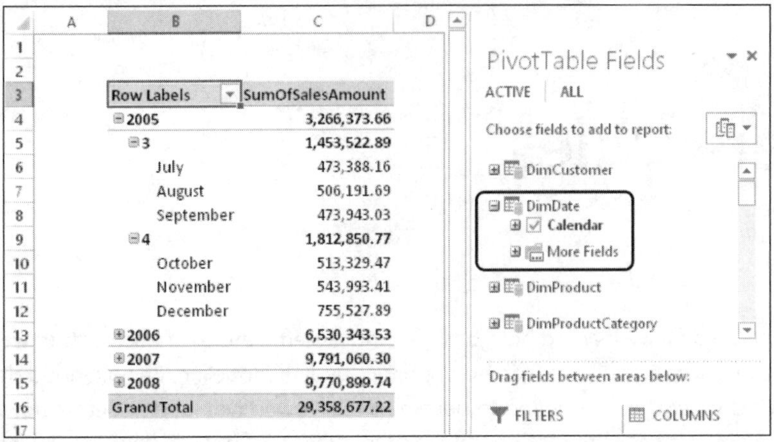

FIGURE 9-1 The Calendar hierarchy makes it easier to select a predefined navigation path.

A hierarchy like this can save you a lot of time by helping to find what you are looking for quickly. With a hierarchy, there is only one thing to drag to a PivotTable, and once you have done this, you just have to double-click an item to go to it, and repeat the process until you get to the level of detail you require.

Hierarchies turn out to be useful in Power View reports too. By clicking a hierarchy, you can add all columns of the hierarchy to a report, greatly enhancing the user experience, because a standard report can be created with fewer clicks and without having to worry about which columns are the more appropriate for the report. In Figure 9-2, you can see that you can simply select the Calendar hierarchy to add Year, Quarter, and Month to a Power View report.

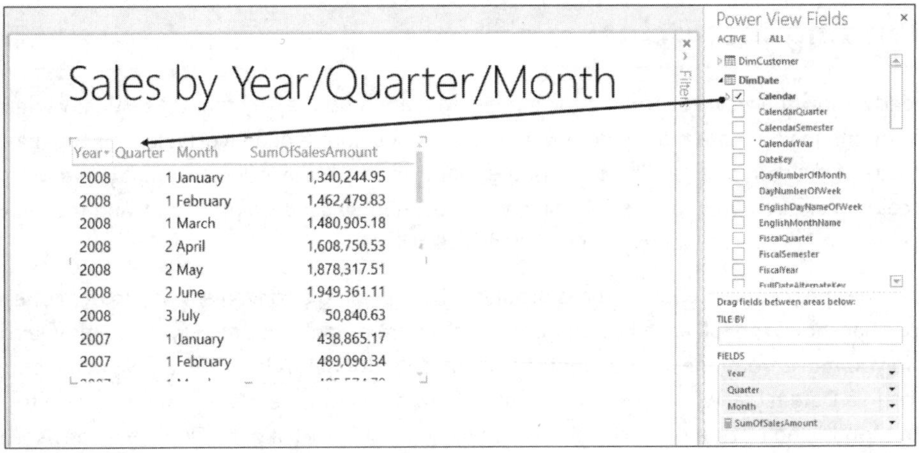

FIGURE 9-2 Hierarchies are useful for Power View too.

When to build hierarchies

There are several advantages in building hierarchies, but that does not mean you should build hundreds of them in every table. Here are a few guidelines on when to build hierarchies and when not to:

- Hierarchies should be built when there is an underlying pattern in the data itself, because it represents a natural way for you to explore the data. You have already seen a hierarchy going from Year to Quarter to Month to Date; other common examples include hierarchies going from Country to State to City to ZIP Code to Customer, or going from Product Category to Product SubCategory to Product.

- Hierarchies tend to be more useful the more levels they have. There is no point in building a hierarchy with just one level in it; hierarchies with two levels may not provide much benefit either. Clearly, a hierarchy with 15 levels is probably too complex, and you will find yourself having to expand too many levels before you reach the level of detail that is useful for the report.

- With the ease of use that hierarchies bring, there is also rigidity. If you have defined a hierarchy that goes from Product Category to Brand and the underlying columns are hidden, then you will not be able to define a report that places Brand before Product Category, nor will you be able to place Product Category and Brand on opposing axes in a report.

Building hierarchies

Essentially two steps are involved in building a hierarchy. First, you need to prepare your data appropriately; once you have done that, you can build the hierarchy in your table. The initial data preparation step may be performed inside the Excel model itself; in this chapter, we will demonstrate a number of techniques to do this.

The main advantages of doing your data preparation inside the Excel model are that you do not need to ask IT to shape the data for you when building a hierarchy, and that you have the power of DAX at your disposal, which may make it easier and faster to write the logic involved. Alternatively, if you do not feel comfortable preparing data yourself, that task may be performed by your IT department, in a view or in the SQL query used to load data into the tables in your Excel model.

Hierarchies are designed in the Diagram view of the PowerPivot window. To create a hierarchy in a table, you can either click the Create Hierarchy button at the upper-right corner of the table, or select one or more columns in the table and then right-click and select Create Hierarchy to use those columns as the levels in a new hierarchy. To add a new level to an existing hierarchy, you can drag a column into it at the appropriate position, or you can right-click the column and select Add To Hierarchy, and then select the name of the hierarchy you wish to add it to. Once a hierarchy has been created, the levels in it can be moved up or down or deleted by right-clicking them. A hierarchy can also be renamed by right-clicking its name.

Tip The levels of the hierarchy are created in the same order that the columns were selected prior to the hierarchy creation. Thus, if you know in advance that you want to create a year-month-date hierarchy, it is a good practice to select first the year, then the month, then the date (holding the Shift key during selection) and, finally, click Create Hierarchy. This will save you from having to reorder the hierarchy levels later.

In Figure 9-3, you can see what a hierarchy looks like in the PowerPivot window.

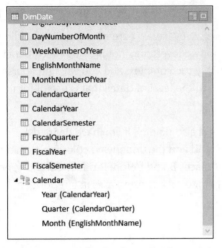

FIGURE 9-3 A hierarchy shown in Diagram view of the PowerPivot window.

Once a column from a table has been included as a level in a hierarchy, the column can be hidden by right-clicking it and selecting Hide From Client Tools. This means that it is only visible as a level in the hierarchy. The decision whether to hide columns is always hard because if you hide a column, then you will only be able to select it using the hierarchy, and you will have a more rigid data model. On the other hand, doing this reduces the number of columns visible in the PivotTable, making it easier to select columns. If you make the wrong decision, you can always change your mind and unhide columns from the PowerPivot window.

Columns included in a hierarchy can be renamed by clicking the level and selecting Rename. Renaming is sometimes useful when you build technical columns (remember that technical columns are columns useful for the data model, but not for the analysis) that are shown in the hierarchy and then hidden. On the other hand, it is not a good idea to rename a column if you keep it visible in the table; then you would find it hard to remember that the two names actually refer to the same column.

Creating hierarchies on multiple tables

A hierarchy can be created on a single table only. If you have the need to create a hierarchy using columns from many tables, then you will need to merge the needed columns in a single table to create the hierarchy. The tables used in the hierarchy are usually linked by a chain of relationships.

A good example of this is the DimProduct table. In fact, as shown in Figure 9-4, the product category and subcategory names are stored in different tables.

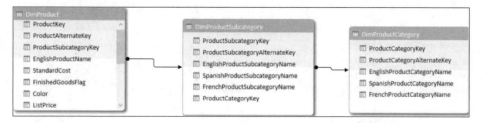

FIGURE 9-4 The Product hierarchy is made of three tables in the *AdventureWorks* database.

If you want to create a hierarchy of products that lets you move from category to subcategory, and then to product, then you need to add the product category name and the product subcategory name to the DimProduct table, using the *RELATED* function. To perform this operation, you can define two new calculated columns in the DimProduct table using this code:

```
DimProduct[ProductSubcategory] =
RELATED ( DimProductSubcategory [EnglishProduct SubcategoryName] )

DimProduct[ProductCategory] =
RELATED ( DimProductCategory [EnglishProductCategoryName] )
```

In Figure 9-5, you can see the DimProduct table with these two new columns.

ProductKey	ProductAlternateKey	ProductCategory	ProductSubcategory
230	LJ-0192-M	Clothing	Jerseys
231	LJ-0192-M	Clothing	Jerseys
232	LJ-0192-L	Clothing	Jerseys
233	LJ-0192-L	Clothing	Jerseys
234	LJ-0192-L	Clothing	Jerseys
235	LJ-0192-X	Clothing	Jerseys
236	LJ-0192-X	Clothing	Jerseys
237	LJ-0192-X	Clothing	Jerseys
391	FK-1639	Components	Forks

FIGURE 9-5 The DimProduct table contains the columns needed to build the hierarchy.

Now that the product category and subcategory are stored inside the DimProduct table, you can easily create a hierarchy using these columns. Because the DimProductCategory and DimProductSubcategory tables are no longer useful, you can safely hide both of them.

In Figure 9-6, you can see the resulting hierarchy in a PivotTable.

Row Labels	SumOfSalesAmount
⊟Accessories	700,759.96
⊞Bike Racks	39,360.00
⊞Bike Stands	39,591.00
⊞Bottles and Cages	56,798.19
⊞Cleaners	7,218.60
⊞Fenders	46,619.58
⊞Helmets	225,335.60
⊞Hydration Packs	40,307.67
⊞Tires and Tubes	245,529.32
⊟Bikes	28,318,144.65
⊞Mountain Bikes	9,952,759.56
⊞Road Bikes	14,520,584.04
⊞Touring Bikes	3,844,801.05
⊞Clothing	339,772.61
Grand Total	29,358,677.22

FIGURE 9-6 The hierarchy simplifies the task of browsing data, gathering columns from different tables.

Performing calculations using hierarchies

One of the best features of hierarchies is the fact that you can create calculations using them. For instance, in the previous example, you have created a hierarchy using product category, subcategory, and the product to show the amount of sales. A common measure to show is the ratio-to-parent that displays, for each row, the percentage of that row against its parent. In other words, it shows the percentage of a category against the grand total, of a subcategory against the total of its category, and of a product against its subcategory.

You can see an example of this report in Figure 9-7.

Color		Row Labels	SumOfSalesAmount	Perc on Parent
Black		⊟Accessories	700,759.96	2.39%
Blue		⊞Bike Racks	39,360.00	5.62%
Multi		⊞Bike Stands	39,591.00	5.65%
NA		⊞Bottles and Cages	56,798.19	8.11%
Red		⊞Cleaners	7,218.60	1.03%
Silver		⊞Fenders	46,619.58	6.65%
White		⊞Helmets	225,335.60	32.16%
Yellow		⊞Hydration Packs	40,307.67	5.75%
		⊞Tires and Tubes	245,529.32	35.04%
		⊟Bikes	28,318,144.65	96.46%
		⊞Mountain Bikes	9,952,759.56	35.15%
		⊞Road Bikes	14,520,584.04	51.28%
		⊞Touring Bikes	3,844,801.05	13.58%
		⊞Clothing	339,772.61	1.16%
		Grand Total	29,358,677.22	100.00%

FIGURE 9-7 The *Perc on Parent* field is useful to better understand the values in a table.

You can create such a report in two different ways:

- Using the PivotTable feature Show Values As, so that the computation is performed by Excel

- Creating a new calculated field that performs the computation, so that the value is computed in the data model

There are advantages and disadvantages in both solutions. Thus, it is worthwhile to look at both of them in order to decide, for each project, which one is better. Let's start with the Excel way, which is easier to learn.

Using Excel only, you can create a PivotTable putting the Category-Subcategory hierarchy on rows and the SumOfSalesAmount on values. At this point, you need to drag once again the SumOfSalesAmount field to the values area. By doing this, you obtain the report shown in Figure 9-8.

Row Labels	SumOfSalesAmount	SumOfSalesAmount2
⊟ Accessories	700,759.96	700,759.96
⊞ Bike Racks	39,360.00	39,360.00
⊞ Bike Stands	39,591.00	39,591.00
⊞ Bottles and Cages	56,798.19	56,798.19
⊞ Cleaners	7,218.60	7,218.60
⊞ Fenders	46,619.58	46,619.58
⊞ Helmets	225,335.60	225,335.60
⊞ Hydration Packs	40,307.67	40,307.67
⊞ Tires and Tubes	245,529.32	245,529.32
⊟ Bikes	28,318,144.65	28,318,144.65
⊞ Mountain Bikes	9,952,759.56	9,952,759.56
⊞ Road Bikes	14,520,584.04	14,520,584.04
⊞ Touring Bikes	3,844,801.05	3,844,801.05
⊞ Clothing	339,772.61	339,772.61
Grand Total	29,358,677.22	29,358,677.22

FIGURE 9-8 You can put a field into the VALUES area more than once—which looks strange, but it is useful.

To change the number shown by SumOfSalesAmount2, right-click it (any row is fine) and choose the Value Field Settings menu option. This will open the Value Field Settings dialog box, from which you can change several properties of the field. These properties are applied only to the current PivotTable; they do not affect the way the field is computed in the data model. In Figure 9-9, you can see the Value Field Settings dialog box with the properties already set.

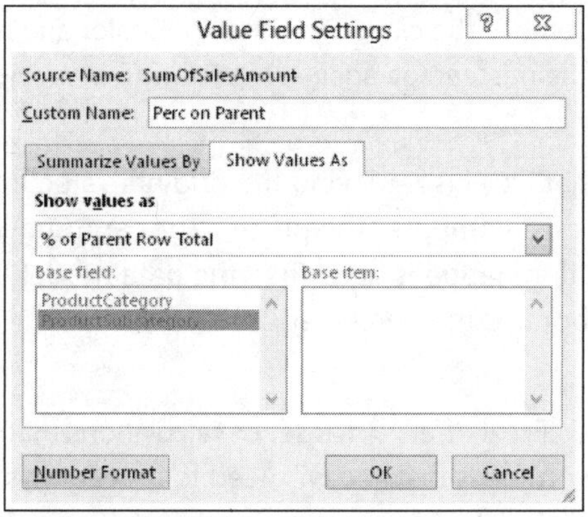

FIGURE 9-9 The Value Field Settings window lets you modify the way a field is shown in the PivotTable.

Two properties need to be updated:

- **Custom Name**   You can set a different name for the field, which is valid only in this PivotTable. Here, you should use "Perc on Parent," to indicate that the value shown is not the sales amount, but the percentage against its parent.

- **Show Values As**   From this list, you can choose one of many different calculations that Excel can perform. It is not useful to explain all of them. Rather, you can try them by yourself and find the one that is most useful for your business or report. In the example, we chose % of Parent Row Total, which is exactly what we need.

Another useful property is the number format, which you can use to assign specific formatting to a field in a PivotTable. Once you click OK, the PivotTable looks like Figure 9-10.

Row Labels	SumOfSalesAmount	Perc on Parent
⊟ Accessories	700,759.96	2.39%
⊞ Bike Racks	39,360.00	5.62%
⊞ Bike Stands	39,591.00	5.65%
⊞ Bottles and Cages	56,798.19	8.11%
⊞ Cleaners	7,218.60	1.03%
⊞ Fenders	46,619.58	6.65%
⊞ Helmets	225,335.60	32.16%
⊞ Hydration Packs	40,307.67	5.75%
⊞ Tires and Tubes	245,529.32	35.04%
⊟ Bikes	28,318,144.65	96.46%
⊞ Mountain Bikes	9,952,759.56	35.15%
⊞ Road Bikes	14,520,584.04	51.28%
⊞ Touring Bikes	3,844,801.05	13.58%
⊞ Clothing	339,772.61	1.16%
Grand Total	29,358,677.22	100.00%

FIGURE 9-10 The Perc on Parent column now shows the percentage against the parent in the hierarchy.

The interesting point of using Excel to perform this calculation is that it will work on any hierarchy you put into the rows. If, for example, you decide to remove the categories, then put color and model into the rows, the calculation still works, computing the percentage against the shown hierarchy.

> **Note**   What is happening under the surface is that Excel is retrieving the original value from the data model and, after it gathers all the values, it computes the percentages and shows them in the PivotTable. Thus, a two-step calculation happens here: first, the data model computes the sales amount, and then Excel elaborates the percentages.

The Excel technique is useful and simple. Moreover, Excel offers a rich set of calculations that solve nearly all your reporting needs. The only drawback with this is that you will need to repeat the same operation for all the PivotTables where you want this calculation to happen. Another drawback is that this feature is not available in SharePoint. If you publish the workbook on SharePoint, the calculation works fine, but if you try creating the percentage column directly in SharePoint, you will not be able to do it. Thus, you might want to make this calculation available among the many calculated fields of your data model, so that users will be able to simply drag the field to the values area and create the report.

Unfortunately, as you will soon see, performing the same calculation in DAX is not easy at all, even if it is a technique worth learning. First of all, it is worth pointing the first big limitation that we will have in DAX; that is,there is no way to build a generic percentage-to-parent calculated field. The reason is that, inside DAX, there is no way to know how the PivotTable has been created.

> **Note** To understand why this happens, you need to remember that the Excel data model is really a local instance of PowerPivot (that is, the SQL Server Analysis Services engine running inside Excel). Even if, from the user's point of view, the data model is Excel, it is really a completely different piece of software that runs inside Excel. Excel executes queries against the data model and retrieves results from there, but the two components are clearly separated by a wall. For this reason, the PowerPivot engine does not know how the PivotTable is built.

Even if you cannot write a generic formula, you can create some fields that compute the correct percentages. Because the hierarchy has three levels (category, subcategory, and product), you can start with three different measures, one for each level, as in the following code:

```
PercOnSubcategory :=
    [SumOfSalesAmount]
    /
    CALCULATE (
        [SumOfSalesAmount],
        ALL ( DimProduct[EnglishProductName] )
    )

PercOnCategory :=
    [SumOfSalesAmount]
    /
    CALCULATE (
        [SumOfSalesAmount],
        ALL ( DimProduct[ProductSubcategory] )
    )

PercOnTotal :=
    [SumOfSalesAmount]
    /
    CALCULATE (
        [SumOfSalesAmount],
        ALL ( DimProduct[ProductCategory] )
    )
```

These three measures compute the needed percentages. Putting them into a PivotTable leads to the result shown in Figure 9-11.

Row Labels	SumOfSalesAmount	PercOnSubcategory	PercOnCategory	PercOnTotal
⊟ Accessories	700,759.96	100.00 %	100.00 %	2.39 %
⊞ Bike Racks	39,360.00	100.00 %	5.62 %	100.00 %
⊞ Bike Stands	39,591.00	100.00 %	5.65 %	100.00 %
⊞ Bottles and Cages	56,798.19	100.00 %	8.11 %	100.00 %
⊞ Cleaners	7,218.60	100.00 %	1.03 %	100.00 %
⊞ Fenders	46,619.58	100.00 %	6.65 %	100.00 %
⊟ Helmets	225,335.60	100.00 %	32.16 %	100.00 %
Sport-100 Helmet, Black	72,954.15	32.38 %	100.00 %	100.00 %
Sport-100 Helmet, Blue	74,353.75	33.00 %	100.00 %	100.00 %
Sport-100 Helmet, Red	78,027.70	34.63 %	100.00 %	100.00 %
⊞ Hydration Packs	40,307.67	100.00 %	5.75 %	100.00 %
⊞ Tires and Tubes	245,529.32	100.00 %	35.04 %	100.00 %
⊟ Bikes	28,318,144.65	100.00 %	100.00 %	96.46 %
⊞ Mountain Bikes	9,952,759.56	100.00 %	35.15 %	100.00 %
⊞ Road Bikes	14,520,584.04	100.00 %	51.28 %	100.00 %
⊞ Touring Bikes	3,844,801.05	100.00 %	13.58 %	100.00 %
⊞ Clothing	339,772.61	100.00 %	100.00 %	1.16 %
Grand Total	29,358,677.22	100.00 %	100.00 %	100.00 %

FIGURE 9-11 The three Calculated fields you have written work fine, but only at the level where they have meaning.

You can see that the calculated fields show correct values, but only where they are meaningful. Otherwise, they show a useless 100 percent. Moreover, as of now, we have three different calculated fields but our goal is to have only one that shows different percentages at different levels.

Let's start clearing the 100 percent out of the *PercOnSubcategory* field. What you need to do is avoid performing the calculation if the hierarchy is not showing the EnglishProductName column on rows. You might recall from Chapter 7, "Understanding Evaluation Contexts," that you can test whether a column is filtered by using *ISFILTERED*. In fact, when the product name is on the rows, it is filtered (that is, it shows only one value out of all its possible ones). Thus, you can change the formula with this new expression:

```
PercOnSubcategory :=
    IF (
        ISFILTERED ( DimProduct[EnglishProductName] ),
        [SumOfSalesAmount]
        /
        CALCULATE (
            [SumOfSalesAmount],
            ALL ( DimProduct[EnglishProductName] )
        )
    )
```

Figure 9-12 shows the PivotTable using this new formula.

Row Labels	SumOfSalesAmount	PercOnSubcategory	PercOnCategory	PercOnTotal
⊟Accessories	700,759.96		100.00%	2.39%
⊞Bike Racks	39,360.00		5.62%	100.00%
⊞Bike Stands	39,591.00		5.65%	100.00%
⊞Bottles and Cages	56,798.19		8.11%	100.00%
⊞Cleaners	7,218.60		1.03%	100.00%
⊞Fenders	46,619.58		6.65%	100.00%
⊟Helmets	225,335.60		32.16%	100.00%
Sport-100 Helmet, Black	72,954.15	32.38%	100.00%	100.00%
Sport-100 Helmet, Blue	74,353.75	33.00%	100.00%	100.00%
Sport-100 Helmet, Red	78,027.70	34.63%	100.00%	100.00%
⊞Hydration Packs	40,307.67		5.75%	100.00%
⊞Tires and Tubes	245,529.32		35.04%	100.00%
⊟Bikes	28,318,144.65		100.00%	96.46%
⊞Mountain Bikes	9,952,759.56		35.15%	100.00%
⊞Road Bikes	14,520,584.04		51.28%	100.00%
⊞Touring Bikes	3,844,801.05		13.58%	100.00%
⊞Clothing	339,772.61		100.00%	1.16%
Grand Total	29,358,677.22		100.00%	100.00%

FIGURE 9-12 Using *ISFILTERED,* we have removed the useless 100 percent values from the PercOnSubcategory column.

Using the same technique, you can remove the 100 percent from other calculated fields. Beware of the fact that, in PercOnSubcategory, you need to check that ProductSubcategory is filtered and EnglishProductName is not. This is because when EnglishProductName is filtered, so is ProductSubcategory; but when both are filtered, you are displaying a product rather than a subcategory.

It is now time to solve the other issue by merging all three values into a single calculated field. The code is somewhat cumbersome, but it is not difficult to write because you have to check only one column of the hierarchy at a time and stop when you find the correct level. Here is the code for *PercOnParent:*

```
PercOnParent:=

IF (
    ISFILTERED ( DimProduct[EnglishProductName] ),
    [SumOfSalesAmount]
    /
    CALCULATE (
        [SumOfSalesAmount],
        ALL ( DimProduct[EnglishProductName] )
    ),
    IF (
        ISFILTERED ( DimProduct[ProductSubcategory] ),
        [SumOfSalesAmount]
        /
        CALCULATE (
            [SumOfSalesAmount],
            ALL ( DimProduct[ProductSubcategory] )
        ),
        IF (
            ISFILTERED ( DimProduct[ProductCategory] ),
            [SumOfSalesAmount]
```

```
        /
        CALCULATE (
            [SumOfSalesAmount],
            ALL ( DimProduct[ProductCategory] )
        )
    )
  )
)
```

Using the *PercOnParent* calculated field, you obtain the desired result, which you can see in Figure 9-13.

Row Labels	SumOfSalesAmount	PercOnSubcategory	PercOnCategory	PercOnTotal	PercOnParent
⊟ Accessories	700,759.96			2.39%	2.39%
⊞ Bike Racks	39,360.00		5.62%		5.62%
⊞ Bike Stands	39,591.00		5.65%		5.65%
⊞ Bottles and Cages	56,798.19		8.11%		8.11%
⊞ Cleaners	7,218.60		1.03%		1.03%
⊞ Fenders	46,619.58		6.65%		6.65%
⊟ Helmets	225,335.60		32.16%		32.16%
Sport-100 Helmet, Black	72,954.15	32.38%			32.38%
Sport-100 Helmet, Blue	74,353.75	33.00%			33.00%
Sport-100 Helmet, Red	78,027.70	34.63%			34.63%
⊞ Hydration Packs	40,307.67		5.75%		5.75%
⊞ Tires and Tubes	245,529.32		35.04%		35.04%
⊟ Bikes	28,318,144.65			96.46%	96.46%
⊞ Mountain Bikes	9,952,759.56		35.15%		35.15%
⊞ Road Bikes	14,520,584.04		51.28%		51.28%
⊞ Touring Bikes	3,844,801.05		13.58%		13.58%
⊞ Clothing	339,772.61			1.16%	1.16%
Grand Total	29,358,677.22				

FIGURE 9-13 The *PercOnParent* calculated field merges into a single column the three columns computed before.

Obviously, the three calculated fields that you have created can be deleted because now you have a single field which computes everything, putting the right value in a single column, detecting the level at which you are browsing the PivotTable using *ISFILTERED*.

> **Note** The order of the *IF* is important. You need to start testing the innermost level of the hierarchy and then go one step at a time. Otherwise, if you reverse the order of the conditions, you will get incorrect results. You need to remember that when the ProductSubcategory is filtered through the hierarchy, the ProductCategory is filtered too.

This calculation has some interesting features compared to the Excel one. First of all, this calculation is stored inside a calculated field, so it works in SharePoint reports and can be used in any report, always yielding the same result. Therefore, you have added information to the data model, which is a big advantage compared to adding the information to a report. The data model is more widely available than the calculation in reports.

Finally, there are two differences in how this field and the Excel calculation behave:

- The *PercOnParent* written in DAX works only if the correct hierarchy is put on rows. If you replace the category hierarchy with the color, for example, then the numbers will no longer be correct.

- Because *PercOnParent* uses the *ISFILTERED* function to detect the current level of the hierarchy, it might be fooled by the presence of any additional filter (created for example, by a slicer).

The latter issue is the bigger one. If, for instance, you put a slicer on EnglishProductName on the report and select a couple of products, belonging to the same subcategory, you will produce a report similar to the one shown in Figure 9-14.

EnglishProductName		Row Labels	SumOfSalesAmount	PercOnParent
Classic Vest, L	^	⊟Clothing	25,019.00	7.36%
Classic Vest, M		⊟Vests	25,019.00	70.11%
Classic Vest, S		Classic Vest, L	12,382.50	34.70%
Fender Set - Mount...		Classic Vest, M	12,636.50	35.41%
	v	Grand Total	25,019.00	0.09%

FIGURE 9-14 The *PercOnParent* calculated field does not work if you filter the product name with a slicer.

You can easily see in Figure 9-14 that *PercOnParent* does not show correct percentages. To solve this problem, you might use a DAX trick, which is worth learning because it can prove useful in many other scenarios.

First of all, let's try to get a better understanding of why the calculated field does not work. The percentage shown for Classic Vest computes the percentage of sales amount for the product against all the products of the same category and, to perform this, it uses ALL (DimProduct[EnglishProductName]). By doing this, it is actually removing both the filter introduced by the product on rows and the filter created by the slicer. Thus, it is removing too many filters. In fact, the sum of all percentages for products does not yield 100 percent because there are other products, not shown in the report, that cover the remaining percentage.

What we would like to do is to remove the filter from the EnglishProductName introduced by the rows but still keep the filter introduced by the slicer. Unfortunately, because both filters operate on the same column, there is no way to differentiate between the two using the *ISFILTERED* function. In fact, *ISFILTERED* tells you whether a column is filtered, but it has no way to detect whether the filter comes from the slicer of from rows or columns.

> **Note** The *ALLSELECTED* function is not useful here. You might try to detect if a column is filtered by counting the values of the column for the current filter and for the ALLSELECTED filter, mixing *COUNTROWS* and *ALLSELECTED*. This test, anyway, will fail in the special case where a hierarchy has a level with a single value. In that case, the result will always be 1 because you are selecting, on the rows, the only visible value of the column.

The solution, which is not very intuitive, is to make the two filters operate on different columns. You create three new columns, called HProductName, HProductCategory, and HProductSubcategory, where the initial *H* stands for "Hierarchy." Then you build the hierarchy using the H columns, renaming them inside the hierarchy, and finally, you hide the H columns from client tools so that they cannot be used on slicers, rows, or columns.

In Figure 9-15, you can see the DimProduct table with all these duplicated columns. You can note that the H ones are hidden from client tools.

ProductKey	EnglishProductName	HProductName	ProductCategory	HProductCategory	ProductSubcategory	HProductSubcategory
445	Men's Sports Shorts, S	Men's Sports Shorts, S	Clothing	Clothing	Shorts	Shorts
447	Cable Lock	Cable Lock	Accessories	Accessories	Locks	Locks
448	Minipump	Minipump	Accessories	Accessories	Pumps	Pumps
449	Mountain Pump	Mountain Pump	Accessories	Accessories	Pumps	Pumps
450	Taillights - Battery-Powered	Taillights - Battery-Powered	Accessories	Accessories	Lights	Lights
451	Headlights - Dual-Beam	Headlights - Dual-Beam	Accessories	Accessories	Lights	Lights
452	Headlights - Weatherproof	Headlights - Weatherproof	Accessories	Accessories	Lights	Lights
453	Men's Sports Shorts, M	Men's Sports Shorts, M	Clothing	Clothing	Shorts	Shorts
454	Men's Sports Shorts, L	Men's Sports Shorts, L	Clothing	Clothing	Shorts	Shorts

FIGURE 9-15 In order to solve the scenario, you had to duplicate many columns in the DimProduct table.

In Figure 9-16, you can see the newly created hierarchy, which is now based on the H columns.

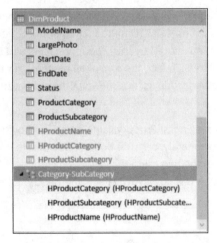

FIGURE 9-16 The hierarchy on DimProduct is now based on the H columns.

Finally, you need to update the formula of *PercOnParent* so that it uses the H columns instead of the original ones:

```
PercOnParentCorrect :=
IF (
    ISFILTERED ( DimProduct[HProductName] ),
    [SumOfSalesAmount]
    /
    CALCULATE (
        [SumOfSalesAmount],
        ALL ( DimProduct[HProductName] )
    ),
    IF (
        ISFILTERED ( DimProduct[HProductSubcategory] ),
        [SumOfSalesAmount]
        /
        CALCULATE (
            [SumOfSalesAmount],
            ALL ( DimProduct[HProductSubcategory] )
        ),
        IF (
            ISFILTERED ( DimProduct[HProductCategory] ),
            [SumOfSalesAmount]
            /
            CALCULATE (
                [SumOfSalesAmount],
                ALL ( DimProduct[HProductCategory] )
            )
        )
    )
)
```

With this new data model, the user will be able to put EnglishProductName on the slicer, but this will not filter the HProductName column directly. Thus, ISFILTERED ([HProductName]) will return *False* on all the rows that do not display the product name.

In Figure 9-17, you can see both calculated fields in the same PivotTable.

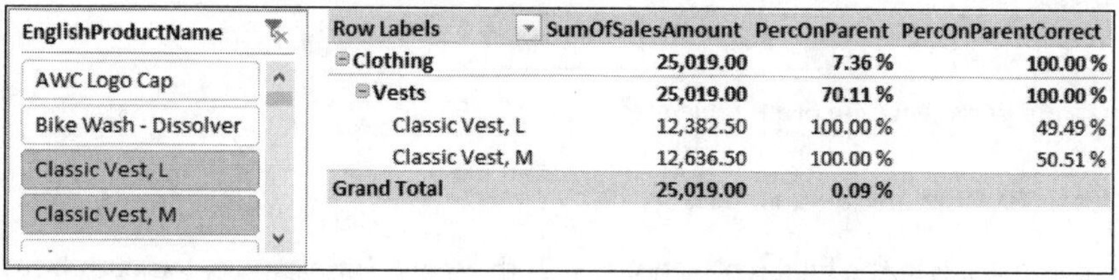

EnglishProductName		Row Labels	SumOfSalesAmount	PercOnParent	PercOnParentCorrect
AWC Logo Cap		⊟Clothing	25,019.00	7.36 %	100.00 %
Bike Wash - Dissolver		⊟Vests	25,019.00	70.11 %	100.00 %
Classic Vest, L		Classic Vest, L	12,382.50	100.00 %	49.49 %
Classic Vest, M		Classic Vest, M	12,636.50	100.00 %	50.51 %
		Grand Total	25,019.00	0.09 %	

FIGURE 9-17 PercOnParentCorrect now computes the correct results.

Note This approach works only if the user selects regular columns for the slicer and selects the Category-Subcategory hierarchy on PivotTable rows. If the user selects one or more levels from the hierarchy and puts them in one or more slicers, the same issue shown previously in Figure 9-14 will happen. Unfortunately, DAX does not offer you more control with that; you have to instruct the user to select the correct columns for the slicers.

From the point of view of the filter contexts, there is no practical difference between filtering a column from the hierarchy or from the visible ones. In fact, if the user filters a product category, only products of that category will be visible. The only notable difference is internal to DAX; that is, *ISFILTERED* will return *TRUE* only when a column of the hierarchy has been used to filter the table. Otherwise, it will return *FALSE,* even if not all the values of the column are visible.

As you have seen, solving the scenario with DAX is neither easy nor intuitive. Nevertheless, it gives you some advantages over the Excel solution. Choosing the right one really depends on your needs. If you work mainly with Excel on a few reports, then the Excel way is easier to use. If, on the other hand, you need to create a data model that is mainly used in SharePoint by people who cannot use Excel to create their reports, then the DAX way is the only viable one.

Using parent/child hierarchies

Hierarchies are useful, and a carefully designed set of hierarchies will make the browsing of your data model a much better experience. A special type of hierarchy appears very often in accounting data models; namely, the parent/child hierarchy, often abbreviated as P/C.

You can see a classical P/C hierarchy in Figure 9-18.

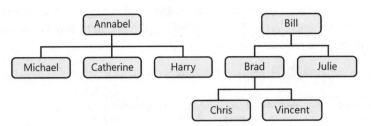

FIGURE 9-18 A graphical representation of a P/C hierarchy.

P/C hierarchies have some unique qualities:

- The number of levels in the hierarchy is not always the same. For example, the path from Annabel to Michael has a depth of two levels, whereas in the same hierarchy, the path from Bill to Chris has a depth of three levels.

- The hierarchy is normally represented in a single table, storing for each row a link to the parent.

The canonical representation of P/C hierarchies can be seen in Figure 9-19. You can find this data model in the companion workbook "CH09-02-Parent Child.xlsx."

NodeId	Node	ParentNodeID
1	Bill	
6	Annabel	
7	Catherine	6
8	Harry	6
9	Michael	6
2	Brad	1
3	Julie	1
4	Chris	2
5	Vincent	2

FIGURE 9-19 An Excel table containing a P/C hierarchy.

It is easy to see that the ParentNodeId is the ID of the parent of each node. In fact, for Catherine, it stores 6, which is the ID of Annabel, her parent. The issue with this data model is that, this time, the relationship is a self-referenced one; that is, the two tables involved in the relationship are really the same table.

PowerPivot does not support self-referencing relationships. Thus, there is no way to create such a relationship inside the data model, and we will need to use different functions here. Moreover, because PowerPivot does not handle P/C hierarchies either, we will need to modify the data model, removing the P/C hierarchy and turning it into a classical hierarchy.

Before delving into the details of how to handle the P/C hierarchies, it is worth noting one last point. Take a look at the table containing the values we want to aggregate using the hierarchy, shown in Figure 9-20.

NodeID	InvoiceID	Amount	City
2	3	200	Chicago
2	4	200	Seattle
3	5	300	Chicago
4	6	400	Seattle
5	7	500	Chicago
6	8	600	Seattle
7	9	600	Seattle
7	10	600	Chicago
8	11	400	Chicago
8	12	400	Seattle
9	13	300	Chicago
9	14	300	Seattle

FIGURE 9-20 This table contains the data for the P/C hierarchy.

The rows in the fact table contain references to both leaf-level and middle nodes in the hierarchy. For example, the sixth row references NodeId number 6, which is Annabel. Annabel has three children nodes, so when we look at her data, we will need to aggregate both her numbers and her children's values.

Figure 9-21 displays the final result we want to achieve.

Row Labels	WithDataMember
⊟ Annabel	3,200.00
Annabel	600.00
Catherine	1,200.00
Harry	800.00
Michael	600.00
⊟ Bill	1,600.00
⊟ Brad	1,300.00
Brad	400.00
Chris	400.00
Vincent	500.00
Julie	300.00
Grand Total	4,800.00

FIGURE 9-21 This PivotTable shows the final result of browsing a P/C with a PivotTable.

There are many steps to cover before reaching the final goal. Let's start from the beginning (that is, loading the tables inside the Excel data model). Once the tables have been loaded, the first step is to create a calculated column that contains, for each node, the path to reach it. In fact, because we cannot use standard relationships, we will need to use a set of special functions, available in DAX, designed for handling P/C hierarchies.

The new calculated column uses the *PATH* function:

```
HPath = PATH ( PC[NodeId], PC[ParentNodeId] )
```

PATH is a function that receives two parameters. The first is the key of the table (in this case, the table name is PC), and the second is the name of the column that holds the parent node ID. The *PATH* function performs a recursive traversal of the table and for each node, it builds the path as a list of keys separated by the pipe (|) character. In Figure 9-22, you can see the PC table with the HPath calculated column.

NodeId	Node	ParentNodeID	HPath
1	Bill		1
6	Annabel		6
7	Catherine	6	6|7
8	Harry	6	6|8
9	Michael	6	6|9
2	Brad	1	1|2
3	Julie	1	1|3
4	Chris	2	1|2|4
5	Vincent	2	1|2|5

FIGURE 9-22 The HPath column contains, for each node, the complete path to reach it.

The HPath column, by itself, is not useful. It is so important because it is the basis for another set of calculated columns, which you will use to build the hierarchy. In fact, the next step is to build three calculated columns (one for each level of the hierarchy) by following this pattern:

```
Level1 = LOOKUPVALUE ( PC[Node], PC [NodeId], PATHITEM ( PC [HPath], 1 ) )
```

The three columns will be Level1, Level2, and Level3 and the only change is in the second parameter to *PATHITEM*, which will be 1, 2, and 3. The calculated column uses *LOOKUPVALUE* to search a row where the NodeId equals the result of *PATHITEM* inside the PC table. *PATHITEM* returns the *n*th item in a column built with *PATH* (or *BLANK* if there is no such item), because you are requesting a number higher than the length of the path. The resulting table is shown in Figure 9-23.

NodeId	Node	ParentNodeID	HPath	Level1	Level2	Level3
1	Bill		1	Bill		
6	Annabel		6	Annabel		
7	Catherine	6	6|7	Annabel	Catherine	
8	Harry	6	6|8	Annabel	Harry	
9	Michael	6	6|9	Annabel	Michael	
2	Brad	1	1|2	Bill	Brad	
3	Julie	1	1|3	Bill	Julie	
4	Chris	2	1|2|4	Bill	Brad	Chris
5	Vincent	2	1|2|5	Bill	Brad	Vincent

FIGURE 9-23 The Level columns contain the values to show in the hierarchy.

In this example, you have used three columns because the maximum depth of the hierarchy is three. In a real-world scenario, you need to count the maximum number of levels of your hierarchy and build the number of columns that is big enough to hold all the levels. Thus, you can see that even if the number of levels in a P/C hierarchy should be flexible, in order to implement them in PowerPivot, you will need to fix it by setting its maximum number. It is a good practice to add a couple more levels to create space for a future growth of the hierarchy without needing to update the data model.

Now, you need to transform the set of level columns into a hierarchy and, because none of the other columns in the P/C is useful, you should hide everything else from the client tools. Your data model will look like Figure 9-24.

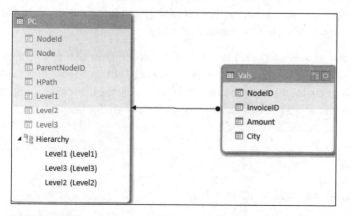

FIGURE 9-24 Here, you can see the data model containing the final P/C structure.

At this point, you can create a PivotTable using the hierarchy and putting the sum of amounts on the values. Figure 9-25 displays the result.

Row Labels	Sum of Amount
⊟ Annabel	3,200
⊟ (blank)	600
(blank)	600
⊟ Catherine	1,200
(blank)	1,200
⊟ Harry	800
(blank)	800
⊟ Michael	600
(blank)	600
⊟ Bill	1,600
⊟ Brad	1,300
(blank)	400
Chris	400
Vincent	500
⊟ Julie	300
(blank)	300
Grand Total	4,800

FIGURE 9-25 The P/C hierarchy is not exactly what we want because it shows too many rows.

There are several problems with this P/C hierarchy:

- Under Annabel, two blank rows contain the value of Annabel herself.

- Under Catherine, there is a blank row containing the value of Catherine herself.

- The hierarchy always shows three levels, even for paths where the maximum depth should be two (such as Harry, who has no children).

Apart from these issues, which are basically visualization problems, the hierarchy computes correct values because, under the Annabel node, you can see the values of all of Annabel's children. Thus, the important aspect of this solution is that you have been able to mimic a self-chain relationship by using the *PATH* function to create a calculated column. The remaining part is to solve the aesthetic issues, but now, at least, you are moving toward the correct solution.

The first problem to solve is the removal of all the blank values. The second row of the PivotTable, for example, accounts for an amount of 600 that should be visible for Annabel, not for (blank). This can be easily solved by modifying the formula for the Level columns. You remove all the blanks, repeating the previous level if you reached the end of the path. Here, you can see the pattern for Level2:

```
Level2 =
IF (
    PATHLENGTH ( PC[HPath] ) >= 2,
    LOOKUPVALUE ( PC[Node], PC[NodeId], PATHITEM ( PC[HPath], 2 ) ),
    PC[Level1]
)
```

With this new formula, the table looks like Figure 9-26.

No...	Node	ParentNodeID	HPath	Level1	Level2	Level3
1	Bill		1	Bill	Bill	Bill
6	Annabel		6	Annabel	Annabel	Annabel
7	Catherine	6	6|7	Annabel	Catherine	Catherine
8	Harry	6	6|8	Annabel	Harry	Harry
9	Michael	6	6|9	Annabel	Michael	Michael
2	Brad	1	1|2	Bill	Brad	Brad
3	Julie	1	1|3	Bill	Julie	Julie
4	Chris	2	1|2|4	Bill	Brad	Chris
5	Vincent	2	1|2|5	Bill	Brad	Vincent

FIGURE 9-26 With the new formula, the Level columns never contain a blank.

If you look at this point at the PivotTable, the blank rows are gone. Yet, there are still too many rows. In Figure 9-27, you can see the PivotTable, and, beside it, the filter context for each row.

Row Labels	Sum of Amount		Level1	Level2	Level3
⊟ Annabel	3,200		Annabel		
⊟ Annabel	600		Annabel	Annabel	
Annabel	600		Annabel	Annabel	Annabel
⊟ Catherine	1,200		Annabel	Catherine	
Catherine	1,200		Annabel	Catherine	Catherine
⊟ Harry	800		Annabel	Harry	
Harry	800		Annabel	Harry	Harry
⊟ Michael	600		Annabel	Michael	
Michael	600		Annabel	Michael	Michael
⊟ Bill	1,600		Bill		
⊟ Brad	1,300		Bill	Brad	
Brad	400		Bill	Brad	Brad
Chris	400		Bill	Brad	Chris
Vincent	500		Bill	Brad	Vincent
⊟ Julie	300		Bill	Julie	
Julie	300		Bill	Julie	Julie
Grand Total	4,800				

FIGURE 9-27 Here, you can see the PivotTable, and beside it, the filter context of each row.

Let's focus on the second and third rows of the PivotTable. In both cases, a single row of the hierarchy is shown (that is, the row of Annabel). You might want to show the second row because it contains a good value for Annabel, but you do not want to see the third row, since the hierarchy is browsing too deep and the path of Annabel is no longer valid. We need to make a more accurate search for a correct way to hide columns.

If we assign to each row of the hierarchy the length of the path needed to reach it, it is easy to see that Annabel is a root node, which means it is a node of level 1. Catherine, on the other hand, is a node of level 2 because she is a daughter of Annabel. Thus, the path of Catherine is of length 2. Moreover, even if it might not be so evident, Catherine is visible at level 1 because her value is aggregated under the first node of Annabel.

At this point, we can say that each node should be visible whenever we are browsing the hierarchy up to its level. Then, when the PivotTable shows a level that is too deep, we want to hide the node. In order to check this algorithm, we need two values:

- The depth of each node, which can be stored in a calculated column, because it is a fixed value for each row of the hierarchy

- The current browsing depth of the PivotTable, which is a dynamic value that depends on the current filter context, meaning that you will need a calculated field, because the value changes depending on the PivotTable and has different values for each row. For example, Annabel is a node at level 1, but it appears in three rows, where the current depth of the PivotTable has three different values.

If you could compute these two values, then the solution to the problem would be much closer. Yes, you will still need a way to hide the rows, but we can forget about this issue for now. Let's focus on the identification of the unwanted rows.

The depth of each node is easy to compute. You can add a new calculated column to the PC table with this simple expression:

```
NodeDepth = PATHLENGTH ( PC[HPath] )
```

PATHLENGTH returns the length of a column computed by *PATH*, and you can see that there is nothing complex here. The resulting calculated column is shown in Figure 9-28.

NodeId	Node	ParentNodeID	HPath	NodeDepth
1	Bill		1	1
6	Annabel		6	1
7	Catherine	6	6|7	2
8	Harry	6	6|8	2
9	Michael	6	6|9	2
2	Brad	1	1|2	2
3	Julie	1	1|3	2
4	Chris	2	1|2|4	3
5	Vincent	2	1|2|5	3

FIGURE 9-28 The NodeDepth column stores the depth of each node in a calculated column.

The NodeDepth column is easy to create. Computing the browsing depth is more difficult because you need to compute it in a calculated field. Nevertheless, the logic behind it is not very complex, and it is similar to the technique you have already learned for standard hierarchies: it uses the *ISFILTERED* function, to let you discover whether a Level column is filtered or not.

The formula takes advantage of the fact that a *TRUE/FALSE* value can be converted to a number, where *TRUE* has a value of 1 and *FALSE* has a value of zero.

```
BrowseDepth :=
ISFILTERED ( PC[Level1] ) +
ISFILTERED ( PC[Level2] ) +
ISFILTERED ( PC[Level3] )
```

Thus, if only Level1 is filtered, then the result is 1. If both Level1 and Level2 are filtered, but not Level3, then the result is 2. You can see the result for the BrowseDepth column in Figure 9-29.

Row Labels	Sum of Amount	BrowseDepth	Level1	Level2	Level3
Annabel	3,200	1	Annabel		
Annabel	600	2	Annabel	Annabel	
Annabel	600	3	Annabel	Annabel	Annabel
Catherine	1,200	2	Annabel	Catherine	
Catherine	1,200	3	Annabel	Catherine	Catherine
Harry	800	2	Annabel	Harry	
Harry	800	3	Annabel	Harry	Harry
Michael	600	2	Annabel	Michael	
Michael	600	3	Annabel	Michael	Michael
Bill	1,600	1	Bill		
Bill		2	Bill	Bill	
Bill		3	Bill	Bill	Bill
Brad	1,300	2	Bill	Brad	
Brad	400	3	Bill	Brad	Brad
Chris	400	3	Bill	Brad	Chris
Vincent	500	3	Bill	Brad	Vincent
Julie	300	2	Bill	Julie	
Julie	300	3	Bill	Julie	Julie
Grand Total	4,800	0			

FIGURE 9-29 The BrowseDepth calculated field computes the depth of browsing in the PivotTable.

It is interesting to see that this new PivotTable shows more rows than before. Now you can see that Bill has three rows, whereas in the previous PivotTables, Bill had a row only. The reason is that in the previous PivotTable, these additional Bill rows were hidden because the value for the sum of amounts returned a blank value. By default, the PivotTable automatically hides rows that results in a blank value for all the displayed measures. This may look like a small piece of information, but it is going to turn into a much more valuable one. In fact, it shows the path to hide a row: if the value of the measure is a BLANK, then the row will be hidden. Thus, you now have all the necessary pieces of information to complete the formula:

- The depth of each node, in the NodeDepth calculated column

- The depth of the current cell in the PivotTable, in the BrowseDepth calculated field

- A way to hide unwanted columns, by means of blanking the value of the result

It is time to merge all this information into a single calculated field, as follows:

```
PC_Amount :=
IF (
    MAX ( PC[NodeDepth] ) < [BrowseDepth],
    BLANK (),
    SUM ( Vals[Amount] )
)
```

To understand how this calculated field works, look at the PivotTable in Figure 9-30, where we put all the values that are useful to grab the formula behavior.

Row Labels	Sum of Amount	BrowseDepth	MaxNodeDepth	PC Amount	Level1	Level2	Level3
⊟Annabel	3,200	1	2	3,200	Annabel		
⊟Annabel	600	2	1		Annabel	Annabel	
Annabel	600	3	1		Annabel	Annabel	Annabel
⊟Catherine	1,200	2	2	1,200	Annabel	Catherine	
Catherine	1,200	3	2		Annabel	Catherine	Catherine
⊟Harry	800	2	2	800	Annabel	Harry	
Harry	800	3	2		Annabel	Harry	Harry
⊟Michael	600	2	2	600	Annabel	Michael	
Michael	600	3	2		Annabel	Michael	Michael
⊟Bill	1,600	1	3	1,600	Bill		
⊟Bill		2	1		Bill	Bill	
Bill		3	1		Bill	Bill	Bill
⊟Brad	1,300	2	3	1,300	Bill	Brad	
Brad	400	3	2		Bill	Brad	Brad
Chris	400	3	3	400	Bill	Brad	Chris
Vincent	500	3	3	500	Bill	Brad	Vincent
⊟Julie	300	2	2	300	Bill	Julie	
Julie	300	3	2		Bill	Julie	Julie
Grand Total	4,800	0	3	4,800			

FIGURE 9-30 This PivotTable shows the final result and all the partial results used by the formula.

If you look at the first row, which is Annabel, you see that *BrowseDepth* equals 1, because this is the root of the hierarchy. MaxNodeDepth, which is defined as MAX(PC[NodeDepth]), has a value of 2, meaning that the current node is showing not only data at level 1, but also data for some children that are at level 2. Thus, the current node is showing data for some children too, and for this reason, it needs to be visible. The second line of Annabel, on the other hand, has a *BrowseDepth* of 2 and *MaxNodeDepth* of 1. The reason is that the filter context filters all the rows where Level1 equals Annabel and Level2 equals Annabel, and there is only one row in the hierarchy satisfying this condition, which is Annabel herself. But Annabel has a *NodeDepth* of 1 and, because the PivotTable is browsing at level 2, then we need to hide the node. In fact, the *PC Amount* calculated field returns a *BLANK*.

It is useful to verify the behavior for other nodes by yourself so you can improve your understanding of how the formula is performing and of its behavior. Although it is clear that you can simply return to this part of the book and copy the formula whenever you need to, understanding it is a good exercise because it forces you to think in terms of how the filter context interacts with various parts of the formula.

To reach the final result, you only need to remove from the PivotTable all the columns that are not needed, leaving PC Amount alone, and the visualization will be the desired one, as shown in Figure 9-31.

Row Labels	PC Amount
Annabel	3,200
Catherine	1,200
Harry	800
Michael	600
Bill	1,600
Brad	1,300
Chris	400
Vincent	500
Julie	300
Grand Total	4,800

FIGURE 9-31 Once the measure is left alone in the PivotTable, all unwanted rows disappear.

As you might imagine at this point, you will need to use the same pattern for any calculated field you might want to add to your PivotTable when the P/C hierarchy is in place. If you put in a single calculated field that does not have a *BLANK* value for unwanted rows, then all of them will suddenly appear and disrupt our pattern.

At this point, the result is already satisfactory. Yet there is still a small problem. In fact, if you look at the total of Annabel, it is 3,200. Her children, summed up, show a total of 2,600. There is a missing amount of 600, which is the value of Annabel herself. You might already be satisfied by this visualization, because the value of a node is detectable by looking at the difference between its total and the total of its children. However, if you compare this figure to the original goal (we compare them for you, in Figure 9-32), you see that, there, the value of each node was clearly visible as a child of the node itself.

Row Labels	WithDataMember		Row Labels	PC Amount
Annabel	3,200		Annabel	3,200
Annabel	600		Catherine	1,200
Catherine	1,200		Harry	800
Harry	800		Michael	600
Michael	600		Bill	1,600
Bill	1,600		Brad	1,300
Brad	1,300		Chris	400
Brad	400		Vincent	500
Chris	400		Julie	300
Vincent	500		Grand Total	4,800
Julie	300			
Grand Total	4,800			

FIGURE 9-32 The original goal is not yet reached—you still need to show some rows.

At this point, the technique should be clear enough. In order to show the value for Annabel, you only need to find a suitable condition that lets you identify it as a node that should be made visible. In this case, the condition is somewhat complex. You need to note that the nodes that need to be visible are non-leaf nodes (that is, they have some children) that have values. These nodes will be made visible for one additional level. All other nodes (that is, leaf nodes or nodes with no value associated) will follow the original rule.

First, you need to create a calculated column in the PC table that indicates whether a node is a leaf. The DAX expression is easy: leaves are nodes that are not parents of any other node. In order to check the condition, you can count the number of nodes that have the current node as the parent. If it equals zero, then you know that the current node is a leaf. The following code does this:

```
IsLeaf =
CALCULATE (
    COUNTROWS ( PC ),
    ALL ( PC ),
    PC[ParentNodeID] = EARLIER ( PC[NodeId] )
) = 0
```

In Figure 9-33, the IsLeaf column has been added to the data model.

NodeId	Node	ParentNodeID	HPath	IsLeaf
1	Bill		1	FALSE
6	Annabel		6	FALSE
7	Catherine	6	6|7	TRUE
8	Harry	6	6|8	TRUE
9	Michael	6	6|9	FALSE
2	Brad	1	1|2	FALSE
3	Julie	1	1|3	TRUE
4	Chris	2	1|2|4	TRUE
5	Vincent	2	1|2|5	TRUE

FIGURE 9-33 The IsLeaf column indicates which nodes are leaves.

Now that you can identify leaves, it is time to write the final formula for handling the P/C hierarchy (numbers have been added to the lines to make them easier to identify):

```
FinalFormula :=
1.      IF (
2.          [MaxNodeDepth] + 1 < [BrowseDepth],
3.          BLANK (),
4.          IF (
5.              [MaxNodeDepth] + 1 = [BrowseDepth],
6.              IF (
7.                  VALUES ( PC[IsLeaf] ) = FALSE && SUM ( Vals[Amount] ) <> 0,
8.                  SUM ( Vals[Amount] ),
9.                  BLANK ()
10.             ),
11.             SUM ( Vals[Amount] )
12.         )
13.     )
```

The beginning of this formula is identical to the previous one: there is only a +1 in [MaxNode-Depth] at line 3, to take into account the next level. The reason why we add 1 to [MaxNodeDepth] is to allow certain nodes to show at specified browse levels; without it, the nodes that we are interested in showing will always be hidden as the [MaxNodeDepth] is less than their [BrowseDepth]. Not all the nodes should be visible at the next level—only the ones that are not leaves and have some value to show. This is the purpose of the remaining lines. On line 6, we check the special case of a node that should be made visible for one more level. If it is on that special level, then we check whether it is not a leaf (using *VALUES*, because here we are sure that only a single row is visible in the P/C hierarchy) and whether there is some value to show. If this is the case, then the calculated field returns the sum of the amounts; otherwise, it returns a blank, hiding the row.

This is not an easy formula to digest, so take your time and read it repeatedly until you are sure you get it. The interesting part of this formula is that it clearly shows the power of DAX and the difficulty of "thinking in DAX." DAX is a beautiful language because it has a simple structure, yet it also possesses an incredible power. But, in order to fully exploit the power of DAX, you need to master the concepts of evaluation contexts and data modeling. At that point, even complex formulas like this one for P/C hierarchies become feasible.

It is clear that, if PowerPivot had the ability to handle P/C hierarchies natively, then all this hard work could have been avoided. But the good news is that you have witnessed an example where you have created a self-relationship with a table and then decided precisely what to show and what to hide in a report by modifying the formula of a calculated field. This is great, and it shows how, by mastering DAX, one can create custom calculations that can be used to tackle a huge number of business scenarios.

CHAPTER 10

Using Power View

You already looked briefly at Power View in Chapter 1, "Introduction to PowerPivot." There, you just scratched the surface of the new, beautiful reporting engine that now is part of Microsoft Excel 2013. Power View lets you perform graphical analysis of data, making the search for insights in your datasets more fun.

Power View was designed with simplicity in mind. Nevertheless, even if it looks like a toy, Power View is amazingly powerful, resulting in a unique blend of simplicity and power that makes graphical exploration a unique experience.

In this chapter, you learn the capabilities of Power View. We are not going to explain all the features in great detail, at least partly because there are plenty of good books and resources where you can learn much more information about Power View. Our goal here is to introduce this new tool and show the most important information about the role it plays in graphical exploration.

What is Power View?

Power View was originally an additional reporting system in SQL Server Reporting Services that was integrated into SharePoint. Thus, before the advent of Microsoft Office 2013, you needed to buy and install Microsoft SharePoint, Reporting Services, and PowerPivot for SharePoint in order to use Power View.

The feedback of users has been so enthusiastic that Microsoft decided to add Power View to Excel 2013 too, and when they did it, they did not create a subset of Power View. Instead, they took all the functionalities of the tool and added much more power to it. Thus, Excel 2013 contains the best data exploration tool that Microsoft offers, without needing any modification.

You already saw in Chapter 1 that, like PowerPivot, Power View needs to be activated because it comes as a disabled add-in. We imagine that, at this point of the book, you have probably already tried some Power View reports on your own data, just because reading the first part of this book has stimulated your interest in it. If not, we strongly suggest you to do so now for two reasons:

- Power View is not only a technical tool. It fosters a wonderful experience that we will not be able to describe adequately on the printed page. Looking at static figures, you can learn new techniques to create useful reports, but you will lack the feeling of doing it yourself.

- If you have alread used Power View without reading about how to write correct metadata for it, you will probably have seen some limitations and some operations that look hard to perform; and you will have a greater appreciation of the hints in this chapter.

Power View basics

To create a Power View report, you need a data model in the Excel workbook. If you want to follow the examples in this chapter, use the data model in the "CH10-01-Power View.xlsx" file, which contains the *AdventureWorks* structure of products, categories, sales, and geography.

To create your first Power View report, you need to choose Power View from the INSERT tab of the ribbon. A new worksheet is created in your workbook, containing a Power View report.

The Power View editor, shown in Figure 10-1, is a white canvas where you will draw your analysis. The Power View Fields panel contains the elements of your data model.

FIGURE 10-1 The Power View editor is made of a white canvas (left) and the Power View Fields panel (right).

In order to start creating a report, you need to choose the values you are interested in. In the beginning, you do not need to worry about the layout; just focus on data. Imagine that you are interested in performing an analysis of sales in different territories.

You start clicking the Territory hierarchy from DimSales and then click the *Sales* calculated field in FactInternetSales. Your report looks like Figure 10-2.

Sales Territory Group	Sales Territory Country	Sales Territory Region	Sales
Europe	France	France	$2,644,017.71
Europe	Germany	Germany	$2,894,312.34
Europe	United Kingdom	United Kingdom	$3,391,712.21
North America	Canada	Canada	$1,977,844.86
North America	United States	Central	$3,000.83
North America	United States	Northeast	$6,532.47
North America	United States	Northwest	$3,649,866.55
North America	United States	Southeast	$12,238.85
North America	United States	Southwest	$5,718,150.81
Pacific	Australia	Australia	$9,061,000.58
Total			$29,358,677.22

FIGURE 10-2 Adding columns to the report results in a table with the required information.

Power View added the columns of the hierarchy to a table, computed the calculated field for each row, and provided a total at the bottom. You can click the title of the report and type **Sales Analysis** to give it a name. Now, the numbers are fine and already show some relevant insights, but they are not easy to read. Can you easily compare United States with Europe in this report? The answer is "No" because the report mixes information at different granularities. Europe and North America are territory groups, and the report shows values at the region level, without providing subtotals. Moreover, if you are interested in comparing data quickly, then a chart is definitely a better option. Since this first table looks useful anyway, it is better to add a chart to the report instead of replacing the current table. To add a chart with only SalesTerritoryGroup and sales, click an empty area of the canvas and select SalesTerritoryGroup and Sales again. At this point, your report looks like Figure 10-3.

Sales Analysis

Sales Territory Group	Sales Territory Country	Sales Territory Region	Sales		Sales Territory Group	Sales
Europe	France	France	$2,644,017.71		Europe	$8,930,042.26
Europe	Germany	Germany	$2,894,312.34		North America	$11,367,634.37
Europe	United Kingdom	United Kingdom	$3,391,712.21		Pacific	$9,061,000.58
North America	Canada	Canada	$1,977,844.86		Total	$29,358,677.22
North America	United States	Central	$3,000.83			
North America	United States	Northeast	$6,532.47			
North America	United States	Northwest	$3,649,866.55			
North America	United States	Southeast	$12,238.85			
North America	United States	Southwest	$5,718,150.81			
Pacific	Australia	Australia	$9,061,000.58			
Total			$29,358,677.22			

FIGURE 10-3 Adding new columns when no table is selected creates a new table.

Now, you have two tables in the same report: one with detailed information and another with summary information. Since the second table has been created to make a quick comparison of data, you now want to turn it into a chart. To do this, you simply need to change the way this second table is shown. You do this by clicking the Bar Chart button on the DESIGN tab of the ribbon (see Figure 10-4).

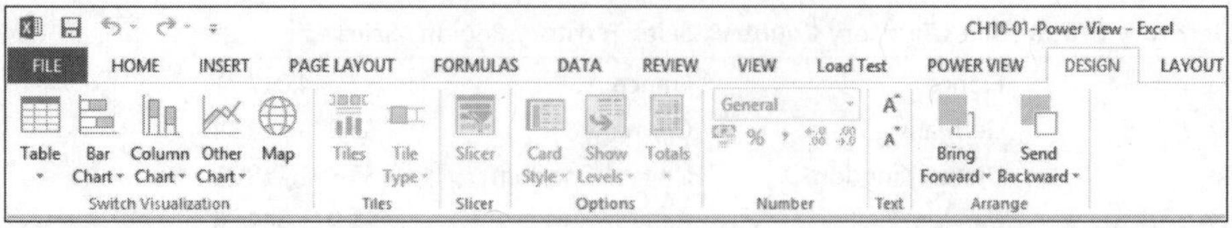

FIGURE 10-4 The DESIGN tab of the Excel ribbon shows different options to format Power View elements.

Clicking it once will turn the table into a chart, which you can see in Figure 10-5.

Sales Analysis

Sales Territory Group	Sales Territory Country	Sales Territory Region	Sales
Europe	France	France	$2,644,017.71
Europe	Germany	Germany	$2,894,312.34
Europe	United Kingdom	United Kingdom	$3,391,712.21
North America	Canada	Canada	$1,977,844.86
North America	United States	Central	$3,000.83
North America	United States	Northeast	$6,532.47
North America	United States	Northwest	$3,649,866.55
North America	United States	Southeast	$12,238.85
North America	United States	Southwest	$5,718,150.81
Pacific	Australia	Australia	$9,061,000.58
Total			**$29,358,677.22**

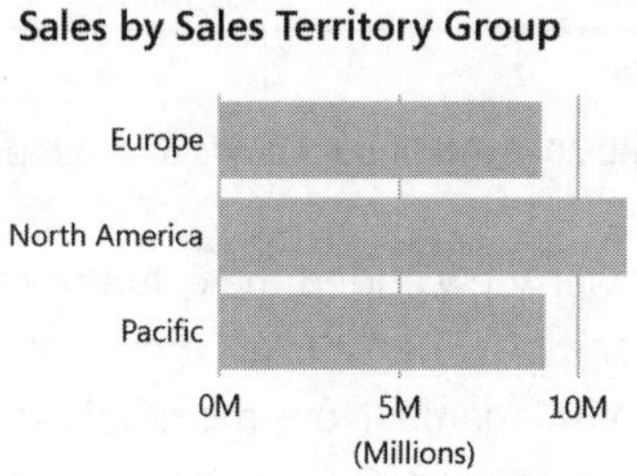

FIGURE 10-5 With the chart representation, the report looks much better.

Up to now, you have not done anything that cannot be done in Excel too, even if you are already seeing the simplicity of Power View. You do not need to follow complex procedures to create a chart; just select the data that you want to show and then select the way to represent them.

One of the most interesting features of Power View is activated by clicking one of the bars of your chart. In Figure 10-6, you can see the report as it appears after you click Europe.

Sales Analysis

Sales Territory Group	Sales Territory Country	Sales Territory Region	Sales
Europe	France	France	$2,644,017.71
Europe	Germany	Germany	$2,894,312.34
Europe	United Kingdom	United Kingdom	$3,391,712.21
Total			**$8,930,042.26**

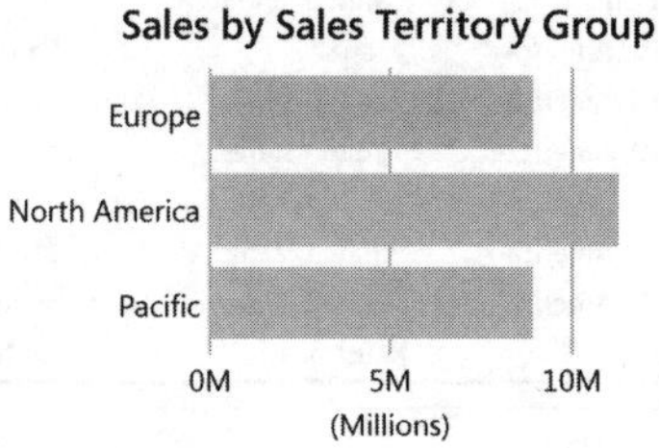

FIGURE 10-6 Clicking Europe immediately filters both the chart and the table.

The chart acts as a filter, and the filter is applied to all the tables in the same report. By clicking Europe, we are now showing sales of Europe only. If your report contains multiple charts, they will all show the effect of the filter on their data, too. A figure can help to explain this concept. For example, if you add a new chart that shows sales divided by color, the final result will be as shown in Figure 10-7.

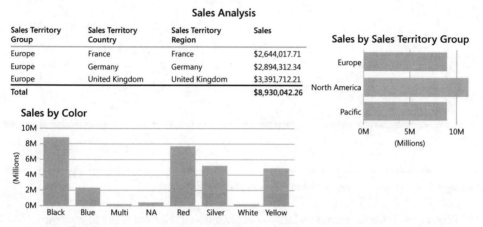

FIGURE 10-7 The filter on territory group is reflected on the colors chart too.

You can see that the color chart on the bottom shows the contribution of sales in Europe to total sales all over the world. This is an interesting feature because it means that any chart can be used as a slicer right away. The auto-filter feature of bar and column charts is not working in tables. In fact, when you select a row in a table, this selection does not filter the data model. You can turn a table made up of a single column into a slicer and then using it as a filter, as you will learn in the "Using a table as a slicer" section, later in this chapter.

Using the Filters pane

In the previous section, you saw that many charts can be used as slicers. Power View offers another tool to apply filters to a report: the Filters pane. The Filters pane is a panel that appears on the right of the report canvas. If the Filters pane is not visible, you can activate it by clicking the small filter icon that appears on the upper-right corner of each table in your report.

In Figure 10-8, you can see a report with the Filters pane open and the small filter button on the bar chart.

FIGURE 10-8 The Filters pane shows different filters applied to the report.

The Filters pane is useful because it lets you apply different kinds of filters to your report. Adding a column to the Filters pane is as easy as dragging it there from the field list. You can easily filter values using the check boxes for the different values of the column, or you can switch to Advanced Filtering mode using the button highlighted in Figure 10-9.

FIGURE 10-9 The Advanced Filter mode lets you create complex filter expressions easily.

For example, in Figure 10-9, you can see that we created a complex filter that shows values containing "America" or that are equal to Europe. The filters created in the Filters pane can be applied to the entire report (VIEW) or to a part of it (TABLE, CHART, or MAP) by selecting the appropriate area before adding the column to the Filters pane.

Another useful feature of the Filters pane is the calculated field filter. Imagine that you want to see all the products that sold more than a certain amount of dollars (for example, $1 million). This time, the filter is not on a column in the table but on a calculated field. This kind of filter can be applied only using the Filters pane on an item; it cannot be used to filter the entire report.

You can see in Figure 10-10 that the Filters pane is open on the table, and it shows both the columns of the table and the calculated fields that are computed for each row of the table. In the example, *Sales* is the only calculated field.

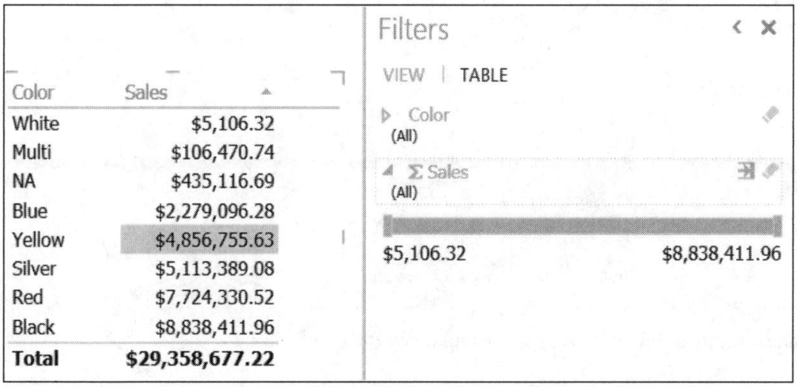

Color	Sales	
White	$5,106.32	
Multi	$106,470.74	
NA	$435,116.69	
Blue	$2,279,096.28	
Yellow	$4,856,755.63	
Silver	$5,113,389.08	
Red	$7,724,330.52	
Black	$8,838,411.96	
Total	**$29,358,677.22**	

Filters

VIEW | TABLE

▷ Color
(All)

◢ Σ Sales
(All)

$5,106.32 $8,838,411.96

FIGURE 10-10 The Filters pane lets you filter both columns and calculated fields.

In order to filter the *Sales* calculated field, you can either drag the slicer (which shows the minimum and maximum values of the field as boundaries) or click the Advanced Filtering button to specify a filter. Filtering of calculated fields is available only for the table, not for the view.

Note You can drag columns to the Filters pane from the Power View Fields panel; this creates a filter on that column. Columns that have the Σ symbol before their name (such as Σ Sales) represent automatic calculations, but if you drag such a column to the Filters pane, you are creating a filter on the column, not on the sum of the column.

Decorating your report

If you need to polish and decorate your reports, you have a couple of options. You can add images in any location using the Picture button on the Power View tab of the ribbon, and you can add and format a background image to the report using the Background Image button group on the same ribbon. Finally, you can use text boxes to add notes.

For example, in Figure 10-11, you can see a report with a gray background, the company logo on the bottom, and a note near the sales of black products.

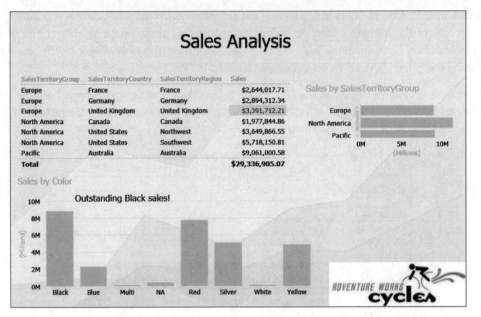

FIGURE 10-11 You can decorate a Power View report using many different tools.

Understanding table, matrix, and cards

Now that you have learned the basics of Power View, it is time to delve a bit deeper into the different tools you can use to show data. As you have seen, you always start building your report with a table, which is the default visualization that Power View uses when you start adding table columns to the report.

Even if you always start with a table, you can then switch to different tabular or graphical visualizations and, in this section, you are going to explore them in more detail. After you select a table, you can change the visualization using the Switch Visualization button group on the DESIGN tab of the Excel ribbon, as shown in Figure 10-12.

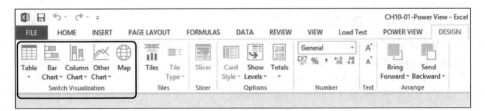

FIGURE 10-12 The Switch Visualization button group lets you change the visualization of data.

The Table button contains three visualizations: Table, Matrix, and Card. Table is the visualization that you are already familiar with; it shows data in a simple, tabular format. Matrix is more like a PivotTable, showing data sliced into rows and columns and highlighting the hierarchical structure of your model.

Using the matrix visualization

In Figure 10-13 you can see a matrix visualization where the Territory hierarchy is placed on rows and the Year on columns, and the Sales is the value to show.

Matrix View

Sales Territory Group	Sales Territory Country	Sales Territory Region	2005	2006	2007	2008	Total
Europe	France	France	$180,571.69	$514,942.01	$1,026,324.97	$922,179.04	$2,644,017.71
		Total	$180,571.69	$514,942.01	$1,026,324.97	$922,179.04	$2,644,017.71
	Germany	Germany	$237,784.99	$521,230.85	$1,058,405.73	$1,076,890.77	$2,894,312.34
		Total	$237,784.99	$521,230.85	$1,058,405.73	$1,076,890.77	$2,894,312.34
	United Kingdom	United Kingdom	$291,590.52	$591,586.85	$1,298,248.57	$1,210,286.27	$3,391,712.21
		Total	$291,590.52	$591,586.85	$1,298,248.57	$1,210,286.27	$3,391,712.21
	Total		$709,947.20	$1,627,759.71	$3,382,979.27	$3,209,356.08	$8,930,042.26
North America	Canada	Canada	$146,829.81	$621,602.38	$535,784.46	$673,628.21	$1,977,844.86
		Total	$146,829.81	$621,602.38	$535,784.46	$673,628.21	$1,977,844.86
	United States	Central			$2,768.12	$232.71	$3,000.83
		Northeast			$3,966.81	$2,565.66	$6532.47
		Northwest	$415,203.49	$847,839.26	$1,094,829.47	$1,291,994.33	$3,649,866.55
		Southeast		$782.99	$3,013.46	$8,442.40	$12,238.85
		Southwest	$685,345.96	$1,278,074.30	$1,733,934.50	$2,020,796.06	$5,718,150.81
		Total	$1,100,549.45	$2,126,696.55	$2,838,512.36	$3,324,031.16	$9,389,789.51
	Total		$1,247,379.26	$2,748,298.93	$3,374,296.82	$3,997,659.37	$11,367,634.37
Pacific	Australia	Australia	$1,309,047.20	$2,154,284.88	$3,033,784.21	$2,563,884.29	$9,061,000.58
		Total	$1,309,047.20	$2,154,284.88	$3,033,784.21	$2,563,884.29	$9,061,000.58
	Total		$1,309,047.20	$2,154,284.88	$3,033,784.21	$2,563,884.29	$9,061,000.58
Total			$3,266,373.66	$6,530,343.53	$9,791,060.30	$9,770,899.74	$29,358,677.22

FIGURE 10-13 The Matrix visualization looks more like a PivotTable than a simple table.

The matrix visualization is remarkable, but due to the limited real estate available on a single page, it might be somewhat dispersive because not enough data will fit into the report. A good option to increase the number of rows and columns shown in a report is to remove the totals. On the DESIGN tab of the Excel ribbon, you have the option to show totals for rows, columns, both, or neither of them, as shown in Figure 10-14.

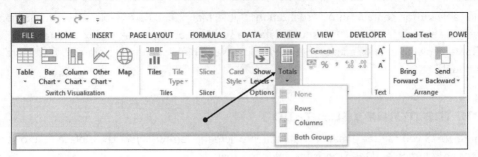

FIGURE 10-14 You can choose to show totals for rows, columns, both, or neither for a Matrix view.

For example, in Figure 10-15, you can see the same report without the totals, which looks much more compact and easy to read.

Sales Territory Group▲	Sales Territory Country	Sales Territory Region	2005	2006	2007	2008
Europe	France	France	$180,571.69	$514,942.01	$1,026,324.97	$922,179.04
	Germany	Germany	$237,784.99	$521,230.85	$1,058,405.73	$1,076,890.77
	United Kingdom	United Kingdom	$291,590.52	$591,586.85	$1,298,248.57	$1,210,286.27
North America	Canada	Canada	$146,829.81	$621,602.38	$535,784.46	$673,628.21
	United States	Central			$2,768.12	$232.71
		Northeast			$3,966.81	$2,565.66
		Northwest	$415,203.49	$847,839.26	$1,094,829.47	$1,291,994.33
		Southeast		$782.99	$3,013.46	$8,442.40
		Southwest	$685,345.96	$1,278,074.30	$1,733,934.50	$2,020,796.06
Pacific	Australia	Australia	$1,309,047.20	$2,154,284.88	$3,033,784.21	$2,563,884.29

FIGURE 10-15 Removing totals, the Matrix view is much more compact and easier to read in Power View.

The most interesting feature of a Matrix view without the subtotals is the ability to put a table column (the year, in this example) as a column header. In fact, in a normal table, you can only slice using the rows, whereas a matrix lets you slice on columns too, resulting in a convenient way to show data for different time frames.

Using the card visualization

The third table visualization is the Card view. When data is shown in Card mode, each row is like an index card. Card view is great to use when your dataset contains pictures. For example, in Figure 10-16, you can see a report showing products and sales in card format.

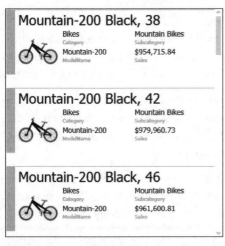

FIGURE 10-16 Card view is effective when a table has a picture in a column, like the Products table.

Values are automatically arranged in rows and columns based on the width of the table. The smaller the width, the larger the number of rows used for the card. If a picture is added to the card, then it is shown in the first position, making it very visible.

The heading of Card view is the table default label, if there is one. You can set the table default label in the PowerPivot window, using the Table Behavior button on the Advanced tab of PowerPivot. The Table Behavior button opens a window that you can use to set a few properties for the table, among which you will find the Default label and Default image. You will learn more about the default behavior in the next chapter, but for now, it is enough to remember that the header of the Card view can be set by selecting a column as the table default label.

In Figure 10-17, you can see the Table Behavior dialog box for the product table.

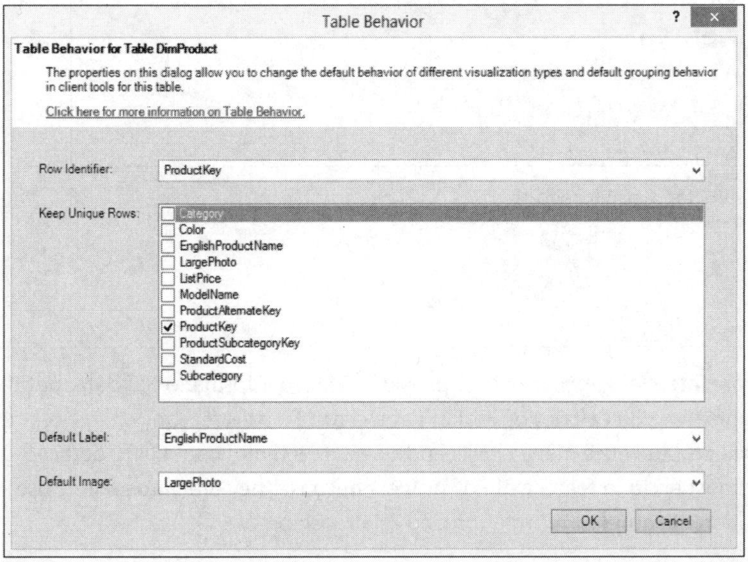

FIGURE 10-17 The Table Behavior window contains, among other properties, the default label of the table.

Using a table as a slicer

Previously in this chapter, you saw that a chart can be used to filter the report automatically by clicking one of the items of the chart. Table visualizations do not have this property. You can click and move the cursor on the rows of a table, but this operation does not apply any filtering to the report.

Nevertheless, you can use a table as a filter by converting it into a slicer. Not all the tables can be converted into slicers, though. If you want to turn a table into a slicer, it needs to contain a single column. Once you have created a table containing a single column, you can convert it into a slicer using the Slicer button on the DESIGN tab of the Excel ribbon.

Once a table has been converted to a slicer, you will not be able to add columns and calculated fields to it anymore because a slicer contains only a single column. Nevertheless, you can always convert it back to a table visualization. At that point, you will be free to modify its content.

In Figure 10-18, you can see a Card view with two slicers: one for the color and another one for the model name. Please note that the slicers affect each other. In fact, once the model name has been selected, only the valid colors for the selected model name become available for further selection.

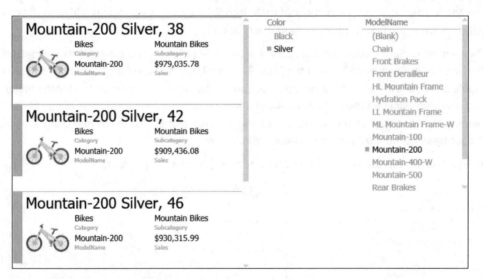

FIGURE 10-18 Slicers are useful for dynamic reports.

Using charts

The table visualizations are interesting because they provide detailed information of data, but they lack the immediate insights that you can get by looking at a chart. For this reason, when working with summary reports, you will probably use many charts and only a few tables containing detailed data. Charts are probably the most exciting feature of Power View because they are immediately useful and provide a great visualization of complex information and relationships.

The most commonly used charts are bar and column charts, which you can select by using the correspondent buttons in the Switch Visualization button group of the DESIGN tab of the Excel ribbon. Charts can be used as automatic slicers by simply clicking a value. For example, in Figure 10-19, you can see two charts (one column and one bar) where the user clicked the Black bar in the Sales by Color chart. The charts clearly show both the global value and the selected ones very effectively.

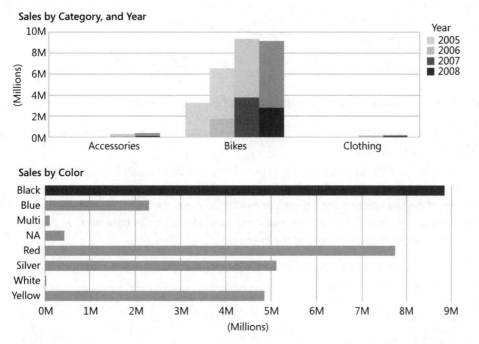

FIGURE 10-19 Bar and column charts are useful for both visualizing and slicing data.

The choice between whether to use a column chart or a bar chart really depends on the kind of data you are analyzing.

Using the line chart

Another chart visualization is the line chart, which is mainly used to show the behavior of a measure over time. You can place many measures on the same chart. For example, in Figure 10-20, you can see a simple line chart showing sales and revenues for several months.

> **Tip** In Chapter 11, "Shaping the reports," you will learn some useful data modeling techniques to draw charts that cover a broad time span. In this example, we are showing only one year of data. Putting many years on a single chart will result in some issues that will require some attention and are explained in the next chapter.

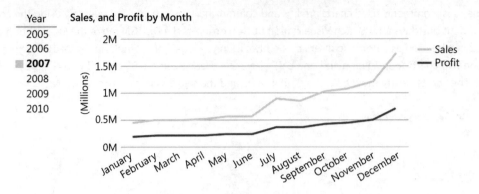

FIGURE 10-20 Line charts are useful to show the behavior of a measure over time.

Using the pie chart

Another type of chart visualization is the pie chart. Many professionals discourage the use of pie charts because they are not easy to read at first glance. They make it difficult to compare the relative size of different sections of a given pie chart or to compare data across different pie charts. Nevertheless, pie charts are very popular, and many users request them because they want to compare the size of a single slice against the entire pie.

For example, in Figure 10-21, you can see a simple pie chart that shows the contribution of different categories to total sales.

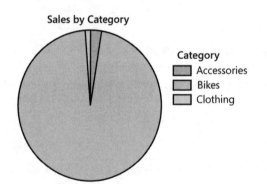

FIGURE 10-21 Simple pie charts are compact and might be a good representation for simple data.

Pie charts in Power View can be simple or sophisticated, depending on the kind of data you want to show. You have the option to select one column to define the slice size and a different column to color them. Moreover, when slicers are active in the chart, the pie highlights the selected area, as other charts do.

In Figure 10-22, you can see a sophisticated pie chart that uses the territory group to define the color of the slices. The slices are then created using the territory country, resulting in many slices rendered with the same color. The interesting fact is that when you click a year to select one, the inner highlighted part shows the contribution for that year and for each country to the total of the territory group.

Sales by Sales Territory Group, and Sales Territory Country

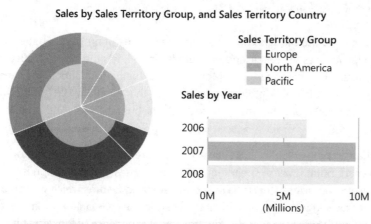

Sales Territory Group
- Europe
- North America
- Pacific

Sales by Year

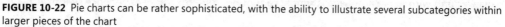

FIGURE 10-22 Pie charts can be rather sophisticated, with the ability to illustrate several subcategories within larger pieces of the chart

It is worth noticing that the bar chart used as a slicer is graphically placed inside the pie chart in Figure 10-22, resulting in a single, interactive, and compact report.

Using the scatter chart

The scatter chart (also known as the *bubble chart,* in its more advanced format) is probably the most fascinating (and most complex) feature among the charting capabilities of Power View. Scatter and bubble charts are a great way to display a lot of related data in one chart. In this type of chart, the x-axis displays one measure and the y-axis displays another, making it easy to see the relationship between the two values for all the items in the chart.

In a bubble chart, a third measure controls the size of the data points. Figure 10-23 displays an example of the visualization power of bubble charts.

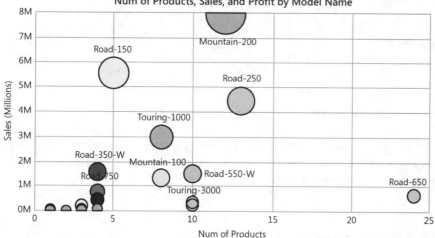

FIGURE 10-23 A bubble chart shows many related pieces of information in a single visualization.

To create this chart, you need to use the sales on the *y*-axis, the number of products on the *x*-axis, and the product model name as the detail, and the bubble size reflects the size of profits. By reading the chart, it is easy to see that the top seller is Mountain-200, the biggest bubble of all, thus producing the most of the revenues. It is also interesting to compare the Mountain-200 bubble with the Road-650 bubble. The Road-650 model has many more products, but it sells less and produces less revenues.

Working with bubble charts is not easy. It will take some time before you find a good way of showing the numbers in a chart, but it is worth spending that time. The final representation is compact, yet informative. Moreover, scatter charts have another amazing feature, which we can only try to describe here. We strongly suggest that you look at the chart in the companion workbook and play around with it, because words simply cannot describe the visual experience of looking at it.

In a bubble chart, you can drop a calendar attribute into the play area. It can be the year, the month, or the date, depending on the granularity you want to look at. For example, in Figure 10-24, we put the year in the play axis. At this point, the chart shows data for only the year 2008, the last year for which there are data, but a stimulating play button appears in the lower-left corner of the chart.

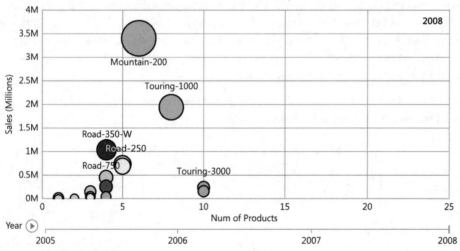

FIGURE 10-24 Using the play axis, there is a play button in the bubble chart.

Clicking the play button starts an animation that shows how values changed over time, resulting in a sort of race between the bubbles to reach the best position. In Figure 10-25, you can see the animation at the point when it reached 2007.

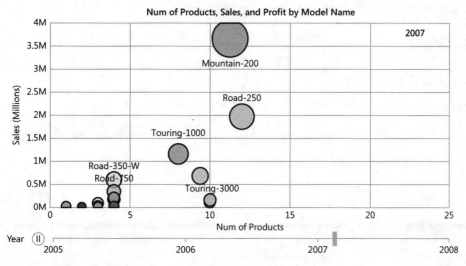

FIGURE 10-25 When the animation arrives at 2007, it shows a different layout.

As already stated, there is no way to express in just words the feeling of looking at this effect, so stop reading at this point and play with the animation on your PC. We are sure that the experience will push you to study this chart and all its options further.

Using maps

All the charts you have seen in Power View up to now are somewhat familiar to Excel users because they exist, although with some differences, in standard Excel. The map chart is a wonderful addition to Power View and, as you might imagine, it lets you draw charts on a map. Like all other Power View features, the beauty of the map chart is its simplicity.

To build a map chart, you need to have information about the locations of sales. In *Adventure-Works*, each customer contains the complete address through the DimGeography table, and you are going to use this information to create a map out of it. You find this data model in the companion workbook "CH10-02-Power View Map.xlsx."

> **Note** To complete this demo, you are not using just the information in DimSalesTerritory, which was already present in the previously used data model, because DimSalesTerritory contains only information at the country level. For the map chart, you want to get complete addresses. Thus, you are going to use customer addresses to find precise points on the map.

In Figure 10-26, you can see the data model for this demo.

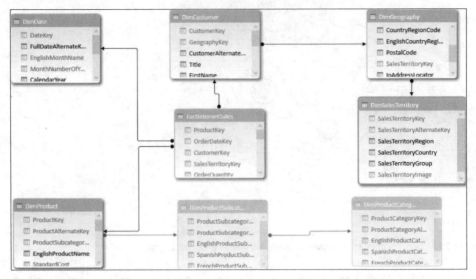

FIGURE 10-26 The data model for the map demo contains the DimGeography table.

To start, simply select the *Sales* calculated field in a newly created Power View report and convert the table into a map by clicking the Map button on the DESIGN tab of the ribbon. After a bit of resizing, you end up with a map of the world that does not contain any information about sales. If you look at the field list, you will note that some columns have a world icon beside them; namely, City, EnglishCountryRegionName, and PostalCode.

In fact, Excel analyzed the content of the table and, having detected city and location names inside these objects, marked them as geographical columns. To draw circles on the map and start looking at the map, it is enough at this point to select EnglishCountryRegionName and put it into the LOCATIONS panel to project data using the geographical location of the region.

> **Important** The first time you create a map using the data mode, a privacy warning appears, saying that the data need to be sent to Bing in order to be geocoded. This is because Excel does not contain a map of the world, with cities and addresses. In order to take the latitude and longitude of your addresses, Excel sends them to Bing, which in turn returns the coordinates of the addresses. For this reason, you can create map charts only if you have an active Internet connection, which is also required to download the map from Bing.

At this point, your chart will look like Figure 10-27.

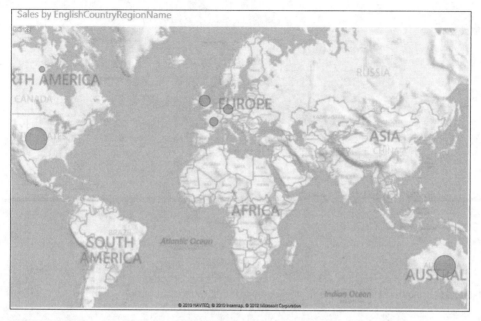

FIGURE 10-27 The map chart is incredibly easy to create using geographical names as the source.

This chart is amazingly simple to create. When you zoom into Europe, you will see that the points drawn are at the country level only—there is no information about the cities. The reason for this is pretty obvious: you used the country name as the slicer. To get more detailed information, you can try to add the city after the country in the LOCATION panel, but surprisingly, nothing changes in the report after you do this. In fact, even if you are able to add many columns to the LOCATION panel, only the first one is shown on the map. All the remaining ones are used for drill-down operations, which you will learn later.

A way to get more detailed information might be to remove the country and leave the city in the LOCATION pane. After a few seconds, during which geographical resolution happens, you will see many points in the map, and if you zoom on Paris in France, you will see the report shown in Figure 10-28.

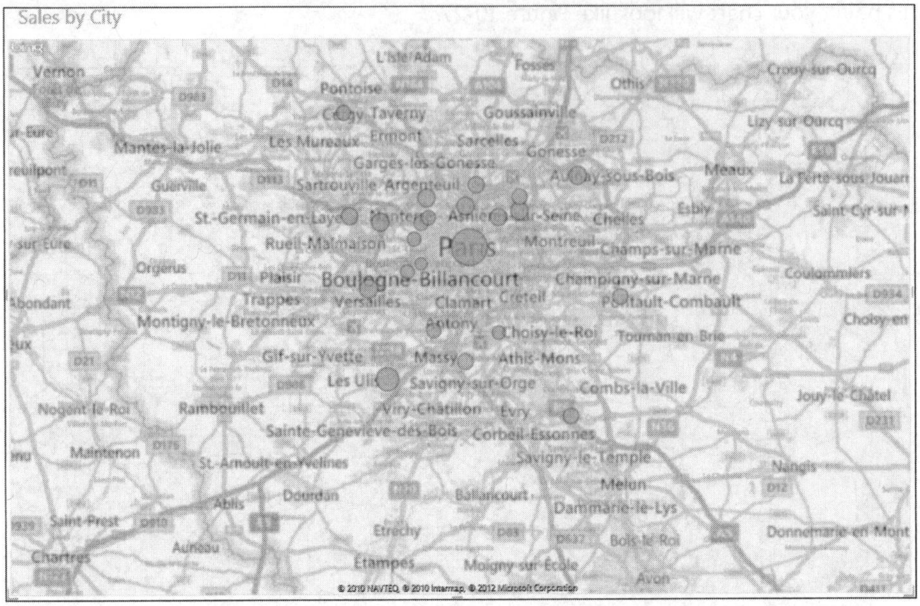

FIGURE 10-28 Using the city, the map is much more detailed, showing cities instead of countries.

Unfortunately, there are at least two cities named Paris in the world: there is one in France, and there is another in Texas. When you say that you want to plot data for the city of Paris, which one do you mean? You clearly need a way to distinguish between these two (and possibly others as well).

Because only one column can be used on the map, the solution is to create a calculated column that concatenates the various pieces of the address into a single place. The expression for the calculated column is as follows:

```
FullCityName =

    DimGeography[City] & ", " &
    DimGeography[StateProvinceName] & ", " &
    DimGeography[EnglishCountryRegionName]
```

Now each column contains the full specification of the city (that is, the city, the state or province, and the country). By using this column, you will get detailed information about locations, with no ambiguity.

When drawing maps, you can even add more information to your chart by using a separation by color. In Figure 10-29, you can see a map where we assigned the category to the color axis and added a slicer for the country region. You can see that each point in the map has turned into a small pie chart, colored as the legend indicates.

FIGURE 10-29 When you add a color axis, each point is turned into a small pie chart and colored by category.

You can modify the way a map chart is shown on the LAYOUT tab of the Excel ribbon. You can change the map background to make the map look like satellite view or look like a road map, modify the legend, and other cosmetic options.

Understanding drill-down

In previous sections of this chapter, you learned the basic tools to build a Power View report. Now it is time to learn another feature, which will liven up your reports by adding much more interactivity: the drill-down. *Drill-down* is the action of analyzing a chart in more detail, following a predefined path.

For example, let's consider the map chart. You have seen that it is possible to plot circles at the country level or at the city level, and that, to plot the cities, you need to create a calculated column to uniquely identify the cities. The problem with this approach is that by plotting data at the city level, you produce many points on the world map, resulting in a scattered view of data that makes it hard to get high-level insights. You can obviously generate two reports: a high-level one and a summary, so that you can get both views. However, with Power View, you have a better option—merge the two reports into a single one and use the drill-down feature.

Using drill-down, you can prepare the report at the country level and create a navigation path that starts with the country and moves down to the state province, then to the city and, finally, to the customer address. This is the drill-down path. You start with a report like the one in Figure 10-30.

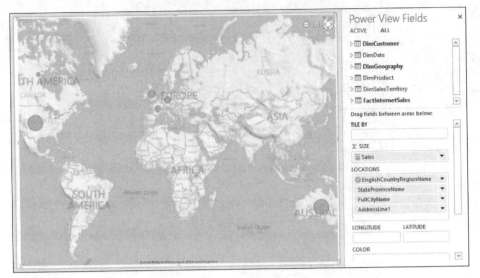

FIGURE 10-30 The drill-down path for a map is created in the LOCATIONS panel.

The initial chart is showing only the country names, with circles that represent the sales for the whole country. To activate drill-down, you only need to double-click one of the circles (for example, Australia). The map automatically zooms into Australia and shows the next level, which is the state province name, as shown in Figure 10-31.

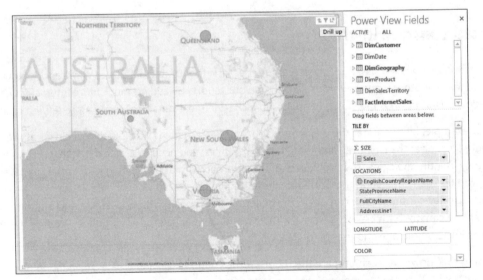

FIGURE 10-31 Double-clicking Australia shows the next level of the drill-down path.

After you start drilling-down, you will notice that a small button with an arrow appears in the upper-right corner of the map: this is the drill-up button, which you use to go back one level at a time in the hierarchy. If you click when you are at the state province, Power View will redraw the map at the country level. You can use drill-down to reach the address level and find the exact address of your customers, if needed.

The drill-down feature is not limited to maps. It works on any type of chart. For example, you can easily create a column chart that shows the sales divided by year, and when double-clicking the year, it drills down to the month, and finally to individual days. The beauty of drill-down is that the chart is no longer a static chart; it becomes a live analysis that moves along a predefined path.

Using tiles

You have seen that drill-down is useful to spice up a report. There is a feature in Power View that is amazingly powerful, even if it is not so evident: the ability to use tiles. To see tiles in action, you start with a simple Power View report, containing only month and sales, like the one in Figure 10-32.

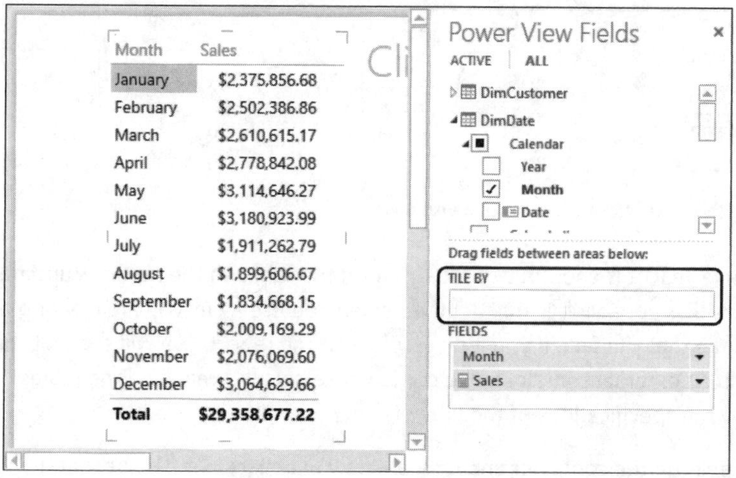

FIGURE 10-32 The TILE BY panel lets you add tiles to your visualization.

Because this report does not contain any selection for the year, it is showing sales divided by month and taking all the years into account. If you want to filter a single year, you can either use the Filters pane or you can use tiles. If you drag the year to the TILE BY panel, the report will be sliced by year and a selector appears on top of it, as shown in Figure 10-33.

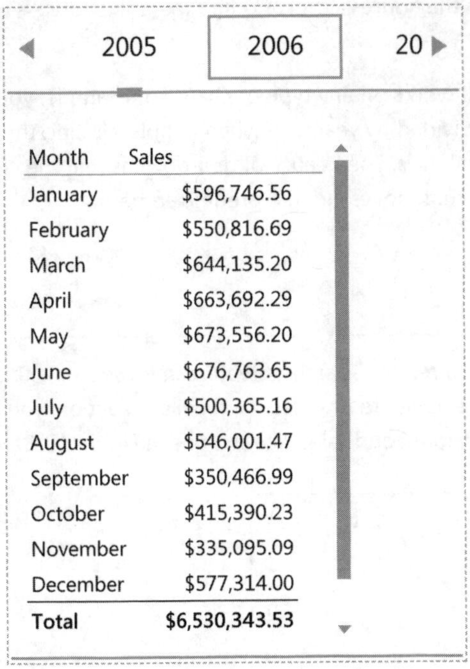

Month	Sales
2005	2006	20 ▶

Month	Sales
January	$596,746.56
February	$550,816.69
March	$644,135.20
April	$663,692.29
May	$673,556.20
June	$676,763.65
July	$500,365.16
August	$546,001.47
September	$350,466.99
October	$415,390.23
November	$335,095.09
December	$577,314.00
Total	**$6,530,343.53**

FIGURE 10-33 Tiles are selectors that filter the report in a visual way.

To show data for a single year, it is enough to click a year on the top, and the report is updated automatically. What makes tiles appealing is the fact that, when you use a tile, you are creating a container that surrounds the table. In fact, if you look carefully at the report, you will see that the table has been included in an external container. The container selects the year, and the tables contained into it will obey the specifications of the filter.

At this point, you can enlarge the container and create a new bar chart in it. The bar chart will be filtered by the same year, simply because it is in the same tile section, as shown in Figure 10-34.

2005 2006 **2007** 2008

Month	Sales
January	$40,726.26
February	$41,060.21
March	$65,006.95
April	$59,362.06
May	$54,488.01
June	$91,487.83
July	$100,639.36
August	$86,964.96
September	$106,927.58
October	$76,469.09
November	$104,172.80
December	$199,019.87
Total	**$1,026,324.97**

(Bar chart: Sales in Millions by country — Australia, Canada, France, Germany, United Kingdom, United States — 0M to 3M)

FIGURE 10-34 All the charts and tables inside a tile section will be filtered by the tile.

Using this feature, you can build interactive reports, like the one in Figure 10-35.

Sales Analysis

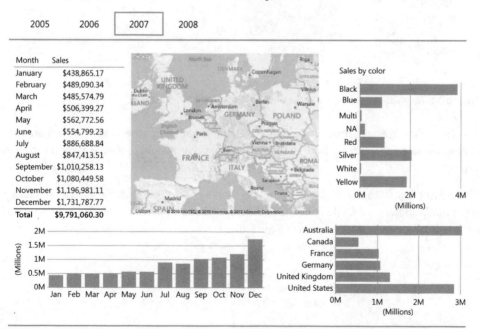

FIGURE 10-35 Using tiles, you can group any kind of visualization into a single container.

Understanding multipliers

In the previous section, you learned how to use tiles to create reports that are automatically filtered. Another common scenario is that you do not want the report to be filtered by year, but you want to repeat it many times, once for each year.

For example, you can create a pie chart that shows sales by country. If you want to take a quick look at the values for different years, you can use the VERTICAL MULTIPLIER section of the field list. Putting the year in that section will make Power View repeat the chart for different years.

The result is a larger chart (you will probably use full window for a multiplied chart) that gives quick insights into the full set of data, as shown in Figure 10-36.

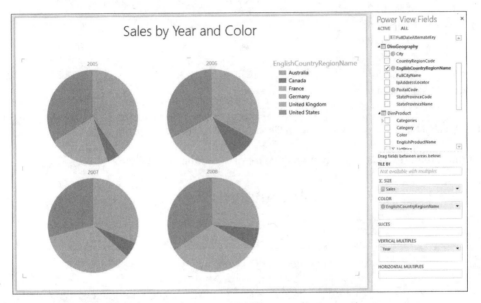

FIGURE 10-36 The multiplier section lets you repeat the same chart many times.

You cannot mix tiles and multipliers. Tiles are meant for filtering, whereas multipliers are meant for repeating the same chart. Using both of them in a single chart would probably make it too complex to use.

You are not limited to using multipliers only in simple charts. For example, you can repeat a map chart so that it shows on a single page many different locations, with full detailed information about where items have been sold, as shown in Figure 10-37.

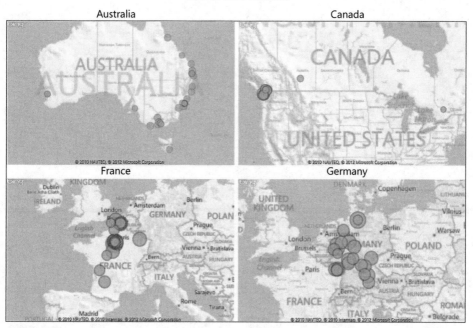

FIGURE 10-37 You can multiply any chart; this example shows different maps.

Using Power View effectively

Power View is an amazing tool when it comes to get insights from data in a visual way. You normally start your investigation by putting some columns and calculated field into a table, then project the data into different charts until you get the visualization that makes the pattern you are searching for more evident.

At this point, you add more charts, drill-down, and use tiles and other analytical items to go into additional detail and, when you are finished, you will have created an interactive report that can be used many times to perform the same analysis on updated data.

Keep in mind that for the data model to be used in an efficient way in Power View, you need to pay attention to some small details. You will learn more about these in the next chapter, which covers several advanced topics about reporting with Excel.

Using Power Views Effectively

CHAPTER 11

Shaping the reports

In the previous chapters, you have learned some data modeling techniques that greatly help in the building of reports. Data modeling is very important, and we cannot overstress the fact that, although you will not need to become a master in data modeling, you need at least to understand the basic techniques to achieve optimal results using Microsoft Excel to create complex reports. But data modeling, alone, is only useful to compute numbers. Once a number is computed, it still needs to be shown to the user in a report so that it is easy to understand and leads to good insights in the data.

You have learned the tools available in Power View to design a report; now, it is time to merge the two topics and learn some techniques that you will find useful when designing a data model to build reports. There are several minor points that you need to care about when designing a data model that is easy to use, like the sorting of values in the PivotTable, number formats, the creation of sets, visual Key Performance Indicators (KPIs), and columns that will make reporting easier. This chapter is dedicated to some of the most useful techniques of this art.

Key Performance Indicators (KPIs)

Up to now, you have learned the basics of Microsoft PowerPivot and of the DAX language to compute values (that is, numbers). In most of the examples, we focused on simple calculations because the focus was on the way these calculations work, not on the real content of the calculations.

When you define a data model, you should not only create simple calculations like the sum of sales amounts, but more complex ones that provide a strategy for the analysis. In fact, even if the sales amount is a good indicator of how sales are going, it does not tell you anything about whether you are following the right strategy in achieving your goals. Before you can define a strategy, you need to define a goal and then check if the numbers are bringing you closer to your goal.

The definition of the goals is up to you, and it really depends on the business you are analyzing. In this section, you are going to learn the most important tool available in the Excel data model to perform goal-oriented analysis (that is, the KPI). As has already been said, the KPI is a useful feature in itself, but you will get the most out of it if you use it to start thinking in terms of strategic analysis instead of simple "number crunching."

Imagine that you are responsible for tracking and monitoring sales at AdventureWorks, and you have created the report shown in Figure 11-1. You can find this example in the companion workbook "CH11-01-KPI.xlsx."

Categories	Bikes			

Sum of SalesAmount	Column Labels			
Row Labels	Europe	North America	Pacific	Grand Total
⊟ 2007	$3,262,529.32	$3,148,783.82	$2,947,789.48	$9,359,102.62
⊞ January	$140,385.68	$112,241.26	$186,238.23	$438,865.17
⊞ February	$168,726.52	$112,581.78	$207,782.04	$489,090.34
⊞ March	$179,588.64	$107,197.66	$198,788.49	$485,574.79
⊞ April	$181,942.10	$119,104.09	$205,353.08	$506,399.27
⊞ May	$180,535.03	$178,079.89	$204,157.65	$562,772.56
⊞ June	$212,462.84	$139,701.12	$202,635.26	$554,799.23
⊞ July	$333,201.66	$284,811.89	$247,679.23	$865,692.78
⊞ August	$284,417.71	$313,087.61	$174,516.19	$772,021.51
⊞ September	$323,856.12	$298,111.52	$309,996.31	$931,963.95
⊞ October	$326,268.27	$347,098.00	$326,562.61	$999,928.88
⊞ November	$354,261.68	$444,124.90	$318,234.32	$1,116,620.90
⊞ December	$576,883.06	$692,644.09	$365,846.09	$1,635,373.24
⊟ 2008	$3,044,696.49	$3,676,699.92	$2,440,928.44	$9,162,324.85
⊞ January	$395,828.51	$484,544.09	$374,195.67	$1,254,568.27
⊞ February	$469,545.40	$520,284.83	$387,588.90	$1,377,419.13
⊞ March	$476,525.46	$537,930.03	$377,582.58	$1,392,038.07
⊞ April	$502,636.62	$584,167.07	$427,245.04	$1,514,048.73
⊞ May	$554,627.44	$805,193.09	$415,476.42	$1,775,296.95
⊞ June	$645,533.06	$744,580.81	$458,839.83	$1,848,953.70
Grand Total	$6,307,225.81	$6,825,483.74	$5,388,717.92	$18,521,427.47

FIGURE 11-1 Here is a sample PivotTable showing the sales amounts for different periods.

The report already contains a lot of information, but extracting strategic information from it requires some time and patience. Try to ask yourself some simple questions, like:

- Are sales in Europe growing at the same rate as sales in the Pacific, or in North America?

- Which region is growing the fastest?

- How is the growth in March, compared with other months? Was that a good month?

You can clearly answer these questions by analyzing the numbers and drawing conclusions about them, but if you want to answer these questions quickly, it is much better if you add some features to your data model to make it easier to get these insights.

First, you need to better understand the concept of "growth." You will use the growth in percentage against the previous year as the main indicator of growth in sales. Thus, you need a measure such as the following code for Sales Growth:

```
Sales := SUM ( FactInternetSales[SalesAmount] )

SalesLastYear := CALCULATE ( [Sales], SAMEPERIODLASTYEAR ( DimDate[FullDateAlternateKey] ) )

[Sales Growth] := ( [Sales] - [SalesLastYear] ) / [SalesLastYear]
```

Note You will learn to use the *SAMEPERIODLASTYEAR* function in Chapter 12, "Performing date calculations in DAX," but for the moment, you can safely assume that *SalesLastYear*, as its name suggests, computes the sales of the same period, but from the previous year. Thus, for March 2008, it will return the sales of March 2007.

You can test these calculated fields in a PivotTable, which you can see in Figure 11-2.

Categories	Bikes ⫪		
Row Labels ⫪	**Sales**	**SalesLastYear**	**Sales Growth**
⊟ 2007	$9,359,102.62	6,530,343.53	43.32%
⊞ January	$438,865.17	596,746.56	-26.46%
⊞ February	$489,090.34	550,816.69	-11.21%
⊞ March	$485,574.79	644,135.20	-24.62%
⊞ April	$506,399.27	663,692.29	-23.70%
⊞ May	$562,772.56	673,556.20	-16.45%
⊞ June	$554,799.23	676,763.65	-18.02%
⊞ July	$865,692.78	500,365.16	73.01%
⊞ August	$772,021.51	546,001.47	41.40%
⊞ September	$931,963.95	350,466.99	165.92%
⊞ October	$999,928.88	415,390.23	140.72%
⊞ November	$1,116,620.90	335,095.09	233.23%
⊞ December	$1,635,373.24	577,314.00	183.27%
⊟ 2008	$9,162,324.85	9,359,102.62	-2.10%
⊞ January	$1,254,568.27	438,865.17	185.87%
⊞ February	$1,377,419.13	489,090.34	181.63%
⊞ March	$1,392,038.07	485,574.79	186.68%
⊞ April	$1,514,048.73	506,399.27	198.98%
⊞ May	$1,775,296.95	562,772.56	215.46%
⊞ June	$1,848,953.70	554,799.23	233.27%
⊞ July		865,692.78	-100.00%
⊞ August		772,021.51	-100.00%
⊞ September		931,963.95	-100.00%
⊞ October		999,928.88	-100.00%
⊞ November		1,116,620.90	-100.00%
⊞ December		1,635,373.24	-100.00%
Grand Total	**$18,521,427.47**	**15,889,446.14**	**16.56%**

FIGURE 11-2 Here, you can see the three calculated fields previously defined working in a PivotTable.

Although the numbers are correct, there are some points that still need attention:

- The months from July to December 2008 need to be removed because they have no sales in 2008, so the growth is not computable.

- The grand total does not make any sense, at least not in terms of the growth.

- The figure showing growth in 2008 is incorrect because it takes into account the sales of the entire year 2007, while it should only be computing the months before July.

These issues can be corrected using this formula for the *SalesLastYear* calculated field:

```
SalesLastYear :=
IF (
    HASONEVALUE ( DimDate[CalendarYear] ),
    SUMX (
        VALUES ( DimDate[EnglishMonthName] ),
        IF (
            CALCULATE ( [Sales] ) > 0,
            CALCULATE (
                [Sales],
                SAMEPERIODLASTYEAR ( DimDate[FullDateAlternateKey] )
            )
        )
    )
)
```

You now check that the computation is executed for a single year, and you return only values for the months where there are sales. If there were no sales in a particular month, then a *BLANK* is returned, resulting in the line being removed from the PivotTable.

Moreover, using *SUMX* over the months, you compute a correct value at the Year level, taking into account only the months where there are sales. Finally, the *SalesGrowth* calculated field needs to check that the grand total is not computed:

```
SalesGrowth :=
IF (
    HASONEVALUE ( DimDate[CalendarYear] ),
    ( [Sales] - [SalesLastYear] ) / [SalesLastYear]
)
```

With these definitions, the PivotTable looks much better, as Figure 11-3 shows.

Categories	Bikes		
Row Labels	**Sales**	**SalesLastYear**	**Sales Growth**
⊟ 2007	$9,359,102.62	6,530,343.53	43.32%
⊞ January	$438,865.17	596,746.56	-26.46%
⊞ February	$489,090.34	550,816.69	-11.21%
⊞ March	$485,574.79	644,135.20	-24.62%
⊞ April	$506,399.27	663,692.29	-23.70%
⊞ May	$562,772.56	673,556.20	-16.45%
⊞ June	$554,799.23	676,763.65	-18.02%
⊞ July	$865,692.78	500,365.16	73.01%
⊞ August	$772,021.51	546,001.47	41.40%
⊞ September	$931,963.95	350,466.99	165.92%
⊞ October	$999,928.88	415,390.23	140.72%
⊞ November	$1,116,620.90	335,095.09	233.23%
⊞ December	$1,635,373.24	577,314.00	183.27%
⊟ 2008	$9,162,324.85	3,037,501.36	201.64%
⊞ January	$1,254,568.27	438,865.17	185.87%
⊞ February	$1,377,419.13	489,090.34	181.63%
⊞ March	$1,392,038.07	485,574.79	186.68%
⊞ April	$1,514,048.73	506,399.27	198.98%
⊞ May	$1,775,296.95	562,772.56	215.46%
⊞ June	$1,848,953.70	554,799.23	233.27%
Grand Total	**$18,521,427.47**		

FIGURE 11-3 The test PivotTable now shows correct values for all of the formulas.

This PivotTable has been useful to check the values, and you will probably follow the same procedure whenever you create your formulas: you start with a PivotTable that shows all the numbers used in the formula to check easily that the computation is correct. Then, when you trust your formulas, you remove intermediate columns and return to the original PivotTable you were working on.

You can look at the SalesGrowth measure in the original PivotTable in Figure 11-4.

Categories	Bikes			
Sales Growth	**Column Labels**			
Row Labels	**Europe**	**North America**	**Pacific**	**Grand Total**
⊟ 2007	100.43%	14.57%	36.83%	43.32%
⊞ January	23.56%	-56.83%	-16.53%	-26.46%
⊞ February	34.76%	-56.94%	26.57%	-11.21%
⊞ March	28.93%	-60.63%	-14.53%	-24.62%
⊞ April	39.95%	-61.48%	-8.51%	-23.70%
⊞ May	42.60%	-47.82%	-0.74%	-16.45%
⊞ June	59.23%	-58.13%	-3.35%	-18.02%
⊞ July	168.01%	16.23%	89.08%	73.01%
⊞ August	103.35%	22.11%	16.55%	41.40%
⊞ September	133.99%	211.15%	166.66%	165.92%
⊞ October	158.68%	243.65%	73.47%	140.72%
⊞ November	184.67%	314.27%	207.65%	233.23%
⊞ December	179.46%	319.95%	77.64%	183.27%
⊟ 2008	186.25%	378.17%	102.57%	201.64%
⊞ January	181.96%	331.70%	100.92%	185.87%
⊞ February	178.29%	362.14%	86.54%	181.63%
⊞ March	165.34%	401.81%	89.94%	186.68%
⊞ April	176.26%	390.47%	108.05%	198.98%
⊞ May	207.21%	352.15%	103.51%	215.46%
⊞ June	203.83%	432.98%	126.44%	233.27%

FIGURE 11-4 Here, you can see the Sales Growth measure working in the initial PivotTable.

Even though we now have a clear idea of what sales growth means, we still need to understand how to evaluate the sales growth. What does it mean to say that a month was "good"? You can define a specific target (for example, 50 percent more than the same month in the previous year); or you can define a more generic target (for example, "better than average growth"). Clearly, the insights that come from these two definitions are different and you are going to learn both techniques.

Let's start with a comparison against the 50 percent growth target. Instead of using only two values (that is, less than or more than 50 percent), you can use a more granular definition: if it is less than 40 percent, then it is bad; if it is between 40 and 80 percent, it is good; and if it is more than 80 percent it is outstanding. It would be desirable to use images to show the three situations, and this is exactly what the KPI feature of PowerPivot is designed to do.

What is a KPI? A *KPI* is a graphical and intuitive representation of the relationship existing between a measure and a value, either a fixed value or another measure. To create a new KPI, you will need to choose the New KPI option from the KPIs menu of the PowerPivot tab on the Excel ribbon (see Figure 11-5).

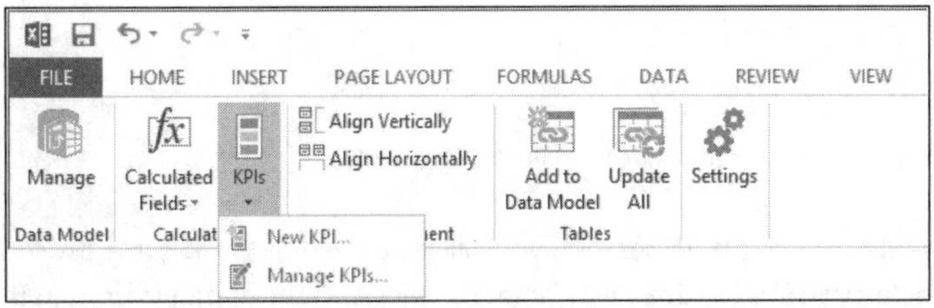

FIGURE 11-5 You need to use the New KPI option to create a new KPI.

Choosing New KPI will open the Key Performance Indicator (KPI) dialog box, shown in Figure 11-6.

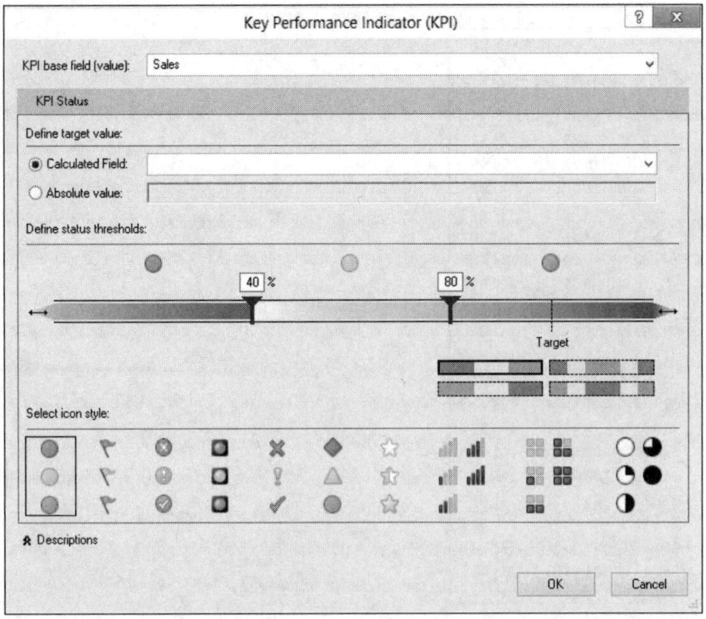

FIGURE 11-6 The Key Performance Indicator (KPI) dialog box lets you create new KPI.

Because a KPI shows the relationship between a calculated field and a value, you need to provide a calculated field as the base field for the KPI, and then the target of the KPI, which can be an absolute value or another calculated field. For now, you are going to use an absolute value. Because our calculated field is already a ratio, its value is represented as a percentage: 1 means 100 percent, 2 means 200 percent, and so on. When defining the KPI, you need to use Sales Growth as the base calculated field and 1 as the absolute value to check. You can leave all other fields with their default value and click OK to close the window and define the KPI.

> **Tip** You can modify the values of the thresholds either by clicking on the values (40 and 80 in the example) and typing the values with the keyboard or by dragging the black indicators left or right until you find the value that fits your needs.

Once the KPI is defined, it will appear as a new folder under the FactInternetSales table and the base measure used to define the KPI will disappear from the available calculated fields. In fact, once a calculated field is used to define a KPI, it becomes the KPI value and is no longer considered a "normal" calculated field. In Figure 11-7, you can see the KPI folder in the FactInternetSales table.

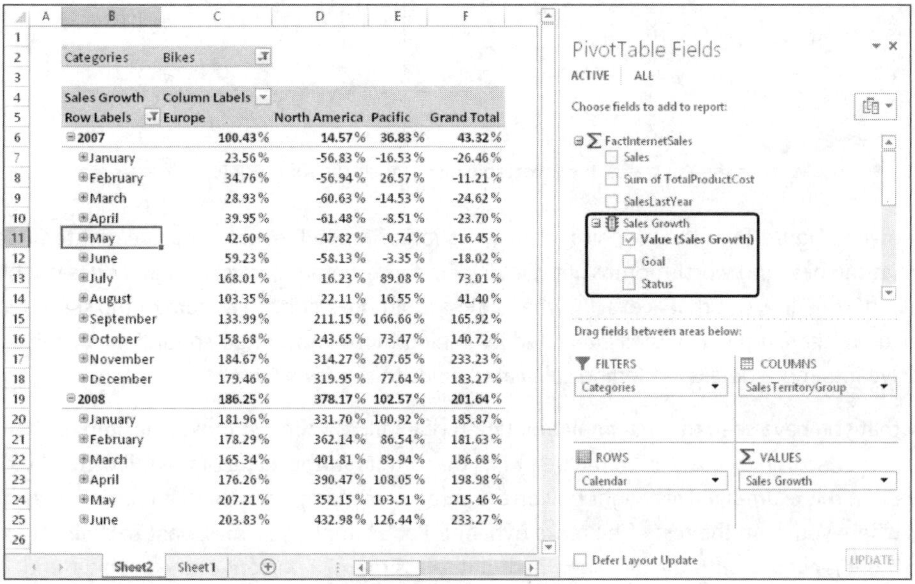

FIGURE 11-7 Once a calculated field is used for a KPI, it is shown as a folder in the table where it is defined.

If you now select the status of the KPI and remove the value, the PivotTable appears as shown in Figure 11-8.

Categories   Bikes

Sales Growth Status   Column Labels

Row Labels	Europe	NA	North America	Pacific	Grand Total
⊟ 2007					
⊞ January					
⊞ February					
⊞ March					
⊞ April					
⊞ May					
⊞ June					
⊞ July					
⊞ August					
⊞ September					
⊞ October					
⊞ November					
⊞ December					
⊟ 2008					
⊞ January					
⊞ February					
⊞ March					
⊞ April					
⊞ May					
⊞ June					
⊞ July					
⊞ August					
⊞ September					
⊞ October					
⊞ November					
⊞ December					
Grand Total					

FIGURE 11-8 Once you use the KPI status, the PivotTable gives much clearer insights.

As shown in Figure 11-8, the graphical representation of the KPI makes it much easier to understand what the best and worst months are. Clearly, the representation is concise and does not provide complete information, but that is exactly what a KPI should be: a concise picture of the status of a strategic goal. Then, if the analyst is interested in gaining more knowledge about it, he or she can easily delve into more details by adding calculated fields to the PivotTable.

Now that you have seen the first implementation of a KPI, it is time to move one step further and perform a more complex analysis. In the first KPI, you compared the value of the KPI with a fixed number (1, in this example). This might be correct in many scenarios, but there are other kinds of analysis where you want the test to be more dynamic. For example, you may want to define a month as "good" if it is aligned with the average, "bad" if it is less than 70 percent of the average, and "outstanding" if it is more than the average. Clearly, to define such a set of conditions, you first need to specify what you mean by "average."

When performing analysis at the month level, the average can be the average of the year. But, when analyzing many years, the average can be the average over many years. It is not that one number is more correct than the other—it is a matter of what kind of analysis you want to perform. When defining KPI, you need to have a clear idea of what you are analyzing.

As an example of a suitable formula to determine whether a month is good or not, you can use the yearly growth of the selection. What does this mean? If there is a slicer filtering only a specific country in the PivotTable, you take the yearly growth for that country, and for each month, you create the KPI so that it shows whether that month grew more than the defined average. Clearly, if the PivotTable selects a color too, then the average will change, and so will the KPI status.

A picture might clarify this concept. In Figure 11-9, you can see two PivotTables side by side.

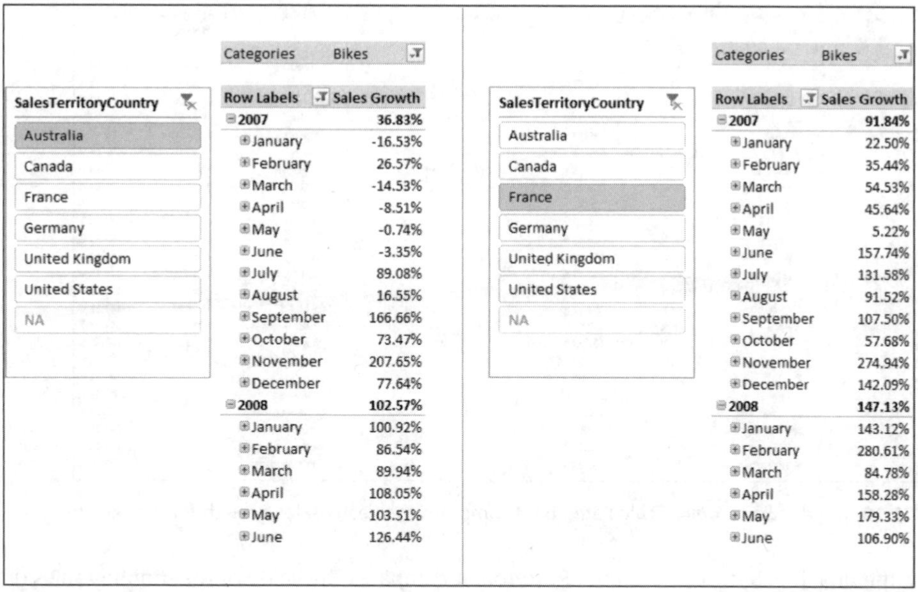

FIGURE 11-9 These two PivotTables show data for different countries, so the average sales growth is different.

In the left PivotTable, the slicer selects Australia, while in the right one, the slicer selects France. For example, in 2007, you want to compare the value of January with the growth for the whole year 2007. However, the growth in 2007 is different in Australia and France, and you want to compare the monthly growth with the yearly one in the same selection. Thus, September 2007 is strong in Australia (166.66 percent compared to 36.83 percent) and just all right in France (107.50 percent against 91.84 percent).

Now that you have learned DAX, the formula for a measure that computes the correct average to use as the comparison base is not hard to come up with. You want to compute, for the current year, the value of the grand total for all other columns. In other words, you fix the year and leave all other columns in the database unconstrained. (Well, not completely unconstrained—you want them to still obey the original filter context of the PivotTable.) You might recall that the *ALLSELECTED* function does exactly this: it removes filters from columns, restoring the original filter context of the PivotTable. With this in mind, the following formula is not hard to read:

```
[Avg SalesGrowth] :=
CALCULATE (
    [Sales Growth],
    ALLSELECTED (),
    VALUES ( DimDate[CalendarYear] )
)
```

ALLSELECTED without any parameter restores the original filter context, whereas VALUES
(DimDate[CalendarYear]) restricts the filter to only the current year. You can see the result of this new
calculated field in Figure 11-10.

SalesTerritoryCountry		Row Labels	Sales Growth	Avg Sales Growth
Australia		⊟2007	36.83 %	36.83 %
Canada		⊞January	-16.53 %	36.83 %
France		⊞February	26.57 %	36.83 %
Germany		⊞March	-14.53 %	36.83 %
NA		⊞April	-8.51 %	36.83 %
United Kingdom		⊞May	-0.74 %	36.83 %
United States		⊞June	-3.35 %	36.83 %
		⊞July	89.08 %	36.83 %
		⊞August	16.55 %	36.83 %
		⊞September	166.66 %	36.83 %
		⊞October	73.47 %	36.83 %
		⊞November	207.65 %	36.83 %
		⊞December	77.64 %	36.83 %
		⊟2008	102.57 %	102.57 %
		⊞January	100.92 %	102.57 %
		⊞February	86.54 %	102.57 %
		⊞March	89.94 %	102.57 %
		⊞April	108.05 %	102.57 %
		⊞May	103.51 %	102.57 %
		⊞June	126.44 %	102.57 %
		⊞July		102.57 %
		⊞August		102.57 %
		⊞September		102.57 %
		⊞October		102.57 %
		⊞November		102.57 %
		⊞December		102.57 %

Categories: Bikes

SalesTerritoryCountry		Row Labels	Sales Growth	Avg Sales Growth
Australia		⊟2007	91.84 %	91.84 %
Canada		⊞January	22.50 %	91.84 %
France		⊞February	35.44 %	91.84 %
Germany		⊞March	54.53 %	91.84 %
NA		⊞April	45.64 %	91.84 %
United Kingdom		⊞May	5.22 %	91.84 %
United States		⊞June	157.74 %	91.84 %
		⊞July	131.58 %	91.84 %
		⊞August	91.52 %	91.84 %
		⊞September	107.50 %	91.84 %
		⊞October	57.68 %	91.84 %
		⊞November	274.94 %	91.84 %
		⊞December	142.09 %	91.84 %
		⊟2008	147.13 %	147.13 %
		⊞January	143.12 %	147.13 %
		⊞February	280.61 %	147.13 %
		⊞March	84.78 %	147.13 %
		⊞April	158.28 %	147.13 %
		⊞May	179.33 %	147.13 %
		⊞June	106.90 %	147.13 %
		⊞July		147.13 %
		⊞August		147.13 %
		⊞September		147.13 %
		⊞October		147.13 %
		⊞November		147.13 %
		⊞December		147.13 %

Categories: Bikes

FIGURE 11-10 The *Avg SalesGrowth* calculated field computes the yearly sales growth for the selection.

Now, the final touch is to define the KPI so that it compares the value of the monthly sales growth
to the result of this new calculated field. Doing so, you will get a dynamic and meaningful KPI that
quickly draws the user's attention to months that performed worse than average. In Figure 11-11, you
can see the KPI definition.

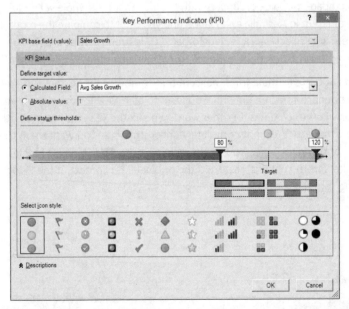

FIGURE 11-11 Instead of comparing to a fixed value, you compare Sales Growth to a calculated field.

At this point, you can add other fields to the PivotTable and build a report like the one shown in Figure 11-12, where the KPI is used to bring your attention to the months that performed worse than average, and other numbers help you get more insight into the scenario.

	Categories	Bikes .T		

SalesTerritoryCountry ⊼	Row Labels .T	Sales Growth	Sales	SalesLastYear	Sales Growth Status
Australia	⊟2007	36.83 %	$2,947,789.48	2,154,284.88	◯
Canada	⊞January	-16.53 %	$186,238.23	223,109.11	◯
France	⊞February	26.57 %	$207,782.04	164,161.08	◯
Germany	⊞March	-14.53 %	$198,788.49	232,584.98	◯
United Kingdom	⊞April	-8.51 %	$205,353.08	224,451.06	◯
United States	⊞May	-0.74 %	$204,157.65	205,688.58	◯
NA	⊞June	-3.35 %	$202,635.26	209,659.38	◯
	⊞July	89.08 %	$247,679.23	130,989.75	◯
	⊞August	16.55 %	$174,516.19	149,740.46	◯
	⊞September	166.66 %	$309,996.31	116,250.79	◯
	⊞October	73.47 %	$326,562.61	188,257.15	◯
	⊞November	207.65 %	$318,234.32	103,439.43	◯
	⊞December	77.64 %	$365,846.09	205,953.11	◯
	⊟2008	102.57 %	$2,440,928.44	1,204,954.73	◯
	⊞January	100.92 %	$374,195.67	186,238.23	◯
	⊞February	86.54 %	$387,588.90	207,782.04	◯
	⊞March	89.94 %	$377,582.58	198,788.49	◯
	⊞April	108.05 %	$427,245.04	205,353.08	◯
	⊞May	103.51 %	$415,476.42	204,157.65	◯
	⊞June	126.44 %	$458,839.83	202,635.26	◯
	Grand Total		$5,388,717.92		

FIGURE 11-12 KPIs are normally used to attract the user's attention to lines that already contain more information.

Creating data models for Power View

You have already had a brief overview of Power View in Chapter 1, "Introduction to PowerPivot." There, you just scratched the surface of the new, beautiful reporting engine now available in Excel 2013. Then, in Chapter 10, "Using Power View," you learned the building blocks of Power View reporting. Power View lets you do graphical analysis of data, making the search for insights in your datasets easier and maybe even a little fun.

We imagine that at this point of the book, you have already tried some Power View reports with your own data, just because we have succeeded in piquing your interest. If not, we strongly suggest that you do so now, for two reasons:

- Power View is not only a technical tool. It creates a wonderful experience that is hard to describe in print. Looking at static figures, you learn new techniques to create interesting reports, but you lack the feeling of doing it yourself.

- Using Power View without reading the explanation of how to write correct metadata for it, you will probably see some limitations and some operations that look hard to perform, and you will appreciate the hints in the rest of this chapter more.

When you design your data model, you need to pay special attention to Power View for many reasons, which you are going to learn here. In fact, a data model that does not take into account the peculiarities of Power View will provide a suboptimal experience when creating charts. An example may help to clarify this.

Imagine that you have a simple data model with a calendar table with a year-month-day hierarchy, which is the perfect choice for a PivotTable. In Figure 11-13, you can see the data model that you are going to use as a starting point. You can find this model in the companion workbook "CH11-02-Power View.xlsx."

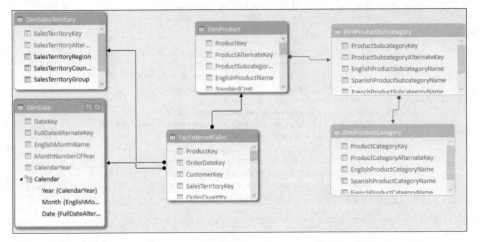

FIGURE 11-13 Here is an example of a data model that is correctly designed for a PivotTable.

Having created a hierarchy, you have hidden the columns of the calendar to reduce the number of fields shown in the field list. Now, using this data model, you can create a new Power View report and, when you click on the Calendar hierarchy, you get the list of all the years, months, and dates in a list. At this point, you can add the *Sales* calculated field, which is the sum of sales amounts, and you get the result shown in Figure 11-14.

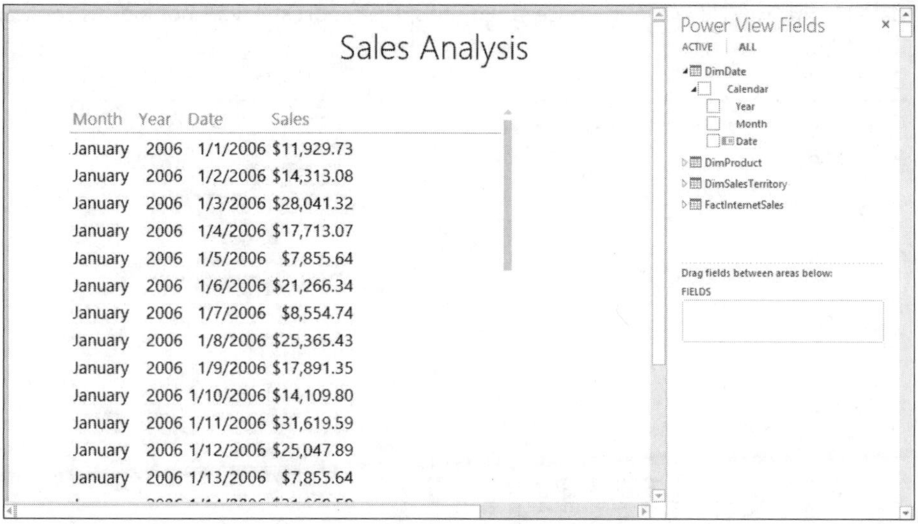

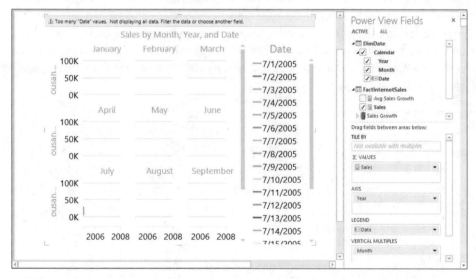

FIGURE 11-14 The default visualization of Power View is always a table.

This is the starting point of your Power View project, but, in this example, you are not interested in numbers. Rather, you want to generate a line chart that shows sales over several years. Thus, you click the Line chart of Power View. However, the result, shown in Figure 11-15, is definitely not what you would like to see.

FIGURE 11-15 Drawing the data in a line chart does not provide you a good representation of data.

The issue here is very clear: the columns of the hierarchy have been used in the wrong places: the year is on the axis, the month is a vertical multiplier, and the date has been used for the legend. Fixing all these problems is easy: just remove the year from the axis and the month from the multiplier, and use the date for the axis. Nevertheless, once you do this, the report still does not look as you want (see Figure 11-16).

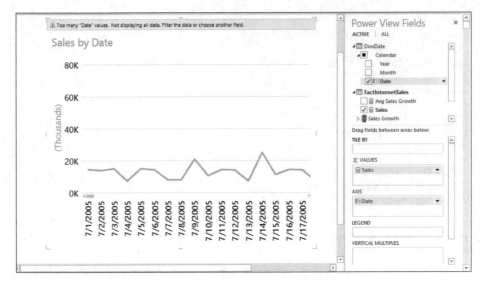

FIGURE 11-16 Even after making some changes, the chart does not represent the desired insights into the data.

You can see that on the chart, only dates from July 1 to July 17 are visible. You wanted to show many years, but you do not see that because Power View does not automatically scale data to make it fit the screen. The problem here is with the data model, which has been designed with a PivotTable in mind and is now being used with Power View. You can try to reduce the visualization by putting the month on the axis, but at this point, you will discover that each month shows the data for all the years. There is no difference between January 2007 and January 2008; the two numbers are aggregated inside January, as shown in Figure 11-17.

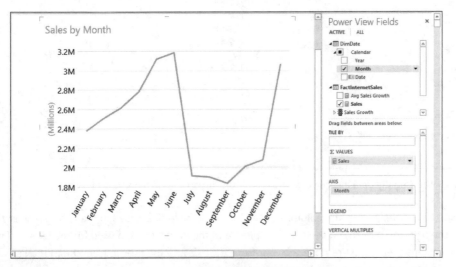

FIGURE 11-17 Using the month, you lose the year level of the hierarchy, so the result is still not correct.

The problem here is that in Power View, you can have only one column on the axis, so there is no way to put a hierarchy on the axis. Additional columns in the AXIS area will be used for drill-through purposes, but for visualization, Power View always uses a single column. With this limitation in mind, it is not so difficult to create a new calculated column in the calendar table that contains the combination of year and month. You achieve this using this simple expression:

```
YearMonth = YEAR ( [FullDateAlternateKey] ) * 100 + MONTH ( [FullDateAlternateKey] )
```

This column works much better on the axis because it does not contain too many values and includes the hierarchy year/month in a single column. Nevertheless, if you use this column on the axis, you still do not get an optimal result, as shown in Figure 11-18.

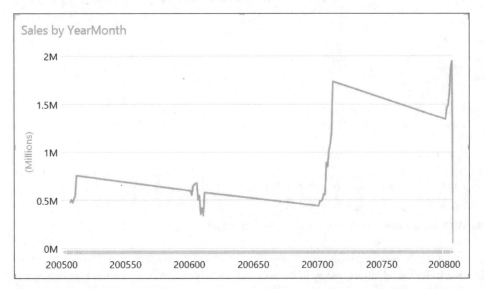

FIGURE 11-18 The YearMonth column works better, but it still is not the perfect choice.

What is wrong with this chart? Well, can you guess which month is represented by 200500? January 2005 should be 2005-01, and, worse, do you think there exists a month like 2005-50? Not at all. Here you are facing another issue; that is, since the column is a number, Power View thinks that it contains values covering the whole range and, not being able to show all of them on the axis, it uses standard mathematics to include values in the middle, which simply do not exist in the database.

To solve this issue, you simply need to convert the number into a string, or use a slightly different formula for the column, like the following one:

```
YearMonth =
    YEAR ( [FullDateAlternateKey] ) &
    "-" &
    RIGHT ( "00" & MONTH ( [FullDateAlternateKey] ), 2 )
```

Using this column for the axis, you get the desired result (see Figure 11-19).

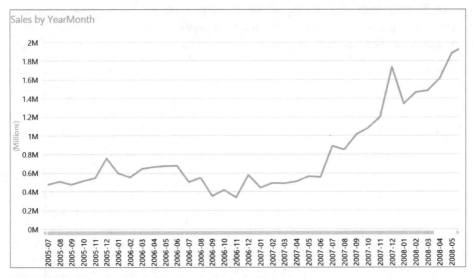

FIGURE 11-19 Using a string for YearMonth yields the desired result.

If the data model were designed with Power View in mind, then the YearMonth column as a string would have been already there, ready to be selected, and this chart could be built using a few clicks: select the YearMonth column, then add Sales and turn the table into a chart. Thus, you can see that there is a big difference in terms of usability between a data model designed for Power View and a data model designed only for PivotTables. For this reason, we strongly suggest that you become confident working with Power View and get a good understanding of its characteristics and its limitations, so that when you create data models, you will have a clearer picture of which columns will be useful to generate Power View reports.

Understanding Power View metadata

In the previous section, you saw that the data model needs to be designed with Power View in mind, to create the smoothest possible experience for the user. To make things easier for those who must build data models, Excel provides a rich set of information that you can store in the data model to facilitate the Power View experience. This set of information is known as *metadata* (that is, data about data). You have already seen an example of metadata; namely, hierarchies. When you build a hierarchy, you can click it in Power View to use all the columns of the hierarchy in a report, eliminating the need to select these columns one after the other. Small things like this save a lot of time in report creation, and this is why it is advisable to create a complete set of metadata for Power View usage.

You can find the metadata sets on the Advanced tab of the PowerPivot ribbon, which you can see in Figure 11-20. The companion workbook for this section is "CH11-03-Power View Metadata.xlsx."

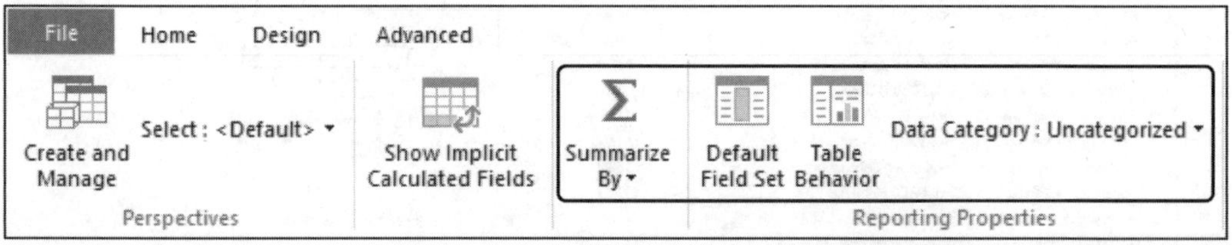

FIGURE 11-20 You can find the Power View metadata on the Advanced tab of the ribbon.

There are four sets of metadata:

- **Column summarization** For each column, you can choose the default function to use when data need to be summarized. The default, for numeric columns, is *SUM* because most of the times you want to sum values (for example, the sales amount for a year is the sum of the individual sales). For string columns, the default is *COUNT*. There are scenarios where you do not want to use *SUM;* in these cases, you can modify the default behavior from here.

- **Default field set** You can define, for each table, the set of columns that are selected by default when you double-click the table name to generate a report.

- **Table behavior** From here, you can choose different behaviors of the table and set some special columns, like the default image.

- **Data category** You can tag some columns in your table with special categories so that Power View knows how to handle them. If, for example, you use localized names for the columns, then Power View will have a hard time detecting where you placed the country name. In such a case, it is useful to categorize the column as type *Country,* to make it easier for Power View to find geographical information in the table.

Let us review these features in more detail.

Using Summarize By

For each column, you can choose the default function for summarize using the Summarize By feature. Even if this is an interesting function, we do not think you should use it for what it was meant for. In fact, imagine that you want to aggregate the product cost in FactInternetSales using the *MIN* function. You can choose *MIN* as the default aggregator and, when you put the column in a Power View report, you will see the minimum value of the current selection instead of the sum. This looks intriguing, so why not use it? The first reason is that if you do this, you will see the column in the

Power View fields with a summation symbol in front of it (see Figure 11-21), and it is only when you add it to a report when it will have "Min of" in front of it to show that, in reality, it contains the minimum value.

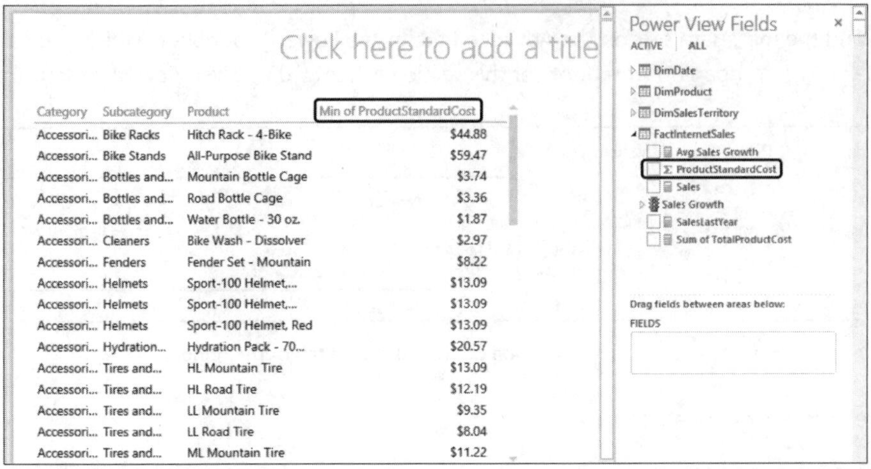

FIGURE 11-21 The summation symbol in front of the column name is somewhat misleading.

Moreover, if you aggregate using *MIN*, there is an excellent chance that at some point, you will want to aggregate using *MAX* or some other aggregation function. Finally, if you want to have some special handling for grand totals, you will have no control over it, because the query that Power View sends to the data model is built directly by Power View using the default aggregation function. Thus, if you want to aggregate a column using a specific function, it is much better to create a calculated field that contains the aggregation function in its name. Then, you can safely hide the original column from the client tools to avoid confusing the user. In Figure 11-22, you can see the final result, which is much easier to use than the previous one.

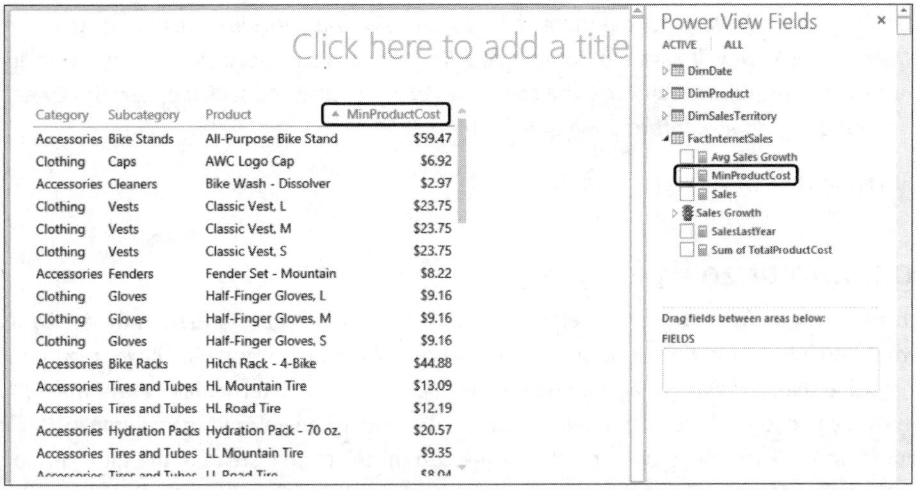

FIGURE 11-22 Using calculated fields instead of default summarization leads to a better user experience.

If you need to add *MAX* as another summarization function, you can easily define a new calculated field with *MaxProductCost,* and it is much easier to maintain the data model.

However, there is a situation where the default summarization function proves to be very useful: when you want to use the Do Not Summarize option. Some numeric columns need to be used as slicers and not as values. A good example of this is the Year column in the DimDate table. Even if the year is a numeric value, there is no point in summing years. Yet, this is what Power View does by default if you select the year, as shown in Figure 11-23, where we selected the category hierarchy and then the year.

Category	Subcategory	Product	CalendarYear
		Touring End Caps	4398433
		Touring Rim	4398433
Accessories	Bike Racks	Hitch Rack - 4-Bike	4398433
Accessories	Bike Stands	All-Purpose Bike Stand	4398433
Accessories	Bottles and...	Mountain Bottle Cage	4398433
Accessories	Bottles and...	Road Bottle Cage	4398433
Accessories	Bottles and...	Water Bottle - 30 oz.	4398433
Accessories	Cleaners	Bike Wash - Dissolver	4398433
Accessories	Fenders	Fender Set - Mountain	4398433
Accessories	Helmets	Sport-100 Helmet,...	4398433
Accessories	Helmets	Sport-100 Helmet,...	4398433
Accessories	Helmets	Sport-100 Helmet, Red	4398433
Accessories	Hydration...	Hydration Pack - 70...	4398433
Accessories	Lights	Headlights - Dual-...	4398433
Accessories	Lights	Headlights -...	4398433
Accessories	Lights	Taillights - Battery	4398433

FIGURE 11-23 Being a numeric column, the year is summarized as if it were a value instead of a slicer.

To avoid this undesirable behavior, you can set the Summarize By Property option of the Year column to Do Not Summarize, so that Power View will never attempt to summarize the column but will use it only as a slicer. The result is what you would expect (see Figure 11-24).

Category	Subcategory	Product	CalendarYear
Accessories	Bike Racks	Hitch Rack - 4-Bike	2007
Accessories	Bike Racks	Hitch Rack - 4-Bike	2008
Accessories	Bike Stands	All-Purpose Bike Stand	2007
Accessories	Bike Stands	All-Purpose Bike Stand	2008
Accessories	Bottles and...	Mountain Bottle Cage	2007
Accessories	Bottles and...	Mountain Bottle Cage	2008
Accessories	Bottles and...	Road Bottle Cage	2007
Accessories	Bottles and...	Road Bottle Cage	2008
Accessories	Bottles and...	Water Bottle - 30 oz.	2007
Accessories	Bottles and...	Water Bottle - 30 oz.	2008
Accessories	Cleaners	Bike Wash - Dissolver	2007
Accessories	Cleaners	Bike Wash - Dissolver	2008
Accessories	Fenders	Fender Set - Mountain	2007
Accessories	Fenders	Fender Set - Mountain	2008
Accessories	Helmets	Sport-100 Helmet,...	2007
Accessories	Helmets	Sport-100 Helmet,...	2008

FIGURE 11-24 Setting the correct value for the Summarize By Property option, you get the desired result.

Using the default field set

The default field set is the set of columns that is selected by default when you double-click a table, which makes it easy to produce recurring reports. For example, if you frequently analyze the products using category, subcategory, model name, product name, and list price, you can set the default field set as it appears in Figure 11-25.

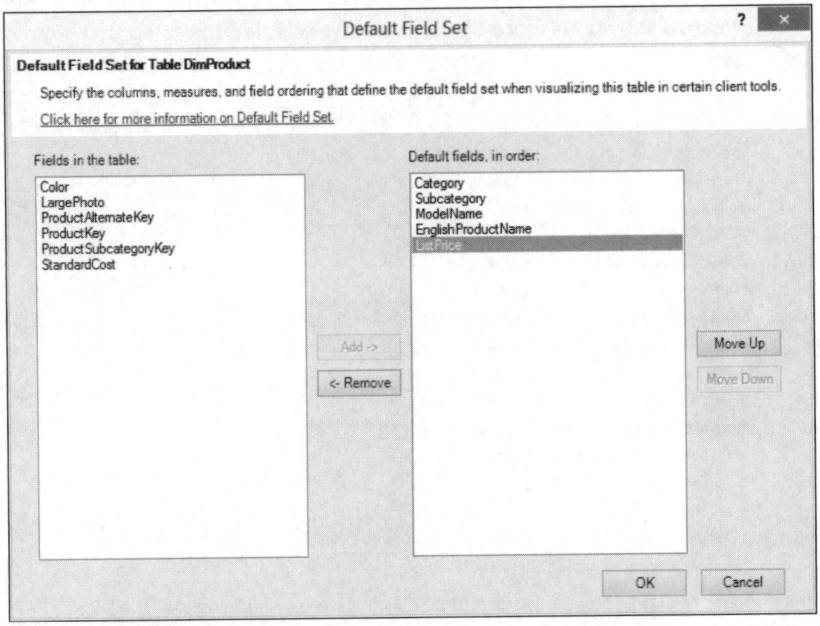

FIGURE 11-25 The default field set makes it easier to create reports just by double-clicking.

Once the field set is defined, the columns included in it will be selected for a report when you double-click the table name in Power View.

> **Tip** Even if you can add hidden columns to the field set, only the visible ones will be shown in the report; hidden columns will not be added to it automatically. This behavior is different from that of hierarchies. Using hierarchies, you will be able to show hidden columns in a report because clicking a hierarchy always adds all its columns to the report.

The default field set was the only feature to define a field set in the first release of Power View, which did not incorporate the handling of hierarchies. Now that you can use multiple hierarchies as a way to define field sets (whereas you have only one default set available for each table), you should put only the more important fields of a table into the default field set.

Using the Table Behavior dialog box

In the Table Behavior dialog box, you can set several behaviors of the table, again to make it easier to browse the table with Power View. In Figure 11-26, you can see the Table Behavior dialog box opened on the DimProduct table, already filled with some values.

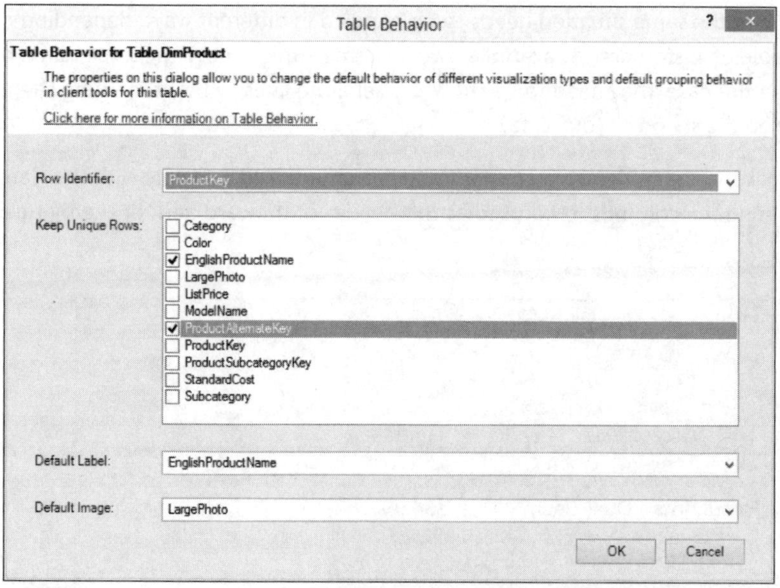

FIGURE 11-26 The Table Behavior dialog box lets you select some default behaviors for a table.

The first setting is Row Identifier. The Row Identifier needs to be a column with a different value for each row of the table and becomes the key that uniquely identifies a row. In data warehouses, this is normally a numeric value, but for other kind of databases, it might contain strings, dates, or any other data type. If the table has a row identifier, then you can modify the behavior of other columns using the Keep Unique Rows panel.

If you flag a column using Keep Unique Rows, you mean that the column needs to be aggregated using the Row Identifier, even if the value displayed will be that of the column. This is not an easy concept to explain, so an example will be of great help.

The DimProduct table contains some rows that seem to be duplicates. The reason is that the table keeps track of changes in some columns. For example, if the product changes the price or the standard cost, then there will be many rows for the same product with different prices and costs. You can see this in Figure 11-27, where we filtered the DimProduct table showing only a single product, with its versions, highlighted by the presence of StartDate, EndDate, and Status.

Produc...	ProductAlternateKey	EnglishProductName	ListPrice	StartDate	EndDate	Status
226	LJ-0192-S	Long-Sleeve Logo Jersey, S	$48.07	7/1/2005	6/30/2002	
227	LJ-0192-S	Long-Sleeve Logo Jersey, S	$48.07	7/1/2006	6/30/2003	
228	LJ-0192-S	Long-Sleeve Logo Jersey, S	$49.99	7/1/2007		Current

FIGURE 11-27 The same product can have many versions, due to different costs and prices.

With this table, there are three rows that actually represent a single product. For example, what do you want to happen when the EnglishProductName column is put on a report? Power View can show either a single line for all three rows or three different ones. In this case, the choice is clearly to merge all the lines into a single one because, in reality, they represent the same product and need not be separated.

There are cases where the same situation needs to be handled in different ways, depending on the situation. For a table of customers, for example, two customers might have the same name but different codes, and in this case, they need to be shown as separate lines, without merging them. The choice depends only on the shape of your data.

Finally, default label and default picture are parameters that are useful mainly with the Card view because they define the columns to be used as the header of the card and for the picture (see Figure 11-28).

FIGURE 11-28 The Card view takes advantage of Power View metadata to show an informative card for each row.

Defining sets

Now let's continue our coverage of advanced modeling techniques for reporting by analyzing another useful option of Excel: the ability to define sets. Before we discuss about how sets work, we probably should explain what a set is.

Intuitively, a set is a list of items, where an item might be anything we would like to think about. You can define a set by enumerating the items inside it, as you normally do with your shopping list, where each item is categorized separately; or you can define a set by giving a description of what belongs to it, like the set of all countries in North America. Both are valid definitions of a set.

Nevertheless, since this is a PowerPivot book, we need to understand the meaning that PowerPivot gives to a set. For example, look at a PivotTable; it is made of cells, and each cell defines a filter as the set of rows used to build the result of the cell itself. It does so by filtering some fields (that is, the ones present on the rows, columns, slicers, and report filter).

In Figure 11-29, you can see a PivotTable over some data. You can find this example in the companion workbook "CH11-05-Sets.xlsx."

Sales	Column Labels				
Row Labels	⊞ 2005	⊞ 2006	⊞ 2007	⊞ 2008	Grand Total
Europe	**$709,947.20**	**$1,627,759.71**	**$3,382,979.27**	**$3,209,356.08**	**$8,930,042.26**
⊞ Accessories			$84,458.16	$117,811.25	$202,269.41
⊞ Bikes	$709,947.20	$1,627,759.71	$3,262,529.32	$3,044,696.49	$8,644,932.72
⊞ Clothing			$35,991.79	$46,848.34	$82,840.13
North America	**$1,247,379.26**	**$2,748,298.93**	**$3,374,296.82**	**$3,997,659.37**	**$11,367,634.37**
⊞ Accessories			$151,870.08	$207,929.84	$359,799.92
⊞ Bikes	$1,247,379.26	$2,748,298.93	$3,148,783.82	$3,676,699.92	$10,821,161.92
⊞ Clothing			$73,642.92	$113,029.61	$186,672.53
Pacific	**$1,309,047.20**	**$2,154,284.88**	**$3,033,784.21**	**$2,563,884.29**	**$9,061,000.58**
⊞ Accessories			$57,381.47	$81,309.16	$138,690.63
⊞ Bikes	$1,309,047.20	$2,154,284.88	$2,947,789.48	$2,440,928.44	$8,852,050.00
⊞ Clothing			$28,613.26	$41,646.69	$70,259.95
Grand Total	**$3,266,373.66**	**$6,530,343.53**	**$9,791,060.30**	**$9,770,899.74**	**$29,358,677.22**

FIGURE 11-29 Each cell of a PivotTable like this one can be defined in terms of sets.

Let's analyze Figure 11-29 in terms of sets. The sales in North America in year 2007 have a value of 3,374,296.82. Excel computes this value by analyzing "the set of all the sales that were made in North America in the year 2002." You can apply the same technique to each cell, and you will discover that Excel computes each cell by analyzing a set. This way of thinking will lead you to our first definition of set, which identifies a set with a filter context.

It might be tempting to believe that a set is nothing but a filter context. Even if this were true, however, we think that it is better to think of a filter context as one element of a set. Thus, when we define a set, we can enumerate a list of filter contexts, and the list of all those filters will define a set. As an example of this, let's return to Figure 11-29.

We can define a set containing both "Accessories in Europe for the year 2007" and "Clothing in North America in 2006." Each item in the set defines a filter context, and the union of both filter contexts (which is, in turn, a more complex filter context) is the set.

As you might have noticed, the definition of a set is given, providing values for some attributes of the data model. For example, you can set the year as 2007 and define the set of all sales in 2007. In addition, you can fix another attribute (such as setting the territory group to "North America") and define the "sales in North America in the year 2007." Each time you fix the value of an attribute, you narrow the number of elements covered by the set. Whenever you do not restrict the value of an attribute, you mean that "all values are good."

With all this in mind, you can now learn how to define a set with Excel. On the Options ribbon of Excel, you will find a button named Fields, Items, & Sets, which contains the links to the feature that we are interested in. Figure 11-30 shows the details of this button, including a drop-down menu of options.

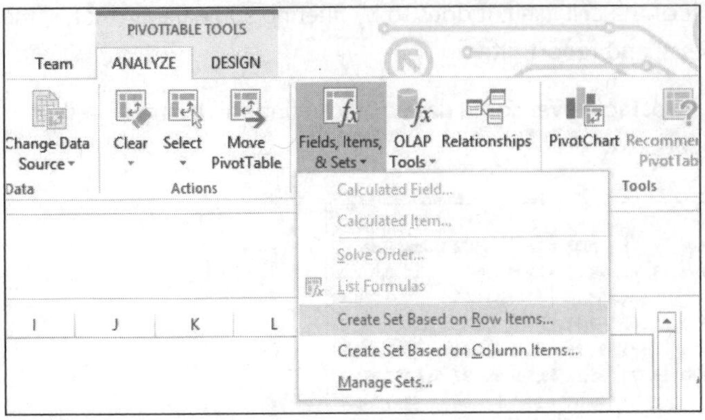

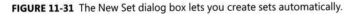

FIGURE 11-30 A menu with various options to create sets in Excel can be seen by clicking the Fields, Items, & Sets button on the ANALYZE tab of the ribbon.

Through this menu, you can create a set using the values in the rows or columns of the PivotTable. If you select Create Set Based On Row Items... in your PivotTable, Excel will open the New Set dialog box shown in Figure 11-31.

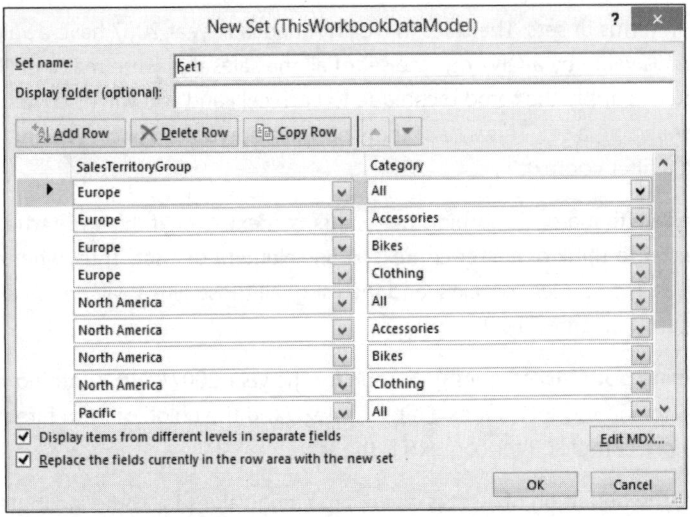

FIGURE 11-31 The New Set dialog box lets you create sets automatically.

Because you have two attributes on the rows (SalesTerritoryGroup and Category), the dialog box contains two columns. Each row in the set contains a filter context that will define one of the members of the set. All filter contexts together will define the set.

It is interesting to see that the first row in the set sets the following definitions:

- SalesTerritoryGroup = Europe

- Category = All

This means that the first element forces one constraint on the SalesTerritoryGroup and another on the Category to select all the possible values. In fact, if you look carefully at the first row of the PivotTable, it contains sales made in Europe for all the categories together.

Thus, since there are three values for SalesTerritoryGroup and three values for Category, our set will contain 12 elements: 9 for the different combinations of sales territory and product category, and 3 for the different sales territory with an unconstrained category. These elements are the exact number of rows of the PivotTable. If you open this dialog box on a complex PivotTable with hundreds (or thousands) of rows, the number of elements in the set would become large and hard to manage.

Using this dialog box, you have the option to name the set, provide it with a folder where to show it, and update the set definition. To show an example, we will edit the set to leave only four elements in it (see Figure 11-32).

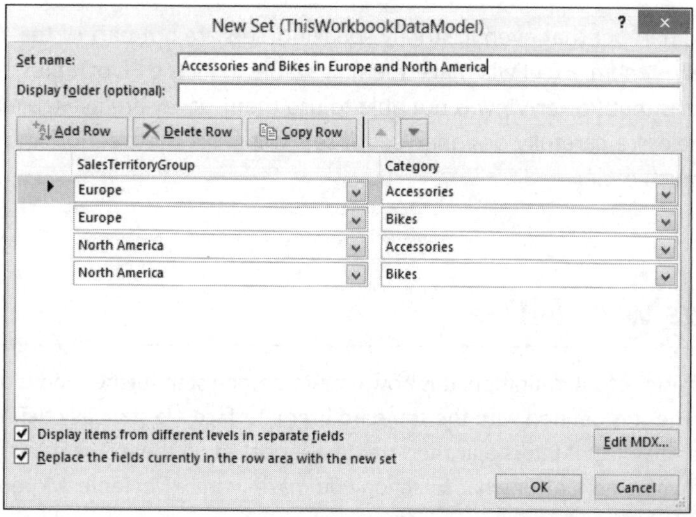

FIGURE 11-32 Here, you can see the definition of a set made of four elements.

Now the set represents a selection of combinations of sales territories and product categories, as its name indicates. You can save it and look at what happens to the PivotTable field list. Once you have defined a set, it appears under a special folder called Sets at the top of the table list, just below the calculated fields. In Figure 11-33, you can see the PivotTable with the set put on the rows.

Sales	Column Labels				
Row Labels	⊞2005	⊞2006	⊞2007	⊞2008	Grand Total
Europe					
Accessories			$84,458.16	$117,811.25	$202,269.41
Bikes	$709,947.20	$1,627,759.71	$3,262,529.32	$3,044,696.49	$8,644,932.72
North America					
Accessories			$151,870.08	$207,929.84	$359,799.92
Bikes	$1,247,379.26	$2,748,298.93	$3,148,783.82	$3,676,699.92	$10,821,161.92

FIGURE 11-33 This PivotTable is based on the set that you have defined.

When putting a set on rows or columns, you filter the data by imposing a filter context that makes only the data inside the set visible.

If you look carefully at the PivotTable, you can note that something is missing: you have no total for the territory group, nor any grand total. As strange as it might appear, this is the perfectly expected result. You have removed from the set the items containing the member All for the Category. This means that the set does not contain a filter context for "Europe, any category." Thus, the PivotTable does not show the total for category. The same obviously applies to the grand total.

Sets are commonly used with dates. If, for example, you define a set containing the last two years, then it will be easy to select the last two years in a report quickly. Moreover, when you want to update all the reports (to show, for example, the last three years), it will be enough to update the set, and then all the reports will be updated automatically to reflect the change in the underlying set.

> **Note** It is important to remember that even if, strictly speaking, sets are not part of the data model, once you define them, Excel will make them available to all the PivotTables. The only drawback of sets is that Power View is not able to use them—they are available in PivotTables only. Nevertheless, a carefully designed set of sets will make the creation and handling of PivotTables much easier.

Creating dynamic sets with MDX

So far, you have learned the basics of set definition. It is now time to go one step further and look at some advanced uses of sets. The sets defined with the standard user interface are statically defined, which means that you enumerate a list of filters and then create a set based on them. The items contained in the set do not change, no matter what selection you make in the PivotTable. Moreover, to create the set, you need to know in advance which items to put in.

Even if this condition might seem obvious, there is sometimes the need to define a set that changes dynamically based on the selection, without knowing what it will contain in advance. For example, suppose that you could define a set containing the top 10 selling products. You do not know in advance what these products will be. Moreover, the set will change depending on your filtering, since you expect that the top-selling products in 2006 are different from the top-selling products in 2007.

These kind of sets are called *dynamic sets,* because they can change their content based on user selection. To create them, you will need explore the internal workings of PowerPivot and discover the OLAP cube that is well hidden inside it. Because PowerPivot can look to Excel like an OLAP cube, you will need to use MDX to create dynamic sets. In this section, we will show a simple demonstration of what can be done using MDX to query PowerPivot and create dynamic sets.

Note The topic of MDX can fill up a book by itself, so we are not going to show all the details of what can be done using this exciting query language. Our goal is just to bring the attention of the interested reader to what can be done by using PowerPivot with MDX and dynamic sets. You can achieve the same results using different techniques or using the DAX language, but MDX can be useful in some scenarios.

To create a dynamic set, you need to select the Manage Set option of the Fields, Items, & Sets button, which opens the Set Manager dialog box shown in Figure 11-34.

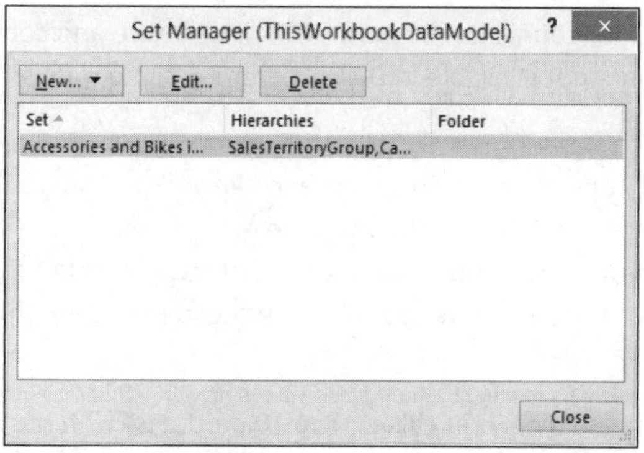

FIGURE 11-34 The Set Manager dialog box is the place where you can edit sets and create new MDX sets.

Using this dialog box, you can create, delete, or update set definitions. Moreover, using the New button, you can create new sets based on rows and columns. You can also do this by using the MDX editor. You already know what happens with the simpler options of using rows and columns, so it is time to go deeper and choose the MDX option. Excel will open the Modify Set dialog box, which is shown in Figure 11-35.

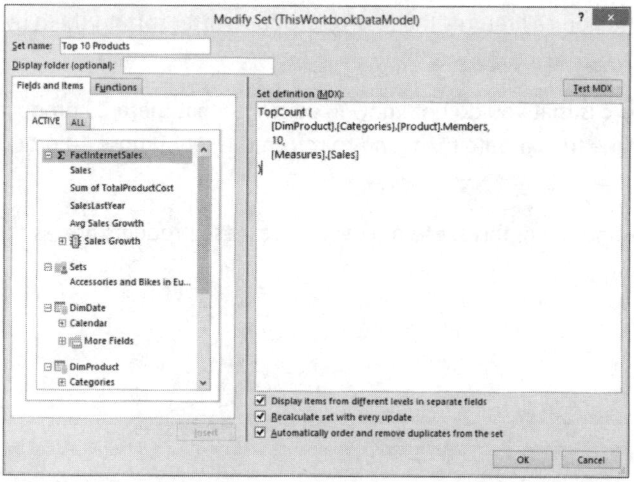

FIGURE 11-35 The Modify Set dialog box lets you design MDX sets.

This dialog box lets you create an MDX expression that will query the PowerPivot OLAP cube inside the PowerPivot database. But what does an OLAP cube have to do with PowerPivot? As we have said, you are now delving into some of the internal features of PowerPivot, one of which is the fact that the PowerPivot database can be queried as an OLAP cube based on the tables and relationships that it holds. In fact, PivotTables always use MDX to query the PowerPivot data model, even if they show the data model as being composed of tables. The OLAP cube that PowerPivot makes visible to Excel is called Model, and it is visible in Excel using the connection "ThisWorkbookDataModel," which is completely managed by Excel internally.

If you need to create dynamic sets, you need to query the Model cube directly and use the full power of MDX. It is not an easy task, and to get the best from it, you need to know the MDX language. Nevertheless, it exploits some useful functionalities because MDX is a mature and complete language, and it contains some functions that are not available in DAX. Therefore, some queries might be easier to write in MDX than in DAX.

The OLAP cube contains one dimension and one measure group for each PowerPivot table. The dimensions contain the fields used to perform slicing, whereas the measure groups contain the values that can be aggregated. In our example, you have a DimProduct fact table that lets you count the products (count is a measure that can be shown in cells), as well as a DimProduct dimension, which contains the attributes used to slice data.

With a bit of knowledge of MDX, you can define a new set called "Top 10 products" with this formula:

```
TopCount (
    [DimProduct].[Categories].[Product].Members,
    10,
    [Measures].[Sales]
)
```

In this example, the *TopCount* function call returns the first 10 products after sorting them by the *Sales* calculated field.

Now, the real power of this feature is that you do not know in advance what these 10 products will be. You have to ask the OLAP cube to compute them and to return the set of those 10 products, whatever they are.

You can now create a PivotTable and select this set to discover what these products are, as shown in Figure 11-36.

Color		Sales	Column Labels ▾				
		Row Labels	⊞ 2005	⊞ 2006	⊞ 2007	⊞ 2008	Grand Total
Black ⌃		Mountain-200 Black, 38		$106,553.11	$600,795.59	$587,517.44	$1,294,866.14
Red		Mountain-200 Black, 42		$159,829.66	$627,269.94	$576,042.49	$1,363,142.09
Silver		Mountain-200 Black, 46		$163,927.86	$679,399.00	$530,142.69	$1,373,469.55
Blue		Mountain-200 Silver, 38		$136,713.69	$613,471.64	$589,277.46	$1,339,462.79
Grey		Mountain-200 Silver, 42		$136,713.69	$584,803.19	$535,917.69	$1,257,434.57
Multi		Mountain-200 Silver, 46		$103,570.98	$617,531.62	$579,997.50	$1,301,100.10
NA		Road-150 Red, 48	$547,475.31	$658,401.68			$1,205,876.99
Silver/Black ⌄		Road-150 Red, 52	$472,331.64	$608,305.90			$1,080,637.54
		Road-150 Red, 56	$486,644.72	$568,944.93			$1,055,589.65
		Road-150 Red, 62	$593,992.82	$608,305.90			$1,202,298.72

FIGURE 11-36 In this PivotTable, you can see the set of top 10 products at work.

In this PivotTable, we added a slicer to filter for product color. Nevertheless, if you select Red (for example), the PivotTable does not compute the top 10 red products. Instead, it filters the top 10 products, but it shows only the red ones, as shown in Figure 11-37.

Color		Sales	Column Labels ▾		
		Row Labels	⊞ 2005	⊞ 2006	Grand Total
Black ⌃		Road-150 Red, 48	$547,475.31	$658,401.68	$1,205,876.99
Red		Road-150 Red, 52	$472,331.64	$608,305.90	$1,080,637.54
Silver		Road-150 Red, 56	$486,644.72	$568,944.93	$1,055,589.65
Blue		Road-150 Red, 62	$593,992.82	$608,305.90	$1,202,298.72
Grey					
Multi					
NA					
Silver/Black ⌄					

FIGURE 11-37 When a color is selected, the set of top 10 products is filtered but not recomputed.

The reason for this behavior is that by default, the set is still static, even if it is defined with MDX. Even if you do not know its content in advance and used MDX to define it, the set is evaluated once during the first query after data are refreshed into the PowerPivot workbook. Thus, it is not recomputed for each query. When you apply a filter, that filter is applied to the set too, reducing its content.

You can convert a standard set to a dynamic one using the Recalculate Set With Every Update check box in the Modify Set dialog box. If you select this box, then the set will be marked as a dynamic one and will be computed for each query, reflecting the filtering made on the PivotTable.

In Figure 11-38, you can see the same query with Red selected, but this time with the set marked as dynamic. Its behavior is different: the set now contains the top 10 sellers that are red.

Color		Sales	Column Labels				
		Row Labels	2005	2006	2007	2008	Grand Total
Black		Sport-100 Helmet, Red			$31,421.02	$46,606.68	$78,027.70
Red		Road-150 Red, 44	$500,957.80	$504,536.07			$1,005,493.87
Silver		Road-150 Red, 48	$547,475.31	$658,401.68			$1,205,876.99
Blue		Road-150 Red, 52	$472,331.64	$608,305.90			$1,080,637.54
Grey		Road-150 Red, 56	$486,644.72	$568,944.93			$1,055,589.65
Multi		Road-150 Red, 62	$593,992.82	$608,305.90			$1,202,298.72
NA		Road-250 Red, 44		$175,921.20	$175,921.20		$351,842.40
Silver/Black		Road-250 Red, 48		$219,901.50	$175,921.20		$395,822.70
		Road-250 Red, 52		$202,798.05	$122,167.50		$324,965.55
		Road-250 Red, 58		$235,608.75	$313,097.85	$153,931.05	$702,637.65

FIGURE 11-38 The top 10 products dynamic set is correctly recomputed when a color is selected.

Using this feature, you will be able to produce a report that will provide the set of the top 10 selling products and that will change whenever you change the filtering condition.

> **Note** The set is conditioned by the filters and the slicers, but not by the selection on rows and columns. This means that the set produces the top 10 selling products for all time, and then the PivotTable shows the sales in the different years. If you are interested in the top-selling products in a specific year, you will need to move the year to a slicer or to the filter part of the PivotTable, so that the year acts as a filter and operates over the dynamic set, too. Dynamic sets obey the filter context imposed by the filters over the whole PivotTable, not the ones imposed by the rows and columns to each single cell.

This small example just scratches the surface of the power of MDX. Using MDX to query a cube, you can produce complex and useful reports, so it is worth learning MDX and the structure of an OLAP cube, which are required for doing this. We believe that the PowerPivot power user will want to buy one of the many helpful books about MDX and start learning it, to get the best out of PowerPivot. Nevertheless, PowerPivot can still produce great reports without ever opening an MDX editor, so in general, we are saying that if you decide to use MDX, then be prepared to undergo a long, fairly arduous period of study; on the other hand, if you can get the results you need with just the PowerPivot user interface, then life will certainly be easier. The choice is yours, and will be based on your particular needs.

Using perspectives

Using the techniques you have learned so far, you can build complex reporting systems, and as time goes by, you will find yourself creating bigger and bigger solutions. Chances are that, at some point, you will need to deal with many tables and models loaded into the same workbook, and then the simple operation of finding the correct table to put in a PivotTable may be an issue. The rule of thumb of business intelligence (BI) professionals regarding the usability of PivotTable is that you should have no more than 10 tables in the fields list. Otherwise, users will start to complain about its complexity.

One feature that can help in reducing the complexity of PivotTable is that of perspectives. In this section, you will learn how to create and use perspectives.

Imagine that you have created a workbook that contains Internet sales, reseller sales, and sales quota for employees. You merged everything into the same data model because sometimes you need to create reports that grab data from all these entities, but in your everyday work, you focus on a single topic. Your data model (shown in Figure 11-39) is not going to be easy to work with. You can see the data model in the companion workbook "CH11-06-Perspectives.xlsx."

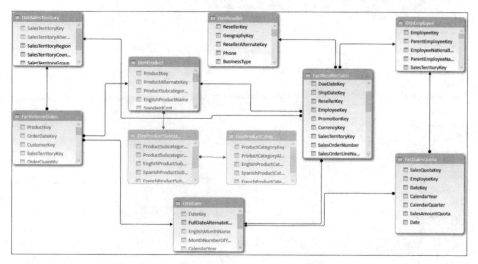

FIGURE 11-39 The data model of a complex solution is hard to read and use.

The data model contains three fact tables: FactInternetSales, FactResellerSales, and FactSalesQuota. Each one is related to several dimensions, and some dimensions (like DimDate) are used by all the fact tables. But when you are working on FactResellerSales, it would be nice to remove from the view all the tables that are not linked to the reseller sales so you can have a clearer picture of your model.

On the Advanced tab of the PowerPivot ribbon, the first button group is Perspectives (see Figure 11-40). From there, you can create and manage perspectives or choose the one to use when browsing the model.

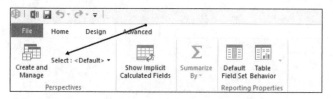

FIGURE 11-40 You can manage perspectives using the Advanced tab of the PowerPivot ribbon.

If you click the Create And Manage button, you open the Perspectives dialog box, where you can create a new perspective, modify its content, or delete it. Adding tables or columns to a perspective is as easy as using the check box that appears beside each table and column. In Figure 11-41, you can see that we have defined three different perspectives for our data model.

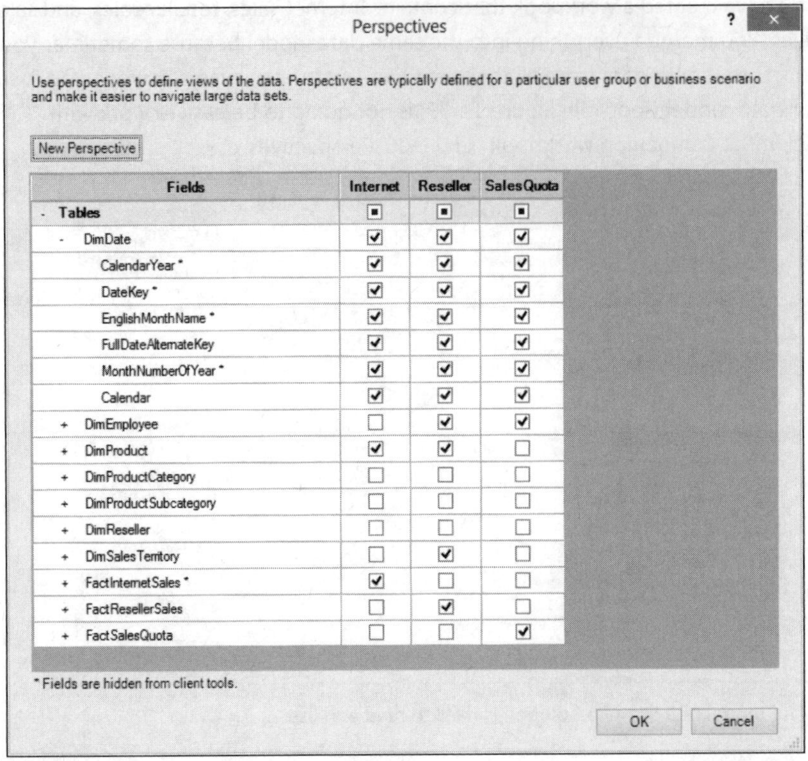

FIGURE 11-41 The Perspectives dialog box is useful to create and manage perspectives.

Once you defined some perspectives for your model, you can select them using the Select button in the same button group. Doing this will filter the PowerPivot window, making visible only the tables that belong to the perspective. For example, in Figure 11-42, you can see how the diagram view of the model looks like when you select the Reseller perspective.

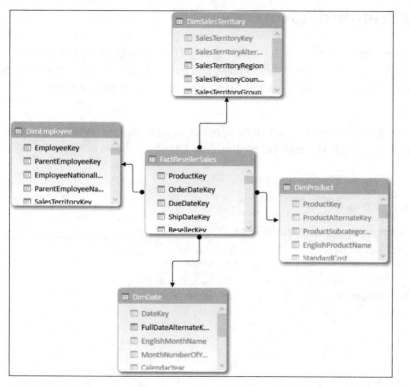

FIGURE 11-42 Once you select a perspective, the Diagram view shows only the tables belonging to the perspective.

Unfortunately, perspectives can only be used to filter the data model from inside the PowerPivot window. There is no support in the PivotTable Fields list to filter tables and columns based on a perspective, as it was the case in the previous version of PowerPivot.

The only scenario where perspectives are useful to reduce the number of items in the PivotTable Fields list is when you publish a workbook containing perspectives on Microsoft SharePoint. In that case, if you open a workbook connected to the SharePoint data model containing perspectives, Excel prompts you to choose the perspective to use to browse the model, as shown in Figure 11-43.

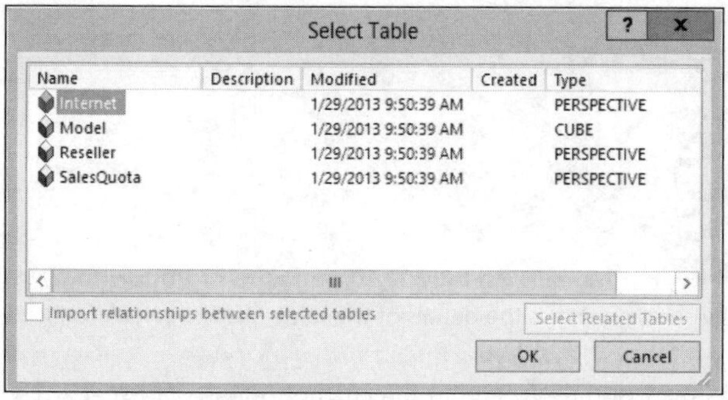

Name	Description	Modified	Created	Type
Internet		1/29/2013 9:50:39 AM		PERSPECTIVE
Model		1/29/2013 9:50:39 AM		CUBE
Reseller		1/29/2013 9:50:39 AM		PERSPECTIVE
SalesQuota		1/29/2013 9:50:39 AM		PERSPECTIVE

FIGURE 11-43 You can choose the perspective to connect to when browsing a PowerPivot for SharePoint model.

Understanding drill-through

The last topic regarding reports in this chapter is drill-through. *Drill-through* is the operation of looking at detailed data of a specific cell of a PivotTable, and it is useful both for debugging purposes and for investigation because it shows the source of data used to compute a specific cell of a PivotTable.

You can start a drill-through operation in two ways: either you double-click a cell in a PivotTable, or you open the context (right-click) menu and choose Show Details, as shown in Figure 11-44.

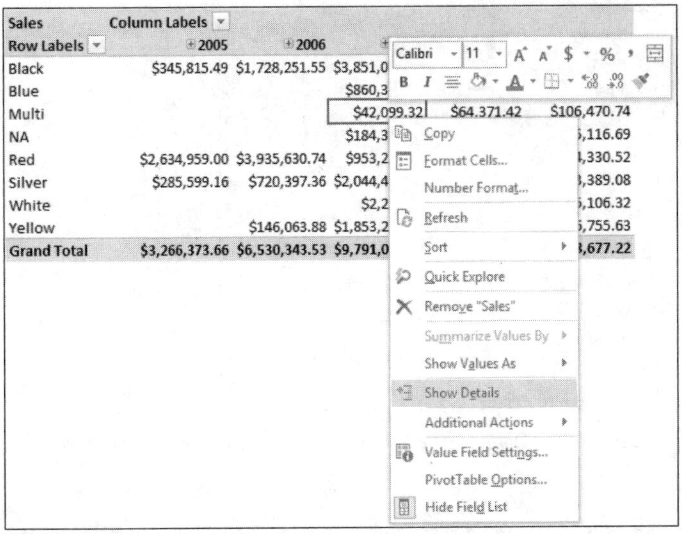

Sales	Column Labels				
Row Labels	2005	2006			
Black	$345,815.49	$1,728,251.55	$3,851,0		
Blue			$860,3		
Multi		$42,099.32	$64,371.42	$106,470.74	
NA		$184,3		,116.69	
Red	$2,634,959.00	$3,935,630.74	$953,2	,330.52	
Silver	$285,599.16	$720,397.36	$2,044,4	,389.08	
White		$2,2		,106.32	
Yellow		$146,063.88	$1,853,2	,755.63	
Grand Total	$3,266,373.66	$6,530,343.53	$9,791,0	,677.22	

Context menu items:
- Copy
- Format Cells...
- Number Format...
- Refresh
- Sort ▸
- Quick Explore
- Remove "Sales"
- Summarize Values By ▸
- Show Values As ▸
- Show Details
- Additional Actions ▸
- Value Field Settings...
- PivotTable Options...
- Hide Field List

FIGURE 11-44 The context menu in a PivotTable contains the Show Details option for drill-through.

The result of a drill-through operation is that Excel creates a new worksheet containing an Excel table with all the rows of the table containing the selected calculated field and that are visible under the filter context defined by the selected cell. In Figure 11-45, you can see the result of drill-through on the cell selected in Figure 11-44.

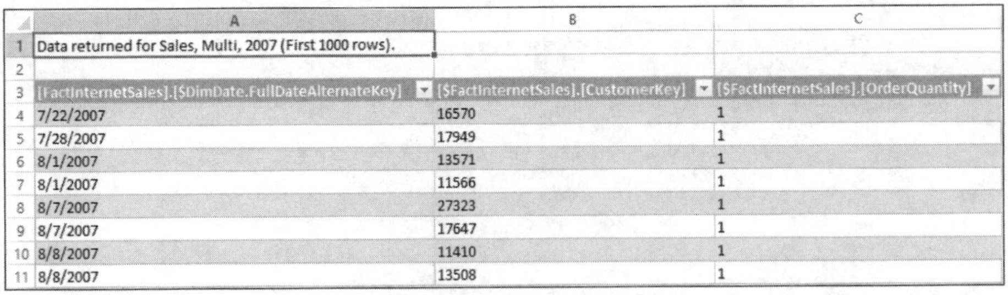

	A	B	C
1	Data returned for Sales, Multi, 2007 (First 1000 rows).		
2			
3	[FactInternetSales].[$DimDate.FullDateAlternateKey]	[$FactInternetSales].[CustomerKey]	[$FactInternetSales].[OrderQuantity]
4	7/22/2007	16570	1
5	7/28/2007	17949	1
6	8/1/2007	13571	1
7	8/1/2007	11566	1
8	8/7/2007	27323	1
9	8/7/2007	17647	1
10	8/8/2007	11410	1
11	8/8/2007	13508	1

FIGURE 11-45 The result of a drill-through operation shows the details of the table used to calculate the cell.

By default, drill-through returns the first 1,000 rows, and in the current release of Excel 2013, there is no way to customize this value when you query a data model.

CHAPTER 12

Performing date calculations in DAX

M any analyses of data involve dates. In fact, most, if not all, business reports require calculations like Year to Date, Month to Date, Same Period Last Year, and similar computations. These kinds of calculations are often called *time intelligence*. Microsoft PowerPivot for Excel offers a number of functions that simplify many calculations on dates that are typical in a business scenario. In this chapter, you are going to learn the techniques needed to handle time intelligence, and in the meantime, learn some DAX techniques that will prove useful in different scenarios.

Building a calendar table

To work with time intelligence, you need to have a calendar table inside the data model. Sometimes the data source from which you load information already has a calendar table (as it is the case for the *AdventureWorks* data warehouse), but other times, you can find yourself in a scenario where you will need to create this table from scratch. For this reason, we will now describe how to build a correct calendar table in PowerPivot.

Before starting, it is worth mentioning why you need a calendar table at all. In some examples in the previous chapters, we defined calculated columns that extracted parts of the date, such as the year and the month, and then we used them to group dates. This technique might be applied to each table containing a date, but it would quickly become hard to manage. It is better to create a separate table containing a row for each date, using the date as a key to link that calendar table with other tables that contain data related to a date. In this way, you obtain a model wherein all attributes about dates are included in a separate table and are easy to access when you browse data with a PivotTable, as shown in Figure 12-1.

A calendar table is also useful for making calculations using many of the DAX functions that operate on dates. These functions, of which *DATEADD* is an example, often require that all the days in a given range exist in the table—otherwise, a missing day will result in a wrong calculation. You might have no sales for a day (in fact, it is pretty common to have no sales on nonworking days), so the separate calendar table allows you to make the right calculations without requiring any modification to the original table that contains measures to analyze.

Sum of SalesAmount	Column Labels				
Row Labels	**Black**	**Red**	**Silver**	**Yellow**	**Grand Total**
⊟2005	$345,815.49	$2,634,959.00	$285,599.16		$3,266,373.66
⊟Q3	$135,722.61	$1,178,400.69	$139,399.59		$1,453,522.89
July	$50,166.75	$362,021.59	$61,199.82		$473,388.16
August	$65,764.01	$392,827.82	$47,599.86		$506,191.69
September	$19,791.84	$423,551.28	$30,599.91		$473,943.03
⊟Q4	$210,092.89	$1,456,558.31	$146,199.57		$1,812,850.77
October	$55,518.54	$417,011.06	$40,799.88		$513,329.47
November	$52,264.05	$427,129.55	$64,599.81		$543,993.41
December	$102,310.30	$612,417.71	$40,799.88		$755,527.89
⊟2006	$1,264,769.51	$936,801.19	$376,998.37	$146,063.88	$2,724,632.94
⊟Q3	$642,026.90	$537,423.12	$155,356.47	$62,027.13	$1,396,833.62
July	$230,157.83	$205,557.24	$47,642.65	$17,007.44	$500,365.16
August	$263,854.81	$203,208.27	$55,928.33	$23,010.06	$546,001.47
September	$148,014.26	$128,657.62	$51,785.49	$22,009.63	$350,466.99
⊟Q4	$622,742.61	$399,378.07	$221,641.90	$84,036.75	$1,327,799.32
October	$188,598.83	$133,282.53	$72,499.69	$21,009.19	$415,390.23
November	$120,538.50	$145,904.75	$47,642.65	$21,009.19	$335,095.09
December	$313,605.28	$120,190.79	$101,499.56	$42,018.38	$577,314.00
Grand Total	$1,610,585.00	$3,571,760.19	$662,597.53	$146,063.88	$5,991,006.60

FIGURE 12-1 The presence of a calendar table simplifies PivotTable creation.

A correct calendar table for PowerPivot needs to have two characteristics:

- It contains the full date range, from January 1 to December 31 of the years in question.

- It contains a column of *Date* type, representing the date. This need not be the key column used to relate other tables in the data model; it just needs to be present to make the time intelligence function in DAX work.

You can easily create a Microsoft Excel table with these characteristics. Figure 12-2 displays the calendar table that we are going to use as the starting point for this chapter. You can find this data in the companion workbook "CH12-01-Calendar Table.xlsx."

FullDate	DateKey	Year	Quarter	Month	MonthNumber	Day	WeekDay
1/1/2005	20050101	2005	Q1	January	1	1	Saturday
1/2/2005	20050102	2005	Q1	January	1	2	Sunday
1/3/2005	20050103	2005	Q1	January	1	3	Monday
1/4/2005	20050104	2005	Q1	January	1	4	Tuesday
1/5/2005	20050105	2005	Q1	January	1	5	Wednesday
1/6/2005	20050106	2005	Q1	January	1	6	Thursday
1/7/2005	20050107	2005	Q1	January	1	7	Friday
1/8/2005	20050108	2005	Q1	January	1	8	Saturday
1/9/2005	20050109	2005	Q1	January	1	9	Sunday
1/10/2005	20050110	2005	Q1	January	1	10	Monday
1/11/2005	20050111	2005	Q1	January	1	11	Tuesday

FIGURE 12-2 A simple calendar table can be built using Excel.

> **Tip** The FullDate column can be created easily by preparing the first two rows and then dragging with the Alt key pressed down to fill the full table, up to the desired extent.

To prepare this table, we started from the FullDate column, and then we used the formulas in Table 12-1.

TABLE 12-1 Formula definitions for the Dates table in Excel

Column	Formula
DateKey	=[@Year] * 10000 + [@MonthNumber] * 100 + [@Day]
Year	=YEAR ([@FullDate])
Quarter	="Q" & ROUNDUP (MONTH ([@FullDate]) / 3, 0)
Month	=TEXT ([@FullDate], "MM - mmmm")
MonthNumber	=MONTH ([@FullDate])
Day	=DAY ([@FullDate])
WeekDay	=TEXT ([@FullDate], "dddd")

Note Table 12-1 does not include a column for week number because there are several techniques for calculating the week number in a year, and different businesses have different ways to make this calculation. More important, sometimes a week belongs to a year that is different from the calendar year—the fiscal year, for example—even if only for a few days of that year. In such a case, you also need to define a WeekYear column, which must be used to browse the weeks in a meaningful way. We preferred not to include a specific week calculation to keep the calendar table simple and to avoid possible confusion introducing an algorithm that might be different from that used in your company.

At this point, name the table Calendar, and now that it is ready in Excel, you can add it to the data model. The data model we have used to produce the first report of this chapter contained other tables loaded from the *AdventureWorks* data warehouse; namely, DimCustomer, DimProduct, and FactInternetSales. To make the calendar table work as a slicer for the sales, you only need to create the correct relationship, using DateKey in Calendar as the target and OrderDateKey in FactInternetSales as the source of the relationship. You can see the resulting diagram in Figure 12-3.

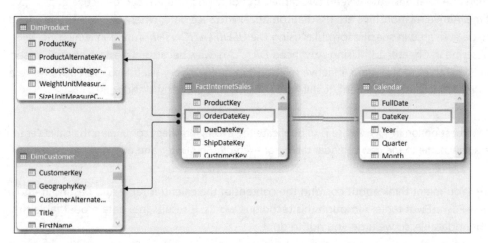

FIGURE 12-3 Here, you can see the data diagram of the example, where the relationship with Calendar is correctly set.

Now that the relationship is set correctly, you can use any column of the Calendar table to slice your sales. Clearly, if you need additional columns to handle fiscal year, fiscal month, week number, or any other column you might need for your report.

When it is time to decide whether to use a database table to hold the calendar or to create it in Excel, you should think about the full lifetime of your data model. In a standard Excel report, the difference is really negligible. If, at some point, you need more dates because you created the report in 2012 and you are now in 2013, just update the calendar table and you are ready to go.

If, on the other hand, your report is uploaded to Microsoft SharePoint and users expect it to be automatically updated every day, without any manual intervention, then using a table is a much better technique because your report will load every day from the correct calendar table and you will rely on the database for the updated information.

Moreover, if you have many reports using Calendar (as it is very often the case), then using a database table guarantees that all your reports use the same algorithm to compute week numbers, fiscal years, working days, and, in general, all the columns of the calendar.

Thus, the best practice is to use a calendar table in your database. If you cannot rely on this, then using a linked table in Excel is still a good solution. Just keep in mind the limitations that come with it.

Working with multiple calendar tables

In the model you saw in the previous section, each order has several dates. If you want to analyze not only the order date, but also the ship date, you need to define a second table in PowerPivot because the same table (that is, the calendar table) cannot have more than one relationship with a given table (FactInternetSales, in our example).

> **Note** To be precise, the previous statement is not completely true. You *can* have more than one relationship between two tables, but only one of them can be active at any given time. Active relationships are used automatically to slice data, whereas inactive ones need to be activated in specific formulas using the *USERELATIONSHIP* function, which we will describe in Chapter 13, "Using Advanced DAX." Anyway, because dates are normally used in PivotTables to slice data, inactive relationships are not very useful, so even if we make a formally incorrect statement, it still holds true from a practical standpoint.

Your best option in such a case is to duplicate the Excel worksheet containing the calendar table, give a new name to the new calendar table (for example, ShipDate), and add it to the data model.

> **Tip** You might think about copying the content of the calendar table and pasting it into a new PowerPivot table. Although this technique works, it results in a data model table that is not updatable, so we urge you not to do it.

The final operation is to create a relationship between the FactInternetSales table and the new ShipDate table. The data model in Figure 12-4 illustrates this. You can find this data in the companion workbook "CH12-02-Multiple Calendar Table.xlsx."

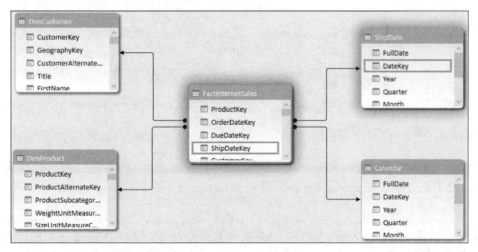

FIGURE 12-4 You can have many calendar tables in your data model.

Date columns in different tables

You must define a separate calendar table to distinguish the meaning of different dates in your data. This is certainly true whenever different date columns belong to the same table, as in the case of OrderDate and ShipDate in the FactInternetSales table. However, when you have date columns in different tables, you have to evaluate whether the meaning of these dates is the same or not.

Every time you have a different role for a date, you have to create separate calendar tables to browse data, just as you saw in this section. On the other hand, you have to use the same calendar table whenever these dates have the same meaning, at least for your analysis.

For example, if you have an OrderDate in the Sales table and a CallDate in a CallCenterCalls table, you might decide to create two separate data tables named OrderDate and CallDate. But you might also want to create a single calendar table that connects both events, which would ease the browsing over time of data from both tables in the same report. If you have no other dates in your model, no ambiguities arise from that arrangement, but if there are other dates involved in the same model, you should consider a separate PowerPivot model for doing correlation analysis, avoiding misleading names in your model.

At this point, you have two different calendar tables in the model. Duplicating the same table multiple times in a data model makes the resulting PivotTable difficult to read whenever the same attributes from different tables are used. For example, in Figure 12-5, you can see a PivotTable in which the Year from

OrderDate data has been put in rows in the first slicer, and the Year from ShipDate data has been put in columns in the second slicer. The problem is that there is no evidence of the table that a column belongs to whenever it is moved into slicers, filters, rows, or columns of the PivotTable.

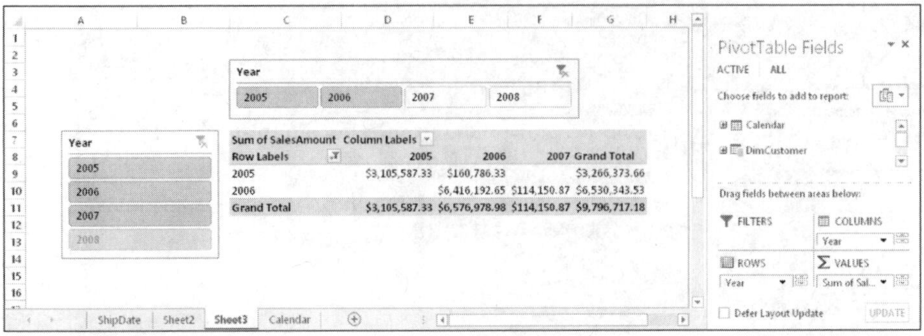

FIGURE 12-5 Having multiple columns with the same name leads to hard-to-understand reports.

So in case you create a model with multiple copies of the same table, you should differentiate the names of the columns so that they are immediately recognizable in a report. You can edit the table names in Excel by adding a prefix to each column. In Figure 12-6, you can see the heading of the ShipDate table, wherein each column has been prefixed with the word *Ship*. You can do the same for the OrderDate column by using the *Order* prefix.

ShipFullDate	ShipDateKey	ShipYear	ShipQuarter	ShipMonth	ShipMonthNumber	ShipDay	ShipWeekDay
1/1/2005	20050101	2005 Q1	January		1	1	Saturday
1/2/2005	20050102	2005 Q1	January		1	2	Sunday
1/3/2005	20050103	2005 Q1	January		1	3	Monday
1/4/2005	20050104	2005 Q1	January		1	4	Tuesday
1/5/2005	20050105	2005 Q1	January		1	5	Wednesday
1/6/2005	20050106	2005 Q1	January		1	6	Thursday
1/7/2005	20050107	2005 Q1	January		1	7	Friday
1/8/2005	20050108	2005 Q1	January		1	8	Saturday

FIGURE 12-6 The ShipDate table should have column names prefixed with *Ship* to make them easier to recognize.

In Figure 12-7, you can see a PivotTable based on this ShipDate table.

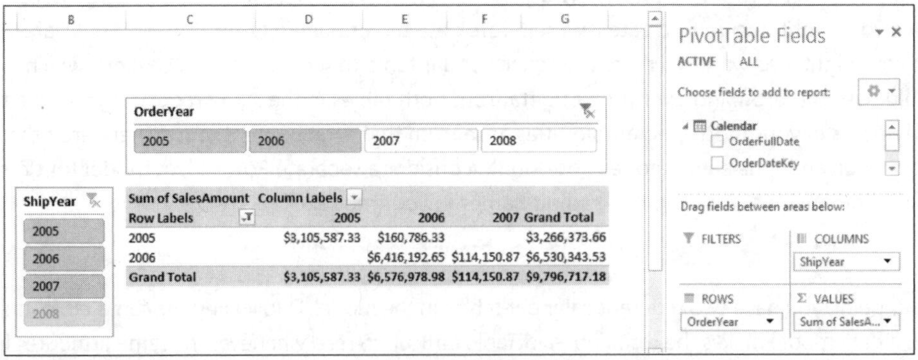

FIGURE 12-7 Using *Ship* as a prefix, column names and slicers are much easier to understand.

Using this new naming convention, the resulting PivotTable has several advantages:

- The slicer title clearly indicates which year it is filtering.

- The COLUMNS area shows the ShipYear name, making it easier to understand the report.

- It is now clear that the highlighted value of $160,786.33 represents orders shipped in 2006 and made in 2005, which is the main information that the report is meant to communicate.

This may look like a small digression about naming conventions (after all, we have been discussing calendar tables), but it is actually rather important. The same care in choosing a naming convention should be taken for all the tables in the data model. A good choice of names for tables and columns is very important if you want to create a usable data model.

Calculating working days

Now that you have learned how to create a calendar table, it is worth pointing out some columns that can be very useful in data analysis and that can be conveniently stored in the calendar table. For example, you might be interested in defining a measure that calculates the average of sales per working days in a given period. To do that, you have to calculate the number of working days, which in turn requires knowing whether a day is a working day or not.

The simplest way to do this is to add a WorkingDays column to the Excel calendar table. That column should have the value 1 for working days and 0 for holidays, weekends, and other nonworking days. Instead of compiling this column by hand, you might define it using the following Excel formula, which assigns 1 to all weekdays, leaving 0 to Saturday and Sunday:

```
= IF ( WEEKDAY ( [@FullDate], 2 ) > 5, 0, 1 )
```

> **Tip** You might want to use a separate NonWorkingDays table to configure the working days in the week. In that case, you use the *VLOOKUP* Excel function in this expression. You see a similar example later in this section, when we discuss how to create a table that defines public holidays that must be differentiated from working days.

This formula is automatically copied into all the rows of the OrderDate table, as shown in Figure 12-8. You can find this data in the companion workbook "CH12-04-Working Days.xlsx."

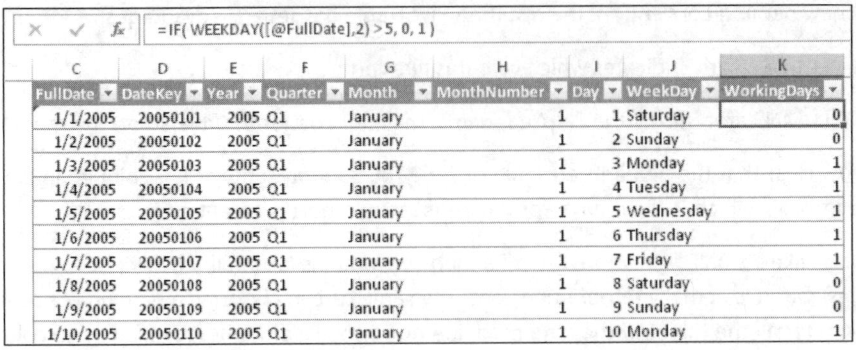

	C	D	E	F	G	H	I	J	K
	FullDate	DateKey	Year	Quarter	Month	MonthNumber	Day	WeekDay	WorkingDays
	1/1/2005	20050101	2005	Q1	January	1	1	Saturday	0
	1/2/2005	20050102	2005	Q1	January	1	2	Sunday	0
	1/3/2005	20050103	2005	Q1	January	1	3	Monday	1
	1/4/2005	20050104	2005	Q1	January	1	4	Tuesday	1
	1/5/2005	20050105	2005	Q1	January	1	5	Wednesday	1
	1/6/2005	20050106	2005	Q1	January	1	6	Thursday	1
	1/7/2005	20050107	2005	Q1	January	1	7	Friday	1
	1/8/2005	20050108	2005	Q1	January	1	8	Saturday	0
	1/9/2005	20050109	2005	Q1	January	1	9	Sunday	0
	1/10/2005	20050110	2005	Q1	January	1	10	Monday	1

The formula bar shows: `= IF( WEEKDAY([@FullDate],2) > 5, 0, 1 )`

FIGURE 12-8 The WorkingDays column is very useful for counting the number of working days in a date range.

You can modify single values for other nonworking days, such as public holidays, overriding the formula with a forced fixed value (usually 0) just for these days.

You can refresh the linked table in the Excel data model, and the WorkingDays column shows up in the PivotTable too. At this point, you can define a calculated field belonging to the FactInternetSales table named *DailySales,* which divides the sum of *SalesAmount* by the sum of working days, as shown in Figure 12-9.

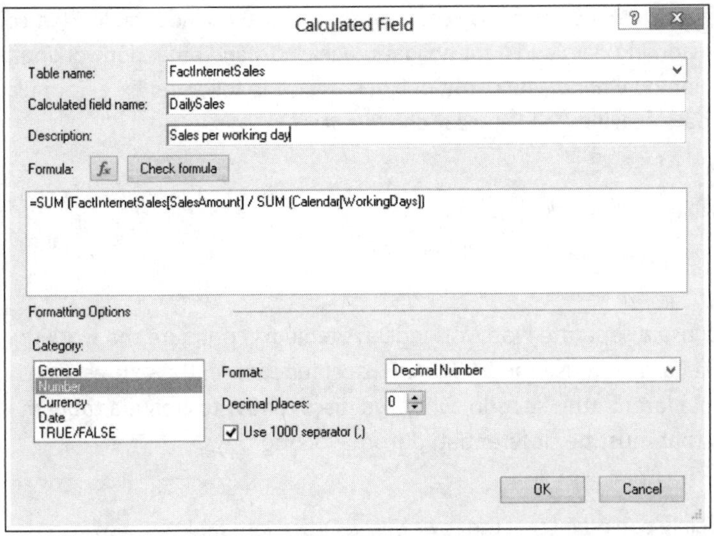

FIGURE 12-9 Here you can see the definition of the *DailySales* calculated field.

The final result is shown in Figure 12-10, where both WorkingDays and DailySales measures are exposed in the PivotTable. However, in a real report, you usually do not show the working days number but just the average measures, such as Daily Sales.

Row Labels	Sum of SalesAmount	Sum of WorkingDays	DailySales
⊞ 2005	$3,266,373.66	260	12,563
⊟ 2006	$6,530,343.53	260	25,117
January	$596,746.56	22	27,125
February	$550,816.69	20	27,541
March	$644,135.20	23	28,006
April	$663,692.29	20	33,185
May	$673,556.20	23	29,285
June	$676,763.65	22	30,762
July	$500,365.16	21	23,827
August	$546,001.47	23	23,739
September	$350,466.99	21	16,689
October	$415,390.23	22	18,881
November	$335,095.09	22	15,232
December	$577,314.00	21	27,491

FIGURE 12-10 Here you can see the PivotTable showing results for *WorkingDays* and *DailySales*.

This simple calculation works fine for years like 2005 and 2006, where there is data for the whole year. If you use it on years that are not completely filled with data, however, you will see incorrect numbers. For example, in Figure 12-11, you can see that the value for 2008 is 37,294, which is lower than all the monthly values. Thus, it is certainly not the correct average.

Year		Row Labels	Sum of SalesAmount	Sum of WorkingDays	DailySales
2005		⊟ 2008	$9,770,899.74	262	37,294
2006		January	$1,340,244.95	23	58,272
2007		February	$1,462,479.83	21	69,642
2008		March	$1,480,905.18	21	70,519
		April	$1,608,750.53	22	73,125
		May	$1,878,317.51	22	85,378
		June	$1,949,361.11	21	92,827
		July	$50,840.63	23	2,210
		August		21	
		September		22	
		October		23	
		November		20	
		December		23	
		Grand Total	**$9,770,899.74**	**262**	**37,294**

FIGURE 12-11 At the year and grand total level, the computation shown here is wrong.

The problem here is that when you are computing the average at the year level, you take into account sales for the first 7 months only while you take the working days for the whole 12-month period. In fact, the result is 9,770,899.74 divided by 262. To solve this issue, you simply need to avoid computing the value of working days for months where there are no sales. Moreover, it is worthwhile to note that this test (the lack of sales) needs to be done at the month level. Thus, the formula will iterate over the months in the filter context and, for each one, check if there are sales. If no sale is present in a specific month, than the number of working days for that month will be ignored. The following code shows the correct formula:

```
CorrectedDailySales =
SUM ( FactInternetSales[SalesAmount] )
/
```

```
SUMX (
    VALUES ( Calendar[Month] ),
    CALCULATE (
        IF (
            COUNTROWS ( FactInternetSales ) > 0,
            SUM ( Calendar[WorkingDays] )
        )
    )
)
```

Finally, in Figure 12-12, you can see the correct formula showing the desired result.

Row Labels	Sum of SalesAmount	Sum of WorkingDays	DailySales	CorrectedDailySales
⊟2008	$9,770,899.74	262	37,294	63,862
January	$1,340,244.95	23	58,272	58,272
February	$1,462,479.83	21	69,642	69,642
March	$1,480,905.18	21	70,519	70,519
April	$1,608,750.53	22	73,125	73,125
May	$1,878,317.51	22	85,378	85,378
June	$1,949,361.11	21	92,827	92,827
July	$50,840.63	23	2,210	2,210
August		21		
September		22		
October		23		
November		20		
December		23		
Grand Total	**$9,770,899.74**	**262**	**37,294**	**63,862**

Year slicer: 2005, 2006, 2007, 2008

FIGURE 12-12 The CorrectedDailySales column now shows the correct values.

Working days in different countries

In the examples included in this section, we are making some wrong assumptions for a database like *AdventureWorks*, but that might work for your own data. In fact, because we are accounting for sales in stores located in different countries, we should consider a different number of working days for each of these countries. This would make the *DailySales* measure harder to calculate. In fact, we should accomplish all of the following as well:

■ Define a separate table to calculate working days, based on country and date.

■ Make a calculation of the required *DailySales* average by country.

■ Aggregate that number for all countries by using a weighted average based on the sales amount for that country in a given period.

Although this calculation is still possible, it is very complex, and it is seldom used because this measure is probably not the same for different countries in the same report.

The technique up to this point is quite error-prone because you write directly into a cell a value of 0 to indicate a holiday, without any further explanation. If you make an error, it is really hard to identify; furthermore, you make no distinction between weekend days (which are calculated automatically) and holidays. A better solution is to define a separate Holidays table, which is easier to check and to maintain because it moves into a single calculated column the logic to merge weekend evaluation and holiday definition using a single formula. In Figure 12-13, you can see such a Holidays table, defined in Excel. You can find this data in the companion workbook "CH12-05-Working Days - Holidays.xlsx."

Date	Holiday
1/1/2005	New Year's Day
1/15/2005	Birthday of Martin Luther King, Jr.
2/19/2005	Washington's Birthday
5/28/2005	Memorial Day
7/4/2005	Independence Day
9/3/2005	Labor Day
10/8/2005	Columbus Day
11/12/2005	Veterans Day

FIGURE 12-13 Here is an example of a holiday table in Excel.

Suppose that you use simple *VLOOKUP* logic, like the following code:

```
=IF (
    ISNA ( VLOOKUP ( [@FullDate], Holidays, 2 ) ),
    IF (
        WEEKDAY ( [@FullDate], 2 ) > 5,
        "Weekend",
        ""
    ),
    VLOOKUP ( [@FullDate], Holidays, 2 )
)
```

In this way, you can bring this information into the original calendar table and build a more complete calendar table like the one shown in Figure 12-14.

FullDate	DateKey	Year	Quarter	Month	MonthNumber	Day	WeekDay	WorkingDays	HolidayReason
1/1/2005	20050101	2005	Q1	January	1	1	Saturday	0	New Year's Day
1/2/2005	20050102	2005	Q1	January	1	2	Sunday	0	Weekend
1/3/2005	20050103	2005	Q1	January	1	3	Monday	1	
1/4/2005	20050104	2005	Q1	January	1	4	Tuesday	1	
1/5/2005	20050105	2005	Q1	January	1	5	Wednesday	1	
1/6/2005	20050106	2005	Q1	January	1	6	Thursday	1	
1/7/2005	20050107	2005	Q1	January	1	7	Friday	1	
1/8/2005	20050108	2005	Q1	January	1	8	Saturday	0	Weekend
1/9/2005	20050109	2005	Q1	January	1	9	Sunday	0	Weekend
1/10/2005	20050110	2005	Q1	January	1	10	Monday	1	
1/11/2005	20050111	2005	Q1	January	1	11	Tuesday	1	
1/12/2005	20050112	2005	Q1	January	1	12	Wednesday	1	
1/13/2005	20050113	2005	Q1	January	1	13	Thursday	1	
1/14/2005	20050114	2005	Q1	January	1	14	Friday	1	

FIGURE 12-14 Adding holidays to the calendar table is a simple operation in Excel.

Holidays are just an example of what kind of information you can bring inside the calendar table. Once the column is computed and put inside the Excel data model, you will be able to use it to slice your data and compute useful values.

Before we leave this topic, we should look at why we decided to use Excel and *VLOOKUP* to compute the HolidayReason column instead of relying on DAX and the data model. After all, this book is about learning DAX, not learning the Excel language, which you probably already know very well. The reason is that, from a modeling point of view, computing these values in DAX is harder and does not have any advantages.

If you use only the data model to compute HolidayReason, then you need to bring the Holidays table into the data model and then define relationships correctly. Once the table is in the data model, you can go to Diagram view, create the first relationship between the Calendar and the Holidays table, and then create the relationship between ShipDate and the holidays table. The resulting diagram is shown in Figure 12-15.

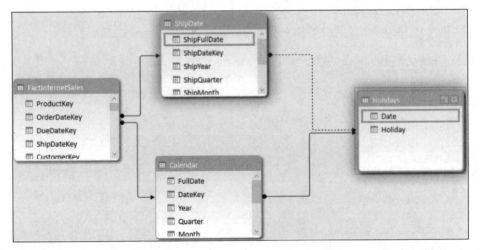

FIGURE 12-15 The holidays table has two incoming relationships from the two calendar tables.

Even if everything seems to work correctly, it really is not. You can see that the line connecting ShipDate and Holidays is dotted, whereas the one between Calendar and Holidays is continuous. PowerPivot did not raise any warning, but it decided that the relationship that we created as the second one could not be activated. In fact, if it were active, then we would have created an ambiguity in the data model because there would be two different paths starting from FactInternetSales and moving toward Holidays.

In fact, try to answer this simple question: what is the result of RELATED (Holidays[Holiday]) written inside a calculated column in FactInternetSales? The engine could start from FactInternetSales, follow the relationship with Calendar, and then reach Holidays, but it also could follow the relationship with ShipDate and, from there, reach Holidays. Thus, the correct answer is: "It cannot be safely computed if there are multiple paths connecting two tables."

There are two solutions to such a scenario: you can duplicate the Holidays table creating one copy for the Calendar and one copy for the ShipDate, or you can avoid relationships completely and use only calculated columns in DAX using the *LOOKUPVALUE* function. Neither of these solutions is really suitable, because each one requires complex DAX or a complex data model, with no advantage. On the other hand, using *VLOOKUP* inside the Excel table leads to a very simple implementation that comes only with benefits. For this reason, we preferred to use Excel in this scenario instead of DAX.

> **Tip** Another possible solution is to create several inactive relationships and then use the *USERELATIONSHIP* function to compute the holiday information in the calendar table, still using a single holiday table. Nevertheless, in PowerPivot, the Excel solution is the easiest one to implement. Moreover, it is more important to note that just because you can do something does not mean you need to do it. Having the ability to use DAX does not mean that DAX is the solution to all modeling problems. Each decision in your data model requires attention, and you always need to choose the best option, which in this case is Excel.

Computing the difference in working days

You learned how to compute the number of working days in a specific range by using the PivotTable. There is another common calculation involving working days: the delta between two dates. For example, the FactInternetSales table contains three different dates:

- **OrderDate**   The date of the order

- **DueDate**   When the customer expects the order to be delivered

- **ShipDate**   The date an order is shipped

Calculating whether an order has been shipped on time seems pretty easy: you could just compare the DueDate and ShipDate columns. However, if you consider a standard delivery time to be four working days, you should calculate how many orders have been shipped after DueDate minus four working days. If you ship on Friday, you cannot expect the item to be delivered on Tuesday because only two working days have passed. You need to consider that Friday plus four working days means the item will arrive the following Thursday. This calculation requires the support of the calendar table and of the WorkingDays column that you looked at in the previous sections of this chapter.

Finally, we want to point out that this calculation is easy to perform with Excel, but this time, we want to focus on DAX only, for two reasons. The first is educational: we want to start using DAX. The second one is that the pattern we are using for the delta in working days has several different variations that are very useful in many other scenarios. Thus, learning it is valuable not only for working days, but for many other scenarios. You can find this data in the companion workbook "CH12-07-Working Days Delay.xlsx."

To address this scenario, we start by making it more general. Instead of focusing on the difference between ShipDate and DueDate, we work on computing the difference in working days between any two dates. Performing the calculations using only the Date column turns to be very complex, but if we could compute a new column that starts at 1 and increases only during working days, then the calculation would be much easier. This column is shown in Figure 12-16.

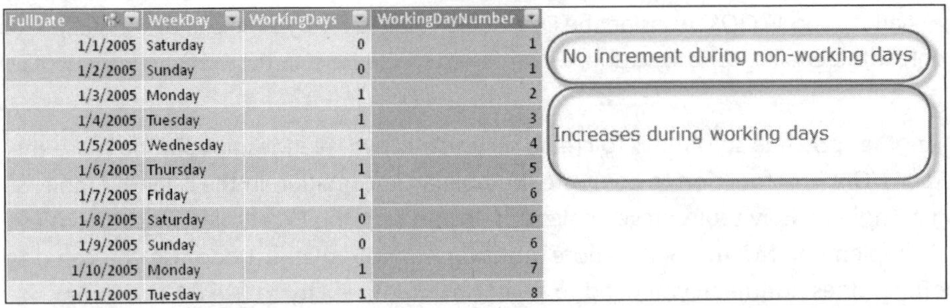

FIGURE 12-16 The *WorkingDayNumber* value increases only during working days.

With the WorkingDayNumber column available, computing the difference between any two days is much easier: it is enough to subtract the *WorkingDayNumber* value of the two dates to compute it. As you have seen, we have switched the problem from computing the difference to computing the WorkingDayNumber column. It is clear that this column will be a calculated column in DAX—we only need to create the formula.

If we were to solve this scenario using Excel, then finding *WorkingDayNumber* would have been very easy; once the calendar table is sorted by FullDate, the value can be computed as "the value of the previous row plus WorkingDays." Unfortunately, DAX has no concept of "the previous row." In DAX, we can only use table functions and evaluation contexts. Thus, to write this formula, we need to start thinking in DAX terms, finding a suitable expression that will compute *WorkingDayNumber* without relying on table sorting.

The definition of such an expression can be the following: Count the number of rows that have a previous date than the current one and that are working days, and then add 1 so that there will never be zeros in the expression. In other words, we want to count the number of rows (*COUNTROWS*) of a table (that is, we need a table function) that shows only some rows from a table (*FILTER*) satisfying a condition (hence, the *FILTER* condition). With this approach, the formula is pretty easy to write:

```
        WorkingDayNumber =
1.      COUNTROWS (
2.          FILTER (
3.              Calendar,
4.              Calendar[FullDate] <= EARLIER ( Calendar[FullDate] ) &&
5.              Calendar[WorkingDays] = 1
6.          )
7.      ) + 1
```

Even for this small exercise, the formula is using many of the concepts that you have learned so far. *FILTER* is in charge of computing the table for which we want to count the number of rows. It does this by filtering out of the complete calendar table only the rows that are working days (see row 5) and that are before the current date (see row 4). Note the use of *EARLIER* to address the value of the date in the current row (that is, in the row where the calculated column is being computed) and compare it to the value of the date currently iterated by *FILTER*. Take your time to understand this formula; the pattern used here will be very useful in more advanced scenarios.

Because you want to subtract the *WorkingDayNumber* of ShipDate from the one in DueDate, you should define the same calculation in both tables to perform the calculation. We called these columns ShipWorkingDayNumber (in ShipDate) and DueWorkingDayNumber (in DueDate).

At this point, all you need to do is compute the difference in working days between the two dates, storing the result in the FactInternetSales table. Because there is a relationship between FactInternetSales and both calendar tables, as shown in Figure 12-17, the *RELATED* function will come in handy here.

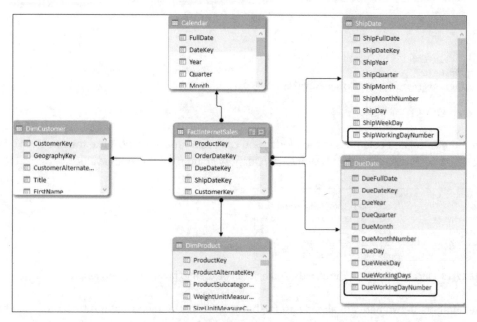

FIGURE 12-17 The data model has relationships starting from FactInternetSales and reaching the calendar tables.

In fact, you can easily define a calculated column in FactInternetSales with this definition:

```
WorkingDaysDelay =
    RELATED ( ShipDate[ShipWorkingDayNumber] )
    - RELATED ( DueDate[DueWorkingDayNumber] )
```

The *RELATED* function will take care of finding the related working day number for the ship and due dates. The difference between the two is a positive number if the good has been shipped with a delay, and negative otherwise. It turns out that at *AdventureWorks*, no order is ever shipped later than expected because the result is always a negative value. But we have not yet taken into account the shipment days, which are four working days. Thus, the correct expression should be

```
WorkingDaysDelay =
    RELATED ( ShipDate[ShipWorkingDayNumber] )
    - RELATED ( DueDate[DueWorkingDayNumber] )
    + 4
```

where the last 4 represents the number of actual shipping days. The final touch is to create a new calculated column that makes it easy to read this value. In fact, if the WorkingDaysDelay column has a negative value, then the order was shipped on time; otherwise, there was a delay. A new calculated column will make this fact clearer:

```
Delay =
IF (
    FactInternetSales[WorkingDaysDelay] <= 0,
    "No Delay,"
    FactInternetSales[WorkingDaysDelay] & " Days of Delay"
)
```

Once the calculated column is in the model, you can easily create a report like the one shown in Figure 12-18, where we used the SUM of OrderQuantity column to display the value.

SumOfQuantity	Column Labels				
Row Labels	2005	2006	2007	2008	Grand Total
1 Days of Delay		605	1,451	13,968	18,789	34,813
2 Days of Delay		13	96	965		1,074
No Delay		395	1,130	9,510	13,476	24,511
Grand Total		1,013	2,677	24,443	32,265	60,398

FIGURE 12-18 Once a delay is in a calculated column, it can be used to build interesting reports.

The numbers shown here are already useful, but to get a better picture of this trend, it would be better to show them as a percentage of the total number of items sold. You can easily achieve such a result by using a simple *CALCULATE* with the *DelayPct* calculated field:

```
DelayPct :=
    SUM ( FactInternetSales[OrderQuantity] )
    /
    CALCULATE (
        SUM ( FactInternetSales[OrderQuantity] ),
        ALL ( FactInternetSales[Delay] )
    )
```

This calculated field shows the percentage of orders with some delay based on the total of all orders, without taking the Delay column into account. The resulting report is much easier to read, as shown in Figure 12-19.

DelayPct	Column Labels				
Row Labels	2005	2006	2007	2008	Grand Total
1 Days of Delay	59.72%	54.20%	57.15%	58.23%	57.64%
2 Days of Delay	1.28%	3.59%	3.95%		1.78%
No Delay	38.99%	42.21%	38.91%	41.77%	40.58%
Grand Total	100.00%	100.00%	100.00%	100.00%	100.00%

FIGURE 12-19 Using the percentage instead of the absolute value leads to a better understanding of trends.

Aggregating and comparing over time

Calculating working days is only the first step in the benefits that you can obtain by using a calendar table. In the next sections, we introduce other useful techniques. It is often required that you analyze particular aggregations of values over time. For example, you might want to calculate the aggregated value of a column (for example, Sales Amount) from the beginning of the year up to the period that you are selecting. This is commonly called *year-to-date aggregation*. You might want to look at the Sales Amount for the month of March but also want to look at the total Sales Amount from January to March. Having a calendar table is an important prerequisite for making this calculation in the Excel data model.

Year-to-Date (YTD), Quarter-to-Date (QTD), and Month-to-Date (MTD)

The calculation of year-to-date (YTD), quarter-to-date (QTD), and month-to-date (MTD) are all very similar. Obviously, MTD is meaningful only when you are looking at data at the day level, whereas YTD and QTD calculations are often used to look at data at the month level.

For example, in Figure 12-20, you can see the *SalesAmount* value aggregated by year, quarter, and month. You can find this data in the companion workbook "CH12-08-YTD.xlsx."

Row Labels	Sum of SalesAmount
⊟ 2005	$3,266,373.66
⊟ Q3	$1,453,522.89
July	$473,388.16
August	$506,191.69
September	$473,943.03
⊟ Q4	$1,812,850.77
October	$513,329.47
November	$543,993.41
December	$755,527.89
⊟ 2006	$6,530,343.53
⊟ Q1	$1,791,698.45
January	$596,746.56
February	$550,816.69
March	$644,135.20
⊟ Q2	$2,014,012.13
April	$663,692.29
May	$673,556.20
June	$676,763.65
⊟ Q3	$1,396,833.62

FIGURE 12-20 Sales amount values can be easily aggregated using the calendar table.

You can calculate the YTD value of *SalesAmount* for each month and quarter by using a specific function: *TOTALYTD*. You can define a new calculated field using this formula:

```
SalesAmountYTD =
TOTALYTD (
    SUM ( FactInternetSales[SalesAmount] ),
    Calendar[FullDate]
)
```

Unfortunately, this formula does not yield the desired result, as shown in Figure 12-21.

Row Labels	Sum of SalesAmount	SalesAmount YTD
⊟ 2005	$3,266,373.66	3,266,373.66
⊟ Q3	$1,453,522.89	1,453,522.89
July	$473,388.16	473,388.16
August	$506,191.69	506,191.69
September	$473,943.03	473,943.03
⊟ Q4	$1,812,850.77	1,812,850.77
October	$513,329.47	513,329.47
November	$543,993.41	543,993.41
December	$755,527.89	755,527.89
⊟ 2006	$6,530,343.53	6,530,343.53

FIGURE 12-21 *TOTALYTD* does not work unless you define the calendar table correctly.

You can see that the same value is shown for both the simple sum and *TOTALYTD*. The problem is that in order for the time intelligence functions to work correctly, PowerPivot needs to know that the Calendar is a "date table." Unless this information is provided, all time intelligence functions will provide incorrect results. To fix the issue, click the Mark As Date Table button on the Design tab of the PowerPivot ribbon, as shown in Figure 12-22.

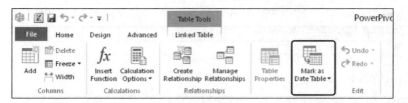

FIGURE 12-22 The Mark As Date Table button lets you inform PowerPivot that a table is a date table.

A date table needs to have a Date column. Thus, when you mark a table as a date table, PowerPivot asks for the column containing the date with the dialog box shown in Figure 12-23.

Mark as Date Table

Select a column to be used as unique identifier for the date table. The selected column must be of the date data type and must contain unique values only.

Date: FullDate

OK   Cancel

FIGURE 12-23 The Mark As Date Table dialog box lets you specify the column containing the date.

The dialog box defaults to the first column in your table of type Date and, in the example, it already shows the correct value. If your calendar table contains more than one column of Date type, you will need to choose the correct one. Once the table is marked as a date table, the previous formula using *TOTALYTD* computes the correct result, as shown in Figure 12-24.

Row Labels	Sum of SalesAmount	SalesAmount YTD
⊟ 2005	$3,266,373.66	3,266,373.66
⊟ Q3	$1,453,522.89	1,453,522.89
July	$473,388.16	473,388.16
August	$506,191.69	979,579.85
September	$473,943.03	1,453,522.89
⊟ Q4	$1,812,850.77	3,266,373.66
October	$513,329.47	1,966,852.36
November	$543,993.41	2,510,845.77
December	$755,527.89	3,266,373.66
⊟ 2006	$6,530,343.53	6,530,343.53
⊟ Q1	$1,791,698.45	1,791,698.45
January	$596,746.56	596,746.56
February	$550,816.69	1,147,563.25
March	$644,135.20	1,791,698.45

FIGURE 12-24 Once the calendar table is marked as a date table, time intelligence functions will work correctly.

TOTALYTD has some companion functions that compute different aggregations over time. They are *TOTALQTD* for QTD and *TOTALMTD*, for MTD.

What Date Column to Use

One important thing to remember is that the date column that you must use when calling *TOTALYTD* (and other similar functions) is the date column of the calendar table, not the date column of the table that is the object of analysis. In this example, we used the Calendar[FullDate] column and not the FactInternetSales[OrderDate]. If we had used the latter, the calculation would have been wrong, showing the same value as the simple *SUM*.

To calculate a YTD measure over the fiscal year, you need to use an optional parameter that specifies the end day of the fiscal year. For example, you can calculate the fiscal YTD for *SalesAmount* by using the following expression:

```
FiscalYtdLineTotal :=
TOTALYTD (
    SUM ( FactInternetSales[SalesAmount] ),
    Calendar[FullDate],
    "06-30"
)
```

The last parameter corresponds to June 30, which in our calendar corresponds to the end of the fiscal year. The format of this string follows the locale settings, so you will have to use "30-06" in case the current international setting requires dates to be specified with the *DD-MM* format instead of *MM-DD*, as it is the case for English-US locale setting. You can find several Time Intelligence functions that have a last, optional parameter for this purpose: *STARTOFYEAR, ENDOFYEAR, PREVIOUSYEAR, NEXTYEAR, DATESYTD, TOTALYTD, OPENINGBALANCEYEAR,* and *CLOSINGBALANCEYEAR,* most of which will be treated in this chapter.

In Figure 12-25, you can see the difference between YTD on the solar and on the fiscal calendar.

Row Labels	Sum of SalesAmount	SalesAmount YTD	FiscalYtdLineTotal
⊟ 2006	$6,530,343.53	6,530,343.53	2,724,632.94
⊟ Q1	$1,791,698.45	1,791,698.45	5,058,072.11
January	$596,746.56	596,746.56	3,863,120.21
February	$550,816.69	1,147,563.25	4,413,936.91
March	$644,135.20	1,791,698.45	5,058,072.11
⊟ Q2	$2,014,012.13	3,805,710.59	7,072,084.24
April	$663,692.29	2,455,390.74	5,721,764.40
May	$673,556.20	3,128,946.94	6,395,320.59
June	$676,763.65	3,805,710.59	7,072,084.24
⊟ Q3	$1,396,833.62	5,202,544.20	1,396,833.62
July	$500,365.16	4,306,075.74	500,365.16
August	$546,001.47	4,852,077.21	1,046,366.63
September	$350,466.99	5,202,544.20	1,396,833.62
⊟ Q4	$1,327,799.32	6,530,343.53	2,724,632.94
October	$415,390.23	5,617,934.44	1,812,223.85
November	$335,095.09	5,953,029.53	2,147,318.94
December	$577,314.00	6,530,343.53	2,724,632.94
Grand Total	$6,530,343.53	6,530,343.53	2,724,632.94

FIGURE 12-25 Using the fiscal calendar, many time intelligence functions can aggregate over the fiscal year.

Time intelligence with *CALCULATE*

In the previous section, you learned the usage of *TOTALYTD* and that it is important to mark a calendar table as a date table to make it work correctly. The *TOTALYTD* function is internally implemented using *CALCULATE*. It is useful to learn *TOTALYTD* because it is very easy to read, but at the same time, it is important to learn the *CALCULATE* version of time intelligence. In fact, using *CALCULATE*, you will be able to create many interesting patterns, even when there is no built-in function like *TOTALYTD*.

The *CALCULATE* version of YTD uses the following formula:

```
Calc YTD :=
CALCULATE (
    SUM ( FactInternetSales[SalesAmount] ),
    DATESYTD ( Calendar[FullDate] )
)
```

This formula uses the *DATESYTD* function, which returns all dates in a calendar table. *DATESYTD* analyzes the current filter context and returns all the dates starting from January 1 of the currently selected year (that is, the one visible in the filter context) up to the last selected date (that is, the last date visible in the current filter context). The new set of dates is used to filter the calendar table; thus, the expression of *CALCULATE* is evaluated for all those dates. You can better understand the behavior of *DATESYTD* by rewriting it using standard functions, as in the following formula:

```
    Calc YTD Std :=
1.  IF (
2.      HASONEVALUE ( Calendar[Year] ),
```

```
3.          CALCULATE (
4.              SUM ( FactInternetSales[SalesAmount] ),
5.              FILTER (
6.                  ALL ( Calendar ),
7.                  Calendar[FullDate] <= MAX ( Calendar[FullDate] )
8.                  && Calendar[Year] = VALUES ( Calendar[Year] )
9.              )
10.         )
11.     )
```

There are a few interesting patterns used in this formula, which are worth studying:

- You test whether only one year is selected, using *HASONEVALUE,* at line 2. This is useful to avoid showing a grand total for many years, because it does not make sense. It is worth to note that the built-in functions do not perform this operation; that is, they show a grand total that might be hard to understand because it is the last YTD value, not a real grand total.

- The *FILTER* function iterates on ALL (Calendar) at line 6. This is needed because you need to expand the filter on the calendar table, returning rows that are not visible in the current filter context. If, for example, March 2012 is selected, you will need to return all the rows from January to March and the ones of January and February are outside the current filter context.

- On row 7, you can see that the formula makes a comparison between Calendar[FullDate] and MAX (Calendar[FullDate]). The two expressions are evaluated under different conditions. In fact, Calendar[FullDate] references the current row in the row context introduces by *FILTER,* whereas MAX (Calendar[FullDate]) does not use the row context, but it uses the filter context and, being a condition of the *CALCULATE* at row 3, it is evaluated in the original filter context, effectively returning the last date selected in the cell of the PivotTable currently being computed.

- The same scenario of row 7 is visible at row 8, but this time, instead of using *MAX,* you are using *VALUES. VALUES* returns a table of one column, but because you have previously tested with *HASONEVALUE* at row 2 that there is only one year visible, then *VALUES* will return that year only. Thus, the condition at row 7 checks that the date is in the same year as the one selected.

With these points in mind, you can now read the condition of *FILTER* at rows 5–9 as "return the dates that are in the same year as the selected one and that are previous than or equal to the last visible date." If you have selected March 2012, this set is the set of all the dates from January 1 to the end of March, exactly what you need to compute the YTD.

You can see in Figure 12-26 that the *Calc YTD Std* field returns exactly the same values of the other *YTD* fields you have seen before. The only notable (and desired) difference is at the grand total, where your last formula results in a *BLANK*, whereas the previous one shows a value that is not really useful.

Row Labels	Sum of SalesAmount	SalesAmount YTD	Calc YTD	Calc YTD Std
⊟2005	$3,266,373.66	3,266,373.66	3,266,373.66	3,266,373.66
⊟Q3	$1,453,522.89	1,453,522.89	1,453,522.89	1,453,522.89
July	$473,388.16	473,388.16	473,388.16	473,388.16
August	$506,191.69	979,579.85	979,579.85	979,579.85
September	$473,943.03	1,453,522.89	1,453,522.89	1,453,522.89
⊞Q4	$1,812,850.77	3,266,373.66	3,266,373.66	3,266,373.66
⊟2006	$6,530,343.53	6,530,343.53	6,530,343.53	6,530,343.53
⊞Q1	$1,791,698.45	1,791,698.45	1,791,698.45	1,791,698.45
⊞Q2	$2,014,012.13	3,805,710.59	3,805,710.59	3,805,710.59
⊟Q3	$1,396,833.62	5,202,544.20	5,202,544.20	5,202,544.20
July	$500,365.16	4,306,075.74	4,306,075.74	4,306,075.74
August	$546,001.47	4,852,077.21	4,852,077.21	4,852,077.21
September	$350,466.99	5,202,544.20	5,202,544.20	5,202,544.20
⊞Q4	$1,327,799.32	6,530,343.53	6,530,343.53	6,530,343.53
Grand Total	$9,796,717.18	6,530,343.53	6,530,343.53	

FIGURE 12-26 The *Calc YTD Std* field behaves exactly as *Calc YTD* and *SalesAmount YTD* do.

At this point, you might wonder why you should learn a more complex way to accomplish what can be easily done with built-in functions. The reason is that understanding the more difficult way of writing the formula lets you create more complex expressions for which there is no built-in function. For example, if you want to compute a useful calculation like the running total, built-in functions are of no use. Since now you know how to write them from scratch, you can easily write (and understand) the code of *RunningTotal*, which is similar to *YTD* but avoids filtering the year:

```
RunningTotal :=
CALCULATE (
    SUM ( FactInternetSales[SalesAmount] ),
    FILTER (
        ALL ( Calendar ),
        Calendar[FullDate] <= MAX ( Calendar[FullDate] )
    )
)
```

You can see the behavior of *RunningTotal* in Figure 12-27.

Row Labels	Sum of SalesAmount	SalesAmount YTD	Calc YTD	Calc YTD Std	RunningTotal
⊟2005	$3,266,373.66	3,266,373.66	3,266,373.66	3,266,373.66	3,266,373.66
⊟Q3	$1,453,522.89	1,453,522.89	1,453,522.89	1,453,522.89	1,453,522.89
July	$473,388.16	473,388.16	473,388.16	473,388.16	473,388.16
August	$506,191.69	979,579.85	979,579.85	979,579.85	979,579.85
September	$473,943.03	1,453,522.89	1,453,522.89	1,453,522.89	1,453,522.89
⊞Q4	$1,812,850.77	3,266,373.66	3,266,373.66	3,266,373.66	3,266,373.66
⊟2006	$6,530,343.53	6,530,343.53	6,530,343.53	6,530,343.53	9,796,717.18
⊟Q1	$1,791,698.45	1,791,698.45	1,791,698.45	1,791,698.45	5,058,072.11
January	$596,746.56	596,746.56	596,746.56	596,746.56	3,863,120.21
February	$550,816.69	1,147,563.25	1,147,563.25	1,147,563.25	4,413,936.91
March	$644,135.20	1,791,698.45	1,791,698.45	1,791,698.45	5,058,072.11
⊞Q2	$2,014,012.13	3,805,710.59	3,805,710.59	3,805,710.59	7,072,084.24
⊟Q3	$1,396,833.62	5,202,544.20	5,202,544.20	5,202,544.20	8,468,917.86
July	$500,365.16	4,306,075.74	4,306,075.74	4,306,075.74	7,572,449.40
August	$546,001.47	4,852,077.21	4,852,077.21	4,852,077.21	8,118,450.87
September	$350,466.99	5,202,544.20	5,202,544.20	5,202,544.20	8,468,917.86
⊞Q4	$1,327,799.32	6,530,343.53	6,530,343.53	6,530,343.53	9,796,717.18
Grand Total	$9,796,717.18	6,530,343.53	6,530,343.53		9,796,717.18

FIGURE 12-27 Using *CALCULATE*, you can create a *RunningTotal* field even if no built-in function is available.

You can see that this time the *RunningTotal* field has a grand total, which makes sense because the running total does not depend on the year.

Now that you know how to write time intelligence functions using *CALCULATE*, do not assume that you will always need to do it this way. In reality, the built-in functions are useful because they are easy to read and make the formula much more readable and easier to maintain. Nevertheless, when needed, you will have a new tool in your toolset to handle more complex scenarios.

Computing periods from the prior year (PY)

Reports commonly need to get a value from a period of the prior year (PY). This can be useful for comparing trends, say, during a period last year to the same period this year. You can find this data in the companion workbook "CH12-09-Previous Year.xlsx." This is the DAX expression you need to calculate that value:

```
PySales :=
CALCULATE (
    SUM ( FactInternetSales[SalesAmount] ),
    SAMEPERIODLASTYEAR ( Calendar[FullDate] )
)
```

The *CALCULATE* function changes the filter by using the *SAMEPERIODLASTYEAR* function, which returns a set of dates from one year ago. The *SAMEPERIODLASTYEAR* function is a specialized version of the more generic *DATEADD* function, which can be used by specifying the number and type of periods to shift. For example, the same *PySales* field can be defined by this equivalent expression:

```
PySales :=
CALCULATE (
    SUM ( FactInternetSales[SalesAmount] ),
    DATEADD ( Calendar[FullDate], -1, YEAR )
)
```

Sometimes you must look at the total amount of a measure for the previous year, usually to compare it with the *YTD* total. To do that, you can use the *PARALLELPERIOD* function, which is similar to *DATEADD* but returns the full period specified in the third parameter instead of the partial period returned by *DATEADD*. The *PyTotSales* field that calculates the total sum of sales amounts for the complete previous year can be defined this way:

```
PyTotSales :=
CALCULATE (
    SUM ( FactInternetSales[SalesAmount] ),
    PARALLELPERIOD ( Calendar[FullDate], -1, YEAR )
)
```

In Figure 12-28, you can see the result of the *PySales* and *PyTotSales* fields. The quarter's data in 2006 for the Sum Of SalesAmount column has been copied into the respective quarters of year 2007 in the PySales column. The PyTotSales reports, for every period, the total amount of the SalesAmount column for the year before.

Row Labels	Sum of SalesAmount	PySales	PyTotSales
⊟ 2006	$6,530,343.53	3,266,373.66	3,266,373.66
⊞ Q1	$1,791,698.45		3,266,373.66
⊞ Q2	$2,014,012.13		3,266,373.66
⊟ Q3	$1,396,833.62	1,453,522.89	3,266,373.66
July	$500,365.16	473,388.16	3,266,373.66
August	$546,001.47	506,191.69	3,266,373.66
September	$350,466.99	473,943.03	3,266,373.66
⊞ Q4	$1,327,799.32	1,812,850.77	3,266,373.66
⊟ 2007	$9,791,060.30	6,530,343.53	6,530,343.53
⊞ Q1	$1,413,530.30	1,791,698.45	6,530,343.53
⊞ Q2	$1,623,971.06	2,014,012.13	6,530,343.53
⊟ Q3	$2,744,340.48	1,396,833.62	6,530,343.53
July	$886,668.84	500,365.16	6,530,343.53
August	$847,413.51	546,001.47	6,530,343.53
September	$1,010,258.13	350,466.99	6,530,343.53
⊞ Q4	$4,009,218.46	1,327,799.32	6,530,343.53
Grand Total	$16,321,403.82	9,796,717.18	9,796,717.18

FIGURE 12-28 Here, you can see the *PySales* and *PyTotSales* calculated fields in action.

Using the *CALCULATE* version of time intelligence, the only limit to the power you have is your imagination. For example, you might want to calculate the *YTD* of the prior year because, typically, you want to compare it with the current *YTD*. In this case, you have to mix the two techniques. Instead of passing the Calendar[FullDate] parameter to *SAMEPERIODLASTYEAR*, which corresponds to the list of dates that are active in the current filter context, you can use the *DATESYTD* function to transform these dates, defining the YTD group first. However, you might also invert the order of these calls. In fact, the two following definitions of *PyYtdLineTotal* are equivalent:

```
PyYtdSales :=
CALCULATE (
    SUM ( FactInternetSales[SalesAmount] ),
    SAMEPERIODLASTYEAR ( DATESYTD ( Calendar[FullDate] ) )
)

PyYtdSales :=
CALCULATE (
    SUM ( FactInternetSales[SalesAmount] ),
    DATESYTD ( SAMEPERIODLASTYEAR ( Calendar[FullDate] ) )
)
```

You can see the results of *PyYtdSales* in Figure 12-29. The values of *YtdSales* are reported for *PyYtdSales* shifted by one year.

Row Labels	Sum of SalesAmount	YtdSales	PyYtdSales
⊟ 2006	6,530,343.53	6,530,343.53	3,266,373.66
⊞ Q1	1,791,698.45	1,791,698.45	
⊞ Q2	2,014,012.13	3,805,710.59	
⊟ Q3	1,396,833.62	5,202,544.20	1,453,522.89
July	500,365.16	4,306,075.74	473,388.16
August	546,001.47	4,852,077.21	979,579.85
September	350,466.99	5,202,544.20	1,453,522.89
⊞ Q4	1,327,799.32	6,530,343.53	3,266,373.66
⊟ 2007	9,791,060.30	9,791,060.30	6,530,343.53
⊞ Q1	1,413,530.30	1,413,530.30	1,791,698.45
⊞ Q2	1,623,971.06	3,037,501.36	3,805,710.59
⊟ Q3	2,744,340.48	5,781,841.84	5,202,544.20
July	886,668.84	3,924,170.20	4,306,075.74
August	847,413.51	4,771,583.71	4,852,077.21
September	1,010,258.13	5,781,841.84	5,202,544.20
⊞ Q4	4,009,218.46	9,791,060.30	6,530,343.53
Grand Total	16,321,403.82	9,791,060.30	6,530,343.53

FIGURE 12-29 *SAMEPERIODLASTYEAR* works with *YTD* too, resulting in complex calculations made easy.

Computing the moving annual total

Another commonly requested calculation that eliminates seasonal changes in sales is the moving annual total (MAT), which always considers the last 12 months (for this reason, it is sometimes known as Last Twelve Months, or LTM). For example, the value of *MatSales* for January 2007 is calculated by summing the range of dates from February 2006 to January 2007. Consider the following *MatSales* measure definition, which calculates the MAT for *SalesAmount*:

```
     MatSales :=
1.     CALCULATE (
2.         SUM ( FactInternetSales[SalesAmount] ),
3.         DATESBETWEEN (
4.             Calendar[FullDate],
5.             NEXTDAY (
6.                 SAMEPERIODLASTYEAR (
7.                     LASTDATE ( Calendar[FullDate] )
8.                 )
9.             ),
10.            LASTDATE ( Calendar[FullDate] )
11.        )
12.    )
```

The implementation of this calculated field requires some attention. You need to use the *DATESBETWEEN* function, which returns the dates from a column included between two specified dates. Because this calculation is always made at the day level even if the PivotTable is browsing data at the month level, you must calculate the first day and the last day of the interval you want. The last day can be obtained by calling the *LASTDATE* function, which returns the last date of a given column (always considering the current filter context). Starting from this date, you can get the first day of the interval by requesting the following day (by calling *NEXTDAY*) of the corresponding last date one year before. (You can do this by using *SAMEPERIODLASTYEAR*, as we did before.)

In Figure 12-30, you can see a PivotTable using the MAT calculation. The *MatSales* of January 2007 is the sum of *SalesAmount* from February 2006 to the end of January 2007.

Row Labels	Sum of SalesAmount	MatSales
2006	6,530,343.53	6,530,343.53
January	596,746.56	3,863,120.21
February	550,816.69	4,413,936.91
March	644,135.20	5,058,072.11
April	663,692.29	5,721,764.40
May	673,556.20	6,395,320.59
June	676,763.65	7,072,084.24
July	500,365.16	7,099,061.24
August	546,001.47	7,138,871.02
September	350,466.99	7,015,394.98
October	415,390.23	6,917,455.73
November	335,095.09	6,708,557.42
December	577,314.00	6,530,343.53
2007	9,791,060.30	9,791,060.30
January	438,865.17	6,372,462.14
February	489,090.34	6,310,735.78
March	485,574.79	6,152,175.37

FIGURE 12-30 *MatSales* computes a MAT, which is useful to draw charts and take averages.

The value of 2007 is the value of December 2007. If you want to compute the value only at the month level, clearing the total for the year, you can use an *IF* with the same pattern used for the *YTD:*

```
MatSales :=
IF (
    HASONEVALUE ( Calendar[EnglishMonthName] ),
    CALCULATE (
        SUM ( FactInternetSales[SalesAmount] ),
        DATESBETWEEN (
            Calendar[FullDate],
            NEXTDAY (
                SAMEPERIODLASTYEAR (
                    LASTDATE ( Calendar[FullDate] )
                )
            ),
            LASTDATE ( Calendar[FullDate] )
        )
    )
)
```

Using other aggregation functions

In all the examples so far, we have used the *SUM* aggregation function. You might need to use other aggregation functions, such as *AVERAGE,* or more complex formulas. Whenever you saw SUM (FactInternetSales[SalesAmount]) in the previous example, consider that you can always replace such expressions with another DAX formula by simply replacing the aggregation function.

If your calculation becomes more complex, you might prefer to specify that calculation, which can be shared across several other measures, as a separated measure containing just this operation. In this way, you can avoid the duplication of the aggregation function in all the formulas for measures that make special calculations for dates.

For example, you might want to calculate the average price with the following formula, assigned to measure *AveragePrice:*

```
AveragePrice :=
SUM ( FactInternetSales[SalesAmount] )
/
SUM ( FactInternetSales[OrderQuantity] )
```

You can use a direct reference to that measure, without using an aggregation function, whenever you use formulas such as *CALCULATE* or special time intelligence functions that behave like *CALCULATE*, as in the *YTD* calculation defined in the *YtdAveragePrice* measure:

```
YtdAveragePrice := TOTALYTD ( [AveragePrice], Calendar[FullDate] )
```

The calculation for the prior year can be written using the *CALCULATE* function:

```
PyAveragePrice :=
CALCULATE (
    [AveragePrice],
    SAMEPERIODLASTYEAR ( Calendar[FullDate] )
)
```

If you want to make a monthly average of the total sales, you should use the number of months in the denominator of the ratio, as in the following expression, which you can use to define the *MonthlyAverage* measure:

```
MonthlyAverage :=
    SUM ( FactInternetSales[SalesAmount] )
    /
    COUNTROWS ( VALUES ( Calendar[Month] ) )
```

To figure out a monthly average of the YTD sales, you have to replace the corresponding *YtdSales* measure at the numerator and put a *CALCULATE* expression into the denominator so you can calculate the number of months included in the YTD calculation:

```
YtdMonthlyAverage =
    [YtdSales]
    /
    CALCULATE (
        COUNTROWS ( VALUES ( Calendar[Month] ) ),
        DATESYTD ( Calendar[FullDate] )
    )
```

The expression might be different according to the calculation you have to do. You have to pay particular attention to the calculation necessary for numerators and denominators of any ratio and average measure.

Computing difference over a previous year

A common operation that compares a measure with its value in the prior year is to calculate the difference of these values. That difference might be expressed as an absolute value or by using a percentage. To make these calculations, you need the value for the prior year that you already defined in *PySales*:

```
PySales :=
CALCULATE (
    SUM ( FactInternetSales[SalesAmount] ),
    SAMEPERIODLASTYEAR ( Calendar[FullDate] )
)
```

The absolute difference of sales over a previous year (year-over-year, or YOY) is a simple subtraction. You can define a *YoySales* measure with the following expression:

```
YoySales := SUM ( FactInternetSales[SalesAmount] ) - [PySales]
```

You calculate the value of the selected year by using the *SUM* aggregation; the measure corresponding to the value of the prior year does not need to be summed because the aggregation has already been done as part of the underlying measure expression.

The analogous calculation for comparing the YTD measure to a corresponding value in the prior year is a simple subtraction of two calculated fields, following the same pattern.

Most of the time, the YOY difference is better expressed as a percentage in a report. You can define this calculation by dividing *YoySales* by *PySales;* in this way, the difference uses the prior read value as a reference for the percentage difference (100 percent corresponds to a value that is doubled in one year). The following expression defines the *YoyPercSales* calculated field. The *IF* statement avoids a divide-by-zero error if there is no corresponding data in the prior year:

```
YoyPercSales :=
IF (
    [PySales] = 0,
    BLANK (),
    [YoySales] / [PySales]
)
```

In Figure 12-31, you can see the results of these measures in a PivotTable.

Row Labels	Sum of SalesAmount	PySales	YoySales	YoyPercSales
⊟2006	6,530,343.53	3,266,373.66	3,263,969.87	99.93%
January	596,746.56		596,746.56	
February	550,816.69		550,816.69	
March	644,135.20		644,135.20	
April	663,692.29		663,692.29	
May	673,556.20		673,556.20	
June	676,763.65		676,763.65	
July	500,365.16	473,388.16	26,976.99	5.70%
August	546,001.47	506,191.69	39,809.78	7.86%
September	350,466.99	473,943.03	-123,476.04	-26.05%
October	415,390.23	513,329.47	-97,939.24	-19.08%
November	335,095.09	543,993.41	-208,898.32	-38.40%
December	577,314.00	755,527.89	-178,213.89	-23.59%
⊟2007	9,791,060.30	6,530,343.53	3,260,716.77	49.93%
January	438,865.17	596,746.56	-157,881.39	-26.46%
February	489,090.34	550,816.69	-61,726.36	-11.21%
March	485,574.79	644,135.20	-158,560.41	-24.62%
April	506,399.27	663,692.29	-157,293.02	-23.70%
May	562,772.56	673,556.20	-110,783.63	-16.45%
June	554,799.23	676,763.65	-121,964.42	-18.02%
July	886,668.84	500,365.16	386,303.69	77.20%
August	847,413.51	546,001.47	301,412.04	55.20%
September	1,010,258.13	350,466.99	659,791.14	188.26%
October	1,080,449.58	415,390.23	665,059.35	160.10%
November	1,196,981.11	335,095.09	861,886.02	257.21%
December	1,731,787.77	577,314.00	1,154,473.77	199.97%
Grand Total	16,321,403.82	9,796,717.18	6,524,686.64	66.60%

FIGURE 12-31 YOY comparisons are useful and easy to implement.

Closing balance over time

In a PivotTable, each cell contains the result of applying an aggregation function to a measure. Whenever that function is *SUM*, the measure is called an *additive measure* because *SUM* is applied over all dimensions. Whenever another function is applied, such as *AVERAGE, MIN,* or *MAX,* the measure is called a *nonadditive measure* because an aggregation function other than *SUM* is applied over all dimensions. However, it is important to note that for both additive and nonadditive measures, the same aggregation function is always applied over all column values in the current filter context, without exception. You can find this example in the companion workbook "CH12-10-SemiAdditive.xlsx."

Semiadditive measures

Some measures should behave in a different way. For example, think about the balance of a bank account. If you consider several accounts, you can calculate the total balance for an occupation by summing all the balances of customers, grouped by occupation. However, you must not sum the same balance twice, and you probably have several balances of the same account that measure it over time. For example, in Figure 12-32, you can see a Balance table in Excel: the same account has a balance value for each date. This type of measure is called a *semiadditive measure* because it can be aggregated using *SUM* over some dimensions but requires a different aggregation algorithm over other dimensions.

Name	Occupation	Country	Date	Balance
Katie Jordan	Farmer	USA	1/31/2010	1,687.00
Luis Bonifaz	IT Consultant	Argentina	1/31/2010	1,470.00
Maurizio Macagno	IT Consultant	Italy	1/31/2010	1,500.00
Katie Jordan	Farmer	USA	2/28/2010	2,812.00
Luis Bonifaz	IT Consultant	Argentina	2/28/2010	2,450.00
Maurizio Macagno	IT Consultant	Italy	2/28/2010	2,500.00
Katie Jordan	Farmer	USA	3/31/2010	3,737.00
Luis Bonifaz	IT Consultant	Argentina	3/31/2010	3,430.00
Maurizio Macagno	IT Consultant	Italy	3/31/2010	3,500.00

FIGURE 12-32 Here you can see a sample of data that is useful for implementing semiadditive measures.

In the case of account balance data, the only dimension that cannot be summed is the calendar. By the term *dimension calendar,* we include all the attributes of a calendar table related to the table containing the real measures. The logic that has to be implemented for the calendar attributes is to consider only the values belonging to the last date in the evaluated period. In other words, you must implement a logic that can produce the same results shown in Figure 12-33.

LastBalance	Column Labels		
Row Labels	Farmer	IT Consultant	Grand Total
⊟Q1	3,737.00	6,930.00	10,667.00
01 - January	1,687.00	2,970.00	4,657.00
02 - February	2,812.00	4,950.00	7,762.00
03 - March	3,737.00	6,930.00	10,667.00
⊟Q2	2,700.00	4,752.00	7,452.00
04 - April	2,250.00	3,960.00	6,210.00
05 - May	2,025.00	3,564.00	5,589.00
06 - June	2,700.00	4,752.00	7,452.00
⊟Q3	2,812.00	4,950.00	7,762.00
07 - July	3,600.00	6,336.00	9,936.00
08 - August	5,062.00	8,910.00	13,972.00
09 - September	2,812.00	4,950.00	7,762.00
⊟Q4			
10 - October	2,250.00	3,960.00	6,210.00
11 - November	2,081.00	3,663.00	5,744.00

FIGURE 12-33 Semiadditive calculated fields do not use *SUM* over some dimensions (the calendar, in this example).

The *LastBalance* measure used in Figure 12-31 calculates the total of a quarter by using just the last month available in that period. For each month, only the last date for that month is considered. So the total of a quarter is calculated using only the last day of that quarter. You can define the *LastBalance* measure in this way:

```
LastBalance :=
CALCULATE (
    SUM ( Balances[Balance] ),
    LASTDATE ( BalanceDate[Date] )
)
```

The definition of the *LastBalance* calculated field uses the *LASTDATE* function to keep just the last date that is active in the current filter context. Therefore, only the last date in the selected period is considered in the *CALCULATE* call.

Remember that the last date in a period is the last date available in the BalanceDate table (mentioned in the preceding formula), not the last date for which there is raw data. This might have unwanted consequences. If your data does not have values for the last day of a month and the Dates table contains all the days for that month, the *LastBalance* formula that you have used returns no data (a blank value) for that month. Consider the last two months available in the Balances table, as shown in Figure 12-34.

Name	Occupation	Country	Date	Balance
Katie Jordan	Farmer	USA	11/30/2010	2,081.00
Luis Bonifaz	IT Consultant	Argentina	11/30/2010	1,813.00
Maurizio Macagno	IT Consultant	Italy	11/30/2010	1,850.00
Katie Jordan	Farmer	USA	12/15/2010	2,531.00
Luis Bonifaz	IT Consultant	Argentina	12/15/2010	2,205.00
Maurizio Macagno	IT Consultant	Italy	12/15/2010	1,950.00

FIGURE 12-34 Here you can see the last two months of balance account data.

The Balances table contains a balance for each account and each last day of the month, but for December, the last day available is December 15. If the BalanceDate table contains all the days for the year 2010, including 31 days for December, the *LastBalance* measure tries to filter balance data for December 31, which is not available. The result is a PivotTable like the one shown in Figure 12-35, where the row for December is missing.

LastBalance Row Labels	Column Labels Farmer	IT Consultant	Grand Total
⊟ Q1	**3,737.00**	**6,930.00**	**10,667.00**
01 - January	1,687.00	2,970.00	4,657.00
02 - February	2,812.00	4,950.00	7,762.00
03 - March	3,737.00	6,930.00	10,667.00
⊟ Q2	**2,700.00**	**4,752.00**	**7,452.00**
04 - April	2,250.00	3,960.00	6,210.00
05 - May	2,025.00	3,564.00	5,589.00
06 - June	2,700.00	4,752.00	7,452.00
⊟ Q3	**2,812.00**	**4,950.00**	**7,762.00**
07 - July	3,600.00	6,336.00	9,936.00
08 - August	5,062.00	8,910.00	13,972.00
09 - September	2,812.00	4,950.00	7,762.00
⊟ Q4			
10 - October	2,250.00	3,960.00	6,210.00
11 - November	2,081.00	3,663.00	5,744.00

FIGURE 12-35 Using this implementation of *LastBalance*, the data for December is missing.

A possible solution is to delete rows from *BalanceDate* from December 16 through December 31. In this way, the *LastBalance* measure returns correct values. The problem is that, if you have a single calendar table in your data model, it might not be possible to delete rows from there without affecting other calculations.

Another option is to use the *LASTNONBLANK* function, which returns the last date for which a particular expression is not blank. The use of this function is not very intuitive when the calendar column and the expression that you want to evaluate take different tables into account. First, here is a formula for a *LastBalanceNonBlank* measure that also works with *BalanceDate*, complete with all dates through December 31:

```
LastBalancaNonBlank :=
CALCULATE (
    SUM ( Balances[Balance] ),
    LASTNONBLANK (
        BalanceDate[Date],
        COUNTROWS ( RELATEDTABLE ( Balances ) )
    )
)
```

Using the *FIRSTNONBLANK* and *LASTNONBLANK* functions

The *LASTNONBLANK* function you have just seen has a particular behavior, shared also by *FIRSTNONBLANK*. The syntax of these functions is as follows:

```
FIRSTNONBLANK ( <column>, <expression> )
LASTNONBLANK ( <column>, <expression> )
```

These functions return the first or last value in *<column>*, filtered by the current context, wherein the *<expression>* is not blank. So these functions behave like *SUMX* or similar functions in this regard. They set a row context for a value of *<column>* and then evaluate the *<expression>* by using that row context. If *<expression>* and *<column>* manage data from the same table, everything works fine. However, whenever *<expression>* uses columns of tables other than the one to which *<column>* belongs, you need to make a context transition by using *RELATEDTABLE* or *CALCULATE*. This situation occurs every time you have a separate calendar table, which is the best practice for every date-related calculation; so it happens a lot.

To get the right value for the last nonblank date for a given measure/table, you have to use something like this:

```
= LASTNONBLANK ( Dates[Date], CALCULATE ( COUNT ( Balances[Balance] ) ) )
```

This code returns the last date (in the current filter context) for which there are values for the Balance column in the Balances table. You can also use the following:

```
= LASTNONBLANK ( Dates[Date], COUNTROWS ( RELATEDTABLE ( Sales ) ) )
```

This equivalent formula returns the last date (in the current filter context) for which there is a related group of rows in the Sales table.

OPENINGBALANCE and *CLOSINGBALANCE* functions

DAX provides several functions to get the first and last date of a period (year, quarter, or month) that are useful whenever you need to get that value of a selection that is smaller than the whole period considered. For example, if you are dealing with the month level (which may be displayed in rows), you might also want to display the value of the end of the quarter and the end of the year in the same row, as shown in Figure 12-36. You can find this example in the companion workbook "CH12-11-ClosingBalance.xlsx."

Note The raw data used in this example include balances for dates through December 31. For this reason, the DAX function that we are going to use provides complete results because the data based on the *LASTDATE* function would not work if the last day of a period (such as month, quarter, or year) were missing.

Row Labels	LastBalance	ClosingBalanceMonth	ClosingBalanceQuarter	ClosingBalanceYear
⊟ 2010	6,686.00	6,686.00	6,686.00	6,686.00
⊟ Q1	10,667.00	10,667.00	10,667.00	6,686.00
01 - January	4,657.00	4,657.00	10,667.00	6,686.00
02 - February	7,762.00	7,762.00	10,667.00	6,686.00
03 - March	10,667.00	10,667.00	10,667.00	6,686.00
⊟ Q2	7,452.00	7,452.00	7,452.00	6,686.00
04 - April	6,210.00	6,210.00	7,452.00	6,686.00
05 - May	5,589.00	5,589.00	7,452.00	6,686.00
06 - June	7,452.00	7,452.00	7,452.00	6,686.00
⊟ Q3	7,762.00	7,762.00	7,762.00	6,686.00
07 - July	9,936.00	9,936.00	7,762.00	6,686.00
08 - August	13,972.00	13,972.00	7,762.00	6,686.00
09 - September	7,762.00	7,762.00	7,762.00	6,686.00
⊟ Q4	6,686.00	6,686.00	6,686.00	6,686.00
10 - October	6,210.00	6,210.00	6,686.00	6,686.00
11 - November	5,744.00	5,744.00	6,686.00	6,686.00
12 - December	6,686.00	6,686.00	6,686.00	6,686.00
Grand Total	6,686.00	6,686.00	6,686.00	6,686.00

FIGURE 12-36 For each month, this PivotTable shows the balance data at the end of the month, quarter, and year.

The formulas used to calculate *ClosingBalanceMonth, ClosingBalanceQuarter,* and *ClosingBalanceYear* measures are the following:

```
ClosingBalanceMonth :=
    CLOSINGBALANCEMONTH ( SUM ( Balances[Balance] ), BalanceDate[Date] )

ClosingBalanceQuarter :=
    CLOSINGBALANCEQUARTER ( SUM ( Balances[Balance] ), BalanceDate[Date] )

ClosingBalanceYear :=
    CLOSINGBALANCEYEAR ( SUM ( Balances[Balance] ), BalanceDate[Date] )
```

These formulas use the *LASTDATE* function internally, but they operate on a set of dates that can extend the current selection in the PivotTable. For example, the *CLOSINGBALANCEYEAR* function considers the *LASTDATE* of Balance[Date], which is applied to the last year period of the dates included in the filter context. So for February 2010 (and for any month or quarter of 2010), this date is December 31, 2010. The *CLOSINGBALANCEYEAR* function behaves like a *CALCULATE* expression using the *ENDOFYEAR* function as a filter. As usual, the use of *CALCULATE* is more generic and flexible, but specific DAX functions like *CLOSINGBALANCEYEAR* better express the intention of the measure designer. The following are measures equivalent to the ones previously shown using *CALCULATE* syntax.

```
ClosingBalanceEOM :=
    CALCULATE ( SUM ( Balances[Balance] ), ENDOFMONTH ( BalanceDate[Date] ) )

ClosingBalanceEOQ :=
    CALCULATE ( SUM ( Balances[Balance] ), ENDOFQUARTER ( BalanceDate[Date] ) )

ClosingBalanceEOY :=
    CALCULATE ( SUM ( Balances[Balance] ), ENDOFYEAR ( BalanceDate[Date] ) )
```

Tip The DAX functions *OPENINGBALANCEMONTH, OPENINGBALANCEQUARTER,* and *OPENINGBALANCEYEAR* use *FIRSTDATE* internally, instead of the *LASTDATE* of the considered period. They correspond to the *CALCULATE* formula, which uses *STARTOFMONTH, STARTOFQUARTER,* and *STARTOFYEAR,* respectively, as its filter.

An important consideration has to be made about dates for which there is available data in your model. You can see this if you look at data at the day level in the PivotTable. Before doing that, consider the raw dataset used in this example, shown in Figure 12-37.

Name	Occupation	Country	Date	Balance
Katie Jordan	Farmer	USA	1/8/2010	1,540.00
Luis Bonifaz	IT Consultant	Argentina	1/8/2010	2,310.00
Maurizio Macagno	IT Consultant	Italy	1/8/2010	1,450.00
Katie Jordan	Farmer	USA	1/15/2010	1,230.00
Luis Bonifaz	IT Consultant	Argentina	1/15/2010	2,020.00
Maurizio Macagno	IT Consultant	Italy	1/15/2010	1,120.00
Katie Jordan	Farmer	USA	1/22/2010	980.00
Luis Bonifaz	IT Consultant	Argentina	1/22/2010	1,850.00
Maurizio Macagno	IT Consultant	Italy	1/22/2010	630.00
Katie Jordan	Farmer	USA	1/31/2010	1,687.00
Luis Bonifaz	IT Consultant	Argentina	1/31/2010	1,470.00
Maurizio Macagno	IT Consultant	Italy	1/31/2010	1,500.00
Katie Jordan	Farmer	USA	2/10/2010	2,150.00

FIGURE 12-37 The balances appear many times for each month, making calculations more difficult.

As shown in Figure 12-37, there is more than one balance for each month. For example, in January, there are balances for days 8, 15, 22, and 31.

Note In this example, we always have a balance value for each account, as if we took a snapshot on a certain date for every account available, even if nothing has changed since the previous date. We see in the next section what to do whenever this condition is not true (that is, when data is present only when updated).

If you browse this data at the day level in the PivotTable by using the same measures as the previous example, you get the results shown in Figure 12-38.

Row Labels		LastBalance	ClosingBalanceMonth	ClosingBalanceQuarter	ClosingBalanceYear
⊟ 2010		6,686.00	6,686.00	6,686.00	6,686.00
⊟ Q1		10,667.00	10,667.00	10,667.00	6,686.00
⊟ 01 - January		4,657.00	4,657.00	10,667.00	6,686.00
1/1/2010			4,657.00	10,667.00	6,686.00
1/2/2010			4,657.00	10,667.00	6,686.00
1/3/2010			4,657.00	10,667.00	6,686.00
1/4/2010			4,657.00	10,667.00	6,686.00
1/5/2010			4,657.00	10,667.00	6,686.00
1/6/2010			4,657.00	10,667.00	6,686.00
1/7/2010			4,657.00	10,667.00	6,686.00
1/8/2010		5,300.00	4,657.00	10,667.00	6,686.00
1/9/2010			4,657.00	10,667.00	6,686.00
1/10/2010			4,657.00	10,667.00	6,686.00
1/11/2010			4,657.00	10,667.00	6,686.00
1/12/2010			4,657.00	10,667.00	6,686.00
1/13/2010			4,657.00	10,667.00	6,686.00
1/14/2010			4,657.00	10,667.00	6,686.00
1/15/2010		4,370.00	4,657.00	10,667.00	6,686.00
1/16/2010			4,657.00	10,667.00	6,686.00

FIGURE 12-38 Browsing data at the day level displays rows with no balance data.

As shown in Figure 12-38, the calculated fields defined to display values at the end of the period suffer an unpleasant side effect: all the dates are visible, even those for which there are no balance data available. If you want to display just the rows corresponding to dates with balance data defined, you have to modify the measures, checking the existence of data in the Balances table, in this way:

```
ClosingBalanceMonth2 :=
IF (
    COUNTROWS ( Balances ) > 0,
    CLOSINGBALANCEMONTH ( SUM ( Balances[Balance] ), BalanceDate[Date] ),
    BLANK ()
)

ClosingBalanceQuarter2 :=
IF (
    COUNTROWS ( Balances ) > 0,
    CLOSINGBALANCEQUARTER ( SUM ( Balances[Balance] ), BalanceDate[Date] ),
    BLANK ()
)

ClosingBalanceYear2 : =
IF (
    COUNTROWS ( Balances ) > 0,
    CLOSINGBALANCEYEAR ( SUM ( Balances[Balance] ), BalanceDate[Date] ),
    BLANK ()
)
```

Browsing data using these measures results in a report like the one shown in Figure 12-39.

Row Labels	LastBalance	ClosingBalanceMonth2	ClosingBalanceQuarter2	ClosingBalanceYear2
⊟2010	6,686.00	6,686.00	6,686.00	6,686.00
⊟Q1	10,667.00	10,667.00	10,667.00	6,686.00
⊟01 - January	4,657.00	4,657.00	10,667.00	6,686.00
1/8/2010	5,300.00	4,657.00	10,667.00	6,686.00
1/15/2010	4,370.00	4,657.00	10,667.00	6,686.00
1/22/2010	3,460.00	4,657.00	10,667.00	6,686.00
1/31/2010	4,657.00	4,657.00	10,667.00	6,686.00
⊟02 - February	7,762.00	7,762.00	10,667.00	6,686.00
2/10/2010	6,210.00	7,762.00	10,667.00	6,686.00
2/19/2010	5,190.00	7,762.00	10,667.00	6,686.00
2/28/2010	7,762.00	7,762.00	10,667.00	6,686.00

FIGURE 12-39 This PivotTable is using measures that display only days for which there is balance data.

By default, the PivotTable in Excel does not display empty rows and columns. For this reason, the days containing no balance date are not shown: all the measures used in the PivotTable return *BLANK* for those days, removing them from the report.

Updating balances by using transactions

The balance account model you saw in the previous section makes an important assumption: for a given date, either data is not present at all or all the accounts have a balance value for that date. If an account does not have a balance value for a date that other accounts are measured, that account is considered to have a zero balance for that date. This assumption is good for certain data structures, which are generated by a system that makes a snapshot of the situation (all balance account values) on a given date.

However, some scenarios have a different data model in which the previous assumption is not valid. For example, consider this other way to collect data about balance accounts. In the Balances table shown in Figure 12-40, data has been normalized by means of an Accounts table, which can be seen on the right. Moreover, you can find a balance row for an account only for dates when a transaction made some changes in the account balance. You can find this example in the companion workbook "CH12-12-ClosingTransaction.xlsx."

Account	Date	Balance
A001	1/1/2010	1,540.00
A002	1/1/2010	2,310.00
A003	1/1/2010	1,450.00
A001	1/12/2010	1,230.00
A002	1/14/2010	2,020.00
A003	1/15/2010	1,120.00
A001	1/20/2010	980.00
A002	1/21/2010	1,850.00
A003	1/22/2010	630.00
A001	1/25/2010	1,687.00
A002	1/26/2010	1,470.00
A003	1/30/2010	1,500.00
A001	2/8/2010	2,150.00
A002	2/9/2010	1,230.00
A003	2/10/2010	2,830.00

Account	Name	Occupation	Country
A001	Katie Jord	Farmer	USA
A002	Luis Bonif	IT Consultant	Argentina
A003	Maurizio	IT Consultant	Italy

FIGURE 12-40 Here, you can see raw balance account data updated for transactions and not in snapshots.

Account A001 changes its value on January 1, 12, 20, and 25; account A002 changes on January 1, 14, 21, and 26; and account A003 changes on January 1, 15, 22, and 30. There is no data at the end of the month (January 31), and there is no data for all accounts on a given date (for example, January 12 has an account balance only for account A001). So neither the *LastBalance* nor the *ClosingBalance* measure can work with this data because their initial assumptions are no longer valid. We must create a more complex calculation.

The basic idea is that, for each account, you must get the last nonblank date included in the selected period. The calculation for a single account can be made by using the *CALCULATE* function and filtering data on the *LASTNONBLANK* date included in the period between the first date available and the last date in the period. Notice that the date range considered begins even outside the period: you might request the balance for February and there might be no rows in that month, so previous dates also must be considered for the interval. You use a *SUMX* function to iterate all the available accounts:

```
SUMX (
    ALL ( Balances[Account] ),
    CALCULATE (
        SUM ( Balances[Balance] ),
        LASTNONBLANK (
            DATESBETWEEN (
                BalanceDate[Date],
                BLANK (),
                LASTDATE ( BalanceDate[Date] )
            ),
            CALCULATE ( COUNT ( Balances[Balance] ) )
        )
    )
)
```

This expression calculates a value for each date in the BalanceDate table. To get the calculation only for dates that have at least one transaction (for any account), you must make a test similar to the one shown in the previous section for *ClosingBalance* measures. Finally, you can define the complete *LastBalanceTx* measure by using this DAX formula:

```
LastBalanceTx :=
IF (
    COUNTX (
        BalanceDate,
        CALCULATE (
            COUNT ( Balances[Balance] ),
            ALLEXCEPT ( Balances, BalanceDate[Date] )
        )
    ) > 0,
    SUMX (
        ALL ( Balances[Account] ),
        CALCULATE (
```

```
                SUM ( Balances[Balance] ),
            LASTNONBLANK (
                DATESBETWEEN (
                    BalanceDate[Date],
                    BLANK (),
                    LASTDATE ( BalanceDate[Date] )
                ),
                CALCULATE ( COUNT ( Balances[Balance] ) )
            )
        )
    ),
    BLANK ()
)
```

This formula produces the result shown in Figure 12-41, in which you can see the balance updated for each account (one for each column) only for days in which at least one new balance is present in the Balances table.

LastBalanceTx	Column Labels			
Row Labels	Argentina	Italy	USA	Grand Total
⊟ 2010	2,205.00	1,950.00	2,531.00	6,686.00
⊟ Q1	3,430.00	3,500.00	3,737.00	10,667.00
⊟ 01 - January	1,470.00	1,500.00	1,687.00	4,657.00
1/1/2010	2,310.00	1,450.00	1,540.00	5,300.00
1/12/2010	2,310.00	1,450.00	1,230.00	4,990.00
1/14/2010	2,020.00	1,450.00	1,230.00	4,700.00
1/15/2010	2,020.00	1,120.00	1,230.00	4,370.00
1/20/2010	2,020.00	1,120.00	980.00	4,120.00
1/21/2010	1,850.00	1,120.00	980.00	3,950.00
1/22/2010	1,850.00	630.00	980.00	3,460.00
1/25/2010	1,850.00	630.00	1,687.00	4,167.00
1/26/2010	1,470.00	630.00	1,687.00	3,787.00
1/30/2010	1,470.00	1,500.00	1,687.00	4,657.00
⊟ 02 - February	2,450.00	2,500.00	2,812.00	7,762.00
2/8/2010	1,470.00	1,500.00	2,150.00	5,120.00
2/9/2010	1,230.00	1,500.00	2,150.00	4,880.00
2/10/2010	1,230.00	2,830.00	2,150.00	6,210.00

FIGURE 12-41 This PivotTable shows the correct result computed by the *LastBalanceTx* calculated field.

Keep in mind that the Balances[Account] column used to make the relationship with the Accounts table is used in the *LastBalanceTx* formula and should not be selected in the PivotTable. Instead, you should use the Accounts[Account] column; otherwise, you could see incorrect data in the PivotTable. The reason is similar to the case for which we suggest you use a Dates table instead of denormalizing all date information in the same table that contains the measures. So a best practice is to hide in a PivotTable all the columns that you use to relate Balances (the table containing measures) to other tables such as BalanceDate and Accounts (which are the tables containing attributes for browsing data).

Computing moving averages

An interesting calculation related to time is that of a moving average. A *moving average* is the average of a measure over a moving time period. For example, you can compute the moving average of the price of a stock over 50 periods or the moving average of the price of gasoline over the last 365 days. Moving averages are useful because they draw a smooth trend line, which might be useful to spot meaningful patterns, which are easier to see after removing the frequent price variations.

To show this technique, we are going to use the price of some stocks as an example. The main reason is that this scenario offers some unique challenges that are useful for learning new DAX techniques.

Let's start by looking at the source of data. Figure 12-42 shows an Excel table that lists the prices of several stocks for the last 10 years. You can find this example in the companion workbook "CH12-13-Stocks Moving Average.xlsx."

Stock	ID	Date	Open	MaxIntr	MinIntra	Close	VarPerc	Volume
MICROSOFT	1	1/4/2001	23.9100	25.2500	23.4400	24.2200	-	112,398,400
APPLE	2	1/4/2001	9.0700	9.2500	8.4100	8.5300	-	26,407,000
MICROSOFT	3	1/5/2001	24.2500	24.9400	23.7800	24.5600	1.42	93,416,400
APPLE	4	1/5/2001	8.4700	8.6900	8.0300	8.1900 -	4.03	14,727,400
MICROSOFT	5	1/8/2001	24.4700	24.8800	23.3400	24.4700 -	0.38	79,784,600
APPLE	6	1/8/2001	8.4700	8.4900	7.9700	8.2800	1.15	13,346,800
MICROSOFT	7	1/9/2001	25.0000	26.3100	24.8800	25.9100	5.87	114,965,400
APPLE	8	1/9/2001	8.4100	8.8200	8.2800	8.5900	3.77	21,033,200
MICROSOFT	9	1/10/2001	25.5000	26.9100	25.3800	26.4400	2.05	90,243,400
APPLE	10	1/10/2001	8.3400	8.5000	8.0300	8.2800 -	3.64	20,742,600
MICROSOFT	11	1/11/2001	26.5000	27.8800	26.1600	27.5000	4.02	101,862,200
APPLE	12	1/11/2001	8.1200	9.2500	8.1200	9.0000	8.68	28,706,800

FIGURE 12-42 The data source contains prices of different stocks, with daily granularity.

The dataset contains much useful information, but for the purpose of this demonstration, we are interested only in the date and the closing value of the price.

> **Note** It is interesting to note that the table has a row identifier (that is, a column called ID that has a different value for all the rows). The reason for this column is that we plan to create many calculated columns in the table that use *CALCULATE* and, as you might recall from Chapter 8, "Understanding *CALCULATE*," if you need to create more than one calculated column using *CALCULATE*, a row identifier is strongly recommended to avoid circular dependencies. The formulas could have been written even without adding this column to the data model, but it would have become much more complex than the ones shown here.

Moreover, because you are interested in performing analysis over this dataset using time as one of the main analytical dimensions, it is always a good idea to add a calendar table, like the one shown in Figure 12-43.

Date	Day	MonthNumber	MonthName	Year
1/1/2001	1	1	01-January	2001
1/2/2001	2	1	01-January	2001
1/3/2001	3	1	01-January	2001
1/4/2001	4	1	01-January	2001
1/5/2001	5	1	01-January	2001
1/6/2001	6	1	01-January	2001
1/7/2001	7	1	01-January	2001
1/8/2001	8	1	01-January	2001
1/9/2001	9	1	01-January	2001
1/10/2001	10	1	01-January	2001
1/11/2001	11	1	01-January	2001

FIGURE 12-43 A basic calendar table is always useful to add to any data model.

You want to perform analysis of this dataset plotting the chart of the price and, on the same chart, the average over 50 and over 200 periods. The result will be a chart like the one shown in Figure 12-44.

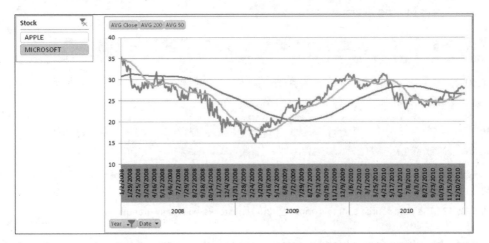

FIGURE 12-44 You need to plot this chart as the final step of this exercise on time intelligence.

Before starting to think about the solution, it is worthwhile to highlight a few considerations:

- The moving average should always consider 50 or 200 periods. It is not a moving average over the last 50 or 200 days; rather, it is more like the last 50 or 200 "working days." In fact, you will need to ignore all the dates where the stock price is not present when computing the average.

- Due to the presence of errors in the database, it might be the case that the last 200 periods for one stock are not the same 200 periods for another stock. In fact, if the price of a stock on a single day is not known for any reason, then that day will be ignored during the average calculation.

- Because the chart will span several years and have a daily granularity, it would be a good idea to avoid performing the calculation of the moving average in a calculated field because this could be slow. Instead, you will use calculated columns to store the moving average, so as to obtain a responsive system.

The first step is obviously that of adding both tables to the data model. Once the tables are there, you can start working on the moving average problem. You will do the following:

- Detect, for each date and stock, the starting date of the 50-period window. This information will be stored in a calculated column.

- Compute, for each date and stock, the moving average of the last 50 periods, using the previously computed calculated column to determine the period to average. This value, too, will be stored in a calculated column.

The first step is pretty easy to complete if you remember the technique you previously learned when you had to compute the difference, in working days, between two dates. You created a WorkingDayNumber calculated column that increased on working days only. In this case, you do not need a value that increases on working days only because all the dates stored in the fact table are working days. This time, you want a value that assigns a unique number to each date and stock. Thus, the first date where you have the price for Microsoft will be assigned the value of 1, the second date will be number 2, and so on. The numbering will be different for different stocks, so each stock can be counted separately.

The formula for this first calculated column is straightforward:

```
DayNumber =
COUNTROWS (
    FILTER (
        Fixing,
        Fixing[Date] <= EARLIER ( Fixing[Date] )
            && Fixing[Stock] = EARLIER ( Fixing[Stock] )
    )
)
```

This formula simply counts the number of rows that have a date earlier than the current one and share the same stock name. The result is a unique number assigned to each stock/date (see Figure 12-45).

ID	Stock	Date	DayNumber
1	MICROSOFT	1/4/2001	1
2511	APPLE	1/4/2001	1
2	MICROSOFT	1/5/2001	2
2512	APPLE	1/5/2001	2
3	MICROSOFT	1/8/2001	3
2513	APPLE	1/8/2001	3
4	MICROSOFT	1/9/2001	4
2514	APPLE	1/9/2001	4
5	MICROSOFT	1/10/2001	5
2515	APPLE	1/10/2001	5

FIGURE 12-45 The DayNumber column assigns a unique, increasing number to each stock/date.

Now you need to compute, for each day, the date to start computing the average for the 50-day moving average. This is easily accomplished by using a mix of *VALUES* and *CALCULATE*, in a common pattern: You define an expression that filters a single row from a table and then use *VALUES* to compute the value of a column:

```
FirstDateOfRange50 =
CALCULATE (
    VALUES ( Fixing[Date] ),
    FILTER (
        Fixing,
        Fixing[DayNumber] = EARLIER ( Fixing[DayNumber] ) - 50
            && Fixing[Stock] = EARLIER ( Fixing[Stock] )
    )
)
```

You can see from the formula that the *FILTER* searches the only row in the Fixing table that has the same stock name as the current one and a *DayNumber* equal to the current one minus 50. If it exists, this row is only one. When this filter is applied, VALUES (Fixing[Date]) will return a table with only one row, and *VALUES* can convert the table into a single value (that is, the date at which to start computing the average).

Figure 12-46 shows the resulting table at this point.

ID	Stock	Date	DayNumber	FirstDateOfRange50
2559	APPLE	3/15/2001	49	
50	MICROSOFT	3/16/2001	50	
2560	APPLE	3/16/2001	50	
51	MICROSOFT	3/19/2001	51	1/4/2001 12:00:00 AM
2561	APPLE	3/19/2001	51	1/4/2001 12:00:00 AM
52	MICROSOFT	3/20/2001	52	1/5/2001 12:00:00 AM
2562	APPLE	3/20/2001	52	1/5/2001 12:00:00 AM
53	MICROSOFT	3/21/2001	53	1/8/2001 12:00:00 AM
2563	APPLE	3/21/2001	53	1/8/2001 12:00:00 AM
54	MICROSOFT	3/22/2001	54	1/9/2001 12:00:00 AM
2564	APPLE	3/22/2001	54	1/9/2001 12:00:00 AM

FIGURE 12-46 The FirstDateOfRange50 column contains the first date to use for the moving average over 50 days.

You can see that the column is empty for the first 50 days and then the values start being computed. The final touch is to add a calculated column that computes the average over the period starting at *FirstDateOfRange50* and ending with the current date. The formula is not complex:

```
MovingAverage50 =

CALCULATE (
    AVERAGE ( Fixing[Close] ),
    FILTER (
        Fixing,
```

```
          Fixing[Date] >= EARLIER ( Fixing[FirstDateOfRange50] )
          && Fixing[Date] <= EARLIER ( Fixing[Date] )
          && Fixing[Stock] = EARLIER ( Fixing[Stock] )
    )
)
```

As in the previous formula, the logic is inside the inner *FILTER,* which returns all the rows from the Fixings table with a date included in the range starting from *FirstDateOfRange50* and ending with the current date, for the current stock. This range always contains 50 dates, and the *AVERAGE* is computed against it. In Figure 12-47, you can see the final shape of the table.

ID	Stock	Date	DayNumber	FirstDateOfRange50	MovingAverage50
2559	APPLE	3/15/2001	49		9.6369
50	MICROSOFT	3/16/2001	50		28.8516
2560	APPLE	3/16/2001	50		9.6894
51	MICROSOFT	3/19/2001	51	1/4/2001 12:00:00 AM	28.8184
2561	APPLE	3/19/2001	51	1/4/2001 12:00:00 AM	9.7010
52	MICROSOFT	3/20/2001	52	1/5/2001 12:00:00 AM	28.8600
2562	APPLE	3/20/2001	52	1/5/2001 12:00:00 AM	9.7267
53	MICROSOFT	3/21/2001	53	1/8/2001 12:00:00 AM	28.8692
2563	APPLE	3/21/2001	53	1/8/2001 12:00:00 AM	9.7633
54	MICROSOFT	3/22/2001	54	1/9/2001 12:00:00 AM	28.9188
2564	APPLE	3/22/2001	54	1/9/2001 12:00:00 AM	9.8129
55	MICROSOFT	3/23/2001	55	1/10/2001 12:00:00 AM	28.9653
2565	APPLE	3/23/2001	55	1/10/2001 12:00:00 AM	9.8700

FIGURE 12-47 The MovingAverage50 column contains the average over 50 periods.

At this point, we should note that the moving average is computed using a calculated column, not a calculated field. This is important because the computation of such a number can be time-consuming for large datasets (much larger than the example provided here), and because you want to show the value in a chart, you do not want to perform the calculation as the chart is being drawn. Being a calculated column, this value will be computed only when the data model is refreshed, and then returning its value to the chart will be a fast operation.

To complete this scenario, you only need to define, in a similar way, the formulas to compute the first date of the range 200 and the moving average over 200 days. Once the calculated columns have been created, you create a new PivotChart (in Line mode), and add the year and the date to the *x*-axis. On the chart, you will plot both the moving averages and the value of the close. The last step is to add a slicer for the stock name. In Figure 12-48, you can see the final result.

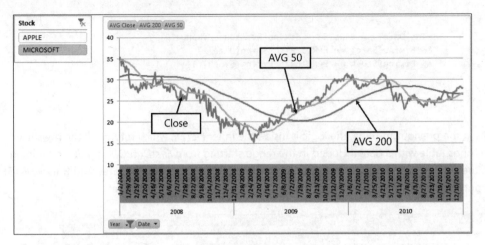

FIGURE 12-48 The final result shows the different averages and the value of the stock over time.

This example clearly shows the incredible power of calculated columns. By performing a calculation in a calculated column, you end up with much faster queries. As a result, users have a good experience when browsing the data model with a PivotTable.

CHAPTER 13

Using advanced DAX

Now that you have gotten this far, you have learned many different aspects of DAX, data modeling, and report building, and, in general, you have learned the basics of self-service Business Intelligence (BI). Yes, you read that right: We have been able to teach only the basics up to now. You will need to master many other skills before you can qualify for the Microsoft PowerPivot gurus club. You will learn how to create a good BI solution only with experience: the more scenarios you work on, the more your skills become refined.

This chapter helps you get some of that experience, by virtue of our sharing our experience with you. Here, we analyze several common scenarios and, for each one, we show some useful techniques to solve them. You might find them immediately useful (if you are lucky enough that we describe your scenario exactly), or you may find that the pattern is somewhat similar to your situation, in which case you will need to adapt the DAX code and the data model to your needs.

Banding

A common situation is that you have to convert continuous values into separated bands, to make it easier to perform analysis on them. An example of banding is the analysis of sales divided into price ranges. You might be interested in grouping different prices into categories (for example, high, medium, and low) and analyze sales of products using those categories.

In Figure 13-1, you can see that by using a standard PivotTable, you can put the product price in rows and group sales by product price. Nevertheless, you end up with many rows in which each single price is separated by others. This makes the analysis difficult and the report nearly useless. Moreover, the item price that you use to slice data is the list price, and you cannot use the discounted one, if applicable. You can find this workbook in the file "CH13-01-Banding.xlsx."

Sum of SalesAmount	Column Labels				
Row Labels	2005	2006	2007	2008	Grand Total
1.3282			15.62		15.62
1.374			612.80	296.78	909.59
2.495			58.38		58.38
2.7445			784.79	125.15	909.94
2.8942			638.17	558.75	1,196.93
2.994			2,999.99	2,311.37	5,311.36
3.975			89.44		89.44
4.3221		97.25			97.25
4.3725			938.78	141.23	1,080.01
4.495			218.46	113.27	331.73
4.611			1,202.00	994.13	2,196.13
4.75	111.15	136.80			247.95
4.7543		894.28	144.53		1,038.81

FIGURE 13-1 Using the list price, we can get a complex PivotTable.

The price that you want to use to slice data is the actual price at which the product was sold, which is stored in the FactResellerSales table and may change over time. Let's show you an example to make the scenario clearer. If you define a price band to range from $10 to $20 U.S. dollars (USD), you might find that the same product is sometimes sold at $19 and other times at $22 because of discounts or price changes over time. So we want to separate these sales into different bands, even if they belong to the very same product.

In Figure 13-2, you can see that after you load the FactResellerSales table into PowerPivot, the discounted prices make the product with code 470 fall into different price bands as the real price changes over time.

Produc...	OrderDat...	OrderQuantity	UnitPrice	ProductStandardCost
470	20061201	26	$19.00	$15.67
470	20070301	14	$22.03	$15.67
470	20070601	12	$22.03	$15.67
470	20060701	27	$19.00	$15.67
470	20061201	31	$19.00	$15.67
470	20070501	25	$19.00	$15.67
470	20060801	17	$20.89	$15.67
470	20060901	18	$20.89	$15.67
470	20061001	20	$20.89	$15.67
470	20060701	14	$22.03	$15.67
470	20060801	12	$22.03	$15.67

FIGURE 13-2 The same product is sold under different price bands over time.

To aggregate different prices into bands, you first need a place in which to define the bands. A Microsoft Excel table is the perfect place to create the price bands, as shown in Figure 13-3.

BandCode	BandName	MinPrice	MaxPrice
1	VERY LOW	0	20
2	LOW	20	100
3	MEDIUM	100	250
4	HIGH	250	500
5	VERY HIGH	500	99999

FIGURE 13-3 Here, you can see the Excel table that defines price bands.

The PriceBand table contains both a code and a description. You will need the code to sort bands properly, as you will see later in this chapter. At this point, it might occur to you to bring the price bands table into the data model, make a relationship between this new table and the sales, and then slice the sales by price band. As easy as this solution seems, it cannot work. You need to base the relationship on the price range, not on a single key. In fact, there is no column in the sales table that can act as a key for the price band; for example, the discounted price ($28.50) does not point to any row in the bands table. We definitely need some advanced technique to handle banding because standard PowerPivot relationships are not enough.

The solution is not to try to define a relationship that cannot be created, but to mimic one using calculated columns. In fact, you can create a calculated column in the FactResellerSales table with the following expression:

```
1.    PriceBand =
2.    CALCULATE (
3.        VALUES ( PriceBands[BandName] ),
4.        FILTER (
5.            PriceBands,
6.            PriceBands[MinPrice] <= FactResellerSales[UnitPrice]
7.                && PriceBands[MaxPrice] > FactResellerSales[UnitPrice]
8.        )
9.    )
```

The relevant parts of the formula are the following:

- Line 3, where you use *VALUES* to compute the value of the band name. Here, you rely on the fact that if *VALUES* returns a table with a single row only, such a table can be converted in the column content, returning not a table, but the band name.

- The *FILTER* expression at lines 5–8 ensures that the PriceBands table is filtered so that a single row will be returned. If there is some error in the formula and more than a single row is filtered by *FILTER*, then the formula will return an error.

The *VALUES* call is required because there is no row context on PriceBands that would resolve the column name into a value. But because you know that *FILTER* always returns one single row, then *VALUES* will return a one-row table that is then transformed into a single value. The result is that this column contains the price band of each sale, and you can use that column to slice sales, as shown in Figure 13-4.

Sum of SalesAmount	Column Labels				
Row Labels	2005	2006	2007	2008	Grand Total
HIGH	1,090,612.93	4,376,654.11	5,572,490.43	2,278,695.34	13,318,452.81
LOW	48,280.58	672,657.51	1,451,419.62	674,159.43	2,846,517.14
MEDIUM	157,168.95	1,362,078.87	1,660,224.26	610,789.10	3,790,261.18
VERY HIGH	6,763,041.73	17,663,075.43	23,388,826.86	12,429,667.13	60,244,611.15
VERY LOW	6,331.12	69,963.74	129,708.26	44,751.59	250,754.71
Grand Total	8,065,435.31	24,144,429.65	32,202,669.43	16,038,062.60	80,450,596.98

FIGURE 13-4 You can use the PriceBand column in a PivotTable to slice by price band.

The only drawback of this PivotTable is sorting. Excel has used alphabetical sorting which, for price bands, is clearly the wrong choice. You can use the Sort By Column option of Power Pivot, but as you might remember, that feature works only for columns belonging to the same table. Thus, the solution is to bring the *BandCode* value into the FactResellerSales table, using a slight variation of the previous column (the updated part of the formula is in bold):

```
BandCode =
CALCULATE (
    VALUES ( PriceBands[BandCode] ),
    FILTER (
        PriceBands,
        PriceBands[MinPrice] <= FactResellerSales[UnitPrice]
            && PriceBands[MaxPrice] > FactResellerSales[UnitPrice]
    )
)
```

Once the column has been stored in the fact table, you can use Sort By Column to sort the band name using the band code, and you finally achieve your desired result (see Figure 13-5).

Sum of SalesAmount	Column Labels				
Row Labels	2005	2006	2007	2008	Grand Total
VERY LOW	6,331.12	69,963.74	129,708.26	44,751.59	250,754.71
LOW	48,280.58	672,657.51	1,451,419.62	674,159.43	2,846,517.14
MEDIUM	157,168.95	1,362,078.87	1,660,224.26	610,789.10	3,790,261.18
HIGH	1,090,612.93	4,376,654.11	5,572,490.43	2,278,695.34	13,318,452.81
VERY HIGH	6,763,041.73	17,663,075.43	23,388,826.86	12,429,667.13	60,244,611.15
Grand Total	8,065,435.31	24,144,429.65	32,202,669.43	16,038,062.60	80,450,596.98

FIGURE 13-5 Using Sort By Column bands, you have got the entire table sorted correctly now.

The significant point of this solution is that, by using an Excel table to store the price band configuration, you are free to modify it to suit your needs, adding or removing rows and changing the band boundaries. Because you used the *VALUES* function, if you enter an incorrect configuration, the workbook will show an error that is not very easy to understand and fix. For example, you can enter the configuration shown in Figure 13-6 for the price bands.

BandCode	BandName	MinPrice	MaxPrice
1	VERY LOW	0	20
2	LOW	10	30
3	MEDIUM	100	250
4	HIGH	250	500
5	VERY HIGH	500	99999

FIGURE 13-6 The configuration of the bands is wrong in this table, and this leads to complex errors.

The problem with this configuration is that the Low band overlaps the Very Low one on values from 10 to 20. Moreover, there is a gap between Low and Medium because Low ends at 30 and Medium starts at 100. If you refresh the data model with this table, you will see the error that appears in Figure 13-7.

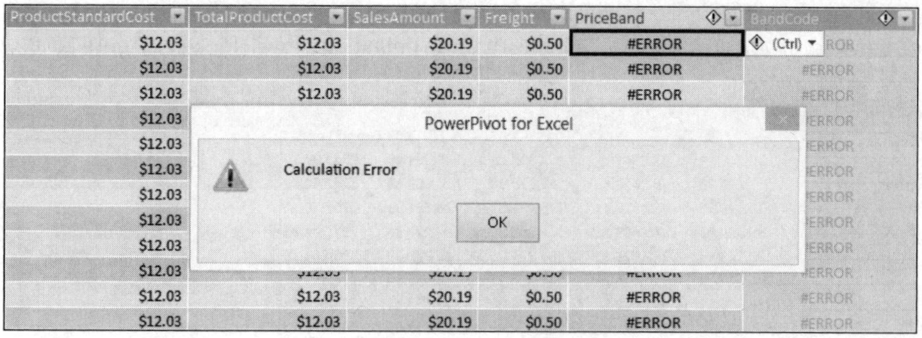

FIGURE 13-7 An incorrect configuration leads to errors that are hard to find and correct.

It is not a good idea to leave the handling of these errors to PowerPivot because a user changing the band configuration might not have the necessary skills and knowledge to fix the problem. In such a case, it is better to protect your formula using the *IFERROR* function (shown in bold in the next formula), which will guarantee that, in the presence of configuration errors, you will return a default value anyway:

```
PriceBand =
CALCULATE (
    IFERROR (
        VALUES ( PriceBands[BandName] ),
        "Wrong Configuration"
    ),
    FILTER (
        PriceBands,
        PriceBands[MinPrice] <= FactResellerSales[UnitPrice]
          && PriceBands[MaxPrice] > FactResellerSales[UnitPrice]
    )
)
```

You can see that by surrounding the *VALUES* function with *IFERROR*, you can always return a default value, which in this case is "Wrong Configuration." You need to fix the BandCode column too, using a default value for sorting. You can achieve the desired result with the following formula, where the *IFERROR* check is highlighted in bold:

```
BandCode =
CALCULATE (
    IFERROR ( VALUES ( PriceBands[BandCode] ), -1 ),
    FILTER (
        PriceBands,
        PriceBands[MinPrice] <= FactResellerSales[UnitPrice]
          && PriceBands[MaxPrice] > FactResellerSales[UnitPrice]
    )
)
```

This time, the default value is –1, which forces the "Wrong Configuration" message to the top of the price band list. If you create a PivotTable with these definitions, it will look like Figure 13-8.

Sum of SalesAmount	Column Labels				
Row Labels	2005	2006	2007	2008	Grand Total
(blank)		426,967.57	1,087,358.23	539,681.46	2,054,007.26
Wrong Configuration	210.36	57,436.62	93,270.70	24,066.68	174,984.37
VERY LOW	6,120.76	12,527.11	36,437.55	20,684.91	75,770.34
LOW	48,280.58	245,689.93	364,061.39	134,477.98	792,509.88
MEDIUM	157,168.95	1,362,078.87	1,660,224.26	610,789.10	3,790,261.18
HIGH	1,090,612.93	4,376,654.11	5,572,490.43	2,278,695.34	13,318,452.81
VERY HIGH	6,763,041.73	17,663,075.43	23,388,826.86	12,429,667.13	60,244,611.15
Grand Total	8,065,435.31	24,144,429.65	32,202,669.43	16,038,062.60	80,450,596.98

FIGURE 13-8 Using error handling functions in columns leads to a much better experience when browsing data.

Looking at the PivotTable, you can detect the presence of errors in the first two rows. One is blank, meaning that for some sale, the price band has not been computed (the range from 30 to 100), and the other contains "Wrong Configuration," meaning that there are overlapping values. You can change the error messages and provide other descriptions, but the technique remains the same.

Ranking

Another common request in reporting is that of performing ranking. Imagine, for example, that you want to find the top 10 products in a specific year; in such a case, ranking will be invaluable. Ranking functions in DAX are powerful and somewhat complex to understand. In this section, you are going to learn all you need to know to use them effectively.

We are going to use as an example the simple set of data shown in Figure 13-9.

ProductId	Product
1	Bike
2	Helmet
3	Shirt
4	Shoe

ProductId	Sale
1	10
1	20
2	30
2	40
3	50
3	60
4	70
4	80
4	90
1	100

FIGURE 13-9 This is the simple dataset that we will use to learn the ranking capabilities of PowerPivot.

As shown in Figure 13-9, you have products and sales: only four products and some sales info, and the only number is the amount sold, shown in the Sale column.

The DAX function that computes ranking is *RANKX* and, as its name suggests, *RANKX* is an iterator; that is, it iterates a table and, during iteration, creates a row context. In its simplest form, *RANKX* is used with two parameters: a table and an expression. *RANKX* computes the expression for each row of the table and then sorts the result. Finally, it evaluates the expression again, for the current cell, and searches for the place where the value fits in the ordered table.

Thus, you can define a calculated field with the following formula:

```
RankOnSales := RANKX ( Products, [SumOfSales] )
```

Using the previous description, *RANKX* does the following:

1. It creates a table with the sum of sales for each product.

2. It evaluates the sales for the current cell.

3. It finds the place of the value computed during step 2 in the table.

Thus, if you put the *SumOfSales* and *RankOnSale* calculated fields in a PivotTable, you get the result shown in Figure 13-10.

SumOfSales	RankOnSale
550.00	1

FIGURE 13-10 This PivotTable shows the result (1) for RankOnSale when no product is used to slice data.

This result, by itself, is not very useful. Nevertheless, before computing better results, it is useful to understand what happened exactly, under the surface, because this knowledge will help greatly later, when the formulas will be more complex.

1. *RANKX* iterated the Products list and computed, for each product, *SumOfSales*. Because *SumOfSales* is a calculated field, it has been automatically surrounded by *CALCULATE,* causing context transition. Thus, the value computed for each row is the sales of the current product. At the end, *RANKX* created a table like the one you can see in Figure 13-11.

Shoe	240.00
Bike	130.00
Shirt	110.00
Helmet	70.00

FIGURE 13-11 This is the table created by *RANKX*.

2. Once the table has been created, *RANKX* computed the expression for the current cell again and, because there is no filter on the data model, it computed the sum of all sales, resulting in the value of 550.00.

3. Finally, *RANKX* searched for the place of 550.00 in the list and found that it is the biggest value of all, so the function assigned it the rank value of 1. Note that *RANKX* does not require the value to be present in the list; rather, it searches for the place where the value would be if inserted in the list.

At this point, it is time to bring the product name into the PivotTable to see what happens. In Figure 13-12, you can see the result.

Product		Row Labels ↓	SumOfSales	RankOnSale
Bike		Shoe	240.00	1
Helmet		Bike	130.00	1
Shirt		Shirt	110.00	1
Shoe		Helmet	70.00	1
		Grand Total	**550.00**	**1**

FIGURE 13-12 Putting the product in the PivotTable yields to incorrect results.

The result from Figure 13-12 is always 1, which is clearly wrong. To understand what happened, you need to compute the *RANKX* function in each cell. Take, for example, the first row, where Shoe is shown in the PivotTable. There, *RANKX* is invoked, passing *Product* as the first parameter. This time, *Product* does not contain all of the products, because the filter context of the first row shows only the *Shoe* product. Thus, in that cell, *Product* contains a single row and *RANKX* will first create its lookup table, which will contain a single row [that is, (Shoe, 240,00)]. Then, it evaluates *SumOfSales* in the current filter context and computes the value of 240, which is at the first (and only) place. The same happens for all subsequent rows, and this is the reason why you always see 1 as the result. In a filter context containing a single product, that product is always ranked first. The only cell where many products are visible is the grand total, where the lookup table contains all of the product, but *SumOfSales* is computed for the grand total, yielding, again, a rank of 1.

To make the formula work in the desired way, you need to pass to *RANKX* a table that does not contain a single product, but all the products. A first step in the right direction is to modify the formula using this code:

```
RankOnSales := RANKX ( ALL ( Products ), [SumOfSales] )
```

By using *ALL* on Products, you always force the ranking of the current cell to be computed against all the products. The result is much better (see Figure 13-13).

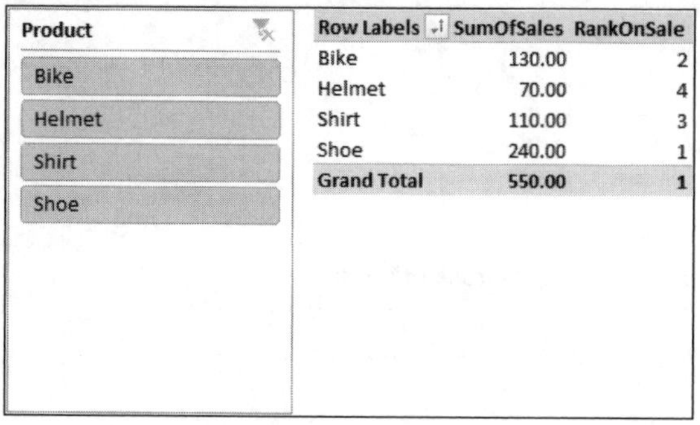

FIGURE 13-13 Using *ALL* on *Products,* the *RANKX* function now computes correct values.

There are still a couple of problems with this measure. First, the grand total value of 1 is not meaningful; it would be better to have it be blank. This is easy to accomplish by using *HASONEVALUE* or *ISFILTERED.* The other issue, which is a bigger problem, is that if you select some values in the slicer, then the ranking is no longer correct, as shown in Figure 13-14.

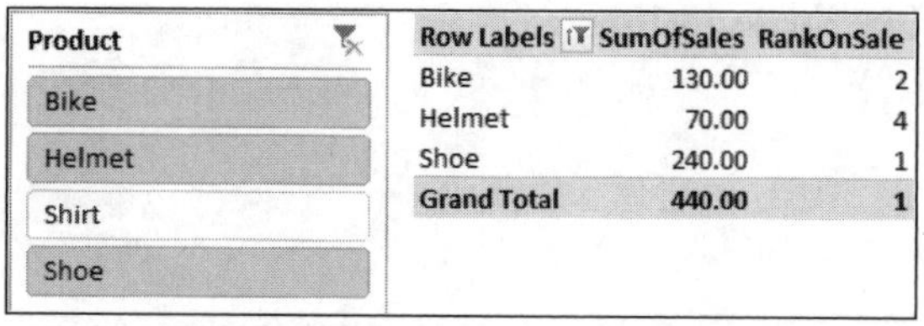

FIGURE 13-14 If the slicer selects some products, then the ranking is missing number 3: only 1, 2, and 4 are displayed.

As in the previous example, this time you are having issues due to the filter context. In fact, by using ALL (Products), you are ranking the current row against all the products, while it would be better to rank the current product against the visible ones. This will lead to the final formulation for the ranking function:

```
RankOnSales :=
IF (
    HASONEVALUE ( Products[Product] ),
    RANKX ( ALLSELECTED ( Products ), [SumOfSales] )
)
```

In this final formula, we have blanked the grand total using *HASONEVALUE* and used the *ALLSELECTED* function to take into account only the visible products. The result is what you expect from a basic ranking (see Figure 13-15).

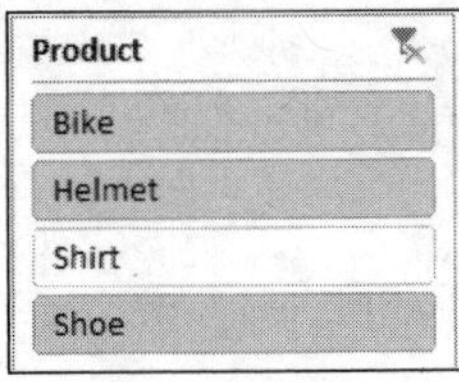

Row Labels	SumOfSales	RankOnSale
Bike	130.00	2
Helmet	70.00	3
Shoe	240.00	1
Grand Total	440.00	

FIGURE 13-15 The final formula works correctly in computing the rank of products.

RANKX and context transition

It is important to always remember that *RANKX* is an iterator. The reason you are ranking a product against other products is the context transition that happens due to an implicit *CALCULATE* function surrounding any calculated field evaluation inside a row context.

Suppose that you rewrite *RankOnSales* using this formula:

```
RankOnSalesWrong := RANKX ( ALL ( Products ), SUM ( Sales[Sales] ) )
```

In that case, the result will be wrong (see Figure 13-16).

Row Labels	SumOfSales	RankOnSalesWrong
Bike	130.00	1
Helmet	70.00	1
Shirt	110.00	1
Shoe	240.00	1
Grand Total	550.00	1

FIGURE 13-16 If you are not relying on context transition, the result here is wrong.

The reason the result is wrong is that, with no context transition, the expression SUM (Sales[Sales]) is always computed in the current filter context and returns the value of the product of the current cell for all the products iterated by *RANKX*. Then the value of the cell is compared with this table (that contains the same value for all the rows), and the result is 1 for all rows. Even if the result is similar to the absence of *ALL* on Products, as noted at the beginning of this section, the reason that it is always 1 in this case is different.

RANKX has some optional parameters. The third parameter is probably the hardest to understand and use. To help you understand how to work with it, you can add a column to the Products table, holding the product price. The Products table now looks like Figure 13-17.

ProductId	Product	Price
1	Bike	100
2	Helmet	200
3	Shirt	300
4	Shoe	400

FIGURE 13-17 We now have added the price column to the Products table.

At this point, you might want to add a new ranking based on the product price. Armed with your knowledge so far, you can write the final format of the formula using this code:

```
RankOnPrice :=
IF (
    HASONEVALUE ( Products[Product] ),
    RANKX ( ALLSELECTED ( Products ), Products[Price] )
)
```

If you try to create this formula, though, you will get an error (see Figure 13-18).

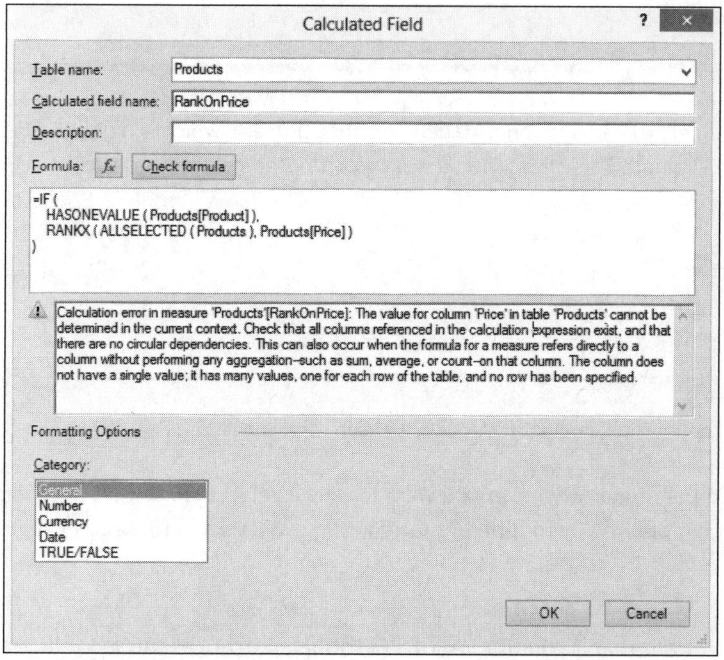

FIGURE 13-18 Ranking on a simple column seems not to work.

Again, to understand what is happening, it is important to remember the single steps of *RANKX*. First, the expression Products[Price] is evaluated in the row context introduced by *RANKX*, and this will compute the price for each product because it is a direct reference to the Price column of the Products table. Then, when it is time to compute the ranking of the current row, the same expression Products[Price] is evaluated in the current filter context, without an active row context. As you already know, the expression Products[Price] is a column reference that has no meaning unless a row context is active and, for the current cell, no such row context exists. For this reason, you get the error shown in Figure 13-18. This issue was avoided before by using a calculated field that contained an aggregation expression.

This is where the third parameter of *RANKX* comes in handy. The second parameter is the expression used to build the ranking table, and the third is the expression evaluated to find the rank.

They are identical by default, but they can be different expressions. There are many reasons for that, but in this example, it is that you cannot compute Products[Price], due to the lack of a row context. However, you can compute VALUES (Products[Price]), which yields the same value but can be computed in a filter context without a row context. Thus, the correct expression is

```
RankOnPrice :=
IF (
    HASONEVALUE ( Products[Product] ),
    RANKX (
        ALLSELECTED ( Products ),
        Products[Price],
        VALUES ( Products[Price] )
    )
)
```

This time, for the current cell, the expression VALUES (Products[Price]), which is highlighted in bold in the formula, will be evaluated and the formula will be computed correctly, as shown in Figure 13-19.

Row Labels	SumOfSales	RankOnPrice
Bike	130.00	4
Helmet	70.00	3
Shirt	110.00	2
Shoe	240.00	1
Grand Total	550.00	

FIGURE 13-19 Using the third optional parameter of *RANKX* is useful in some scenarios.

You can specify the third parameter whenever you want to rank a value against a set of other values, or when, as in the example, you need different formulas to evaluate in a row and in a filter context.

Note It is worthwhile to state that if you use VALUES (Products[Price]) as the second parameter, you will get an incorrect result—again. The reason for this, again, is the fact that VALUES (Products[Price]) is computed in a row context but ignores it. Rather, *VALUES* uses only the filter context. Thus, for all the rows iterated by *RANKX*, VALUES (Products[Price]) is always the value of the product of the current cell instead of the product iterated by *RANKX*, and the result will be wrong.

As you might already have noticed, we have shown several wrong formulas to illustrate the issues that you are likely to encounter when creating your own ranking expressions. Looking at the possible problems in advance will probably illuminate the issue whenever you will see wrong results, and you will go back and reread this section. *RANKX* is not an easy function. It takes time to master. We suggest that you learn the *RANKX* function by examining the examples provided in the book, before trying ranking on a real data model. That will make it much easier to understand this concept.

The last two parameters of *RANKX* are much easier to use and understand. You have the option to use descending or ascending sort for the ranking (fourth parameter) and to use dense or nondense ranking (fifth parameter). *Dense ranking* refers to how to compute ranking in the case of a tie. If there is a tie, all the cells with the same value will have the same ranking number and the next one will be increased by the number of ties (if dense ranking is off) or by 1 (if dense ranking is on).

In Figure 13-20, you can see three formulas that compute the ranking on the Cost column using standard *RANKX,* descending order (third parameter), and dense ranking (fourth parameter).

Row Labels	RankOnCost	RankOnCostDense	RankOnCostDesc
Bike	4	3	1
Helmet	2	2	2
Shirt	2	2	2
Shoe	1	1	4

ProductId	Product	Cost	Price
1	Bike	100	100
2	Helmet	200	200
3	Shirt	200	300
4	Shoe	300	400

FIGURE 13-20 Optional parameters of *RANKX* provide slightly different results.

The formulas used for the three measures are the following:

```
RankOnCost :=
=IF (
    HASONEVALUE ( Products[Product] ),
    RANKX ( ALLSELECTED ( Products ), Products[Cost], VALUES ( Products[Cost] ) )
)

RankOnCostDense :=
IF (
    HASONEVALUE ( Products[Product] ),
    RANKX (
        ALLSELECTED ( Products ),
        Products[Cost],
        VALUES ( Products[Cost] ),
        FALSE,
        DENSE
    )
)

RankOnCostDesc :=
=IF (
    HASONEVALUE ( Products[Product] ),
    RANKX (
        ALLSELECTED ( Products ),
        Products[Cost],
        VALUES ( Products[Cost] ),
        TRUE
    )
)
```

Using many-to-many relationships

In most of the scenarios and examples we have shown up to now, we always used simple one-to-many relationships, which PowerPivot handles easily. One-to-many relationships are easy to understand and to handle: one product is related to a single category, and one sale is related to a sales territory and to a customer. Finally, one-to-many relationships have the great characteristic that they usually produce additive measures, meaning that the total products sold in a year is the sum of the products sold in 12 months. This characteristic leads to reports that are easy to read and interpret.

But the truth is that one-to-many relationships are not the only kind of relationships in the real world. Another kind of relationship appears often, and that one is much harder to use, understand, and program: many-to-many relationships. A *many-to-many relationship* exists between two tables when many rows in one table are related to many rows in the other one.

Many-to-many relationships appear often in a data model, even when it seems not to contain any. To illustrate this, we are going to study the example shown in Chapter 7, "Understanding evaluation contexts." In Figure 13-21, the sample data model is laid out:

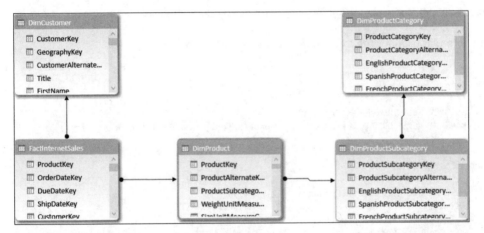

FIGURE 13-21 This simple data model seems to contain only one-to-many relationships, but in reality, many-to-many relationships are well hidden inside it.

In this data model, you define these three calculated fields:

```
NumOfSales      := COUNTROWS ( FactInternetSales )
NumOfProducts   := COUNTROWS ( DimProduct )
NumOfCustomers  := COUNTROWS ( DimCustomer )
```

Once the calculated fields are defined, you can try to create a PivotTable with a slicer on product color, model name, and product name on the rows and three calculated fields in the values area. The result is not what you might want because NumOfCustomers always shows the total number of customers (see Figure 13-22).

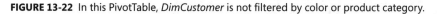

Color		Row Labels	NumOfSales	NumOfProducts	NumOfCustomers
Black	^	⊟Cycling Cap	2,190	3	18,484
Blue		AWC Logo Cap	2,190	3	18,484
Grey		⊟Long-Sleeve Logo Jersey	1,736	12	18,484
Multi		Long-Sleeve Logo Jersey, L	452	3	18,484
NA		Long-Sleeve Logo Jersey, M	442	3	18,484
Red		Long-Sleeve Logo Jersey, S	429	3	18,484
Silver		Long-Sleeve Logo Jersey, XL	413	3	18,484
Silver/Black	v	⊟Men's Bib-Shorts		3	18,484
		Men's Bib-Shorts, L		1	18,484
		Men's Bib-Shorts, M		1	18,484
		Men's Bib-Shorts, S		1	18,484
		Grand Total	3,926	18	18,484

FIGURE 13-22 In this PivotTable, *DimCustomer* is not filtered by color or product category.

In Chapter 7, you learned that the filter context is not propagated from products to customers because of the direction of relationships. Filter context is propagated from the one to the many side, but not from the many side to the one. Thus, the filters on products effectively filter the product table (directly) and the sales table (indirectly), but not the customer table. That said, you might object that there is a relationship between products and customers; that is, you want to see the number of customers who bought the selected product. And you are perfectly right. The fact is that the relationship between products and customers is a many-to-many relationship: many customers can buy a single product, and one customer can buy several products. Yet, PowerPivot is not able to traverse many-to-many relationships with simple DAX formulas.

Figure 13-23 shows the scenario in a graphical way: You can see that the original filter of products has been propagated (cross-filtered) to the sales table because of the direction of the relationship. Thus, the sales table is filtered too. *Customers* is not filtered because the relationship linking sales to customers goes in the opposite direction.

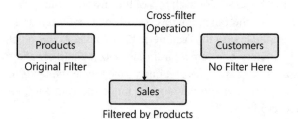

FIGURE 13-23 Cross-filtering flows from the one side to the many side, but not in the opposite direction.

To solve this scenario of traversing the many-to-many relationship, you need to apply a filter context to the customers manually so only the customers who bought one of the selected products are shown. In other words, the customers you want to count are only those for which there is at least one row in the sales table that states that the customer bought one of the selected products.

Now, the sales table is already filtered by product. You only need a way to filter the sales table by customer and then check if some specific row exists in the sale table, after the two filters are applied together. The idea is starting to shape at this point: for each customer, filter the sales table to show only his or her sales and, at this point, check if any row survived both filters (the one from Products, still alive, and the one from Customers, which we are creating now).

In Figure 13-24, you can see what will happen: The sales table will be filtered by both products and customers, and the formula will simply check if there is any row inside it that satisfies both conditions.

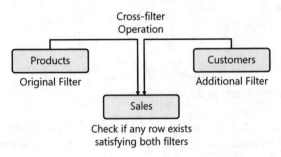

FIGURE 13-24 The many-to-many formula will apply two filters to the Sales table.

At this point, it is time to look at the formula:

```
NumOfCustomers :=
COUNTROWS (
    FILTER (
        DimCustomer,
        CALCULATE ( COUNTROWS ( FactInternetSales ) ) > 0
    )
)
```

The magic of this formula happens inside the *FILTER*. For each row of the customer table, we force the context transition using *CALCULATE*. At this point, the row context on *DimCustomer* is transformed into a filter context, which is propagated to the FactInternetSales table. At this point, the FactInternetSales table is affected by two filters: one coming from the PivotTable (slicer and row) and one coming from the context transition. If there is still at least one visible row in the table, it means that there is a sale match for both the customer and the product. If not, then it means that the customer never bought one of the selected products.

This is not the best formula to work with many-to-many relationships, so it is not important to memorize it right now, but it is the easiest to understand, even if it has suboptimal performances.

The result of this measure can be seen in Figure 13-25.

FIGURE 13-25 With the many-to-many formula, the number of customers is now correct.

It is important to note that whenever many-to-many relationships come into play in a formula, the additive nature of the formula is lost. In fact, if you sum the values of the cells, you will see that the total is not equal to the grand total. In fact, if a customer bought both a cap and a pair of shorts, it will be counted in both cells once, and only once, in the grand total. Thus, you will see a nonadditive behavior, where 1 + 1 = 1.

There is a better way to express the same formula:

```
NumOfCustomers :=
CALCULATE (
    COUNTROWS ( DimCustomer ),
    FILTER (
        DimCustomer,
        CALCULATE ( COUNTROWS ( FactInternetSales ) ) > 0
    )
)
```

The reason why this new way of writing the same expression is better is that you can put any expression inside *CALCULATE,* not only a simple *COUNTROWS* function as in the example. *DimCustomer* does not contain interesting information that can be used for aggregation, but in the next section of this chapter, you will see different examples where the many-to-many pattern is used to compute more complex expressions, and then you will need this pattern.

> **Note** Many-to-many relationships are not easy to understand at first sight. Take the necessary time to gain a good understanding of the formula before moving on to more advanced topics like counting new customers or basket analysis, and try the formula with the workbook in the companion material. Even if they are not easy, many-to-many relationships are among the most powerful tools to model complex scenarios and compute interesting values. You can find a longer discussion about many-to-many relationships in the white paper "The many-to-many revolution 2.0," which is available at *http://www.sqlbi.com/articles/many2many/.*

A simpler and faster way to write the same formula is using the FactInternetSales table as a filter in the *CALCULATE* statement:

```
NumOfCustomers :=
CALCULATE (
    COUNTROWS ( DimCustomer ),
    FactInternetSales
)
```

Because the presence of a table in the filters of a *CALCULATE* statement applies a filter to the related lookup tables as well, by putting the *FactInternetSales* table in the context, you obtain a filter on *DimCustomer* that shows only the customers who bought a product. This syntax works fine—like magic. Unfortunately, explaining exactly how and why it works would require a long digression about DAX internals, which is beyond the scope of this book.

Computing new and returning customers

Now that you learned the basics of many-to-many relationships, it is time to look at some scenarios that can be solved with the knowledge that you gained so far. One common pattern is that of not only counting the customers, but finding, in a specific time period, how many of them are new customers and how many are returning customers.

A customer is new if he or she never bought anything before, and a returning one if he or she bought some products in the past and is now returning to continue shopping. Obviously, the same customer is a new one in a specific time period and may become a returning one later. Thus, you cannot store the status of a customer in the customer table itself, and this is what makes this analysis challenging.

Figure 13-26 displays a PivotTable showing the number of buying customers (computed with the many-to-many pattern you learned before) sliced with the date dimension.

At the risk of being tedious, we think it is important to remember how the number of customers is computed: it is the number of customers that have some corresponding lines in the FactInternetSales table, once that table has been filtered using all other filters in the PivotTable. The formula is

```
NumOfCustomers :=
CALCULATE (
    COUNTROWS ( DimCustomer ),
    FILTER (
        DimCustomer,
        CALCULATE ( COUNTROWS ( FactInternetSales ) ) > 0
    )
)
```

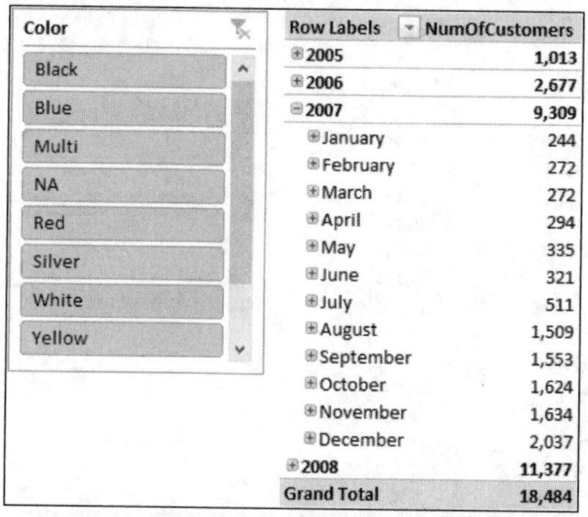

Color		Row Labels	NumOfCustomers
Black	∧	⊞ 2005	1,013
Blue		⊞ 2006	2,677
Multi		⊟ 2007	9,309
NA		⊞ January	244
Red		⊞ February	272
Silver		⊞ March	272
White		⊞ April	294
Yellow	∨	⊞ May	335
		⊞ June	321
		⊞ July	511
		⊞ August	1,509
		⊞ September	1,553
		⊞ October	1,624
		⊞ November	1,634
		⊞ December	2,037
		⊞ 2008	11,377
		Grand Total	**18,484**

FIGURE 13-26 *NumOfCustomers* is easy to write, but how many of these customers are new ones?

Because we know that the new customers are the ones who did not buy anything before the currently selected time period, we can start thinking at the formula to use. Before writing the complete formula, let's start with a simpler exercise: count the customers who did not buy anything in the current period. You know that a customer bought something if there are rows in FactInternetSales related to the customer. Checking the opposite condition, then, is easy: you simply need to check that there are no rows in FactInternetSales related to the customer.

Thus, the formula for *NotBuyingCustomers* is a simple variation of the formula for *NumOfCustomers*, where the only difference is the test = 0 instead of > 0:

```
NotBuyingCustomers :=
CALCULATE (
    COUNTROWS ( DimCustomer ),
    FILTER (
        DimCustomer,
        CALCULATE ( COUNTROWS ( FactInternetSales ) ) = 0
    )
)
```

In Figure 13-27, you can see the measure in a PivotTable. You can easily check that each row generates a total of 18,484, which is the total number of customers.

Color		Row Labels	NumOfCustomers	NotBuyingCustomers
Black		⊞ 2005	1,013	17,471
Blue		⊞ 2006	2,677	15,807
Grey		⊟ 2007	9,309	9,175
Multi		⊞ January	244	18,240
NA		⊞ February	272	18,212
Red		⊞ March	272	18,212
Silver		⊞ April	294	18,190
Silver/Black		⊞ May	335	18,149
		⊞ June	321	18,163
		⊞ July	511	17,973
		⊞ August	1,509	16,975
		⊞ September	1,553	16,931
		⊞ October	1,624	16,860
		⊞ November	1,634	16,850
		⊞ December	2,037	16,447
		⊞ 2008	11,377	7,107
		⊞ 2009		18,484
		⊞ 2010		18,484
		Grand Total	18,484	

FIGURE 13-27 Computing the number of not-buying customers is easy as the number of buying ones.

The next step is to compute the number of customers who did not buy anything before the current time period. For example, if the current selection on the rows is February 2005, you need to check that the customer never bought anything before February 1, 2005. This is easily accomplished by computing a different filter context for the DimDate table, one that contains all the dates that are before the current selection:

```
NeverBoughtBefore :=
CALCULATE (
    COUNTROWS ( DimCustomer ),
    FILTER (
        DimCustomer,
        CALCULATE (
            COUNTROWS ( FactInternetSales ),
            FILTER (
                ALL ( DimDate ),
                DimDate[FullDateAlternateKey]
                    < MIN ( DimDate[FullDateAlternateKey] )
            )
        ) = 0
    )
)
```

You can see the result of this new calculated field in Figure 13-28.

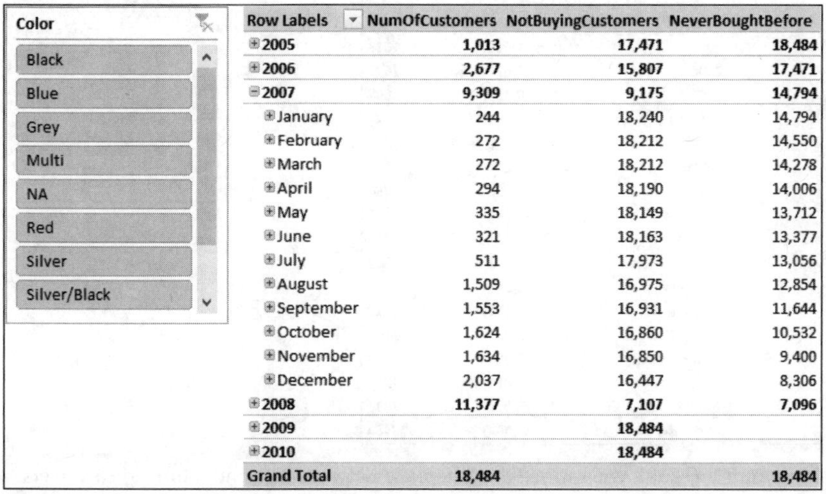

Color		Row Labels	NumOfCustomers	NotBuyingCustomers	NeverBoughtBefore
Black	^	⊞ 2005	1,013	17,471	18,484
Blue		⊞ 2006	2,677	15,807	17,471
Grey		⊟ 2007	9,309	9,175	14,794
Multi		⊞ January	244	18,240	14,794
NA		⊞ February	272	18,212	14,550
Red		⊞ March	272	18,212	14,278
Silver		⊞ April	294	18,190	14,006
Silver/Black	v	⊞ May	335	18,149	13,712
		⊞ June	321	18,163	13,377
		⊞ July	511	17,973	13,056
		⊞ August	1,509	16,975	12,854
		⊞ September	1,553	16,931	11,644
		⊞ October	1,624	16,860	10,532
		⊞ November	1,634	16,850	9,400
		⊞ December	2,037	16,447	8,306
		⊞ 2008	11,377	7,107	7,096
		⊞ 2009		18,484	7,096
		⊞ 2010		18,484	
		Grand Total	18,484		18,484

FIGURE 13-28 The new calculated field computes the number of customers who never have bought anything before.

At this point, the number of new customers is easy to compute: it is a mix of the previous formulas; you need only filter all the customers who bought something in the current period and did not buy anything before it, in the same *FILTER* expression:

```
NewCustomers:=
CALCULATE (
    COUNTROWS ( DimCustomer ),
    FILTER (
        DimCustomer,
        CALCULATE ( COUNTROWS ( FactInternetSales ) ) > 0
        && CALCULATE (
            COUNTROWS ( FactInternetSales ),
            FILTER (
                ALL ( DimDate ),
                DimDate[FullDateAlternateKey]
                    < MIN ( DimDate[FullDateAlternateKey] )
            )
        ) = 0
    )
)
```

In Figure 13-29, you can see the *NewCustomer* calculated field, along with *NumOfCustomers*, which clearly shows the number of new customers compared to buying customers. If you need the number of returning customers, they can be easily computed using a difference function.

Color		Row Labels	NumOfCustomers	NewCustomers
Black	∧	⊞ 2005	1,013	1013
Blue		⊞ 2006	2,677	2677
Multi		⊟ 2007	9,309	7698
NA		⊞ January	244	244
Red		⊞ February	272	272
Silver		⊞ March	272	272
White		⊞ April	294	294
Yellow		⊞ May	335	335
	∨	⊞ June	321	321
		⊞ July	511	202
		⊞ August	1,509	1210
		⊞ September	1,553	1112
		⊞ October	1,624	1132
		⊞ November	1,634	1094
		⊞ December	2,037	1210
		⊞ 2008	11,377	7096
		Grand Total	18,484	18484

FIGURE 13-29 Starting from July 2007, you can see the difference between new and returning customers.

One of the most interesting aspects of this formula is that you can use it with other filters too. If, for example, you filter a color with the slicer, then you see how many customers never bought a red product and are buying it now, and you can obviously use it for other significant analysis, like seeing how many new customers are buying the newly introduced products on the market.

Later in this chapter, you will learn how to use a similar technique to perform basket analysis and more powerful reports.

Understanding *KEEPFILTERS*

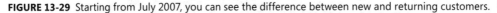

You are now going to take a small break from your tour of scenarios to spend some time learning an important function, one of many that exist in DAX: *KEEPFILTERS*. *KEEPFILTERS* is a simple function, but to understand why it is needed, you need to get a very clear idea about the concepts of evaluation context and context transition. This is the reason why the function is explained here, in the section dedicated to advanced DAX.

Let's start with a simple PivotTable, like the one in Figure 13-30.

Row Labels	Sum of SalesAmount
⊟ 2006	$912,409.09
⊞ November	$335,095.09
⊞ December	$577,314.00
⊟ 2007	$927,955.51
⊞ January	$438,865.17
⊞ February	$489,090.34
Grand Total	$1,840,364.60

FIGURE 13-30 Here, you can see sales over a few months spanning 2006 and 2007.

The interesting part of the PivotTable is the selection of the last two months of 2006 and the first two of 2007, which is obtained by filtering the hierarchy on the DimDate table (see Figure 13-31).

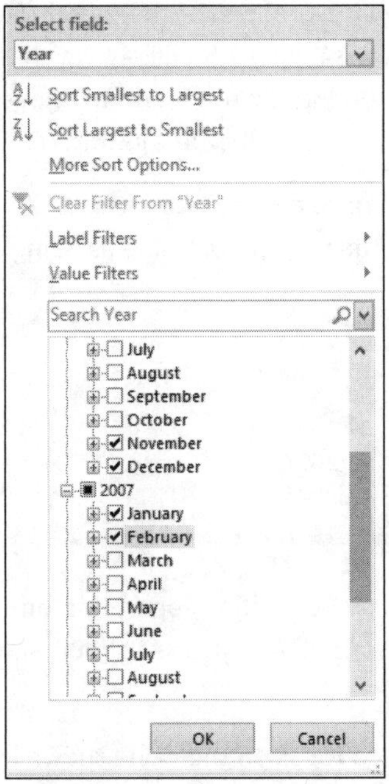

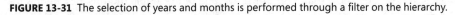

FIGURE 13-31 The selection of years and months is performed through a filter on the hierarchy.

There is absolutely nothing wrong with the numbers shown in the PivotTable. But imagine that you want to show the average monthly sales instead of the sum of sales. You can easily obtain this result using the *AVERAGEX* function in a new calculated field, as in the following code:

```
MonthlyAverageSales =
AVERAGEX (
    VALUES ( DimDate[EnglishMonthName] ),
    [Sum of SalesAmount]
)
```

Note that we are relying on context transition when using the calculated field *[Sum of SalesAmount]* from inside the row context introduced by *AVERAGEX*. Thus, we are making the average of sales of every month included in the filter. You can see the resulting PivotTable in Figure 13-32.

Row Labels	Sum of SalesAmount	MonthlyAverageSales
2006	$912,409.09	$456,204.54
November	$335,095.09	$335,095.09
December	$577,314.00	$577,314.00
2007	$927,955.51	$463,977.75
January	$438,865.17	$438,865.17
February	$489,090.34	$489,090.34
Grand Total	$1,840,364.60	$1,479,174.18

FIGURE 13-32 The average sales amount looks correct inside the PivotTable, but at the grand total level, it is definitely wrong.

If you look at monthly and yearly sales, they are correct, but what happened at the grand total? You would expect an average of less than 500,000.00, yet the result is nearly 1.5 million, which is clearly not the average of the values shown in the PivotTable. Something is wrong, and to understand what this is, you need to explore deeply how evaluation contexts work together in this formula.

Let's start with the filter context of the PivotTable. Because you have filtered two months of 2006 and two months of 2007, you can think the filter context on the entire PivotTable as being the following:

```
(DimDate[EnglishMonthName] = "November" && DimDate[Year] = 2006)
|| (DimDate[EnglishMonthName] = "December" && DimDate[Year] = 2006)
|| (DimDate[EnglishMonthName] = "January"  && DimDate[Year] = 2007)
|| (DimDate[EnglishMonthName] = "February" && DimDate[Year] = 2007)
```

It is important to note that the complete expression is a mix of two conditions operating on different columns. In strictly technical terms, this is known as an *arbitrarily shaped set;* that is, a set that cannot be expressed as the intersection of two simpler sets.

Now, the first step needed to understand what is happening is to focus on the value shown in the grand total. You already know that it is not the average of the visible months, but what is that number? To find out, you create a new PivotTable, and this time, instead of filtering the hierarchy, you select *CalendarYear* and *EnglishMonthName* from the DimDate table using two slicers. You create a different layout like the one shown in Figure 13-33, which now shows eight months instead of the four that were selected.

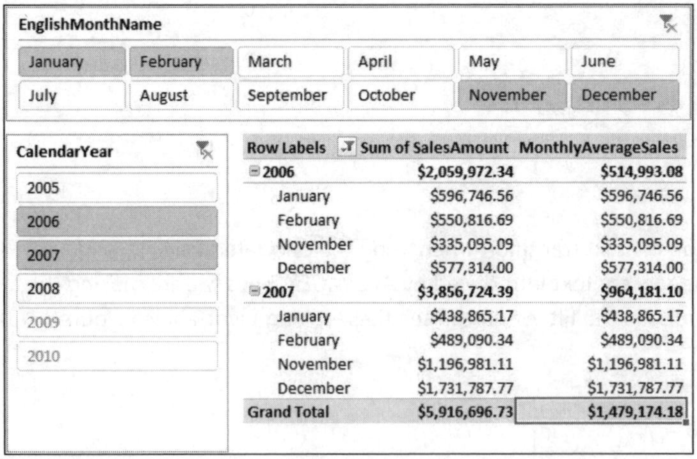

Row Labels	Sum of SalesAmount	MonthlyAverageSales
⊟ 2006	$2,059,972.34	$514,993.08
January	$596,746.56	$596,746.56
February	$550,816.69	$550,816.69
November	$335,095.09	$335,095.09
December	$577,314.00	$577,314.00
⊟ 2007	$3,856,724.39	$964,181.10
January	$438,865.17	$438,865.17
February	$489,090.34	$489,090.34
November	$1,196,981.11	$1,196,981.11
December	$1,731,787.77	$1,731,787.77
Grand Total	$5,916,696.73	$1,479,174.18

EnglishMonthName: January, February, March, April, May, June, July, August, September, October, November, December

CalendarYear: 2005, 2006, 2007, 2008, 2009, 2010

FIGURE 13-33 Selecting all eight months, you can see that the grand total is the same, so it is not yet correct.

The grand total corresponds to the previous one in Figure 13-30, and this time, it looks more like a correct value because if you take into account all eight months, sales of November and December 2007 bring the average to a much higher value. But . . . wait a moment. While it is true that December 2007 is very high, it is also true that that the value still looks a bit too high. It is time to stop trusting the formula and use a calculator. If you manually compute the average of those eight months (or let Excel do the calculation, which is easier), the result is 739,587.09. In other words, the result is still wrong.

To discover the real meaning of the value, you need to remove the year from the rows so that each month shows the sum of both years. While the report (shown in Figure 13-34) is not very meaningful, this time the average is correct.

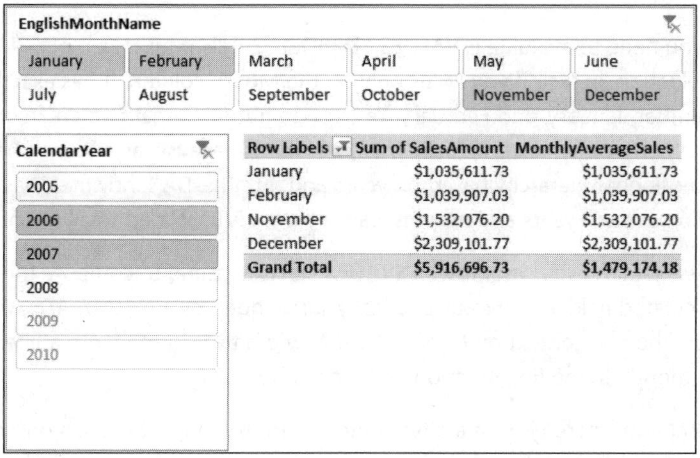

FIGURE 13-34 The grand total shows the correct average of the sum of both years for each month.

Now we can understand what the number represents. The question is: Why do we see this number? Or, if you prefer, why does DAX compute the average in such a strange way? The reason is that if you do not pay attention to them, arbitrarily shaped sets can lead to incorrect results when they are mixed with context transition.

Let's focus on the grand total cell of Figure 13-30 and try to follow exactly what happened to the filter context. The original one, in which the PivotTable is computed, contains four months spanning two years, as shown in Table 13-1.

TABLE 13-1 The four selected months in the original filter context of the grand total

Year	Month
2006	November
2006	December
2007	January
2007	February

Inside this original filter context, you evaluate the expression, as before:

```
MonthlyAverageSales =
AVERAGEX (
    VALUES ( DimDate[EnglishMonthName] ),
    [Sum of SalesAmount]
)
```

The first expression that you need to evaluate is VALUES (DimDate[EnglishMonthName]). This is the trickiest part of the evaluation. In fact, if you focus only on the Month column, it has exactly four values: November, December, January, and February. Yes, you might think that two are in one year and other two are in another year (which is actually true), but this is because, as a human being, you are used to thinking of a calendar hierarchy based on years and months. DAX, however, has no knowledge of the relationship between years and months: each column is unrelated to all the others.

Once *VALUES* computes its result for four months, *AVERAGEX* starts iterating to compute the *[Sum of SalesAmount]*. This is a calculated field and it is automatically surrounded by a *CALCULATE*, which induces the context transition: the row context on *EnglishMonthName* is transformed into a filter context containing only one month. In the first iteration, the month is January.

Thus, PowerPivot is in a scenario where there is a filter context with this original expression, which we will call the "original filter context":

Original Filter Context

```
(DimDate[EnglishMonthName] = "November" && DimDate[Year] = 2006)
|| (DimDate[EnglishMonthName] = "December" && DimDate[Year] = 2006)
|| (DimDate[EnglishMonthName] = "January"  && DimDate[Year] = 2007)
|| (DimDate[EnglishMonthName] = "February" && DimDate[Year] = 2007)
```

And there is also another filter context, induced by the context transition and filtering only January, which we will call the "new filter context":

New Filter Context

```
DimDate[EnglishMonthName] = "January"
```

To merge the two contexts, DAX removes the part of the filter on *EnglishMonthName* from the original filter context and replaces that part with the new filter context. Let's do this now: take the original filter context and remove from there all the conditions set on *EnglishMonthName*. The result is easy to compute but somewhat astonishing:

```
Original Filter Context Without the Conditions on EnglishMonthName

DimDate[Year] = 2006
|| DimDate[Year] = 2006
|| DimDate[Year] = 2007
|| DimDate[Year] = 2007
```

You see that, without the *EnglishMonthName* condition, this filter now filters two years and can be simplified to:

```
DimDate[Year] = 2006 || DimDate[Year] = 2007
```

The final step is to combine the two filters into an *AND* condition. The result is:

```
DimDate[EnglishMonthName] = "January"
&& ( DimDate[Year] = 2006 || DimDate[Year]= 2007 )
```

If you read this filter, it says: "Filter the month of January in both 2006 and 2007." The DAX engine evaluates the first step of the *AVERAGEX* iteration under this filter context. Inside this filter context, *AVERAGEX* computes the sum of sales amount (that is, the sales of January in two years).

The same process happens again for the remaining three months: Each time, PowerPivot computes the sum of the month in both years, and at the end, it computes the average of the four values computed.

This scenario happens whenever you mix iterations, context transitions, and arbitrarily shaped sets, and it is somewhat complex to understand and identify. Moreover, even though we have demonstrated the issue at the grand total in this example, it can happen on any cell, so long as you have, for that cell, the correct (and dangerous) mix of ingredients.

To address this issue, you need to use the *KEEPFILTERS* function. *KEEPFILTERS* modifies the behavior of the *CALCULATE* function. In fact, *CALCULATE*, by default, replaces existing filters for each column. Using *KEEPFILTERS*, you instruct *CALCULATE* to take into account previously existing filters and intersect them with the new filter.

The correct formulation for the monthly average is as follows:

```
MonthlyAverageCorrect =
AVERAGEX (
    KEEPFILTERS ( VALUES ( DimDate[EnglishMonthName] ) ),
    [Sum of SalesAmount]
)
```

You can see that in this new formula, the *VALUES* function is now surrounded by *KEEPFILTERS*. When *CALCULATE* will be used in the evaluation of *[Sum of SalesAmount]*, it will perform context transition and create the new filter context, containing one month for two years, exactly as outlined before, but before using it, it will put it in a logical *AND* with the original filter. The complete expression will be:

```
(
    (DimDate[EnglishMonthName] = "November" && DimDate[Year] = 2006)
    || (DimDate[EnglishMonthName] = "December" && DimDate[Year] = 2006)
    || (DimDate[EnglishMonthName] = "January"  && DimDate[Year] = 2007)
    || (DimDate[EnglishMonthName] = "February" && DimDate[Year] = 2007)
)
&& DimDate[EnglishMonthName] = "January"
&& (DimDate[Year]=2006 || DimDate[Year]=2007)
```

This expression can be simplified to:

```
DimDate[EnglishMonthName] = "January" && DimDate[Year] = 2007
```

The result this time uses both the original and new filters and contains only one month: January 2007. In fact, using this new formula in a PivotTable, you now obtain the correct result (see Figure 13-35).

Row Labels	Sum of SalesAmount	MonthlyAverageSales	MonthlyAverageCorrect
2006	$912,409.09	$456,204.54	$456,204.54
November	$335,095.09	$335,095.09	$335,095.09
December	$577,314.00	$577,314.00	$577,314.00
2007	$927,955.51	$463,977.75	$463,977.75
January	$438,865.17	$438,865.17	$438,865.17
February	$489,090.34	$489,090.34	$489,090.34
Grand Total	$1,840,364.60	$1,479,174.18	$460,091.15

FIGURE 13-35 Using *KEEPFILTERS*, the MonthlyAverageCorrect column now shows correct values.

The grand total now shows the correct value because it iterated only the correct four months, two for each year, thanks to the *KEEPFILTERS* function. As you have seen, it is more difficult to understand and identify the issue than to solve it. Adding *KEEPFILTERS* is enough to handle arbitrarily shaped sets in DAX and perform correct calculations.

Now that you have understood the basics of *KEEPFILTERS*, it is important to see some other scenario in which *KEEPFILTERS* can be useful. In fact, you can create arbitrarily shaped sets with many filtering options using Excel and you need to understand when they can break your formulas.

Imagine that you have created a simple PivotTable that shows years and sales of products, as in Figure 13-36, but, instead of looking at all the products, you want to focus only on the top seller for each year.

Row Labels	Sum of SalesAmount
2005	$3,266,373.66
Mountain-100 Black, 38	$70,874.79
Mountain-100 Black, 42	$60,749.82
Mountain-100 Black, 44	$97,874.71
Mountain-100 Black, 48	$70,874.79
Mountain-100 Silver, 38	$98,599.71
Mountain-100 Silver, 42	$57,799.83
Mountain-100 Silver, 44	$84,999.75
Mountain-100 Silver, 48	$44,199.87
Road-150 Red, 44	$500,957.80
Road-150 Red, 48	$547,475.31
Road-150 Red, 52	$472,331.64
Road-150 Red, 56	$486,644.72
Road-150 Red, 62	$593,992.82

FIGURE 13-36 This simple PivotTable shows too many products, and you want to focus only on the top seller.

To show only the best seller of each year, you can use the advanced filtering options of the Excel PivotTable. You right-click a line containing a product name and then choose Filter | Top 10..., to select only the top sellers, as in Figure 13-37.

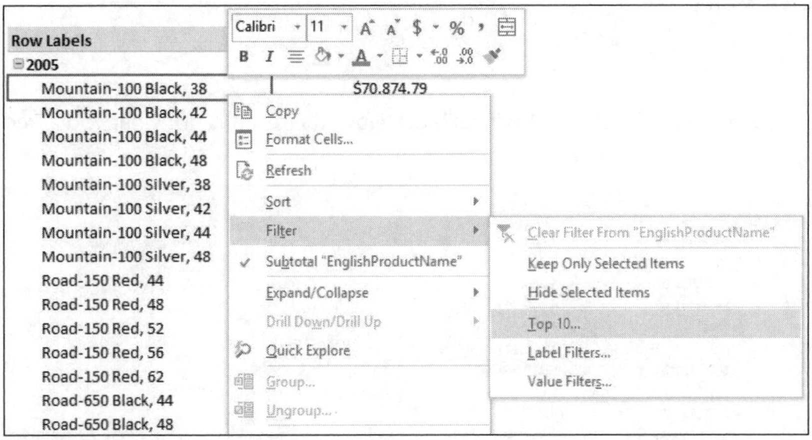

FIGURE 13-37 Advanced filtering options let you select only the top-selling items from a long list.

Excel opens the Top 10 Filter dialog box, shown in Figure 13-38, from which you can choose the exact number of items to show and the value to use to sort them.

FIGURE 13-38 The Top 10 Filter dialog box lets you choose various options of the top filter.

After you click OK, the PivotTable looks exactly as you want, showing only the top seller for each year (see Figure 13-39).

Row Labels	Sum of SalesAmount
⊟ 2005	$593,992.82
Road-150 Red, 62	$593,992.82
⊟ 2006	$658,401.68
Road-150 Red, 48	$658,401.68
⊟ 2007	$679,399.00
Mountain-200 Black, 46	$679,399.00
⊟ 2008	$589,277.46
Mountain-200 Silver, 38	$589,277.46
Grand Total	$2,521,070.96

FIGURE 13-39 The PivotTable with top filtering shows only the top seller for each year.

Up to now, nothing strange has happened. You obtained exactly what you asked for. Now, you want to enrich your report by adding, for each product, the daily average of the sales amount. You can accomplish this by using the *AVERAGEX* function to iterate on the selected dates of the year. The formula is straightforward:

```
AverageSalesAmount :=
AVERAGEX (
    VALUES ( DimDate ),
    [Sum of SalesAmount]
)
```

You create the calculated field, add it to the PivotTable. Now, the result is not what you asked for (see Figure 13-40).

Row Labels	Sum of SalesAmount	AverageSalesAmount
⊟ 2005	$593,992.82	7,660.86
Road-150 Red, 48		5,420.55
Road-150 Red, 62	$593,992.82	5,603.71
⊟ 2006	$658,401.68	6,075.00
Mountain-200 Black, 46		2,602.03
Mountain-200 Silver, 38		2,629.11
Road-150 Red, 48	$658,401.68	5,352.86
Road-150 Red, 62		5,685.10
⊟ 2007	$679,399.00	4,684.31
Mountain-200 Black, 46	$679,399.00	3,363.36
Mountain-200 Silver, 38		3,245.88
⊟ 2008	$589,277.46	6,623.79
Mountain-200 Black, 46		4,381.34
Mountain-200 Silver, 38	$589,277.46	4,332.92
Grand Total	$2,521,070.96	6,010.69

FIGURE 13-40 Adding the *AverageSalesAmount* calculated field breaks the PivotTable, making it show incorrect values.

Again, something strange is happening here. Instead of seeing only the top seller, now each year shows the sales of the top seller plus some additional rows with the average sales amount of all the products that are top sellers in at least one of the years. In fact, in 2006, you can see all four products that are top products in one year, whereas in 2005, there are only a couple of them (that is, products that were sold at least once during that year).

Another important consideration is that the sum of sales amount is visible only for the top seller, whereas it is empty for other products, even if they have sales during the year. It is clear that something weird is happening with the *AverageSalesAmount* formula.

To understand what is happening here, you need to take this a step further and understand that, to show only the top seller, Excel has created a filter on the data model that filters both the year and the products, making visible only the top seller for each product and year. Thus, the filter will show a different product for each year. The scenario is similar to the previous one, but this time, the filter works on different tables. Yet, it is a single filter working on two separate columns.

Inside your formula, you iterate the dates and compute, for each date, the sum of the sales amounts. Because *Sum Of SalesAmount* is a calculated field, a context transition happens, replacing the filter on *DimDate* with the currently iterated one. The replacement of the filter on *DimDate* removes the dependency between year and product from the filter context and, as happened in the previous example, Excel computes the measure for all the selected products, iterating more rows than necessary.

What you want to do, even in this case, is to tell DAX to iterate the current date and not replace the original filter, but keep it in place. You want to iterate *DimDate*, taking into account any previously existing filter and iterating the dates only for the products that were previously selected (that is, the top-selling product for the year considered in the PivotTable). If you rewrite the formula using *KEEPFILTERS* in this way, here is what the code looks like:

```
AverageSalesAmount :=
AVERAGEX (
    KEEPFILTERS ( VALUES ( DimDate ) ),
    [Sum of SalesAmount]
)
```

The result is exactly what you wanted, as shown in Figure 13-41.

Row Labels	Sum of SalesAmount	AverageSalesAmount
⊟ 2005	$593,992.82	5,603.71
Road-150 Red, 62	$593,992.82	5,603.71
⊟ 2006	$658,401.68	5,352.86
Road-150 Red, 48	$658,401.68	5,352.86
⊟ 2007	$679,399.00	3,363.36
Mountain-200 Black, 46	$679,399.00	3,363.36
⊟ 2008	$589,277.46	4,332.92
Mountain-200 Silver, 38	$589,277.46	4,332.92
Grand Total	$2,521,070.96	4,446.33

FIGURE 13-41 Using *KEEPFILTERS,* the PivotTable works the way you want.

Now the average of the sales amounts takes into account only the top seller, ignoring other products, because the filter on *DimDate* does not replace the entire previously selected filter context, but rather merges with it, producing the correct result.

KEEPFILTERS is not an easy function to master. It is useful whenever a filter is set by Excel on more than one column and, inside your formula, you override the filter context on one of the columns by using a *CALCULATE* function. In such a case, the entire original filter context is lost, and you are likely to get incorrect values as a result. Once you have detected the issue, correcting it is simple: You need to use *KEEPFILTERS* to modify the behavior of *CALCULATE* so that it merges the new filter context with the old one, preserving the original filtering.

The key to using *KEEPFILTERS* effectively lies in understanding why and when it is needed. Moreover, it is hard to forecast in advance if *KEEPFILTERS* will be required for a specific formula. In fact, the need for using *KEEPFILTERS* comes from both the shape of the DAX formula and the filtering that happens in the query sent to PowerPivot.

Implementing basket analysis

In previous sections of this chapter, you have learned the basics of many-to-many relationships. In this section, you can apply this knowledge to a common scenario in which many-to-many relationships are not so evident: performing basket analysis using the many-to-many pattern. Because this formula is very complex, you develop it in many steps, starting from simpler expressions and then increasing the complexity of both the data model and of the formulas.

First, let's focus on the scenario. A data analyst at Adventure Works is interested in answering a simple question: "Of all the customers who bought a mountain bike, how many have never bought a mountain bike tire tube?" This scenario is worth looking at for a couple of reasons:

- You will use the DimCustomer and DimProduct tables to perform this analysis. This time, the sales table will be a bridge table to create a many-to-many relationship between these two tables, resulting in a creative way of using many-to-many relationships.

- You want to search for missing values, which are customers who bought a mountain bike (this is existing information) but did not buy a mountain tire tube (a missing piece of information).

Let's start by looking at the data model, shown in Figure 13-42, which is simple.

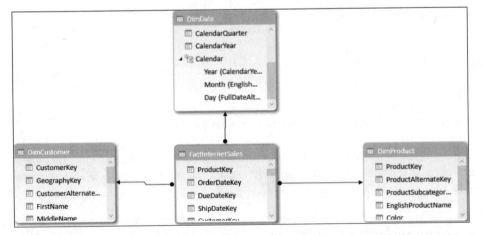

FIGURE 13-42 For this example, you use this data model to perform basket analysis using many-to-many relationships.

Using this data model, you already know how to count the number of customers who bought a specific product. There are many ways to perform this calculation. One good option is the following:

```
BuyingCustomers :=
CALCULATE (
    COUNTROWS ( DimCustomer ),
    FILTER (
        DimCustomer,
        CALCULATE ( COUNTROWS ( FactInternetSales ) ) > 0
    )
)
```

This expression is rather simple: you count the number of customers after you filtered only the ones that have some rows in the FactInternetSales (that is, they have sales associated with them).

Note Previously, we said that the many-to-many pattern can be expressed easily using just the table name instead of the *FILTER*. We have not used the optimized version here because, later in this section, you will modify the formula; you will need the expanded version with *COUNTROWS*.

Using this formula, you create a PivotTable like the one in Figure 13-43.

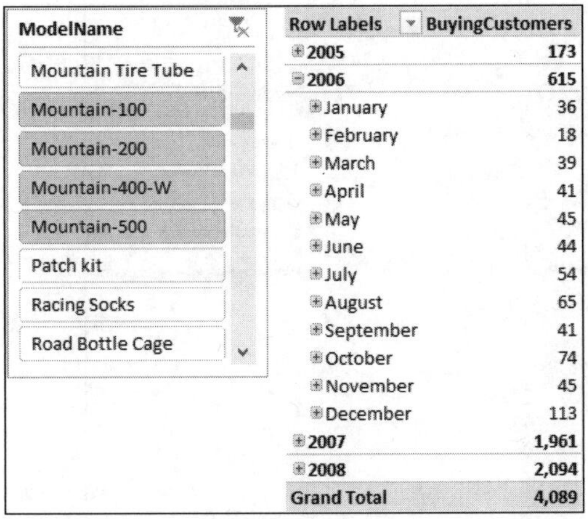

ModelName		Row Labels	BuyingCustomers
Mountain Tire Tube		2005	173
Mountain-100		2006	615
Mountain-200		January	36
Mountain-400-W		February	18
Mountain-500		March	39
Patch kit		April	41
Racing Socks		May	45
Road Bottle Cage		June	44
		July	54
		August	65
		September	41
		October	74
		November	45
		December	113
		2007	1,961
		2008	2,094
		Grand Total	4,089

FIGURE 13-43 The *BuyingCustomers* calculated field works in the presence of slicers on product models.

From this starting solution, you can count the number of customers who bought a specific product or family of products. You already learned how to write similar expressions, so here is where it gets more challenging—when the scenario starts to change.

For the needs of our analysis, the data model is not enough. In fact, using the DimProduct table, you can select one product by using a slicer or a filter. If you look carefully at what the analysis needs, it turns out that you must select two products: one is the mountain bike (the product sold); the other one is the mountain bike tire tube (the product you want to analyze). There is no way to select two products for different roles by using a single slicer.

Therefore, the data model must include a new instance of the DimProduct table, which is needed to perform the second filtering. Because you are loading the DimProduct table twice, it will be hard to follow the formulas if you call them DimProduct and DimProduct1. It is a good idea, then, to rename both tables and call one ProductBought (the mountain bike) and the other one ProductToCheck (the mountain tire tube).

Figure 13-44 shows the resulting diagram.

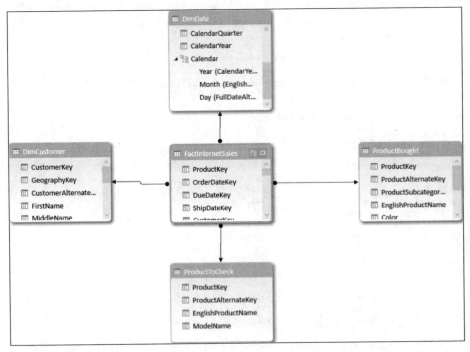

FIGURE 13-44 The new instances of DimProduct, with the more descriptive names for both DimProduct tables, is useful to filter two products.

Now this data model has two product tables, both of which are linked to the ProductKey column in the FactInternetSales table. PowerPivot, by default, keeps these relationships active, as the diagram indicates. In such a scenario, if you select two different products in the two tables, you will always end up with an empty result because both tables will try to filter the fact table, and since no product is equal to another one, they will conflict with each other.

Because you want to activate the relationships only when needed, it is better to designate both of them as inactive. You can do this by using the Manage Relationship button on the Design tab of the PowerPivot ribbon. This will open the Manage Relationship dialog box, where you see all the relationships in the data model. Figure 13-45 shows the Manage Relationship dialog box, with the relationships already disabled.

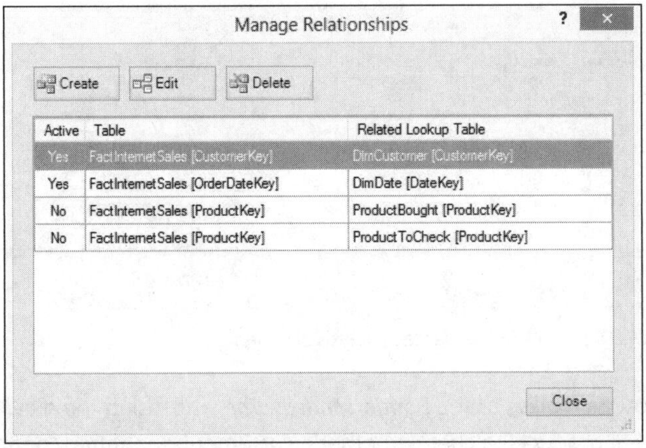

FIGURE 13-45 The relationships between FactInternetSales and the two product tables should be disabled in the Manage Relationships dialog box.

Because you define the relationships in the data model but mark them as inactive, they are used only when requested through *USERELATIONSHIP*, as you will do next.

> **Important** Always pay attention when there are many relationships starting from a single key in a table and pointing to different lookup tables. PowerPivot leaves them active by default, but there are few cases in which you want two lookup relationships active on the same key. We personally find that it is better to disable them and activate only the ones we need inside the formulas. Otherwise, there is always the risk of incurring complex side effects due to the interactions between the relationships. An interesting exercise would be to leave one of these two relationships (for example, the one with DimProduct) active and try to make the formula work. We suggest the brave reader take some time to do it, after learning the easier version that we provide here.

Before learning the solution, it might be worth looking at the final result you want to reach. Recall the original question: "Of all the customers who bought a mountain bike, how many have never bought a mountain bike tire tube?" In Figure 13-46, you see a report using this data model.

ML Road Front Wheel	ML Road Handlebars	ML Road Pedal	ML Road Rear Wheel
ML Road Seat/Saddle 2	ML Road Tire	ML Touring Seat/Sad...	Mountain Bike Socks
Mountain Bottle Cage	Mountain Pump	Mountain Tire Tube	Mountain-100
Mountain-200	Mountain-300	Mountain-400-W	Mountain-500

BoughtModelName

Mountain Tire Tube
Mountain-100
Mountain-200
Mountain-400-W
Mountain-500
Patch kit
Racing Socks
Road Bottle Cage
Road Tire Tube
Road-150
Road-250

BoughtProduct — Column Labels

Row Labels	July	August	September	October	November	December	2007 Total	2008	Grand Total
Mountain-100	364	346	326	317	312	310	310	291	291
Mountain Bottle Cage	373	358	343	337	334	333	333	321	321
Mountain Pump	396	396	396	396	396	396	396	396	396
Mountain Tire Tube	387	384	379	376	374	373	373	365	365
Mountain-200	1,144	1,195	1,254	1,284	1,324	1,408	1,408	1,951	1,951
Mountain Bottle Cage	1,163	1,234	1,306	1,352	1,416	1,533	1,533	2,275	2,275
Mountain Pump	1,202	1,304	1,424	1,515	1,629	1,829	1,829	3,011	3,011
Mountain Tire Tube	1,182	1,264	1,370	1,444	1,532	1,698	1,698	2,668	2,668
Mountain-400-W	13	31	53	78	104	159	159	415	415
Mountain Bottle Cage	19	42	67	98	131	192	192	496	496
Mountain Pump	20	45	73	107	141	205	205	543	543
Mountain Tire Tube	14	34	59	87	114	172	172	460	460
Mountain-500	12	25	39	53	69	102	102	251	251
Mountain Bottle Cage	13	27	44	59	78	120	120	307	307
Mountain Pump	23	47	75	103	132	193	193	479	479
Mountain Tire Tube	22	45	70	96	122	173	173	421	421
Grand Total	1,490	1,532	1,566	1,608	1,677	1,836	1,836	2,698	2,698

FIGURE 13-46 This Excel PivotTable shows the result of the basket analysis scenario.

Note that we selected several mountain bikes as the *BoughtModelName,* and, using the slicer for *CheckModelName,* selected several products to check whether a customer bought both or not. The number shown is the number of customers who bought a mountain bike in the selected list (Mountain-100 through Mountain-500) and not any of the selected *CheckModelNames*. For example, the highlighted cell means that 396 customers bought a Mountain-100 bike but no mountain pump. At the aggregated level of Mountain-100, the number is lower (364) because it is the number of customers that did not buy a bottle cage, pump, or tire tube.

There is a little issue with the handling of dates. When a time period has been selected, do you want to detect the customer who bought the mountain bike during that time period, or at any time before it? The correct solution (or, at least, the one we are talking about) is "before or during this period." After all, if we are analyzing customers in 2008, we want to count customers that bought a mountain bike either in 2007 or 2008, yet did not buy a mountain pump, bottle cage, or tire tube in that same period.

The problem can be analyzed in two steps:

1. Detect all the customers who bought a Mountain bike before or within the date range selected.

2. Check whether these customers have bought one of the products selected in *CheckProductName* in the same date range (before or within the specific period of time).

You already solved the first part of this scenario, but now you have added a few conditions that make the formula a bit harder to write; that is, the handling of dates (check if the customer bought the bike any time before the current period) and the relationship status, which is now inactive. To solve both problems, you need to update the formula using this code (the updated part is shown in bold):

```
BuyingCustomers :=
CALCULATE (
    COUNTROWS ( DimCustomer ),
    CALCULATETABLE (
        FILTER (
            DimCustomer,
            CALCULATE (
                COUNTROWS ( FactInternetSales ),
                USERELATIONSHIP (
                    FactInternetSales[ProductKey],
                    ProductBought[ProductKey]
                )
            ) > 0
        ),
        FILTER (
            ALL ( DimDate ),
            DimDate[FullDateAlternateKey] <= MAX ( DimDate[FullDateAlternateKey] )
        )
    )
)
```

Even if this formula looks complex, it is really a simple variation of the previous one. We added *CALCULATETABLE* on top of the *FILTER* on *DimCustomer* so to add the condition on the DimDate table (see the bold code), which changes the filter context for *DimDate* showing all the time periods before (and including) the currently selected one. Thus, in January 2010, the DimTime table will show all years before and including January 2010.

Finally, we extended the check of existence of any row in the sales table (done with *COUNTROWS*) with the *USERELATIONSHIP* function. *USERELATIONSHIP* makes a calculation using a specific relationship. Because the relationship between FactInternetSales and ProductBought is inactive, by means of using *USERELATIONSHIP* we activate it during the calculation of *COUNTROWS* (FactInternetSales). This is the standard way of activating inactive relationships during a formula evaluation.

With this new (and more complex) formula, we are now able to compute the number of customers who bought a particular product. Yet, point number 2 still needs addressing: We want to see if the same customer bought one of the ProductToCheck items.

It is now time to look at the complete formula:

```
BoughtProduct :=
CALCULATE (
    COUNTROWS ( DimCustomer ),
    CALCULATETABLE (
        FILTER (
            DimCustomer,
            AND (
                CALCULATE (
                    COUNTROWS ( FactInternetSales ),
                    USERELATIONSHIP (
                        FactInternetSales[ProductKey],
                        ProductBought[ProductKey]
                    )
                ) > 0,
                CALCULATE (
                    COUNTROWS ( FactInternetSales ),
                    USERELATIONSHIP (
                        FactInternetSales[ProductKey],
                        ProductToCheck[ProductKey]
                    )
                ) = 0
            )
        ),
        FILTER (
            ALL ( DimDate ),
            DimDate[FullDateAlternateKey] < MAX ( DimDate[FullDateAlternateKey] )
        )
    )
)
```

The selected part (shown in bold) is the addition to the previous expression. If you look at it carefully, you see that it performs the same check as the previous *COUNTROWS* but, this time, there are two important differences:

1. The *USERELATIONSHIP* function activates the relationship between FactInternetSales and the ProductToCheck table. This means that *COUNTROWS* will act on FactInternetSales under a filter propagated from ProductToCheck, not ProductBought.

2. The test does not check if *COUNTROWS* is greater than zero. This time, it checks if the result is zero; that is, it checks that there are no rows visible in FactInternetSales. This is the reason we have not used the optimized version of the many-to-many pattern here: the optimized version cannot find missing values.

The sum of these conditions can be read, in English, as "Check that there are no sales for the selected customer and any product in the ProductToCheck table." The formula, at the end, solves the scenario, showing the number of customers who bought one product but did not buy another one.

This scenario is worth looking at because it has some peculiarities:

- It uses the many-to-many relationships pattern, even if the pattern was not evident in the first formulation of the scenario. In fact, in this case, we used FactInternetSales as the bridge table between products and customers.

- It used the many-to-many pattern to find negative information. You have seen that by simply changing the condition from greater than zero to equal to zero, you have been able to find customers who did or did not buy a product.

Understanding the power of calculated columns: ABC analysis

Calculated columns are stored inside the database. You learned this during the first chapters of this book, and at this point, it should no longer surprise you. That said, this simple fact opens the door to new ways of modeling data, and this section looks at some scenarios that you can solve efficiently with calculated columns.

As an example of using calculated columns, you will learn how to handle the scenario of ABC analysis using PowerPivot. ABC analysis is based on the Pareto principle. In fact, it is sometimes known as *ABC/Pareto analysis,* and it is a common technique to determine the core business of a company, typically in terms of best products or best customers. In this example, we focus on products.

The goal of ABC analysis is to assign to each product a category (A, B, or C) by which the following is true:

- Products in class A account for 70 percent of the revenues.

- Products in class B account for 20 percent of the revenues.

- Products in class C account for the remaining 10 percent of the revenues.

The goal of ABC analysis is to identify which products have a significant impact on the overall business so that managers can focus their effort on them. You can find more information on ABC analysis at *http://en.wikipedia.org/wiki/ABC_analysis.*

The *ABC* class of a product needs to be stored in a calculated column because you want to use it to perform analysis on products slicing information by class. For example, in Figure 13-47, you can see a simple PivotTable using the *ABC* class on the rows.

Row Labels ▾	NumOfProducts	Sum of SalesAmount
A	35	$20,305,686.47
B	29	$6,048,561.50
C	542	$3,004,429.25
Grand Total	606	$29,358,677.22

FIGURE 13-47 The *ABC* class is used in this PivotTable to show products and sales.

As it often happens with ABC analysis, you can see that only a few products are in class A. This is the core business of Adventure Works. Products in class B are less important but still vital for the company, whereas products in class C are good candidates for removal because there are many of them and their share of revenues is tiny compared to the core products.

Let's start reviewing the data model for this scenario, shown in Figure 13-48.

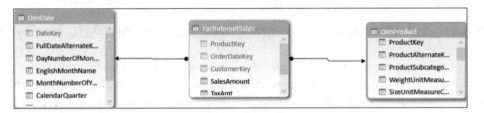

FIGURE 13-48 The data model to compute *ABC* classes for products is simple.

The data model in this scenario is simple because you need only sales and products.

To compute the *ABC* class of a product, you must compute the total sales of that product and compare it with the grand total. This gives you the percentage of the overall sales for which that single product accounts. Then, you sort products based on that percentage and perform a rolling sum. As soon as the rolling sum reaches 70 percent, you have identified products in class A. The remaining products will be in class B until you reach 90 percent (70+20), and then any further products will be in class C. You will build the complete calculations using only calculated columns.

First, you need a calculated column in the DimProduct table that contains the sales for that product. This can be easily accomplished using this expression:

```
TotalSales = CALCULATE ( SUM ( FactInternetSales[SalesAmount] ) )
```

In Figure 13-49, you see the DimProduct table with this new calculated column, in which data is sorted by *TotalSales* in descending order.

EnglishProductName	ModelName	TotalSales
Road-150 Red, 62	Road-150	$1,202,298.72
Road-150 Red, 52	Road-150	$1,080,637.54
Road-150 Red, 56	Road-150	$1,055,589.65
Road-150 Red, 44	Road-150	$1,005,493.87
Mountain-200 Black, 42	Mountain-200	$979,960.73
Mountain-200 Silver, 38	Mountain-200	$979,035.78
Mountain-200 Black, 46	Mountain-200	$961,600.81
Mountain-200 Black, 38	Mountain-200	$954,715.84
Mountain-200 Silver, 46	Mountain-200	$930,315.99
Mountain-200 Silver, 42	Mountain-200	$909,436.08
Touring-1000 Blue, 46	Touring-1000	$421,980.39
Road-350-W Yellow, 40	Road-350-W	$418,443.54
Mountain-200 Black, 46	Mountain-200	$411,868.74

FIGURE 13-49 TotalSales is included as a calculated column in the DimProduct table.

The next step is to compute a running total of *TotalSales* over the DimProduct table ordered by *TotalSales*. Because there is no way to sort a table and iterate over it in DAX, you need a different approach, which has to be set-based. If you think in terms of sets, the running total of each product is the sum of all the products that have a value for *TotalSales* that is greater than or equal to the current one. Clearly, this definition is not iterative and thus is harder to imagine. Nevertheless, this is the DAX way to produce running totals. You can define a new calculated column, RunningTotalSales, with the following formula:

```
RunningTotalSales =
SUMX (
    FILTER (
        DimProduct,
        DimProduct[TotalSales] >= EARLIER ( DimProduct[TotalSales] )
    ),
    DimProduct[TotalSales]
)
```

In Figure 13-50, you see the DimProduct table with this new column.

EnglishProductName	ModelName	TotalSales	RunningTotalSales
Road-150 Red, 62	Road-150	$1,202,298.72	$2,408,175.71
Road-150 Red, 52	Road-150	$1,080,637.54	$3,488,813.25
Road-150 Red, 56	Road-150	$1,055,589.65	$4,544,402.90
Road-150 Red, 44	Road-150	$1,005,493.87	$5,549,896.77
Mountain-200 Black, 42	Mountain-200	$979,960.73	$6,529,857.50
Mountain-200 Silver, 38	Mountain-200	$979,035.78	$7,508,893.28
Mountain-200 Black, 46	Mountain-200	$961,600.81	$8,470,494.09
Mountain-200 Black, 38	Mountain-200	$954,715.84	$9,425,209.93
Mountain-200 Silver, 46	Mountain-200	$930,315.99	$10,355,525.92
Mountain-200 Silver, 42	Mountain-200	$909,436.08	$11,264,962.00
Touring-1000 Blue, 46	Touring-1000	$421,980.39	$11,686,942.39
Road-350-W Yellow, 40	Road-350-W	$418,443.54	$12,105,385.93
Mountain-200 Black, 46	Mountain-200	$411,868.74	$12,517,254.67

FIGURE 13-50 The RunningTotalSales column lists a running total over rows sorted by the values in the TotalSales column.

The final point is to compute the running total sales as a percentage of the grand total of sales. A new calculated column easily solves this problem. You can add a RunningPct column with this formula:

```
RunningPct = DimProduct[RunningTotalSales] / SUM ( DimProduct[TotalSales] )
```

Because *SUM,* computed at the denominator, lies outside any *CALCULATE,* that sum is the grand total of sales, whereas the *RunningTotalSales* is the running total of the row inside which the formula is evaluated. In Figure 13-51, you see the new calculated column, which has been formatted as a percentage to make the result more understandable.

EnglishProductName	ModelName	TotalSales	RunningTotalSales	RunningPct
Road-150 Red, 48	Road-150	$1,205,876.99	$1,205,876.99	4.11 %
Road-150 Red, 62	Road-150	$1,202,298.72	$2,408,175.71	8.20 %
Road-150 Red, 62	Road-150	$1,202,298.72	$2,408,175.71	8.20 %
Road-150 Red, 52	Road-150	$1,080,637.54	$3,488,813.25	11.88 %
Road-150 Red, 56	Road-150	$1,055,589.65	$4,544,402.90	15.48 %
Road-150 Red, 44	Road-150	$1,005,493.87	$5,549,896.77	18.90 %
Mountain-200 Black, 42	Mountain-200	$979,960.73	$6,529,857.50	22.24 %
Mountain-200 Silver, 38	Mountain-200	$979,035.78	$7,508,893.28	25.58 %
Mountain-200 Black, 46	Mountain-200	$961,600.81	$8,470,494.09	28.85 %
Mountain-200 Black, 38	Mountain-200	$954,715.84	$9,425,209.93	32.10 %
Mountain-200 Silver, 46	Mountain-200	$930,315.99	$10,355,525.92	35.27 %
Mountain-200 Silver, 42	Mountain-200	$909,436.08	$11,264,962.00	38.37 %
Touring-1000 Blue, 46	Touring-1000	$421,980.39	$11,686,942.39	39.81 %

FIGURE 13-51 Here, the RunningPct column includes the percentage of running total based on the grand total.

The work is almost complete now. The final touch is to categorize the percentages into the various classes. If you use the values of 70, 20, and 10, the formula for the ABC class is straightforward:

```
ABC Class =
IF (
    DimProduct[RunningPct] <= 0.7,
    "A",
    IF (
        DimProduct[RunningPct] <= 0.9,
        "B",
        "C"
    )
)
```

You can see the result in Figure 13-52.

EnglishProductName	ModelName	TotalSales	RunningTotalSales	RunningPct	ABC Class
Road-150 Red, 48	Road-150	$1,205,876.99	$1,205,876.99	4.11 %	A
Road-150 Red, 62	Road-150	$1,202,298.72	$2,408,175.71	8.20 %	A
Road-150 Red, 52	Road-150	$1,080,637.54	$3,488,813.25	11.88 %	A
Road-150 Red, 56	Road-150	$1,055,589.65	$4,544,402.90	15.48 %	A
Road-150 Red, 44	Road-150	$1,005,493.87	$5,549,896.77	18.90 %	A
Mountain-200 Black, 42	Mountain-200	$979,960.73	$6,529,857.50	22.24 %	A
Mountain-200 Silver, 38	Mountain-200	$979,035.78	$7,508,893.28	25.58 %	A
Mountain-200 Black, 46	Mountain-200	$961,600.81	$8,470,494.09	28.85 %	A
Mountain-200 Black, 38	Mountain-200	$954,715.84	$9,425,209.93	32.10 %	A
Mountain-200 Silver, 46	Mountain-200	$930,315.99	$10,355,525.92	35.27 %	A
Mountain-200 Silver, 42	Mountain-200	$909,436.08	$11,264,962.00	38.37 %	A
Touring-1000 Blue, 46	Touring-1000	$421,980.39	$11,686,942.39	39.81 %	A
Road-350-W Yellow, 40	Road-350-W	$418,443.54	$12,105,385.93	41.23 %	A

FIGURE 13-52 The result of the ABC class is the calculated column called ABC Class.

Because ABC Class is a calculated column, it is stored inside the database, and you can use it on slicers, filters, and rows or columns to produce interesting reports.

In Chapter 14, "Using DAX as a query language," you will learn how to compute ABC analysis with a different approach, which requires the linking back of DAX queries. Both examples are useful, and we suggest that you study both so you have more ways to solve the same scenario.

Handling currency conversion

Another common pattern is currency conversion. There are many techniques to implement currency conversion in a PowerPivot report, and we do not pretend to explain the definitive one, even because requirements are very different when it comes to this scenario. We are going to describe a possible solution to a specific scenario, based on the techniques that you have learned so far for complex relationships.

Three possible scenarios involve currency conversion:

- Data have been collected in a single currency and you want to include results in different currencies in a report or other document. For example, you collected data in USD and want to show values as their corresponding values in British pounds (GBP).

- Data have been collected in many different currencies, and you want to display results in a single one so you can make comparisons. For example, you collected data both in USD and GBP, but you want to show results as their corresponding USD values.

- Data have been collected in many different currencies and you want to display results in many currencies, letting the user decide which currency to use (for example, through a slicer selection) for a report. For example, you collected data both in USD and GBP, and you want the user to decide whether to show results as the corresponding USD or GBP values, using a single currency for the whole report.

This list is just the beginning of the complexity that you need to delve into when handling currency conversion, but more complex scenarios are often harder and will require you to be even more precise in the definition of the algorithms. Because all three scenarios require currency conversion, the first question is: Which date are you going to use to perform the conversion? Here, the business rules become very complex. If the order was placed in euros on December 1, you might be tempted to use the currency exchange in place on December 1 to perform the conversion. But what if the customer paid in euros on December 12, the money was left in a euro account until the end of the month, and then, only on December 31 was it converted to USD? In that situation, which date would be the right one—December 1, 12, or 31? Only a deep analysis can guide you to make the right decision. Nevertheless, because we need to define a scenario and we want to use the *AdventureWorks* database, we will use the following rules:

- Amounts stored in the table are always in USD. Conversion happened at some point during the population of the table, and it used the currency exchange rate in place on the date of the order.

- You want to report information about sales in original currencies using two different currency exchange rates:

  - On the date of the order, there is a different exchange rate for each order.

  - You want to use the last available exchange rate (which should be the current exchange rate).

As we said, this is an educational example. In the real world, business rules might be different, and in each particular case, you will need to change the formulas and the techniques described here to fit your specific needs. You can find this model in the companion workbook "CH13-11-Currency Conversion.xlsx."

You start by loading DimDate, DimCurrency, FactInternetSales, and FactCurrencyRate into a new Excel workbook, and you end up with a data model like the one shown in Figure 13-53.

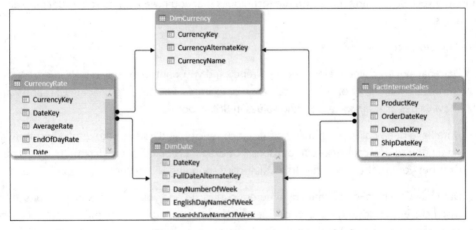

FIGURE 13-53 This is the data model that you are going to use for currency conversion in this example.

If you recall the basics of data modeling explained in Chapter 4, "Understanding data models," you will recognize that the data model is a star schema, where the fact table is related to two dimensions (DimDate and DimCurrency). The CurrencyRate table expresses, for each date and currency, the exchange rate. In this schema, where a single dimension is linked to many fact tables (two, in this case), BI professionals use the term *conformed dimensions*.

Amounts in the FactInternetSales table always represent USD values. Thus, a simple *SUM (FactInternetSales[SalesAmount])* expression will return the result in USD, as shown in Figure 13-54.

Sum of SalesAmount Row Labels	Column Labels 2005	2006	2007	2008	Grand Total
Australian Dollar	$1,309,047.20	$2,154,284.88	$3,033,784.21	$2,554,871.79	$9,051,988.08
Canadian Dollar	$146,829.81	$459,801.97	$536,262.23	$663,623.43	$1,806,517.44
Deutsche Mark	$237,784.99				$237,784.99
French Franc	$180,571.69				$180,571.69
United Kingdom Pound	$291,590.52	$591,586.85	$1,298,339.11	$1,206,833.21	$3,388,349.69
US Dollar	$1,100,549.45	$3,324,669.81	$4,922,674.74	$5,345,571.31	$14,693,465.32
Grand Total	$3,266,373.66	$6,530,343.53	$9,791,060.30	$9,770,899.74	$29,358,677.22

FIGURE 13-54 All the values shown in this PivotTable are in USD, even if the currency shows a different name.

The problem here is that you want to show the amounts in the original currencies using different exchange rates, and to perform this, you will need to create some calculated fields.

With this data model, it is easy to define a formula that computes each sales amount in terms of the original currency at the date of the order by using the *LOOKUPVALUE* function:

```
[OriginalCurrencyAmount] :=
SUMX (
    FactInternetSales,
    FactInternetSales[SalesAmount]
      * LOOKUPVALUE (
            CurrencyRate[EndOfDayRate],
            CurrencyRate[DateKey], FactInternetSales[OrderDateKey],
            CurrencyRate[CurrencyKey], FactInternetSales[CurrencyKey]
        )
)
```

LOOKUPVALUE is similar to *VLOOKUP:* it performs a search in the CurrencyRate table for the EndOfDayRate column, where DateKey in the CurrencyRate table equals OrderDateKey in the FactInternetSales table and the CurrencyKey columns in both tables are equal. It is more powerful than *VLOOKUP* because it can search using multiple conditions, all of which need to be equalities.

The formula iterates over all the orders, and for each order, it searches the correct currency rate in the CurrencyRate table so it can multiply the *SalesAmount* by the correct exchange rate. You can see the *OriginalCurrencyAmount* calculated field in Figure 13-55.

OriginalCurrencyAmount	Column Labels				
Row Labels	2005	2006	2007	2008	Grand Total
Australian Dollar	813,892.60	1,185,508.64	1,577,067.88	1,413,562.07	4,990,031.20
Canadian Dollar	100,183.70	305,393.40	340,559.13	425,551.42	1,171,687.65
Deutsche Mark	118,672.09				118,672.09
French Franc	26,914.37				26,914.37
United Kingdom Pound	466,779.48	865,911.80	1,865,021.06	1,856,667.71	5,054,380.05
US Dollar	1,100,549.45	3,324,669.81	4,922,674.74	5,345,571.31	14,693,465.32
Grand Total	2,626,991.70	5,681,483.66	8,705,322.81	9,041,352.52	26,055,150.69

FIGURE 13-55 The OriginalCurrencyAmount column shows the values using the original currency instead of USD.

There is still an issue with this formula at the grand total level. Because the values in different rows represent amounts expressed in different currencies, summing them has no meaning at all. The best option here is to blank out the grand total, adding an *IF* condition that removes the result if more than one currency is selected, as in the following code:

```
[OriginalCurrencyAmount] :=
IF (
    HASONEVALUE ( CurrencyRate[CurrencyKey] ),
    SUMX (
        FactInternetSales,
        FactInternetSales[SalesAmount]
        * LOOKUPVALUE (
            CurrencyRate[EndOfDayRate],
            CurrencyRate[DateKey], FactInternetSales[OrderDateKey],
            CurrencyRate[CurrencyKey], FactInternetSales[CurrencyKey]
        )
    )
)
```

The initial *IF* removes the grand total row, returning *BLANK ()* where many currencies are used, as in Figure 13-56.

OriginalCurrencyAmount	Column Labels				
Row Labels	2005	2006	2007	2008	Grand Total
Australian Dollar	813,892.60	1,185,508.64	1,577,067.88	1,413,562.07	4,990,031.20
Canadian Dollar	100,183.70	305,393.40	340,559.13	425,551.42	1,171,687.65
Deutsche Mark	118,672.09				118,672.09
French Franc	26,914.37				26,914.37
United Kingdom Pound	466,779.48	865,911.80	1,865,021.06	1,856,667.71	5,054,380.05
US Dollar	1,100,549.45	3,324,669.81	4,922,674.74	5,345,571.31	14,693,465.32

FIGURE 13-56 The grand total is cleared out using the *IF (HASONEVALUE ())* function.

On small data volumes, this formula is easy and works fine, but if you care about performance, it is not optimal. The reason for this is that *LOOKUPVALUE* is a complex formula that might slow computation to a crawl. If you have 100 million orders, you will start noticing that the formula is not as fast as it could be.

A better solution reduces the number of iterations. If you divide the FactInternetSales table into segments, each of which has a fixed exchange rate, then you can perform a massive computation the sum of the sales amount and multiply it by the single exchange rate. Looking at the formula should make the algorithm clearer. The following is a first shape for the formula:

```
[OriginalCurrencyAmount] :=
SUMX (
    DimCurrency,
    SUMX (
        DimDate,
        CALCULATE (
            VALUES ( CurrencyRate[AverageRate] )
                * SUM ( FactInternetSales[SalesAmount] )
        )
    )
)
```

The number of iterations is now much lower because it is equivalent to the number of dates and of currencies. For each combination of <Date, Currency>, there is a massive computation over the fact table that can be better optimized by the engine, thanks to its internal algorithms.

Now, what should you change in the formula to take into account the fact that you might want to use a different exchange rate? One of the requirements we had in mind was to be able to compute the value using the last available exchange rate. The formula, thanks to the power of DAX, is easy to create. This time, you do not need to iterate over DimDate because the value of the date does not change. You just have to iterate DimCurrency because the value of the exchange rate is different for each currency:

```
[OriginalCurrencyAmountLastDate] :=
CALCULATE (
    SUMX (
        DimCurrency,
        CALCULATE (
            VALUES ( CurrencyRate[AverageRate] )
                * SUM ( FactInternetsales[SalesAmount] )
        )
    ),
    FILTER (
        VALUES ( CurrencyRate[DateKey] ),
        CurrencyRate[DateKey] = MAX ( CurrencyRate[DateKey] )
    )
)
```

The last *FILTER* makes it visible only for the last available date in the currency rate table, and thus, the last available exchange rate. Inside *SUMX*, which iterates over the currencies, the inner *CALCULATE* further restricts the filter on *CurrencyRate* so that only one row is visible (that is, the one containing the exchange rate of the current currency for the last available date). It is clear that this formula outperforms the previous one in terms of speed because the number of iterations is reduced since there is no need to iterate over DimDate.

In this example, you have learned how to use DAX to implement basic currency conversion. Clearly, your scenario might be different from what we have been discussing, but these formulas can be the basis on which you can meet your specific needs.

CHAPTER 14

Using DAX as a query language

Throughout this book, you have learned that DAX is a powerful programming language that you can use to write formulas of different complexity and to build simple to complex Business Intelligence (BI) solutions. Chapter 13, "Using Advanced DAX," provided many examples that you can use in your daily work to build useful reports.

In this chapter, you will learn that DAX is a powerful querying language too. Up to this point in this book, you never worried about querying, mainly because in Microsoft Excel you use the PivotTable tool or the Power View reporting system to build queries. You never needed to create your own queries to build a report. So, what is the point in learning that DAX is a querying language, if you will never need to use it to query a data model? There are a few insights that you will get from knowing the querying options of DAX:

- You will learn to run DAX queries against your data model, load their result into Excel tables, and eventually push them back into the data model, discovering the tremendous power of double-step computation, where you mix Excel and DAX to create complex analysis.

- You will get better insights into the way that a PivotTable or a Power View report compute their results by taking information out of the data model. This will help you understand better what happens beneath the surface and, for some subtle scenarios, give you the weapons you need to understand why a specific formula behaves in a particular way.

Finally, there are many DAX functions that are useful to make queries and that are seldom used in formulas. That said, you can use the same functions to write complex formulas. In this chapter, we have grouped many of these functions, like *ROW, ADDCOLUMNS,* and *SUMMARIZE* that you have already used, for example, to handle many-to-many relationships.

Understanding *EVALUATE*

Querying DAX is a simple operation: you need to learn only a single statement, which is *EVALUATE*. *EVALUATE*, followed by any valid DAX expression that returns a table, will result in a valid DAX query that returns the table result.

For example, this is a simple DAX query:

```
EVALUATE
    FILTER (
        DimProduct,
        DimProduct[Color] = "Black"
    )
```

In this query, *FILTER* returns a table (that is, the table containing all the black products) and *EVALUATE* simply returns the result to the caller. *EVALUATE* has other options too, which will prove useful in specific scenarios even if, for an Excel user, they are not mandatory to learn. The full syntax of *EVALUATE* is the following:

```
[DEFINE { MEASURE <tableName>[<name>] = <expression> }]
EVALUATE <table>
[ORDER BY {<expression> [{ASC | DESC}]} [, …]
    [START AT {<value>|<parameter>} [, …]] ]
```

With *DEFINE*, you can create calculated fields that are local to the query (they are called *measures* in pure DAX terminology), *ORDER BY* is useful to specify the sort order of the result, and *START AT* is useful for paging. None of these options is important, with the notable exception of *ORDER BY*, which sometimes can be useful in Excel too.

Creating an Excel table with *EVALUATE*

Now that you know how to write a DAX query, it is interesting to see where you can use this new knowledge. You cannot use *EVALUATE* either in a calculated column or in a calculated field. The reason is simply that the result of EVALUATE is a table, and calculated columns and fields need a single value as their result. Because *EVALUATE* returns a table, a good place where to put its result might be an Excel table. You can use *EVALUATE* to fill an Excel table with the result of a DAX query, even if the procedure to follow is not very intuitive.

To fill an Excel table with a DAX query, you need to perform these steps:

1. Import data from a PowerPivot table into an Excel table. This operation loads the content of an entire PowerPivot table into an Excel table. You can think at this as a "reverse-linked table": instead of filling a PowerPivot table with the content of an Excel table, you do the opposite.

2. Modify the DAX code that fills the Excel table with your own DAX expression. This is the trickiest part of the procedure: not intuitive, but amazingly powerful.

Let's start with the first step. To reverse-link a PowerPivot table in Excel, you need to use the Existing Connections button on the DATA tab of the Excel ribbon, highlighted in Figure 14-1. You can follow this exercise using the companion workbook "CH14-01-Simple Query.xlsx."

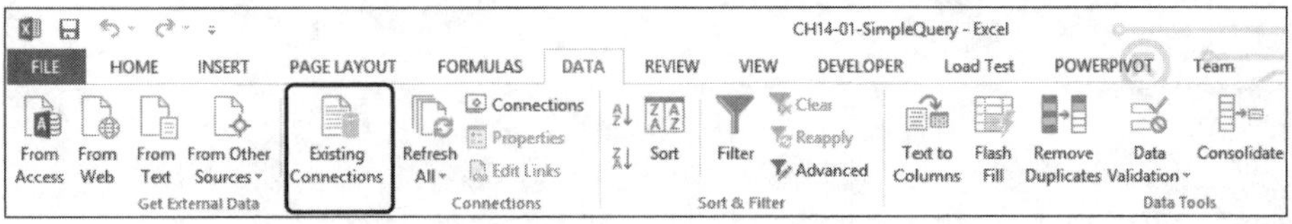

FIGURE 14-1 Here, you can see the Existing Connections button to load data from existing connections.

Clicking the button will open the Existing Connections dialog box, which lists all the connections that have already been created in this workbook or saved on your computer. There are two tabs in the dialog box: the second one, called Tables, is the one shown in Figure 14-2.

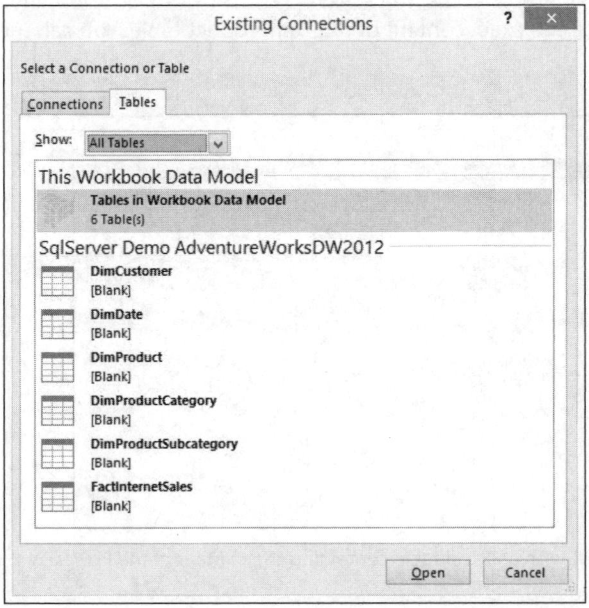

FIGURE 14-2 The Tables tab shows the tables available as connections in the current workbook.

Under the SqlServer Demo AdventureWorksDW2012 title (which happens to be the name of the connection used to load data in PowerPivot), you see the list of the tables of your data model. If you select DimProduct and click Open, Excel presents you with the Import Data dialog box, shown in Figure 14-3.

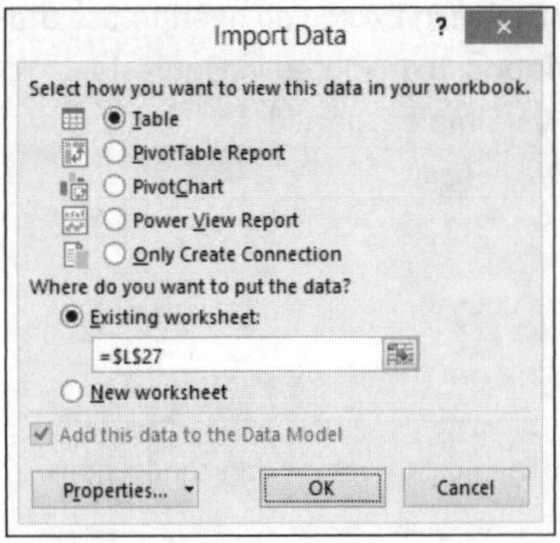

FIGURE 14-3 In the Import Data dialog box, you choose where to save the table that you selected previously.

Because you want to fill an Excel table with the DimProduct table, you can leave the selection on Table and then click OK to start the loading procedure. The process lasts for a few seconds, and then you will see a new Excel table containing the exact content of the DimProduct table. You can see the result in Figure 14-4.

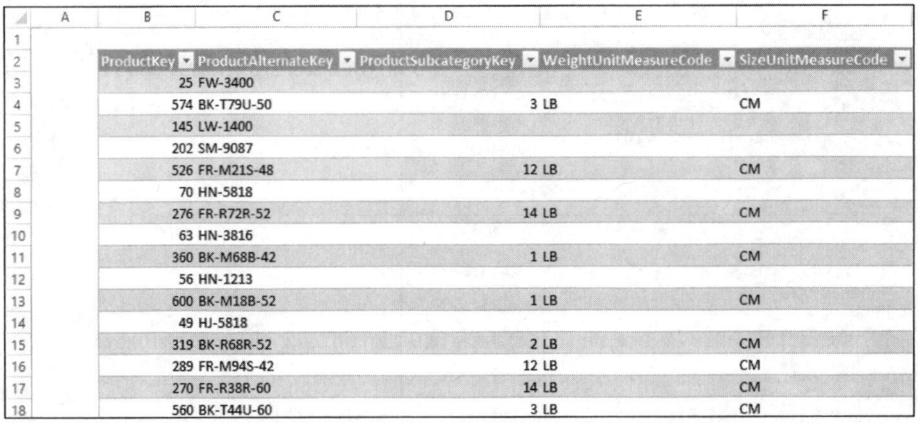

ProductKey	ProductAlternateKey	ProductSubcategoryKey	WeightUnitMeasureCode	SizeUnitMeasureCode
25	FW-3400			
574	BK-T79U-50	3	LB	CM
145	LW-1400			
202	SM-9087			
526	FR-M21S-48	12	LB	CM
70	HN-5818			
276	FR-R72R-52	14	LB	CM
63	HN-3816			
360	BK-M68B-42	1	LB	CM
56	HN-1213			
600	BK-M18B-52	1	LB	CM
49	HJ-5818			
319	BK-R68R-52	2	LB	CM
289	FR-M94S-42	12	LB	CM
270	FR-R38R-60	14	LB	CM
560	BK-T44U-60	3	LB	CM

FIGURE 14-4 The reverse-link operation ends with an Excel table containing the content of the PowerPivot table.

At this point, you have finished the reverse-link operation, and you have the content of a PowerPivot table in Excel.

> **Tip** You need to select a specific table to import it into Excel. Later, you will modify the source of the Excel table. Thus, the table you select at the beginning is not very important, but you need to select one. To save time, it is a good practice to always choose a small one during this first step, so that you do not need to wait for too many rows to be loaded in Excel before continuing with the rest of the steps.

This operation, alone, is already interesting because the Excel table is not a copy of the current content of the PowerPivot table. In reality, it is a live connection with the PowerPivot table and will be refreshed automatically as soon as the PowerPivot table is refreshed. Because it is an Excel table, you have the full power of Excel formulas available to investigate it or compute results. But from our point of view, this is only a partial result. What we really wanted to do is fill the Excel table with a DAX query.

Note Excel has a limit of 1 million rows for a table, whereas PowerPivot can handle much larger tables. Thus, trying to perform this operation with a PowerPivot table that contains more than 1 million rows will result in an error.

To perform the second step, you simply right-click inside the table and open the menu. Under the Table drop-down menu, you will find the Edit DAX option (see Figure 14-5), which is worth trying.

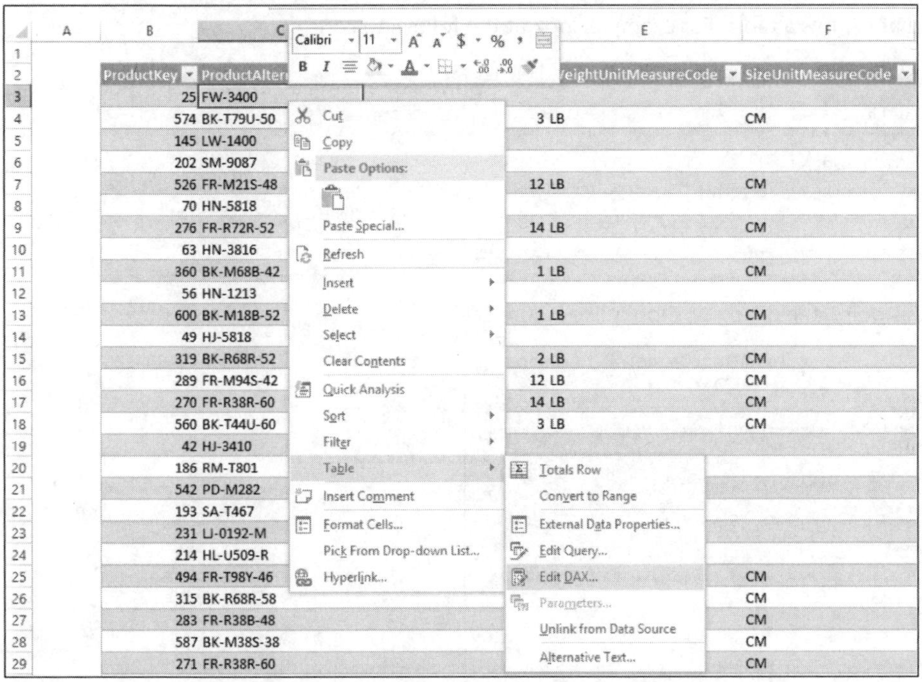

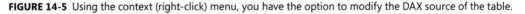

FIGURE 14-5 Using the context (right-click) menu, you have the option to modify the DAX source of the table.

Choosing Edit DAX, you will open the Edit DAX dialog box (see Figure 14-6), which is the place where you can modify the source of the Excel table. The Edit DAX dialog box is basic, offering only a combo box where you can choose Table or DAX.

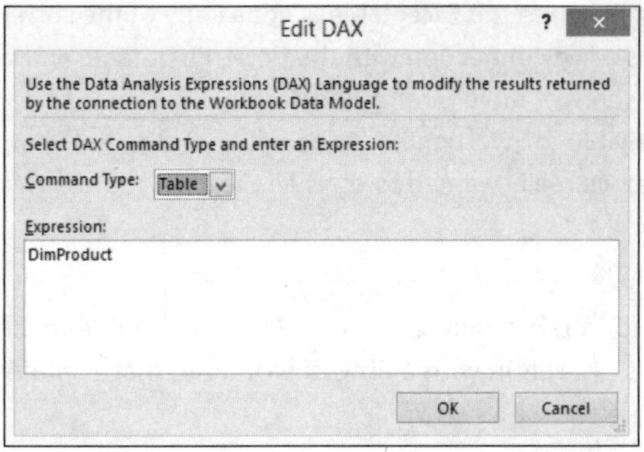

FIGURE 14-6 The Edit DAX dialog box is basic, yet it can be used for complex scenarios.

If you choose Table, then you need to provide the name of a table in the Expression text box. On the other hand, if you choose DAX, then you can write in the Expression text box any valid DAX query that returns a table. For example, look at the following code:

```
EVALUATE
    FILTER (
        DimProduct,
        DimProduct[Color] = "Black"
    )
```

At this point, the dialog box looks like Figure 14-7.

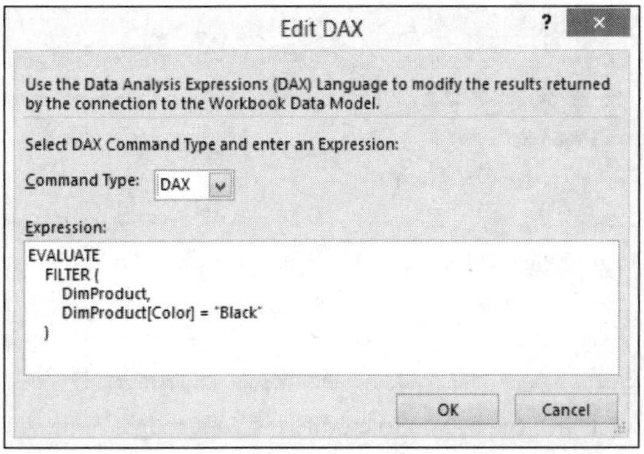

FIGURE 14-7 Using a DAX query will load the result of the query in the Excel table.

As soon as you click OK, Excel will refresh the table, and it will show only the black products. Moreover, if you refresh the data model with the most current information from the database, the table will be refreshed too because the query will be executed again on the new data.

It is clear that this feature, used with *FILTER*, is not very useful. We have used a simple expression just to show the procedure, but this tool becomes more useful as soon as you start learning more about DAX as a query language and you enrich your toolset of DAX functions to create queries that are better.

Using common functions in queries

Before you learn new functions, it is interesting to take a brief tour of functions that you already learned about in previous chapters. They will prove extremely useful in queries.

Using *FILTER*

As of now, you know all the secrets of the *FILTER* function, which can be very useful in queries. Before now, you probably thought of *FILTER* as an easy way to find some interesting rows inside a table that will be processed further by other functions. You can find this example in the companion workbook "CH14-02-FILTER.xlsx."

For example, if you wanted to count the number of red products in a table, you could use code like the following:

```
NumOfRedProducts := COUNTROWS ( FILTER ( DimProduct, DimProduct[Color] = "Red" ) )
```

In the calculated field, the result of *FILTER* is processed by *COUNTROWS* because the final result you want to obtain is a number, not a table. This is the common pattern of how *FILTER* is used in formulas: you are not really interested in the result of *FILTER,* but in a further computation of that result.

What makes *FILTER* a useful function in queries is the fact that you can retrieve the full result of *FILTER* and put it inside an Excel table. You already did this when you loaded your first Excel table with the black products.

But can you do even more with *FILTER?* The answer is yes, and it is because *FILTER* is an iterator, and you can use context transition to perform complex filtering and see the result easily.

Let's take as an example a common scenario: you want to see the list of products that sold more than twice as many in 2008 than in 2007. You can produce this report using a PivotTable, of course, but this would mean creating some nontrivial calculated fields, and you will need to handle the display of only the relevant products in the PivotTable. Such a result can be obtained easily by using a DAX query like the following:

```
EVALUATE
    FILTER (
        DimProduct,
        CALCULATE (
```

```
            SUM ( FactInternetSales[SalesAmount] ),
            DimDate[CalendarYear] = 2008
        )
        > CALCULATE (
            SUM ( FactInternetSales[SalesAmount] ),
            DimDate[CalendarYear] = 2007
        ) * 2
    )
```

The formula is simple to read: *FILTER* iterates all the products and, for each one, it checks if the sales in 2008 are greater than the sales in 2007 multiplied by 2. The resulting dataset is a list of products that fills an Excel table, as shown in Figure 14-8.

ProductKey	ProductAlternateKey	ProductSubcategoryKey	WeightUnitMeasureCode	SizeUnitMeasureCode	EnglishProductName
600	BK-M18B-52		1 LB	CM	Mountain-500 Black, 52
582	BK-R79Y-44		2 LB	CM	Road-350-W Yellow, 44
573	BK-T79U-46		3 LB	CM	Touring-1000 Blue, 46
599	BK-M18B-48		1 LB	CM	Mountain-500 Black, 48
575	BK-T79U-54		3 LB	CM	Touring-1000 Blue, 54
567	BK-T18U-62		3 LB	CM	Touring-3000 Blue, 62

FIGURE 14-8 Using DAX queries, you can easily produce a list of products with complex conditions.

This table contains all the columns in the DimProduct table. When producing a report, you will probably be interested in a selection of the columns, like the product name and product code. Later in this chapter, you will learn how to perform this selection using *SUMMARIZE*.

Using *CALCULATETABLE*

CALCULATETABLE is the companion of *CALCULATE*. Whereas *CALCULATE* returns a value, *CALCULATETABLE* returns a table. Even if you are probably used to working with *CALCULATE*, there have not been many examples in this book where *CALCULATETABLE* proved to be useful. The reason for this is that we were mainly interested in computing values as results.

Using *EVALUATE* and DAX as a query language, *CALCULATETABLE* becomes more interesting because you can use it whenever you want to apply filters to the data model and retrieve a list as a result. For example, if you are interested in the list of products of the Clothing category, you can use this simple query:

```
EVALUATE
    CALCULATETABLE (
        DimProduct,
        DimProductCategory[EnglishProductCategoryName] = "Clothing"
    )
```

As usual, it is important to note that the filter is on the DimProductCategory table, and the result is DimProduct, automatic context propagation makes the magic of showing only the products that belong to the requested category.

CALCULATETABLE behaves in a similar way to *FILTER*, but it is generally faster, and you can specify many filters on different tables in a single statement with relatively simple syntax. Generally, *CALCULATETABLE* is the preferred filtering function as the outermost function call in a DAX query, whereas *FILTER* is useful when you want to filter on columns that are computed in the inner functions or when you need to generate a row context using the iteration capabilities of *FILTER*.

Using *ADDCOLUMNS*

The first function that you learn in this chapter is *ADDCOLUMNS*. *ADDCOLUMNS* is an iterator that returns a table containing the same columns as its first parameter, enriched with a set of new columns that you specify as further parameters. An example is easier to understand than a theoretical explanation, so let's look at one. You can find this example in the companion workbook "CH14-03-ADDCOLUMNS.xlsx."

Take a look at the following example:

```
EVALUATE
    ADDCOLUMNS (
        DimProductCategory,
        "NumOfProducts",
        CALCULATE ( COUNTROWS ( DimProduct ) )
    )
```

The result of this code is a list of categories with a new column, NumOfProducts, containing the number of products in that category (see Figure 14-9).

ProductCategoryKey	ProductCategoryAlternateKey	EnglishProductCategoryName	NumOfProducts
1	1	Bikes	125
2	2	Components	189
3	3	Clothing	48
4	4	Accessories	35

FIGURE 14-9 *ADDCOLUMNS* adds new calculated columns to the result of a query.

The NumOfProducts column behaves like a calculated column, but it is not stored in the data model, it exists only for the lifetime of the query. You can add as many columns as you want to a table; for each column, you need to provide a name and an expression. The expression is evaluated in the row context created by the *ADDCOLUMNS* iterator, which, in our example, we convert to a filter context by using *CALCULATE*.

It is interesting to note at this point that the calculated column introduced by *ADDCOLUMNS* can be used in further expressions. Imagine that you want to filter, out of all the categories, only the ones that have more than 100 associated products. You can modify the expression in this way:

```
EVALUATE
    FILTER (
        ADDCOLUMNS (
            DimProductCategory,
            "NumOfProducts",
            CALCULATE ( COUNTROWS ( DimProduct ) )
        ),
        [NumOfProducts] > 100
    )
```

The outermost *FILTER* uses the NumOfProducts column to filter the categories that have less than 100 products. Even if the NumOfProducts column does not exists in the data model, you can use it inside the *FILTER* expression because it is created by *ADDCOLUMNS*, and during the time that the query is being executed, the column exists and can be used.

The same behavior is valid for other functions that add temporary columns to the model, like *SUMMARIZE*. It is important to note, however, that temporary columns created by functions like *SUMMARIZE* are available only if you create a row context, which is done by iterators like *FILTER*, but not by *SUMMARIZE*. For example, to test the result of a column added by *SUMMARIZE*, you need to use its result in a *FILTER* call:

```
EVALUATE
    FILTER (
        SUMMARIZE (
            DimProductCategory,
            DimProductCategory[EnglishProductCategoryname],
            "NumOfProducts",
            CALCULATE ( COUNTROWS ( DimProduct ) )
        ),
        [NumOfProducts] = > 100
    )
```

Using *VALUES* with *ADDCOLUMNS*

In previous chapters, you have learned about the *VALUES* function, which returns the values of a column filtered by the current filter context. As with other functions, you learned how to use *VALUES* with *CALCULATE* to push the outer filter context inside the *CALCULATE* one, or to count the number of values of a column. And, as with other functions, you are about to discover that *VALUES* can be useful in other scenarios, as soon as you start thinking at DAX as a query language.

Imagine that you want to create a simple table containing a product category name and the number of products for that category in each row. You already have learned the *ADDCOLUMN* syntax, but the result included all the columns of the DimProductCategory table.

You can use *VALUES* to retrieve a table containing the product category names only, and then extend this single-column table with the count. Look at this DAX query:

```
EVALUATE
    ADDCOLUMNS (
        VALUES ( DimProductCategory[EnglishProductCategoryName] ),
        "NumOfProducts",
        CALCULATE ( COUNTROWS ( DimProduct ) )
    )
```

This returns, as a result, the table shown in Figure 14-10.

EnglishProductCategoryName	NumOfProducts
Bikes	125
Components	189
Clothing	48
Accessories	35
	209

FIGURE 14-10 Using *VALUES*, you can use a single-column table and then extend it with new calculated columns.

You can see that the result does not contain all the columns of the DimProductCategory table, but only the EnglishProductCategoryName one, originally computed by *VALUES*.

> **Note** You may have noticed a blank row at the end of the table in Figure 14-10. That row contains the products that are not associated with a particular category. In fact, *VALUES* returns the set of values of a column, and if there are rows in related tables that reference no row in the current table, it adds a blank row to guarantee that all the possible "values" are represented, even invalid ones. Thus, you can think of *VALUES* as returning both valid and invalid values. If you want to see only the valid values, you can use *DISTINCT* instead of *VALUES*. *DISTINCT* does not return blank rows created by the engine for referential integrity.

Using *SUMMARIZE*

SUMMARIZE is probably the most commonly used function to create queries. It is extremely powerful and performs many meaningful tasks. Mastering it takes some time, but once you start using it, it will become your best friend in query writing.

Instead of starting with the full syntax of *SUMMARIZE*, which might be intimidating, it is better to start using it, look at the results, and show the many features of this function one step at a time. You can find the examples in this section in the companion workbook "CH14-04-SUMMARIZE.xlsx."

The first example of *SUMMARIZE* is simple. Look at the following query:

```
EVALUATE
    SUMMARIZE (
        DimProduct,
        DimProduct[Color]
    )
```

The result is very simple: the list of distinct values of DimProduct[Color], shown in Figure 14-11.

Color
NA
Black
Silver
Red
White
Blue
Multi
Yellow
Grey
Silver/Black

FIGURE 14-11 A simple *SUMMARIZE* function on a column returns the distinct values of the column.

SUMMARIZE performed a full scan of the DimProduct table and built the set of distinct values of the Color column. So far, you may not find this very exciting, but it starts to become more interesting if you provide additional parameters, as in the following expression:

```
EVALUATE
    SUMMARIZE (
        DimProduct,
        DimProduct[Color],
        DimProduct[SizeRange]
    )
```

The result is the set of distinct values of both columns. In Figure 14-12, you can see the first few rows of the resulting table.

Color	SizeRange
Black	38-40 CM
Black	42-46 CM
Grey	NA
Multi	L
Multi	M
Multi	NA
Multi	S
Multi	XL
NA	NA
Red	42-46 CM

FIGURE 14-12 Using *SUMMARIZE* on two columns returns the distinct combinations of the two columns.

You can see that only the valid combinations of Color and SizeRange are shown, while combinations that are not present in the DimProduct table are not returned. If you know the SQL language, this is exactly like using a *GROUP BY* clause in a *SELECT* statement. You can pass as many columns as you want after the initial table. These are known as GroupBy columns because they are the columns used to create the summary table returned as a result.

Note This first feature is already very useful in itself, but there is more. In fact, if you ever need to compute the number of distinct combinations of some columns, you can rely on *COUNTROWS* (*SUMMARIZE* (...)) to perform the calculation, without having to search for other, more complex solutions.

You are not limited to GroupBy columns, though. You can enrich the summary table with new columns, using a syntax similar to *ADDCOLUMNS*. For example, the following expression returns the distinct combinations of Color and SizeRange and, for each combination, the total sales (see results in Figure 14-13):

```
EVALUATE
    SUMMARIZE (
        DimProduct,
        DimProduct[Color],
        DimProduct[SizeRange],
        "Total Sales",
        SUM ( FactInternetSales[SalesAmount] )
    )
```

Color	SizeRange	Total Sales
Black	38-40 CM	1486160.171
Black	42-46 CM	4019104.826
Black	48-52 CM	2187284.353
Black	54-58 CM	860360.9476
Black	60-62 CM	106207
Black	L	36255.44

FIGURE 14-13 *SUMMARIZE* can add columns to the summary table.

The Total Sales column has been added to the summary table. It is important to note that *SUMMARIZE* is not an iterator, and therefore it does not create a row context. Instead, it creates a filter context under which the expression for the new columns is evaluated. This is the reason why you do not need a surrounding *CALCULATE* for the SUM (FactInternetSales[SalesAmount]) expression.

Another important feature of *SUMMARIZE* is the fact that you do not need to use GroupBy columns that belong to the same table that you are summarizing. Any column that can be reached through a chain of many-to-one relationships works fine. For example, if you want to show the total sales summarized by product category, you can run this query:

```
EVALUATE
    SUMMARIZE (
        DimProduct,
        DimProductCategory[EnglishProductCategoryName],
        "Total Sales",
        SUM ( FactInternetSales[SalesAmount] )
    )
```

The result can be seen in Figure 14-14.

EnglishProductCategoryName	Total Sales
Bikes	28318144.65
Components	
Clothing	339772.61
Accessories	700759.96

FIGURE 14-14 *SUMMARIZE* works with related columns too.

The reason why *SUMMARIZE* is so popular is that it is the only function in DAX that lets you reduce the number of columns returned as the result. In fact, you have seen that you can query the DimProduct table without needing to retrieve all its columns. *SUMMARIZE* does not really remove columns from the dataset. Rather, it creates a summary table that contains only the columns you need, providing grouped information for other columns that can be calculated.

Because you will often need to build reports based on the Excel data model, the chances are excellent that most of your queries will start with *SUMMARIZE,* so you can shape the final dataset the way you want.

Using the *ROLLUP* option

You have seen that with *SUMMARIZE,* you can define many GroupBy columns easily. Another kind of GroupBy column is available, which is the Rollup column. You define the Rollup column in a specific *ROLLUP* section of *SUMMARIZE*. Rollup columns produce the same behavior as the GroupBy column, but they also add subtotal rows.

For example, look at the following query:

```
EVALUATE
    SUMMARIZE (
        FactInternetSales,
        ROLLUP (
            DimProductCategory[EnglishProductCategoryName],
            DimDate[CalendarYear]
        ),
        "Total Sales",
        SUM ( FactInternetSales[SalesAmount] )
    )
```

Here, the category name and the calendar year are defined as Rollup columns. The resulting dataset is shown in Figure 14-15, where we have formatted the numbers to make them easier to read.

EnglishProductCategoryName	Total Sales	CalendarYear
Bikes	3,266,373.66	2005
Bikes	6,530,343.53	2006
Bikes	9,359,102.62	2007
Bikes	9,162,324.85	2008
Clothing	138,247.97	2007
Clothing	201,524.64	2008
Accessories	293,709.71	2007
Accessories	407,050.25	2008
Bikes	28,318,144.65	
Clothing	339,772.61	
Accessories	700,759.96	
	29,358,677.22	

FIGURE 14-15 Rollup columns produce additional subtotal rows.

You can see that there are some rows, near the bottom of the table, that contain blank values for the CalendarYear and for the EnglishProductCategoryName columns. These columns contain the subtotal for each category (the rows without the CalendarYear) and the grand total (the only row with blank values for both CalendarYear and EnglishProductCategoryName).

Using *SUMMARIZE* with *ROLLUP* returns a dataset that is similar to a PivotTable. Although *ROLLUP* is useful in many scenarios for BI professionals, Excel users do not use it very often because if the result you want to obtain looks so similar to a PivotTable, then maybe a PivotTable will be a better tool for producing the report. On the other hand, *SUMMARIZE* (without *ROLLUP*) is probably the most frequently used function to retrieve datasets because of the linking-back option that you will learn about in the next section.

Linking back a DAX query

Even though we have not yet covered all the DAX functions that are useful to build queries, it is time to introduce what we believe is the main reason why you will probably want to learn DAX as a query language—namely, the option to link back the result of a DAX query.

What is linking back? Before we go into detail about it, let's establish some terminology:

- A *linked table* is an Excel table that is linked to a PowerPivot table, meaning that the content of the Excel table is copied into the PowerPivot data model and refreshed whenever the original Excel table is updated.

- A *reverse-linked table* is a DAX query used as the source for an Excel table. Whenever the PowerPivot data model is updated, the query is executed again against the new data, and the Excel table is refreshed.

Thus, linked tables move data from Excel to PowerPivot, whereas reverse-linked tables move data from PowerPivot to Excel. It would be handy to have the option to take a reverse-linked table and create a new linked table from it. In fact, this can be done, and when you do that, you create a linked-back table.

A *linked-back table* is a DAX query used to fill an Excel table, which is then used as a linked table so that its content is pushed inside the PowerPivot data model again. Practically speaking, you store in the data model the result of a DAX query, which you can use to compute other calculated columns, calculated fields, or both.

This option opens the door to a completely new way of thinking about your solution. In fact, you can start from data in Excel, push it inside PowerPivot, and perform some computation. Then you build a query that retrieves data from the PowerPivot model and fill a new Excel table with its result. At this point, because the new table is an Excel table, you have the full power of the Excel language to build new cells with Excel formulas. At the end, you return the result to PowerPivot, so your new table can be used in PivotTables as if it were originally present in the data model.

Excel handles all the complexity of performing the refresh operations in the correct order to ensure that all your numbers are correctly computed. As a first example of linking back, let's see a simple example of its usage. You can find this example in the companion workbook "CH14-05-Link Back.xlsx."

Imagine that you want to see the top 25 sellers among your products. You can easily compute this query using the *TOPN* function, which returns the top *N* items out of a table:

```
EVALUATE
    SUMMARIZE (
        TOPN (
            25,
            DimProduct,
            CALCULATE ( SUM ( FactInternetSales[SalesAmount] ) )
        ),
        DimProduct[ProductKey],
        DimProduct[EnglishProductName],
        "Sales",
        SUM ( FactInternetSales[SalesAmount] )
    )
ORDER BY [Sales]
```

This query returns the 25 top-selling products, as shown in Figure 14-16, where the numbers are formatted to make it easier to read them.

ProductKey	EnglishProductName	Sales
312	Road-150 Red, 48	1,205,876.99
310	Road-150 Red, 62	1,202,298.72
313	Road-150 Red, 52	1,080,637.54
314	Road-150 Red, 56	1,055,589.65
311	Road-150 Red, 44	1,005,493.87
361	Mountain-200 Black, 42	979,960.73
353	Mountain-200 Silver, 38	979,035.78
363	Mountain-200 Black, 46	961,600.81
359	Mountain-200 Black, 38	954,715.84
357	Mountain-200 Silver, 46	930,315.99
355	Mountain-200 Silver, 42	909,436.08
573	Touring-1000 Blue, 46	421,980.39
580	Road-350-W Yellow, 40	418,443.54
362	Mountain-200 Black, 46	411,868.74
561	Touring-1000 Yellow, 46	410,060.04
581	Road-350-W Yellow, 42	399,732.65
369	Road-250 Red, 48	395,822.70
583	Road-350-W Yellow, 48	394,629.68
376	Road-250 Black, 48	383,605.95
360	Mountain-200 Black, 42	383,181.36
575	Touring-1000 Blue, 54	381,451.20
563	Touring-1000 Yellow, 54	376,683.06
371	Road-250 Red, 58	375,228.75
377	Road-250 Black, 52	375,228.75
356	Mountain-200 Silver, 46	370,784.11

FIGURE 14-16 Computing the top sellers using a query is straightforward.

Because this is an Excel table, you can then enrich the table with other calculations in Excel. For example, you can assign to each line a ranking number, using the Excel *RANK* function, and then perform a simple banding using the *IF* statement, obtaining a table like the one shown in Figure 14-17.

ProductKey	EnglishProductName	Sales	Position	Ranking
312	Road-150 Red, 48	1,205,876.99	1	TOP 5
310	Road-150 Red, 62	1,202,298.72	2	TOP 5
313	Road-150 Red, 52	1,080,637.54	3	TOP 5
314	Road-150 Red, 56	1,055,589.65	4	TOP 5
311	Road-150 Red, 44	1,005,493.87	5	TOP 5
361	Mountain-200 Black, 42	979,960.73	6	TOP 10
353	Mountain-200 Silver, 38	979,035.78	7	TOP 10
363	Mountain-200 Black, 46	961,600.81	8	TOP 10
359	Mountain-200 Black, 38	954,715.84	9	TOP 10
357	Mountain-200 Silver, 46	930,315.99	10	TOP 10
355	Mountain-200 Silver, 42	909,436.08	11	TOP 25
573	Touring-1000 Blue, 46	421,980.39	12	TOP 25
580	Road-350-W Yellow, 40	418,443.54	13	TOP 25
362	Mountain-200 Black, 46	411,868.74	14	TOP 25
561	Touring-1000 Yellow, 46	410,060.04	15	TOP 25
581	Road-350-W Yellow, 42	399,732.65	16	TOP 25
369	Road-250 Red, 48	395,822.70	17	TOP 25
583	Road-350-W Yellow, 48	394,629.68	18	TOP 25
376	Road-250 Black, 48	383,605.95	19	TOP 25
360	Mountain-200 Black, 42	383,181.36	20	TOP 25
575	Touring-1000 Blue, 54	381,451.20	21	TOP 25
563	Touring-1000 Yellow, 54	376,683.06	22	TOP 25
371	Road-250 Red, 58	375,228.75	23	TOP 25
377	Road-250 Black, 52	375,228.75	23	TOP 25
356	Mountain-200 Silver, 46	370,784.11	25	TOP 25

FIGURE 14-17 You can enrich an Excel table with other Excel-calculated columns.

The formulas used in the table, which has the name Top25Products, are as follows:

```
Position = RANK ( [@Sales], [Sales] )
Ranking = IF ( [@Position] <= 5, "TOP 5",
          IF ( [@Position] <= 10,"TOP 10", "TOP 25" ) )
```

At this point, it might be a good idea to use this result (that is, the Ranking column) and store it as an attribute of the DimProduct table, so that any PivotTable can use the Ranking column to perform filtering. You can achieve this by linking the table to the data model and creating the correct relationship. You can either link the table or simply create the relationship from inside Excel using the Relationship button on the Data tab of the Excel ribbon. In this latter case, you can create the new relationship shown in Figure 14-18.

FIGURE 14-18 Creating a relationship automatically adds the tables to the data model, if they are not already there.

If, at this point, you go back to the PowerPivot window, you will see that the Top25Products table has been added to the data model, and it is as available as any other table. Figure 14-19 shows the resulting data model.

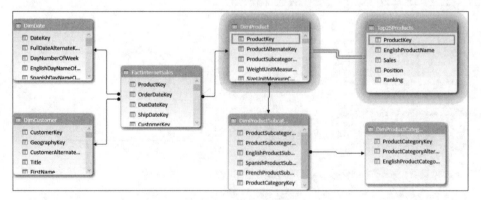

FIGURE 14-19 The Top25Products table is now part of the data model.

The big difference between the Top25Products table and all the rest is that this is a calculated table, not one that has been imported from any database. At this point, you can easily create a

PivotTable showing the number of orders and the quantity sold for the top five products, like the one shown in Figure 14-20.

Ranking		Row Labels ▼	Count of SalesOrderNumber	Sum of OrderQuantity
Ranking 🔽		Road-150 Red, 44	281	281
TOP 10		Road-150 Red, 48	337	337
TOP 25		Road-150 Red, 52	302	302
TOP 5		Road-150 Red, 56	295	295
(blank)		Road-150 Red, 62	336	336
		Grand Total	**1551**	**1551**

FIGURE 14-20 The Ranking column is now available to filter the data model.

You can see that the PivotTable shows the top five products by sales amount and the sales amount column is not visible in the PivotTable. In fact, it does not need to be there because the Ranking column is a calculated one and belongs to the data model. It is not computed using the *TOP10* function of PivotTables.

This example was very easy, but you probably can already imagine the incredible power of such an approach. Mixing Excel calculations and the DAX modeling options opens new, exciting possibilities and the key to exploiting this power is using DAX as a query language.

If you refresh the data source, Excel reloads tables from external connections, and then refreshes the Excel tables based on DAX queries. Then, if they are linked back, it refreshes the PowerPivot tables linked to the DAX queries. All those operations happen automatically; you do not need to perform any manual operation to refresh linked-back tables.

Computing ABC analysis with a linked-back table

As a further example of the power of linking back, we want to show you a scenario that you already have solved—that is, the calculation of the *ABC* class for products. In Chapter 13, you used DAX and calculated columns to add the *ABC Class* attribute to the Product table. The DAX code was not very complex, but the very fact that we included it in a chapter called "Using Advanced DAX" indicates that we do not consider it easy, either.

Using the link-back capability, you are now going to solve the same scenario using Excel code only, with a straightforward technique. You can find this example in the companion workbook "CH14-06-ABC in Excel.xlsx."

You might remember from Chapter 13 that ABC analysis assigns class A to products that are responsible for 70 percent of your sales, class B to products for the next 20 percent, and class C for the products that, together, account for the remaining 10 percent of your sales. To compute these classes, you first need a table that shows, for each product, the total sales for that product.

This can be easily accomplished using a DAX query like the following:

```
EVALUATE
    SUMMARIZE (
        DimProduct,
        DimProduct[ProductKey],
        DimProduct[EnglishProductName],
        "Total Sales",
        SUM ( FactInternetSales[SalesAmount] )
    )
ORDER BY
    [Total Sales] DESC
```

The reason for *ORDER BY* is that it will make it much easier to compute the running total, a point that will become clearer shortly. This query produces a table like the one in Figure 14-21.

ProductKey	EnglishProductName	Total Sales
312	Road-150 Red, 48	1,205,876.99
310	Road-150 Red, 62	1,202,298.72
313	Road-150 Red, 52	1,080,637.54
314	Road-150 Red, 56	1,055,589.65
311	Road-150 Red, 44	1,005,493.87
361	Mountain-200 Black, 42	979,960.73
353	Mountain-200 Silver, 38	979,035.78
363	Mountain-200 Black, 46	961,600.81
359	Mountain-200 Black, 38	954,715.84
357	Mountain-200 Silver, 46	930,315.99
355	Mountain-200 Silver, 42	909,436.08
573	Touring-1000 Blue, 46	421,980.39
580	Road-350-W Yellow, 40	418,443.54

FIGURE 14-21 The query produces a list of products, along with their total sales, arranged in descending order by total sales.

The next step is to compute a running total that shows, for each product, the sum of the sales of all the products that are above it. In DAX, this step was not very easy to do, because that language has no concept of sort ordering of a table. In Excel, on the other hand, it is easy to compute such a value, because it is always the row above plus the sales of the current product (that is, of the current row). The only exception is the first row, because it has no "row above." But handling this kind of exception in Excel is simple—it is just a matter of adding an *IF* condition in front of the formula. Thus, you can add a column named RunningTotal to this Excel table with the following formula:

```
= IF (
    ISNUMBER ( OFFSET( [@RunningTotal], -1, 0 ) ),
    OFFSET ( [@RunningTotal], -1, 0 ) + [@[Total Sales]],
    [@[Total Sales]]
)
```

This column simply checks if the previous row (using *OFFSET*) contains a number in the Running Total column. If so, then it takes that value and adds the current total sales; otherwise, it returns the total sales. The only exception is the first row, where the previous one is the header containing the RunningTotal string (that is, not a number). The result is shown in Figure 14-22.

ProductKey	EnglishProductName	Total Sales	RunningTotal
312	Road-150 Red, 48	1,205,876.99	1,205,876.99
310	Road-150 Red, 62	1,202,298.72	2,408,175.71
313	Road-150 Red, 52	1,080,637.54	3,488,813.25
314	Road-150 Red, 56	1,055,589.65	4,544,402.90
311	Road-150 Red, 44	1,005,493.87	5,549,896.77
361	Mountain-200 Black, 42	979,960.73	6,529,857.50
353	Mountain-200 Silver, 38	979,035.78	7,508,893.28
363	Mountain-200 Black, 46	961,600.81	8,470,494.09
359	Mountain-200 Black, 38	954,715.84	9,425,209.93
357	Mountain-200 Silver, 46	930,315.99	10,355,525.92
355	Mountain-200 Silver, 42	909,436.08	11,264,962.00
573	Touring-1000 Blue, 46	421,980.39	11,686,942.39
580	Road-350-W Yellow, 40	418,443.54	12,105,385.93

FIGURE 14-22 The RunningTotal amount is much easier to compute using Excel than using DAX.

The next step is to transform the running total into a percentage of the grand total of sales. This operation is easily accomplished by using a new column (RunningPct) in the Excel table with the following formula:

```
= [@RunningTotal] / SUM ( [Total Sales] )
```

Figure 14-23 shows the resulting table.

ProductKey	EnglishProductName	Total Sales	RunningTotal	RunningPct
312	Road-150 Red, 48	1,205,876.99	1,205,876.99	4.11%
310	Road-150 Red, 62	1,202,298.72	2,408,175.71	8.20%
313	Road-150 Red, 52	1,080,637.54	3,488,813.25	11.88%
314	Road-150 Red, 56	1,055,589.65	4,544,402.90	15.48%
311	Road-150 Red, 44	1,005,493.87	5,549,896.77	18.90%
361	Mountain-200 Black, 42	979,960.73	6,529,857.50	22.24%
353	Mountain-200 Silver, 38	979,035.78	7,508,893.28	25.58%
363	Mountain-200 Black, 46	961,600.81	8,470,494.09	28.85%
359	Mountain-200 Black, 38	954,715.84	9,425,209.93	32.10%
357	Mountain-200 Silver, 46	930,315.99	10,355,525.92	35.27%
355	Mountain-200 Silver, 42	909,436.08	11,264,962.00	38.37%
573	Touring-1000 Blue, 46	421,980.39	11,686,942.39	39.81%
580	Road-350-W Yellow, 40	418,443.54	12,105,385.93	41.23%

FIGURE 14-23 The RunningPct column shows RunningTotal as a percentage of the grand total of sales.

The last operation is the easiest: a simple *IF* condition will transform the RunningPct column into the *ABC* class, assigning class A to all the rows where RunningPct is less than 0.7, class B to rows where RunningPct is between 0.7 and 0.9, and class C to all other rows. The formula for the ABC Class column is straightforward:

```
= IF ( [@RunningPct] <= 0.7, "A", IF ( [@RunningPct] <= 0.9, "B", "C" ) )
```

Figure 14-24 shows the result.

ProductKey	EnglishProductName	Total Sales	RunningTotal	RunningPct	ABC Class
312	Road-150 Red, 48	1,205,876.99	1,205,876.99	4.11%	A
310	Road-150 Red, 62	1,202,298.72	2,408,175.71	8.20%	A
313	Road-150 Red, 52	1,080,637.54	3,488,813.25	11.88%	A
314	Road-150 Red, 56	1,055,589.65	4,544,402.90	15.48%	A
311	Road-150 Red, 44	1,005,493.87	5,549,896.77	18.90%	A
361	Mountain-200 Black, 42	979,960.73	6,529,857.50	22.24%	A
353	Mountain-200 Silver, 38	979,035.78	7,508,893.28	25.58%	A
363	Mountain-200 Black, 46	961,600.81	8,470,494.09	28.85%	A
359	Mountain-200 Black, 38	954,715.84	9,425,209.93	32.10%	A
357	Mountain-200 Silver, 46	930,315.99	10,355,525.92	35.27%	A
355	Mountain-200 Silver, 42	909,436.08	11,264,962.00	38.37%	A
573	Touring-1000 Blue, 46	421,980.39	11,686,942.39	39.81%	A
580	Road-350-W Yellow, 40	418,443.54	12,105,385.93	41.23%	A

FIGURE 14-24 Once RunningPct is computed, transforming it into the *ABC* class is very simple.

At this point, you have a table in Excel that contains, for each product, the *ABC* class designation. Now it is time to exploit the power of linking back and push this table into the data model, creating a relationship from DimProduct to this new table using the ProductKey column. The resulting data model is shown in Figure 14-25.

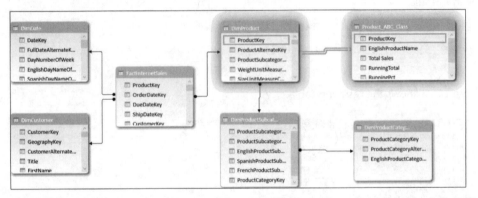

FIGURE 14-25 The Product_ABC_Class table is now placed inside the data model, linked back from Excel.

You can immediately use the *ABC* class from the new table in a PivotTable. If you are a purist of data modeling, as we are, you can create a new calculated column in DimProduct using the *RELATED* function to denormalize the ABC Class column. At this point, you can hide the Product_ABC_Class table, which is just a technical table.

We hope this small example has shown you the power of linking back. The idea is not that you should always try to mix Excel and DAX. There are arguments in favor of DAX and others in favor of Excel; the choice you make will depend on the specific scenario you are facing. Roughly speaking, we think it is always best to write the formulas in the language that makes them easier to create because you end up writing and debugging less code. In this specific scenario, the running total is simple to write in Excel, while doing so in DAX would require some complex effort. Thus, the Excel solution looks easier to implement.

Using *CROSSJOIN*

Another function that is useful in query authoring is *CROSSJOIN*. *CROSSJOIN* takes two parameters as input (they must be table expressions) and produces the Cartesian product of the two tables. The two tables can be created using any table function, which lends you the ability to create complex table expressions.

As an example, consider this query:

```
EVALUATE
    ADDCOLUMNS (
        CROSSJOIN (
            VALUES ( DimDate[CalendarYear] ),
            VALUES ( DimProductCategory[EnglishProductCategoryName] )
        ),
        "Total Sales",
        CALCULATE ( SUM ( FactInternetSales[SalesAmount] ) )
    )
```

CROSSJOIN takes the values of *CalendarYear* and *EnglishProductCategoryName* and produces every possible pair of the two values. Then, when the Cartesian product is created, it computes for each pair the total sales for that category and year. The resulting output contains many rows that result in blank sales, as shown in Figure 14-26. It is useful to note that blank rows sometimes have a meaning. In fact, you might be interested both in categories that sold and in categories that did not sell anything. If you do not show blank lines, then products that did not generate sales would be missing. You can find this example in the companion workbook "CH14-07-CROSSJOIN.xlsx."

EnglishProductCategoryName	CalendarYear	Total Sales
Bikes	2005	3,266,373.66
Bikes	2006	6,530,343.53
Bikes	2007	9,359,102.62
Bikes	2008	9,162,324.85
Bikes	2009	
Bikes	2010	
Components	2005	
Components	2006	
Components	2007	
Components	2008	
Components	2009	
Components	2010	

FIGURE 14-26 Using *CROSSJOIN*, all pairs are evaluated, even blank ones.

You can compare that result with the following query:

```
EVALUATE
    SUMMARIZE (
        FactInternetSales,
        DimDate[CalendarYear],
```

```
        DimProductCategory[EnglishProductCategoryName],
        "Total Sales",
        SUM ( FactInternetSales[SalesAmount] )
    )
```

The result of *SUMMARIZE* is different because it takes into account only pairs of category and year where some sales exist in the FactInternetSales table (see Figure 14-27).

EnglishProductCategoryName	CalendarYear	Total Sales
Bikes	2005	3,266,373.66
Bikes	2006	6,530,343.53
Bikes	2007	9,359,102.62
Bikes	2008	9,162,324.85
Clothing	2007	138,247.97
Clothing	2008	201,524.64
Accessories	2007	293,709.71
Accessories	2008	407,050.25

FIGURE 14-27 Using *SUMMARIZE*, the result shows only pairs that have some value.

Using *GENERATE*

The last function you need to learn before you can count yourself among the legion of DAX query gurus, is *GENERATE*. *GENERATE* is a simple yet powerful function that can be used to encapsulate a complex behavior in a single query.

Imagine that you want to produce a report that shows, for each year, the top three sellers among your company's products. You can build such a report with a PivotTable and the *TOP10* Excel function, but because this chapter is about DAX queries, now you want to build the dataset using a query. Moreover, always keep in mind that if you build the report with a query, you will be able to link it back to the data model, making it the basis for more advanced analysis.

You need to take the *VALUES* of *CalendarYear* and, for each year, run a subquery that evaluates the three top sellers among the various products. Then you need to merge everything into a single dataset. This is exactly what *GENERATE* does. You can find this example in the companion workbook "CH14-08-GENERATE.xlsx."

Let's start by looking at this query:

```
EVALUATE
    ADDCOLUMNS (
        GENERATE (
            VALUES ( DimDate[CalendarYear] ),
            TOPN (
                3,
                VALUES ( DimProduct[EnglishProductName] ),
                CALCULATE ( SUM ( FactInternetSales[SalesAmount] ) )
```

```
            )
        ),
        "Total Sales",
        CALCULATE ( SUM ( FactInternetSales[SalesAmount] ) )
    )
ORDER BY
    DimDate[CalendarYear], [Total Sales] DESC
```

The resulting dataset can be seen in Figure 14-28.

CalendarYear	EnglishProductName	Total Sales
2005	Road-150 Red, 62	593,992.82
2005	Road-150 Red, 48	547,475.31
2005	Road-150 Red, 44	500,957.80
2006	Road-150 Red, 48	658,401.68
2006	Road-150 Red, 62	608,305.90
2006	Road-150 Red, 52	608,305.90
2007	Mountain-200 Black, 46	679,399.00
2007	Mountain-200 Black, 42	627,269.94
2007	Mountain-200 Silver, 46	617,531.62
2008	Mountain-200 Silver, 38	589,277.46
2008	Mountain-200 Black, 38	587,517.44
2008	Mountain-200 Silver, 46	579,997.50
2009	Crown Race	
2009	Chain Stays	
2009	Decal 1	
2009	Decal 2	
2009	Down Tube	

FIGURE 14-28 *GENERATE* is useful for merging a query and its subquery.

Let's analyze this query in detail:

- The outermost *ADDCOLUMNS* is needed to add the *Total Sales* values to the dataset, which is meaningful to see in the final result but does not add complexity to the query.

- *GENERATE* evaluates its first parameter, which is *VALUES (DimDate[CalendarYear])*. It takes all the years, and for each one, it evaluates its second parameter, which is the *TOPN* call.

- *TOPN* computes the top three products after arranging the products by the sum of sales amount, returning the top three sellers among the products. *TOPN* is the subquery here because it is evaluated once for each year.

- *GENERATE* merges the main table (the years) and the subquery (the top three sellers) in a single dataset, repeating the value of the year for each row in the subquery, resulting in a single dataset being returned as the result.

In fact, you can see that the resulting dataset contains three products for each year. The exceptions are the years after 2008, because there are no sales in 2009 and later years. For this reason, all the products lead to a result of zero and, in the case of a tie, *TOPN* returns all the products with the same ranking.

In fact, in Figure 14-28, you can see that there are many rows for year 2009, and in the companion workbook, you will see many more of them. You can get rid of them by filtering the result using *FILTER* or limiting the years to only the ones where there are sales. An example of this latter technique is the following, where instead of using *VALUES (DimDate[CalendarYear])*, you use *SUMMARIZE* to take only the years in which there are some sales:

```
EVALUATE
    ADDCOLUMNS (
        GENERATE (
            SUMMARIZE (
                FactInternetSales,
                DimDate[CalendarYear]
            ),
            TOPN (
                3,
                VALUES ( DimProduct[EnglishProductName] ),
                CALCULATE ( SUM ( FactInternetSales[SalesAmount] ) )
            )
        ),
        "Total Sales",
        CALCULATE ( SUM ( FactInternetSales[SalesAmount] ) )
    )
ORDER BY
    DimDate[CalendarYear], [Total Sales] DESC
```

The resulting dataset of this latter query is shown in Figure 14-29.

CalendarYear	EnglishProductName	Total Sales
2005	Road-150 Red, 62	593,992.82
2005	Road-150 Red, 48	547,475.31
2005	Road-150 Red, 44	500,957.80
2006	Road-150 Red, 48	658,401.68
2006	Road-150 Red, 52	608,305.90
2006	Road-150 Red, 62	608,305.90
2007	Mountain-200 Black, 46	679,399.00
2007	Mountain-200 Black, 42	627,269.94
2007	Mountain-200 Silver, 46	617,531.62
2008	Mountain-200 Silver, 38	589,277.46
2008	Mountain-200 Black, 38	587,517.44
2008	Mountain-200 Silver, 46	579,997.50

FIGURE 14-29 After filtering the years, the resulting output contains only three products for each year.

Again, it is important to stress the fact that, by using a query to generate this output, you will be able to link back the result to the data model and produce more complex reports. In that case, it will be useful to put the ProductKey column in the dataset, so you will be able to add relationships to this table and use its result in the data model.

Querying with DAX Studio

As you have learned in this chapter, using DAX as a query language is a powerful technique that lets you create complex and powerful reports. The major drawback of using DAX as a query language, however, is that you do not have any tool in Excel to help you create the query. You need to write it in a simple text box, with no syntax highlighting, no way to see partial results and, in general, without the necessary tools you might expect from a modern query writing environment.

Luckily, there is a free Excel add-in called DAX Studio, which is designed to simplify the creation of DAX queries. You can download this add-in from *http://daxstudio.codeplex.com*. In Figure 14-30, you can see a simple query in DAX Studio.

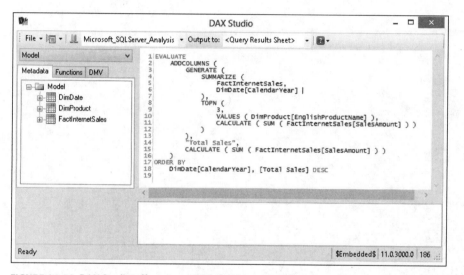

FIGURE 14-30 DAX Studio offers syntax highlighting, a Help function, and many useful tools to create DAX queries.

If you plan to use DAX as a query language, or if you simply want a free environment that makes it easier to write DAX code, we suggest that you try this add-in by downloading and installing the latest version.

Automating operations using VBA

Microsoft Visual Basic for Applications (VBA) is a powerful language included in Microsoft Excel that you can use to automate many operations. In Excel 2013, Microsoft extended the VBA library of objects with the *DataModel* object, which you can use to perform some operations with the PowerPivot data model. Not all the PowerPivot features are available in this first version; many operations (such as adding a calculated column or a calculated field) are still available only through the user interface. But there are some useful features you can use to build interactive and automated reports.

In this chapter, you are going to see some examples of VBA usage. We will not describe in full detail in this book how to write VBA code. This chapter only deals with features and techniques that are specific to the new data model in Excel 2013, on the assumption that you already have a basic knowledge of VBA and programming techniques. If you are completely new to VBA coding, we suggest that you read a book on advanced Excel that will introduce you to the magic of VBA. Even if you are new to VBA, though, you can still get some insights from this chapter, and perhaps you will want to learn more about VBA after seeing what you can do by combining it with PowerPivot.

Before learning how to use VBA to perform operations, we need to give you a warning: VBA scripts are not supported in SharePoint. Thus, all the techniques you are learning here will not work correctly if deployed on a SharePoint server.

Enabling the DEVELOPER tab of the ribbon

Before you can start learning VBA, you will need to enable the DEVELOPER tab of the Excel ribbon. This tab, which contains all the features needed to write VBA code, is hidden by default. To activate it, you need to access the Excel Options dialog box by going to the FILE tab of the ribbon and selecting Options. At this point, you need to select the Customize Ribbon page, as shown in Figure 15-1.

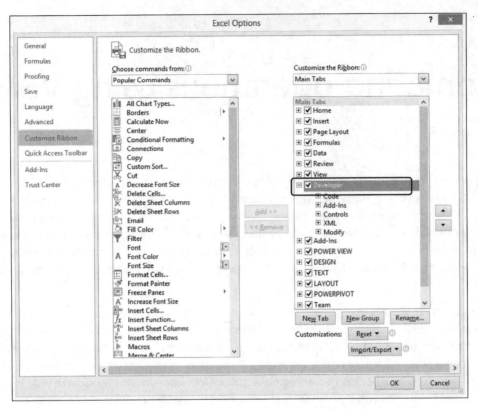

FIGURE 15-1 The Excel Options dialog box lets you modify most Excel behaviors.

You need to make sure the Developer item is selected if you want to see the DEVELOPER tab on the ribbon. Once you enable it, you will see a new tab on the ribbon (see Figure 15-2).

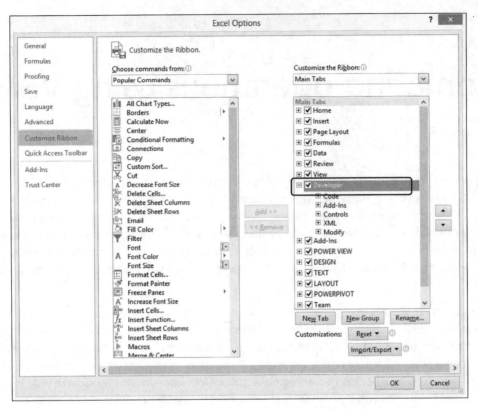

FIGURE 15-2 The DEVELOPER tab contains many useful features to develop VBA code.

The most useful feature of the DEVELOPER tab is the Record Macro button. You will find this button handy whenever you want to automate an operation. In fact, if you want to learn the VBA code that performs an operation, the easiest way is to start recording a macro, perform the operation, and then stop recording. At this point, looking at the code in the macro, you will be able to understand what happened and, if needed, you can modify the code to make it fit your needs.

Let us see an example of this flow of operations. You can open the companion workbook "CH15-01-RecordingMacro.xlsm," which contains a data model with a few tables and no PivotTable. Using this workbook, you will record a macro that creates a PivotTable to understand how VBA works.

Click the Record Macro button. Excel will open the Record Macro dialog box (see Figure 15-3), where you will enter the name of the new macro.

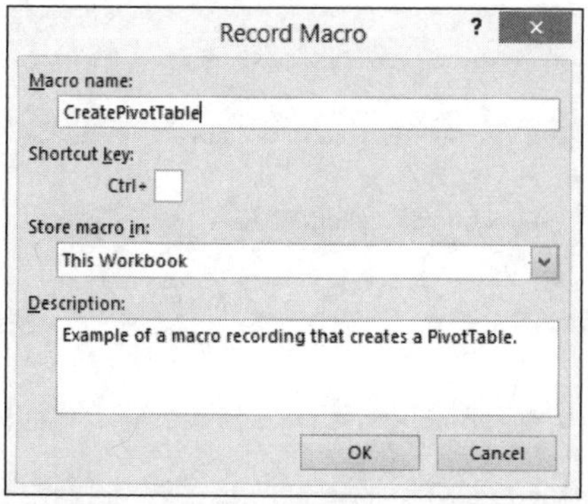

FIGURE 15-3 The Record Macro dialog box lets you specify several properties of a new macro being recorded.

Once you click OK, Excel will start recording all the operations you perform. At this point, you can create a new PivotTable putting the product color on the rows, the calendar year on the columns, and the sales amount on the values area.

> **Note** You need to create the PivotTable from Excel, not from the PowerPivot window; otherwise, the recording will not happen correctly. The macro recorder does not track what happens inside the PowerPivot window.

The result should look like Figure 15-4.

Sum of SalesAmount	Column Labels				
Row Labels	2005	2006	2007	2008	Grand Total
Black	$345,815.49	$1,728,251.55	$3,851,090.66	$2,913,254.25	$8,838,411.96
Blue			$860,380.78	$1,418,715.50	$2,279,096.28
Multi			$42,099.32	$64,371.42	$106,470.74
NA			$184,354.22	$250,762.47	$435,116.69
Red	$2,634,959.00	$3,935,630.74	$953,203.05	$200,537.73	$7,724,330.52
Silver	$285,599.16	$720,397.36	$2,044,406.89	$2,062,985.67	$5,113,389.08
White			$2,229.52	$2,876.80	$5,106.32
Yellow		$146,063.88	$1,853,295.85	$2,857,395.90	$4,856,755.63
Grand Total	$3,266,373.66	$6,530,343.53	$9,791,060.30	$9,770,899.74	$29,358,677.22

FIGURE 15-4 This is the final result you should obtain before you finish recording your macro.

Once the PivotTable is finished, you can go back to the DEVELOPER tab and click Stop Recording. Then the macro has been recorded. To see it in action, you will need to open the Microsoft Visual Basic for Applications window using the Visual Basic button on the DEVELOPER tab of Excel.

The Visual Basic window shows all the macros and the functions that are present in your workbook, and you should see a single function named CreatePivotTable with some code that looks like the following (here, we have formatted the code slightly to make it more readable):

```
Sub CreatePivotTable()
    ActiveWorkbook.PivotCaches.Create( _
        SourceType:=xlExternal, _
        SourceData:=ActiveWorkbook.Connections("ThisWorkbookDataModel"), _
        Version:=xlPivotTableVersion15) _

    _
    .CreatePivotTable _
        TableDestination:="Sheet1!R2C7", _
        TableName:="PivotTable1", _
        DefaultVersion:=xlPivotTableVersion15

    With ActiveSheet.PivotTables("PivotTable1").CubeFields("[DimProduct].
[Color]")
        .Orientation = xlRowField
        .Position = 1
    End With
    With ActiveSheet.PivotTables("PivotTable1").CubeFields("[DimDate].
[CalendarYear]")
        .Orientation = xlColumnField
        .Position = 1
    End With
    ActiveSheet.PivotTables("PivotTable1").CubeFields.GetMeasure _
        "[FactInternetSales].[SalesAmount]", _
        xlSum, _
        "Sum of SalesAmount"
    ActiveSheet.PivotTables("PivotTable1").AddDataField _
        ActiveSheet.PivotTables("PivotTable1").CubeFields("[Measures].[Sum of
SalesAmount]"), _
        "Sum of SalesAmount"
End Sub
```

There is no space here to describe in detail what this code performs, but if you are familiar with VBA and know some programming, you will recognize in this piece of code the operations that create a PivotTable:

- At the beginning, a PivotCache is created, using the ThisWorkbookDataModel connection (that is, the internal connection of PowerPivot).

- Based on this PivotCache, a new PivotTable is created at the coordinated R2C7, with the name "PivotTable1."

- The product color is put on the rows.

- The calendar year is put on the columns.

- Because you added the Sales Amount column to the values area, an implicit calculated field is created to hold the sum of sales amount, which is then put on the cube fields (that is, on the values area of the PivotTable).

You will not normally use the code of a macro as it is. Rather, you record a macro to better understand how Excel is performing an operation. Then it is up to you to spend some time polishing the code, making it behave the way you want, and adding parameters to it.

The interesting part, for the sake of this demo, is to see how to use the code generated by the macro to automate a procedure. To follow the demo, now you should delete the PivotTable and start again with the empty sheet. On this sheet, you will place a button and link the button to the macro so that when you click the button, the entire PivotTable will be generated automatically.

To add a button to your worksheet, you should use the Insert button on the DEVELOPER tab of the Excel ribbon and select the Button from the rich list of controls you can use, as shown in Figure 15-5.

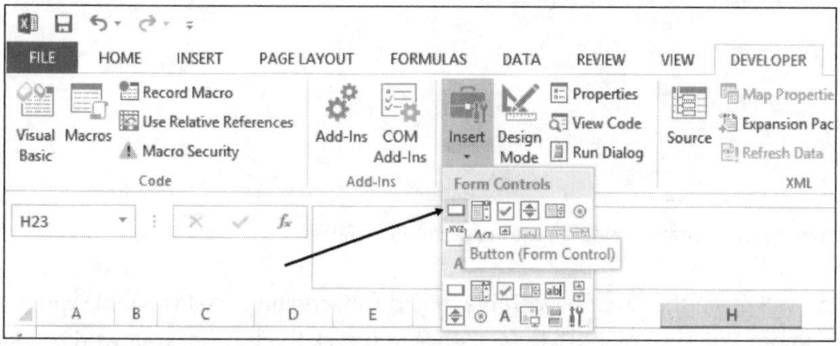

FIGURE 15-5 The Insert button lets you add user interface elements to a worksheet.

Once you clicked the button, select an area in the worksheet where you want to put the button. Once you have selected the area, Excel will open the Assign Macro dialog box (see Figure 15-6), which lists the macros available in the workbook.

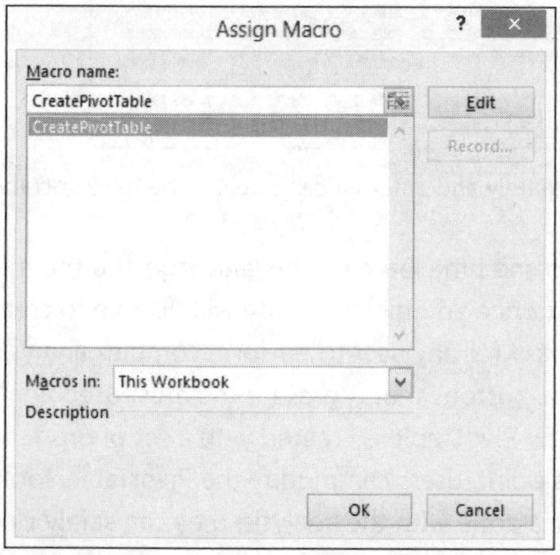

FIGURE 15-6 The Assign Macro dialog box lets you assign a macro to a button.

The only macro available should be the one you just recorded. Select it and click OK. At this point, your workbook should contain a single button on an empty canvas, as shown in Figure 15-7.

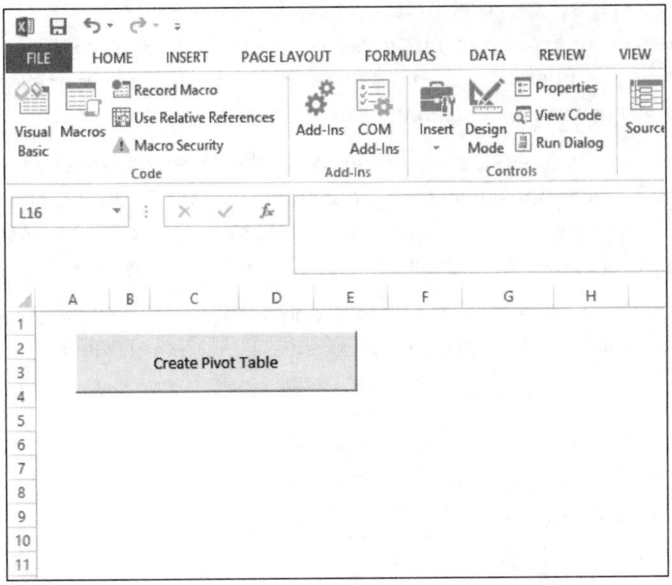

FIGURE 15-7 The workbook now contains a single button and no PivotTable.

Clicking this button will make the CreatePivotTable macro run, creating the PivotTable with color, year, and sales amount on the columns. In fact, once you click the button, your workbook will instantly show a new PivotTable (see Figure 15-8).

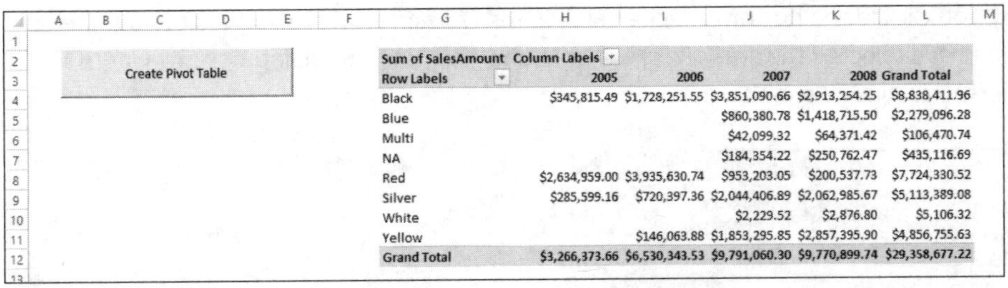

		Sum of SalesAmount	Column Labels				
	Create Pivot Table	Row Labels	2005	2006	2007	2008	Grand Total
		Black	$345,815.49	$1,728,251.55	$3,851,090.66	$2,913,254.25	$8,838,411.96
		Blue			$860,380.78	$1,418,715.50	$2,279,096.28
		Multi			$42,099.32	$64,371.42	$106,470.74
		NA			$184,354.22	$250,762.47	$435,116.69
		Red	$2,634,959.00	$3,935,630.74	$953,203.05	$200,537.73	$7,724,330.52
		Silver	$285,599.16	$720,397.36	$2,044,406.89	$2,062,985.67	$5,113,389.08
		White			$2,229.52	$2,876.80	$5,106.32
		Yellow		$146,063.88	$1,853,295.85	$2,857,395.90	$4,856,755.63
		Grand Total	$3,266,373.66	$6,530,343.53	$9,791,060.30	$9,770,899.74	$29,358,677.22

FIGURE 15-8 Clicking the Create Pivot Table button immediately and automatically creates the full PivotTable.

This is the power of macros and VBA. You spend some time learning the language and the many different objects that are involved in its behavior, but once you master it, you will be able to create completely automated workbooks that will make it easy for any user to perform complex analysis. For example, you can create a command panel with a few buttons that represent the most used analysis in your company. When the user clicks a button, a new PivotTable is created with a set of predefined columns and values, showing the full analysis. At this point, users can modify the PivotTable, look at data, and discover remarkable insights. When they are done with the analysis, they can safely close the workbook knowing that if they want to rebuild the original PivotTable, it is just one click away.

Updating a linked-back DAX query through VBA

In Chapter 14, "Using DAX as a query language," you saw how to compute the *ABC* class of a product using a DAX query and some Excel code, linking back the result of the query in the data model. That example was significant because it demonstrated how to link back queries. In this section, you learn how to build on that example by using VBA code to make the query dynamic.

In fact, in the example from Chapter 14, you used a query that computes, for each product, its *ABC* class using the sales over the whole history available in the database. In fact, a product can have a different class depending on the year you are looking at; so a better approach in a real-world scenario would be to compute the *ABC* class for one year and use the information to analyze sales in other years. You can obviously hard-code the year selection in the query, but because this chapter is about VBA, we are going to show you a way to use VBA code to make the query dynamic.

The result of this section is available in the companion workbook "CH15-02-Dynamic ABC.xlsm." We suggest that you look at the companion workbook to learn the technique, because we are not providing full detailed explanations here on how to re-create it.

In Figure 15-9, you can see the query worksheet, which, this time, contains a combo box to select the year to use for the calculation and a button that will refresh the query and update the data model.

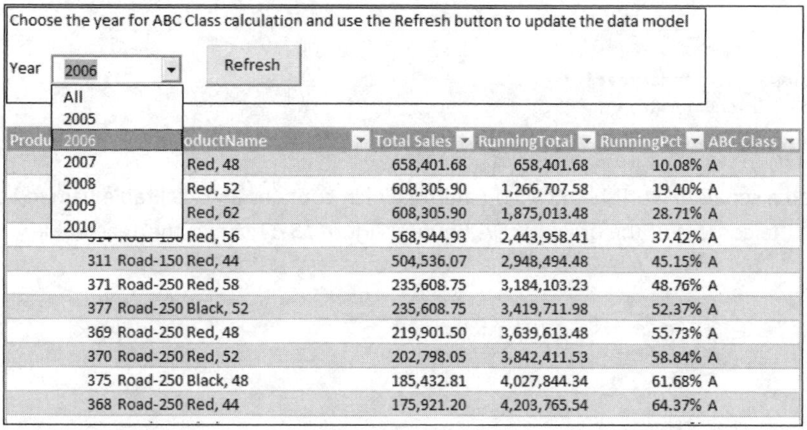

FIGURE 15-9 Using VBA, you will create a macro that updates the DAX query that underlies the Excel table.

There are a few relevant things to note about this example:

- You should populate the combo box for the year using the years available in the data model, so that it dynamically changes when you refresh the data model.

- The Refresh button will create a new DAX query using the parameter set in the combo box, update the Excel table, and refresh the data model.

To create this workbook, we started from the workbook containing the fixed query that you learned in Chapter 14. In this way, we started with an Excel table that already has the necessary columns and calculations.

Then, you need to add a combo box using the ActiveX combo box control from the Insert menu of the DEVELOPER tab of the Excel ribbon (see Figure 15-10).

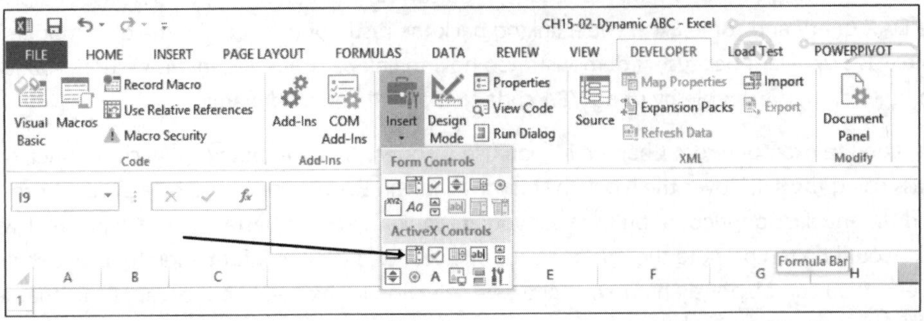

FIGURE 15-10 The Insert menu lets you select user interface controls to add to a worksheet.

Now you add the combo box to the worksheet. By doing this, you create a simple combo box with no list attached to it, because at this stage, Excel does not know how to fill the list of values of the combo. To fill the list of values, you need to retrieve the years available in the DimDate table. Because you already have learned how to run a DAX query, you know that you can retrieve this list in Excel by running this query:

```
EVALUATE
    VALUES ( DimDate[CalendarYear] )
ORDER BY DimDate[CalendarYear]
```

Thus, we created a separate worksheet called Params, which contains an Excel table named Years, which is filled with the content of the previous DAX query. Figure 15-11 shows the Years table.

CalendarYear
2005
2006
2007
2008
2009
2010

FIGURE 15-11 The Years Excel table contains the years available in the database.

At this point, you need to write some code to fill the list of values of the combo box with the content of the table:

```
Sub ReloadComboBoxYearValue()
    Dim oldValue As String
    Dim years As Range
    oldValue = Sheet1.ComboBoxYear.Value
```

```
    Sheet1.ComboBoxYear.Clear
    Set years = Worksheets("Params").Range("Years")
    Sheet1.ComboBoxYear.AddItem "All"
    For i = 2 To years.ListObject.Range.Rows.Count
        Sheet1.ComboBoxYear.AddItem years.ListObject.Range.Cells(i, 1)
    Next i
    Sheet1.ComboBoxYear.Value = oldValue
End Sub
```

This procedure first saves the content of the combo box, then it fills it with the content of the Years table, row by row, and finally, it sets the value of the combo box to its previous content. This can be useful if you plan to run the macro when the combo box already contains a value because of a previous user selection. We designed the code in this way so that you can attach it to the AutoStart macro of the workbook and refresh the content of the combo box each time you open the workbook.

Because you want the user to be able to select each single year, and even a special value meaning: "use all available years," the first item added to the list is the string "All," which the procedure will consider as "do not filter years."

The next step is to add a button to the workbook and write the code that will update the Excel table. To filter the year, you will need to use a slightly more complex query than the one you used in Chapter 14:

```
EVALUATE
    CALCULATETABLE (
        SUMMARIZE (
            DimProduct,
            DimProduct[ProductKey],
            DimProduct[EnglishProductName],
            "Total Sales",
            SUM (FactInternetSales[SalesAmount])
        ),
        DimDate[CalendarYear] = 2006
    )
ORDER BY
    [Total Sales] DESC
```

This query contains an outer *CALCULATETABLE* function, which places a filter on DimDate[CalendarYear]. The value of the year should not be hard-coded in the query; it needs to be dynamically computed by the code attached to the button. In fact, this is exactly what the next procedure does:

```
Sub Recompute()
    Dim AbcTable As ListObject
    Dim Year As String
```

```
    Dim FilterYear As String

    Set AbcTable = Sheet1.ListObjects("Product_ABC_Class")
    Year = Sheet1.ComboBoxYear.Value

    If (Year <> "All") Then
        FilterYear = " , DimDate[CalendarYear] = " & Year
    Else
        FilterYear = ""
    End If
    With AbcTable.TableObject.WorkbookConnection.OLEDBConnection
        .CommandText = Join( _
            Array( _
                "EVALUATE ", _
                "    CALCULATETABLE (", _
                "        SUMMARIZE (", _
                "            DimProduct,", _
                "            DimProduct[ProductKey],", _
                "            DimProduct[EnglishProductName],", _
                "            ""Total Sales"","", _
                "            SUM (FactInternetSales[SalesAmount])", _
                "        )", _
                FilterYear, _
                "    )", _
                "ORDER BY ", _
                "    [Total Sales] DESC" _
            ), _
            vbLf)
        .Refresh
    End With
    ActiveWorkbook.Model.ModelTables("Product_ABC_Class").Refresh
End Sub
```

Looking at the code, you can see that this procedure does the following:

1. It checks the year selected in the combo box. If the year is "All," then it stores a blank string in *FilterYear*; otherwise, it assigns to the variable *FilterYear* a string that will represent the correct filter to apply inside the outermost *CALCULATE*.

2. It updates the *CommandText* value of the connection of the table. Doing this will modify the content of the query as if it were entered using the Edit DAX menu of the table. The dynamic condition on the year is set using the *FilterYear* variable, so it contains the year selected in the combo box.

3. After the query is in place, the table needs to be refreshed, and the Refresh statement does this. Refreshing the table has the effect of executing the DAX query against the data model, updating its content.

4. Once the Excel table is updated, it is time to refresh the data model with the new content of the query. This is the goal of the last statement, which executes the *Refresh* method of the

Product_ABC_Class table in the data model. Because the data model table is linked to the Excel table, refreshing it makes PowerPivot reread the Excel table and update the data model.

Note In this example, we used a combo box to select the year, but that is not your only alternative. You can choose to use a slicer, which might look more appealing. The issue with slicers to be aware of is that they are slightly harder to use from code because they are designed to be integrated with PivotTables. However, the decision depends only on your personal taste.

All these operations happen when the user clicks the Refresh button, and they take no more than a couple of seconds to execute on a modern PC. Clearly, your personal situation will probably be different from what we have described here. As always, we try to show techniques that you can adapt to your specific needs to automate the production of a report.

Using the *Model* object

In Excel 2013, the object model of VBA has been enriched with a new entity: the *Model* object. You can access the *Model* object using the ActiveWorkbook.Model and, using the model, you can perform the operations that are available to program PowerPivot through VBA.

Unfortunately, there are not many operations available using the *Model* object. As a rule of thumb, you can perform all the operations that are available through the standard Excel interface using the *Model* object, but you cannot automate any of the operations that are available solely in the PowerPivot add-in. For example, you can create a relationship using *Model* because the creation of relationships is available in standard Excel, but you cannot create a calculated column, a calculated field, or a hierarchy because these operations are available only in the PowerPivot window.

You can see the methods available for the *Model* object using the VBA editor: As soon as you finish typing **ActiveWorkbook.Model**, IntelliSense will show the list of methods available for the *Model* object (see Figure 15-12).

```
Sub Test()
    ActiveWorkbook.Model.|
End Sub
```
AddConnection
Application
CreateModelWorkbookConnection
Creator
DataModelConnection
Initialize
ModelRelationships

FIGURE 15-12 Using IntelliSense in the VBA editor, you can look at the various functionalities of the *Model* object.

The complete list of the functionalities of the *Model* object is available in Microsoft Help online. For now, we just want to cite the most useful ones:

- **AddConnection**   This functionality allows you to add Excel connections to the data model. You will learn more about Excel and PowerPivot connections in the "Understanding data connections" section later in this chapter.

- **ModelRelationships**   This functionality allows you to browse the relationships in the model using this collection. You can even create new relationships using the *Add* method or delete relationships using the *Delete* method of a relationship.

- **ModelTables**   This functionality allows you to access the tables in the model using this collection. There is no functionality to add, delete, or modify a table. This collection is read-only. One useful feature of a ModelTable is the *Refresh* method.

- **Refresh**   This is probably the most useful functionality because it lets you refresh the data model by reloading all the tables and then computing calculated columns.

If, for example, you want to refresh the DimProduct table programmatically, you can easily do it using the following code:

```
ActiveWorkbook.Model.ModelTables( "DimProduct" ).Refresh
```

Importing data into the data model using VBA

Another operation that you can automate using VBA code is the loading of tables into the data model. There are many ways to load data into Excel tables and then push data into the model, but for this discussion, we are mainly interested in loading information directly inside the data model, avoiding the extra step of loading an Excel table. In the "Loading data from external sources" section of Chapter 2, "Using the Unique Features of PowerPivot," we discussed the many reasons why it is better to avoid loading data in Excel before pushing it to the PowerPivot data model.

To load data into the model, first you need to create a workbook connection using a connection string that points to the data source. Then, you have a few options to load data into the model: you can use a SQL query or load from tables. If you load from tables, you can choose to load the relationships in the model if you want.

The following piece of code will load three tables into the data model from the *AdventureWorksDW2012* database:

```
Sub LoadTables()
    Dim ConnString As Variant
    Dim ComnandText As Variant
```

```
    ConnString = Array( _
        "OLEDB;Provider=SQLOLEDB.1", _
        "Integrated Security=SSPI", _
        "Initial Catalog=AdventureWorksDW2012", _
        "Data Source=Demo;" _
        )
    CommandText = Array( _
        "dbo.DimCustomer", _
        "dbo.DimProduct", _
        "dbo.FactInternetSales" _
        )
    ActiveWorkbook.Connections.Add2 _
        Name:="Multiple Tables from AdventureWorks", _
        Description:="Multiple Tables from AdventureWorks", _
        ConnectionString:=Join(ConnString, ";"), _
        lCmdtype:=xlCmdTableCollection, _
        CommandText:=Join(CommandText, ", "), _
        CreateModelConnection:=True, _
        ImportRelationships:=True
End Sub
```

Here is what is important about this code:

- The *ConnString* variable contains the connection string, which is used by Excel to connect to the database. In the example, we used an OleDB connection with the *AdventureWorksDW2012* database on the SQL Server instance Demo.

- The *CommandText* variable contains the command that will be executed against the SQL Server instance. In this example, we used a xlCmdTableCollection command type; that is, we provide the list of tables to load from the connection. You can use the command type xlSQL to specify a single SQL query instead.

- To load the data effectively, you use the *Add2* method of the *Connection* object in the workbook. *Add2* is an enhanced version of the *Add* method (which will not load data into the model, just into Excel tables).

  Note that we used the *JOIN* function to transform the arrays in strings, which are needed as parameters of the *Add2* method. Semicolons separate parts of the connection string, whereas commas separate table names in the command text.

  Finally, the last two parameters of the *Add2* method are *CreateModelConnection* and *ImportRelationships*. *CreateModelConnection*, if set to *True*, creates not only the workbook connection, but a PowerPivot data model connection. *ImportRelationships* specifies whether you want to import relationships from the database.

If you execute the code above, Excel will create three connections. Two of them are workbook connections, and the other is a model connection. You can see the workbook connections by using the Connections button on the DATA tab of the Excel ribbon, as shown in Figure 15-13.

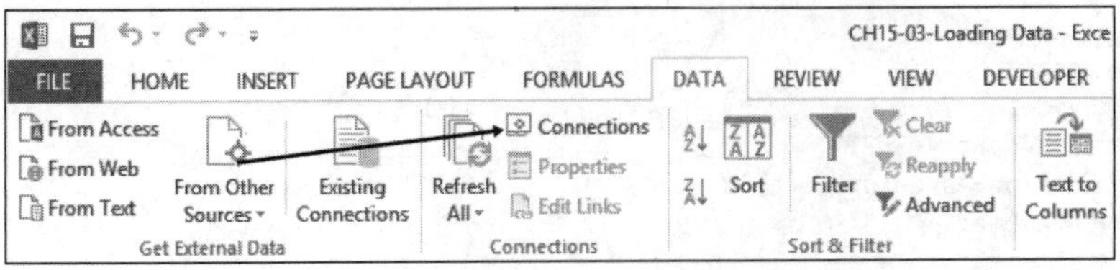

FIGURE 15-13 The Connections button is useful to see the data connections of the workbook.

Clicking the Connections button opens the Workbook Connections dialog box, where you can look at the connections in the workbook (see Figure 15-14).

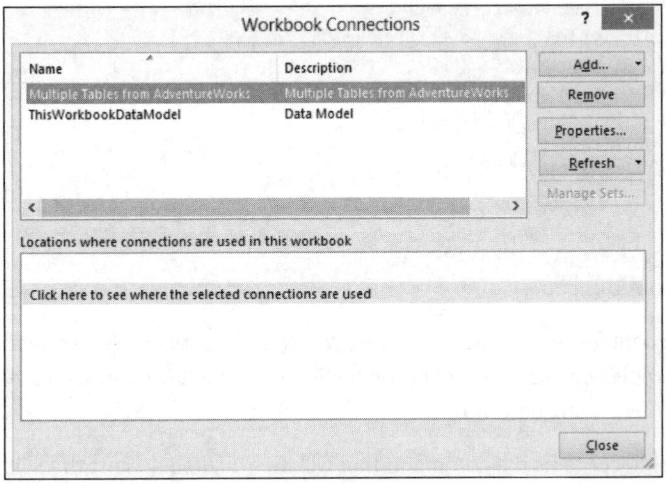

FIGURE 15-14 There are two connections in the workbook, even though we created only one.

There are two connections in the workbook. The first one is the one created by your code, which you can easily recognize by its name (Multiple Tables From AdventureWorks). The other connection, named ThisWorkbookDataModel, is a special connection created by Excel whenever your workbook contains a PowerPivot data model. It is the connection used by the PivotTable tool to create PivotTables, or by Power View to surface reports, to cite just two examples.

None of these connections is used in the workbook. In fact, no Excel table was created after you executed the code. But if you open the PowerPivot window, you will see that the three tables are present in the data model (see Figure 15-15).

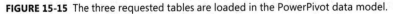

FIGURE 15-15 The three requested tables are loaded in the PowerPivot data model.

We have said that three connections were created, so where is the third one? It is the data model connection in PowerPivot. In fact, PowerPivot does not load data from workbook connections. Rather, it uses its own connections, which you can see by clicking the Existing Connections button on the Home tab of the PowerPivot ribbon. The Existing Connection dialog box of PowerPivot (see Figure 15-16) shows the third connection.

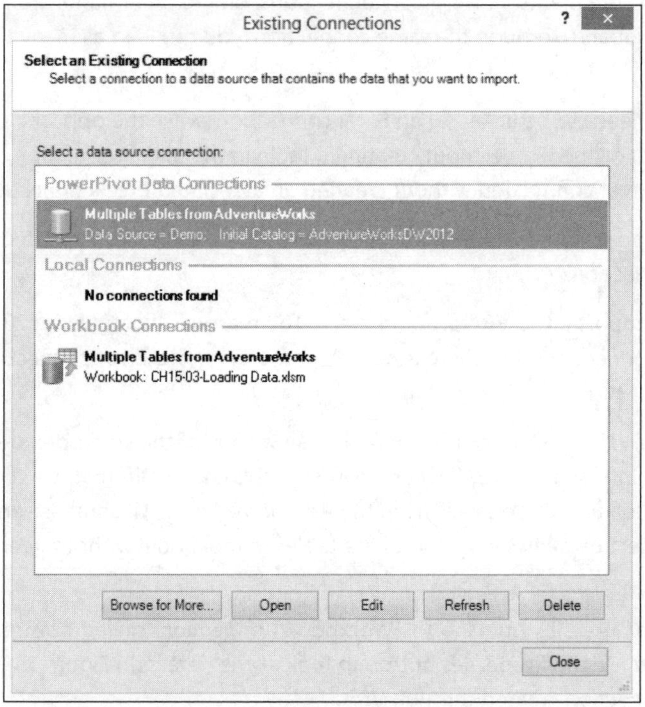

FIGURE 15-16 The PowerPivot Existing Connections dialog box shows the PowerPivot connections.

Excel created this connection because you set the *CreateModelConnection* parameter to *True* when calling *Add2*. When creating the connection, Excel loaded the three tables in the model too.

Unfortunately, there is no way to use VBA to add calculated columns or calculated fields to your model. This is a serious limitation in the ability of VBA to create analytical workbooks from code. You can create a skeleton of the data model, but not a complete workbook with all the necessary calculations. We hope that, in future releases of Excel, Microsoft will solve this problem.

Understanding data connections

In the previous example, you loaded three tables from the database directly inside PowerPivot, and as you have seen, by creating an Excel connection, you also created a PowerPivot connection. The opposite happens as well: when you create a PowerPivot connection (something you can do only using the user interface), an Excel connection is created too.

Here, it is important to learn more about the interactions between Excel and PowerPivot connection, because this behavior, which works very well when using the user interface, might lead to unexpected results when using VBA to work with the model. Here are the most significant points:

- Excel connections and PowerPivot connections are not the same. Excel connections are used to load data into Excel, and each connection can load a single query, a table, or a set of tables by using different types of statements. PowerPivot connections, on the other hand, are used to load data into PowerPivot and, through the same connection, you can load as many tables or queries as needed.

- A PowerPivot connection needs to be linked to an Excel connection, while the opposite is not true. You can have an Excel connection without creating a table in the data model for it, but you cannot have a PowerPivot connection without creating an associated Excel connection.

- Some properties can be updated in an Excel connection, whereas others can be updated only using the PowerPivot connection.

Why are these considerations important to VBA programmers? The reason is that, in Excel 2013, VBA lets you interact with Excel connections, but there is no way to modify PowerPivot connections in a programmatic way.

In the companion workbook "CH15-04-Connections.xlsx," there is a copy of the workbook used in the "Importing data into the data model using VBA" section earlier in this chapter. In that workbook, there is a single Excel connection loading three tables from the *AdventureWorksDW* database and, as you have seen, creating that connection allows you to load the tables in the model without needing to load data in Excel first.

You can look at the connection details by opening the Workbook Connections dialog box (see Figure 15-13). From there, you can use the Properties button to look at the details. In Figure 15-17, you can see the details of the connection created through VBA.

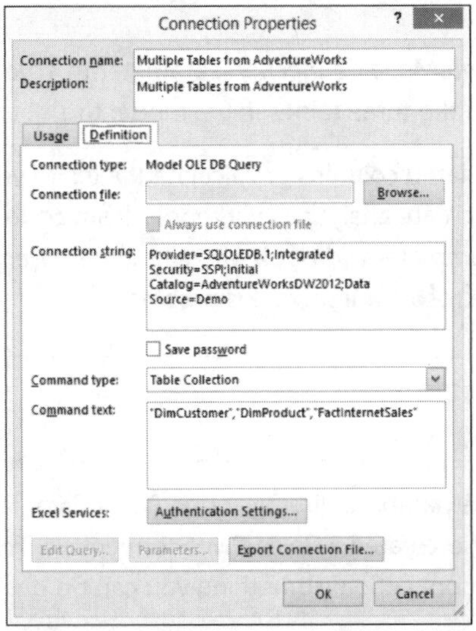

FIGURE 15-17 The Connection Properties dialog box shows the details of a connection.

You can modify the properties of the connection using the Connection Properties dialog box. If, for example, you want to load the DimProductCategory table, you can modify the Command text box by adding a new table name to it. The result is this code:

```
"DimCustomer","DimProduct","FactInternetSales","DimProductCategory"
```

Once you click OK, the new table will be loaded into the data model, without using the PowerPivot add-in. This example shows that it is possible to use the Excel connection to modify the PowerPivot data model. From the VBA point of view, this means that you can load tables and modify the data model structure by using code because you can obtain the same result by using a script. Nevertheless, before relying on this feature, you need to be aware of the fact that the relationship between the Excel data connection and the PowerPivot one breaks as soon as you modify anything about the data model from inside PowerPivot.

For example, suppose that you open the PowerPivot add-in and rename one table (for example, renaming DimProduct to Products). After that, go back to the Connection Properties dialog box to see the Excel connection. You will see a warning message, shown in Figure 15-18.

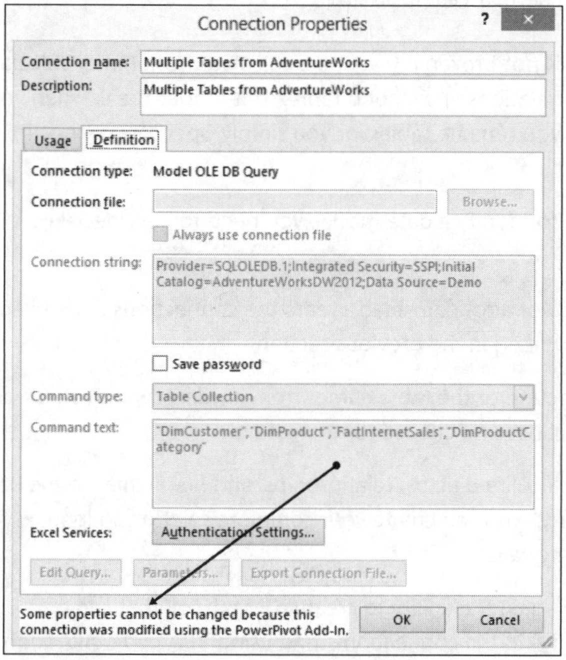

FIGURE 15-18 Once the PowerPivot connection is modified, the Excel connection becomes read-only.

Once you modify the connection inside PowerPivot, the link between the Excel and the PowerPivot connections is broken. In fact, you can no longer modify the connection properties in Excel and, if you want to load another table, then you have to use the PowerPivot add-in. Needing to use the add-in means that the option of modifying the connection is no longer available in VBA because (as you have seen) there is no way to modify the PowerPivot connections using VBA.

Look at this code:

```
With ActiveWorkbook.Connections("Multiple Tables from AdventureWorks")
    .OLEDBConnection.CommandText = "DimCustomer"
End With
```

If you execute it, the result is the error message shown in Figure 15-19.

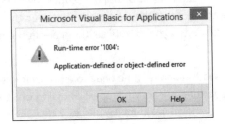

FIGURE 15-19 Trying to modify a read-only connection leads to an error.

The link between the two connections is not broken if you add a calculated column or calculated field, or if you modify the structure of the relationships among tables, but it does break when you load more tables from inside PowerPivot, you rename tables, or you simply open the connection with the Table Import Wizard.

This means that if you plan to use VBA to modify a data model, you need to pay special care to some aspects of your workbook:

- Do not load data from the PowerPivot add-in. Instead, create the connections in Excel and add them to the data model (as outlined in the previous section).

- Never touch either the data connection or the table names from inside PowerPivot; otherwise, the link will be broken, and you will have no chance to re-create it.

- You can add calculated columns, calculated fields, relationships, and hierarchies to the data model without worry. In other words, you can create your complete solution so long as you do not modify the data structure in any way.

By following these simple rules, you will gain the ability to create a workbook that can be connected to different databases by modifying the connection string using VBA code. Although this feature might not be important to information workers, independent software vendors (ISV) or IT people might find it useful to create a skeleton solution that is customizable to different scenarios.

Comparing Excel and SQL Server Analysis Services

This chapter is devoted to comparing Microsoft PowerPivot in Excel 2013 with its siblings in the family of analytical engines in the Microsoft Business Intelligence (BI) stack: PowerPivot for SharePoint and SQL Server Analysis Services (SSAS) 2012.

In fact, in 2012, Microsoft expanded its software offering with several products dedicated to the BI world. Moreover, it treads a clear path that starts with PowerPivot for Excel 2013, for self-service BI; moves to PowerPivot for SharePoint, for team BI; and then continues to SSAS, for corporate BI and complex solutions. The good news is that everything you have learned about Microsoft Excel in terms of data modeling techniques, the DAX language, and different ways to approach different scenarios remains valid for these other members of the family. Thus, you invest time only once, and then you use it to scale your system from self-service to corporate.

The goal of this chapter is not to teach you how to create an SSAS solution using Microsoft Visual Studio; that task would be complicated and not of great interest for any Excel user. What we want to cover is the difference between PowerPivot for Excel, Microsoft SharePoint, and SSAS, to help you better understand what the characteristics of the engines are and which of the more powerful features you can expect to use if you choose one of the other products.

In this way, you will realize what you can do with Excel alone, as well as the requirements that are needed if you decide to use the other products.

Understanding the different versions of the engine

PowerPivot for Excel is the analytical engine that you have been learning to use in this book. It consists of the VertiPaq database, which stores the PowerPivot tables, and the xVelocity in-memory analytical engine, which executes DAX code and answers queries coming from PivotTables, Power View reports, or DAX queries saved in Excel tables. The same engine powers three different products in the BI offering:

- **PowerPivot for Excel 2013**   We have already discussed pretty much everything about this at this point.

- **PowerPivot for SharePoint** This is a special version of the more complete SSAS engine, optimized to work side by side with SharePoint 2013. If offers the ability to store Excel workbooks containing PowerPivot data, surface them in HTML using Excel Services, and answers queries as if they were complete SSAS databases.

- **SQL Server Analysis Services 2012 Tabular** This is the most powerful edition of the engine; it works as a server, and you use Visual Studio to create data models. It offers advanced features like partitioning, security, and full programmability.

Even if these three software programs run the same engine and share most of their functionalities, they are different in terms of pricing and complexity. Thus, the question arises naturally: Why buy SSAS and pay more to buy separately the same engine that is included in Excel 2013? Are the extra features really worth the money?

As you might already imagine, we cannot provide you with a clear answer. It really depends on how important a specific feature is for your business. Because we want to leave the decision to you, and that decision depends on the presence of specific features, in the next sections, we will analyze all the differences among the three products.

Feature matrix

It might seem strange to provide a conclusive matrix at the beginning of a chapter, yet we think it is useful to see it here. Table 16-1 lists the features we are comparing in the different versions of PowerPivot, to give you an immediate view of what the relevant differences are among them.

Each feature listed in table 16-1 is discussed in much more detail in subsequent sections.

TABLE 16-1 Features of different BI tools

Feature	Excel	SharePoint	SSAS
Security	None.	Document level.	Full security options.
Programmability	Using VBA.	None available.	Full options using XMLA.
Flexibility	Great options with linked and linked-back tables.	Somewhat limited.	Very rigid; needs coding to implement almost anything.
Extensibility	Only the workbook consumes the data.	Any suitable tool can consume the data and improve reporting.	Any suitable tool can consume the data and improve reporting.
Drill-through	Available, but not customizable.	Not available.	Fully customizable.*
Partitioning	Not available.	Not available.	Available, useful for large tables.

Translations	Not available.	Not available.	Available, for metadata only.*
Database size	Suggested for small datasets, can handle medium datasets.	Small and medium datasets.	Capability to handle huge datasets.
Number of databases	One database per workbook.	One database per workbook, option to build a central model.	One central model serves all the reporting needs.

* Feature is available by using BIDS Helper (*http://bidshelper.codeplex.com/*).

Securing your data

Let's be very clear about this: Excel does not handle security, in any way. If you load information from a database and store it inside an Excel workbook, it is no longer secure. Any users who have access to the workbook can open the PowerPivot window and look at all the information stored there. Worse, because now DAX is a query language, they can query the PowerPivot database, store the results in an Excel table, and from there, save the information wherever they want.

This is not unique to PowerPivot. The same level of security always has existed in Excel. The reason why we stress this fact is that you can load huge amounts of data in a single PowerPivot workbook. Thus, security requirements are more important now than ever.

> **Warning** Think twice before sending a workbook containing sensitive information to anybody, whether it contains PowerPivot data or not: You are not sharing with this person just the content of a PivotTable; you are sharing the full database that you used to create that PivotTable. We are not trying to scare you by saying this; we just want you to be aware of the level of security that you can handle with PowerPivot for Excel—that is, no security at all.

This might or might not be an issue in your specific scenario. If you mainly use Excel to create workbooks that remain safely inside your company, then security is not a big issue. But if you need to share a report, and sharing the workbook is the only way you have to show data to somebody, then it is better if you stop for a moment and think about security issues.

SharePoint moves one step toward providing you a secure environment. Using SharePoint, you do not need to send the workbook to anybody to share its content. Forget about sending analysis as email attachments. As you learned in Chapter 5, "Publishing to SharePoint," you can upload a workbook on SharePoint so that other users can see its content using a browser. Being a SharePoint document, your report is subject to the security rules of SharePoint, which let you give access to the report only to selected users. Moreover, using SharePoint, you have the ability to let a user browse the content of the report using the browser, but deny this person the ability to download a copy of the data inside it. Finally, you can hide part of the report, so that only the results of the analysis are visible, hiding everything else.

SharePoint provides a level of security to your data. Its only drawback is that the security rules need to be set at the document level. Thus, either a user can look at a report, or he or she cannot look at it at all. There is no way to let different users look at the same report with different data depending on user credentials. Imagine, for example, that you build a report for sales analysis and, being the general sales manager, you build it while looking at the entire database. You might want to share the report with local managers, but in such a way that each manager can see only the data of his or her region and does not have access to other regions. While this is a common scenario, you cannot implement it in SharePoint. In fact, if a report loads data for the entire database, its results will always contain the whole database, no matter who is browsing it.

There is a workaround to this limitation; that is, creating many reports, one for each homogeneous group of users with the same security rules. Doing it this way, each user sees the report of his or her group. Obviously, this solution is handy if and only if the number of reports in your solution is small. If, on the other hand, you plan to build many reports, then implementing security using this system is not advisable because you would multiply each report by the number of security groups. Finally, keep in mind that once you start using Excel to build reports, you will build many of them, if only because it is so easy to do.

When it comes to security, SSAS is clearly your best option. Using SSAS, you build a database and query it using Excel or any other client. SSAS requires the user to provide credentials and implements a sophisticated security system that lets you hide data to users at the single-row level. For example, you can build a database in such a way that one user sees only sales for Europe and another user, when running the same report, sees only sales for the United States.

We do not want to spend time here describing the details of the security system of SSAS because it is a complex topic beyond the scope of this book. It is enough to note that SSAS provides you all the tools needed to hide the content of the database to unauthorized users, while permitting authorized users the ability to browse all the data you allowed them to see.

To draw some conclusions regarding security, each of these three tools adhere to its nature:

- PowerPivot for Excel is good for self-service BI, serving a single user or a group of users who do not care about security. You completely lack security, yet you are happy with that: PowerPivot for Excel is perfect in your scenario.

- PowerPivot for SharePoint is good for teamwork. All the workbooks accessible to a team share the same security layer and see the same data. If you want to keep something private, you deny access to the SharePoint document to any user who does not have permission to look at that report. In case you need slightly more complex security, you have some workarounds that are not perfect, but could be good enough in some scenarios.

- SSAS provides complete security. Each user has a personal vision of the database, carefully filtered so that he or she cannot see any data he or she does not have permission to see. You do not need to build different reports; security is stored inside the database, and the same report will show different results to different people.

Programmability and flexibility

When it comes to programmability and flexibility, the comparison among the three systems is somewhat hard to make. Regarding programmability, you learned in Chapter 15 that you might use Microsoft Visual Basic for Applications (VBA) to program PowerPivot for Excel. You also learned that there are many limitations in controlling PowerPivot through VBA because the *Model* object does not expose the needed methods and properties to perform relatively simple operations like creating a calculated column or a calculated field.

Although programmability is somewhat limited in PowerPivot for Excel, when it comes to flexibility, Excel is second to none. Two powerful features are available only in Excel:

- Linked tables provide a simple, effective way of customizing the data model.

- Linked-back tables bring the power of multiple-step calculations, materialization of DAX queries, and mixing of the Excel and DAX languages.

Neither feature is available in PowerPivot for SharePoint or in SSAS. This is in line with the goal of using Excel for self-service BI: limited programmability, but great flexibility and freedom to build and modify data models.

In PowerPivot for SharePoint, you cannot use VBA, so from the programmability point of view, using SharePoint brings some limitations. Moreover, linked tables are not supported for direct update because you cannot update a table using PowerPivot for SharePoint. PowerPivot for SharePoint has some flexibility advantages because you can download a workbook from the SharePoint store, modify it with Excel, and then save it back to SharePoint. However, that does not mean that PowerPivot for SharePoint is the right choice in all situations. The ability to share workbooks and interact with them using a web browser comes with some limitations, and you need to be aware of them before relying on the PowerPivot for SharePoint architecture.

When it comes to SSAS, the scenario becomes more complex. Regarding flexibility, SSAS is the most rigid of the three products. There are no linked tables, no VBA, and no way to update a data model spontaneously. Every update has to be carefully designed and deployed by BI professionals using Visual Studio. On the other hand, SSAS can be programmed completely through using the XMLA language and a set of .NET libraries provided by Microsoft to manage an SSAS instance using a programming language.

No BI professional will really complain about the lack of flexibility in SSAS because flexibility and corporate BI do not go together naturally. In corporate BI, every modification to the model has to be carefully prepared, so to ensure that the data is still correct, all the reports work fine, and the values computed by the analytical system can be trusted. BI professionals reduce the need for flexibility thanks to the power of programmability. By writing custom code, you can manage SSAS to perform virtually any kind of calculation and operation, and while writing such a code is not an option for Excel users, it is the everyday work of BI professionals.

Finally, there are some programmability features in SSAS that are not available in PowerPivot for Excel or in PowerPivot for SharePoint, such as drill-through customization. You learned in Chapter 11,

"Shaping the reports," that by double-clicking a PivotTable cell, you can see the details of the rows underneath the current cell using a drill-through operation. Using SSAS, you can define many drill-through operations, and for each one, you can decide which columns to show from different tables. This feature is useful because it let users create reports in a very detailed and convenient way. For example, in Figure 16-1, you can see how different drill-through actions appear in an Excel PivotTable.

Sales	Column Labels				
Row Labels	⊞ 2005	⊞ 2006	⊞ 2007	⊞ 2008	Grand Total
⊟ Europe	$709,947.20				$8,930,042.26
⊟ France	$180,571.69				$2,644,017.71
France	$180,571.69				$2,644,017.71
⊟ Germany	$237,784.99			$1,076,890.77	$2,894,312.34
Germany	$237,784.99			$1,076,890.77	$2,894,312.34
⊟ United Kingdom	$291,590.52			$1,210,286.27	$3,391,712.21
United Kingdom	$291,590.52			$1,210,286.27	$3,391,712.21
⊟ North America	$1,247,379.26			$3,997,659.37	$11,367,634.37
⊟ Canada	$146,829.81			$673,628.21	$1,977,844.86
Canada	$146,829.81			$673,628.21	$1,977,844.86
⊟ United States	$1,100,549.45			$3,324,031.16	$9,389,789.51
Central				$232.71	$3,000.83
Northeast				$2,565.66	$6,532.47
Northwest	$415,203.49			$1,291,994.33	$3,649,866.55
Southeast				$8,442.40	$12,238.85
Southwest	$685,345.96				3,150.81
⊟ Pacific	$1,309,047.20				1,000.58
⊟ Australia	$1,309,047.20				1,000.58
Australia	$1,309,047.20			$2,563,884.29	$9,061,000.58
Grand Total	$3,266,373.66			$9,770,899.74	$29,358,677.22

Context menu:
Calibri · 11 · A˙ A˙ $ · % , ▦
B I ≡ ◇ · A · ▦ · ⁺⁰⁰ ⁰⁰⁺ ✦
- Copy
- Format Cells...
- Number Format...
- Refresh
- Sort ▸
- Quick Explore
- Remove "Sales"
- Show Values As ▸
- Show Details
- Additional Actions ▸ → Customer List / Product List
- Value Field Settings...
- PivotTable Options...
- Show Field List

FIGURE 16-1 The Additional Actions drop-down menu shows all the actions defined in the SSAS database.

Customer List and Product List are drill-through operations defined in the SSAS data model that produce different datasets: one returns product information about the sales related to the current cell, while the other shows the details of related products.

In conclusion, regarding programmability and flexibility, keep the following in mind about these three options:

- PowerPivot for Excel is easy to program in VBA, but it is somewhat limited. In terms of flexibility, it is the top performer.

- PowerPivot for SharePoint is less flexible than PowerPivot for Excel and does not offer the same level of programmability.

- SSAS is the most rigid environment, but it offers such a high level of programmability that, in the hands of professionals, it can be the foundation of complex, highly performing systems.

Translations

If you work for a multinational company that needs to share reports with people in different cultures all over the world, chances are that you will need to translate your report into different languages. Usually, you will need translations for the table and column names and, less frequently, you will need them for the data as well.

Translations are not supported in either PowerPivot for Excel or in PowerPivot for SharePoint. In SSAS, you have the option to define different localized names for tables, columns, and calculated fields, making life much easier for foreign readers of your report. However, translations are available only by using the BIDS Helper add-in (available free from *http://bidshelper.codeplex.com/*). This feature is not built into the SSAS development environment.

It is unlikely that self-service BI users need translations. However, if you plan to use PowerPivot for SharePoint, keep in mind that it does not offer translations. If you need to do them, then SSAS with BIDS Helper is your only option.

Database size

In the 64-bit version of Excel 2013, the limit of the size of a workbook is the amount of memory installed on the PC. On 32-bit systems, the hard limit is 2 GB of virtual memory, which in reality means less than 1 GB of data because the memory is shared with Excel. Thus, you might think that you do not need to worry about the size of the database when deciding whether it is better to use PowerPivot for Excel, PowerPivot for SharePoint, or SSAS. Unfortunately, this is not true. The size of the database is important for several reasons, which we are going to analyze in this section.

First, you need to consider that, while it is true that you can build a workbook of, say, 20 GB, to run on your powerful workstation, in a practical world, you would not consider it easy to handle. You will have to wait a few minutes every time you want to open the workbook, modify anything, or save your work. Each of these operations will last for some time, leading to a poor user experience.

However, this is not the real issue. Much worse is the time it would take to refresh it, reloading everything from the database. You can store several billion rows in 20 GB of a PowerPivot workbook, but when it comes to refreshing this amount of data, waiting a few hours for the refresh operation to complete should not come as a surprise. Thus, we think that a practical limit of PowerPivot for Excel is more like 500 to 600 MB of data. If you go over this size, chances are that you are asking too much from self-service BI, and it is time to go a step further and use one of the higher-level tools.

PowerPivot for SharePoint is slightly different. The data refresh operation can be scheduled to run at nighttime, when nobody is querying the data model. Even if it takes a long while, that time is computer time, not generally something humans need to worry about too much. However, when using PowerPivot for SharePoint, you need to look at other considerations:

- SharePoint 2013 has a hard limit of 2 GB for a file, so you cannot upload Excel workbooks larger than 2 GB, even if they can work locally on your workstation.

- Many people share a SharePoint server. When you create a large workbook of hundreds of megabytes, then you need to remember that a larger amount of memory is required during queries. If many users are querying different reports at the same time, you might need a server dedicated to PowerPivot for SharePoint, with enough memory to satisfy all the requests. You might find that performance will suffer if there is not enough memory.

- If you want to update the report structure, you will need to download the workbook locally, modify it, and finally upload it again on SharePoint. For big workbooks, this might be more of an issue, again leading to a poor user experience, as with PowerPivot for Excel. However, as a workaround for that, you can create a regular Excel workbook connected to an external PowerPivot workbook already saved on SharePoint. In this way, you can share a single PowerPivot model with many Excel workbooks, paying the cost for storing data only once. In the next section of this chapter, you will see more details about this option.

Thus, the limit on the size of the database can be slightly higher than the one suggested for PowerPivot for Excel, but not too high. We can picture a team working happily with workbooks of sizes up to 2 GB (remember you cannot upload files larger than 2 GB to SharePoint).

SSAS is the clear winner in this category. In fact, SSAS is a corporate BI tool, and it implements a feature that is a lifesaver for big databases—that is, partitioning. You can split a big table into smaller segments, called *partitions*, each of which can be handled independently from the others. If a BI professional is working on a database with 10 billion rows, for example, he or she will certainly implement some kind of partitioning so that the server will never need to reload the full database (except in a few rare situations). By implementing sophisticated processing algorithms, you can load on the server only the last set of rows, reprocess them, and then move the database online. This technique is called *incremental loading*.

Partitioning is available only in SSAS; neither version of PowerPivot has it. Handling partitions should be done only by BI professionals. When it comes to memory usage, the sizing of the server has to be done correctly, and, again, you would expect IT people to know better how to ensure that a server has enough memory and CPU power to execute the activities gracefully on databases that it needs to manage.

Using SSAS and partitions, the limit of the database is really the amount of memory installed on the server, and it is common to see databases of tenths of gigabytes that work smoothly, providing a good user experience.

Thus, regarding database size, we can draw a few conclusions:

- Both PowerPivot for Excel and PowerPivot for SharePoint share the same practical limits, more or less, even if there is no technical limit on PowerPivot for Excel other than the memory available. Handling more than 1 GB of data is unlikely to work well, in any case. Keep in mind that you can fit a huge amount of data in such a size; it is just a matter of knowing the limits and obeying them. (There are many ways to optimize the memory impact of a PowerPivot data model, but they are too complex to cover here.)

- SSAS has no practical limit other than the memory available. BI professionals have all the tools to ensure that big databases can run smoothly. IT people handle these tools better than information workers.

Finally, we want to give you a small word of caution about an important point, if you ever face medium to big databases: that is, performance tuning. While you can count yourself among the elite number of DAX experts once you have finished this book, you need to be aware of the fact that when the size of a database grows, the performance of your formulas might suffer if you do not write them correctly. In this book, we did not cover optimization and query monitoring, mainly because of their complexity and limited usefulness for information workers. If your database is growing to be over 1 GB, then performance starts to be an issue, and whenever you write a formula, you need to be careful to use the best practices for the engine you are using.

Number of databases

In the previous section, we discussed database size. Even if size, as measured in gigabytes or memory used, is worth considering, a more important topic to understand is the complexity of the business model and the number of reports that you need to produce.

With PowerPivot for Excel, you can easily create a data model to produce some reports. However, in the real world, you do not create a single report; you probably have dozens of reports, which are useful for different goals and people. Using Excel, you have to make an important decision: how many workbooks do you create?

If you create a separate workbook for each report, then you will duplicate both the database and the business logic; that is, the set of formulas and calculations, in your workbooks. This has several drawbacks:

- You use more space, because you have duplicate data in several databases.

- If you need to change a formula, you need to do it in all your workbooks.

- At some point, you will have different formulas in different workbooks, and this can be confusing and lead to incorrect reports.

- When it is time to refresh the model, all your workbooks need to be refreshed.

This is an issue in both PowerPivot for Excel and PowerPivot for SharePoint. In the case of PowerPivot for SharePoint, it is a bigger problem because there, many models can be loaded at once if different users are browsing different reports (something that is less likely to happen with plain Excel). Unfortunately, there is no way to build a single data model and many different reports, in different workbooks, using PowerPivot for Excel only.

With PowerPivot for SharePoint, there is a better option. You can create a single workbook containing the data model with all the calculations and the business logic and, once you publish it in SharePoint, you can create many Excel workbooks that use the data model in SharePoint instead of building their own data model. This architecture, known as *hub/spoke,* is a convenient way of organizing your reporting system, but it requires you to spend more time building the central data model in such a way that it can serve all your reports. Moreover, you need to be careful whenever you update the central model because any update to it will have an impact on all the existing reports.

In this respect, SSAS behaves exactly the same way as PowerPivot for SharePoint in this last scenario. In SSAS, you build the central model and use it for all your reports. The only difference here is that BI professionals handle the central model, and they are used to making decisions and changing the data model, taking into account all the needs of the different reporting systems.

PowerPivot as a prototyping system

One interesting thing to note about the three varieties of PowerPivot is that a complete upgrade path is available. That is, you can start a project with PowerPivot for Excel and be able to upgrade to higher levels without having to restart from scratch. Once you feel the need to share data with colleagues or partners, you can move your data to PowerPivot for SharePoint seamlessly: it is just a matter of checking that you did not use any feature that is not supported by SharePoint and then uploading the workbook to SharePoint.

If, later, your needs are growing because you hit the limits of PowerPivot for SharePoint, it is at least somewhat easy to move to the next level (that is, SSAS). It is not as easy as moving from PowerPivot for Excel to PowerPivot for SharePoint, but it is not that difficult. Keep in mind that SSAS is not intended for Excel users. Rather, it requires a BI professional to manage it. Nevertheless, you can transform a PowerPivot workbook into a Visual Studio solution by simply opening the Excel workbook with Visual Studio. All the calculated columns, calculated fields, KPI definitions, and metadata are transferred from the workbook into the solution, so that BI professionals do not need to reinvent the wheel. They can start right where you left off and move the solution to corporate BI.

In fact, BI professionals commonly use PowerPivot for Excel as a prototyping tool. Using its user interface and its simplicity and rapid development, they can create a simple prototype along with the customer, and then, when it is time to build a complete solution from it, move their prototype into a Visual Studio solution.

Index

Symbols

& (ampersand)
&& (AND) operator, 53, 395
string concatenation operator, 51, 53
* (asterisk), multiplication operator, 53
. (commas), in DAX code, 66
= (equals sign)
equal to operator, 53
in calculated column and calculated field
definitions, 67
! (exclamation mark), NOT operator, 53
> (greater than) operator, 53
>= (greater than or equal to) operator, 53
< (less than) operator, 53
>= (less than or equal to) operator, 53
- (minus sign), subtraction/negation operator, 53
<> (not equal to) operator, 53
( ) (parentheses), precedence or grouping operator, 53
+ (plus sign), addition operator, 53
' ' (quotation marks, single) in DAX literals, 53
/ (slash), division operator, 53
∑ symbol before column names, 267
∑ Values field, 38
| (vertical bar), OR operator, 53

A

ABC analysis, 407–411
computing with linked-back table, 435–438
data model to compute ABC classes for
products, 408
dynamic, using VBA, 451–455
ABS function, 74
Access, loading data from, 143–144
actions defined in SSAS database, showing, 468
ADDCOLUMNS function, 441

using in DAX queries, 425–427
using VALUES with, 426
AddConnection function, 456
additive measures, 353
additive nature of formula, many-to-many relationships
and, 385
Add To Data Model button, 159
AdventureWorks sample database, 5
aggregate functions, 68–71
A-suffixed, 69
changing, 46
using for date calculations, 349–351
X-suffixed, 71
aggregating and comparing over time, 339–352
ALL function, 193
filter context and, 209
parameter of CALCULATE, 212
removal of filters with, 194
using in FILTER expression in CALCULATE, 219
ALLSELECTED function, 230–232
detecting if column is filtered in hierarchy, 246
restoring original filter context of table, 297
using with RANKX, 377
Analysis Services. *See* SSAS
AND function, 71
AND operator, 53
combining filters, 395
conditions for filtering with CALCULATE, 218
TRUE/FALSE arguments in CALCULATE, 221
animation (in a bubble chart), 276
arithmetical operations in DAX, 61
arithmetic operators, 53
Assign Macro dialog box, 449
A-suffixed aggregate functions, 69
.atomsvc file extension, 156
technical information about source data feeds, 168
AVERAGE function, 68

Q

About the Authors

Alberto Ferrari (*alberto.ferrari@sqlbi.com*) and **Marco Russo** (*marco.russo@ sqlbi.com*) are the two founders of SQLBI.COM, where they regularly publish articles about Microsoft PowerPivot, DAX, and SQL Server Analysis Services Tabular. They have worked with PowerPivot since the first beta version in 2009.

They both provide consultancy and mentoring on business intelligence (BI), with a particular specialization in the Microsoft technologies related to BI. They have written several books and papers about these topics, with a particular mention of "SQLBI methodology," which is a complete methodology for designing and implementing the back end of a BI solution; and "The Many-to-Many Revolution," which is a paper dedicated to modeling patterns using many-to-many dimension relationships in SQL Server Analysis Services and PowerPivot.

Marco and Alberto are also regular speakers at major international conferences, such as TechEd, PASS Summit, SQLRally, and SQLBits.

What do you think of this book?

We want to hear from you!
To participate in a brief online survey, please visit:

microsoft.com/learning/booksurvey

Tell us how well this book meets your needs—what works effectively, and what we can do better. Your feedback will help us continually improve our books and learning resources for you.

Thank you in advance for your input!